The Continuing Crisis

U.S. Policy in Central America and the Caribbean

MARK FALCOFF is a professional staff member with the Senate Foreign Relations Committee. He worked on this book while a resident fellow at the American Enterprise Institute for Public Policy Research. He received his M.A. and Ph.D. from Princeton University and has taught at the universities of Illinois, Oregon, and California (Los Angeles), as well as at the U.S. Foreign Service Institute. His books include (with Ronald H. Dolkart) *Prologue to Perón: Argentina in Depression and War, 1930–43* (1976) and (with Frederick B. Pike) *The Spanish Civil War, 1936–39: American Hemispheric Perspectives* (1982).

ROBERT ROYAL, a research associate at the Ethics and Public Policy Center, was formerly editor-in-chief of *Prospect* magazine, published in Princeton, New Jersey. He holds an M.A. from Brown University, where he also taught. He spent 1979 in Italy as a Fulbright Fellow, has done extensive research in Latin languages, literatures, and cultures, and has written essays and reviews for several publications.

The Continuing Crisis

U.S. Policy in Central America and the Caribbean

Thirty Essays by Statesmen, Scholars, Religious Leaders, and Journalists

Edited by

Mark Falcoff

and

Robert Royal

ETHICS AND PUBLIC POLICY CENTER

THE ETHICS AND PUBLIC POLICY CENTER, established in 1976, conducts a program of research, writing, publications, and conferences to encourage debate on domestic and foreign policy issues among religious, educational, academic, business, political, and other leaders. A nonpartisan effort, the Center is supported by contributions (which are tax deductible) from foundations, corporations, and individuals. The authors alone are responsible for the views expressed in Center publications. The founding president of the Center is **Ernest W. Lefever.**

Distributed by arrangement with
University Press of America, Inc.
4720 Boston Way
Lanham, MD 20706

3 Henrietta Street
London WC2E 8LU England

Library of Congress Cataloging in Publication Data
The Continuing crisis.
  Bibliography: p.
  Includes index.
  1. Central America—Foreign relations—United States.
  2. United States—Foreign relations—Central America.
  3. United States—Foreign relations—1981–
  I. Falcoff, Mark.   II. Royal, Robert, 1949–
  F1436.8.U6C67   1986   327.730728   86-24145
  ISBN 0-89633-105-9
  ISBN 0-89633-106-7 (pbk.)

© **1987 by the Ethics and Public Policy Center.** All rights reserved.
Printed in the United States of America.

Contents

Foreword   **vii**
Senator Richard G. Lugar

Preface   **ix**
The Editors

PART ONE: GLOBAL PERSPECTIVES

Map of the Region   2

Chronology   3

1. The Threat in Central America   9
   Ronald Reagan

2. The Global Peoples' Revolution   19
   Fidel Castro

3. The Crisis and Our Opportunity   41
   Kissinger Commission

4. Soviet Arms and Central American Turmoil   59
   Alberto R. Coll

5. Views of the U.S. Catholic Bishops   79
   John J. O'Connor

PART TWO: REGIONAL PERSPECTIVES

6. The Development Alternative   93
   Abraham F. Lowenthal

7. Caribbean Basin Initiative: Pros and Cons   113
   Richard E. Feinberg, Richard Newfarmer, Bernadette Orr

8. The English-Speaking Caribbean   129
   Anthony P. Maingot

9. A Plea for Contadora   147
   Eight Latin American Foreign Ministers

10. Demystifying Contadora   151
    Susan Kaufman Purcell

11. A Costa Rican Perspective   175
    Oscar Arias Sánchez

12. The Elections in Guatemala and Honduras   181
    Richard L. Millett

PART THREE: EL SALVADOR

Map   191

Chronology   193

13. A Culture of Violence   195
    John Kurzweil

14. What Duarte Won   211
    Julia Preston
15. Rebel Factions   231
    Shirley Christian
16. The Divided Military   245
    Shirley Christian
17. Why I Broke With the Guerrillas   261
    José Napoleón Romero
18. The State of Human Rights   267
    U.S. State Department

PART FOUR: NICARAGUA

Map   293

Chronology   295

19. Somoza, Sandino, and the United States   297
    Mark Falcoff
20. A New Deal for the Nicaraguan People   321
    Gabriel Jackson
21. The Slow Road to Communism   337
    Joshua Muravchik
22. North America's Crimes   363
    Daniel Ortega
23. The Sandinistas' Tangled Elections   375
    Robert S. Leiken
24. The Sandinistas Have Bound and Gagged Us   401
    Miguel Obando y Bravo
25. The Nature of the Insurgency   409
    Michael S. Radu
26. Nicaragua and International Law   433
    John Norton Moore
27. An Alternative to Contra Aid   445
    Michael Walzer
28. The Newest Political Pilgrims   453
    Paul Hollander
29. Don't Abandon the Nicaraguan People   465
    Jaime Chamorro
30. A Revolution Betrayed   471
    Edén Pastora Gómez

Appendixes
   A. Caribbean Basin Initiative   479
   B. Contadora Proposals for Peace   489
   C. The Seventy-two Hour Document   493
   D. The Nicaraguan Constitution – First Draft   519

Bibliographical Essay   541

Index of Names   547

Foreword

By SENATOR RICHARD G. LUGAR

THE TERM "crisis" is too much used in our discussions of American foreign policy, but it often describes the environment in which we abruptly discover neglected countries or entire regions. The United States has many strengths as a society, but so far it has not found a way to combine global responsibilities with a clear set of priorities and a capacity to carry out commitments over a relatively long time. The result is what some of our foreign friends call "brushfire diplomacy," which sometimes works, but often at enormous cost in time, energy, and money. Since the tragic experience of Vietnam, the problem has become even more complex, since many people believe that any security commitment anywhere in the world, but especially the Third World, must automatically lead to a quagmire and, ultimately, a military and political defeat for the United States.

Few areas demonstrate this twin dilemma more clearly than Central America and the Caribbean. There the conflict is not only between us and our adversaries but also among Americans themselves—over the facts on the ground, and their meaning for our national values and interest. In a way this is paradoxical, for the Caribbean Basin constitutes the oldest area of our foreign policy interest. Until 1914, most American overseas investment, all our naval stations, and most of our diplomatic service were in this region. Most of the important episodes of American diplomatic history in the nineteenth century took place in Mexico, Cuba, or what is now the Republic of Panama. Some of these included the use of American troops, under the Roosevelt corollary to the Monroe Doctrine—in the Dominican Republic, Haiti, and Nicaragua.

World War II brought about two important changes in American foreign policy. First, it became global rather than merely regional. And second, the United States, which had withdrawn its troops from Central America and the Caribbean during the 1930s, developed a virtually unchallenged hegemony throughout the entire Basin. This encouraged a long period of neglect, which ended dramatically in 1959 with a Communist revolution in Cuba and the eventual establishment of a Soviet military and naval presence in what had been an "American sea." Unlike earlier challengers to U.S. predominance in the region—Napolean's Second Empire in France, or Imperial Germany—the Soviets were armed with an ideology calculated to appeal to the dispossessed and the thwarted middle classes of these small, backward, and vulnerable countries. Meeting that challenge requires an understanding of and sympathy for the genuine struggle of these peoples for a better life.

The need for this understanding—combined, of course, with a clear appreciation of the strategic issues at stake—has been underlined by events in Nicaragua since 1979, which have been profoundly unsettling for the whole of Central America. In the meantime, a quiet crisis has been brewing in the Caribbean islands that were formerly vestigial portions of the French, British, and Dutch Empires. To the extent that Americans are aware of these microstates at all, they regard them as havens from our winters, or sources of tropical products or dance music; but, as recent events in Grenada illustrate, for Fidel Castro and his allies they are a living archipelago of frustration that can be exploited for revolutionary purposes.

Keeping strategic and humanitarian considerations in proper balance is never easy, but those of us who labor in the U.S. Congress know there is no other way to forge a successful bipartisan policy. At the same time, we need to listen carefully both to our friends and to our adversaries in the region, so that we have a clear picture of their needs, their goals, and the threat that some of them represent to our values and interest. We Americans also need to listen carefully to one another—and to address the hard issues for which Central America and the Caribbean are dramatic metaphors, involving the use of military power in the Third World, the utility (or limits) of negotiation, and the relation between revolutionary change and democracy. In this collection of essays, Mark Falcoff and Robert Royal make a signal contribution to that end, bringing into focus a region that, for all its geographical proximity, is still too far from our attention and our creative imagination.

RICHARD G. LUGAR, *Chairman*
Committee on Foreign Relations
United States Senate

October 10, 1986

Preface

ALTHOUGH CENTRAL AMERICA appears to be mired in centuries-old conditions, it is a rapidly changing region. In the last few years, it has undergone highly visible large-scale political shifts, as well as more obscure and subtle social developments. These changes may be characterized as a continuing crisis, if we take crisis in its original meaning as a turning point or a moment of decision. The remaining years of the 1980s may well set the whole region on a new course.

In 1984, when we published *Crisis and Opportunity: U.S. Policy in Central America and the Caribbean*, three of the seven Central American countries were ruled by military dictatorships. During the past two years, Honduras and Guatemala have elected civilian presidents; El Salvador has turned back a guerrilla threat to its democratic government; and Nicaragua has become an ever more vexed question for U.S. policy. *Crisis and Opportunity* went through three printings and continues to be used as a classroom text. But we thought the present collection of essays, three-quarters of which have appeared in the last two years, was necessary to keep pace with the rapidly unfolding events in Central America.

These changes do not point to an early resolution of the crisis. Slow economic growth and lack of foreign investment still plague Central American societies. Marxist-Leninist forces, allied with Cuba and Nicaragua, are still seeking ways to exploit social unrest when they are not engaged in outright guerrilla warfare. Democratic traditions in the region are weak in proportion to the problems to be solved. Under the best circumstances, it will take years of struggle for the region to achieve social, economic, and political stability.

Probably the most crucial factor affecting the struggle is the foreign policy of the United States. Under President Reagan, that policy has been one of strong support for democracies and heavy pressure on the Marxist-Leninist rulers of Nicaragua. By the spring of 1986, when increased aid to the contras fighting the Sandinista regime was being debated in Congress, all but a handful of senators and representatives had come to see that Nicaragua was oppressive at home and a threat to its neighbors. This was a big shift from congressional opinion of only a few years earlier. But agreement on U.S. policy toward the Sandinistas remained hampered by a number of questions: Can the U.S. use of force, even by support to native rebels, be morally justified? Are economic and political pressures and rewards, or regional defense treaties like Contadora, likely to achieve U.S. goals without risking security? Will current policy lead to U.S. military involvement in Central America and another "Vietnam"? Although Congress eventually voted $100 million in aid to the contras in June 1986, these and other questions continue to play a major role in the debate on Central America.

Doubts about the wisdom of military solutions are among the characteristic virtues of democratic systems. But caution can often shade imperceptibly into indecision, and inconsistent and shifting policy badly suited to the long-term needs for stability of regions like Central America. As De Tocqueville observed of the foreign policy of democratic states: "A democracy finds it difficult to coordinate the details of a great undertaking and to fix on some plan and carry it through in spite of obstacles. It has little capacity for combining measures in secret and waiting patiently for the result."

The Central American debate may have demonstrated that so-called covert measures are no longer possible for the United States. For better or worse, U.S. policy debates on Central America will continue to take place in the open and will, therefore, remain subject to political expediency. The Congress has become better acquainted with Central America as a result of the crisis, but the electorate as a whole still remains poorly informed. After over seven years of intense news coverage, more than two-thirds of the U.S. public still does not even know which side we are on in Nicaragua and El Salvador. As the country seeks ways to limit the federal budget, voters' pressure to deal first with domestic issues, coupled with this widespread ignorance, may influence many congressmen to vote for measures inadequate to Central American problems.

This collection of essays is aimed at making a contribution to better understanding of Central America. As in our earlier volume, we have tried to select a balanced, comprehensive range of opinion on the key issues. Because El Salvador's problems, though still acute, are less pressing than they once were, the section on El Salvador has been slightly shortened. Regional solutions and the views of regional actors have emerged into greater prominence with the return of civilian governments and the ongoing debate over the Contadora peace treaty. As a result, we have added a section on regional views.

Part One deals with Global Perspectives. Since conflicts in the modern world seem almost inevitably to involve the two superpowers, this section presents long-range views of the Central American struggle and differing large-scale solutions.

Part Two examines Regional Perspectives. Since the formation of the Contadora Four—Mexico, Venezuela, Panama, and Colombia—Latin American governments outside as well as inside Central America have been actively seeking a peaceful resolution of conflicts.

Part Three is devoted to El Salvador. Death-squad killings in that country have dropped off sharply. President José Napoleón Duarte has instituted land reform and has even gone so far as to meet with guerrilla leaders to begin a national dialogue. But the insurgency continues, aided by forces outside El Salvador. Duarte badly needs economic growth and time to heal deep social rifts if his program is to succeed.

Part Four, the largest section, encapsulates the debate on Nicaragua. Although there is growing awareness in Congress and among journalists of the unpleasant nature of the Sandinista regime, no consensus has been reached on the general or specific aims of U.S. policy toward Nicaragua. This debate will influence our basic approach to questions about America's commitments and responsibilities around the world.

As in our earlier volume, we have tried to make the complicated history and little-known geography of Central America more understandable by including chronologies and maps. The four appendixes contain some of the essential documents for study of the region. One of the criticisms of the first volume was that a fuller bibliographical guide to the vast literature on Central America was needed. The bibliographical essay at the back of this volume should satisfy that demand.

We would like to thank the president of the Ethics and Public Policy Center, Ernest W. Lefever, for his enthusiasm and sage suggestions for this new undertaking. The Center's editor, Carol Friedley Griffith, brought her usual standards of excellence to the at times exasperating task of making thirty authors coexist peacefully within the covers of one book.

The editors also thank the publications in which this material first appeared for permission to reprint. Any remaining errors or omissions are solely our responsibility.

MARK FALCOFF
ROBERT ROYAL

Washington, D.C.
September 15, 1986

Part One

Global Perspectives

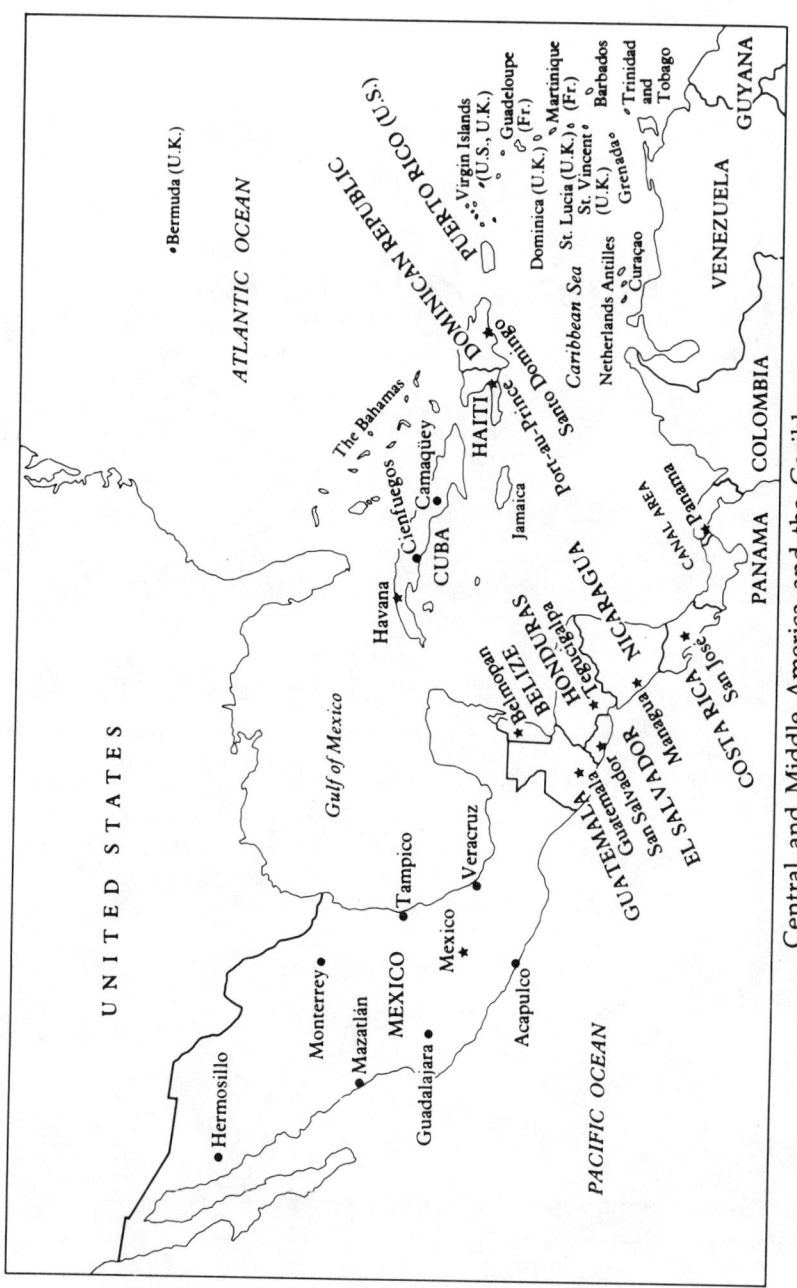

Central and Middle America and the Caribbean

Reprinted by permission from *Latin American Politics and Development* (second edition), edited by Howard J. Wiarda and Harvey F. Kline (© 1985 by Westview Press, Boulder, Colorado).

Chronology

1812–1899

1812   Constitutional monarchy established in Spain; colonial rule liberalized. Election of town councils in Central America marks beginning of national political life.

1814   Fernando VII restored to Spanish throne; annuls 1812 constitution and all its outgrowths in the New World.

1821   Guatemala and other provinces of Central America declare independence from Spain, but differ on subsequent course of action.

1822   Central American provinces annex themselves to independent Mexican Empire under General Augustín de Iturbide, later Emperor Augustín I.

1823–24   Augustín I overthrown; Mexico becomes a republic. Costa Rica, Guatemala, Honduras, Nicaragua, and El Salvador form Central American Federation, with capital in Guatemala City (later, briefly, San Salvador).

1825   United States and Central American Federation sign treaty of friendship, ratified following year.

1829–38   Political conflict between federation members and the capital increases. In 1838, Central American Congress allows states to leave federation; Nicaragua, Honduras, and Costa Rica secede.

1847   Guatemala declares itself a "republic" rather than a "state," foreclosing possibility of reunion. Other Central American states follow suit.

1850–55   Trans-Panama railway built. Most Central American commerce moved from Caribbean to Pacific ports.

1895–99   Major efforts to restore Central American Federation fail.

1900–1986

1903	**Panama** declares independence from Colombia; United States quickly recognizes it and negotiates favorable treaty to build interoceanic canal.
1914	**Panama Canal** opened.
1917	**Attempted union** of five Central American states, on Honduran initiative, fails when Nicaragua refuses to cooperate.
1927	Peace accord among fighting factions in **Nicaragua** provides basis for U.S. occupation and subsequent elections.
1927–34	General Augusto C. **Sandino** leads Nicaraguan guerrillas against U.S. occupation.
1934	**Sandino** murdered by members of Nicaraguan National Guard; Guard chief Anastasio **Somoza** dominates country until 1956.
1936	U.S.-**Panama** Canal Treaty abrogated; United States abandons protectorate powers over Panama and agrees to non-intervention.
1944	Dictator Jorge Ubico in **Guatemala** resigns under pressure of violence and protests.
1944–50	"Spiritual socialist" Juan José Arévalo heads reformist administration in **Guatemala**.
1948	Fraudulent conservative government in **Costa Rica** overthrown by José Figueres and his Army of National Liberation; start of long period of democratic institutions and dominance of Figueres in Costa Rican politics.
1948	**Organization of American States** (OAS) created.
1950–54	Jacobo Arbenz elected president of **Guatemala**. Revolutionary reforms intensify; Communist infiltration of government increases.
1952	Fulgencio Batista seizes power in **Cuba** and establishes repressive dictatorship.
1953	Cuban revolutionary leader Fidel **Castro** imprisoned after unsuccessful attack on army post in Santiago de Cuba.

CHRONOLOGY 5

1954	OAS "Declaration of Solidarity" against intervention of International Communism is directed against Arbenz government in **Guatemala**. After Eastern European arms arrive, Colonel Carlos Castillo Armas overthrows Arbenz with aid of Honduras, Nicaragua, and U.S.
1955	Fidel **Castro** released from Cuban prison; goes to Mexico.
1956	Anastasio **Somoza** assassinated. His sons, Luis and Anastasio, Jr., continue family domination of Nicaragua to 1979.
1956	Fidel **Castro** and several dozen companions arrive in Cuba from Mexico to begin guerrilla struggle.
1957	Castillo Armas assassinated. Period of instability and violence begins in **Guatemala**.
1958–63	Conservative Miguel Ydígoras Fuentes elected president of **Guatemala**.
1959	**Castro** overthows Cuban dictator Batista; establishes totalitarian regime.
1961	U.S.-sponsored exile invasion of **Cuba** fails to establish beachhead at Bay of Pigs; Castro declares himself Marxist-Leninist and ally of Soviet Union.
1962	U.S.-Soviet crisis over placement of strategic missiles in **Cuba** resolved by compromise: Soviet Union agrees to remove the weapons; U.S. promises not to invade the island.
1964	Riots in **Panama Canal Zone** lead to new canal treaty negotiations.
1965	U.S. intervention in **Dominican Republic** restores order after left-wing insurgency.
1972	Earthquake devastates Managua, **Nicaragua**. Poor handing of crisis and mishandling of international relief aid by Anastasio Somoza Debayle increase opposition to his dictatorship.
1972	Michael Manley of pro-socialist People's National Party begins first term as prime minister of **Jamaica**.
1972	Christian Democrat José Napoleón Duarte wins plurality in **El Salvador** election. Legislature, however, acting within constitu-

	tion, chooses Colonel Arturo Armando Molina as president. Duarte charges fraud, is arrested and exiled.
1974	Election fraud in **Nicaragua** ensures Somoza's reelection to six-year term.
1977	New Panama Canal treaties establishing means for eventually ceding canal to **Panama** ratified by U.S. Senate after long fight.
1979	Somoza overthrown in **Nicaragua**; new governing coalition dominated by Marxist FSLN (Sandinista National Liberation Front) assumes power.
1979	Young military officers overthrow **El Salvador** dictator General Carlos Humberto Romero.
1979	Maurice Bishop seizes control of **Grenada** while elected prime minister Eric Gairy is out of country.
1980	New government of **El Salvador** declares land, tax, and banking reforms. Carter administration suspends U.S. aid to Nicaragua because of evidence that FSLN is arming Salvadoran insurgents. In December, José Napoleón Duarte becomes president of military-civilian junta.
1980	Anti-Communist **Jamaica** Labor Party defeats Michael Manley; Edward Seaga becomes prime minister.
1981	Guerrillas in **El Salvador** launch unsuccessful "final offensive" early in year. Carter administration resumes arms sale to Salvadoran government.
1981	U.S. Congress requires semi-annual certification of progress in human rights in **El Salvador** as condition for military aid.
1982	Elections for constitutent assembly in **El Salvador** draw record turnout despite guerrilla threats. Alvaro Magaña named provisional president.
1982	President Reagan launches **Caribbean Basin Initiative**.
1982	Military coup in **Guatemala** replaces civilian president Ríos Montt with a military government.

1983	Marxist dictator Maurice Bishop and other government officials in **Grenada** murdered in October by hard-line Marxists led by Bernard Coard. U.S. forces restore peace and parliamentary democracy; Coard imprisoned, Cuban "advisors" expelled.
1983	**Kissinger Commission** formed.
1984	José Napoleón Duarte elected president of **El Salvador**.
1984	Daniel Ortega elected president of **Nicaragua**.
1985	Democracy returns to **Guatemala** and **Honduras** with the election of civilian presidents.
1986	U.S. Congress approves $100 million aid to contras in **Nicaragua**.

1. The Threat in Central America

By RONALD REAGAN

Focus "This is not some narrow partisan issue; it is a national security issue, an issue on which we must act not as Republicans, not as Democrats, but as Americans." With this nationally televised appeal for bipartisan support, President Reagan sought $100 million in aid to the Nicaraguan contras in the spring of 1986. The President built his case on two assertions: that the Sandinistas have become oppressive totalitarians at home, and that they seek to export their revolution abroad. Three months later, Congress approved the aid.

Citing Sandinista repression of the Catholic and Protestant churches, the flight of Nicaragua's Jewish community, censorship and shutdowns of the independent press, elimination of independent labor groups, and intimidation of other sectors of Nicaraguan society, the President asked: "Will we give the Nicaraguans' democratic resistance the means to recapture their betrayed revolution, or will we turn our backs and ignore the malignancy in Managua until it spreads and becomes a mortal threat to the entire New World?"

As evidence of the international dimension of the Sandinistas' program, the President refers to the Sandinistas' own "Seventy-two Hour Document" (see appendix C), which calls for support of revolutions throughout Latin America and the world and identifies the enemy as the United States. In addition to Nicaragua's export of subversion to neighboring El Salvador, Costa Rica, Honduras, and Guatemala, says the President, the presence of Libyan, Italian, German, and Palestinian terrorists in Managua is cause for concern for the entire Free World.

Furthermore, the Sandinistas' East German, Bulgarian, Cuban, and Soviet advisors show the types of regimes with which Managua has already aligned itself.

Reagan supporters seized on this speech as a warning of the gravity of the situation. Critics called it overstatement or downright falsehood. The President's remarks should be compared with those of Fidel Castro (selection 2), Alberto Coll (selection 4), Costa Rican president Arias (selection 11), and Part Four, on Nicaragua.

Ronald Reagan was re-elected president of the United States in 1984.

MY FELLOW AMERICANS, I must speak to you tonight about a mounting danger in Central America that threatens the security of the United States. This danger will not go away; it will grow worse, much worse, if we fail to take action now.

I am speaking of Nicaragua, a Soviet ally on the American mainland only two hours' flying time from our own borders. With over a billion dollars in Soviet-bloc aid, the Communist government of Nicaragua has launched a campaign to subvert and topple its democratic neighbors.

Using Nicaragua as a base, the Soviets and Cubans can become the dominant power in the crucial corridor between North and South America. Established there, they will be in a position to threaten the Panama Canal, interdict our vital Caribbean sea lanes, and, ultimately, move against Mexico. Should that happen, desperate Latin peoples by the millions would begin fleeing north into the cities of the southern United States, or to wherever some hope of freedom remained.

The United States Congress has before it a proposal to help stop this threat. The legislation is an aid package of $100 million for the more than 20,000 freedom fighters struggling to bring democracy to their country and eliminate this Communist menace at its source. But this $100 million is not an additional $100 million. We are not asking for a single dime in new money. We are asking only to be permitted to switch a small part of our present defense budget — to the defense of our own southern frontier.

Gathered in Nicaragua already are thousands of Cuban military advisors, contingents of Soviet and East Germans, and all the elements of international terror — from the PLO to Italy's Red Brigades. Why are they there? Because, as Colonel Qaddafi has publicly exalted: "Nicaragua means a great thing, it means fighting America near its borders. Fighting America at its doorstep."

For our own security the United States must deny the Soviet Union a beachhead in North America. But let me make one thing plain. I am not talking about American troops. They are not needed; they have not been requested. The democratic resistance fighting in Nicaragua is only asking

---

Address to the nation on March 16, 1986.

America for the supplies and support to save their own country from Communism.

The question the Congress of the United States will now answer is a simple one: Will we give the Nicaraguans' democratic resistance the means to recapture their betrayed revolution, or will we turn our backs and ignore the malignancy in Managua until it spreads and becomes a mortal threat to the entire New World?

Will we permit the Soviet Union to put a second Cuba, a second Libya, right on the doorstep of the United States?

The Sandinistas' Intentions

How can such a small country pose such a great threat? It is not Nicaragua alone that threatens us, but those using Nicaragua as a privileged sanctuary for their struggle against the United States.

Their first target is Nicaragua's neighbors. With an army and militia of 120,000 men, backed by more than 3,000 Cuban military advisors, Nicaragua's armed forces are the largest Central America has ever seen. The Nicaraguan military machine is more powerful than all its neighbors combined.

This map represents much of the Western Hemisphere. Now let me show you the countries in Central America where weapons supplied by Nicaraguan Communists have been found: Honduras, Costa Rica, El Salvador, Guatemala. Radicals from Panama — to the south — have been trained in Nicaragua. But the Sandinista revolutionary reach extends well beyond their immediate neighbors. In South America and the Carribbean, the Nicaraguan Communists have provided support in the form of military training, safe haven, communications, false documents, safe transit, and sometimes weapons to radicals from the following countries: Colombia, Ecuador, Brazil, Chile, Argentina, Uruguay, and the Dominican Republic. Even that is not all, for there was an old Communist slogan that the Sandinistas have made clear they honor: the road to victory goes through Mexico.

If maps, statistics, and facts aren't persuasive enough, we have the words of the Sandinistas and Soviets themselves. One of the highest-level Sandinista leaders was asked by an American magazine whether their Communist revolution will — and I quote — "be exported to El Salvador, then Guatemala, then Honduras, then Mexico?" He responded, "That is one historical prophecy of Ronald Reagan's that is absolutely true."

The Soviets have been no less candid. A few years ago, then Soviet foreign minister Gromyko noted that Central America was "boiling like a cauldron" and ripe for revolution. In a Moscow meeting in 1983, Soviet chief of staff Marshal Ogarkov declared: "Over two decades ago there was only Cuba in Latin America. Today there are Nicaragua, Grenada, and a serious battle is going on in El Salvador."

But we don't need their quotes; the American forces who liberated Grenada captured thousands of documents that demonstrated Soviet intent to bring Communist revolution home to the Western Hemisphere.

The Nature of the Regime

So, we are clear on the intentions of the Sandinistas and those who back them. Let us be equally clear about the nature of their regime. To begin with, the Sandinistas have revoked the civil liberties of the Nicaraguan people, depriving them of any legal right to speak, to publish, to assemble, or to worship freely. Independent newspapers have been shut down. There is no longer any independent labor movement in Nicaragua or any right to strike. As AFL-CIO leader Lane Kirkland has said, "Nicaragua's headlong rush into the totalitarian camp cannot be denied by anyone who has eyes to see."

Like Communist governments everywhere, the Sandinistas have launched assaults against ethnic and religious groups. The capital's only synagogue was desecrated and firebombed—the entire Jewish community forced to flee Nicaragua. Protestant Bible meetings have been broken up by raids, by mob violence, by machine guns. The Catholic Church has been singled out—priests have been expelled from the country, Catholics beaten in the streets after attending mass. The Catholic primate of Nicaragua, Cardinal Obando y Bravo, has put the matter forthrightly: "We want to state clearly that this government is totalitarian. We are dealing with an enemy of the church." [See also selection 24.]

Evangelical pastor Prudencio Baltodano found out he was on the Sandinista hit list when an army patrol asked his name. "You don't know what we do to the evangelical pastors. We don't believe in God," they told him. Pastor Baltodano was tied to a tree, struck in the forehead with a rifle butt, stabbed in the neck with a bayonet—finally his ears were cut off, and he was left for dead. "See if your God will save you," they mocked. Well, God did have other plans for Pastor Baltodano. He lived to tell the world his story—to tell it, among other places, right here in the White House.

I could go on about this nightmare—the blacklist, the secret prisons, the Sandinista-directed mob violence. But, as if all this brutality at home were not enough, the Sandinistas are transforming their nation into a safe house, a command post, for international terror.

The Sandinistas not only sponsor terror in El Salvador, Costa Rica, Guatemala, and Honduras—terror that led last summer to the murder of four U.S. marines in a cafe in Salvador—they provide a sanctuary for terror. Italy has charged Nicaragua with harboring its worst terrorists, the Red Brigades.

The Sandinistas have been involved themselves in the international drug trade. I know every American parent concerned about the drug problem will be outraged to learn that top Nicaragua government officials are deeply involved in drug trafficking. This picture, secretly taken at a military airfield outside Managua, shows Federico Vaughn, a top aide to one of the nine *comandantes* who rule Nicaragua, loading an aircraft with illegal narcotics, bound for the United States.

No, there seems to be no crime to which the Sandinistas will not stoop—this is an outlaw regime.

If we return for a moment to our map, it becomes clear why having this regime in Central America imperils our vital security interests.

Through this crucial part of the Western Hemisphere passes almost half our foreign trade, more than half our imports of crude oil, and a significant portion of the military supplies we would have to send to the NATO alliance in the event of a crisis. These are the choke points where the sea lanes could be closed.

Central America is strategic to our Western alliance, a fact always understood by foreign enemies. In World War II, only a few German U-boats, operating from bases 4,000 miles away in Germany and occupied Europe, inflicted crippling losses on U.S. shipping right off our southern coast.

Today, Warsaw Pact engineers are building a deep-water port on Nicaragua's Caribbean coast, similar to the naval base in Cuba for Soviet-built submarines. They are also constructing, outside Managua, the largest military airfield in Central America—similar to those in Cuba, from which Russian Bear bombers patrol the U.S. East Coast from Maine to Florida.

The Sandinista History

How did this menace to the peace and security of our Latin neighbors—and ultimately ourselves—suddenly emerge? Let me give you a brief history. In 1979, the people of Nicaragua rose up and overthrew a corrupt dictatorship. At first the revolutionary leaders promised free elections and respect for human rights. But among them was an organization called the Sandinistas. Theirs was a Communist organization, and their support of the revolutionary goals was sheer deceit. Quickly and ruthlessly, they took complete control.

Two months after the revolution, the Sandinista leadership met in secret, and, in what came to be known as the "Seventy-two Hour Document" [see appendix C], described themselves as the "vanguard" of a revolution that would sweep Central America, Latin America, and finally the world. Their true enemy, they declared: the United States.

Rather than make this document public, they followed the advice of Fidel Castro, who told them to put on a façade of democracy. While Castro viewed the democratic elements in Nicaragua with contempt, he urged his Nicaraguan friends to keep some of them in their coalition — in minor posts — as window dressing to deceive the West. That way, Castro said, you can have your revolution and the Americans will pay for it.

And we did pay for it. More aid flowed to Nicaragua from the United States in the first eighteen months under the Sandinistas than from any other country. Only when the mask fell, and the face of totalitarianism became visible to the world, did the aid stop.

Confronted with this emerging threat, early in our administration I went to Congress and, with bipartisan support, managed to get help for the nations surrounding Nicaragua. Some of you may remember the inspiring scene when the people of El Salvador braved the threats and gunfire of Communist guerrillas — guerrillas directed and supplied from Nicaragua — and went to the polls to vote decisively for democracy. For the Communists in El Salvador it was a humiliating defeat.

A Second Chance for Nicaragua

But there was another factor the Communists never counted on, a factor that now promises to give freedom a second chance — the freedom fighters of Nicaragua.

You see, when the Sandinistas betrayed the revolution, many who had fought the old Somoza dictatorship literally took to the hills and, like the French Resistance that fought the Nazis, began fighting the Soviet-bloc Communists and the Nicaraguan collaborators. These few have now been joined in the struggle by thousands of other Nicaraguans.

With their blood and courage, the freedom fighters of Nicaragua have pinned down the Sandinista army and bought the people of Central America precious time. We Americans owe them a debt of gratitude. In helping to thwart the Sandinistas and their Soviet mentors, the resistance has contributed directly to the security of the United States.

Since its inception in 1982, the democratic resistance has grown dramatically in strength. Today it numbers more than 20,000 volunteers, and more come every day. But now the freedom fighters' supplies are running short, and they are virtually defenseless against the helicopter gunships Moscow has sent to Managua.

Now comes the crucial test for the Congress of the United States. Will they provide the assistance the freedom fighters need to deal with Russian tanks and gunships—or will they abandon the democratic resistance to its Communist enemy?

What the Fight Is Against

In answering this question, I hope Congress will reflect deeply upon what it is the resistance is fighting against in Nicaragua.

Ask yourselves, what in the world are Soviets, East Germans, Bulgarians, North Koreans, Cubans, and terrorists from the PLO and the Red Brigades doing in our hemisphere, camped on our own doorstep? Is that for peace?

Why have the Soviets invested $800 million to build Nicaragua an armed force almost the size of Mexico's, a country fifteen times as large and twenty-five times as populous? Is that for peace?

Why did Nicaragua's dictator, Daniel Ortega, go to the Communist Party Congress in Havana and endorse Castro's cause for the worldwide triumph of Communism? Was that for peace?

Some members of Congress asked me, Why not negotiate? Good question—let me answer it directly. We have sought—and still seek—a negotiated peace and a democratic future in a free Nicaragua. Ten times we have met and tried to reason with the Sandinistas. Ten times we were rebuffed. Last year, we endorsed church-mediated negotiations between the regime and the resistance. The Soviets and the Sandinistas responded with a rapid arms buildup of mortars, tanks, artillery, and helicopter gunships.

Clearly, the Soviet Union and the Warsaw Pact have grasped the great stakes involved, the strategic importance of Nicaragua. The Soviets have made their decision—to support the Communists. Fidel Castro has made his decision—to support the Communists. Arafat, Qaddafi, and the Ayatollah have made their decision—to support the Communists. Now, we must make our decision. With Congress's help, we can prevent an outcome deeply injurious to the national security of the United States.

If we fail, there will be no evading responsibility. History will hold us accountable.

This is not some narrow partisan issue; it is a national security issue, an issue on which we must act not as Republicans, not as Democrats, but as Americans.

Forty years ago, Republicans and Democrats joined together behind the Truman Doctrine. It must be our policy, Harry Truman declared, to support peoples struggling to preserve their freedom. Under that doctrine, Congress sent aid to Greece just in time to save that country from the closing grip of a Communist tyranny. We saved freedom in Greece then—and with that same bipartisan spirit we can save freedom in Nicaragua today.

Over the coming days, I will continue the dialogue with members of Congress, talking to them, listening to them, hearing out their concerns. Senator Scoop Jackson, who led the fight on Capitol Hill for an awareness of the danger in Central America, said it best: On matters of national security, the best politics is no politics.

History's Single Sentence

You know, recently one of our most distinguished Americans, Clare Boothe Luce, had this to say about the coming vote.

"In considering this crisis," Mrs. Luce said, "my mind goes back to a similar moment in our history—back to the first years after Cuba had fallen to Fidel. One day during those years, I had lunch at the White House with a man I had known since he was a boy—John F. Kennedy. 'Mr. President,' I said, 'no matter how exalted or great a man may be, history will have time to give him no more than one sentence. George Washington—he founded our country. Abraham Lincoln—he freed the slaves and preserved the union. Winston Churchill—he saved Europe.'

" 'And what, Clare,' John Kennedy said, 'do you believe my sentence will be?'

" 'Mr. President,' she answered, 'your sentence will be that you stopped the Communists—or that you did not.' "

Tragically, John Kennedy never had the chance to decide which that would be. Now, leaders of our own time must do so. My fellow Americans, you know where I stand. The Soviets and the Sandinistas must not be permitted to crush freedom in Central America and threaten our own security on our own doorstep.

Now the Congress must decide where it stands. Mrs. Luce ended by saying: "Only this is certain. Through all time to come, this, the 99th Congress of the United States, will be remembered as that body of men and women that either stopped the Communists before it was too late—or did not."

So tonight I ask you to do what you have done so often in the past. Get in touch with your representatives and senators and urge them to vote yes. Tell them to help the freedom fighters—help us prevent a Communist takeover of Central America.

I have only three years left to serve my country, three years to carry out the responsibilities you have entrusted to me, three years to work for peace. Could there be any greater tragedy than for us to sit back and permit this cancer to spread, leaving my successor to face far more agonizing decisions in the years ahead? The freedom fighters seek a political solution. They are willing to lay down their arms and negotiate to restore the original goals of the revolution. A democracy in which the people of Nicaragua choose their own government, that is our goal also, but it can come only if the democratic resistance is able to bring pressure to bear on those who have seized power.

We still have time to do what must be done so history will say of us, We had the vision, the courage, and the good sense to come together and act—Republicans and Democrats—when the price was not high and the risks were not great. We left America safe, we left America secure, we left America free, still a beacon of hope to mankind, still a light unto the nations.

Thank you, and God bless you.

2. The Global Peoples' Revolution

By FIDEL CASTRO

Focus "U.S. imperialism, especially the Reagan administration, is entirely responsible for the worsening of the international situation," says Fidel Castro in this address to the Third Congress of the Cuban Communist Party in February 1986. He speaks of the Communist Party of the Soviet Union as "our closest friend and our best political ally." The Soviet Union "has initiated a kind of economic relations with Cuba that might be considered the New International Economic Order to which we of the world's underdeveloped countries aspire."

The Cuban president sees the current situation in Central America as symptomatic of a new predicament for the United States. In the past five years "the imperialist plans to govern our America through genocidal military tyrannies went into a crisis." In Castro's view, the return to democracy in Argentina, Uruguay, Brazil, Guatemala, and elsewhere represents a rejection of U.S.-sponsored tyrannies.

In El Salvador, says Castro, a proud band of rebels has shown the limits of U.S. power despite the "crude and brutal" Latin American policy President Reagan revealed in Grenada. U.S. support for Britain in the Malvinas conflict "confirmed that the imperialists are capable of trampling the feelings of an entire continent as often as their interests require," he says, though he previously cited the Argentina junta as one of the "genocidal tyrannies" working the will of the United States.

In Nicaragua, "the firm and brave Sandinista decision of not retreating has made it clearly evident that what happened in Cuba is not exceptional." Throughout Latin America the rising resistance to foreign domination and the refusal to be satellites of the United States signify a maturing revolutionary spirit.

Castro speaks positively of "the theology of liberation" and says that Christians who see the value of socialism both are vital to building socialism and cannot achieve their own liberation without it.

As a way out of the Latin debt crisis, Castro counsels a unified refusal to pay. The creditor states, he says, should assume the debt burden contracted by Latin governments and amortize it by cutting their military spending 12 per cent.

This speech stands in stark contrast to the theses of the Kissinger Commission (selection 3) and Alberto R. Coll (selection 4).

Fidel Castro has ruled Cuba since his takeover of the island in 1959.

Durinc the years we are analyzing [1980–85], the international situation has been one of the most tense and complex of the post-war period. It has been characterized by a growing threat to world peace and by the growing danger of a nuclear war in the midst of one of the worst economic crises of the capitalist system, which mercilessly unloaded on the Third World nations the catastrophic consequences of this crisis.

U.S. imperialism, especially the Reagan administration, is entirely responsible for the worsening of the international situation. In our report to the Second Congress, a few days before President Reagan initiated his first term in office, we warned that we had to be prepared to face the serious difficulties the world would face. We based our opinion on the policy that the new U.S. administration had proclaimed. This administration's program was flooded with a fascist foreign policy based on chauvinistic and militarist concepts. It included the manipulation of U.S. public opinion and stirring up the ghost of an alleged Soviet threat.

This would be used as a premise to back the security theory of military supremacy as the only guarantee for defending what they call U.S. interests. This policy was necessarily accompanied by the reaffirmation of the global role the United States has adopted, in open alliance with reactionaries and counter-revolutionaries everywhere.

The Reagan administration's foreign policy was complemented domestically by measures that give privileges to the richer sectors of U.S. society, and that have resulted in cuts in the budgets for U.S. health, education, and social assistance, cuts that negatively affected lower-income groups, including the elderly people, the unemployed, and broad sectors of blacks and Latin Americans.

This domestic policy was accompanied by a decapitalization of the economies of Third World countries by means of a brutal increase in interest rates—and all this to obtain a huge increase in military expenditures and to

---

Excerpt (the final fifth) from an address to the Third Congress of the Communist Party of Cuba, February 4, 1986, as recorded and translated by the U.S. Foreign Broadcast Information Service. Bracketed interpolations in italics are from the FBIS text; others are by the editors.

pay for rearmament without having to impose new taxes, while promising that there would be a well-balanced budget.

Reagan and his aides thought that while military expenditures would serve to reactivate the flat U.S. economy, they would also simultaneously secure the objective of imposing on the Soviet Union and the other socialist countries unsustainable tension on their economic, scientific, and technological resources, and that this would delay the advances of socialism.

The U.S. administration exerted pressure on its European, NATO, and Japanese allies to have them implement this policy. This is how new and increasingly more costly arms buildup projects began. The U.S. government began installing 572 medium-range missiles in Europe aimed at the Soviet Union. All this recently culminated with the proclamation of the so-called Star Wars.

In the face of a growing and powerful pro-peace movement that comprises the most dissimilar forces—which initially included workers and student groups in Europe as well as important U.S. sectors—the march toward a nuclear confrontation went on. Only in recent months have signs appeared, still weak, of the possibility of a return to détente.

The sinister path of U.S. foreign policy has been importantly obstructed by the unflinching position in favor of peace of the Soviet Union and the socialist countries, by the firm opposition of the progressive masses of Europe and elsewhere, and by the firm resistance put up by all the revolutionary movements and countries and the Third World to the positions of force and blackmail adopted by the United States during these years.

The clear, brave, and flexible proposals that the CPSU [Communist Party of the Soviet Union] leadership has repeatedly presented to safeguard peace and to stop the arms race have taken the initiative from the United States and its aggressive policy; this forced Reagan, who had declared his decision not to negotiate with the Soviet Union, to accept the Geneva meeting and to talk for many hours—extensively, beyond the official meetings held by the representatives of the two countries—with the head of the Soviet delegation, Comrade Mikhail Gorbachev. [*Applause.*] No solution came out of Geneva, but hopes did arise for a change that could lead to an increase in communication, and this, to serious steps toward détente and peace.

The fact that those who once based their policy on a search for military supremacy have now said that this supremacy cannot be secured, and that such a search is senseless, and the fact that those who one day proclaimed that there was the possibility to win an atomic war are now admitting that this is impossible and that therefore there should be no nuclear war – these facts are an indication that there have been slight changes.

The Gorbachev Proposal

On 15 January, Comrade Gorbachev, responsibly sustaining the line and position he held in Geneva, proposed a program of action for the remainder of this century to secure the total elimination of nuclear weapons in the world. Not since the emergence of these fearsome weapons of massive destruction, which have become a terrible nightmare for mankind, had there been a proposal so categoric, firm, and specific to eliminate those weapons.

The same type of proposal has been made regarding chemical weapons. The principle of on-site inspections has been accepted. All the pretexts imperialism has presented in the past in this regard have been refuted. This program has been received with satisfaction everywhere.

The U.S. President himself has not been able to prevent the acknowledgment of what his spokesmen have called positive aspects of that proposal. Reagan's policies have not only endangered world peace and threatened mankind as a whole, but in the unfolding of Reagan's hegemonistic goals and of his function as an imperialist gendarme, he has aggravated the world situation, especially in areas that are potential and dangerous foci of tension.

In some cases, such as in Central America, Angola, South Africa, and other countries, the imperialist aggression has increased since Geneva.

Return to the Big Stick

One dramatic example of the return to the Big Stick Policy, proclaimed by Theodore Roosevelt almost a century ago and now being implemented by Reagan at the world level, is the unscrupulous and brutal occupation of Grenada, a tiny Caribbean island of approximately 400 square km and 120,000 people that is thousands of kilometers from the United States. The U.S. government sent a powerful military force against the government of that country, thus exercising its self-appointed international gendarme function.

It is true that, unfortunately, the errors of the revolutionaries of Grenada made it easier for imperialism to accomplish its filthy task. However, this does not make the U.S. government's crime against international law and the rights of the people less serious, and it does not diminish the meaning of the death of the unforgettable founder of that fatherland, our Comrade Maurice Bishop, of his *compañeros* [comrades] who died with him, and of the Cuban internationalist workers who were compelled by the brutal occupation forces to defend their honor and lives in an unequal battle for which they were not prepared. This was a lesson for us.

But Grenada was hardly an expression of the crude and brutal policy of President Reagan for Latin America. Reagan dumped billions of dollars in arms, military assistance, and economic aid on El Salvador, a small and underdeveloped Central American country whose people for decades endured the most brutal and corrupt despotism and whose pro-Yankee and Yankee-made regimes have tortured, made disappear, and murdered tens of thousands of citizens. He put this in the hands of genocidal people who want to uproot the revolution and to impose at all costs a military solution on the conflict. This is being done, as it happened in Santo Domingo, Guatemala, Vietnam, and other places, while invoking the defense of democracy in the world and the security of the United States.

The admirable resistance that the Salvadoran revolutionaries have presented, and the ability with which they have been able to adapt themselves to the war conditions imposed by the flood of sophisticated military technology and by the advice given by the best U.S. experts, have sent down the drain the imperialist dreams of smashing rebelliousness [*rebeldía*] in that country. The Salvadorans have given the imperialists an example of the heroism, intelligence, and capabilities for the struggle of the Latin American people, whom they have always considered a strange and scornful mixture of arrogant blacks, people who in El Salvador — one of the smallest countries on this continent — are now showing the empire what its limits of might and power are. [*Applause.*]

The U.S.–Nicaragua Conflict

Nicaragua, and its young Sandinista revolution, however, were meant to endure the most visible and sinister evidence of the return to the days of the imperialist stick and carrot. The current U.S. administration wants to materialize its aggressive and reactionary ideology by destroying the Sandinista revolution, forcing it to capitulate and to accept U.S. conditions. With this, the U.S. administration wants to teach a lesson and issue a warning to the entire continent.

Nicaragua is enduring a war financed, directed, and implemented by the

Pentagon and the CIA by means of a mercenary army that has bases in Honduras and Costa Rica. However, no one can make history march backward. The firm and brave Sandinista decision of not retreating has made it clearly evident that what happened in Cuba is not exceptional, that no power—regardless of how powerful it might be—can impose its arbitrary will on a nation willing to resist.

After years of heroic struggle to maintain its identity and to respect the will of the people, Nicaragua is there, unbeatable, and exhibiting important achievements, such as the agrarian reform, and great progress in the educational and health services in spite of the bleeding and destruction it is enduring, a bleeding that already amounts to more than 12,000 dead and a destruction that amounts to more than $1 billion in property damage. The U.S. equivalent to the Nicaraguan death toll resulting from Reagan's dirty war would be 900,000 dead; the property losses would be unbearable.

Enduring the economic burden that the war imposes, and mourning its dead daily, but firmly maintaining its plan for a new independent, democratic, non-aligned, and pluralistic Nicaragua, the Sandinista revolution stands. [*Applause.*]

U.S. Failures in Latin America

The Yankee incapacity to impose its policy in Central America by force is symptomatic of a more important predicament. In the past five years, the period we are analyzing, the imperialist plan to govern our America through genocidal military tyrannies went into a crisis. The crumbling of the Argentine military junta and the victory of Alfonsin; the return of Uruguay to democratic life after many years of bloodshed; the democratic opening of a country as important as Brazil; the arrival in power of a civilian government in Guatemala, where the represssion of the military regimes installed by the CIA in 1954 has produced a toll of more than 80,000 either missing, tortured, or dead among a valiant people, and a revolutionary movement that has unselfishly struggled and resisted for years and is now hoisting the banner of a negotiated political solution for its country—these as well as other evident changes in the continent have left Pinochet, Stroessner, and Duvalier as the solitary representatives of a sinister imperialist scheme whose fate is to disappear.

The formation of the so-called Contadora Group, where Mexico has played an outstanding and positive role, is part of this framework because in spite of its weaknesses and instability and of the tendency of some of its members to make concessions to Washington, Contadora is an expression of Latin America's growing will to demand respect for its countries' sovereignty, to resolve its problems by peaceful means without intervention or demands from the United States, and to safeguard the right of the people to have whatever social and political system they view as suitable. The support for that effort by the Support Group—made up of Uruguay, Argentina, Brazil, and Peru—strengthens its Latin American spirit.

Since the beginning, Cuba has expressed solidarity and unrestricted support for the Sandinista revolution and for its young teachers, doctors, construction workers, and technicians in general. We do not conceal this. The military and security advisors have been a modest expression of our solidarity.

Cuba has also played a role in the search for a negotiated solution to the Central American conflict, which must also involve a U.S. commitment to give up its aggressive actions against the Nicaraguan people. To demand that Nicaragua assume commitments, without complying with this prerequisite first, is equivalent to requesting a negotiated surrender of the Sandinista revolution and renunciation of the country's sovereignty and independence. In addition, we must not forget the need to seek negotiated political solutions to the wars in El Salvador and Guatemala.

The Malvinas incident confirmed that the imperialists are capable of trampling the feelings of an entire continent as often as their interests require. They are even capable of insulting the integrity of Latin America rather than contradict their NATO allies. That was an unforgettable lesson for the gullible. Only a few days before the war, relations between the United States and Argentine military intelligence, at the service of the CIA, trained the first Somozist groups in Honduras that would soon attack Nicaragua. The Yankees preferred the Gurkha mercenaries of the British Army over those mercenaries.

The unified Latin American and Caribbean conscience is making some progress. SELA [Latin American Economic System], in which Cuba has participated since its inception despite existing differences, is evidence of this. The recent declaration in Caracas and the previous one in Quito express this common spirit.

Most current governments in Latin America that refuse to accept Washington's demands do not advocate the disappearance of imperialism, much less question the capitalist system. Some advocate structural changes; others do not. The economic reform on which they are willing to embark varies in degree; in some cases, it is minimal.

This involves resistance against foreign domination—the repugnance that any self-respecting government feels toward being used as a satellite. The objective contradictions between the economic interests of the empire and of our peoples are increasingly more evident. This reinforces the necessary historical inclination of Latin America toward its development and final liberation, which is an indispensable preamble for the most profound transformations required by our region.

The Non-Marxist Role in Liberation

In this Latin American position, even non-Marxist currents, such as the Social Democrats, can play a certain positive role. In the face of the most negative aspects of U.S. policy, the European Social Democrats allow themselves to assume more progressive positions. The European Christian Democrats do not show the same trend, however, and it would be wrong not to note that among Christian Democratic and Christian Socialist forces in Latin America, we can find progressive elements, and it would be neither correct nor valid to describe all Christian Democratic governments that might emerge in the area as necessarily negative forces. Not all are constantly called to play the ominous role of the Christian Democratic government of Duarte in El Salvador.

In addition to the Christian Democrats there are the Christians who are not necessarily Christian Democrats, those who are represented in Latin America by a mass of hundreds of millions, most of them laborers, peasants, and middle-class members who will not be able to liberate themselves unless they build socialism. In turn, socialism cannot be built without their support.

The theology of liberation has emerged as an important force in Latin America. We value it as a sincere experience committed to the poor and involving those who in this way express their authentic Christianity. However, we also value its potential political significance as the expression of the will of many Christians—based on their own religious convictions—to build a world in which fraternity, equality, and justice prevail among all men.

In the struggle for the independence of Latin America, the military officers should not be forgotten. Although the prestige of the men in uniform was shamefully tarnished in many of the countries in the hemisphere, in others, such as Peru during the times of Velasco Alvarado and in Panama—to which we must add many personal cases in various corners of our America—these military men showed the patriotic, popular attitude that many officers can adopt and claimed the right not to be excluded in this struggle for the second and final liberation of our peoples.

Third World Debt: The Problem

The nations of the Caribbean are also struggling under the effects of the capitalist crisis. The U.S. protectionist measures and the constant drop in the price of their main exports has prompted social unrest with a painful toll of victims in countries such as the Dominican Republic, Jamaica, and Haiti. The much publicized Caribbean Basin Initiative has only served as a mechanism to consolidate U.S. military, political, and economic control in this region without doing anything to solve its abysmal crisis. The Caribbean countries experiencing difficulties include Puerto Rico, the sister Latin American nation that is still moaning under the Yankee colonial boot.

The crisis that has shaken the economies of Latin America and the Caribbean has made the region regress to the levels of the per capita product existing in 1977. Between 1980 and 1985 the growth rate of the Latin American economies was a meager 0.5 per cent per year, which in per capita terms represented a 2.4 per cent drop. The inflation rate increased 5.9 times. The foreign debt of Latin America and the Caribbean reached $368 billion in 1975. In that year alone, Latin American countries turned over $35 million to foreign capitalists in interest and profits. In the three years they transferred $106 billion in cash in interest and profits.

Latin America and the Caribbean are now the regions with the highest debt in the world. The magnitude and seriousness of this problem has been thoroughly discussed in our country, the site of the meeting of personalities and the meetings of labor leaders, women, youths, and intellectuals. The underdevelopment and poverty these nations received as a legacy from colonialism and neocolonialism—and the historical plundering they were victims of when they financed the development of the capitalist world with centuries of blood and sweat—have been joined, in the past decades, by the increasingly abusive unequal exchange, the protectionist measures, the dumping [*preceding word in English*], the flight of capital to the centers of economic power, and the monetary and financial manipulations that are within the origins of the debt and that paved the way for the current economic and social catastrophe afflicting these countries.

The increase in interest rates implemented by the government of Reagan, who even ignored the protests of his Western allies, whom he engulfed in recessions with that action, made the problem worse and converted the foreign debt into an insurmountable obstacle not only for development, but for maintaining the minimum levels of survival that had been reached.

Third World Debt: The Solution

When we announced that the debt could not be paid, we were using as a basis calculations and arguments that cannot be refuted. On the contrary, the debt becomes more unpayable with each day and each hour that passes. The most recent drops in the price of oil, as brutal as its rise has been since late in 1974, must completely persuade even those oil-exporting countries in our hemisphere that one day dreamed such a giant debt was payable. We are sure that debtors and creditors alike will sooner or later reach the conviction that it is absolutely impossible to pay the debt. I hope that it will be through a dialogue and not through catastrophic crises that these debts will receive their death certifications and be buried once and for all.

If one tried to apply the inhuman IMF [International Monetary Fund] formulas for paying debt, no one could predict the magnitude of the social unrest and the consequences that would result from it, still without this impossible goal even being reached. The formula proposed by Cuba is simple, understandable, and perfectly applicable: Let the states of the creditor developed countries assume the Third World countries' debt with their own banks. Cuba proposes that 12 per cent of what is invested in military expenditures be used for amortization of the debt. We do not propose a break for the international financial system, or that depositors in capitalist industrialized countries lose money, or that taxpayers must pay more taxes.

To this we add that simple annulment of the debt would not solve the profound economic crisis in the Third World countries. There is a need to apply the principles of the New International Economic Order approved by the United Nations to put an end to unequal exchange, protectionism, the dumping [*preceding word in English*], the usurious interest, and the monetary and financial manipulations by a few developed capitalist powers. We propose the practicing of economic solidarity, without any conditions, with the poorest countries and those with the greatest economic backwardness.

We have insisted that a correct solution to the foreign debt problem and a New International Order would increase the purchasing power of the Third World, which has many needs. It would also put to work at full capacity a large part of the factories of the developed capitalist world, which has many unemployed.

As for the development and future of Latin America, we say that an annulment of the debt and a New International Economic Order are not enough; economic integration is indispensable if we want to have a place in the world in the twenty-first century. To those who shed crocodile tears for the financial resources of developed capitalist countries, it suffices to remind them that, with price reductions of petroleum last year, those countries will save no less than $80 billion in 1986, which is enough to service the interest of the Third World's foreign debt for an entire year.

As we might surmise, the economic crisis and the enormous, unpayable foreign debt have contributed to the historic convergence of the peoples of Latin America and the Caribbean.

U.S. Policy in Africa

The United States has tried to impose its policy of force in Africa, the Middle East, and Asia, and it is failing in those attempts. In the African southern cone, it offered its decisive support to the ignominious South African regime. At the same time, the United States has tried to promote agreements between South African racists and the People's Republic of Angola to force the latter to accept the withdrawal of Cuban forces. All of this is accompanied with a disregard for and distortion of U.N. Resolution No. 435, which aims to guarantee Namibia's independence. Instead of an independent Namibia, for which its people have fought for long years under the direction of SWAPO [South-West Africa People's Organization], Washington is trying to ensure that Namibia will become an appropriate site for South African and U.S. neocolonial exploitation.

To complement this policy, the United States has promoted an understanding between the MPLA [Popular Movement for the Liberation of Angola] and Jonas Savimbi, a traitor to Africa linked to racist South Africa. A few days ago, Reagan welcomed this mercenary with honors befitting a head of state. His forces have attacked and torched entire villages, murdered defenseless people, and killed thousands of civilians without differentiating among men, women, the elderly, and children. That is the prototype for freedom fighters with which the U.S. President associates himself in Nicaragua and Angola.

This Reagan attitude has encouraged South Africa to maintain an aggressive policy toward Angola; to continue to support the counter-revolutionary bandits of Renamo [the Mozambique National Resistance Movement], despite its hypocritical Nkomati accord with the People's Republic of Mozambique; to attack Lesotho and Bostwana; and to threaten Zimbabwe and Zambia.

Angola, which today, 4 February – the day in which this congress begins – marks the twenty-fifth anniversary of the beginning of its courageous struggle against Portuguese colonialism [*applause*] – Angola has maintained its position based on firm principles, has strengthened and developed its armed forces, and has decisively faced the military escalation. During that period, Cuba has increased its support to that brother country.

However, a negotiated solution is possible. The known phase of the Cuban-Angolan joint declaration of May 1984 for the independence of Namibia, based on the application of U.N. Resolution No. 435, and previous attempts to normalize the situation in southern Angola, have full validity today.

The old attempt to link Namibia's independence with the withdrawal of the Cuban internationalist contingent has faced a decisive rejection from the international community at the United Nations, the OAU [Organization of African Unity], and the Non-Aligned Movement. The independence of Namibia, an end to aggressions against Angola, and an end to aid to UNITA [National Union for the Total Independence of Angola] would make feasible the gradual withdrawal of part of those forces, as Angola and Cuba have proposed. However, whether the remaining forces continue in Angola, and the circumstances and the date when all of them should be withdrawn, is the exclusive prerogative of the peoples of Angola and Cuba. [*Applause.*]

South Africa today faces an irreversible crisis of apartheid and of its own system of domination. The growing work of the ANC [African National Congress] and the increasing rebellion of the masses, which met with the most brutal racist repression and received enormous solidarity in the world, are a reflection of the current situation. We have no doubt that the historic result of this multiple battle will be reaffirmation of the independence and revolution in Angola, the independence of Namibia, and the disappearance of the intolerable system of apartheid. [*Applause.*]

Reagan's policy has gone further. Its unconditional support for Morocco has served to break the process for resolution of the conflict in the western Sahara that was proposed and approved by the OAU. His threats against Libya and the blockade established because of that country's anti-imperialist position create permanent insecurity in the Mediterranean and northern Africa.

U.S. Policy in the Middle East

A little farther beyond, in the Middle East, the desire to make Israel — which Reagan has declared a strategic U.S. ally — prevail in that region has led to making the situation in Lebanon more tense and more difficult, instead of finding a solution to that country's dramatic problems. Reagan's failure was made evident with the rapid withdrawal the U.S. Marines were forced to carry out and the subsequent withdrawal of his Israeli allies.

The complex problems of the Middle East have been aggravated by the differences among the Arab countries, countries that have always had our firm friendship and solidarity. The Palestinians, who through the PLO have had almost universal support, have become dramatically divided and continued to be so. Cuba, like other countries, did everything within its modest capabilities to restore that unity, but without achieving that objective. However, this will not detract from our solidarity with the Palestinian people's struggle for their legitimate and unrenounceable rights.

We have also worked and will continue to work for the unity of the Arab world as an essential part of the progressive forces of the Non-Aligned Movement in the international community. We view our support for the Saharan Democratic Arab Republic and the Polisario Front as a matter of principle in the same way we reject with indignation the policy of blackmail and threats against Libya. [*Applause.*] Ethiopia, its great people, and its great leader, *Compañero* Mengistu Haile Mariam, will also always have our full support. [*Applause.*] Africa in general will continue to have the permanent solidarity of the Cuban revolution.

U.S. Policy in Asia

A rapid review of Asia shows noticeable signs of the ill-fated character of U.S. foreign policy. Were it not been for the political, logistical, and financial U.S. support for the Afghan counter-revolutionary bands, it would have been easier to achieve the political solution advocated by the United Nations, which has been accepted in principle by Afghanistan and Pakistan with the support of the Soviet Union. In a country where 235 out of every 1,000 children born alive died in the first year of life, where 80 per cent of the population was illiterate and 70 per cent of the land was in the hands of only 2,000 families, nothing was more logical, necessary, and just than a revolution. Nevertheless, the U.S. government has invested billions of dollars to try to crush the revolution; but it has not been successful. It is time for imperialist interference in the internal affairs of the Afghan people to stop and for the right of the Afghan people to build a future and live in peace to be respected. [*Applause.*]

India has denounced the manipulations aimed at destabilizing and dividing that country through inflammation of the separatist tendencies, community clashes, and the use of terror. That extreme climate of tension had a tragic culmination with the assassination of our dear and highly esteemed friend, Indira Gandhi. [*Applause.*] Death deprived India of a great stateswoman who deeply understood the problems that, alongside her father, she had learned to handle. She was humane and sensitive, but at the same time firm. All of mankind felt as its own this loss, which we Cubans also felt. The wise and sure action of Rajiv Gandhi, who has continued the family tradition and shown his maturity and own determination, has confirmed that the enemies of India will not be able to impose their designs there.

The U.S. aggressive and war-mongering strategy also acts in Japan for the purpose of strengthening the U.S. military presence in the Pacific and Indian oceans and of taking beyond the Japanese coasts, to which they are limited, the defense forces of that country.

The provocations on the Korean peninsula continue. Seoul was chosen as host for the forthcoming Olympic Games without taking into consideration at all the other part of the country, thus ignoring—undoubtedly as a result of U.S. influence, pressure, and maneuvers—that the nation is cruelly and artificially divided, that not long ago there was a bloody war as a result of which hundreds of thousands of people from various nations died, that South Korea is a Yankee military base, and that that puppet state is ruled by one of the most horrible and repressive regimes in the world.

Cuba supports North-South talks aimed at sharing the Olympic Games. This is the only honorable way out of the situation that has been created. Without that honorable way out, our country cannot possibly participate in those games. [*Applause.*]

The process of dialogue in Southeast Asia between the Indochinese countries and those of ASEAN [Association of Southeast Asian Nations] is shamelessly being obstructed, and Cambodian counter-revolutionaries are being encouraged. Meanwhile, the efforts to isolate Vietnam have continued, but this policy has not succeeded. The dialogue between ASEAN and Indochina continues. Vietnam is consolidating and strengthening its relations with the socialist society and the rest of the world. In Cambodia, there is a process of national rebirth.

Meanwhile, the anti-nuclear and pacifist movement has gained strength in the region and has extended to South Korea, Australia, and New Zealand, a country that has been implementing an anti-nuclear policy that provoked a crisis in ANZUS [the Australia–New Zealand–U.S. treaty].

In the entire Asian continent, the positive position China has been adopting in recent times regarding important international matters has not failed to produce an impact because of the undeniable weight China has in the complex development of situations in the world. Its orientation toward world peace and its commitment, as a nuclear power, not to be the first to use nuclear weapons, its rejection of Reagan's war-of-the-galaxies plan, its support for the demands of the underdeveloped countries in the framework of its international economic relations, and its correct policy for the problems of Central America are part of this position.

Meanwhile, China and the Soviet Union are exchanging delegations and improving their relations. China supports the idea that the Seoul Olympic Games be shared. These are positive facts that we must cheer. The militants of our party know, however, that along with our adequate state relations with China, there are still Chinese Communist Party positions on vital foreign policy with which we do not agree and with which we cannot agree, including its hostility and its actions of force against Vietnam, a country that in its heroic struggle against imperialism spilled its blood for the independence of all Third World countries. [*Applause.*] We hope that some day this animosity will disappear, because it is a shadow and an obstacle for a sincere improvement of relations between Cuba and China.

If to the resistance that the Reagan policy has found and will continue to find in these three continents, we add the reluctance and the lack of enthusiasm with which Reagan's own allies back it, the unreal and anachronistic nature of that policy becomes evident. On the other hand, the catastrophic commercial deficit of the United States in 1985 amounted to the record figure of $148.5 billion. Reagan's promises about a reduction in the budget deficit, which in 1985 was more than $200 billion, were not kept. As a whole, the country spent more than $350 billion that had not been produced in a year. This is something that not even the lucky owners of Aladdin's lamp could have dreamed of.

Cuba and the Non-Aligned Movement

At the beginning of the five-year period, Cuba headed the Non-Aligned Movement, a task that was not easy at a moment as complex as the one that existed. The Cuban efforts to stop the war between Iran and Iraq have been acknowledged. That war has always appeared to us as absurd and of tragic consequences not only for both countries but also for our movement.

We cooperated alongside the non-aligned countries in the struggle to fight the Israeli aggression against Lebanon and to demand respect for the rights of the Palestinian people, victims of brutal massacres such as those at Sabra and Shatila. The movement was present in Central America and in the Malvinas war. At the United Nations, the condemnation of South Africa was due, to a great extent, to the action of the non-aligned countries. The economic problems of the Third World and the struggle for a New International Economic Order were given attention continuously.

Cuba also has decidedly contributed to maintaining the unity of the movement and to promoting an acceptable solution regarding the host country for the seventh Non-Aligned Movement summit that had to be decided upon because of the continuation of the Iran-Iraq war.

We need no higher praise for Cuba's work during that period than a statement by Indira Gandhi upon taking over the presidency of the movement from Cuba. The Non-Aligned Movement continues to maintain its already known heterogeneous nature. In recent years it has continued to be an active and determining force in world policy. The assassination of Indira Gandhi brought about uncertain moments that Rajiv Gandhi has successfully overcome with sagacity and energy. The ministerial meeting in Luanda displayed the strength and unity of the Non-Aligned Movement. The election of Zimbabwe as host of the next summit not only confirmed the prestige of that country and its young leader, Robert Mugabe, but also showed the importance the non-aligned members give to the situation in southern Africa, the apartheid problem, and the dramatic status of the African economy.

Cuba and the Soviet Union

Our party's activity in international circles during these years, the development and strengthening of our ties with Communist parties of the entire world, especially to the members of the socialist community to which we belong, has played a decisive role. To us, the unity of a Communist movement, with absolute reciprocal respect and independent criteria for each member, is an important factor in the struggle to further socialism and in the implementation of a common strategy of peace and development.

The role of the Communist Party of the Soviet Union in this historical task is well known to us. In its capacity as the first socialist country, due to its enormous economic potential, its undoubted military might, and loyalty to the principles of Marxism-Leninism and proletarian internationalism, the U.S.S.R. is a decisive party of the historic contemporary forces.

The CPSU, leader in the East, is our closest friend and our best political ally. Similarly, each party in this important movement, be it big or small, will always be worthy of our greatest respect and consideration. [*Applause.*] Our party's good relations with the other revolutionary, progressive, and democratic forces throughout the world take place in the framework of the political situation that we described. As for state relations, Cuba currently holds diplomatic ties with 121 states and maintains consular relations with two others. This figure is enough for us to be able to see from another angle the failure of the imperialist policy that tried to politically encircle and isolate the Cuban revolution. Pre-revolutionary Cuba had relations with 51 countries.

In the Cuban state's international activities, relations with the Soviet Union also enjoy priority and special attention. The exemplary nature of these relations demonstrates not only the U.S.S.R.'s continued political support and invaluable supply of military matériel that has permitted the defense of Cuba, but also, as we have stressed more than once, the fact that the Soviet Union initiated a kind of economic relations with Cuba that might be considered the New International Economic Order to which we of the world's underdeveloped countries aspire. [*Applause.*] The long-term program for the development of the economic and scientific-technical cooperation between Cuba and the Soviet Union until the year 2000 confirms this.

Cuba and the Socialist Community

Close cooperation with the other countries of the socialist community, CEMA [Council of Economic Mutual Assistance] members, takes place to a different extent and according to particular circumstances. Along with the Soviet Union, the German Democratic Republic, the People's Republic of Bulgaria, the Czechoslovak Socialist Republic, the Hungarian People's Republic, the Mongolian People's Republic, the Polish People's Republic, the Socialist Republic of Romania, and the Socialist Republic of

Vietnam constitute our most important associates. Our joint participation in CEMA permits us to work in coordination and on a long-term basis. A close friendship and mutual identification with the Democratic People's Republic of Korea, Lao People's Democratic Republic, and the People's Republic of Kampuchea also constitute a part of our socialist relations expressed in our firm friendship and cooperation with the SFRY [Socialist Federal Republic of Yugoslavia]. We hold normal relations with the People's Republic of China, with which we maintain important and positive trade and government relations. Our relations with the Socialist People's Republic of Albania have developed favorably.

More than once we have stressed our historical and racial ties with Africa. We are proud to say the revolution has strengthened these ties. Both Cubans and Africans in Angola and Ethiopia have set an example of combative internationalism. With them and numerous African countries, this internationalism has also been applied in the economic, scientific, and technical fields. Angola, Ethiopia, Mozambique, Tanzania, Zambia, Zimbabwe, Congo, Guinea-Bissau, Cape Verde, Madagascar, Seychelles, Benin, and São Tomé are permanent allies in common battles in which we are now accompanied by Ghana and Burkina-Faso after the positive transformations in these countries.

The Sudanese people, subjected for long years to the bloody oppression of the Numayri regime—a pawn of imperialism and Arab reactionaries—broke the chains of tyranny with their vigorous mass actions in the north and the struggle of their guerrilla army in the south, and, with their heroic fighting, opened a promising revolutionary outlook. We harbor the hope that imperialism will not be able to hamper the process of change.

Our friendship with Arab countries like Algeria, the People's Democratic Republic of Yemen, Libya, Syria, and Iraq is traditional. Ties with Iran were strengthening after the popular revolution that deposed the reactionary shah. We hope the dramatic events in the People's Democratic Republic of Yemen, whose tragic consequences we recently witnessed, will not harm the revolutionary process, the indispensable unity, independence, and peace in this sister country.

Cuba and the Capitalist Community

Our relations with developed capitalist countries have been determined by our policy of normal trade and mutually advantageous cooperation based on mutual respect and the independence of different social systems.

Although we have not succeeded in getting the European Economic Community (EEC) countries to amend regulations that hamper or discriminate against our potential exports and they have not been able to relinquish protectionist policies, subsidies, and dumping [*preceding word in English*] that seriously harm the economy of many Third World countries, neither the EEC nor Japan has accepted the U.S.-advocated policy of establishing a virtual economic and financial blockade against us. This has been shown by the way in which these countries, Cuba's creditors, have dealt with the problem of refinancing our foreign debt. We will continue our efforts to make these relations stable and lasting. This, in addition to a firm economic perspective, includes a political dialogue regarding matters related to bilateral relations of the most important international problems.

It will hardly be necessary to explain—because this springs almost naturally from the U.S. policy all over the world—that the accession of the current U.S. administration to the government brought about an extremely aggressive stance toward Cuba. This stance led the U.S. government to strengthen its economic blockade against our country and make even more efforts than the previous administrations to impede our normal commercial and financial operations. At the same time, new plans for military aggression and subversion against our country were shamelessly announced. Stress was laid on confronting us with the possibility of a true military action and going to the source, as one of their leaders described it, attributing to us with marked arbitrariness all that happened against the U.S. plans of dominance in Latin America, the Caribbean, and other places in the world. With unheard of insolence, the United States has continued to violate Cuban airspace with its SR-71 flights. As we have explained already, the Reagan government's threats and organizational measures have only served to strengthen our country's defensive ability and to turn our homeland into an impregnable bastion. [*Applause.*]

In the middle of the U.S. government's permanently aggressive stance against Cuba, an opportunity arose for the two sides to reach a limited immigration accord, and our policy regarding this country was reasserted on the possibility of reaching reasonable agreements for the two parties, independent of the ideological abyss separating our two governments. Such agreements can be reached if our sovereign equality is respected and the absurd and intolerable interventionist plans that have generally marked U.S. policy toward Cuba for more than twenty-five years of revolution are excluded. During the four months that this immigration accord was in force, we scrupulously did our duty. Nevertheless, suddenly and provocatively, with only a few hours' advance notice, and in an action simultaneously unnecessary and offensive, the U.S. government made the decision to carry out its paranoid plans to initiate subversive medium-wave radio broadcasts against our country [Radio Martí]. Even more, the United States cynically used the name of our national hero [José Martí, nineteenth-century leader of the struggle for Cuban independence].

As we have said many times, Cuba is not reluctant to discuss its lengthy disagreement with the United States and seek peace and better relations between our two peoples. Our party reasserts this once again in this congress. [*Applause.*] We believe this would help to improve our area's political climate and would somehow also influence international policy. This, however, would have to be based on the strictest respect for our situation as a country that does not tolerate any shadows over its independence, for whose dignity and sovereignty entire generations of Cubans struggled and sacrificed themselves. This will be possible only when the United States makes up its mind to negotiate in earnest and is willing to deal with us in a spirit of equity, reciprocity, and the fullest mutual respect.

The times when the empire could do its will in our country are long gone. [*Applause.*] The perseverance, tenacity, and firmness with which we have resisted during these twenty-seven years, our proven loyalty to our principles, the determination with which we have engaged in the task of creating a new world and a just homeland, the confidence and certainty with which we lay the foundations of our future, and the heroism with which we have defended and will defend our revolutionary work, entitle us to the right that no one ignore or underestimate our people. [*Applause.*]

In addition, the links that we have established with the billions of human beings in the world who have common interests with us demonstrate that we are not fighting alone, but that we are a part of a humanity that is determined to prevail in its struggle for survival, peace, freedom, and justice.

Like it or not, the United States will have to put up with a revolutionary Cuba. [*Applause.*] It will have to resign itself to this, and to a changing world. [*Prolonged applause.*]

The Solid Ship of Revolution

Compañero delegates, because we have made the right decisions, and have worked tenaciously throughout these years, our fatherland is stronger, our economy more solid, our experience richer, our party more experienced, and our people more mature, more united, more cultured, more self-confident, and more revolutionary. [*Applause.*]

As we near the thirtieth anniversary of the *Granma* [the yacht that brought Castro and several dozen Cuban exiles from Mexico in 1956 to mount a guerrilla offensive against the dictator Fulgencio Bastista], now that we look back on the road that we have covered—back then, there was not even a light to show us the way to our destination—we are pleased to think that these congresses are lighthouses that point the way to safe ports for the ship of the revolution to pause now and again to renew its commitment to its cause, during its lengthy voyage through the seas of history. [*Prolonged applause, rhythmic clapping to shouts of "Granma!"*]

However, we are no longer a handful of men in a small yacht, better equipped with ideas than with weapons; we are now an immense, solid ship that no wave, no wind, no storm can sink. This time, it is loaded with many dreams that have become reality, and many realities that are dreams still to be realized. An entire people is sailing toward the future, to land in it with the knowledge that even if they are faced with mountains of difficulties and obstacles, and even if a perfidious enemy is waiting to pounce, many 1 Januaries [Bastista fled on January 1, 1959] await them, as a reward for their tenacity, their self-confidence, and their effort. [*Applause.*]

Let us pledge to redouble our efforts and promise ourselves that if some day our work should look good to us, we will strive to make it better, and if it is better, we will strive to make it perfect, with the foreknowledge that, for a Communist, nothing is ever good enough, and no human deed can ever be sufficiently perfect. [*Prolonged applause, shouting.*]

3. *The Crisis and Our Opportunity*

By the KISSINGER COMMISSION

Focus
In July 1983, President Reagan set up a bipartisan commission under the chairmanship of former secretary of state Henry Kissinger to draw up a plan for U.S. policy in Central America. After half a year of research, hearings, and visits to key Central American countries, the six Democratic and six Republican commissioners released a 132-page report in early January 1984.

The report emphasized the threat to the region and to U.S. security posed by Soviet, Cuban, and Nicaraguan support for Marxist insurgents. In response to this threat the commission recommended sharp increases in both development and security assistance. More than $8 billion in economic aid alone would be earmarked for the region over the next five years. At a news conference, Henry Kissinger defended the increases: "If present levels of expenditures are continued, we will fail both in economic and social progress and in the security field. There will be lingering deterioration with very grave consequences."

An Emergency Stabilization Program should be adopted immediately, said the report, as a multifaceted response to the severe economic crisis. Continued pressure should be applied to the Sandinista government of Nicaragua, including U.S. aid to the contras. Concerning the stalemate in El Salvador the commission said: "There might be an argument for doing nothing to help the government of El Salvador. There might be an argument for doing a great deal more. There is, however, no logical argument for giving some aid but not enough.

The worst possible policy for El Salvador is to provide just enough aid to keep the war going, but too little to wage it successfully."

The commission proposed that large increases in military aid to El Salvador be dependent upon continuing reforms in the government, the military, and the judiciary. Dr. Kissinger and two other members of the commission noted, however that this recommendation should not be read as allowing a Marxist-Leninist takeover, which would abolish the human rights of a whole people.

For humanitarian reasons as well as for reasons of U.S. self-interest, concludes the report, we cannot turn away: "Central America's crisis is our crisis."

President Reagan strongly supported the general recommendations of the commission, which in important respects coincide with announced initiatives and objectives of the Reagan administration.

The chairman of the commission, **Henry A. Kissinger,** was secretary of state from 1973 to 1977. Other members were: Nicholas F. Brady, Henry G. Cisneros, William P. Clements, Jr., Carlos F. Díaz-Alejandro, Wilson F. Johnson, Lane Kirkland, Richard M. Scammon, John Silber, Potter Stewart, Robert S. Strauss, and William B. Walsh.

MOST MEMBERS of this commission began with what we now see as an extremely limited understanding of the region, its needs, and its importance. The more we learned, the more convinced we became that the crisis there is real, and acute; that the United States must act to meet it, and act boldly; that the stakes are large, for the United States, for the hemisphere, and, most poignantly, for the people of Central America.

In this report, we propose significant attention and help to a previously neglected area of the hemisphere. Some who have not studied the area as we have may think this disproportionate, dismissing it as the natural reaction of a commission created to deal with a single subject. We think any such judgment would be a grave mistake.

TOWARD DEMOCRACY AND ECONOMIC PROSPERITY

Most past U.S. development programs have been predominantly economic. We argue here that the crisis in Central America cannot be considered in solely economic or political or social or security terms. The actions we recommend represent an attempt to address this complex interrelationship in its totality, not just in its parts.

We envision, in the short term, an emergency stabilization program and, in the medium and long term, a new multilateral regional organization to measure performance across the entire political, social, economic, and security spectrum, and to target external aid resources where they can provide the most significant impetus. In support of these efforts, we urge a five-year commitment by the United States to a substantially increased level of economic assistance.

We recognize that it is unlikely that the social inequities and distortions that have accumulated over the last five centuries will be corrected during the next five years. But the groundwork for recovery should be laid as soon as possible. The costs of not meeting the challenge in Central America would be too great, today and for generations to come.

For their part, other countries are also contributing to Central America's

---

Excerpts from the report of the National Bipartisan Commission on Central America, January 1984.

economic recuperation. Mexico and Venezuela have established a major facility to provide oil on concessional terms.

But the outlook, even under optimistic assumptions, is not very promising. Even if economic stabilization policies are consistently implemented, if official capital flows remain at roughly current levels through the rest of the decade, if private capital flows eventually recover, and if international stability returns, unless more is done the economies of Central America will only gradually begin to recover. Without a significant increase in the levels of foreign assistance, improvement in the ways those resources are managed and used, and the introduction of growth-oriented economic policies, economic activity in the region, measured on a per capita basis, would probably reach no more than three-quarters of the 1980 level by 1990. This would mean more unemployment and continued widespread poverty.

An Emergency Stabilization Program

The commission urges the immediate adoption of an emergency stabilization program combining public and private efforts to halt the deterioration. The program includes eight key elements:

- We urge that the leaders of the United States and the Central American countries meet to initiate a comprehensive approach to the economic development of the region and the reinvigoration of the Central American Common Market.
- We encourage the greatest possible involvement of the private sector in the stabilization effort.
- We recommend that the United States actively address the external debt problems of the region.
- We recommend that the United States provide an immediate increase in bilateral economic assistance.
- We recommend that a major thrust of expanded aid should be in labor-intensive infrastructure and housing projects.
- We recommend that new official trade credit guarantees be made available to the Central American countries.
- We recommend that the United States provide an emergency credit to the Central American Common Market Fund (CACMF).

The Central American countries have asked for a credit to refinance part of the accumulated trade deficits among themselves which have contributed to the contraction of intra-regional trade. The United States should use part of the increased economic aid for this purpose; the Central American countries that have been in surplus would be expected to transform the remainder of the deficits into long-term local currency credits. As the Central American countries have proposed, CACMF regulations should then be adjusted to avoid future buildups of large unsettled balances. Since the debts that would be refinanced under this proposal are among central banks, there should be no adverse implications for other rescheduling efforts.

We recognize that support for Common Market institutions benefits all members of the Common Market, regardless of their political orientation or social and economic performance. There is no way to isolate one or two member countries. However, support for the Common Market would be one of the quickest ways to revive intra-regional trade and economic activity. The Common Market continues to enjoy strong support among Central Americans.

We have concluded that the benefits of an infusion of capital into the CACMF outweigh the disadvantages. However, we are convinced that the Common Market will have to change toward a more open trading posture. This will require a basis reorientation of regional trade and industrial policies.

- We recommend that the United States join the Central American Bank for Economic Integration (CABEI).

The Central American countries are opening membership in CABEI to countries outside the region. We urge the United States to join this institution and to encourage other creditor countries to seek membership. The infusion of new resources would help reinvigorate the bank, which could channel much-needed funds to small-scale entrepreneurs and farmers, provide working capital to existing private-sector companies, and encourage the development of new industries.

U.S. Development Support

We urge a major increase in U.S. and other-country financial and economic assistance for Central America.

Reaching that goal will require a significant effort. External financing needs between now and 1990 have been estimated at as much as $24 billion for the seven countries (Belize, Costa Rica, El Salvador, Guatemala, Honduras, Nicaragua, and Panama) as a group. The World Bank, the International Monetary Fund, the Inter-American Development Bank, other official creditors, private investors, and commercial banks are likely to provide at least half of these funds—especially if each Central American country follows prudent economic policies, if there is steady social and political progress, and if outside aggression is eliminated. The balance, as much as $12 billion, would have to be supplied by the United States.

We now propose that economic assistance over the five-year period beginning in 1985 total $8 billion.

This global figure would include direct appropriations as well as contingent liabilities such as guarantees and insurance. In effect, this would represent a rough doubling of U.S. economic assistance from the 1983 level.

We recognize that such a proposal may be viewed with skepticism. However, we firmly believe that without such large-scale assistance, economic recovery, social progress, and the development of democratic institutions in Central America will be set back.

Ultimately, the effectiveness of increased economic assistance will turn on the economic policies of the Central American countries themselves. We agree with what many experts have told us: that unless these reforms are extended, economic performance will not significantly improve, regardless of the money foreign donors and creditors provide. In too many other countries, increased availability of financial resources has undermined reform by relieving the immediate pressure on policy-makers. This must be avoided in Central America.

What is now required is a firm commitment by the Central American countries to economic policies, including reforms in tax systems, to encourage private enterprise and individual initiative, to create favorable investment climates, to curb corruption where it exists, and to spur balanced trade.

We recommend that the United States expand economic assistance for democratic institutions and leadership training.

Key initiatives which either are already under way or should be developed include:

- The encouragement of neighborhood groups, community improvement organizations, and producer cooperatives which provide a training ground for democratic participation and help make governments more responsive to citizen demands.
- The United States Information Service's binational centers provide valuable insight into the advantages of personal freedoms in the United

States. Significantly expanded funding would allow the centers to expand their library holdings, courses, and programs.

- Exchange and training programs for leaders of democratic institutions. The International Visitors Program of USIA and AFL-CIO's George Meany Institute are both examples of effective programs that bring leaders from Central America, as well as from other regions, to the United States for training programs. Additional programs should be established to bring leaders of such democratic institutions as labor unions, local governments, legislatures, and professional associations to work and study in counterpart U.S. organizations.

Expanded Trade Opportunities

Rapid Central American economic growth requires increased foreign-exchange earnings. In the short run the region will continue to rely largely on the earnings which come from the export of commodities.

The solution to this problem will necessarily be a slow one. Over the medium term, the Central American countries should try to broaden their export bases in both the agricultural and manufactured-goods sectors. More diversified exports would help to insulate the region from some of the swings in the international economy.

Central American export-promoting policies will come to naught, however, if the rest of the world fails to open its markets. The United States has taken the lead in this respect, and the Caribbean Basin Initiative (CBI) will provide additional encouragement for the development of new export industries.

We encourage the extension of duty-free trade to Central America by other major trading countries.

We urge the European Community to extend trade preferences to Central America under the Lomé Agreement, since the United States is extending CBI benefits to Lomé beneficiaries in the Caribbean. Other countries of Latin America should also be encouraged to offer special trade benefits to the Central American countries as their own economic recovery progresses.

We urge the United States to review non-tariff barriers to imports from Central America.

We recognize that this issue—which principally applies to products like textiles, sugar, and meat—is highly contentious, both internationally and domestically. All of these products are affected by multilateral agreements which partly determine the degree of access to the United States market. We encourage the President to use whatever flexibility exists in such agreements in favor of Central American producers.

Several initiatives could be undertaken by the United States to encourage U.S. investors to consider projects in Central America.

We encourage the formation of a privately owned venture capital company for Central America.

We recommend that a venture capital company—which might be called the Central American Development Corporation (CADC)—be established for Central America. The CADC, capitalized by private-sector investors, would use its capital to raise funds which, in turn, would be lent to private companies active in Central America. It would be managed and directed by experienced entrepreneurs. Its loans would be made to commercially viable projects in high priority economic sectors for working capital or investment purposes. The U.S. government could support the CADC initiative through a long-term loan as it has for similar initiatives in other areas of the world.

Integrated programs of rural development targeted at the food-producing sector have enormous potential for improving the welfare of large numbers of people while increasing and diversifying agricultural production and lessening dependence on food imports. Such programs require a variety of coordinated measures which would have to be undertaken by the Central Americans themselves.

We recommend that the financial underpinnings of the efforts to broaden land ownership be strengthened and reformed.

In programs of land reform, ways should be found to insure that the redistribution of land provides the new owners with a valid title, that governments promptly allocate resources as they become available to insure that former owners are effectively compensated, and that in the end the system enhances incentives to expand the nation's total agricultural output.

Organizing for Development

We have developed the outline of a structure which we have called the Central American Development Organization, or CADO. We put it forward not as the only design, but as a means of illustrating how the concept could be implemented.

Membership in CADO, as we envision it, would initially be open to the seven countries of Central America—Belize, Costa Rica, El Salvador, Guatemala, Honduras, Nicaragua, and Panama—and to the United States. Associate member status would be available to any democracy willing to contribute significant resources to promote regional development. We would hope that the other Contadora countries would participate actively, as well as the nations of Europe, Canada, and Japan. The organization's chairman should be from the United States with an executive secretary from Central America.

Central American participation in the program should turn on acceptance of and continued progress toward political pluralism, and a process of recurrent elections with competing political parties. Only nations prepared to base their governments on the free choice of their people should be eligible. This does not necessarily mean that each country would institutionalize its political process in the same way as the United States, but it does mean that each would adopt democratic forms appropriate to its own conditions.

We recommend that an economic reconstruction fund be established with CADO and that the United States channel one-quarter of its economic assistance through such a fund. Loans to countries would be in support of development programs and policies including the implementation of growth-oriented economic policies, the establishment of genuine democratic institutions, and the adoption of programs to improve social conditions. They would be quick-disbursing, balance-of-payments support loans.

Governments, including that of the United States, would not be bound to accept the judgments of CADO. The United States would be free to maintain a bilateral economic assistance program in a particular country, regardless of performance. But the present purely bilateral process has its drawbacks. It factors political assessments directly into economic aid decisions. This makes the United States the prosecutor, judge, and jury. It leads to rancorous debate, sometimes poorly informed. This commission's proposal is an effort to explore a new process. The responsibility for assessing development performance would be assumed in the first instance by a respected multilateral body, with donors retaining effective final control of their financial resources. The process should be more effective, more acceptable to Central America, and more compatible with present-day views of how sovereign nations should deal with one another.

Central American Security Issues

Cuba and Nicaragua did not invent the grievances that made insurrection possible in El Salvador and elsewhere. Those grievances are real and acute. But it is important to bear in mind three facts about the kind of insurgencies we confront;

- They depend on external support, which is substantially more effective when it includes the provision of privileged sanctuaries for the insurgents.
- They develop their own momentum, independent of the conditions on which they feed.
- The insurgents, if they win, will create a totalitarian regime in the image of their sponsors' ideology and their own.

Propaganda support, money, sanctuary, arms, supplies, training, communications, intelligence, logistics, all are important in both morale and operational terms. Without such support from Cuba, Nicaragua, and the Soviet Union, neither in El Salvador nor elsewhere in Central America would such an insurgency pose so severe a threat to the government.

Therefore, curbing the insurgents' violence in El Salvador requires, in part, cutting them off from their sources of foreign support.

If reforms had been undertaken earlier, there would almost surely have been no fertile ground for revolution, and thus no effectively developed insurgency. But once an insurgency is fully under way and once the lines of external support are in place, it has a momentum which reforms alone cannot stop. Unchecked, the insurgents can destroy faster than the reformers can build.

One reason for this is that an explicit purpose of guerrilla violence is to make matters worse.

None of this legitimizes the use of arbitrary violence by the right in El Salvador or elsewhere. Indeed, the grim reality is that many of the excesses we have condemned would be present even if there were no guerrilla war supported by outside forces.

Beyond the issue of U.S. security interests in the Central American–Caribbean region, our credibility worldwide is engaged. The triumph of hostile forces in what the Soviets call the "strategic rear" of the United States would be read as a sign of U.S. impotence.

Thus, even in terms of the direct national security interests of the United

States, this country has large stakes in the present conflict in Central American.

The fundamental dilemma is as follows: both the national interests of the United States and a genuine concern for the long-term welfare of Central America create powerful incentives to provide all necessary assistance to defeat totalitarian guerrillas. At the same time one of the principal objectives of the guerrilla forces is to destroy the morale and efficiency of the government's administration and programs.

Progress in El Salvador

Much attention has been paid—correctly—to the shortcomings of the El Salvador government. But it is important—and only fair—to recall the many demands that have been made upon it and the progress that has been made in many fields. It carried out impressive elections in 1982, despite severe intimidations by the guerrillas, and will conduct another one this March [1984]. It has been going forward with an extensive land reform program. It allows debate, freedom of assembly, opposition, and other aspects of democracy, however imperfect. Albeit belatedly and because of U.S. pressure, it is beginning to address the problem of right-wing violence.

There is, of course, a darker side as well in El Salvador. The United States obviously cannot accept, let alone support, the brutal methods practiced by certain reactionary forces in Central America. Some of these actions are related to counterinsurgency. Other violence has, in fact, nothing to do with insurgency at all. It is designed to terrorize opponents, fight democracy, protect entrenched interests, and restore reactionary regimes.

Whatever their aims, these methods are totally repugnant to the values of the United States. The methods of counterinsurgency developed over the last generation by the armed forces of the United States are consistent with such models. They depend upon gaining the confidence and support of the people and specifically exclude the use of violence against innocent civilians.

The present level of U.S. military assistance to El Salvador is far too low to enable the armed forces of El Salvador to use these modern methods of counterinsurgency effectively. At the same time, the tendency in some quarters of the Salvadoran military towards brutality magnifies congressional and executive pressures for further cuts in aid. A vicious cycle results in which violence and denial of human rights spawn reductions in aid, and reductions in aid make more difficult the pursuit of an enlightened counterinsurgency effort.

In the commission's view it is imperative to settle on a level of aid related to the operational requirements of humane anti-guerrilla strategy and to stick with it for the requisite period of time.

Another obstacle to the effective pursuit of anti-guerrilla strategy is a provision of current U.S. law under which no assistance can be provided to law-enforcement agencies. This dates back to a previous period when it was believed that such aid was sometimes helping groups guilty of serious human rights abuses. The purpose of the legislation was to prevent the United States and its personnel from being associated with unacceptable practices. That concern is valid, but, however laudable its intentions, the blanket legal prohibition against the provision of training and aid to police organizations has the paradoxical effect, in certain cases, of inhibiting our efforts to improve human rights performance.

We therefore suggest that Congress examine this question thoroughly and consider whether Section 660 of the Foreign Assistance Act should be amended so as to permit — under carefully defined conditions — the allocation of funds to the training and support of law-enforcement agencies in Central America.

The war is at a stalemate — a condition that in the long term favors the guerrillas. They have relatively little popular support in El Salvador, but they can probably continue the war as long as they receive the sort of external support they are now getting.

In part, the Salvadoran military's difficulties in containing the guerrilla threat are related to manpower problems — their training, their retention, their equipment, and their development.

The Salvadoran armed forces have also suffered from inadequate command and control, coordination, and leadership. A recent major reorganization of the military command structure is designed to achieve needed improvements in command and control and coordination, and to lead to a more aggressive prosecution of the war. But to end the stalemate will require much more in equipment and trained manpower.

Insurgency in Guatemala

The insurgency in Guatemala is at a much lower level. There are about 2,500 guerrillas in four groups loosely organized under an umbrella organization. The guerrillas lost critical ground in the fall of 1982 and have not yet recovered. The guerrillas engage in harassment and terrorism but make no attempt to hold ground or to engage military units in sustained combat.

But an even more serious obstacle in terms of the ultimate containment of armed revolt in Guatemala is the brutal behavior of the security forces. In the cities they have murdered those even suspected of dissent. In the countryside, they have at times killed indiscriminately to repress any sign of support for the guerrillas. Such actions are morally unacceptable. They are also self-defeating — as long as they persist, the conditions in which insurgency can appear and reappear will continue.

Military Aid to El Salvador

While important U.S. interests are engaged in El Salvador, and while we pay a high political price at home and abroad for assisting the armed forces there, the United States has not provided enough military aid to support the methods of counterinsurgency we have urged. At the same time, the United States cannot countenance the brutal alternative methods of counterinsurgency which wreak intolerable violence upon the civilian population. In our judgment, the current levels of military aid are not sufficient to preserve even the existing military stalemate over a period of time. Given the increasing damage — both physical and political — being inflicted on the economy and government of El Salvador by the guerrillas, who are maintaining their strength, a collapse is not inconceivable.

The Salvadoran government's National Campaign Plan combines military operations with follow-up civic actions to restore agriculture and commerce. The plan is designed to provide secure areas within which the Salvadoran *campesino* can grow, harvest, and market his crops, and where industry can again operate. The plan assumes that sufficient security can be established countrywide to reduce the insurgency at least to a low level within two years. But the government's forces must be significantly and quickly strengthened if the plan is to succeed.

There might be an argument for doing nothing to help the government of El Salvador. There might be an argument for doing a great deal more. There is, however, no logical argument for giving some aid but not enough. The worst possible policy for El Salvador is to provide just enough aid to keep the war going, but too little to wage it successfully.

The commission has concluded that present levels of U.S. military assistance are inadequate.

We are not in a position to judge the precise amounts and types of increased aid needed. We note that the U.S. Department of Defense estimates that it would take approximately $400 million in U.S. military assistance in 1984 and 1985 to break the military stalemate and allow the National Campaign Plan to be carried out. The department believes that thereafter assistance levels could be brought down to considerably more modest levels.

The commission recommends that the United States provide to El Salvador—subject to the conditions we specify later in this chapter—significantly increased levels of military aid as quickly as possible so that the Salvadoran authorities can act on the assurance that needed aid will be forthcoming.

To be effective, U.S. military assistance programs require greater continuity and predictability. As we have seen, local commanders are now uncertain whether an adequate supply of such critical support items as ammunition will be on hand. The result in El Salvador has all too often been a less than vigorous prosecution of the war. The commission believes the Administration and the Congress should work together to achieve greater predictability. That could be most effectively achieved through multi-year funding.

Military Aid and Human Rights

The question of the relationship between military aid and human rights abuses is both extremely difficult and extremely important. It involves the potential clash of two basic U.S. objectives. On the one hand, we seek to promote justice and find it repugnant to support forces that violate—or tolerate the violation of—fundamental U.S. values. On the other hand, we are engaged in El Salvador and Central America because we are serving fundamental interests of the United States that transcend any particular government.

The commission believes that vigorous, concurrent policies on both the military and human rights fronts are needed to break out of the demoralizing cycle of deterioration on the one hand and abuses on the other. We believe policies of increased aid and increased pressure to safeguard human rights would improve both security and justice. A slackening on one front would undermine our objective on the other. El Salvador must succeed on both or it will not succeed on either.

The United States government has a right to demand certain minimum standards of respect for human rights as a condition for providing military aid to any country.

With respect to El Salvador, military aid should, through legislation requiring periodic reports, be made contingent upon demonstrated progress toward free elections, freedom of association, the establishment of the rule of law and an effective judicial system, and the termination of the activities of the so-called death squads, as well as vigorous action against those guilty of crimes and the prosecution to the extent possible of past offenders. These conditions should be seriously enforced.

Implementation of this approach would be greatly facilitated through the device of an independent monitoring body, such as the Central American Development Organization.

As an additional measure, the United States should impose sanctions, including the denial of visas, deportation, and the investigation of financial dealings, against foreign nationals in the United States who are connected with death-squad activities in El Salvador or anywhere else.

The Search for Peace

Americans yearn for the end to the bloodshed in Central America. On no issue in the region is there a stronger consensus than on the hope for a diplomatic solution that will stop the killing and nourish freedom and progress. The commission shares this deeply felt goal.

We believe that there is a chance for a political solution in Central America if the diplomacy of the United States is strategic in conception, purposeful in approach, and steadfast in execution. Our broad objectives should be:

- To stop the war and the killing in El Salvador.
- To create conditions under which Nicaragua can take its place as a peaceful and democratic member of the Central American community.
- To open the way to democratic development throughout the isthmus.

El Salvador

The commission has concluded that power-sharing as proposed by the insurgents is not a sensible or fair political solution for El Salvador. There is no historical precedent suggesting that such a procedure would reconcile contending parties which entertain such deeply held beliefs and political goals and which have been killing each other for years. Indeed, precedent argues that it would be only a prelude to a takeover by the insurgent forces.

We believe that a true political solution in El Salvador can be reached only through free elections in which all significant groups have a right to participate.

Thus the El Salvador government must take all appropriate measures to make the March 25 [1984] elections as safe and open as possible. This should include the introduction of outside observers to help insure the security and fairness of the process.

We understand that El Salvador contemplates holding municipal and legislative assembly elections in 1985. The elements of the following approach could be applied to that process.

1. The Salvadoran government would invite the FDR-FMLN [Democratic Revolutionary Front–Farabundo Martí National Liberation Front] to negotiate mutually acceptable procedures to establish a framework for future elections.

2. As part of this framework a broadly representative Elections Commission would be established, including representatives of the FDR-FMLN.

3. Violence should be ended by all parties so that mutually satisfactory arrangements can be developed among the government, pro-government parties, the different opposition groups, and insurgent groups for the period of campaigning and elections.

4. A system of international observation should be established to enhance the faith and confidence of all parties in the probity and equity of arrangements for elections. This might include senior advisors to the Elections Commission drawn from the OAS, Contadora nations, or third countries agreed upon by all parties to the conflict.

Nicaragua

Though the commission believes that the Sandinista regime will pose a continuing threat to stability in the region, we do not advocate a policy of static containment.

Instead, we recommend, first, an effort to arrange a comprehensive regional settlement. This would elaborate and build upon the twenty-one objectives of the Contadora group [see appendix B]. Within the framework of basic principles, it would:

- Recognize linkage between democratization and security in the region.

- Relate the incentives of increased development aid and trade concessions to acceptance of mutual security guarantees.
- Engage the United States and other developed nations in the regional peace system.
- Establish an institutional mechanism in the region to implement that system.

The commission believes that whatever the prospects seem to be for productive negotiations, the United States must spare no effort to pursue the diplomatic route. Nicaragua's willingness to enter into a general agreement should be thoroughly tested through negotiations and actions.

As a broad generality, we do not believe that it would be wise to dismantle existing incentives and pressures on the Managua regime except in conjunction with demonstrable progress on the negotiating front. With specific reference to the highly controversial question of whether the United States should provide support for the Nicaraguan insurgent forces opposed to the Sandinistas now in authority in Managua, the commission recognized that an adequate examination of this issue would require treatment of sensitive information not appropriate to a public report. However, the majority of the members of the commission, in their respective individual judgments, believe that the efforts of the Nicaraguan insurgents represent one of the incentives working in favor of a negotiated settlement and that the future role of the United States in those efforts must therefore be considered in the context of the negotiating process. The commission has not, however, attempted to come to a collective judgment on whether, and how, the United States should provide support for these insurgent forces.

Conclusion

We have concluded this exercise persuaded that Central America is both vital and vulnerable and that whatever other crises may arise to claim the nation's attention, the United States cannot afford to turn away from that threatened region. Central America's crisis is our crisis.

All too frequently, wars and threats of wars are what draw attention to one part of the world or another. So it has been in Central America. The military crisis here captured our attention, but it has also wakened us to many other needs of the region.

As we have studied these nations, we have become sharply aware of how great a mistake it would be to view them in one-dimensional terms. An exceptionally complex interplay of forces has shaped their history and continues to define their identities and to affect their destinies.

We have developed a great sympathy for those in Central America who are struggling to control those forces and to bring their countries successfully through this period of political and social transformation. As a region Central America is in midpassage from the predominantly authoritarian patterns of the past to what can, with determination, with help, with luck, and with peace, become the predominantly democratic pluralism of the future. That transformation has been troubled, seldom smooth and sometimes violent. In Nicaragua, we have seen the tragedy of a revolution betrayed; the same forces that stamped out the beginnings of democracy in Nicaragua now threaten El Salvador. In El Salvador itself, those seeking to establish democratic institutions are beset by violence from the extremists on both sides. But the spirit of freedom is strong throughout the region, and the determination persists to strengthen it where it exists and to achieve it where it does not.

The use of Nicaragua as a base for Soviet and Cuban efforts to penetrate the rest of the Central American isthmus, with El Salvador the target of first opportunity, gives the conflict there a major strategic dimension. The direct involvement of aggressive external forces makes it a challenge to the system of hemispheric security and, quite specifically, to the security interests of the United States. This is a challenge to which the United States must respond.

But beyond this, we are challenged to respond to the urgent human needs of the people of Central America. Central America is a region in crisis economically, socially, and politically. Its nations are our neighbors, and they need our help.

Our task now, as a nation, is to transform the crisis in Central America into an opportunity: to seize the impetus it provides and to use this to help our neighbors not only to secure their freedom from aggression and violence but also to set in place the policies, processes, and institutions that will make them both prosperous and free. If, together, we succeed in this, then the sponsors of violence will have done the opposite of what they intended: they will have roused us not only to turn back the tide of totalitarianism but to bring a new birth of hope and of opportunity to the people of Central America.

Because this is our opportunity, in conscience it is also our responsibility.

4. Soviet Arms and Central American Turmoil

By ALBERTO R. COLL

Focus
"To be sure, if the Sandinista regime were to be removed in Nicaragua—indeed, if all Soviet influence were eradicated from the Western Hemisphere—Central America would still face profound problems," observes Alberto R. Coll. But, he says, this should not divert our attention from the role the Soviets and the Cubans have played in exacerbating existing difficulties.

Between 1968 and 1981, the number of U.S. troops stationed in the Caribbean Basin declined from 25,000 to 16,000. By the end of 1984 the Soviet Union was providing ten times as much military aid to Nicaragua and Cuba as the United States was providing to all of Latin America. Such aid has enabled Cuba to become a regional power and sponsor of revolution throughout the area. Moreover, the Cuban navy when fully operational may have the capacity to operate not only in the Gulf of Mexico and the Caribbean Basin but in part of the Atlantic as well.

Cuba's participation in the military buildup of Nicaragua has included the loan, since 1983, of General Ochoa, a senior commander with experience in Ethiopia and Angola, who is in charge of combat training in Cuba.

Nicaragua has become a conduit for arms to other Central American subversive forces as well as a refuge and strategy center. Several Nicaraguan defectors have confirmed that massive amounts of arms were transferred to El Salvador shortly after the Sandinistas took power. The House Permanent Select Committee on Intelligence concluded in a 1983 report that the Salvadoran guerrilla force depended "for its life-blood—arms, ammunition, financing, logistics, and command-and-control facilities—upon outside assistance from Nicaragua and Cuba." Miguel Bolaños Hunter, a defector from the Sandinista intelligence forces, estimated that the Salvadorans "now have five times more [weapons] than we had against Somoza."

But says Coll, the Soviet-Cuban-Nicaraguan aid to subversion is not restricted to El Salvador. Evidence of support for guerrilla organizations in Costa Rica, Honduras, and Guatemala has made the leaders and peoples of those countries wary of Nicaragua as well.

Coll's analysis of the Soviet role in Central America should be compared with Cardinal John J. O'Connor's statement of the U.S. Catholic bishops' position (selection 5) and the views of Nicaraguan president Daniel Ortega (selection 22).

Alberto R. Coll is an assistant professor of political science at Georgetown University, Washington, D.C.

FOR A LONG TIME, Latin America was an area of remote concern for the Soviet Union. In the past two decades it has become an area of great interest and considerable involvement.[1] Through the establishment and reinforcement of its ties to Cuba and, more recently, to Nicaragua, the U.S.S.R. has gradually expanded its influence in the region. Today, Soviet actions taken in pursuit of "the inevitable march of history"[2] threaten the security of Central America and the United States.

Serious observers of Central America agree that Soviet involvement there has increased, but opinions diverge sharply on what direction U.S. policy should take. As Howard Wiarda has pointed out, the debate "has not always been infused with light."[3] Many Americans do not understand Latin America well and do not want to. The debate has been compromised by the dominance of "instant experts" whose knowledge of the region is superficial. And it has been heavily partisan and politicized, often reflecting trends in U.S. domestic politics.[4]

This article examines one important aspect of that debate: the nature, in quantifiable terms, of Soviet involvement through arms transfers in Central America and the Caribbean Basin.[5]

Until the 1960s, Latin America was outside the "zone of peace" proclaimed by Khrushchev; indeed, Soviet attention in the Third World had gone almost exclusively elsewhere: the Middle East, Africa, and Asia.[6] The Soviets had no long-standing political, cultural, or commercial ties with geographically remote Latin America, believing it to be firmly under U.S. control. They also assumed that Washington would not tolerate leftist regimes or significant Soviet influence in the region.[7] Indicative of this perception was the fact that Latin America had been excluded from Moscow's primary Third World organization, the Afro-Asian People's Solidarity Organization.

Soviet Policy in the 1960s

The Cuban revolution and the unexpected survival of the Castro regime critically altered Moscow's perceptions of three essential elements: U.S.

Reprinted from the Summer 1985 issue of *World Affairs* by permission of the Helen Dwight Reid Educational Foundation (published by Heldref Publications; © 1985). The notes for this essay begin on page 76.

influence in Latin America, the opportunities presented in the hemisphere, and the Soviet ability to take advantage of them. Fidel Castro's successful communization of Cuba prompted Khrushchev to proclaim in 1960 that the Monroe Doctrine had "outlived its times" and had died "a natural death."[8]

Following Castro's successful revolution, Soviet policy in the Western Hemisphere was to exploit all opportunities for the expansion of influence. Having learned by the Cuban missile crisis that it could not without very considerable risk attempt directly to expand its military presence, Moscow turned primarily to augmenting its diplomatic, economic, and cultural links to Latin America and to increasing the sway of indigenous Communist parties in trade unions, universities, and broad electoral fronts.[9]

During this period, the prospect of armed revolutions within Central America was rejected as unviable by the Soviets. Significant tensions arose between Cuba and the Soviet Union in response to Castro's ill-fated revolutionary "adventurism" in Venezuela, Colombia, Guatemala, and several other countries. As Jiri Valenta has noted, as a result of "doctrinal differences," Soviet-Cuban relations during 1966–67 "were strained almost to the breaking point."[10] Castro's revolutionary ardor was, however, dampened by Ernesto "Ché" Guevara's death and the elimination of Castroist guerrillas in Venezuela and Guatemala in 1967.

The Soviets' threat in the spring of 1968 to stop supplying petroleum to Cuba reminded Castro of his dependence on Moscow. Castro, who was now intent on eliminating some of the mild currents of liberalization that had begun to surface in Cuba in 1967, decided to move into an increasingly close relationship with the U.S.S.R. His firm support for the Soviet invasion of Czechoslovakia in August 1968 was a confirmation of this important political decision.

Soviet Policy in the 1970s

In the 1970s, several developments combined to shift the U.S.S.R. toward a bolder approach involving, in the words of the Kissinger Commission [see selection 3], "support for revolutionary armed struggle in Central America."[11] The United States, defeated in Vietnam, became gripped by isolationism and self-doubt, just as Soviet confidence increased as Soviet-backed forces succeeded in gaining power in Angola, Mozambique, Ethiopia, South Yemen, and Cambodia. These triumphs bolstered the Soviet perception that the "correlation of forces" had shifted significantly against the West, and became added incentive for a more aggressive Third World policy. In the Caribbean, a major effort was launched to enhance Soviet military capabilities in the region. This included, according to the Kissinger Commission:

a dramatic buildup of the size and sophistication of the Cuban armed forces, not least their air and naval components; an enlarged direct Soviet military presence in Cuba, with regular port calls by Soviet naval task forces and nuclear missile submarines and the deployment of advanced reconnaissance aircraft; increased numbers of Soviet military advisors; and close operational collaboration between Soviet and Cuban forces, as, for example, when Soviet pilots were sent to Cuba in 1976 and 1978 to replace Cuban pilots aiding pro-Soviet regimes in Angola and Ethiopia.[12]

This increased Soviet presence in the Caribbean Basin coincided with a sharp reduction in the U.S. military presence. Whereas in 1968 the United States had more than 25,000 men stationed there, the figure dropped to fewer than 16,000 in 1981.[13] And just as American military power was decreasing in the 1970s, Central America was undergoing an intensification of the political, social, and economic crises that were to render it highly vulnerable to insurgency.[14]

As in the case of Castro's accession to power two decades earlier, the success of the 1979 Sandinista revolution in Nicaragua led to the Soviets' reassessment of their Central American policy. Victor Volskii, president of the Soviet Association of Friendship with Latin American Countries, called the armed victory in Nicaragua a "model" for other countries to emulate. The chairman of the International Department of the Central Committee of the Communist Party, Boris Ponomarev, began to include the Central American states among Third World states undergoing revolutionary changes of a "socialist orientation."[15] Soviet and Cuban views on revolution in Central America began to coalesce. The U.S.S.R. now perceived that successful revolution in Central America was possible and desirable. In *Kommunist*, the theoretical organ of the Soviet Communist Party, the secretary general of El Salvador's Communist Party, Shafik Jorge Handal, wrote in 1980 that a revolution in El Salvador "will be victorious by the armed road.... There is no other way."[16]

Military Buildup in Cuba

Significant Soviet military aid to Cuba followed the establishment of political and economic ties. In early 1961, Czechoslovak- and Soviet-made weapons began to be displayed openly. Soviet arms transfers to Cuba reached their peak in 1962, the year of the Cuban missile crisis. Seaborne transfers reached their low point in 1968, a time when Soviet relations were at a correspondingly low point. In 1969, arms transfers increased slightly, remaining at a constant level until 1974. New increases in the mid to late 1970s coincided with the Soviet-Cuban actions in Ethiopia and Angola.[17]

By 1983, it was estimated that the U.S.S.R. was delivering twenty times more military assistance to Cuba than the United States was providing to all of Latin America.[18] Within its tactical arsenal, Cuba today has 200 MiG jet fighters, including two squadrons of MiG-23 Floggers, more than 90 helicopters and 650 tanks, a Koni-class frigate, two Foxtrot submarines, two amphibious assault ships, and some 50 torpedo attack boats.[19] The U.S.S.R. provided Cuba with approximately 10,000 metric tons of military supplies from 1969 to 1974, 15,000 in 1975, and 20,000 from 1976 to 1980; this figure leapt to 66,000 in 1981 and 68,000 in 1982. Cuba today is home to a full Soviet army brigade of 2,600 to 3,000 men, 2,500 military advisors, and 6,000 to 8,000 civilian advisors.[20]

According to the U.S. State Department, the Cuban air force is "one of the largest and probably the best equipped in Latin America." Cuba's fighter aircraft, MiG-23s, could be employed effectively in either an air-superiority or ground-attack role, given proper circumstances. With a strength of about 10,000 personnel, the Cuban navy remains essentially a defensive force; once its two Foxtrot-class submarines and single Koni-class frigate are integrated fully into the operational force, however, the navy "will be able to sustain operations through the Caribbean Basin, the Gulf of Mexico, and to a limited extent, the Atlantic Ocean." Since its intervention in Angola, Havana has increased the training of airborne forces, which now consist of a landing and assault brigade and a special troops contingent, and has augmented its air and sealift capacity. Moreover, the introduction of "sophisticated Soviet weapons geared toward mobility and offensive missions has improved Cuban ability to conduct military operations off the island."[21]

The Nicaraguan Buildup

Nicaragua also has received significant military assistance from the Soviet Union and its satellites since 1979: 150 Soviet tanks, the heaviest in Central America, along with 1,000 East German trucks, 200–300 anti-

The Military Buildup in Nicaragua
Since the Overthrow of Somoza (July 1979)

	Forces (Active Duty, Mobilized Militia)	Tanks	Other Armored Vehicles	Fixed-Wing Aircraft/ Helicopters	Airfields	Anti-Aircraft Guns/Missile Launchers
July 1979	6,000	3	31	30/8	4	2/10
December 1979	16,000	3	31	30/8	4	2/1
December 1980	24,000	3	25	40/8	4	39/6
December 1981	39,000	30	45	40/10	4	100/6
December 1982	41,000	50	45	40/15	4	150/30+
December 1983	46,000	50	90	44/15	4	150/30+
October 1984	62,000	150	200	45/17	5	200/300+

SOURCE: U.S. Department of Defense, November 11, 1984

aircraft guns and missile launchers, and Soviet 152-millimeter howitzers with a range of seventeen miles. (See chart.) Nicaraguan military pilots and crews have trained in Bulgaria and other Eastern European countries, and Nicaraguan airfields have been enlarged to accommodate advanced jet fighters. By the end of 1982, the Sandinista regime had received an estimated $125 million worth of military equipment from the U.S.S.R. alone.[22] By the end of 1984, the Soviets were providing to Nicaragua and Cuba ten times as much military aid as the United States was giving to all of Latin America.

At the height of his power, Somoza commanded some 12,000 ill-equipped troops armed mostly with older vintage U.S. arms. By 1982, the Nicaraguan army had reached an estimated strength of 20,000 backed by 80,000 militia and reserve troops. Thirty-nine per cent of all males over eighteen are in uniform, and an armed force of 250,000 is planned, which would put one in ten Nicaraguans in the military or militia. Thirty-six new military bases and garrisons have been added; Somoza had thirteen. There are currently some 8,000 Cubans, 50 Soviets, 35 East Germans, 50 Palestine Liberation Organization and Libyan personnel, and an undetermined number of North Koreans and Bulgarians—that is, roughly one foreign advisor for every 1,000 Nicaraguans—now stationed in Nicaragua.[23] Although many of the Cubans are engaged in military and security affairs, they have 500–700 doctors and several thousand "teachers" involved in propaganda and literacy training, and some 1,000 construction workers erecting bridges and maintaining hydroelectric plants and state-owned telecommunications companies.

In June 1983 Cuba sent one of its senior combat commanders, General Ochoa, to Nicaragua to bolster the Sandinista government and promote Castro's revolutionary image in the Caribbean region. Ochoa, a close friend of Castro, received special training in the Soviet Union in 1976 and went directly to Angola, where Cuban forces were increased from 3,000 to 20,000 in defense of the Marxist government. In December 1977 Ochoa was transferred to Ethiopia as head of Cuban combat and support forces and increased their strength from 2,000 to 17,000 men. Since 1981, he has been in charge of military combat training in Cuba. His presence in Nicaragua is a strong indication that a similar force buildup, with Cuban aid, will continue there.[24]

Such a military buildup undoubtedly facilitates Soviet covert arms transfers. Without the strong foothold in Central America provided by a heavily armed Nicaragua, Soviet efforts to support Communist rebels in the region would be significantly more difficult, if not impossible.

The Flow of Arms From Nicaragua

Soviet arms transfers to Central American revolutionary groups have exhibited two characteristics. First, the U.S.S.R. has abstained from acting as a direct supplier and has used instead allies and client-states such as Eastern European states, Vietnam, and Ethiopia. Second, arms shipments have gone to Cuba and from there to Nicaragua for covert distribution to insurgents in El Salvador, Guatemala, and Honduras.

The covert assistance provided to the Salvadoran and other Central American rebels either directly or indirectly by the Soviet Union and its allies is somewhat difficult to document, since those involved naturally have attempted to keep their operations as clandestine as possible. Moreover, much of the information gathered by U.S. intelligence has remained classified in order to protect the sources and to avoid revealing the operations of the American intelligence network. Nevertheless, considerable material has been made available to selected congressional committees in closed session. On 4 March 1982, the Democratic chairman of the House Intelligence Oversight Committee stated:

> The insurgents are well trained, well equipped with modern weapons and supplies, and rely on the use of sites in Nicaragua for command and control and for logistical support. The intelligence supporting these judgments . . . is convincing.

There is further persuasive evidence that the Sandinista government of Nicaragua is helping train insurgents and is transferring arms and support from and through Nicaragua to the insurgents. They are further providing the insurgents with bases of operation in Nicaragua. Cuban involvement—in providing arms—is also evident.[25]

According to a report of the full committee dated 22 September of the same year, "intelligence had been able to establish beyond doubt the involvement of Communist countries in the insurgency."[26]

In its May 1983 report, the Democratic-controlled Permanent Select Committee on Intelligence of the House of Representatives (chaired by Congressman Boland) concluded that the Salvadoran insurgency depended "for its life-blood—arms, ammunition, financing, logistics, and command-and-control facilities—upon outside assistance from Nicaragua and Cuba." The committee also concluded that the Nicaraguan-Cuban contribution to the Salvadoran insurgency was "long-standing," that it "began shortly after the overthrow of Somoza" in July 1979, and that it had provided by land, sea, and air "the great bulk of the military equipment and support received by the insurgents."[27] This assessment was based upon the committee's review of voluminous intelligence materials collected since the 1979 Sandinista victory in Nicaragua.

Among the classified materials examined by the committee were guerrilla papers captured in El Salvador by the CIA documenting the substantial covert material assistance provided to the Salvadoran and other Central American rebels by Cuba and Nicaragua acting as proxies of the Soviet Union. According to some of the captured documents that the U.S. State Department has made available to the public, Soviet-supported arms transfers to Central America via Cuba began in mid-1980. On 15 August, for example, a major arms shipment from Ethiopia arrived in Cuba.[28] Three weeks later, sixty tons of captured U.S. arms that had been promised by Vietnam to the Salvadoran rebels also arrived in Havana. This Vietnamese shipment included two million rifle and machine gun bullets, 14,500 mortar shells, 1,620 rifles, 210 machine guns, 48 mortars, 12 rocket launchers, and 192 pistols. A captured, undated guerrilla document details other arms that the Salvadoran guerrillas expected soon afterward, including 50 submachine guns, 2,500 rifles, 90,000 submachine gun rounds, and 540,000 rifle rounds.

Ethiopia would have had easy access to Western weapons because before 1976 its army was supplied by the United States; because of the Indochina war, Vietnam would have had similar access.

The guerrillas prefer Western weapons because they are harder to trace to their Eastern-bloc sources. The same captured list indicated that Czechoslovakia would have to send Czech weapons because it had been unable to exchange them for Western ones. Bulgaria was to send 300 German-made submachine guns with 200,000 rounds, 10,000 uniforms, and 2,000 first aid kits; the uniforms and kits were to be sent after specifications were received, suggesting that they were to be manufactured especially for the rebels. Hungary was listed as sending short-wave radio equipment and 10,000 uniforms according to specifications and sizes requested. To gauge the impact of arms shipments of this size, it is worth keeping in mind that El Salvador's total area is 8,124 square miles, approximately the size of Massachusetts, with a 1981 population of 4.6 million, roughly that of Maryland.

The captured documents further revealed a significant increase in the number of flights from Cuba to Nicaragua during September and October 1980. The total cargo capacity of these flights was several hundred tons. Until this time arms had been sent to El Salvador from Nicaragua overland, but by October the quantity of material had become too large for such shipments, and as much as 120 tons of weapons remained in Nicaragua. At this time, Nicaragua, with Cuban support, began airlifting arms to El Salvador. By December, the Salvadoran guerrillas had begun to complain that the volume of arms shipments had become so large that they could no longer absorb it.[29]

Other Forms of Aid

Arms were not the only form of assistance being provided to the rebels at this time. One Salvadoran guerrilla who defected to Honduras in September 1981 stated that he and twelve others had traveled from Nicaragua to Cuba, where they had received extensive military training. He reported that more than 900 Salvadorans were being trained in Cuba. A raid by Salvadoran security forces on a safehouse in November 1981 captured several terrorists who admitted that the Nicaraguan government had given them funding for travel and explosives.[30]

On 6 April 1983, Melida Anaya Montes, one of the Salvadoran insurgent leaders, was assassinated near Managua. Subsequent news stories made it clear that the FMLN [Farabundo Martí National Liberation Front, the Salvadoran guerrilla movement] has a large and sophisticated command-and-control center outside Managua, one that could survive only with the blessing of the Sandinista government. Further evidence is provided by recent accounts of increasing resentment on behalf of some of the Salvadoran guerrillas toward key leaders who safely direct operations from Managua. Also, since December 1980 the Salvadoran guerrillas have been broadcasting from Nicaragua to El Salvador, using a new radio station, Radio Liberación, that has been heavily subsidized by the Sandinista regime.[31]

A raid on a safehouse in Honduras on 22 August 1982 led to the capture of two high ranking FMLN leaders. One of them, Alejandro Montenegro,[32] admitted that he had attended two high-level meetings with Cuban officials in 1981, one in Havana and one in Managua, in order to obtain strategic advice on the Salvadoran civil war. He stated that the vehicles modified to carry concealed weapons travel between Nicaragua and El Salvador with such frequency that the Sandinistas have set up three repair shops for such vehicle modifications, under the direction of a special section of the Nicaraguan Ministry of Defense. Finally, Montenegro confessed that he had personally directed the successful 27 January 1982 raid on the Ilopango air force base in El Salvador, which damaged or destroyed a dozen aircraft, almost half of El Salvador's tiny air force. He said that his eight-man team had received five months of intensive infiltration and sabotage training in Cuba. He also confirmed that Nicaragua remained the primary source of the rebels' weapons and ammunition, although some arms and ammunition had been captured from the Salvadoran army in 1980.

The other captured leader, Lopez Arriola, said that he had attended a platoon leaders' course in Cuba in July 1979, and that he had returned for a strategy meeting in Havana in June 1981 at which Castro himself was present. He added that hundreds of Salvadoran guerrillas had received military training in Cuba, and that the Cubans give special courses for combatants, commanders, staff officers, and intelligence officials. He also revealed that weapons delivered to Nicaragua from Vietnam are controlled by the Sandinistas, and that the Salvadorans must ask for permission to draw on these supplies. The Sandinistas give the rebels an extensive base of operations in and around Managua and provide a school for their children, Arriola said. A third Salvadoran rebel caught in the same safehouse raid admitted making five trips to Managua in 1982 to pick up arms, using a truck that the Sandinistas had modified to carry concealed weapons.[33]

The revelation of Cuban–Nicaraguan support for the Salvadoran insurgency resulted in a repudiation of the former rebel leader Montenegro by the Salvadoran insurgents over their Radio Venceremos. The announcement also contained significant information concerning the goals of the insurgency: "The high morale of our forces is based on the capacity of our strategic commands to conduct war from the very scenes of war, also in the capacity shown by the same strategic commands in meeting the material and political needs of this war with international help." The rebels attempted to explain why their leaders were outside El Salvador by saying, "We have conducted important logistical operations in clandestinity, which have served to provide our forces with arms and ammunition for long periods of time."[34] This rebel admission that ammunition and arms were provided from abroad came only in response to Montenegro's revelations.

Beyond El Salvador

The scope of Nicaraguan and Cuban involvement in Central America has extended well beyond El Salvador. In democratic and peaceful Costa Rica, the police have confiscated weapons and explosives in the homes of Communist party functionaries and members of small terrorist groups supported by the Cubans and the Nicaraguans. On 15 March 1982, Costa Rican judicial police announced the capture of a "sizeable cache of arms, explosives, uniforms, passports, documents, false immigration stamps from more than thirty countries, and vehicles with hidden compartments, all connected with arms smuggling through Costa Rican territory."[35] In March of the following year, a San José newspaper reported that the government had confiscated M-1 and M-14 rifles, ammunition, and grenade launchers in the possession of the brother of a Communist parliamentarian. According to *La Nación*,

> These weapons only represent the small part of the arsenal which the rural guard has been unable to confiscate despite its meritorious and patriotic work. While Nicaragua is preparing aggression against our country, its local accomplices are trying to destabilize the government as part of an overall plan against Costa Rica that was launched by international communism several months ago.[36]

Costa Rica's president, Luis Alberto Monge, was quoted on San José radio on 24 April 1983 as referring to the "repeated aggressions against the nation's sovereignty by the Nicaraguans." The president deemed the "constant violations of Costa Rican territory" by Sandinistas "unlawful, harmful, and therefore unacceptable."[37] One of the most stable democracies in Latin America, Costa Rica has no army and traditionally has pursued a policy of neutrality in most hemispheric conflicts. Concern over the growing extent of leftist subversive activities prompted the Costa Rican foreign minister to complain in September 1983 of "the growing Marxist threat to Costa Rica's national integrity."[38]

On 26 March 1983, a group of subversives in southwest Honduras was forced to retreat after a firefight with police. They left behind equipment and documents confirming that men, weapons, and other supplies were being transported from Nicaragua to El Salvador by way of Honduran territory.[39] Meanwhile, in early 1983, Guatemalan armed forces captured a hidden cache of twenty-four U.S.-made M-16 rifles, twelve of which were confirmed as having originally been shipped from the United States to Vietnam.

A Nicaraguan Defector Speaks

In June 1983 the *Washington Post* published two interviews with a defector from Nicaragua's counterintelligence agency. The testimony of the former security official, Miguel Bolaños Hunter, further corroborates the extent to which the Soviet Union and its close regional allies, Cuba and Nicaragua, have used arms transfers in Central America. Bolaños, who on 7 May 1983 hijacked a plane from Nicaragua to Costa Rica, where he was released into the custody of U.S. authorities, was interviewed for thirteen hours by *Post* reporters, "with no questions barred."[40]

According to Bolaños's testimony, small airplanes had been flying to barricaded sections of highway in guerrilla-controlled areas twice a day since 1980. Each plane carried thirty to forty guns; medicine and ammunition often were dropped by parachute. Other arms went overland through Honduras on mules or concealed in trucks. The arms flow to El Salvador was so heavy that it sometimes became an annoyance to Nicaraguans, Bolaños told reporters. One evening, a navy chief who was a friend of Bolaños complained to him that he had been instructed on short notice to go to an Atlantic coast port at midnight to meet a Cuban boat loaded with guns bound for El Salvador. "He had an arrangement with a woman friend that night and he didn't want to go," said Bolaños. "He said it was too bad that somebody always had to be standing behind these Salvadorans and taking care of them."[41]

Corroborating Alejandro Montenegro's story, related earlier, about the Cuban role in the January 1982 raid that decimated the Salvadoran air force, Bolaños said he had spoken with a Cuban advisor who had supervised the planning and the training for the raid at a Nicaraguan facility eight miles from Managua. Bolaños also explained that his cousin, Miguel

Guzman Bolaños, who oversees arms distribution in Nicaragua, had told him that Luis Carrion, a member of the Sandinista directorate, had visited the U.S.S.R. in 1980 and had then been promised that the Nicaraguans would be given two AK-47 machine guns for every weapon they gave the Salvadoran guerrillas. In 1983, Bolaños reported, the arms flow from Nicaragua to El Salvador almost ceased because the rebels were so enormously oversupplied with weapons that they simply could not absorb any more. "They now have five times more than what we had against Somoza," he said.[42]

Similar evidence surfaced in late 1984 in the testimony of a high-ranking Cuban official, José Luis Llovio Menéndez, who defected to the United States via Canada. Llovio explained that Cuba has aided the Salvadoran guerrillas in two different ways. One has been to send arms to Nicaragua with the understanding that they will be channeled from there to the guerrillas. Another method has been to give the guerrillas money to buy U.S. and other Western arms on the U.S. black market. Llovio, whose high positions in the Cuban bureaucracy included a top post at the Ministry of Finance, indicated that the funds given to the guerrillas came from the Interior Ministry's "exterior expense" budget.[43]

Two Views of Soviet Intentions

What is one to make of the substantial evidence of Soviet activity in Central America and the Caribbean Basin? How significant is such activity? To what degree is it a threat to the security of the United States? Of Central America? The answers to such questions are necessarily colored by one's view of the Soviet Union, its leadership, its capabilities, and its intentions.

Type "A" analysts of Soviet behavior, for example, view the U.S.S.R. as a basically conservative state, whose expansionist moves are caused more by whatever opportunities are available than by any master plan.[44] The Soviet leadership, according to the A school, makes decisions on an *ad hoc* basis, employing no strategic grand design; it is cautious, motivated by a desire for security. The Kremlin, according to proponents of analysis A, relies upon the military, but does so pragmatically; when the perceived risks are low, for example, the Soviets push beyond their strict defense. In the Third World, an "overall shift in the balance may embolden the Soviets to capitalize on new opportunities for intervention when the risk of U.S. counterintervention seems slight."[45] [The quotations about the two types of analysis in this paragraph and the next are from a paper by Robert Osgood of Johns Hopkins University.] In its relations with the Soviet

Union, A analysts argue, the United States must eschew linkage and attempt to maximize its common interests with the other superpower. In the Third World, the United States must deal with states on a case-by-case basis, cognizant of their uniqueness and working with their "local forces of nationalism and socioeconomic change to reduce Soviet opportunities to exploit instability."[46]

Type "B" analysts, in contrast, view the Soviet Union as a revisionist state motivated by Marxist-Leninist ideology. The U.S.S.R. pursues goals with tactical flexibility as part of an overall grand strategy. The Soviet strategy is offense-oriented, its leadership fueled by a relentless drive for superiority and international recognition. According to analysis B, the Soviet goal in the Third World is to gain local preponderance by fostering turmoil; such proponderance is a necessary step to reaching the strategic goal of world domination. B analysts see U.S.-Soviet relations as a seamless web and favor "linkage": "the West must not permit the Soviets to exploit so as to derive the tactical benefits of accommodation while pursuing a strategic offensive."[47] The United States must maximize resistance to the Soviet Union, seeking ultimately the defeat of Soviet grand strategy. "Analysis B is more likely to see the Soviet Union's direct or indirect intervention in local turmoil as the principal source of danger, to view the local and central military balance as decisive factors in the equation of conflict."[48] In the Third World, B analysts assert, the United States must respond to Soviet intervention with counterintervention by providing arms or armed forces.

Although the A and B analyses of Soviet foreign policy can produce sharply divergent interpretations of Soviet intentions in specific contexts, often they converge. In looking at Central America, A analysts would agree with B analysts that Soviet policy has always contained strong elements of caution and opportunism with the U.S.S.R. acting as would a burglar in a hotel, stealing from unlocked rooms and avoiding difficult heists.[49] In Central America, Soviet "burglary" has been facilitated by fighting among the hotel's guests. And the U.S.S.R.'s massive arms buildup of Cuba and, more recently, Nicaragua has served to permit the Soviets to support revolutionary activity in Central America without incurring the serious risk of U.S. retaliation.

To be sure, if the Sandinista regime were to be removed in Nicaragua — indeed, if all Soviet influence were eradicated from the Western Hemisphere — Central America would still face profound problems. As Gary Wynia has observed, the story of Central America "cannot be told entirely on a printed page or in a statistical table."[50] Aside from external influences, internal conditions for revolution exist in Central America. In the words of Thomas Anderson, the "roots of revolution lie in the increasingly bitter competition between political groups and social classes for the scarce resources of the region." The struggle in Central America "is a complex one, and the conditions in no two countries are identical."[51]

Summing Up the Threat

Given the chronic internal problems of most Central American states, Central America presents the United States with a challenge far more difficult and complex than one of simply responding to Soviet actions. Indeed, as Jiri and Virginia Valenta have pointed out, "military concerns about arms levels in the region alone will not lead to resolution of the systemic social and economic crisis visited on those least able to bear the burden."[52] The successful containment of Soviet policy will ultimately require substantial economic and political reforms that will promote economic growth, lift vast numbers of people out of indigence, and create a prosperous middle class that will share fully in the economic and political life of these societies.

But while the record of Soviet arms transfers does not tell the whole story of Central America, it is nevertheless of profound significance. The fact is that Soviet promotion of insurgencies through arms transfers and other kinds of support has more than any other single factor exacerbated the internal problems of Central America. It has contributed to a major escalation of violence in El Salvador and to the resolve of the Sandinista leadership to establish a non-pluralistic economic and political system in Nicaragua.

The first step of Soviet policy was to promote a significant military buildup of Cuba, which then became a bridge between the U.S.S.R. and the Caribbean. Through overt military assistance to Nicaragua, Moscow gained a foothold in Central America, a terminus for a bridge between its ally Cuba and Central America, and ultimately, a link between itself and the Communist rebels of the region. Moreover, the growing military capabilities of Nicaragua and Cuba have a significant offensive dimension that enables them to carry out an open policy of intervention in Central America without incurring serious risks of retaliation.

The United States is now confronted by an urgent situation in Central America. The Sandinista regime in Nicaragua—supported by massive Cuban military strength, backed by Soviet and other Eastern-bloc weapons, guidance, and diplomacy, and integrated into the Cuban network of intelligence and subversion — poses a significant threat to the security of all Central America. The President's Bipartisan Commission on Central America (Kissinger Commission) reported that it "encountered no leader in Central America, including democratic and unarmed Costa Rica, who did not express deep foreboding about the impact of a militarized, totalitarian Nicaragua on the peace and security of the region." Several expressed the view that should the Nicaraguan regime now be consolidated as a totalitarian state, their own freedom and even their independence would be jeopardized.[53] The maintenance of the Sandinista regime is essential for the successful realization of Soviet goals in the hemisphere. Without it, the Soviet ability to support Communist revolution in Central America would be significantly weakened.

More is at stake in Central America than merely a transfer of weapons to insurgents. The consolidation of the Sandinista regime in Nicaragua, combined with the growing turmoil in Central America, economic stagnation and political unrest in several of the Caribbean mini-states, and confusing signals from Washington, has provided the U.S.S.R. with an excellent strategic opportunity. By financing and providing military hardware to Nicaraguan and Cuban surrogates, the Soviets can help to establish and consolidate a group of Marxist states with an anti-American orientation close to American shores, without providing Washington the excuse for forcible action that would exist had the Soviets intervened directly.

In the end, the Soviets could achieve a major strategic breakthrough with profound consequences for the global balance of power: the United States would be exposed to the same circumstances the Soviet Union has had to endure since NATO was created three decades ago and the states of Norway, Turkey, and Greece became major members. A group of Marxist states in the Caribbean region armed as extensively as Cuba is,[54] and as Nicaragua is fast becoming, would limit U.S. security options in the Western Hemisphere, perhaps as effectively as Norway, Greece, and Turkey limit the Soviet Union's freedom of action in the Mediterranean and North Atlantic. The United States' increased strategic and military insecurity would be compounded by the greater economic vulnerability resulting from the exposure of key ocean lanes to easy enemy interdiction in times of conflict.

It is little wonder that the U.S.S.R. seeks to aid insurgencies in El Salvador and the rest of Central America through covert arms transfers as extensively as prudent calculation permits. As the Bipartisan Commission stated, "preserving U.S. interests in Central America and the Caribbean will be a significant concern for years to come."⁵⁵ The challenge of responding to Soviet strategic coercion in Central America in its numerous forms has never been more pressing.

NOTES

1. Robert S. Leiken, "Eastern Winds in Latin America." *Foreign Policy* 42, Spring 1981, pp. 94-113.
2. Morris Rothenberg, "Latin America in Soviet Eyes," *Problems of Communism* XXXII, Sept.-Oct. 1983, p. 1.
3. Howard J. Wiarda, "The Origins of the Crisis in Central America," in Howard Wiarda, ed., *Rift and Revolution: The Central American Imbroglio* (Washington: American Enterprise Institute, 1984), p. 4.
4. Ibid., pp. 4-5.
5. For the purposes of this study, "arms transfers" shall be defined broadly so as to include not only weapons but also military training, clothing, medical supplies, and the like. This article shall examine overt Soviet arms transfers since the fall of 1960, covert transfers since early 1980.
6. For an overview of Soviet policy toward the Third World in general and Latin America specifically, see Joseph L. Nogee and Robert H. Donaldson, *Soviet Foreign Policy Since World War II* (New York; Pergamon Press, 1981), pp. 130-86.
7. "It is interesting to note that Marx and Engels favored the United States in the war against Mexico in 1848. Later Marx wrote a very unflattering essay on Simón Bolívar, which was based on the recollections of the French soldier of fortune Ducoudray Holstein. Marx's negative evaluation of Bolívar colored Soviet writings on Latin America until the 1950s." Jiri and Virginia Valenta, "Soviet Strategies and Policies in the Caribbean Basin," in Wiarda, *Rift and Revolution*, p. 199.
8. Cited by the *Report of the Bipartisan Commission on Central America*, January 1984, p. 88.
9. Leiken, "Eastern Winds in Latin America."
10. Jiri Valenta, "The U.S.S.R., Cuba, and the Crisis in Central America," *Orbis*, Fall 1981, p. 720.
11. *Report of the Bipartisan Commission*, p. 89.
12. Ibid.
13. Ibid.
14. For a discussion of the "Decade of Disappointment" see Gary W. Wynia, "Setting the Stage for Rebellion: Economics and Politics in Central America's Past," in Wiarda, *Rift and Revolution*, pp. 59-68. In the same volume see also Thomas P. Anderson, "The Roots of Revolution in Central America," pp. 49-50; and Roland H. Ebel, "The Development and Decline of the Central American City-state," pp. 95-98. Wynia's analysis is replete with economic and demographic statistics; Anderson's is socio-political. Ebel, arguing that each Central American state is better understood as a "city-state," details the results of industrial employment and mass mobilization upon the Central American policies of the 1970s.
15. Boris Ponomarev, "Sovmestnaya Bor'ba rabochevo i natsional'no-osvobozhditel'nogo dvizhenii protiv imperializma, za sotsial'nii progress" (Joint Struggle of the Labor and National Liberation Movements against Imperialism, for Social Progress), *Kommunist* 16

(November 1980), p. 41. Cited by Robert S. Leiken, *Soviet Strategy in Latin America* (New York: Praeger, 1982).

16. Shafik Jorge Handal, "Na Putik Svobode" (On the Road to Freedom), *Kommunist* 17 (November 1980), p. 103. Cited by Leiken, *Soviet Strategy in Latin America*, p. 35.

17. Jiri and Virginia Valenta, in Wiarda, *Rift and Revolution*, p. 213.

18. For a detailed discussion of recent Soviet arms deliveries see Department of Defense, *The Global Challenge: Soviet Military Power 1984*, pp. 120–22.

19. John F. Copper and Daniel S. Papp, eds., *Communist Nations' Military Assistance* (Boulder, Colo.: Westview Press, 1983), pp. 140–42. See also Jiri and Virginia Valenta, in Wiarda, *Rift and Revolution*, p. 215.

20. Department of State, Bureau of Public Affairs, "Cuban Armed Forces and the Soviet Military Presence," Special Report No. 103, August 1982, pp. 3–4. See also Copper and Papp, *Communist Nations' Military Assistance*, pp. 140–42, 145.

21. Department of State, "Cuban Armed Forces," pp. 3–4.

22. Department of State, Bureau of Public Affairs, "Nicaragua: Threat to Peace in Central America," Current Policy No. 476, 12 April 1983, p. 1. See also *Diario Las Américas*, 8 October 1983 and 16 December 1982.

23. Ibid. See also *Diario Las Américas*, 15 September 1983, p. 1.

24. *New York Times*, 19 January 1983, p. 1. See also Alex Alexiev, *Soviet Strategy in the Third World and Nicaragua*, U.S. Department of State Contract Paper (Santa Monica: Rand Corporation, March 1982), pp. 7–9.

25. U.S. Congress, House of Representatives, Permanent Select Committee on Intelligence, Subcommittee on Oversight and Evaluation, "Staff Reports: U.S. Intelligence Performance on Central America: Achievements and Selected Instances of Concern," 97th Congress, 2nd Session, 22 September 1982, p. 3.

26. Ibid.

27. U.S. Congress, House of Representatives, Permanent Select Committee on Intelligence, Report 98–122, 13 May 1983, p. 2.

28. Department of State, Bureau of Public Affairs, "Communist Interference in El Salvador," Special Report No. 80, 23 February 1981, p. 6. See also *Diario Las Américas*, 22 November 1981, p. 1.

29. Department of State, "Communist Interference in El Salvador," p. 7.

30. Department of State, "Nicaragua: Threat to Peace," p. 4.

31. Department of State, "Communist Interference in El Salvador," p. 7.

32. Montenegro was so important to the insurgents that a Honduran terrorist group aligned with the Salvadoran rebels seized 108 civilian hostages in San Pedro Sula the following month in an effort to force his release. The effort failed because Montenegro had already been transferred to Salvadoran authorities. U.S. Department of State and Department of Defense, "Background Paper: Central America," 27 May 1983.

33. Ibid.

34. C. W. Bill Young, Dissenting View on H.R. 2760, Permanent Select Committee on Intelligence, U.S. House of Representatives, Report 98–122, 13 May 1983, p. 41.

35. Department of State and Department of Defense, "Background Paper: Central America," p. 7.

36. Cited in Young, Dissenting View, p. 43.

37. Ibid.

38. *Diario Las Américas*, 15 September 1983.

39. For Honduran charges of Nicaraguan-supported guerrilla activities in Honduran territory, see *Diario Las Américas*, 23 February 1983, p. 1, and 21 September 1983, p. 6.

40. "Various independent sources here and in Central America confirmed Bolaños's identity," although for obvious reasons "it was impossible to obtain confirmation of the details he provided of the secretive and influential internal security apparatus in Nicaragua." *Washington Post*, 19 June 1983, p. A4.

41. Ibid.

42. Ibid.

43. "Cuban Defector Says Castro Finances Salvadoran Rebels' Arms Purchases," *Washington Post*, 19 November 1984, p. A10.

44. For two excellent discussions of the different schools of analysis of Soviet foreign policy, see Alexander Dallin and Gail W. Lapidus, "Reagan and the Russians: United States Policy Toward the Soviet Union and Eastern Europe," in Oye, Lieber, and Rothchild, eds., *Eagle Defiant: United States Foreign Policy in the 1980s* (Boston: Little, Brown, 1983), p. 206; and Robert Osgood, "Containment, Soviet Behavior, and Grand Strategy," Policy Papers in International Affairs, No. 16 (Berkeley, Calif.: Institute of International Studies, 1981).

45. Osgood, "Containment," p. 9.

46. Ibid., p. 14.

47. Ibid., p. 13.

48. Ibid., p. 14.

49. Analogy suggested by Madelaine Albright, "The Soviet Union and Détente," lecture at Georgetown University, 29 November 1984.

50. Gary W. Wynia, *The Politics of Latin American Development*, 2nd ed. (Cambridge: Cambridge University Press, 1984), p. 304.

51. Anderson, in Wiarda, *Rift and Revolution*, p. 105.

52. Jiri and Virginia Valenta, in Wiarda, *Rift and Revolution*, p. 249.

53. *Report of the Bipartisan Commission*, p. 113.

54. For an assessment of Cuba's military power relative to that of other Latin American states, see International Institute of Strategic Studies (IISS), *The Military Balance 1982-1983* (London: IISS, 1982), and Trevor N. Dupuy et al., *The Almanac of World Military Power* (San Rafael, Calif.: Presidio Press, 1980).

55. *Report of the Bipartisan Commission*, p. 122.

5. Views of the U.S. Catholic Bishops

By CARDINAL JOHN J. O'CONNOR

Focus
In April 1985 the United States Catholic Conference presented this official statement before a House Foreign Affairs subcommittee. Its author, Cardinal John J. O'Connor, archbishop of New York, is chairman of the USCC Department of Social Development and World Peace. As in all its previous congressional testimony on Central America, the USCC recommended political and diplomatic solutions, adding that the first requisite for such solutions is "the recognition that a military solution is neither possible nor desirable."

The bishops argue that there are three principal elements in the Central American crisis: (1) indigenous conditions in each country, (2) the geopolitical confrontation of the superpowers in the region, and (3) the regional nature of the problem and its resolution.

In Nicaragua, for example, say the bishops, a broad and legitimate revolutionary movement overthrew a long-standing dictator. But the democratic aspirations of the Nicaraguan people were soon thwarted by the Sandinistas' increasing reliance on the Soviet Union and the imposition of Marxist-Leninist ideas on crucial social sectors like education. "We cannot ignore trends that so closely resemble the unacceptable developments of the Cuban revolution," say the bishops.

The bishops call for dialogue and reject the de facto intervention of both the Soviet bloc and the United States (in its support of the contras). They call for "an abolition of Soviet and Cuban military activity in Nicaragua" and also condemn U.S. military aid to any force seeking to overthrow the Sandinistas. Instead, they believe, "significant U.S. economic aid should be provided to Nicaragua both as a measure of humanitarian assistance to a people in need and, with appropriate human rights criteria and evidence of a sincere pursuit of a political solution, as a legitimate means of influence."

In El Salvador, they see improvements, especially in President Duarte's dialogue with the Salvadoran guerrillas, but they advise limiting military assistance to 1983 levels. "We consider military aid from the United States justified to the extent that it enables and encourages the Salvadoran government to progress toward a political resolution of the conflict."

In closing, the bishops caution against too large a military buildup in Honduras, reject aid to the Guatemalan government in any form, and advocate more open policies toward refugees and displaced persons.

The bishops' call for dialogue should be compared with the more defense-oriented views of President Reagan (selection 1) and the Kissinger Commission (selection 3), as well as with Susan Kaufman Purcell's analysis of regional proposals (selection 10).

John J. O'Connor, cardinal archbishop of New York, prepared this testimony on behalf of the United States Catholic Conference, a non-canonical body under the direction of the National Conference of Catholic Bishops.

THE UNITED STATES CATHOLIC CONFERENCE has presented testimony on Central America on numerous occasions in the past, dating back to 1977. We have sought, over this period, to lend our voice to the ongoing public discussion of these complex issues that are of such critical concern both to our own society and to the peoples of Central America.

We have sought to address these issues as informed citizens, conscious of the enormous impact our government's policies necessarily have upon smaller nations so close to us; as religious leaders concerned with the moral implications of those policies; and as Catholic bishops intimately associated with the bishops and churches of Central America.

Our ties with the local churches of the region are many and of long standing. As an expression both of our solidarity with the bishops of Central America and of our desire continually to test our analysis of the situation against ever-changing realities, I was recently commissioned by the president of the U.S. bishops' conference to lead a delegation of bishops to Central America. While visiting only Nicaragua and El Salvador in this February [1985] visit, we were able to consult with bishops and many others from the entire region. My testimony today will reflect our long-standing analysis of the general situation as well as insights more recently gained.

The Central American reality can be viewed adequately only if three separate but closely related dimensions are kept in constant focus. These are: (1) the local roots of the crisis in each country, the largely indigenous sources of the several conflicts; (2) the geopolitical reality, which has converted Central America into an arena of superpower competition; and (3) the regional nature of both the problem and its potential resolution.

First, the *indigenous sources* of the conflicts. There is a temptation in this country, because of our justifiable concern about Soviet intrusion in the Americas, to ignore or misread the harsh realities that have brought revolution to Central America. Historic social inequities and brutal repression, accentuated over the past two decades by economic advances that, ironically, deepened the disparity between prosperous minorities and im-

---

Testimony delivered before a subcommittee of the U.S. House Foreign Affairs Committee, April 17, 1985.

poverished majorities, were responsible for social unrest, which was then exploited by Marxist ideology. Masses of people, many of them awakened to a social consciousness by the teachings of the Catholic Church, have sought to assert their God-given rights to live in dignity and freedom. As our government strives to evolve a policy responsive to perceived threats both to our national security and well-being and to the democratic process in the region, we must never lose sight of the still urgent demands for social change throughout much of Latin America.

The *geopolitical dimension* cannot be ignored. Our highly active U.S. presence and the intrusive policies of the Soviet Union and its ally, Cuba, have helped to convert a previously little-noticed region into a global focal point of indirect superpower confrontation. To fail to recognize the geopolitical aspects of the Central American arena is to miss a crucial dimension of the present reality; to overestimate the geopolitical is to distort the policy problem in both its ethical and political dimensions, and dangerously risk ever-higher levels of armed conflict.

The *regional nature* of the problem is, from our perspective, the crucial dimension of the Central American reality today. To be sure, each of the countries has its own special history and circumstances, and each is inescapably affected by external forces of today's world. But the root problems in each country are, with qualifications, the common problems of the Central American region, and they need to be addressed from a regional perspective. The overriding imperative for U.S. policy should be to work toward a political and diplomatic solution of the regional conflict in Central America.

Elements of a Regional Solution

The first requisite of a political and diplomatic solution is the recognition and acknowledgment that a military solution is neither possible nor desirable. To pursue a military solution, even while proclaiming the goals of political settlements, is to fail the test of political realism and of moral action. From the outset, U.S. policy should be defined in political, not in military, terms. This in turn should set the limits on the means used by the United States in pursuing its goals in Central America.

Second, a regional solution requires the active engagement of the other regional actors and U.S. cooperation with their efforts. While there will be no political solution in El Salvador or Nicaragua or the region generally without U.S. participation, there can be no solution by the United States alone. Our solidarity with the countries of the Contadora Group and our support of their process or of similar regional processes is essential to a peaceful outcome.

Third, an overall political and diplomatic solution requires a coordinated approach both to the region as a whole and to problems specific to each country.

Finally, a political-diplomatic solution requires a commitment to dialogue within the region and inside individual countries. Pope John Paul in his 1983 visit to Central America stressed the need for dialogue within El Salvador. The bishops of the region have repeatedly echoed the call for dialogue both within and among nations. The USCC continues to urge our government to make the pursuit of political and diplomatic dialogue in Central America a matter of highest priority.

Troubling Developments in Nicaragua

In addressing the U.S.-Nicaragua relationship it is useful to state some general characteristics of the Nicaraguan reality, to highlight the impact of the war on Nicaragua, and then to assess the main lines of U.S. policy toward Nicaragua.

In broad strokes, the following elements of recent Nicaraguan history seem pertinent to understanding the policy problem facing the United States.

In 1979, a popular and justified insurrection, led by the unified forces of the Sandinista Front for National Liberation with the active support of virtually all sectors of Nicaraguan society, including the church, overthrew an entrenched dictatorship. The justice of their cause and the right of all those who participated in the overthrow of the Somoza government to participate also in the formation of a new government was not in question. Since 1979 significant accomplishments, achieved in the face of daunting obstacles, have taken place. An emphasis on expanding health, literacy, and educational services has resulted in some significant advances. Needed land reform, difficult to accomplish under the best of circumstances, has made some progress, and the private sector is still somewhat active in the economy.

Simultaneously, however, deeply troubling signs have come to overshadow many of these accomplishments. An increasing reliance upon the

Soviet Union and its allies, the imposition of Marxist-Leninist philosophical ideas upon important areas of social life, including education and the media, and an excessive use of state power to monitor and restrict dissident behavior represent one set of these troubling signs. While we can sympathize with the extraordinary difficulties confronting the new government emerging from a fratricidal conflict that claimed 50,000 lives and depleted the economy, we cannot ignore trends that so closely resemble the unacceptable developments of the Cuban revolution. For example, the organization of neighborhood defense committees can have a chilling effect upon the exercise of freedom of expression.

The Church in Nicaragua

A second set of concerns that particularly touches us as Catholic bishops is that of church-state relations and the role of religion in Nicaragua. Time and again we have spoken out against the violation of religious rights and the persecution of church personnel wherever they have occurred, whether in Chile, Guatemala, and the Philippines or in Lithuania, Czechoslovakia, and Poland.

In the case of Nicaragua, we cannot fail to be concerned about the number of incidents that directly affect the freedom and well-being of the Catholic Church. The disturbances of August 1982, the disruption of the papal Mass in 1983, and the expulsion of ten priests in July 1984 are among the number of instances, some of which the USCC has previously denounced publicly in testimony before committees of the Congress.

As Archbishop John R. Roach stated after his visit to Nicaragua last August [1984], the bishops of the United States maintain ecclesial solidarity with the church in Nicaragua and "stand with the bishops of Nicaragua as they carry out their pastoral ministry in the face of significant pressure and tensions." We renew and reaffirm our solidarity with our brother bishops in Nicaragua.

In two separate and extended sessions with President Ortega during our visit, our delegation listed a number of specific instances of government interference in church affairs. Nicaraguan authorities have frankly acknowledged to us the wrongness of certain past actions and state that other problems which we have raised with them are on the way to solution. We fervently hope that to be the case, although we must note, unfortunately, we have as yet seen no evidence of constructive government action concerning these problems.

Still other actions are claimed to be justified, even required, because of the exigencies of the ongoing war. I want now to turn to that issue.

The War in Nicaragua

The war being waged against the government by the insurgent forces (the contras) is the dominant fact of Nicaraguan life today, and its impact is felt throughout the country. The consequences include the following:

   a. The entire society is in a constant state of alert. Restrictions on rights of assembly, publication, and organizing have been extensive. Mobilization for war, as always, provides the opportune occasion for excessive government control of society.

   b. The economic toll is enormous. Both the diversion of limited resources to defense and the severe damage to the economic infrastructure and to the agricultural sector have created great economic hardships in the country.

   c. The universal male conscription law has caused considerable discontent and imposed severe hardship on many families.

   d. The fear of a U.S. invasion, periodically predicted, is a palpable and generalized phenomenon. However much our government protests it has no intention of invading Nicaragua, the general populace cannot fail to be affected by hostile actions of our government and by the Nicaraguan government's repeated "invasion alerts."

Our delegation found that radically different perspectives on the contras are held in Nicaragua as in our country. During our visit in February we heard direct testimony from witnesses to contra atrocities and saw published material detailing these happenings. To refer to the role of the contras simply as "pressure" is to ignore the human cost of this reality—the cost is measured in narratives of death and destruction, some of which we heard while in Nicaragua.

Yet other witnesses presented a different view of the contras. Some in political opposition to the Sandinista government see the contras as providing a threat that deflects government attention from political opponents.

A major point of contention is the composition of the contras. Some focus on the allegedly heavy presence of former Somoza National Guardsmen in the military leadership of some of the contra groups; others on the large percentage of previously uninvolved *campesinos* and Indians among the troops. It seems unhelpful therefore to characterize all the contras as either idealistic freedom fighters or bloodthirsty right-wing terrorists.

The U.S. Role in Nicaragua

As the war has come to dominate Nicaraguan life today, the effect of U.S. policy is ever more central. The U.S. role in organizing, training, and funding the contras is a pervasive and inescapable issue. How, in the final analysis, to evaluate that U.S. aid, what role to assign it in the overall political equation, is at the heart of the policy debate in Nicaragua and here in the United States.

On the one hand there is evidence that to both the government of Nicaragua and the supporters of the contras, the U.S. backing is viewed, not only in terms of its direct military and political impact, but also in terms of its symbolic and psychological importance. On the other hand, it is clear that U.S. support has been instrumental in transforming the contras into a much stronger fighting force, enhancing their logistical capabilities and providing them with an assured line of supplies and equipment. In this sense the U.S. aid has helped intensify the war.

As bishops we seek to bring a moral perspective to this question, not a purely pragmatic view or a purely national one. Our moral responsibilities as a people and our legal obligations as a nation must be constantly and clearly assessed. Government policy is not exempt from ethical scrutiny. We recognize that forms of de facto external intervention exist throughout Central America. In Nicaragua both the United States and the Soviet bloc (especially Cuba) are part of the interventionary syndrome: the United States by providing military and other aid to the contras, and by exerting economic, psychological, diplomatic, and even military pressures against the Nicaraguan government; the Soviet-bloc nations through their programs of military aid and advisors, and through a more subtle but objectionable ideological intervention. We thus examine U.S. policy fully cognizant of the existing patterns of external intervention.

Our central moral concern at this point is for a just and peaceful resolution of the conflict and therefore for an end to all military assistance from any outside party. We must oppose military aid from the United States, the Soviet Union, or any other country to any party to the conflict in Nicaragua, whether the Sandinista government or any irregular military force in conflict with the government.

Our rationale includes the following elements:

- We are convinced that only a political solution can finally be success-

ful in Nicaragua as in Central America generally; there is no acceptable military solution.
- Further intensification of the military conflict must be avoided; the tide must be turned in a new direction.
- Extrahemispheric intervention, whether Soviet or other, is particularly objectionable for its effect of raising a regional conflict to a new, more dangerous level and fomenting ideological conflict; we seek an abolition of Soviet and Cuban military activity in Nicaragua.
- Direct military activity aid to any force attempting to overthrow a government with which we are not at war and with which we maintain diplomatic relations is illegal and, in our judgment, immoral and therefore cannot merit our support. We are convinced that such military aid undercuts the possibilities of a political solution within Nicaragua and jeopardizes the political process elsewhere in the region. We believe that it violates existing treaty obligations and undermines the moral standing of the United States within the international community.

In light of these propositions, we call for a U.S. policy toward Nicaragua with the following dimensions:

- We accept the need for a continuing series of political and diplomatic measures pressuring the government of Nicaragua both to allay U.S. and Central American fears about Soviet intrusions in the area and to respond to the undeniable grievances of many Nicaraguans.
- We urge all parties to accept the principle of dialogue as the preferred method of resolving differences. We urge the continuance and strengthening of regional dialogue on the lines of the Contadora process or something similar; we urge the resumption of bilateral talks between the United States and Nicaragua, even when only a slight hope of progress is evident; and we urge the Nicaraguan authorities to take seriously the call of their episcopate for an inclusive national dialogue and the bishops' offer to mediate or facilitate such dialogue.
- We are convinced that significant U.S. economic aid should be provided to Nicaragua both as a measure of humanitarian assistance to a people in need and, with appropriate human rights criteria and evidence of a sincere pursuit of a political solution, as a legitimate means of influence.
- We counsel a bona fide attempt to settle Nicaraguan problems between and among Nicaraguans. We urge them to a national effort to achieve dialogue with the participation of every element of Nicaraguan society,

governmental, civic, and insurgents under arms. The government of Nicaragua has already granted amnesty to those who lay down their arms; it seems appropriate, therefore, that the same government take the further step of initiating a comprehensive dialogue. This act would be a useful step toward that mutual disarmament and national reconciliation so important to the people of Nicaragua. Such a reconciliation would include, except for those guilty of specific personal crimes, the reintegration into the civic and political life of the nation of those now in armed insurgency.

• There is a need for the Nicaraguan government to achieve a situation in which there is genuine respect for human rights, political pluralism, freedom of expression, freedom of association, and freedom of private enterprise within a mixed economy. We suggest that the steps to be taken not involve the importation of governmental models from outside Nicaragua but rather the development of a system truly reflecting the historic spiritual and political values proper to the Nicaraguan people.

U.S. Policy Toward El Salvador

The USCC has addressed the issue of El Salvador in some detail over the past years. Let me here briefly summarize our positions.

Dialogue within El Salvador. We strongly support the dialogue begun last October [1984] between the government of El Salvador and the FDR-FMLN, facilitated by the bishops of El Salvador. We applaud this initiative of President Duarte. This process is a specification of the general approach we believe should be followed in seeking political-diplomatic solutions to the region's conflicts. We urge the U.S. government to do everything to support and nothing to hinder this dialogue process.

U.S. economic assistance. While we support the continuance of economic aid, we urge that greater care be taken to guard against the instances of graft and corruption that have plagued the administration of parts of the aid program in the recent past. We are particularly concerned that programs of humanitarian aid, intended especially to assist the approximately half million internally displaced persons, not become political instruments of a pacification program.

U.S. military assistance. We continue to oppose the militarization of U.S. policy toward El Salvador and the region. We recognize the right of the government of El Salvador to seek military assistance adequate to ensure its continuance, but we do not want the United States to contribute to the further militarization of the region. We consider military aid from the

United States justified to the extent that it enables and encourages the Salvadoran government to progress toward a political resolution of the conflict.

We specifically oppose increases of U.S. aid substantially greater than the 1983 levels. We firmly oppose the introduction into El Salvador of highly technological weapon systems and weapon systems that intensify the destructive nature of the war and increase the danger to civilians.

We believe that all programs of military aid should be constrained by certain conditions that enhance the progress of democratic and civilian government. Although the number of reported human rights violations has clearly decreased in El Salvador over the past year, we must note both the continued activity of organized death squads with alleged ties to the military and security forces and also terrorist activities on the left. We applaud President Duarte's efforts to bring the armed forces under civilian control and reduce civil rights violations.

We recommend that all U.S. military assistance be conditioned upon human rights criteria and evidence of sincere efforts to pursue a political solution.

Guatemala and Honduras

More briefly still, let me turn to the two other conflicted countries of Central America simply to restate our standing position. I should mention that although our recent delegation did not visit Guatemala and Honduras, we had the opportunity to consult with church leaders from those countries. We anticipate a USCC delegation to those countries later this year.

Given the continued high level of human rights violations in Guatemala despite some evident improvement on the political level, we affirm the position we took before this committee in 1983 that U.S. military assistance should not be provided to Guatemala in any form.

We view with great concern the continued buildup of U.S. military aid in Honduras. We recognize the need for legitimate defense and security, but we are seriously disturbed by the effects of this buildup upon the economy and the fragile civilian government of Honduras as well as the imminent danger of igniting a regional conflict.

Refugees and Displaced Persons

In 1981 the U.S. bishops said, "We believe that as long as the present state of violence and turmoil exists in El Salvador, the citizens of that country, regardless of political philosophy, should not be forced to return home. Hence, we urge that a moratorium be placed on all deportations to El Salvador, at least until such time as the government in power can guarantee the safety of its citizens." That has continued to be the USCC recommendation regarding the half million or so recent arrivals from El Salvador, extended to include the many thousands from other countries of Central America. The conference has been encouraged in this position by members of the Central American episcopates.

The Intergovernmental Commission for Migrants has begun, since last December, a program for the reception and supervision of Salvadorans deported from the United States. This project is laudable and gives great promise for the safety of individual deportees. We urge its continuance.

Nonetheless, in view of the large areas of conflict where ongoing struggle between the government and guerrilla forces renders many villages, farms, and other country areas dangerous, it seems necessary that the U.S. government be urged on humanitarian grounds to grant extended voluntary-departure status to Salvadorans, Guatemalans, and Nicaraguans as it has to citizens from Uganda, Afghanistan, Poland, and others who have taken refuge from countries in conflict.

Conclusion

If I were to summarize our position in one sentence, it would be that we urge our government to direct its powerful influence toward a regional effort to achieve a diplomatic and political settlement.

Our position concerning the indigenous roots of the conflicts, the imperative need for fundamental social change, and the futility of military solutions has been stated often and is well known. As the dominant external actor, but not the only actor, our government must play the creative diplomatic role that uniquely belongs it it, namely, to effect the goals of a regional settlement: dialogue leading to cessation of hostilities, resulting in an end to conflicts and an internationally guaranteed process of political and social reform and economic development. Under no foreseeable circumstances can direct U.S. military intervention in the region be justified.

With the bishops of the region we express our alarm over the growing militarization of the Central American countries, the danger of a more generalized war, violations of fundamental human rights, lack of progress in judicial redress, and the wrenching tragedy of so many refugees and displaced persons.

Part Two

Regional Perspectives

6. *The Development Alternative*

By ABRAHAM F. LOWENTHAL

Focus
"Caribbeans of whatever race, religion, or nationality want economic growth, more equity, full employment, political participation, enhanced national autonomy, and more self-respect," says Abraham F. Lowenthal. The problem is that these goals are not necessarily compatible. Cuba, for instance, "has achieved full employment at the cost of underemployment and severe limits on political freedom. Martinique is prosperous in large part because it is not autonomous" and is dependent on France. No simple solution presents itself for the complex problems of the Caribbean region.

In this essay written shortly after President Reagan's speech to the Organization of American States in February 1982 announcing the Caribbean Basin Initiative (see appendix A), Lowenthal describes in detail some of the more salient problems of particular Caribbean nations. Most of them stem more from economic underdevelopment than from political conflicts. He sees massive American aid, probably at twice the currently budgeted level, as the only likely way to improve the lot of the average person in the region.

Military security, argues Lowenthal, is not as important as it once was. Furthermore, the strategic situation has changed drastically; even the Panama Canal is no longer "essential in the old sense." Consequently, he discerns no major need for U.S. military aid.

Convincing the Congress and the American people of the need for large economic stimulants in the Caribbean will not be easy, he admits. But Americans should also realize that "doing nothing has its costs."

The Kissinger Commission (selection 3) agrees with Lowenthal that economic assistance must be greatly increased, but also argues that increased military aid is vital. Alberto Coll (selection 4) and Anthony Maingot (selection 8) present other views of the military situation. The Caribbean Basin Initiative (appendix A) and the analysis of it by Richard Feinberg and others (selection 7) should be compared with Lowenthal's recommendations.

Abraham F. Lowenthal is a professor of international relations at the University of Southern California. He was formerly secretary of the Latin American Program of the Woodrow Wilson Center for Scholars in Washington, D.C.

THE CARIBBEAN NOW COMPRISES no fewer than thirty-two political entities with a population totaling some 30 million people.[1] Fifteen of these entities are now independent countries, twelve having achieved independence since 1960. The natives in several British territories (including Montserrat, Anguilla, and St. Kitts–Nevis) are actively seeking independence. Residents of other "dependent" islands (France's Guadeloupe and Martinique, for example) seem happy with the status quo. Puerto Rico's future, perennially under discussion, is less clear than ever, after the nearly equal vote registered in the 1980 gubernatorial election by the pro-statehood and pro-commonwealth forces—with the *independentistas* getting less than 6 per cent of the vote.

The Caribbean territories are remarkably diverse, yet they are also surprisingly alike in important ways. As historian Franklin Knight has noted, the people of the region "have more in common than the Texan and the New Yorker, or the Mayan Indian and the cosmopolite of Mexico City."

To begin with, most of the territories are tiny. Two-thirds of the islands of the Caribbean could fit together into the King Ranch in Texas, or inside the Everglades. Cuba is by far the largest island, 745 miles long, but even Cuba is smaller in area than the state of Ohio. Trinidad is smaller than Rhode Island; Grenada is not much larger than the District of Columbia.

None of the territories is ethnically or culturally homogeneous. Five different racial groups (black, white, Oriental, native Indian, and East Indian) and their numerous subgroups and combinations mingle with varying degrees of integration and hostility. A certain color- and shade-consciousness persists. Numerous languages and dialects are spoken within the region, including Dutch, Spanish, French, and English and their derivatives, plus the Creole mixtures with African and Indian tongues. The result is at once a linguist's feast and nightmare. In Barbados, Antigua, and elsewhere, many archaic English words are still in use, augmented by local inventions—*birdspeed* (for "very fast"), for example, or *dont-carish* ("indifferent").

Caribbean religious sects include mixtures of the borrowed and the in-

---

Reprinted by permission of the author from the Spring 1982 issue of the *Wilson Quarterly*. The notes for this essay are on page 112.

vented, the traditional and the ultramodern. A blending of West African religions with French or Spanish Catholicism produced voodoo in Haiti and *Santería* and *Nañiquísmo* in Cuba, Puerto Rico, and the Dominican Republic. In the English and Dutch Caribbean, there are Moravians, Anglicans, Catholics, and Pentecostals; in Trinidad and Guyana, large communities of Muslims and Hindus flourish. Rastafarians, "black Israelites," wear their long hair in braided "dreadlocks" and look to Ethiopia as the Promised Land.

CARIBBEAN ECONOMICS

The economic organization of the Caribbean runs the gamut from the tax havens of the Bahamas, reportedly the largest single Eurocurrency market outside London, to Cuba's brand of socialism (where free market transactions are beginning to be permitted again), with all manner of hybrids in between.

In the Dominican Republic, because dictator Rafael Trujillo's vast personal fiefdom passed to government ownership after his assassination in 1961, a big share of the economy is now in the public sector; the government tries through generous incentives to encourage private investment, domestic and foreign. Jamaica and Guyana, whose leaders chose to build various forms of socialist-oriented "mixed" economies, are now concerned about how to re-attract and stimulate private investment. Grenada, whose principal exports are bananas and nutmeg and whose main economic potential lies in tourism, is apparently opting for Cuban-style "socialism" in a mini-state where no form of economic organization can much alter the obvious constraints on growth: scant resources, a small island, a tiny population.

Economic productivity ranges from the abysmal showing by Haiti—"the land of unlimited impossibilities," whose chief local growth industry may be the smuggling of refugees to the United States (at up to $1,500 a head)—to the uneven but impressive performances of Martinique, Guadeloupe, the Bahamas, Puerto Rico, Trinidad and Tobago, and Barbados. The region includes four out of six of the countries with the lowest GNP per capita in the Western Hemisphere (Haiti, Dominica, Grenada, and Guyana). But it also boasts eight territories with GNP per capita among the highest (Martinique, Trinidad and Tobago, the Netherlands Antilles, Guadeloupe, Puerto Rico, Surinam, the Bahamas, and Barbados).

Trinidad and Tobago has been lucky. It is the only Caribbean nation to have struck oil and today produces 200,000 barrels per day.

The Prevalence of Poverty

Although per capita incomes in the region are high by Third World standards, bitter poverty is still widespread. Two-thirds of Haiti's rural population were reported in 1978 to have annual incomes below $40; 50 per cent of Haiti's children under five suffer from protein-calorie malnutrition, with 17 per cent classified as severely undernourished. Seventy-five per cent of pre-school children in the Dominican Republic suffer from malnutrition, 4 per cent severely. One-third of Jamaica's people have annual incomes under $200, barely enough to cover a tourist's stay for a single night at one of Montego Bay's fancy hotels. In the slums of West Kingston, writes Trinidadian V. S. Naipaul, "hovels of board and cardboard and canvas and tin lie choked together on damp rubbish dumps behind which the sun sets in mocking splendor."

The poverty of the region is highlighted, and its psychological effects aggravated, by the juxtaposition—through migration, tourism, the media—with American affluence. Between 60 and 80 per cent of the programs shown on Caribbean television are U.S. imports—"Sesame Street," "Peyton Place," "Marcus Welby." At the Mallard's Beach Hyatt in Jamaica, a Canadian Club on the rocks costs $4.75, about three times the hourly wage of a local security guard. Shop windows taunt the poor with duty-free items that they cannot afford but that tourists perceive as bargains.

Overall, the island economies are in deep trouble. Caribbean shares of world production of sugar and of bauxite are falling, and even absolute levels are declining in many cases. (This is true of sugar in Barbados, Guadeloupe, Guyana, Haiti, Jamaica, Trinidad and Tobago, and Puerto Rico, and of bauxite in Guyana, Surinam, and the Dominican Republic.) The region's share of world tourism revenues is also dropping.

At the same time, higher prices for oil and other imports burden economies in the Caribbean as elsewhere in the Third World.[2] Jamaica has had seven consecutive years of negative growth. Cuba's economic growth, even by Castro's own account, is not much more impressive. The Dominican Republic's significant progress counters regional trends, but the Dominicans have been hard hit by the price of oil. In 1973, the Dominican Republic earned almost twice as much from sugar exports as it spent on oil imports; by 1979, oil imports cost about $75 million more than the country's total income from sugar.

Other Economic Disabilities

The Caribbean islands share other painful characteristics. They are densely populated and heavily dependent on exporting a few primary products. They are extremely susceptible to international market fluctuations and the vagaries of disease and weather. The epidemic of dengue fever in Cuba in the summer of 1981 (infecting 100,000 people) and the erratic path of Hurricane David in 1978 (sparing Barbados at the last moment and devastating Dominica instead) vividly illustrate this point.

Most islands have few known resources beyond the sun and sea, and this fact will never change; "the pencil of God has no eraser" is an old Haitian proverb. Those places with a broader resource base—Jamaica, for example, with its bauxite (used in aluminum) and the Dominican Republic with its nickel and gold—have seldom been able to exploit these assets fully. Christopher Columbus's assessment of the Arawak Indians on Hispaniola in 1492 remains valid when applied to Caribbeans today: "They very willingly traded everything they had. But they seemed to me a people very short of everything."

All of the islands have limited domestic markets, insubstantial local savings, and inadequate financing capacity. Agriculture is weak and declining through most of the region. "King Sugar" is now, at best, a princely pretender, its dominance undercut during the twentieth century by large cane growers in Louisiana and Brazil and by the thriving European sugar-beet industry. Most of the islands have deliberately sought to diversify their economies, moving toward manufacturing (Puerto Rico, for example), textiles (Barbados), petroleum refining (Aruba and Curaçao), financial services (the Cayman Islands), mining (many places), and tourism (everywhere). As they did elsewhere, people moved off the farm and into the towns. The result: Food production per capita—of pineapples, bananas, beans—has fallen during the past fifteen years in Jamaica, Guyana, Haiti, and Trinidad and Tobago. The region as a whole now imports more than $1 billion worth of food annually, costing the equivalent of at least 10 per cent of total exports.

While agriculture is declining, so is the push toward industrialization. The region-wide burst of industrialization-by-invitation begun during the 1960s has run out of steam. Most of the islands have found that it is easier to "take off" than stay aloft. Constrained by small size, they cannot generate enough power, in the form of capital, local markets, and so on, to sustain altitude. And capital must generally be imported, with much of the profits—from the making of watches or socks, the retreading of tires, the refining of oil—therefore exported. Few Caribbean islands show any growth since the mid-1970s in the share of GNP accounted for by manufacturing. Industrial stagnation, combined with a rural exodus and populations that are growing by 2 and 3 per cent a year (versus 0.7 per cent in the United States), has produced unemployment rates exceeding 30 per cent in some countries—according to *official* statistics.

Politics in the Caribbean

All of the Caribbean countries—including Haiti, which has been independent since 1804—bear the mark of centuries of colonial rule and of plantation societies. Ninety per cent of the region's population are descendants of the four million slaves imported from West Africa, beginning in 1506. The history of the Caribbean has always been largely shaped, and even written, from outside. A few outstanding Caribbean intellectuals— V. S. Naipaul, Frantz Fanon, Aimé Césaire, C.L.R. James, Eric Williams, Juan Bosch, William Demas, and Arthur Lewis among them—have projected the Caribbean condition onto a much broader canvas. Their work, and the common experiences of Caribbean peoples, have reinforced the outsider's notion of this as a region. As Demas, president of the Caribbean Development Bank, has written, "The [Caribbean] countries have a common historical legacy: the sugar plantation, slavery, indentured labor, monocultural economies producing what they did not consume and consuming what they did not produce ... and perhaps the longest period of external political dependence in any part of the Third World."

Most Caribbean societies are still not well integrated internally. Many, indeed, are more fragmented socially and politically now than they were a generation ago. The Dominican Republic's civil war in 1965; Trinidad's 1970 Black Power uprising; Bermuda's 1977 race riots; the 1980 general strike in Martinique; Jamaica's recurrent urban violence—all exemplify this trend. Cuba is not immune. Recall the 10,800 Cubans who sought asylum within the garden walls of the Peruvian embassy in Havana in April 1980, and the subsequent sea lift that brought 125,000 Cuban refugees into the United States.

The Caribbean islands are even less well integrated "horizontally"—with one another, that is. Although a sense of regional identity is slowly emerging—enhanced by the creation of certain regional institutions, such as the University of the West Indies—local efforts to forge a "common market" have come to naught. The West Indies Federation of ten territories established in 1958 lasted only until 1961; it could not survive inter-island rivalries, especially between Jamaica and Trinidad. The eastern Caribbean, the last portion of the Americas to shed colonial rule, is shattering into mini-states so small as to raise the possibility that one or another could be taken over by international criminal elements, such as those involved in the narcotics trade.[3] Interchange between the British Commonwealth Caribbean countries and the Spanish-, Dutch-, and French-speaking countries is still minimal.

The Trend Toward Polarization

Politically, the Caribbean territories face contradictory currents. All but four of the fifteen independent countries are formal democracies. "Nowhere else in the world," Jamaica's Edward Seaga has said, "does a conglomeration of parliamentary democracies exist as it does in the Caribbean." But democracy is not always deeply rooted. For every Barbados, there is a potential Grenada or Surinam. Grenada's prime minister, the eccentric Sir Eric Gairy, was ousted in a 1979 coup while he was in New York to address the United Nations General Assembly on the subject of flying saucers. In 1980, sixteen Surinamese army sergeants occupied several public buildings in a bid for higher pay—and accidentally toppled the government. "We only wanted a union," one of them said, "but ended up with a country."

While Grenada and Surinam have joined Haiti and Cuba as the Caribbean's only nondemocratic sovereign states [the Grenada and Haiti governments have since been ousted] an extended period of deceptive political "stability" elsewhere may be coming to an end. Many long-standing practitioners of "doctor politics"—Lloyd Best's unimprovable phrase to describe the role of Caribbean scholar-statesmen such as Eric Williams (Trinidad and Tobago), Juan Bosch (Dominican Republic), and Luis Muñoz Marín (Puerto Rico)—are either dead or out of power. Their passing has ushered in an era of uncertainty.

Jamaica, once considered highly developed politically, verged on chaos as the 1980 election approached; some 600 persons were killed in pre-election violence. In the Dominican Republic, the first peaceful transition from one elected president to another came in 1978 only after the Carter administration "jawboned" the local military and thereby made sure the ballots were fairly counted. Even Barbadians, who "consider that they and their institutions are perfect," as one nineteenth-century British governor put it, are nervous about the influence of leftist activists on small neighboring islands. Haiti, long ruled by "Papa Doc" Duvalier, is now ruled by his son "Baby Doc"; no one knows when or how this dynasty will end. [It ended with the ouster of Baby Doc in 1986.] And in Cuba, where Fidel Castro has directed a highly authoritarian regime for twenty-two years, overt dissidence is increasingly evident.

Indeed, polarization seems to be the prevailing political trend. Grenada's leftist coup and the quasi-leftist coup in Surinam have been matched by a rightward swing (albeit through elections) in the politics of Dominica, St. Vincent, St. Kitts–Nevis, and Antigua, and especially by the decisive election in 1980 of Edward Seaga as prime minister of Jamaica after eight years of Michael M. Manley's "democratic socialism." The prospects for some sort of "pan-Caribbean" consensus grow dim as the islands' politicians move in diverging directions.

In Search of an Orbit

On the world scene, most of the Caribbean countries are satellites in search of an orbit, or perhaps of multiple orbits, in the sense of regular and predictable relationships with Big Powers. The United States acts increasingly as the principal *métropole*; France and Britain have been slowly withdrawing from the area. Mexico and Venezuela have shown some interest in expanding their relations with the Caribbean, an interest that reached its most concrete expression in mid-1980 with a Venezuelan-Mexican commitment to sell oil to nine Caribbean and Central American states on extremely favorable terms. The Soviet Union's close relationship with Cuba makes the Kremlin a Caribbean actor, although direct Soviet influence has so far been slim outside of Cuba itself, where Moscow underwrites the economy with some $3.4 billion annually and equips the military.[4]

Cuba's situation is not the most extreme case of dependence on a foreign power, contrary to popular belief. Almost all of the island states have special trade and aid agreements with various powers. Martinique, Guadeloupe, and French Guiana, for example, are juridically part of metropolitan France; their citizens participate in French elections and send voting delegates to the National Assembly in Paris. These three territories (combined population: 702,000) receive some $570 per capita a year from France, making their economies, in William Demas's words, "the most highly artificial in an area in which there is considerable artificiality." The residents of the Netherlands Antilles receive about $200 per capita, courtesy of The Hague. The U.S. subsidy to Puerto Rico, in the form of transfer payments, amounts to more in per capita terms than the U.S.S.R.'s subsidy to Cuba. The Caribbean islands receive more foreign aid per capita than any other group of countries.

The volume of trade with the United States—$12 billion in 1980—reflects one characteristic shared by most of the Caribbean: a high degree of dependence on the U.S. mainland. Not counting Puerto Rico, the United States has more than $4.7 billion in direct private investment in the Caribbean. Some 75 per cent of the bauxite that the United States imports (more than half of our total consumption) comes from the Caribbean, as does about $4.5 billion worth of refined petroleum products.

The most significant ties between the United States and the Caribbean involve people. As I have noted, Caribbean economies depend heavily on tourism and cater primarily to U.S. travelers. Thousands of young Americans attend "last chance" medical schools in the Dominican Republic, Grenada, and Dominica. U.S.-based criminal syndicates find in the Caribbean congenial bases for narcotics and gambling operations, more lucrative than the rum and slave traffic of old. And American culture and technology—high and low—pervade the islands, at all levels and in all classes, from top-forty music and college T-shirts to Ford Mustangs and illegal arms shipments.

The most dramatic link of all is the stream of Caribbean migrants to the United States. Migration has long been a fact of life in the region, beginning with the arrival of the Indians from the South American rain forest and augmented, after 1492, by an influx of Europeans, of slaves, and, during the late nineteenth century, of indentured laborers from India, China, and Java. Up until the 1930s, however, Caribbean migration was essentially migration *into* the Caribbean or *within* the Caribbean. Today, the primary trend is migration *out* of the Caribbean.

Since World War II, some 4.5 million Caribbeans have left the islands and entered the United States. (Many others have gravitated towards France, Britain, the Netherlands, and Venezuela.) Puerto Rico has exported 40 per cent of its total population to the mainland since 1945, primarily to New York, Chicago, and other northern cities. More than one million Cubans have come to stay since 1960, more than 400,000 Dominicans, at least 300,000 Haitians, and about one million West Indians—all of this over and above the continuing shift of populations from island to island in the Caribbean itself. These movements of people are not unrelated events. They reflect a fundamental, continuous, and probably irreversible response to regional overpopulation and the magnetic attraction that any stronger economy exerts on any weaker one.

Haitian peasants flock to the Dominican Republic, where they can earn up to $1.50 for every ton of sugar cane cut, stripped, carried, stacked, and loaded—a princely wage compared to the thirty to seventy-five cents offered back home. Dominicans, meanwhile, head for more prosperous Puerto Rico. Citizens of all Caribbean countries seek opportunity in the United States, where jobs that native Americans, black or white, will not accept go begging. The flow of people back and forth between the Caribbean and the United States is today the most salient feature of U.S.-Caribbean relations.

In sum, much of the Caribbean is in turmoil as a new decade begins. Underlying the contemporary uneasiness is a conflict among goals. Caribbeans of whatever race, religion, or nationality all want economic growth, more equity, full employment, political participation, enhanced national autonomy, and more self-respect. These goals are not necessarily compatible. Cuba has achieved full employment at the cost of underemployment and severe limits on political freedom. Martinique is properous in large part because it is not autonomous. Barbados has grown "birdspeed," but not equitably.

The truth is, no single development strategy in the Caribbean has really worked. As Lloyd Best summed up the post-war experience: "We hoped for economic transformation by borrowing capital, by borrowing management, by borrowing technology, by borrowing this and borrowing that, and kowtowing before every manner of alien expert we could find." Yet sustained progress has been elusive, and high expectations have turned, here and there, to frustration and violence.

U.S. Interests and Role

What is at stake for the United States in the Caribbean? What are U.S. interests? How are they changing?

Most discussions of U.S. interests in the Caribbean emphasize our military security and economic ties. The security interest has usually been seen in terms of keeping hostile political and military influences away from this country's "soft underbelly." That was the aim of both the Monroe Doctrine (1823) and the so-called Roosevelt Corollary of 1904. (Theodore Roosevelt stated then that the United States, in the face of "wrongdoing" in Latin America, would act, "however reluctantly," as an "international police force.")

U.S. military installations dot the region, from the Roosevelt Roads naval base in Puerto Rico to Guantánamo Bay in Cuba. The Caribbean provides access to the Panama Canal, long considered vital to U.S. commerce and defense. The sea lanes on which much U.S. trade depends (including one-half of our imported oil) pass through or near the Caribbean. The economic interest, as traditionally conceived, turns on protecting American commerce in the region, as well as U.S. access to various local strategic minerals and raw materials. For all these reasons, it has long seemed crucial that, if nothing else, the United States maintain what Secretary of State Cordell Hull once called "orderly and stable governments" in the Caribbean.

Many U.S. diplomats and scholars continue to think in these terms. They cite the presence of Soviet fleets in the Caribbean (since 1969, twenty-one Soviet naval deployments, varying in size from two to five ships, have visited the Caribbean); the possible construction of a submarine base capable of handling Soviet vessels at Cienfuegos on the southern coast of Cuba; and the KGB's electronic intelligence-gathering installations, also based in Cuba. In addition, they say, U.S. commercial interests in the Caribbean are being threatened by political instability.

Ray Cline, former deputy director of the Central Intelligence Agency, and now on the staff of Georgetown University's Center for Strategic and International Studies, has urged the White House to "reproclaim" the Monroe Doctrine. To support their views, Cline and others have drawn on the writings of Admiral Alfred Thayer Mahan and Sir Halford John Mackinder, leading geopolitical theorists of the nineteenth century.

A Changing Relationship

Other observers, mostly in academe, ask whether the Caribbean is really still so important to the United States.

Changing technology—jet aircraft, long-range missiles—have reduced both the military significance of the Caribbean and the feasibility of excluding foreign influence. U.S. naval bases and other outposts in the region are no longer vital; U.S. power can easily be brought to bear from the mainland. Indeed, most of the remaining U.S. military installations in the Caribbean are currently due for phase-out by the mid-1980s, primarily for budget reasons. The Panama Canal, although still useful, is no longer *essential* in the old sense. A shrinking share of U.S. trade passes through the canal; many of the world's new oil supertankers are too big to negotiate it, as are almost all of the aircraft carriers around which U.S. fleets are organized.

In practical terms, the United States can no longer exert the total control over this region it once enjoyed. From 1898 to 1969, no hostile naval force (aside from German submarines during World War II) entered Caribbean waters. But, as noted, Soviet surface ships and submarines have been visiting regularly to "show the flag." The primary means for protecting U.S. strategic interests now lies in great-power agreements, exemplified by the apparent U.S.-U.S.S.R. "understandings" of 1962, 1970, and 1979, which, seriatim, are said to have banned from Cuba land-based nuclear missiles, Soviet submarines carrying nuclear missiles, and further deployments of Soviet combat troops.

In economic terms, too, the relative significance of the Caribbean for the United States has waned. Before World War II, the region accounted for more than 11 per cent of direct U.S. foreign investment and an even higher share of overseas trade. By 1978, U.S. investment in the Caribbean (excluding Puerto Rico) amounted to only 2.5 per cent of direct U.S. foreign investment, and considerably less if the $2 billion in "paper" investment in the Bahamas is excluded. The share of U.S. petroleum imports coming from or passing through the Caribbean, though still significant, has been declining in recent years, as imports from the Middle East, Nigeria, and Mexico have risen. Today, the United States depends on no commodity imported from the Caribbean. Bauxite, the principal strategic import, is available from many other countries.

The Ongoing Significance

Yet there are other reasons why Washington should keep its eye on the Caribbean.

First, the sovereign Caribbean nations constitute a significant bloc of votes at the U.N. and other international bodies. That puts them in a position to help or hurt. The Caribbean democracies have voted, en bloc, to condemn the Soviet invasion of Afghanistan; they have consistently supported the U.S. position on Israel. Caribbean hostility could prove to be a considerable irritant. One can imagine, for example, the trouble that might ensue if the island nations went on record in the U.N. in favor of Puerto Rican independence.

Second, the Caribbean has become, by reason of its proximity to the United States and the increasing international prominence of the region's leaders, a kind of litmus test of the attitudes and policies that Washington will adopt toward Third World countries generally.

Third, and most important, there remains the sheer scale of the human interpenetration between the Caribbean and the United States. The United States and the Caribbean import from each other music, dance, crime, literature, and political ideas and techniques. Grenada's radical New Jewel movement is led primarily by men who were influenced, as students in U.S. universities during the 1960s, by the Black Power movement. Jamaica's prime minister, Edward Seaga, was born in Boston and educated at Harvard. People of Caribbean descent are making their presence felt in America, as they have, indeed, been doing since the 1920s, when the arrival in New York of some 40,000 black West Indians helped touch off what is now called the "Harlem Renaissance." The large, active, and growing Caribbean communities in this country are already a fact of political life in Florida, New York, and New Jersey, just as the Mexican influence grows in the U.S. Southwest.

In short, an intimate relationship exists between the Caribbean and the United States, whether either party likes it or not. What remains to be determined are its nature and consequences.

Four Policy Approaches

In pursuing its relationship with the Caribbean region, the United States has, in essence, four policies to choose from.

The *first* of these, not now in vogue, is what may be called the "traditional" policy, its chief principle well expressed by Assistant Secretary of State Francis Butler Loomis in 1904: "No picture of our future is complete which does not contemplate and comprehend the United States as the dominant power in the Caribbean Sea." The traditional policy combines studied indifference to the Caribbean's underlying economic and social realities with keen sensitivity to potential threats to the military security of the United States. At its crudest, it appears as the "gunboat diplomacy" of Roosevelt, Taft, and the Republican presidents of the 1920s—or of Democrat Lyndon Johnson during the Dominican civil war in 1965. This is a deceptively attractive policy because it seems cheap and simple. But it is also shortsighted. It amounts, indeed, to putting out the fires while doing nothing to remove the flammable material.

A *second* approach would be for the United States to "disengage" itself from the Caribbean altogether. The assumption here is that the region is economically and strategically irrelevant—and would perhaps fare better if left alone. This policy, too, has a certain appeal. Given all the other issues with which Washington must deal, how tempting to let the Caribbean stew in its own juices, to lavish upon each of these thirty-two struggling entities the "benign neglect" customarily reserved for Burma or Sri Lanka.

Again, such a policy is not really feasible. The United States cannot withdraw from involvement in its border region by a unilateral act of will. Even if the U.S. government tried to tighten restrictions on immigration, the movement of people to the mainland would continue. American businessmen operating in the Caribbean would still demand protection. American tourists would still migrate south in winter.

A *third* Caribbean policy—the "activist" approach—is essentially the one pursued (in different ways) by the Carter and Reagan administrations. Its tenets are two: The United States must retain its special concern for the region's military security and political stability, and it must, at the same time, increase economic and technical aid to the Caribbean.

The activist approach, which underlies the Reagan administration's "Caribbean Basin Initiative" [see appendix A], calls for beefing up the U.S. presence throughout the area: politically, militarily, economically, culturally, through both the public and private sectors. Its proponents favor adjustment in trade and tariff policy (rather than outright injections of money) to facilitate the transfer of capital and technology to the islands. When money changes hands, activists think it should be done via *bilateral* agreements to emphasize the American "partnership."

The activists also hope to turn the Caribbean away from Cuba. From its very first days, the Reagan administration moved to counter Cuban diplomatic efforts and tighten restrictions on commerce and exchange. It is currently planning to establish a Radio Free Cuba. Secretary of State Alexander Haig has threatened repeatedly to "go to the source" to stop Cuban arms shipments to guerrillas in Central America.[5]

The activist policy has some obvious plusses. Focusing more attention—and aid—on the Caribbean gives Washington a certain leverage in the region. Most Caribbean states are so small that even limited American assistance would go a long way. The timing is also good: Cuba's internal difficulties are growing, while general Caribbean trends are toward greater cooperation with the United States.

But there are also some risks. One danger is creation of unrealistic expectations. Jamaica's Prime Minister Seaga hopes for a U.S. commitment of $3 billion annually to the region—perhaps ten to fifteen times what is likely to be forthcoming. (The *total* U.S. foreign economic aid budget is currently $7.5 billion.) Moreover, the preoccupation of the State Department and the White House with Fidel Castro's Cuba does not sit well with most Caribbean leaders, who perceive Castro as only one of many Caribbean actors rather than as a Cold War instrument. Indeed, most of them are not above "playing the Cuba card" to please domestic voters or curry favor in Third World meetings. Washington's obsession with Cuba diminishes the chances of cooperating with Canada, Mexico, and Venezuela—all of which maintain diplomatic (if not cordial) relations with Castro's government—to develop the Caribbean. This issue, more than any other, helped to dampen enthusiasm for any "mini-Marshall Plan" that depended on close U.S. cooperation with the three.

More generally, the activist approach to the Caribbean carries the risk that Washington will become too "interventionist." Even assuming benign intent, active or covert U.S. pursuit of political goals could stifle local initiative or provoke nationalist reactions. And, to the extent that U.S. interest in the Caribbean appears to be merely expedient—really concerned not with the region's people but only with potential threats to the United States—the chances increase that an active U.S. presence in the Caribbean will backfire.

The *fourth* possible U.S. approach—one favored, not surprisingly, by many Caribbean leaders—is the adoption by Washington (and others) of a sustained commitment to Caribbean development. Such a commitment would emphasize underlying economic progress rather than immediate military security; concentrate on the long-term rather than the short-term; and tolerate diverse political and economic approaches.

This "developmentalist" policy would involve large sums of money, channeled primarily through multilateral rather than bilateral channels; imaginative efforts to provide "non-aid" concessions to help Caribbean development; and a scaling down by Washington of its efforts to contain or reverse the Cuban revolution. Rather than building up U.S. visibility, Washington would downplay its own role and lay the foundations for a healthier future U.S.-Caribbean relationship by focusing on the region's economic stagnation, extreme inequities, malnutrition, illiteracy, and poor social and health services.

The developmentalist approach responds to a fundamental U.S. interest—"security," in a broader sense than the strictly military—in having stable, working societies on our third border. It reflects both a moral concern (that one *is*, to an extent, one's brother's keeper) and a practical realization that festering problems in societies so intertwined with our own will eventually affect this country.

Three drawbacks are apparent, however.

One problem is, again, the danger of exaggerated expectations. It is not likely that the high aspirations of Caribbean peoples can all be achieved, even with substantial foreign aid. Some of the obstacles to sustained, equitable growth—meager resources (material and human), insufficient size, extreme vulnerability to bad weather and world market slumps—cannot be wished away.

Second, there is an inevitable tension between accepting any form of economic and social oganization—even Cuba's—and reassuring domestic and foreign investors about the region's prospects. Stanching the flow of capital from the Caribbean (not to mention attracting more investment) depends in part on giving businessmen confidence that their role will be valued and their assets protected. The prospect of nationalization or outright expropriation undermines that confidence, to say the least.

Finally, the developmental approach would be hard to sell at home. Congress is not likely to go along with what would be portrayed as a "no strings" commitment to aid a bewildering cluster of small countries—at least not until Americans come to realize that their own future well-being depends, in some measure, on that of their neighbors. No administration so far has been willing to make that case, and it may be that none can.

Some Positive U.S. Steps

Whether Washington maintains its current policy toward the region or adopts a longer-term developmentalist approach, several steps could be taken to better the Caribbean's lot:

- Strengthen Caribbean agriculture by earmarking aid funds for research and development, improving access to farm credit, and encouraging private U.S. investment in rural areas.
- Improve access to U.S. markets for both farm products and manufactured goods. Tariff barriers could be lowered or even eliminated (as the Reagan administration has suggested). Indeed, Washington has already

done this for one Caribbean country by granting duty-free status to twenty-seven Jamaican products, including peppers and tomatoes. Reduction or elimination of the U.S. tariff on rum and cigars would have a more positive short-term effect on several Caribbean countries than almost anything else Washington could do.

- Stabilize the export earnings of Caribbean countries that depend on the export of one or two major products by bolstering international commodity and stockpiling arrangements.
- Set up regular procedures to help Caribbean territories cope with hurricanes and other natural disasters, as chronic as they are unexpected.
- Expand tourism—and make it more "efficient." Shared air transport facilities, jointly agreed routings, and other measures would help Caribbean countries divide the annual revenue from tourism more equitably—which would be far preferable to the current cut-throat island rivalry. A decision by the United States to increase the dollar value of duty-free imports permitted to returning tourists would be hailed by island merchants. So would a revison of U.S. income tax codes to allow expenses for business-related conventions held in the Caribbean to be treated as are conventions in Canada and Mexico.
- Promote the transfer of U.S. capital and technology. For example, American companies could be induced, via tax and other incentives, to "export" many of their operations to the Caribbean.
- Expand the existing "guest worker" programs and raise current immigration quotas for the Caribbean. (U.S. quotas are now 20,000 annually from any sovereign nation, 600 from any dependency.) This would enlarge the "safety valve" for the many islands plagued by overpopulation and unemployment.
- Help the Caribbean cope with its energy problem. No other region of the world has been harder hit by the rise in the price of oil since 1973. A breakthrough in solar energy, if it ever comes, might do more for Caribbean development than all other steps combined. But a solar collector that is both practical and economical does not yet exist. Because of the research costs involved, developing one is something only the United States and other industrialized nations can hope to achieve.

These steps, taken together, would cost money and stir much opposition. Letting in more agricultural produce would anger growers of winter fruits and vegetables in Florida and California. Lowering the tariff on rum would hurt Puerto Rican firms. A tax deduction for Caribbean conventions would raise the hackles of U.S. innkeepers. Encouraging added American investment in island industries would be labeled "exporting jobs" by the AFL-CIO and could hurt marginal businesses in the United States (although manufacturers in Asia may, in fact, sustain the biggest loss from Caribbean competition). Permitting more migration from the Caribbean would contribute to social tensions and the demand for public services.

What is more, the American taxpayer would certainly have a larger bill to foot. To implement *all* of these measures, the current $600 million aid package to the Caribbean (not including U.S. payments to Puerto Rico) from all non-Communist countries would, I estimate, have to be doubled; as usual, a large share of that increase would have to come from Washington.

The costs are undeniable. On the other hand, because the Caribbean countries are so tiny, the benefit to their economies from these measures would be greatly disproportionate to any expense the United States might incur. And one should not forget that doing nothing also has its costs: unregulated and illegal immigration, regional instability, and the quality of 30 million lives—not to mention the strains put on the health of democracy and free enterprise by the persistent failure of democratic societies to "make it" in the shadow of the United States.

No 'Special Relationship'

Taking a special interest in the economic and social health of the Caribbean countries is the right thing for the United States to do. At the same time, Washington should refrain from proclaiming a "special relationship" and from promising "regional preferences" that significantly contradict basic U.S. polices on trade, finance, immigration, and the like. U.S. stakes in the Caribbean are fairly high, but there is even more at stake *outside* the Caribbean. On a practical level, history suggests that American interests in the Caribbean, however important they may appear from time to time, would not long sustain the adoption of policies and practices that contravene universal rules. Preferential policies that substantially hurt some other region important to the United States simply would not last.

For their part, local leaders in the Caribbean are uneasy about the idea of a special relationship. Historically, U.S. promises of "special treatment" have meant singling out the Caribbean for rhetorical or military attention: the approach either of Arpège ("Promise her anything ...") or of Hallmark Cards ("When you care enough to send the very best"—the Marines).

The Caribbean is too near the United States to take for granted, yet too far—historically and politically—to integrate comfortably into a U.S.

"sphere." The challenge for policy-makers in Washington is to keep that in mind. It is up to U.S. officials to understand how sensitive the Caribbean is to the impact of the United States and how much our country is affected by the Caribbean. It is important for them to understand the Caribbean for what it was, for what it is, and for what it could become. And it is essential to focus on the realistic possibilities that exist for the United States to affect the region positively—for our sake as much as for the Caribbean's.

NOTES

1. Analysts differ about how to define the Caribbean. For the purposes of formulating U.S. policy, it is helpful to conceive of the Caribbean region as that set of territories, in or bordered by the Caribbean Sea, concerning which the United States has historically felt a special security interest, arising primarily from their proximity and their perceived vulnerability to external penetration. All the Caribbean islands, together with Belize on the Central American isthmus and Guyana, Surinam, and French Guiana on the South American mainland, would fit this definition of the region. While there has been much fashionable talk of late about the larger "Caribbean Basin," the experiences of Venezuela, Colombia, Mexico, and most Central American nations differ in significant ways from those of the Caribbean territories I deal with in this essay.

2. Only Trinidad and Tobago is self-sufficient in oil, but many other nations—Surinam, Cuba, Barbados, Guyana, Jamaica, the Dominican Republic—are exploring. Because Caribbean countries are small, even modest discoveries could be of major importance.

3. In 1980, the FBI arrested ten men in New Orleans who were allegedly planning to overthrow the government of Dominica (population: 77,000) using mercenaries drawn from the ranks of the Ku Klux Klan. The plot was reportedly bankrolled by a Texas millionaire (who hoped to establish a free port in Dominica), supposedly with the blessing of a former Dominican prime minister.

4. Cuba has the best air force in the Caribbean and a modern "gunboat navy." The Soviets have supplied the island with MiG-23 "Floggers" and missile attack boats. Russian pilots reportedly help patrol Cuban skies to free Cubans for duty in Angola, Ethiopia, and elsewhere in Africa.

5. Fidel Castro charged in July 1981 that the United States had also employed germ warfare in Cuba, accounting for the dengue epidemic as well as for the appearance of blue mold tobacco blight and roya rust, which attacks sugar cane. I have no evidence to support this, and I do not believe it, but one U.S. official's observation that Castro is "now as paranoid as he was at the time of the Bay of Pigs" was not unambiguously reassuring.

7. Caribbean Basin Initiative: Pros and Cons

By RICHARD E. FEINBERG, RICHARD NEWFARMER, and BERNADETTE ORR

Focus

The controversial Caribbean Basin Initiative (CBI) proposed by the Reagan administration (see appendix A) seeks to promote economic growth and political stability on the Caribbean islands and the Central American mainland. In the Caribbean, some people feel it will benefit only U.S. companies and larger American interests; in the United States, organized labor and certain manufacturers fear that the CBI will export jobs and profit-making opportunities badly needed for full economic recovery at home.

In July 1983 Congress passed the CBI legislation specifying January 1984 as the date of implementation. It promises twenty-eight nations economic assistance and duty-free access to U.S. markets for twelve years. The three authors of this article, writing before the legislation was passed, examine the details of the CBI and the arguments of both its supporters and its opponents. Their main conclusion: "In the coming years, even if the CBI is tremendously successful, economic growth in the United States based upon a sound monetary and fiscal policy will probably have a far greater impact on the region's welfare."

They add, however, that several of the proposals are valuable. Trade incentives such as the Free Trade Area and Investment Tax Credits hold out the possibility of genuine economic growth. Economic assistance, though needed—especially given the debt burden of many of

113

these nations—may otherwise, they say, contribute only to further dependency.

On the Central American mainland, where needs are different from those of the islands, say the authors, President Reagan's policies have sharpened political conflict and have worked at cross-purposes to the economic goals of his CBI. Only political stability will enable these countries to profit from the economic initiatives already under way.

This analysis differs widely from that of Abraham Lowenthal (selection 6), who views massive economic assistance as the principal means for development in the region.

Richard E. Feinberg is director of the Foreign Policy Program at the Overseas Development Council (ODC). **Richard Newfarmer** is director of the Trade and Industrial Policy Program at ODC. **Bernadette Orr** is a freelance journalist.

PRESIDENT REAGAN UNVEILED his plan for the economic recovery of Central America and the Caribbean, the Caribbean Basin Initiative [see appendix A], in a speech before the Organization of American States on February 24, 1982. Economic progress in the Caribbean Basin was "vital to the security interests of this nation and this hemisphere," the President said. He argued that economic growth was a necessary condition for democracy, and warned that "economic disaster has provided a fresh opening to the enemies of freedom."

Since the first presentation of the plan, the CBI has faced strong criticism as well as praise in its long and frustrating journey through Congress. This spring [1983] the new 98th Congress reopened debate on the economic and foreign policy rationale of the measure, its probable impact both domestically and within the beneficiary nations, and its merit at a time of continued economic recession and high unemployment here at home.

As originally proposed by the President, the CBI was to have three legs—trade, investment, and concessional aid—to generate foreign exchange, create new employment, and raise production levels. In brief, the CBI would:

1. Provide $350 million in supplemental assistance to meet balance-of-payments shortfalls in key countries, notably El Salvador (which was scheduled to receive $128 million).

2. Establish one-way, duty-free access to U.S. markets for Caribbean Basin exports for a twelve-year-period—the so-called Free Trade Area.

3. Create an investment tax credit of 10 per cent for U.S. businesses investing in the Caribbean Basin.

Let us examine each component in greater detail.

1. ECONOMIC ASSISTANCE

The Administration proposed $350 million in quick-disbursing funds to help Caribbean Basin countries meet pressing balance-of-payments needs. Shortages of foreign exchange are a major cause of the profound economic

---

Reprinted by permission from the Spring 1983 issue of *Caribbean Review* (© 1983 by Caribbean Review, Incorporated, Florida International University, Miami, Florida).

crisis gripping the region. The cost of imported energy has risen, whereas prices of such key commodities as sugar, coffee, bauxite, and nickel have declined. The drop in export prices in 1981 alone reduced the region's export earnings by roughly $500 million. In addition, high market interest rates have increased the burden of a swollen foreign debt.

The aid portion of the CBI was the only measure to become law, after passing both houses in September 1982. It stirred controversy for several reasons.

First, the $350 million amount provided less than 10 per cent of the external resources needed to cover the region's balance-of-payments shortfalls. Although a substantial addition to the $474 million provided to the region in the 1982 budget, the CBI supplemental aid nonetheless was a small sum relative to the need—or the aid levels of other donors. For example, Venezuelan president Luis Herrera Campíns pointed out that his country's aid program for the Caribbean provided an equivalent amount of money each year, despite the much smaller size of Venezuela's GNP as compared to that of the United States. Certainly, by itself, the supplemental aid was insufficient to stimulate strong growth.

A second objection to the aid portion of the bill was the emphasis on the Central American countries: El Salvador alone was scheduled to receive $128 million, or 37 per cent of the total. Two other Central Americn countries—Costa Rica ($70 million) and Honduras ($35 million)—were also to receive significant aid. Outside Central America, only the Dominican Republic ($40 million) and Jamaica ($50 million) were to be major beneficiaries. The evident slant toward Central America prompted human rights groups and congressional critics of U.S. policy to view the CBI as a means of financing misconceived U.S. security objectives, rather than as a true effort to promote development. The fact that the proposed aid was for general balance-of-payments support reinforced this impression. Aid that is slated for "development projects," for example, in the agriculture or health sectors, is more carefully programmed and monitored.

In its final version of the bill, therefore, Congress made several adjustments. Amounts were reallocated to give more representation to smaller Caribbean countries and to reduce controversial aid to El Salvador. The House also required—and Secretary of State George Shultz agreed—that 12.5 per cent of the total $350 million be spent for basic needs-oriented projects. A Senate proposal to convert the CBI from a bilateral to a multilateral fund administered by the World Bank—where developmental concerns would dominate—passed the Foreign Relations Committee but was eliminated in the final bill.

The second and third components of the CBI were never passed by the 97th Congress, although a revised trade bill was approved by the House in late December.

2. FREE TRADE AREA

President Reagan heralded the Free Trade Area (FTA) as the "centerpiece" of the CBI. Indeed, trade liberalization is potentially the most important development instrument at the disposal of the Administration; development economists contend that trade is a much more important stimulus to sustained growth than development assistance. Coming at a time of rising demands for protectionism, the FTA is a positive step—albeit small—in the direction of a more accessible U.S. market for developing countries.

The FTA, in reality, will affect only slightly more than 5 per cent of the region's total exports to the United States. As the President mentioned in his formal announcement of the CBI before the Organization of American States, 87 per cent of the region's exports into the United States already enter duty free. These exports include petroleum, products covered by the Generalized System of Preferences (GSP), and other goods, mainly agricultural projects not produced in quantity in the United States.

Whether the original or an amended version of the FTA is adopted, it is certain that some categories of goods that are now "dutiable" will not be granted free entry under the CBI. These include textiles, products not eligible for the GSP becaue their value-added in the CBI country of origin is too low, and products not eligible for the GSP because the country exports more than is allowed under the legislation (most of the category is sugar exports). The exclusion of textiles from the program is particularly lamentable because this industry holds the greatest opportunity for expanding exports and creating jobs in the Caribbean.

What the FTA Could Do

The economic impact of the FTA upon the region will depend on two things: how much more United States consumers buy of the imported product because prices fall and goods are cheaper, and how much more consumers buy of the imported product from the region favored with a price advantage and shift away from similar imported goods produced elsewhere. The total amount of new trade generated for the CBI countries therefore depends upon how high the original tariff was prior to cutting, the responsiveness of consumers to changes in prices, and the shift of consumer purchases into CBI imports at the expense of other imports.

Our study (Richard E. Feinberg and Richard Newfarmer, "The Caribbean Basin Initiative: Bold Plan or Empty Promise," in *From Gunboats to Diplomacy: New U.S. Policies for Latin America*) of the FTA revealed that eliminating the tariffs would initially raise only about $45–90 million in foreign exchange for the beneficiary nations. The reason for this is that for many of these products, tariff levels are not high, and consumers are not particularly responsive to price changes.

The new U.S. demand created for imports from the region will amount to only $23 million. But the region will also benefit from consumers shifting from already imported products to those imported from the region. This response will vary widely. For undifferentiated products where brand names are unimportant, such as beef, handbags, and scrap tobacco, the effect could be large, limited only by the capacity of the exporting countries to expand their production. For other products, the effects are likely to be somewhat less. Even relatively large consumer shifts to CBI-country products, however, would generate additional exports of less than $100 million or 1 per cent of the region's 1980 exports.

The Impact of Sugar Quotas

The FTA is only one element in the trade package. A potentially more important change, at least in the short run, was the decision in May 1982 to impose worldwide sugar quotas, a move that undermined some of the beneficial effects the CBI was intended to produce. The CBI had included a provision for sugar quotas. However, the quotas for the Caribbean's three principal sugar producers—the Dominican Republic, Guatemala, Panama—turned out to be even lower than the amounts the Administration had originally proposed.

The Caribbean Basin nations opposed even the higher quota levels originally proposed in the CBI, since this was the first time the United States had imposed quotas since 1974. Since sugar is one of the region's major foreign-exchange earners, the impact of the restrictive quotas implemented in May was severe. The Organization of American States estimated that total losses for Latin America would be about $90 million through the end of 1982. Many officials from the sugar-producing Caribbean nations expressed concern that the losses from lower sugar exports would more than offset the amount of supplemental aid to their countries.

Nonetheless, as part of the political dealing over the 1982 budget cuts, the Administration bowed to the powerful group of U.S. sugar growers and levied the new quotas, thereby supporting a higher domestic sugar price. Their imposition sent contradictory signals to friendly governments in the Caribbean, many of whom questioned the sincerity and depth of the Administration's commitment to assisting their economic growth. Said one Dominican Republic diplomat, "you can be sure" that the President lost some credibility in his country. The $41 million in supplemental aid "is certainly not enough to offset the impact of the quotas."

The emphasis on the tariff-reducing aspects of the CBI obscured one key point: the impact of all the proposed changes in trade regulations would probably be much less than that of renewed U.S. domestic growth. An acceleration in the U.S. growth rate from zero to 3 per cent per year would probably generate over $300 million in new export earnings for the region. Or consider the effects of lowered U.S. interest rates. Debt service not infrequently absorbs from 15 to 25 per cent of export earnings of CBI countries. If interest rates were to fall by five percentage points on the debt of $5.4 billion dollars owed to private creditors (as of December 31, 1980), interest payments would be reduced by more than $250 million. In the coming years, even if the CBI is tremendously successful, economic growth in the United States based upon a sound monetary and fiscal policy will probably have a far greater impact on the region's welfare.

The FTA, then, provides an opportunity for the region to increase in modest measure its domestic employment, export earnings, and growth. Its impact could be greater if it included freer trade in sugar, textiles, and other manufactured products. For this to occur, the Administration would have to reverse its stand on trade adjustment assistance, worker training, and other legitimate trade concerns of domestic labor. Without an appeal to labor, the CBI will face a continuing tough battle, since during 1982 organized labor was the most virulent opponent of the measure.

With the unemployment rate about 10 per cent nationally and even more for industries and regions competing with low-wage imports from the Caribbean, labor's reaction to proposed trade liberalization is understandable. The Administration cannot hope to enlist the support of domestic labor for freer trade in the very industry that would benefit the region if it fails to help American workers make the painful adjustment to alternative employment. In its own statement on the CBI, the AFL-CIO called for the entire trade and tax-incentives portion of the bill to "be sent back to the drawing board." Labor has not changed its position, and its strength in Congress has grown as a result of the November 1982 elections, in which the Democrats gained twenty-six new seats. It remains to be seen whether President Reagan's support for a jobs bill will be able to defuse the strong protectionist sentiments that the domestic recession has provoked.

3. Investment Tax Credit

The third major component in the CBI proposal was a five-year investment tax credit. A U.S. parent corporation may claim a credit against its total tax liabilities for an amount equal to 10 per cent of new investment in plant and equipment in Caribbean Basin countries. These incentives were coupled with increased protection for foreign investment offered through the Overseas Private Investment Corporation. The U.S. private insurance sector was also encouraged to become active in the Caribbean Basin, to reduce the risk associated with investment. The U.S. Treasury Department estimated that the cost of the investment tax credit in forgone tax revenues would be $40 million. No one knows how much new investment would be generated by this $40 million. New investment is highly sensitive to swings in the business cycle, changes in the perception of risk, and changes in overall levels of profitability.

Studies of the U.S. experience with domestic tax credits, however, offer reason for skepticism. Although this experience contains no "substitution" effect, i.e., shifting among regions in response to changes in relative profitability, it does illustrate the uncertainty of this instrument. According to a study by the Office of Tax Analysis in the Department of Treasury of the effect of the 1973 investment tax credit on domestic investment, every dollar of tax expenditure generated only 76 cents of new investment. Using the 76 per cent figure, an investment tax credit in the CBI that costs the U.S. Treasury $40 million can be predicted to generate only $30 million of investment. This may be even less in the case of a foreign tax credit because of increased risks associated with doing business abroad.

Although the exact estimate of the new investment generated varies depending on the assumptions, the relatively small payback for tax expenditures can be traced back to a central weakness of this instrument: much of the new investment would occur anyway because business activity is ongoing. Yet to get an additional investment, the Treasury has to include all investors in the tax credit. Therefore, if U.S. investors in the region currently spend $400 million on new plant and equipment, and an investment tax credit creates an additional $30 million of investment, the total tax expenditure will be $43 million.

Opposition to the Tax Credit

In the course of the CBI's passage through the legislative process, the investment tax-credit provision proved to be the most controversial aspect of the bill. It was unpopular with labor and with congressmen who feared job flight from their districts. Many deficit-minded congressmen were reluctant to endorse a measure reducing Treasury revenues still further. Several economists observed that it was unlikely that the tax incentives would generate a large amount of new investment as long as business conditions in the region remain precarious. Weak domestic economies, a depressed international economy (particularly in the United States), and in some countries high political risk have depressed expected profitability. Without growing markets, businessmen cannot justify new investments. In fact, capital flight now constitutes a serious drain to Caribbean Basin countries. For at least the foreseeable future, U.S. investors in many countries will probably invest only that amount which is absolutely necessary to maintain their ongoing plant and equipment. This investment will occcur anyway, and the investment tax credit would be an unrequited loss to the Treasury. These arguments were responsible for the fact that the investment tax credit was never seriously considered in either house.

At the same time, however, the government has mounted an impressive surge of activity designed to promote U.S. investment and trade. At least eight federal departments or agencies have developed promotional programs focused on the Caribbean. The Department of Agriculture has established an agricultural information center for U.S. businesses interested in Caribbean markets, and is working closely with an Agribusiness Promotion Council to design appropriate investment projects for the region. USAID and the Peace Corps are devoting greater resources to small business ventures and entrepreneurial training in the region. The Department of Commerce has opened a Caribbean Basin Business Information Center, to provide comprehensive economic information to interested U.S. businesses. According to recent State Department statements, the response has been dramatic: "Literally thousands of companies have asked for guidance on trade and investment opportunities." The Center is sponsoring a series of regional seminars throughout the United States on business opportunities in the Caribbean Basin.

Lessening Political Risk

A key agency supporting greater investment in the Caribbean has been the Overseas Private Investment Corporation (OPIC), which provides political-risk insurance to U.S. investors operating in developing countries. Since FY 1980, OPIC has sharply stepped up its activities in the Caribbean, mainly in the politically less volatile islands. OPIC issued insurance policies on forty-seven new projects in FY 1981 and 1982, totaling $361 million in new investment; authorized direct loans to eighteen small and medium-sized joint ventures, also in FY 1981–82, totaling $149 million; and supported investment feasibility studies and missions. Follow-up investment missions to Haiti and Jamaica that occurred in late 1982 and early 1983 may result in new investment for those countries.

Lastly, the government has developed a program of bilateral investment treaties that provide clear rights and obligations for the host government, the U.S. government, and the foreign investor. The State Department, which strongly supports such treaties as a means of improving the investment climate in developing countries, recently concluded a treaty with Panama. Another was successfully negotiated in January 1983 with Costa Rica. Many other Central American and Caribbean nations have expressed an interest in such a treaty, which could serve to attract greater investment while guaranteeing certain rights of their countries vis-à-vis the investor. Thus, with or without the CBI, the Administration has aggressively sought to promote U.S. trade and investment linkages. If a U.S. economic recovery takes firm hold, these efforts could well produce some success at the margin, especially in the insular countries.

ECONOMIC RESPONSE TO POLITICAL PROBLEMS

But there is more to the CBI than economics. In fact, the CBI is an unabashed attempt to use economic assistance to attack the roots of unrest in the area, a foreign policy objective reminiscent of the Alliance for Progress. The concept of a "Caribbean Basin" is more geographical than economic. Central America differs from most Caribbean islands in culture, economic structure, and, most importantly, political institutions. In the

Dominican Republic and much of the English-speaking Caribbean, relatively stable and democratic structures already exist. Since the negotiation of new Panama Canal treaties and the removal of this historic irritant in U.S.-Panamanian relations, Panama too has enjoyed stability and economic prosperity. The Caribbean Basin Initiative has a better chance of success on the Caribbean islands and in Panama, where the requisite political stability exists, than in the rest of Central America, where the political status quo has been challenged by powerful insurgencies.

In Central America, the Administration's economic and political strategies have been working at cross-purposes. The Administration's economic plan aims to stimulate business, but a confrontationist diplomacy threatens to delay restoration of investor confidence. By heightening political conflict, the United States threatens to inflict deeper wounds on already badly mangled economies.

The Flight of Capital

Fearing that political strife will continue and even worsen, frightened Central American businessmen are stashing their savings in Florida's banks and condominium market. Because capital flight often occurs through illegal channels, it is not possible to measure its magnitude exactly. One study sponsored by AID estimated capital flight during 1979 and 1980 to have surpassed $500 million. The investment climate in Central America has certainly deteriorated since then. Informed observers believe capital flight from El Salvador alone has reached $500 million per year.

The investment climate has been so bad in Central America that even U.S. government agencies have hesitated to commit their own resources there. Although it has vastly increased its activity in the Caribbean nations, the Overseas Private Investment Corporation has been virtually closed for business in El Salvador, Guatemala, and Nicaragua, and has been considering only small projects in Honduras and Costa Rica. The proposed changes contained in the CBI will allow for a greater OPIC involvement in the region, but its activities will still be constrained by its own risk criteria.

The Export-Import Bank (Eximbank) has also been unwilling to undertake major new exposures in Central America. It is noteworthy that, according to the language in the legislative package the Administration sent to Congress, the Eximbank promises to expand its activity in the Caribbean Basin only "where its lending criteria allow."

In the absence of peaceful resolutions to conflicts within and between nations, private capital will continue to flee Central America. Without investor confidence, two of the three prongs of the CBI—investment incentives and trade opportunities—will be irrelevant to Central America. The remaining prong—official aid—will in large measure be devoted to maintaining consumption levels and indirectly to purchasing weapons. Investment planning and implementation, whether by the public or by the private sector, cannot proceed safely and efficiently in an environment of political turmoil.

Benefits of a Multilateral Approach

The Administration's diplomacy of confrontation has also prevented the realization of a truly multilateral Caribbean Basin Initiative. The Administration had been consulting with Canada, Mexico, Venezuela, and Colombia. It has not yet, however, been willing to make the political compromise necessary to permit the elaboration of a cooperative and integrated approach to the region's economic problems. Each donor nation is pursuing its own programs, largely as if the CBI had never been announced. As a result of its uncompromising diplomacy and divergent concepts of national interest, the Administration is actually working at cross-purposes to other donors.

There is an alternative to strictly bilateral effort. A genuinely multinational framework, based on a common political vision, would have several economic advantages. A multilateral mechanism would allow for more efficient coordination of scarce resources. It would make donors feel it was in their interests to match contributions made by others, thereby sharing the aid burden more widely. Moreover, multilateralism provides mechanisms for the transfer of aid resources without the political tensions and resentments that accompany bilateral programs. The Caribbean Group for Economic Cooperation and Development has, since 1977, provided such a multilateral vehicle for aid to the insular Caribbean. The Administration's uncompromising bilateral and hardline diplomacy has impeded the formation of a similar group for Central America.

CONGRESSIONAL INACTION ON THE CBI

With so much attention focused on it, why has the CBI languished in Congress for months? After being introduced in Congress on March 17, 1982, the CBI was split into its separate components and sent to the Foreign Affairs and Ways and Means committees in the House, and Foreign Relations and Finance committees in the Senate. Each portion of the bill galvanized a different set of interest groups in favor of or in opposition to the package. In addition to organized labor, which remained the most consistent opponent throughout the process, various aspects of the CBI drew criticism from U.S. sugar growers, textile and shoe manufacturers, church and development organizations, and budget-conscious citizens and congressmen.

Within the Caribbean, businessmen from Puerto Rico and the Virgin Islands sought guarantees that their export position would not be adversely affected by the CBI. CARICOM [Caribbean Common Market] objected to the selective, exclusionary aspects of the bill and the fact that the plan was developed with inadequate consultation with leaders in the affected countries. CARICOM and other nations in the basin also recognized the essential and complementary nature of the trade and investment incentives, and were confused and damaged by the sugar quotas.

Finally, some church organizations, farmers' cooperatives, and small business groups in the Caribbean concluded that the CBI would only enhance American control over local resources, open the door to increased participation of American multinationals in local economies, and increase economic dependence on the United States. At a conference sponsored by the Development Group for Alternative Policies in Jamaica in December 1982, representatives from twelve nations argued that American firms, not local interests, would be the major beneficiaries of the CBI. As Neville Linton of the Caribbean Council of Churches said, "It [the CBI] again means multinationals, large industry, and export to the United States. Do we only industrialize for the United States to meet its needs, or do we move into production and exports which are enhancing our own societies?" And former Salvadoran minister of economy Jorge Sol added, "At least the Alliance for Progress promoted a degree of social progress."

The aid section of the bill was approved in September 1982, once it was agreed to give greater emphasis to basic needs development and reduced amounts to El Salvador. The momentum of the CBI then seemed to come to a halt. The Administration insisted that the CBI remained a "top priority," but House Ways and Means Committee chairman Dan Rostenkowski (D.-Ill.) predicted the bill had virtually no chance of passage. Meanwhile, the chairman of the Senate Finance Commitee, Robert Dole (R.-Kan.), awaited the results from the House before he would take action to move the bill in the Senate.

A major push came just prior to the President's trip to Latin America in early December during the 1982 lame-duck session. It seemed politically undesirable for Reagan, Secretary of State George Shultz, and Assistant Secretary of State Thomas Enders to appear in Central America without offering some encouraging news on their much-heralded and long-awaited initiative. The greatest push came in the House, and the Administration helped arrange a trip to the region for members, including Rostenkowski, to convince them of the critical need for the bill. That trip "had an enormous amount to do with [the chairman's] change of opinion," said one Ways and Means staff member.

Dropping the Investment Tax Credit

Once the members returned to Washington, Rostenkowski became one of the CBI's strongest supporters, moving the bill forward quickly and stifling several attempts to cripple it with amendments. Through his efforts, the CBI passed the full committee on December 9 by a strong 27–6 vote and was sent on to the House for a final decision. But the version passed on to the floor of the House had undergone important alterations from the initial plan. Most significantly, the five-year, 10 per cent tax credit for investment had been removed, because of the apparent ineffectiveness of the measure and the lack of a political constituency. Rostenkowski chose to delete it to give the bill a decent chance of passage by the full House. In its place, the committee voted for tax deductions for businesses holding conventions in beneficiary countries.

Although such a tax break will undoubtedly bring in greater income to the Caribbean nations, and although Special Trade Representative Bill Brock said the new measure "in the short term can be even more beneficial" than the original proposal, it is clear that its impact would be much more limited. Rather than helping to diversify the export base of the Caribbean economies and take advantage of the twelve-year duty-free trade provisions, the tax measure will result in greater income and investment only in tourism and service sectors, and does nothing to promote new manufacturing and light industry in the basin.

More Protectionist Action

Protectionist sentiment in the House also led to the addition of petroleum and its derivatives, leather goods, and footwear to the list of products excluded from the Free Trade Area. And, in its final version, which passed the full House on December 17, tuna was also exempted. The Ways and

Means Committee did manage to reverse an earlier recommendation of the trade subcommittee to place a quota on rum imports from the region. Instead, rum remained eligible for the Free Trade Area, and Puerto Rico and the Virgin Islands were granted rights to all excise tax collected on rum sold in the United States, as compensation for lower shares of the U.S. rum market.

The final measure also raised the local-content requirement to 35 per cent from Reagan's proposed 25 per cent, again in response to labor concern that a flood of imports produced in other countries could be assembled in the Caribbean and then later enter the United States duty free. Lastly, the CBI legislation gave the President the authority he requested in the original bill to exclude any country that does not sign an extradition treaty with the United States or is "Communist."

It was the action in the Senate, or more precisely the lack of action there, that ultimately prevented the CBI from reaching the President's desk. Finance chairman Dole had been waiting to see what happened to the House before acting on it in his committee. The CBI, introduced in March, was not considered in the Senate until December 20, two days after the House adopted the measure. Despite administration pleas to hold back amendments, thereby avoiding the need for a conference with the House, two amendments were adopted.

One amendment eliminated an earlier provision exempting products produced in the Virgin Islands from meeting the local-content requirement for duty-free entry to the United States. The original measure had been intended to give Virgin Island products preferential status over products from elsewhere in the Caribbean. A second amendment also took aim at preferential treatment of the Virgin Islands by requiring Virgin Islands rum distilleries to comply with U.S. federal water pollution controls. The House had earlier voted to exempt the Virgin Islands distilleries from the requirements.

Despite all these compromises, however, the bill was never taken up by the full Senate, which adjourned on December 23. Senator Jesse Helms's (R.-N.C.) filibuster over the Administration's tax bill prevented any work from being accomplished and frustrated the exhausted senators. It was clear soon after the Finance Committee reported on the bill that it had no chance of passage by the 97th Congress.

In the 98th Congress, which opened in January 1983, the CBI must follow the same long path it nearly completed in December. The White House has continued to emphasize the high priority it places on passage of the CBI. In his January 1983 State of the Union address, President Reagan said, "Final passage of the remaining portions of our [CBI] ... is one of this Administration's top legislative priorities for 1983."

Nonetheless, the CBI faces some tough going on Capitol Hill. Buried under labor opposition and scholarly analyses that reveal its inefficiencies, the investment tax incentive is likely to die in Congress. The remaining portion—the Free Trade Area—has already been reintroduced, but at a time of rising protectionist sentiments. On the other hand, the bill enjoys a residue of interest and support among congressmen who worked on it in the 97th Congress. The best guess is that the FTA will eventually reach the President's desk for his signature, but that labor and selective business opposition will succeed in excluding important products from the list of duty-free items.

Whatever eventually transpires in Congress, the CBI cannot begin to contribute substantially to the region's economic growth until the global economy begins to recover and, in Central America, unless peace is restored.

8. *The English-Speaking Caribbean*

By ANTHONY P. MAINGOT

Focus The United States will be most effective in the English-speaking Caribbean, according to Anthony Maingot, "if it accepts, respects, and even encourages the priorities as they are set by the Caribbean leaders themselves." These priorities, as Maingot sees them, are generally in harmony with U.S. interests.

A number of factors have contributed to an acceptance of a greater U.S. role in the region. The withdrawals of the British and the Dutch have left a power vacuum that can be effectively filled only by the United States. "The leaders of the English-speaking Caribbean are keenly aware that together they form one of the largest single blocs of democratic states outside Western Europe," says Maingot. This sense of distinctiveness makes these countries more likely to cooperate with other democracies, especially since "Castro has claimed the right to intervene in those states where, in his opinion, gross social injustice compels him to act."

As statistics show, economic equality and political freedom are much greater in the English-speaking Caribbean than in Cuba. One reason is Cuba's emphasis on military spending: "Cuba, which has made recognized strides in the area of education, spends $114 per capita on the military and $162 per capita on education; the figures for Barbados are $36 for the military and $233 for education. In Trinidad the ratio is 14:170 and in Jamaica 9:76."

The perceived threat of Cuba has contributed to an increasing sense of vulnerability. But, says Maingot, most leaders in the Caribbean do not expect outright invasion. Rather, they believe in the Adams Doctrine, named after a late Barbados prime minister, which holds that "threats to the small democracies will come not from external forces directly but from critically timed assistance to the small groups at home that would subvert democracy." Evidence from Grenada and other islands has reinforced this theory.

In Grenada, Caribbean leaders have also acquired an understanding of what Marxist-Leninism actually means. For them, the term "mixed economy," for example, "is not a Fabian or Keynesian mixing of private and public efforts but a 'stage,' one step on the path to total control of the economy."

The English-speaking nations of the Caribbean are beginning to learn to provide for a common defense. They do not wish, however, to be unnecessarily drawn into struggles between the superpowers. Understanding both their attraction to the United States and their wish to keep themselves a certain distance from it, says Maingot, will help the United States to formulate the most effective cooperation.

Maingot's views should be compared with those of Fidel Castro (selection 2), the Kissinger Commission (selection 3), and Abraham Lowenthal (selection 6).

Anthony P. Maingot is professor of sociology and anthropology at Florida International University and director of the graduate program in international studies.

I N ANY GOVERNMENT, foreign policy tends to be the least controlled area of decision-making. Short-term exigencies and changes can cause fundamental shifts in the best programmed long-range policies. Events can call forth expedient tactics that fly in the face of well argued philosophies and strategies of international relations. The resulting uncertainties that trouble the major actors in the global arena are, if anything, even more daunting for the smallest actors, the new mini-states of the world.

This paper examines the leaders of a group of mini-states of the English-speaking Caribbean (all British colonies prior to 1958), and their perspectives and perceptions on national security matters. The states are British Honduras, Bahama Islands, Turks and Caicos Islands, Virgin Islands, Cayman Islands, Bermuda, Trinidad and Tobago, British Guyana, Jamaica, and the Lesser Antilles. These are, of course, not the only actors in the Caribbean Sea. Islands such as Cuba, Haiti, and the Dominican Republic have long been part of the region's politics. Puerto Ricans are U.S. citizens and are not supposed to operate independently in foreign affairs, though some of their leaders do. The same holds for the Dutch and French territories.[1]

In examining the security of the region, we must take into account four special characteristics: a sense of distinctiveness, an awareness of economic and political incongruity, a feeling of vulnerability, and the feeling of living in an "open" area.

1. A Sense of Distinctiveness

The leaders of the English-speaking Caribbean are keenly aware that together they form one of the largest single blocs of democratic states outside Western Europe. This awareness contributes to their sense of being distinct from other world groupings and enhances their ability and willingness to work together in a number of areas. One need not take sides over the U.S. intervention in Grenada in October 1983 to understand that the eastern Caribbean was able to act in concert—after meetings of each individual is-

---

Reprinted by permission of *Essays on Strategy and Diplomacy*, The Keck Center for International Strategic Studies (Claremont, California), August 1985. Notes for this essay begin on page 144.

Social and Economic Conditions
In the English-Speaking Caribbean

Country	Population Per Sq.Km. 1980–82[1]	GNP Per Capita 1982	Percentage Annual Growth (Average)		Life Expectancy, Birth 1982	Unemployment, Open/Hidden[2]
			1960–70	1960–82		
Antigua/Barbuda	173	$1,740	3.1	−0.2	–	11
Bahamas	15	3,830	3.4	−0.4	69	–
Barbados	572	2,900	2.3	4.5	72	9
Belize	7	1,080	3.4	3.4	–	5
Dominica	99	710	3.8	−0.8	58	–
Grenada	328	760	3.4	1.6	69	7
Guyana	3.7	670	2.4	1.7	68	16
Jamaica	199	1,330	3.8	0.7	73	18
St. Kitts/Nevis	170	750	5.5	1.1	–	6
St. Lucia	198	720	3.6	3.4	–	12
St. Vincent/the Grenadines	319	620	4.0	0.6	–	9
Trinidad/Tobago	207	6,840	3.2	3.1	68	23

SOURCE: World Bank, *World Development Report*, 1984. Also:
1. *The Europa Yearbook*, 1984. 2. World Bank, *The Commonwealth Caribbean*, 1978.

land cabinet—in a matter that touched some of their most crucial national and international views, such as the maintenance of state sovereignty and independence, and opposition to great-power intervention.

The eastern Caribbean sense of distinctiveness also extends to the economic sphere. The socioeconomic standing of these countries is generally consistent with their democratic form of government. Despite their relative poverty of resources, they rank among the world's middle-income nations as regards certain social indices and in some cases among the world's most advanced. (See the table.) Life expectancy is an interesting datum, since it reflects general health standards, including medical and nutritional levels. The countries of Barbados, Trinidad, and much of the eastern Caribbean now have gerontological problems similar to those of the United States and Europe.

Despite their commendable performance in the social area, Caribbean leaders are sometimes accused of ruling unjust societies whose governments are at best merely formal affairs. Cuba's Fidel Castro has claimed the right to intervene in those states where, in his opinion, gross social injustice compels him to act. Castro has maintained that he should act against social injustice in the countries of the English-speaking Caribbean but not in Mexico and Costa Rica.

West Indian leaders can and do make comparisons that challenge Castro's claim. The household income of oil-rich Trinidad compares favorably with that of Costa Rica, a country generally cited as a paragon of democracy. Household income in Trinidad is more evenly distributed than in Costa Rica—and certainly more than in Mexico—at all levels of the social structure. However, Caribbean leaders recognize that their countries have serious economic problems.

2. An Awareness of Economic and Political Incongruity

The pattern of economic and political development in the Caribbean differs from that of Europe and the United States. In the West, capitalism preceded the growth of a centralized bureaucracy. Moreover, industrialization was accompanied by the growth of parliamentary democracy. As a result, Europe experienced a relatively harmonious "fit" between political and economic systems, with a relatively small population.

In the Caribbean this "fit" has not only never existed but might well be becoming more difficult to achieve. There, a system based on slavery and the plantation evolved into appendages of European mercantilism. The parliamentary system was introduced piecemeal in some islands, or introduced only for a limited, propertied, and largely white sector of the population. As the nationalist-independence movement gathered strength, its central goal became control of the state machinery, not merely of political-parliamentary power.

The nationalists' goals had both political and economic ends. The state governed and offered patronage, but more, it became the main employer and driving force in the quest for development after independence. The combination of these two functions (one traditional to the Westminster system and one not) had different results according to the particular social structure of each territory. In ethnically divided states such as Guyana and Trinidad, the political thrust of the leading nationalist movements accentuated racial-ethnic divisions. In other societies, such as Jamaica, the political struggle continues to trigger recurring civil mini-wars. The killing of some 800 people during the 1980 electoral year in Jamaica and the turmoil surrounding the January 1985 rise in the price of gasoline and cooking gas in that country illustrate the volatility of these systems.

Despite these and other problems, recent history indicates that the majority of West Indians are deeply attached to the Westminster system and most of its related institutions. West Indian leaders will argue with different degrees of ardor but always convincingly that, given the performance records of the other systems available, the parliamentary system is best suited to their particular problems and needs. By combining the freedom to experiment with the demand for accountability they have built a cost-accounting system into their politics. West Indians invariably refer to national elections as "the Day of Reckoning." When the recently elected prime minister of Grenada, Herbert Blaize, said "we are undeniably part of the Western World," or the newly elected prime minister of Belize, Manuel Esquivel, immediately spoke of strengthening his relations with the United States and Britain, they were not saying anything their societies would not approve of.[2]

West Indian leaders are aware that their security lies in steady socioeconomic development. "Security," noted St. Kitts–Nevis prime minister Kennedy Simmons, "can't be won at all with force of arms."[3] The distrust of armies runs deep among these civilian politicians. St. Vincent's prime minister, James "Son" Mitchell, is well aware of the area's defense needs but feels that "development needs" must come first. "The age-old lesson," he notes, "is if you live by the sword, you perish by the sword. I would rather be out of politics than have to depend on the military."[4] The only leader in the English-speaking Caribbean in early 1985 who sported a military title and was constitutionally commander-in-chief of the armed forces was President Forbes Burnham of Guyana.

West Indian elites are apprehensive about the future. The crisis in the West Indian economy is structural and is reflected in dropping growth rates, high rates of unemployment, declining agricultural productivity, and increasing indebtedness. In fact, cooperative arrangements such as the Caribbean Community (CARICOM) so painstakingly assembled by these elites are threatened by the crisis in each individual economy. In the words of St. Vincent's prime minister, "We are in a race against time."[5]

3. A Feeling of Vulnerability

Caribbean leaders' attempts to meet their societies' problems have been marked by an intensified search for political formulas and, since the 1960s, more and more economic ones. While this experimentation has been a natural evolution of the political dynamics of democratic systems in moderately developed societies, other factors have made experimentation increasingly conflictive. These are the exogenous factors. West Indian leaders would probably disagree among themselves on the particular weight that should be attached to each of these factors, but they would agree that all are present and influential:

- The shift from a Euro-centric to a U.S.-centered orientation in most areas of life—education, defense, culture, recreation, commerce. With this shift have come, of course, all the U.S. perceptions and definitions of its vital interests. The U.S. conflict with Cuba, for instance, which preceded the entry into independence of all the new Caribbean states, has slowly but surely become an integral part of Caribbean leaders' concerns.
- The entry into the area of other actors: the so-called middle powers—Venezuela, Brazil, Mexico—and the international transnational actors representing ideological interests (Marxist-Leninists, Christian Democrats, Social Democrats, trade union "federations"), as well as transnational corporations. Very often the presence of these actors is more invited than imposed, and this sometimes includes the Cubans, whose presence is used as leverage at various levels of politics.
- Change in the nature of the region's leadership. Particular "generations" of leaders with shared experiences and compatible political ideologies have had a significant impact on the region's political milieu. One such generation was that of Romulo Betancourt, José Figueres, Luis Munoz Marin, and Juan Bosch. In the West Indies, Norman Manley, Eric Williams, Grantly Adams, and many leaders of the Eastern Caribbean formed something of a "club." Their association and relationship went beyond state-oriented instrumentalism and involved a commitment to an ideal called "regionalism." Today that ideal is much weaker, and attachments to institutional arrangements such as CARICOM are based more on self-interest than on any ideological commitment to regionalism.

Taken together, these changes have left the governing elites feeling isolated and unprotected. Contrary to the widely held idea that the United States has adequately replaced the disappearing European military protection, there is rather a sense that it is "each man on his own" in this area.

4. *Living in an 'Open' Area*

There is no perception among West Indian leaders (especially in the eastern Caribbean) that this is an "American lake," perfectly patrolled and controlled by the U.S. Navy. In fact, there is some doubt of the U.S. Navy's region-wide capabilities. Experiences both distant and recent have taught eastern Caribbean leaders to regard the Caribbean as an "open" area.

Aware of their electorates' post-colonial sensibilities as well as of collective Third World opinions, West Indian elites are also very hesitant to enter into any new type of association, military or otherwise, that might appear neo-colonial. Their perceptions of regional security and national opinion encourage West Indian elites to develop their own ideas about and make their own efforts towards national and regional security.

Most West Indian leaders are old enough to have experienced German submarine warfare in the Caribbean. They are aware that German U-boat captains referred to the Caribbean as their "American Turkey Shoot."[6] Just how unprepared the Allies were initially to defend the vital Caribbean sea lanes can be seen from the statistics on Allied tonnage sunk by U-boats. In 1942 Germans operating in the Caribbean sank 1,559,422 tons of Allied shipping; in 1943, 177,945 tons; and in 1944, 14,804 tons.[7] This damage was done by several dozen German submarines that had to travel more than 5,000 miles from their Atlantic coast bases to the Caribbean.[8] The Nazi subs were supported by supply submarines and by collaborators operating from German-owned plantations on Caribbean coastal areas.[9] Today's Caribbean leaders lived through the years when goods could come in only under convoy protection.

The huge U.S. rearmament eventually enabled the Allies to defeat the German U-boats, but the vulnerability of the Caribbean shipping lanes had been made clear. The possibility of a Nazi victory in Europe—and the horrible implications of that—were not lost even on those West Indian intellectuals who found West Indian social structures odious. A young Eric Williams, for instance, could easily observe that the Caribbean islands were "in fact, a vital link in the chain of hemispheric defense" even as he condemned the treatment of the black man in those islands.[10]

Much more recent and equally dramatic in its impact has been the Mariel boatlift of 1980. The U.S. navy failed to control some 4,000 private boats in the Florida Straits, while the Cuban navy kept tight control over the boats in Cuban waters. As a result, the Carter administration had to accept Castro's *fait accompli*.[11] Where the U.S. navy failed West Indian leaders are well aware that they could not succeed in controlling the movements of Caribbean peoples throughout the islands. The porosity of Caribbean borders has become important in West Indian geopolitical thinking.

The "openness" of the Caribbean is also evident in the current "war" against the drug traffic. While the U.S. government has defined the suppression of narcotics traffic in the Caribbean as one of the five goals of its Southern Command, it has achieved little success so far.[12] The United States and Caribbean governments are unable to stop the drug shipments, especially since smugglers have the capacity to alternate their routes and to move by land as well as sea.[13] The situation is similar in some ways to the 1920–35 war against rum-runners in the Caribbean. With Nassau, Bimini, and Havana as their major bases, and with well-organized collaborators located at strategic points in Florida and elsewhere, these smugglers subjected the Coast Guard to a rough test during the Prohibition years created by the Volstead Act.[14] Both the Mariel boatlift and the ongoing battle against drug smugglers demonstrate that the Caribbean remains very much the "open" sea it has always been.

Geography also impinges on the military balance in the region. Caribbean leaders recognize that the major U.S. base in the area, Roosevelt Roads in Puerto Rico, is 1,300 miles or a two-day sail from Nicaragua. This puts Nicaragua out of range of U.S. land-based fighter aircraft without aerial refueling. Many lessons about the geopolitical and geostrategic reality of the area were learned in the 1970s, when Cuban actions became much more important to them. Additional lessons were learned during the four and a half years of the People's Revolutionary Government of Maurice Bishop in Grenada. To understand how and why West Indian elites developed their own means to protect national and regional security it is necessary to understand the role of Cuba and Grenada.

The Growing Fears of Cuba

West Indian suspicion of Cuba increased during the Carter years (1977–81), a period of U.S. emphasis on multilateralism and avoidance of belligerent rhetoric. A growing sense of a threat from Cuba resulted from a series of intra-Caribbean events played out by Caribbean actors themselves. Most important by far was Cuba's surreptitious use of Barbados to airlift some five thousand troops into Angola in 1975. The operation demonstrated Cuban audacity and logistical capabilities. At the same time, it showed how easily these small states could unknowingly be drawn into an East-West tangle. The airlift had a very negative effect on the relations among West Indian leaders. Neither Jamaica's Michael Norman Manley nor Guyana's Forbes Burnham was overly concerned, but Eric Williams of Trinidad was particularly upset by the discovery of what an old Cuba hand called "this ... sensational development in hemispheric history."[15] Most importantly, Cuba's action led to the first discussions on mutual security assistance between Trinidad and Barbados.

West Indian apprehensions escalated when a *coup d'état* toppled the government of Eric Gairy in Grenada in 1979. Cuba immediately sent a resident ambassador to the island, who soon presided over a growing Cuban presence. It seemed to replicate the situation in Guyana, where the Cuban mission took up nearly half a city block and where Cuba's multiple involvements had long been the talk of Georgetown. On November 18, 1979, Prime Minister Maurice Bishop told a rally that he expected 250 Cubans to start building a new international airport. Because he had just been in Canada seeking funds for a feasibility study for the same project, local and international surprise was understandable. Eventually there would be 700 Cuban workers in Grenada. There would also be a full Soviet embassy staffed by a diplomat whose previous post was ambassador to Argentina, the Soviets' most important trading partner in Latin America.

In 1980 an incident in the Bahamas outer islands sent a chill through West Indian Cuba-watchers. A Cuban MiG aircraft sank one of the Bahamas' three gunboats and strafed the sailors while in the water. Cuban military helicopters later landed on Bahamian territory. Although the incident appeared to result from a genuine case of mistaken identity (the Bahamians were thought to be Cuban exile "pirates") and apologies and reparations were eventually made, the harm was already done. A poll taken in the Bahamas showed that 85.9 per cent believed the attack had been deliberate and not a mistake and that 73.3 per cent believed Cuba still posed a threat to the islands.[16] As a writer in Nassau put it, Cuba had attacked a "defenseless neighboring, friendly country." But even more important than this, he continued, Cuba had attacked "a black developing nation" at the same time that it purported to enjoy wide international prestige as a leader of the Non-Aligned Movement.[17]

The 1980s thus began with a number of incidents that fed the growing fears of a Cuban threat in the area. All seemed to confirm the perception of a militarized and aggressive Cuba taking advantage of Carter's *apertura* (opening) toward multilateralism. Virtually anything emanating from Cuba or its ally, Grenada, elicited suspicion.

While developments in Grenada heightened the sense of threat from the Marxist-Leninist left, leaders in the English-speaking Caribbean were very aware that Marxist-Leninist groups in the area enjoyed little public support.[18] However, the groups were well organized and received region-wide organizational support. They were perceived as being capable of utilizing (not causing) popular discontent and manipulating the ongoing social strife that resulted from the general dislocation between economy and politics in these nations. Of the three major conspiracies known to have occurred in the area in recent years, only the one in Grenada in March 1979 was clearly the work of Marxist-Leninists. There was probably some involvement of the "left" in the mutiny and Black Power movement in Trinidad in 1970, but this was never proven in the court martial that followed. The conspiracy in Dominica in 1980 involved a corrupt ex-prime minister, members of the eighty-man army, and U.S. gambling and drug interests. The army was disbanded after the conspiracy was scotched.

The Adams Doctrine

By 1982, the nations of the eastern Caribbean were ready to do something positive about their security. What developed was a set of ideas increasingly called the "Adams Doctrine" after the late Barbados prime minister Tom Adams. The Adams Doctrine holds that threats to the small democracies will come not from external forces directly but from their critically timed assistance to the small groups at home that would subvert democracy. It follows that the need is for a small, mobile force that counts speed as its most effective asset.[19] The doctrine is not a product of Reagan administration thinking but of Tom Adams's own geopolitical views and of events that unfolded in the area during the Carter period.

The first use of the Adams Doctrine was not in Grenada in October 1983 but in Union Island, St. Vincent (ninety-seven miles due east of Barbados), in early December 1979. An invasion of alleged Rastafarians from the Grenadian island of Carriacou led the government of St. Vincent to request assistance. Elements of the Barbadian defense forces intervened to help put down the uprising. This was the first intervention in the name of collective security in the young history of eastern Caribbean sovereignty. It was this incident and the suspicion that the revolutionary government in Grenada was training others for similar acts that led eventually to the signing in September 1982 of a "Memorandum of Understanding" regarding security and military cooperation. The signatories were Barbados and all the independent states of the Organization of Eastern Caribbean States (OECS), except Grenada.[20] The government of Barbados agreed to pay 49 per cent of the costs of a Central Liaison Office. This was established, and a Barbadian holds the post of regional security coordinator.

While the eastern Caribbean states could deal with the St. Vincent episode, they could not intervene effectively against Grenada and its Cuban ally. However, the U.S. intervention in Grenada coincided with the aims of the Adams Doctrine and the area-wide understanding on security and military cooperation. As distinct from so many other U.S. interventions in the Caribbean, this one was widely supported throughout the region.[21]

Right after the Grenada intervention, a regional security organization, proposed in the "Memorandum of Understanding" of 1982, began to take shape. On November 17, 1983, the Barbadian minister for parliamentary affairs told the House of Assembly that there would be a new force headquartered in Barbados with permanent units stationed in each island. The United States, he said, would train and "partially equip" the new force.[22] Despite this talk and a considerable number of short-term training courses conducted by the United States in Antigua and Barbados, there is no evidence yet of any military buildup in the area. To read of a recent "naval exercise" in the eastern Caribbean involving one U.S. destroyer and coast guard cutters from Barbados, Antigua, St. Lucia, Dominica, and St. Vincent—and to know these nations have tiny coast guards—is not to be impressed with claims of a "militarization" of the Eastern Caribbean.[23] In fact, numerous voices oppose any idea of "standing armies" or anything that goes beyond the Adams Doctrine's emphasis on a small, mobile force. Even the idea of such a limited force has to go through the process of democratic decision-making. As the leader of the opposition told the Barbados House of Assembly: "We will not tolerate any decisions on that force taken in an undemocratic way."[24] Responses to the perceived need for greater national security will invariably have to contend with the civilian-democratic nature of the political cultures. It stands to reason, however, that if Eugenia Charles of Dominica tells the *New York Times* there is a definite threat from Cuba, Libya, and North Korea, she will act to meet the threat.[25]

A Multipronged Security Approach

Cuban militancy, the Adams Doctrine, and the Grenada affair have led Caribbean governments to develop a multipronged approach to the issue of security at home and in the region. Several measures give the broad outlines of their actions.

By far the most important has been the leaders' stress on socioeconomic development. Their enthusiastic welcoming of the Reagan administration's Caribbean Basin Initiative (CBI) [see selection 7 and appendix A] stems precisely from an awareness of the need to provide employment through an expansion of non-traditional exports. Even one as tough-minded about Marxist-Leninist penetration as Jamaica's Edward Seaga can minimize the Cuban threat and point to "economic strategies" as the correct path.[26] Similar public positions have been taken by the late Barbados leader Tom Adams, the most committed defender of an Eastern Caribbean regional force, by St. Vincent's James Mitchell, and by St. Kitts–Nevis's Kennedy Simmons.

Second in importance, the Grenada revolution helped to clarify the rules of the game at two levels that the leaders could use politically to their advantage. There has been a clearer identification of those groups in the Caribbean whose commitment to Leninism makes them opponents of democratic pluralism. The roles played by Trevor Munroe's Workers Party of Jamaica before the 1979 coup in Grenada, during the four years of the People's Republic of Grenada (PRG), and during the October 1983 internal Grenada coup led by Bernard Coard have been an eye-opener to even the most unbelieving.

Accompanying this identification came a clarification of some basic concepts. On this score Caribbean leaders acquired an understanding of what Marxist-Leninists actually mean by the term "mixed economy." It is not a Fabian or Keynesian mixing of private and public efforts but a "stage," one step on the path to total state control of the economy.[27] For the first time the Soviet literature on "socialist oriented" states is being discussed in the West Indies, and this is being done in the light of the failures and successes in development of the Grenadian revolution.

Much less important, yet evident and clearly on the increase, are laws aimed at strengthening the security of the state. Various "state security" or "treason" bills have been discussed in the parliaments of the eastern Caribbean states. These have been accompanied by the use of police and intelligence actions. While the steps taken in the islands thus far are well within the legitimate powers of government generally and the state laws specifically, they do indicate a new hardening of attitudes. Denial of visas and of work permits to suspected subversives are two such actions.[28] The withdrawing of Cuban scholarships is another.

There is no evidence of a McCarthyite wave in the area. In fact, by 1984 the "left" parties were busy regrouping throughout the region, and the usual visits of consultation to Havana were evident in the newspaper columns. Even the old Leninist language was again in evidence when Guyana's

Marxist-Leninist Cheddi Jagan accused the independent Marxist Working People's Alliance (WPA) of "right-wing opportunism" for not supporting the coalition with the ruling PNC of Forbes Burnham, which he was urging with strong Cuban support.[29]

A New Interest in Small-State Security

The concerns of small, weak states such as those of the eastern Caribbean have not called forth much security-related thinking. An indication that this may be changing appeared in the decision taken by the heads of government at the 1984 Commonwealth meeting in New Delhi, India, to set up a committee to study the security of small states.

The tragedy of Grenada has had a dramatic impact not only on the thinking of the elites of Caribbean states but also on all who are concerned with the problem of security for small states.[30] As one author put it recently, there is a need for serious thought about this problem to replace the "comic opera relaxation" with which it is often viewed in major capitals of the world.[31]

There is evidence that this has begun to occur. An interesting indication is the difference in tone between two reports on the Caribbean produced by the Foreign Affairs Committee of Britain's House of Commons. While the first tended to see Washington's concerns about Grenada's People's Revolutionary Government as somewhat off target, the second noted that events in Grenada had contributed to a "wider appreciation of the vulnerability of the individual islands of the area," and concluded that there was "the desirability of establishing regional security arrangements to protect individual states from covert infiltration and overt military threat."[32]

Caribbean leaders have a legitimate concern over their vulnerability in a sea awash with national and international conspirators. Their systems are geared towards electoral competition, and their populations are accustomed to mobilizing all means short of the overthrow of regimes to articulate their demands. Although these demands have been moderately well met, as the comparative data on social welfare levels demonstrate, the deteriorating economic base might well slow down that progress.[33]

With the withdrawal of Britain and Holland from the area, West Indian elites are turning toward the United States as the most promising candidate to assist them in dealing with a wide range of problems. The growing U.S. military connection is perhaps a logical result of all this plus the convergence of outlook between the United States and most of the Caribbean leaders and people. To be sure, there will be closer military ties with the United States, but the nature of these ties should not be exaggerated. The eastern Caribbean countries are intrinsically civilian systems, and chances are they will long remain so. The figures speak for themselves. While both Trinidad and Barbados have only one soldier per 1,000 population, the figure is 206 soldiers per 1,000 in Cuba. Trinidad spends the equivalent of 0.5 per cent of its GDP on the military, Jamaica 0.9 per cent, and Cuba 9 per cent.[34]

Cuba, which has made recognized strides in education, spends $114 per capita on the military and $162 per capita on education; the figures for Barbados are $36 for the military and $233 for education. In Trinidad the ratio is 14:170 and in Jamaica 9:76. These ratios will probably remain for another important economic reason: in societies such as these, military structures are expensive simply because the general socioeconomic standards require military salary levels and living conditions that are on a par with those of other civil servants in these heavily bureaucratized societies. It is calculated that each soldier costs Barbados $9,000, Jamaica $5,000, and Trinidad an incredible $16,000.[35] Even violence-prone Jamaica appears to show a resistance to any form of militarization. The emphasis there—as elsewhere in the region—is on the police services. Recent budget estimates for Jamaica (1984–85) show National Security and Justice with 8.4 per cent of the budgetary allocation, and three-fourths of this went to the police and auxiliaries.[36] It is not surprising that these mini-states turn to the major powers for military assistance.

One of the weaknesses in arguments explaining "spheres of influence" is the assumption that there is only one actor involved, the stronger power. In fact, spheres of influence are often desired by weaker states that fear for their security, or legitimately share an ideological position with the stronger nation, or wish to derive material benefits from it. The stronger power thus is often as much invited as self-imposed. This appeared to have been the case with the Grenada revolutionary elite's dealings with Cuba, the Soviet Union, and other members of the socialist bloc. It certainly has been the case with the evolution of the eastern Caribbean into an explicitly U.S. sphere of influence, in matters of security and in other areas. Tom Adams could not have been more candid or accurate than when he told the Royal Commonwealth Society in London in December 1983 that that year was "the watershed year in which the influence of the United States, willy-nilly, came observably to replace that of Great Britain."[37] Although "willy-nilly" might be a cavalier way of describing such a momentous event, its occurrence is a historical certainty.

One of the problems with spheres of influence is that they automatically represent a range of obligations—some unforeseen—for the dominant power. In this regard my analysis suggests that military security might well be the least troublesome and least costly of the U.S. responsibilities toward the Caribbean. Given the civilian nature of the region's elites, they are sure to stress socioeconomic development as the major pillar in any security arrangement. Who knows their countries' needs better than these democratically elected, astute leaders? As they seek to enhance national and regional security, Caribbean leaders emphasize socioeconomic development and what can best be called "democratic political education," or clarifying and internalizing the rules of the democratic game. These are the "positive" defenses of democracy. Military solutions are steps of last resort.

The United States will be most effective in the long run if it accepts, respects, and even encourages the priorities as they are set by the Caribbean leaders themselves.

NOTES

1. Very clearly, this type of analysis will have to proceed at a fairly high level of generality, so that it should be regarded more as provoking thought than as documenting detailed realities. And yet, the generalities are based on more detailed analysis that spans both time and geographical space. Specifically relevant to this analysis are the following items by the author: "Cuba and the English-Speaking Caribbean: Playing the Cuban Card," in Barry B. Levine, ed., *The Changing Cuban Presence* (Boulder, Colo.: Westview Press, 1983), pp. 19–41; "National Pursuits and Regional Definitions: The Caribbean as an Interest Area," in Basil A. Ince et al., eds., *Issues in Caribbean International Relations* (New York: University Press of America, 1983), pp. 309–36; "Perceptions as Realities: The USA, Venezuela, and Cuba in the Caribbean," in Joseph S. Tulchin and Heraldo Munoz, eds., *Latin American Nations in World Politics* (Boulder, Colo.: Westview Press, 1984), pp. 63–82; "Grenada and the Caribbean: Mutual Linkages and Influences," in Herbert Ellison and Jiri Valenta, eds., *Soviet/Cuban Strategy in the Third World*, forthcoming; and "Citizenship and Parliamentary Politics in the English-Speaking Caribbean," in Paul Sutton, ed., *The Contemporary Legacy to the Caribbean*, forthcoming.

2. For Herbert Blaize's remarks, see *Caribbean Insight*, January 1985, p. 10. For George Price's comment, see the *New York Times*, December 12, 1984, pp. 1 and 10. For an analysis of the essentially conservative and pro-Western structure of West Indian value systems, see A. P. Maingot, "The Caribbean: The Structure of Modern-Conservative Societies," in Jan Knippers Black, ed., *Latin America: Its Problems and Its Promise* (Boulder, Colo.: Westview Press, 1984), pp. 362–80. For survey data that show this pro-Western orientation, see Wendell Bell, *Jamaican Leaders: Political Attitudes in a New Nation*

(Berkeley: University of California Press, 1964); Carl Stone, *The Political Opinions of the Jamaican People, 1976-81* (Kingston, Jamaica: Blackett Publishers, 1982); and Selwyn Ryan, Eddie Greene, and Jack Harewood, *The Confused Electorate: A Study of Political Attitudes and Opinions in Trinidad and Tobago* (St. Augustine, Trinidad: University of West Indies, Institute of Social and Economic Research, 1979), pp. 136-41.

3. *Washington Post*, July 26, 1984, p. 23.
4. *Caribbean Insight*, December 1984, p. 10.
5. Ibid.
6. Cf. Wolfgang Frank, *The Sea Wolves: The Story of German U-Boats at War* (New York: Rinehart, 1955); and S. E. Smith, ed., *The U.S. Navy in WWII* (New York: Ballantine Books, 1966).
7. Stetson Conn, Rose Engelman, and Byron Fairchild, *Guarding the United States and Its Outposts* (Washington: Office of the Chief of Military History, Dept. of the Army, 1964), p. 431.
8. Daniel V. Gallery, *Twenty Million Tons Under the Sea* (Chicago: Regnery, 1956), p. 15; Karl Doenitz, *Memoirs: Ten Years and Twenty Days* (Cleveland: World, 1959), pp. 195-200.
9. Frank, *Sea Wolves*.
10. Eric Williams, *The Negro in the Caribbean* (Westport, Conn.: Negro Universities Press, 1942), p. 8.
11. Cf. Victor Palmicri, "Out of Control" (unpublished manuscript, 1983). Palmieri was ambassador for refugee affairs in 1980.
12. General Paul F. Gorman, "Why Maintain a U.S. Military Presence in Central America?," *Caribbean Today*, November 1984, pp. 28-31.
13. See the *Miami Herald*'s account of the up-to-then-secret "Operation Hat Trick" that began on November 1, 1984: *Miami Herald*, November 24, 1984, p. 1.
14. Cf. Malcolm F. Willough, *Rum War at Sea* (Washington: U.S. Treasury Department, Coast Guard, 1964). The smugglers' crafts had speeds up to fifty knots and were often assembled in the Bahamas islands, then a British colony.
15. Herbert L. Matthews, *New York Times*, March 4, 1976, p. 31. Matthews believed that Angola was "as much Fidel Castro's policy as it was Moscow's" and characterized his old friend as a "Napoleon of the Caribbean."
16. Larry Smith, "The Flamingo Affair," *Image*, Summer 1980, p. 48.
17. Ibid., pp. 48-53.
18. For the results of multiple West Indian elections and the dismal showing of radical parties, see Patrick A. M. Emmanuel, *General Elections in the Eastern Caribbean: A Handbook* (Cave Hill: University of West Indies, Barbados, 1979); and Douglas Midgett, *Eastern Caribbean Elections, 1950-1982* (Iowa City: University of Iowa, Center for Development Studies, Institute of Urban and Regional Research, 1983).
19. For a discussion of the Adams Doctrine, see Graham Norton, "Defending the Eastern Caribbean," *The World Today*, June 1984, pp. 254-60.
20. The memorandum was published in the *Caribbean Monthly Bulletin*, November-December 1983).
21. The debate over the legality as well as the particular role and timing of the request to the United States from the Organization of Eastern Caribbean States continues. Anthony Payne, Paul Sutton, and Tony Thorndike, in *Grenada Revolution and Invasion* (New York: St. Martin's Press, 1984), p. 176, see the U.S. invasion as illegal and assert that it "seriously damaged the image of morality in international relations." Gregory Sandford and Richard Vigilante, in *Grenada: The Untold Story* (Lanham, Md.: Madison Books, 1984), make a

case for the legality and morality of the invasion. The present author has argued that it violated international law but met another fundamental requirement of international morality: the overwhelming majority of the Grenadians wanted it. Cf. A. P. Maingot, "The Death of a Caribbean Utopia," *Caribbean Review*, Fall 1983, pp. 24–28.

22. *Barbados Advocate*, November 18, 1983. The minister noted that the purpose of these forces was to "keep the claws of the Russian bear at some future date from entering these beautiful little islands of ours."

23. *New York Times*, November 9, 1984, p. 6.

24. Hon. Erskine Sandiford, quoted in *Caribbean Monthly Bulletin*, November–December 1983, p. 74.

25. *New York Times*, November 8, 1983, p. 10.

26. See his interview with *U.S. News and World Report*, November 5, 1984, p. 42.

27. Jiri and Virginia Valenta, "Leninism in Grenada," *Problems of Communism*, July–August 1984. It is now known that the Grenadian notion of mixed economy was taken from the Soviet idea of "non-capitalist" or "socialist-oriented" countries.

28. The Barbadian lifting of the work permit of the Guyanese editor of *Caribbean Contact*, Ricki Singh, is an unusual step for the eastern Caribbean. While Trinidad had previously refused to renew Singh's work permit, the Barbados action (a suspension), coming on the foot of the Grenada intervention, was a matter of wide discussion. Prime Minister Tom Adams would later explain that Singh had been in contact with Cuban intelligence officers, who were "visiting him at three in the morning." *The Express*, Trinidad, October 28, 1984, p. 10.

29. *Caribbean Insight*, October 1984, p. 1.

30. Cf. Col. Jonathan Alford, "Security Dilemmas of Small States," *The World Today*, August–September 1984, pp. 363–69.

31. George Quester, "Trouble in the Islands: Defending the Micro-States," *International Security*, Fall 1983, p. 175.

32. House of Commons, Fifth Report from the Foreign Affairs Committee, Session 1981–82, "Caribbean and Central America" (London: HMSO, October 21, 1982); Second Report from the Foreign Affairs Committee, Session 1983–84 (London: HMSO, 1984). Lady Young, in charge of Caribbean affairs in the Foreign and Commonwealth Office, told Barbadian journalists that Britain encouraged and supported regional security arrangements in the eastern Caribbean, saying that "prevention is better than the cure." *Trinidad Guardian*, November 15, 1984, p. 1.

33. Ruth Leger Sivard, *World Military and Social Expenditures* (Washington: World Priorities, 1983), pp. 36–37. Barbados ranks 30th in public expenditure per capita on education, spending $233 (U.S. dollars), and Trinidad ranks 38th, spending $170. Barbados ranks first in public expenditure per capita on safe water, while Trinidad ranks 27th and Costa Rica 39th. Cuba ranks 39th in public expenditure per capita on education, 50th in health, and 59th in safe water.

34. Stockholm International Peace Research Institute, *World Armaments and Disarmament: SIPRI Yearbook 1984* (London and Philadelphia: Taylor and Francis, 1984), pp. 129–30; Central Intelligence Agency, *The World Factbook* (Washington: U.S. Department of State, Bureau of Public Affairs); *Background Notes* (Washington: U.S. Department of State, Bureau of Public Affairs, August and September 1984). The Cuban figure is somewhat deceptive because of economic subsidy from the Soviet Union.

35. Sivard, *World Military and Social Expenditures*, pp. 36–37. All dollar amounts are given in U.S. currency.

36. *Jamaican Weekly Gleaner*, May 21, 1984.

37. Quoted in Norton, "Defending the Eastern Caribbean," p. 256 n.

9. A Plea for Contadora

By EIGHT LATIN AMERICAN FOREIGN MINISTERS

Focus On February 10, 1986, Secretary of State George P. Shultz received a delegation of eight Latin American foreign ministers, led by those of the four Contadora countries (Mexico, Venezuela, Panama, and Colombia), who since 1983 have sponsored a multilateral initiative (see appendix B) that they believe will lead to a negotiated solution to the Central American crisis. The communiqué that resulted from this meeting, though worded in the careful language of traditional diplomacy, betrays the irritation and anger that the authors evidently felt towards the United States. Indeed, the Colombian foreign minister, who spoke afterwards for the group to the American and Latin American press, made it clear that its members regarded the United States as the principal obstacle to a peaceful resolution to the civil war in Nicaragua, since the Reagan administration had recently reiterated its determination to seek renewed congressional support for resistance fighters operating against the Sandinista regime.

The document guardedly establishes moral and political equidistance from Washington and Managua, by emphasizing support for both U.S. goals (an end to the Nicaraguan military buildup; a withdrawal for foreign [Cuban and Eastern bloc] military advisors) and the goals of the Sandinista regime (removal of foreign military bases [in Honduras] and respect for self-determination and non-intervention in the internal affairs of individual countries). The ministers' expressions of support for "national reconciliation" and "human rights" are generalizations without any indication of how they apply to the governments in El Salvador and Nicaragua. The declaration is also unclear about how, once the United States has renounced its support of the anti-Sandinista forces, reconciliation and human rights will be advanced. No attempt is made to reconcile the obvious operational contradiction between non-intervention in the internal affairs of states and a drastic alteration in the quality and direction of their political life.

The ministers' impassioned plea needs to be balanced against the careful political analysis of Susan Kaufman Purcell (selection 10) and the legal brief of John Norton Moore (selection 26). Their apparent confidence in the tractability of Nicaragua's political conflicts is sharply at variance with the views of Costa Rica's president Oscar Arias (selection 11) and those of Cardinal Miguel Obando y Bravo (selection 24). Writing from a U.S. perspective, Michael Walzer (selection 27) seconds the views of the Latin American ministers.

THE FOREIGN MINISTERS of the Contadora Group (Colombia, Mexico Panama, and Venezuela), jointly with the Support Group (Argentina, Brazil, Peru, and Uruguay), met today [February 10, 1986] with Secretary of State George P. Shultz with a view toward expediting the Contadora negotiation process, and putting into operation the actions outlined in the Carabelleda Message [statement in support of negotiations issued by the eight foreign ministers in Carabelleda, Venezuela, January 1986]. All of this is envisaged within the framework of a dialogue that the eight Latin American countries propose to bring about between all of the parties involved in the Central American conflict.

That message, which constitutes a Latin American initiative towards the immediate accomplishment of peace, security, and democratic development within Central America, proposes the following fundamental measures:

- Renewal of negotiations leading to the signature of a Contadora Act for Peace and Cooperation in Central America;
- The termination of all foreign assistance to irregular forces operating in the region;
- The termination of support for insurrectionary movements in all of the countries of the region;
- A freeze on further arms acquisitions and a gradual, programmed decrease in their levels;
- A suspension of international military maneuvers;
- A progressive reduction eventually leading to the full elimination of foreign military advisors and foreign military installations;
- A non-aggression pact among the five Central American countries, to be achieved through unilateral declarations;
- Effective steps conducive to the achievement of national reconciliation and the full respect for human rights and individual liberties;
- Promotion of regional and international cooperation to assist in the solution of the pressing economic and social problems that afflict the Central American region.

The foregoing initiative was supported by all of the Central American governments at a meeting in Guatemala this past January 14 [1986] and has received the explicit support of the countries of the European Economic Community and, in general, that of the international community at large.

The Latin American foreign ministers emphasized to Secretary Shultz their view that the aforementioned measures must be taken rapidly and simultaneously. Within that framework, they expressed their view that a termination of support for the irregular military forces operating in the region is an indispensable contribution to the achievement of peace. At the same time, they recalled that the adoption of effective measures of national reconciliation in all the cases where a profound social division exists is of equal importance.

The ministers reaffirmed that stability and regional security demand respect for what the eight Latin American countries defined at Carabelleda as the Permanent Bases for Peace—that is, a Latin American solution; self-determination; non-intervention in the internal affairs of other states; territorial integrity; pluralist democracy; the absence of armaments or military bases; the absence of acts of aggression, of foreign advisors or troops, of support for subversive groups; and support for human rights.

They also expressed their unshakeable determination to continue the efforts directed toward a peaceful solution to the regional crisis with the parties directly involved in the Central American conflict, and with the countries with links and interests in that region.

In a climate of frankness, the Latin American foreign ministers and Secretary of State Shultz expressed their full agreement that the Central American crisis must be resolved through political and diplomatic instruments.

10. *Demystifying Contadora*

By SUSAN KAUFMAN PURCELL

Focus — According to Susan Kaufman Purcell, every country says it likes the Contadora process, but this surface agreement hides deeper conflicting interests. Though it is widely assumed that the United States opposes a Contadora treaty while the Latins favor it, the reality is much more complex. Some of the Contadora countries share U.S. fears but have hidden the fact, because "the domestic political costs of agreeing with the United States in Central American matters are not negligible." Other countries disagree sharply with both their neighbors and the United States. Even in the U.S. government, opinions about Contadora are mixed. But despite these differences and the even greater obstacles among the Central American countries themselves, Purcell believes that Contadora has "increased the possibility of a negotiated settlement in Central America."

Among the four Latin members of Contadora, perhaps the greatest contrast in opinion is between the Mexicans and the Venezuelans. Having lost much of its territory to the North American superpower, Mexico maintains as one of the pillars of its foreign policy strict nonintervention on the part of the United States. Its concern, therefore, has been to focus on ways to improve its own influence in Central America, even at the cost of interventionism of its own. Venezuela has been quick to recognize a military and political threat in Central America and is, therefore, looking for guarantees of its own safety.

Underlying all the negotiations, however, says Purcell, is the assumption of the Contadora Four that "if their security is really threatened, the United States will do something about it. Thus they can take risks in the negotiating process that the United States is unwilling to take."

Differences of opinion on Contadora also exist among the Central American nations. As close U.S. allies, El Salvador and Honduras naturally tend to line up with American views against Nicaragua. Guatemala has been trying to hedge its bets by being more neutral. In democratic Costa Rica, which has no army, fear of the consolidation of Communism in Nicaragua competes with fear of becoming further embroiled in a region-wide conflict.

Among the many points in the draft treaties that continue to be hotly contested are means of verification and enforcement. Although there is common agreement on the need to keep the superpowers out of the Central American conflict and on the necessity of negotiating arms and troop reductions, no adequate mechanisms have yet been proposed. Furthermore, the Nicaraguans have resisted any limitation on what they regard as necessary defensive forces.

"Even if these details are worked out, the problem of what happens if and when treaty provisions are violated still remains," concludes Purcell. "None of the Contadora countries wants the United States to act unilaterally. On the other hand, the regional powers have traditionally been reluctant, if not unwilling, to take collective action, including military action. They cannot have it both ways."

Purcell's views should be compared with those of Costa Rican president Oscar Arias (selection 11) and of Michael Walzer (selection 27).

Susan Kaufman Purcell is the director of the Latin American Program at the Council on Foreign Relations.

CONTADORA IS THE CODE WORD used to mean the pursuit of peace in Central America through negotiations. Its primary alternatives are widely believed to be a U.S. invasion, a regional war, or both. Like motherhood and apple pie, Contadora is liked and supported by everyone.

Why, then, has a negotiated settlement within the Contadora framework proved so elusive? Critics of U.S. Central American policy argue that a diplomatic solution requires support from Washington and that, despite rhetoric to the contrary, Washington opposes Contadora because a Contadora treaty would prohibit unilateral action by the United States in protection of its interests.

The facts are more complex than this reasoning conveys. The U.S. government remains divided, with some saying that an imperfect treaty is better than no treaty and others arguing that no treaty is better. For their part, the countries of the Contadora group—Mexico, Venezuela, Colombia, and Panama—are divided in their interests and strategies. Some of them share the fears and ambivalence of the United States, though they have taken great pains to conceal this fact, since the domestic political costs of agreeing with the United States in Central American matters are not negligible.

The impression that the United States and the Contadora Four have few shared interests leads to two opposite conclusions: either the Contadora process is a waste of time, since the United States will ultimately impose its own solution on Central America, or Contadora still offers a good solution, if only the United States would support it. The reality is somewhere in between. Over the past two and a half years, the Contadora Four have been obliged to move beyond empty rhetoric to deal with the complexities of designing a treaty that takes account of the interests of the Central American countries and of the United States. In the process, despite all the significant obstacles that remain, they have increased the possibility of a negotiated settlement in Central America.

Reprinted by permission from the Fall 1985 issue of *Foreign Affairs* (© 1985 by the Council on Foreign Relations, Incorporated). Notes for this essay are on page 173.

The Origin of Contadora

Contadora refers to both a regional grouping and the negotiating process in which it is engaged. The Contadora group was created in January 1983, at the initiative of Colombian president Belisario Betancur, as a diplomatic alternative to the conflict escalating in the region. Nicaragua was aiding the Salvadoran guerrillas. In response, the United States organized the contras, who were increasing their forays into Nicaragua from Honduras. The U.S. military presence and activities in the region were beginning to expand. The Contadora countries feared that the Sandinistas would retaliate against the contras and draw Honduras, and then the United States, into open armed conflict that might eventually spill over into the rest of Central America.

Contadora aimed to fill a diplomatic vacuum. The Sandinistas have preferred not to work with the Organization of American States (OAS) since they believe the United States still controls its members, despite considerable evidence to the contrary. They favor the United Nations, where the dominant Third World coalition is sure to favor Nicaragua over the United States. For this reason, the United Nations has been an unacceptable mediator for the United States, which strongly advocates hemispheric solutions to hemispheric problems.

By joining forces under the Contadora umbrella, the regional powers believed that they might be able to constrain the United States from its habitual unilateral actions and thereby enhance their own role. They also hoped to offer a different interpretation of events in Central America. They believed that the United States, as a global and non-Latin power, tended to impose an East-West perspective on conflicts that essentially involved such North-South issues as poverty, inequality, and exploitation. Their deemphasis of the Soviet threat was understandable, since the United States, not the Soviet Union, had traditionally been seen as the danger to the countries of the region.

Finally, the Contadora countries had a record of successful joint efforts. In 1976, Omar Torrijos of Panama had enlisted the support of Mexico, Venezuela, and Colombia, as well as Costa Rica, to generate Latin American support for the Panama Canal treaties. Three years later, these same countries persuaded the not-yet-victorious Sandinistas to commit themselves to political pluralism, a mixed economy, and international nonalignment in return for their support. In 1981, Torrijos again brought the group together, shortly before his death, to pressure the Sandinistas to abide by their commitment.

In January 1983, the presidents of Mexico, Venezuela, Colombia, and Panama met on the Panamanian island of Contadora to discuss the deteriorating situation in Central America. Their meeting marked the formal beginning of the Contadora group.

The Contadora Four were not interested in protecting U.S. security interests in Central America. On the contrary, they were reluctant to acknowledge publicly that the United States even *had* legitimate security interests in the region. They had no such qualms about speaking publicly of the legitimate security interests of Nicaragua. In fact, the regional powers had joined forces precisely to counter a real or imaginary U.S. military threat against Nicaragua.

Since then, observers have repeatedly pronounced the Contadora process dead or dying. They take at face value the frustration of the participants, who keep encountering new, seemingly intractable problems each time they solve old ones. They fail to understand that Contadora's mere existence is useful. It allows the four participating governments to affirm that they have kept the United States at bay and have avoided a regional war. This makes it difficult for any of them to desert the negotiating process. At the same time, the costs of failure are relatively low. If diplomacy leads nowhere, the Contadora countries can say that they did their best but the hegemonic pretensions of the United States made their best not good enough.

The Contadora Four had first become active in Central America in the late 1970s. Venezuela, Colombia, and Panama had helped arm Nicaraguan president Anastasio Somoza's opponents, and all four had worked hard to isolate Somoza internationally. Yet the Four's familiarity with Central America remained limited. Contadora has helped teach them about Central America and about one another. It has also shown them that it is far easier to call for a diplomatic solution than to create one.

Drafting a Treaty: The 'Acta'

Contadora has forged a consensus around a number of objectives that could constitute the basis for a negotiated settlement. These are embodied in the twenty-one points of the Document of Objectives of September 1983, calling for democracy and national reconciliation, an end to support for paramilitary forces across borders, control of the regional arms race, reduction of foreign military advisors and troops, and prohibition of foreign military bases. [See appendix B.] These goals were incorporated into the draft treaty or "Acta" of September 7, 1984, which Nicaragua quickly accepted and the United States just as quickly rejected. These starkly different reactions created the impression that Nicaragua favored a negotiated settlement and the United States did not.

In fact the United States rejected the Acta because it was a vague statement of goals without concrete limits on Nicaraguan action. Its provisions for verification and enforcement were totally inadequate, and it deferred negotiations on foreign military and security advisors and arms and troop reductions until after signature of the treaty. On the other hand, it required the United States upon signature to cease military exercises and support for the contras. Further military aid to El Salvador and Honduras was frozen, while Nicaragua was allowed to maintain its military advantage over these two countries. The provisions for democratization and internal reconciliation were hortatory and unenforceable as drafted. They would have allowed the Sandinistas to claim that the Nicaraguan elections scheduled for November 1984 were in compliance with the Acta despite charges by the democratic opposition, led by Arturo Cruz, that the electoral process was rigged.

Nicaragua accepted the Acta as a final document, not a draft for discussion, because it asked little of Nicaragua immediately and left no possibility for Nicaragua to be pressured in post-signature negotiations. Accepting the Acta also improved Nicaragua's image internationally, just as the U.S. Congress was to vote on aid for the contras and Nicaraguan president Daniel Ortega was to address the U.N. General Assembly.

A Substitute: The Tegucigalpa Act

When Nicaragua surprised U.S. friends in Central America by accepting the Acta, Honduras, El Salvador, and Costa Rica began drafting what became the Act of Tegucigalpa of October 1984—a substitute draft that sought to correct what they and the United States had seen as the main problems of the September Acta. The timetable for disarmament and demilitarization procedures was changed to produce more simultaneous action on these issues, and the role of the Central American governments in the verification and enforcement processes was enhanced. The Nicaraguans immediately rejected the October draft and repeated that they would not accept any substantive changes in the September Acta. That is still their position at this writing.

With the process at an impasse, the Contadora countries looked to the bilateral talks in Manzanillo, Mexico, between the United States and Nicaragua to achieve a breakthrough. In the penultimate round in late 1984, Nicaragua hinted that it was willing to be flexible on key security issues in a strictly bilateral agreement. The United States pointed out that Nicaragua logically could not enter into two contradictory agreements, and eventually concluded that Nicaragua was proposing at Manzanillo the substitution of a limited bilateral agreement on security issues for a comprehensive Contadora agreement. It therefore suspended the bilateral talks in January 1985 to emphasize multilateral discussions within Contadora.

This worked for a time. In April 1985 an agreement in principle was reached on revised verification procedures involving concessions by both Nicaragua and the Central American drafters of the Tegucigalpa Act. But the negotiations bogged down again in the summer of 1985, when Nicaragua once more tried to substitute a series of bilateral security agreements for Contadora's comprehensive agenda. Nicaragua favors such an approach to avoid the issue of democratization and internal reconciliation, a shorthand term for talks between the Sandinistas and the armed and unarmed opponents (including the contras) leading to their eventual incorporation into a democratized political process.

The Democratization Issue

Democratization and internal reconciliation may well be the most difficult issue of all, because it would, in the words of President Reagan, "overthrow the Nicaraguan government, in the sense of changing its structure." The Sandinistas, however, say it is a non-issue: they will not deal with the contras, and Nicaragua is already democratic.

The democratization/internal-reconciliation issue is also at the heart of the division within the U.S. government. While there is consensus that a more democratic Nicaragua would be more likely to abide by a negotiated settlement, the debate is over the more fundamental question of whether it is possible to democratize Nicaragua at all. Some argue that Nicaragua can be made to accept democratization and internal reconciliation under pressure and want the United States to hold firm for such an outcome. Others doubt that the Sandinistas will ever incorporate the rebels and democratize. They believe that the United States should therefore accept a treaty that deals with the conventional security issues but not with democratization and internal reconciliation.

The so-called Reagan Peace Plan of April 4, 1985, came out squarely in favor of continuing to press for democratization and internal reconciliation. President Reagan was not about to abandon the Nicaraguan "freedom fighters"; he called for a ceasefire and talks between the Nicaraguan government and the rebels. At the same time, he asked Congress to release an appropriation of $14 million in humanitarian aid for the rebels, which the United States would make available only if the talks did not succeed by June 1, 1985.

The plan failed to obtain sufficient backing from Congress, which denied aid at that time, and from the Contadora Four, who wanted nothing to do with a plan that included aid for the contras. The Reagan administration continues to emphasize the need to include democratization and internal reconciliation in any treaty. Progress thus depends on whether the Contadora process can devise such a treaty.

The Contadora Four enjoy an image of unity. They oppose a military solution and unilateral action by the United States. They seek a negotiated settlement to end the fighting. They also believe that the Sandinista government of Nicaragua is here to stay and that its future, particularly its international alignment, can be influenced by outside actors. Beyond this consensus, however, there are important differences among the Four, which reflect their particular historical experiences as well as the political constraints they face domestically.

Mexico: At Odds With U.S. Policy

Mexico's position has been most at odds with that of the United States. Although critical of Washington for supporting right-wing dictators in Central America and for failing to help eradicate poverty and injustice, in policy terms Mexico has not behaved very differently from the United States. Mexico has not actively supported right-wing dictators, but it did nothing to undermine their rule until the late 1970s, when it withdrew recognition from the disintegrating Somoza regime. Nor did Mexico pursue an active or generous aid program toward the area. In fact, Mexico "discovered" Central America at about the same time the United States did, belying the myth that Mexico knows and understands Central America better than the United States does.

Mexico's policy toward the Sandinistas has been protective and empathetic. As a country that had experienced its own modern revolution, Mexico could not condemn other revolutions. Mexico had also suffered multiple U.S. interventions and lost half its territory to its northern neighbor. It therefore sympathized with the Sandinistas' fear of a U.S. invasion or intervention in their affairs. Precisely because of its historical relationship with the United States, Mexico had earlier adopted a foreign policy based on the principles of non-intervention and self-determination. It applied them to the Nicaraguan revolution when it occurred in July 1979.

Mexico's definition of non-intervention, however, was tailored to its policy preferences. Mexico did not consider itself to be intervening in Central American affairs when it withdrew recognition from Somoza or joined in the Franco-Mexican declaration of August 1981 that recognized the Salvadoran rebels as a "representative political force."

Mexico's support of the Sandinistas and the Salvadoran rebels reflected its belief that revolutionary governments in Central America, including Communist ones, would not threaten Mexico's interests. It felt confident that it could establish friendly relations with such governments, as it had done earlier with Cuba. Mexico might even gain influence if left-wing governments triumphed in Central America. The United States would have little, if any, influence over such governments; Mexico, in contrast, could work with them and possibly replace the United States as the most important power in the region.

Finally, Mexico rejected the theory that it was the "last domino" that would fall if Marxist revolutionaries were successful in Central America. Mexico correctly viewed itself as different from its southern neighbors, considerably larger and more developed, with a more differentiated social structure. And its political system was more effective and responsive than those in Central America, with the exception of Costa Rica.

An Evolution in Mexican Policy

Mexico's actions were, nevertheless, marked by a gap between rhetoric and reality. The Mexicans pursued a very different policy toward the right-wing military regime of Guatemala than toward other right-wing governments in the region. Mexico has neither broken with nor publicly criticized the government in Guatemala City; nor has it called Guatemala's Marxist guerrillas "a representative political force." Also, despite Mexico's rejection of the domino theory, it has reinforced its military presence along its southern border and implemented the so-called Plan Chiapas to help improve the standard of living of Mexican peasants in the lands bordering on Guatemala.[1]

Over the past year, the perception has grown that Mexico's policy toward both the Sandinistas and Central America in general has changed. The presence of Mexico's foreign minister at the inauguration of President José Napoleón Duarte in El Salvador is often cited. The fact that Mexico no longer supplies petroleum on more favorable terms to Nicaragua than to other clients is another example. Mexico also has become less tolerant of the political representatives of the Salvadoran guerrillas operating in Mexico. President Miguel de la Madrid has begun to balance references to U.S. intervention in Central America with references to Cuban intervention.[2] And he seems less eager than his predecessor, José López Portillo, to engage in high-level meetings with Fidel Castro.

Mexico claims that its policy has not changed but that circumstances in Central America and Mexico have changed. Yet the policy has also evolved. Under López Portillo, Mexico's initial unquestioning support for the Sandinistas, as well as its de-emphasis of the need for political pluralism in Nicaragua, had made Mexico ever more isolated within the Contadora group. Also, as growing numbers of refugees crossed the border into Mexico, Central America increasingly became transformed from a foreign policy issue to a domestic one. Ministries other than the Foreign Ministry became involved, weakening the previous consensus behind the government's approach and pushing it to adopt a more balanced policy toward Central America.

This shift does not mean that Mexico has abandoned the Sandinistas. Mexico does not want to drive the Sandinistas out of the negotiating process and into total isolation. Mexico was therefore critical of the October 1984 treaty drafted by the Central American allies of the United States because it feared that Nicaragua would abandon the Contadora process if it did not get favorable treatment. Mexico also supported the Sandinistas' stress on the importance of having bilateral talks with the United States. The Manzanillo talks were in part the result of a personal initiative by President de la Madrid during his visit to Washington in May 1984. Mexico therefore continues to work for a balanced settlement in Central America.

Venezuela: Closest to the U.S. Position

The Contadora country whose position has been most at odds with that of Mexico, and closest to the United States, is Venezuela. Unlike Mexico, Venezuela does not consider itself a revolutionary country; instead, its sense of identity is strongly based on its evolution into one of the most important democracies of the hemisphere. Support for the principle of democratization has been considerably more important in Venezuela, therefore, than in Mexico. Venezuela has also been much more distrustful of Marxist revolutionaries than Mexico, since for years Marxist guerrillas had threatened the survival of Venezuela's democracy. Venezuela believed that democratic government could not develop in El Salvador if the guerrillas remained unchecked.[3] Venezuela also has been wary of Cuba because of Havana's earlier support of Venezuelan guerrillas.

Unlike Mexico, Venezuela admitted from the beginning that the Central American conflict had implications for Venezuelan security and required a strategic, as well as an economic, political, and social, response. For this reason, Venezuela sent military advisors to El Salvador. (The decision was facilitated because Christian Democratic presidents were in power in both Venezuela and El Salvador.) This policy became politically unsustainable after the United States sided with Britain during the 1982 Falklands War. Nevertheless, even after the transfer of the presidency to a Social Democrat, Venezuela's policy toward Central America did not change dramatically. Venezuela distanced itself initially from the interim government of Alvaro Magaña in El Salvador, when right-wing elements seemed ascendant. But once Christian Democrat Duarte was elected president, even Venezuela's Social Democratic regime supported him.

Venezuela also favored the incorporation of the Salvadoran guerrillas into the electoral process and, like the United States, opposed negotiated power-sharing. Venezuela had, after all, successfully incorporated its own guerrillas into its electoral process, and some had even been elected to important public offices.

As the Sandinistas became more authoritarian and closely tied to Cuba and the Soviet Union, Venezuela became more openly critical of them. More recently, it has terminated shipments of subsidized petroleum to Nicaragua and has increased its assistance to democratic elements in the labor movement, the church, the universities, and the private sector in Nicaragua. Former president Carlos Andrés Pérez, a prominent leader of the Latin American Social Democratic movement who has been highly critical of U.S. policy in the region, refused to attend Ortega's inauguration as president of Nicaragua, to express his displeasure with the path that the Sandinistas were taking. Still, Venezuela has not yet given up on the possibility of some degree of political pluralism in Nicaragua.

The dramatic differences between Venezuela and Mexico demonstrate the fallacy in the judgment that the Contadora Four are united in opposition to the U.S. approach to Central America. Venezuela, in fact, shares some of the basic premises that underlie U.S. policy.

Yet neither Venezuela nor Mexico wishes to see the United States return to the highly interventionist role it played in Latin America in the past. Both would like a solution that would avoid U.S. military intervention or other forms of unilateral U.S. action. The main differences between the Venezuelan and Mexican positions is that Venezuela seems more willing and able to cooperate on military-security dimensions with the United States than is Mexico, and Caracas places more importance than does Mexico City on the need to democratize the Nicaraguan government. At the very least, Venezuelans are divided over whether a Marxist regime poses a security threat and, if so, whether Venezuela should play a military role in changing or containing it.

Colombia: Distancing Itself From the U.S.

The country whose attitudes and behavior changed most substantially with a change of governments is Colombia. Under former Liberal Party president Julio César Turbay, Colombia was supportive of U.S. policy toward Central America. In part, this reflected a traditional tendency on the part of his party to work closely with the United States. Turbay himself distrusted the Sandinistas' expansionist inclinations, particularly toward a number of Colombian islands claimed by Nicaragua. President Reagan backed Colombia in its conflict with Nicaragua, which reinforced cooperation between the two governments.

Colombia is the only Contadora country with an immediate guerrilla problem. Turbay had promulgated a National Security Statute less than one month after his inauguration in 1978. The attempted military solution to Colombia's guerrilla problem failed, and so Turbay's successor, Belisario Betancur, tried a completely new tack when he took office in 1982.[4]

Betancur's goal was to negotiate amnesty for the guerrillas in return for their peaceful incorporation into the political system. The new president believed that such a deal would not be possible while Colombia continued to align itself with the United States, whose Central American policy seemed to emphasize defeat of guerrillas by military means. On his inauguration day, he distanced himself from the United States by announcing that Colombia would apply for admission to the Non-Aligned Movement, chaired at that time by Fidel Castro. He also called for the restructuring of the OAS so as to exclude the United States and include Cuba. These steps paved the way for a new strategy for dealing with the guerrillas at home.

In pursuit of his new domestic policy, Betancur successfully engaged the services of Nobel Prize laureate Gabriel García Márquez, who was close to Castro as well as to the Sandinistas. The ideal was to get Castro and the Sandinistas to encourage Colombia's guerrillas to negotiate the terms of an amnesty with the Colombian government. If successful, the strategy would end Colombia's guerrilla problem and neutralize Cuba and Nicaragua, in the sense of ensuring their non-cooperation with guerrilla groups in Colombia.

Betancur was trying to "Mexicanize" Colombia's foreign policy. By pursuing a "progressive" foreign policy that included friendly relations with Cuba and Nicaragua, Betancur hoped to discourage their support for the Colombian guerrillas and encourage them to cooperate with his government.

The Colombian President as Peacemaker

Betancur paralleled his domestic strategy toward the guerrillas with a more active role for Colombia within the Contadora group. Attracted to the role of international peacemaker, Betancur traveled incessantly throughout the region, engaging in marathon talks with governments and rebels, as well as with the other three Contadora countries and the United States. The last effort ended in Washington, D.C., in April 1985, the same day President Reagan announced his peace plan. President Betancur endorsed the plan but qualified (some would say retracted) his endorsement several days later by saying that he could not side with the United States in supporting the contras. Since the plan clearly included a role for the contras from the beginning, Betancur either had endorsed it before reading it carefully or was persuaded to distance himself from the United States once the other Contadora countries objected to it.

Betancur's domestic policies continue to be debated within Colombia. Critics contend that they are failing. Although Betancur succeeded in signing truces with Colombia's two main guerrilla groups, one of them subsequently changed its mind. There is also evidence that some of the guerrilla groups used the amnesty to regroup and rearm. Betancur has so far rejected the use of force or pressure to achieve his objectives at home and abroad. The guerrillas, however, have not. Their use of force has therefore put the Colombian government at a disadvantage.

Presidential elections are scheduled in Colombia for 1986. If guerrilla violence continues to increase, Colombia will probably return to a more hard-line policy toward the guerrillas after the election, whoever is elected. Colombia's role and posture within Contadora would also probably change, toward a lower profile and a more centrist approach.

Panama: Weak and Ambivalent

The fourth Contadora country, Panama, resembles the Central American countries themselves: it is small, poor, and weak. Yet Panama has never regarded itself as part of Central America, and neither can it be considered a regional power like Mexico, Venezuela, and Colombia. Its membership in the Contadora group is mainly a reflection of the leadership qualities of Omar Torrijos, who regarded Panama as too small a stage for his ambitions and talents and so played an active role in regional politics. Since his death, Panama has been governed by four different presidents, a symptom of the domestic political instability that has focused Panama's attention inward.

Panama's diminished role in Contadora also reflects ambivalence regarding developments in Central America and in its relationship with the United States. On the one hand, Panama does not wish to see the Sandinistas extend their influence in the region. The traits that Panama shares with its Central American neighbors, in addition to its geographical proximity, make it more immediately vulnerable than are its Contadora partners to the destabilizing impact of regional conflict. Furthermore, the Panamanian National Guard shares many of the anti-Communist sentiments that underlie U.S. policy toward Central America.

On the other hand, Panama does not want to appear too closely aligned with the United States for fear of fanning domestic anti-U.S. sentiments. The United States has been a kind of colonial power in Panama, where its ownership of the canal gave it extraordinary influence, if not control, over the course of events. Despite a reduction in the U.S. role in Panama since the signing of the canal treaties, the United States remains very involved. The U.S. Southern Command is headquartered in Panama and has grown considerably during the course of the Central American conflict.

Panama has resolved these tensions by focusing within Contadora on getting an agreement that would increase Panama's international prestige. Consistent with this goal, its position on specific issues has been flexible and pragmatic.

How the Four Produced the 'Acta'

In view of these differences among the four Contadora countries, how could they claim to be united in support of the September 1984 Acta that the United States and the Central American countries found unacceptable? Mexico took the lead in pressing for a draft treaty prior to the U.S. presidential election. It hoped that if a draft treaty were in place prior to Ronald Reagan's expected reelection, the chances for unilateral action by the United States would be diminished. Colombia agreed. Venezuela believed it important to have a treaty prior to the Nicaraguan elections, which were also scheduled for November 1984; after the elections it would be difficult to press Nicaragua to democratize. Nicaragua also wanted to move before its elections so the result would seem to be blessed by Contadora.

There was no time to work out a perfect treaty before November. The decision was made, therefore, to leave the most difficult problems, such as arms negotiations, a timetable of withdrawal for security advisors, verification, and processes for implementation, for later negotiations. Meanwhile, a treaty ending U.S. military exercises and support for the contras would protect Nicaragua and reduce the chances of direct intervention.

This strategy involved a decision to win Nicaragua's support at the expense of that of the United States, a reasonable decision in view of the fact that there was considerable doubt among the Contadora Four that the United States would ever find any draft treaty acceptable. Nicaragua's acceptance of the draft, however, could probably be counted on to increase international pressure on the United States to go along as well. This is exactly what happened.

The Contadora Four did not accept the idea that an unenforceable treaty would threaten their security. This highlights a major problem that confronts the United States in the search for a negotiated settlement in Central America. Underlying any negotiations is the assumption on the part of the Contadora Four that if their security is *really* threatened, the United States will do something about it. Thus they can take risks in the negotiating process that the United States is unwilling to take.

The Central American Players

There are, of course, players beyond the Contadora Four. Any negotiated settlement in Central America would have to win the approval of the Central American countries. Yet these countries do not see eye to eye with the

Contadora countries, and the latter, especially Mexico, virtually ignore them in the mediating process. Costa Rica, Honduras, and El Salvador are pitted against Nicaragua; Guatemala is also, but it seeks to project itself as more neutral than the other three.

Because the positions of Costa Rica, Honduras, and El Salvador are congruent with the U.S. position, the conventional wisdom is that the United States has pressured these small, weak countries to do its bidding. This is, at the least, an oversimplification.

The views of the governments of Costa Rica, Honduras, and El Salvador reflect the common reality they face. They all feel vulnerable to the activities of Marxist guerrillas operating in Central America and accept the much maligned "domino theory." They do not trust the Sandinistas and, together with the United States, fear that Nicaragua will continue to support radical insurgents throughout the region. Their support of the contras is due to their belief that the Sandinistas will change only under outside pressure. A negotiated solution to the conflict that requires the United States to stop providing military assistance to them is unacceptable because they need U.S. military, economic, and political support to survive. Thus they agree with the United States on the root of the problem and its solution.

Nevertheless, these countries are ambivalent toward Washington. The United States cannot be too closely supported without undermining the still fragile domestic legitimacy of their governments. They also view U.S. policy toward the region as erratic and undependable. For these reasons, they need to hedge their bets in order not to damage irreparably their relations with the Sandinistas or the Contadora Four.

Toward the Contadora Four, their attitude is quite negative. Mexico, Venezuela, Colombia, and Panama have little understanding of Central America, they feel, and are more interested in protecting their own interests and assuring the survival of the Sandinista government than in protecting them. Like the Contadora Four, these Central American countries want to avoid regional war, but they doubt that the way to do it is by siding with the Sandinistas against the United States.

As the Contadora Four have become more involved with the specifics of a negotiated settlement, the Central American countries have become more resentful of what they regard as unwarranted intervention in their internal affairs. Costa Rica, El Salvador, and Honduras believe that current trends are in their favor; Contadora, therefore, is seen as increasingly obstructionist. This resentment is directed against Mexico, which is their "Colossus of the North."

Despite the consensus that Costa Rica, Honduras, and El Salvador share, there are some differences. As with the four Contadora countries, these varieties grow out of the different historical experiences and current realities of each country.

Costa Rica: Profoundly Anti-Communist

Costa Rica is unique in Central America as the only institutionalized democracy without a military establishment. Costa Rica also has a tradition of distrust of Nicaragua, stemming from Somoza's repeated attempts to intervene in his neighbor's internal affairs. Anti-Somoza sentiments ultimately led Costa Rica to join with Venezuela, Colombia, Panama, and Mexico to help oust the dictator. Costa Rica, however, soon found the Sandinistas to be authoritarian and interventionist as well.

Officially neutral toward the Central American conflict, Costa Rica is not ideologically neutral; it is profoundly anti-Communist. This helps explain the unofficial support that Costa Rica has given to Edén Pastora, the former Sandinista and current leader of the Nicaraguan rebel group that operates in the border region between Costa Rica and Nicaragua. Costa Rica also supports the need to democratize the Nicaraguan government and incorporate the rebels into the political system. It does not want a Contadora agreement that allows the further consolidation of a Communist regime in Nicaragua. Costa Rica distrusts the ability of any treaty to contain the expansionist tendencies of the Sandinistas and believes, as does the United States, that democratization and internal reconciliation are the best guarantors against the export of revolution by the Sandinistas. Finally, without an agreement that integrates the contras into Nicaraguan politics, Costa Rica fears it will receive thousands of refugees in addition to the approximately 40,000 that it already hosts.

El Salvador: Security Concerns

The government of El Salvador is engaged in a civil war and needs uninterrupted military assistance from the United States even to hold its own against the guerrillas, let alone defeat them. The government also needs to prevent the Sandinistas, the Cubans, and their other allies from supplying the rebels with training, munitions, and other supplies. Therefore, the Salvadoran government is most concerned with the security-related issues of the Contadora process. It supports an end to arms trafficking and is against provisions that would limit military assistance from the United States to El Salvador.

El Salvador also supports the need for internal reconciliation and democratization in Nicaragua. It opposes a double standard implicit in much of the Contadora discussions: the belief that pressure is legitimate if used to get the Salvadoran government to democratize, but is interventionist and illegitimate if applied to the Nicaraguan government. Although the process has not yet gone far, the Duarte government has held talks with the Salvadoran guerrillas and sees no reason why the Sandinistas should not be required to do the same with their guerrillas.

Honduras: Fears About Military Might

As the only immediate neighbor of Nicaragua with a military establishment, Honduras is the one most concerned with the strength and size of the Nicaraguan armed forces. Thus Honduras took the lead in Central America in opposing the September 1984 Acta, which provided for a freeze of military force levels. Honduras does not want a freeze, since that would freeze Nicaragua's military superiority over Honduras. It wants reduction.

A reduction would also assuage Honduran fears over the growing strength of the Salvadoran military. Although Honduras and El Salvador are currently cooperating with each other, they have traditionally been competitors, if not enemies. The perception of a common threat from the Sandinistas has enabled them to bury their differences for the moment. The Hondurans believe, however, that the chances of an enduring Honduran-Salvadoran cooperation would be increased if El Salvador's armed forces were not allowed to become vastly superior to those of Honduras.

As the country from which most of the contras operate, Honduras is also strongly supportive of a treaty that does not abandon the Nicaraguan rebels. Like Costa Rica, it supports talks between the contras and the Sandinistas leading to the incorporation of the former into the Nicaraguan political process.

Finally, like El Salvador, Honduras fears a treaty would deprive it of U.S. military support, and has thus sought a bilateral military agreement with the United States. At the same time, Honduras does not wish to be taken for granted, and so periodically attempts to negotiate more favorable terms of cooperation with the United States.

Why had the Central American allies of the United States originally seemed willing to accept the September Acta that Washington opposed? In part, they were posturing. They had serious problems with the Acta, but they chose to adopt a positive stance in order to impress favorably a group of European foreign ministers scheduled to meet in San José, Costa Rica, on September 28, 1984, to discuss economic assistance for the region. They believed that their objections to the Acta could be concealed for the time being, since they were convinced that Nicaragua would reject it. They were wrong. Nicaragua's unexpected acceptance of the Acta, on the condition that it not be changed in any way, led them to withdraw their support and to draft the Act of Tegucigalpa, which more accurately reflected their interests.

Guatemala: Agreement at a Distance

Since October 1984, when Honduras called together the other Central American governments to draft a substitute treaty, Guatemala has sought to distance itself from the others. Appearances are deceiving. The Guatemalan government is as anti-Sandinista as the other three Central American governments. It also does not want to freeze arms levels within Central America at current levels, thereby giving Nicaragua an advantage. It too wants an end to arms shipments to guerrilla movements, and it does not want the United States to withdraw from the region. Furthermore, although Guatemala sent only a vice minister to the October meeting of foreign ministers and failed to endorse the draft treaty publicly, the vice minister participated actively in its drafting.

Guatemala's ambivalence is explained by its unique situation. It is the only Central American country that shares a border with Mexico, the country that has been most sympathetic to the Sandinistas. Relations between Guatemala and Mexico have never been easy. The Guatemalan government's anti-guerrilla campaign created a serious refugee problem in southern Mexico. Because some refugee camps were used as safe havens for the Guatemalan guerrillas, Guatemala wanted the camps removed from the border. To achieve Mexico's cooperation, Guatemala needed to improve its relations with its neighbor.

The Guatemalan government also had been upset with the United States for some time, largely because of U.S. criticism of its human rights performance and the related cutoff of economic and military assistance. Although Guatemala basically agrees with the United States on Nicaragua and its potential threat to the region, it wants the United States to pay a price for Guatemalan cooperation with the other Central American countries.

Finally, the behavior of Guatemala's military rulers has made the country a pariah within Latin America. The civilian governments of Latin America all publicly supported the efforts of the Contadora Four and regarded the opposition of Honduras, Costa Rica, and El Salvador to the September Acta as an obstructionist move masterminded by the United States. By withholding public support from the October draft treaty, Guatemala could partially reintegrate itself into Latin America.

Nicaragua's Bilateral Bias

Nicaragua has consistently preferred bilateral over multilateral negotiations to resolve the conflict in Central America. It has believed it could better protect itself by dealing with its neighbors individually and avoid the issues of democratization/national reconciliation and regional arms control. A series of bilateral agreements would also make it more difficult for the United States to coordinate its policies with its Central American allies. Facing a Central American refusal to accept bilateral negotiations, and therefore a choice between multilateral negotiations or nothing, Nicaragua reluctantly joined the Contadora process. Negotiations would help forestall a U.S. invasion, which the Sandinistas regarded as otherwise inevitable. And multilateral negotiations could possibly produce a treaty that would legitimize the Sandinista regime and formally circumscribe the U.S. military role in Central America.

The Nicaraguan government, however, does not have faith that a multilateral treaty would constrain Washington. It therefore demanded bilateral talks with the United States, toward the goal of a separate U.S.-Nicaragua treaty that would, among other things, prohibit the United States from invading Nicaragua. When these talks began in Manzanillo in June 1984 Nicaragua's purpose was to preclude U.S. support for the contras. Nicaragua was willing to make a number of concessions to achieve that goal; it saw the contras as the main obstacle to the rapid consolidation of Sandinista rule. In the course of the talks, Nicaragua therefore agreed in principle to send home its Cuban advisors, refrain from supporting guerrilla movements in neighboring countries, and prohibit the installation of foreign bases on its territory.

The issues of internal reconciliation and the democratization of the regime were raised by the United States in the first meeting. The Sandinista position, however, was that internal reconciliation between the government and unarmed opposition groups was already occurring, and that the government would never talk to the contras, who were traitors. They added later that there was no need to discuss democratization since Nicaragua already had a democratically elected president and a pluralistic political system. Finally, the Sandinista government argued that the current internal reconciliation and democratization demands went beyond those that former assistant secretary of state Thomas Enders had originally stated to the Sandinistas in August 1981. At that time, the United States had not insisted on talks between the Sandinistas and the rebels. Enders had demanded that the Sandinistas stop sending arms to El Salvador, cease their own military buildup, loosen their ties with Cuba and the Soviets, and generally increase political and economic pluralism. In exchange, the United States would resume economic aid and not help the rebels.

A Halt to the Manzanillo Talks

The United States ultimately suspended the Manzanillo talks in January 1985, after the ninth session. It argued that Nicaragua was using the talks to extricate itself from Contadora and was exploiting fears among Washington's Central American friends of a separate deal between the United States and Nicaragua. Finally, the United States argued that it was demanding more from the Sandinistas than Assistant Secretary Enders had because Nicaragua had become more authoritarian and allied with the Soviet Union since 1981.

The Nicaraguans claimed the the United States suspended the Manzanillo talks because progress toward an acceptable treaty *was* being made, and the United States had no intention of negotiating a settlement of its conflict with Nicaragua. After the suspension of the talks, Nicaragua ostentatiously sent 100 Cuban soldiers home and agreed to halt both the military draft and the acquisition of new weapons systems. It hoped that these gestures would keep the U.S. Congress from supporting the contras and pressure the United States to resume bilateral talks. President Ortega's trip to Moscow undermined the strategy; Congress voted in favor of humanitarian aid for the contras, and Nicaragua then reversed its positions on the draft and the acquisition of new weapons systems.

Within Contadora, Nicaragua holds firm in its support of the September 1984 Acta, as originally drafted, and continues to press for a resumption of bilateral talks with the United States. In the meantime, it has intensified its military campaign against the Nicaraguan rebels. Nicaragua continues to refuse to talk with the contras or consider additional steps to democratize its political system. Instead, the Sandinistas have tightened their control over the country. They also continue to argue that they have the right to ally with the Soviet Union, Cuba, or any other country and to take whatever steps are necessary to protect themselves from their enemies. Nicaragua has reversed its position before. Whether it will do so again will depend on internal and external pressures on the regime.

A Stalemate Over Timing

Contadora is stalemated once again. The immediate stumbling block concerns timing. Nicaragua first wants an end to U.S. support for the contras, and then it would be willing to negotiate both the terms and the timetables of other issues such as a reduction in the number of military advisors, arms control, and maneuvers.

The other Central American countries want "simultaneity." Agreement must first be reached on all outstanding issues, and all should then enter into effect simultaneously. The Nicaraguans do not like the Tegucigalpa draft treaty because they do not want to negotiate under military pressure. The other Central American countries do not like the September Acta because they are convinced that the Sandinistas will not negotiate in good faith if the contras are first disbanded and the U.S. military presence in the region is reduced.

Even if the disagreement over timing could be resolved, much work remains to be done to convert agreement on principles into the detailed provisions of a negotiated settlement. To their credit, Contadora's numerous working groups are already giving serious attention to the question of how to stop arms trafficking and outside support for so-called liberation movements of the right and left. The negotiators are also grappling with the problem of how to verify arms levels, military reductions, and the like.

The Problem of Enforcement

Even in these details are worked out, the problem of what happens if and when treaty provisions are violated still remains. None of the Contadora countries wants the United States to act unilaterally. On the other hand, the regional powers have traditionally been reluctant, if not unwilling, to take collective action, including military action. They cannot have it both ways.

If the Contadora Four want a negotiated settlement in Central America that will be more than cosmetic, they must be willing to take responsibility for assuring compliance with the treaty. They cannot continue to hide behind the principle of non-intervention. They must be prepared to intervene collectively, including militarily, against violators of the treaty.

Once a treaty draft is available that resolves the timing issue and deals adequately with the problems of verification and enforcement, the problems of internal reconciliation and democratization will remain. At that point, what happens at the negotiating table will depend upon what is happening on the ground—and in Washington.

If the Sandinista government is able to resist pressure from the contras, either because it has won the timing issue or because of its own military capabilities, it will also be strong enough to maintain political control of Nicaragua and to refuse to sign a treaty providing for democratization and internal reconciliation. In such a situation, the U.S. government would be hard put to justify an invasion and the casualties and high political costs that it would entail.

More likely, the United States would eventually decide to drop its demand for democratization and internal reconciliation and settle instead for the kinds of security arrangements that are currently being worked out by Contadora. It would not be an ideal solution. Contadora would have produced a negotiated settlement of the Central American conflict, but the United States would have accepted the consolidation of another Communist regime in the Western Hemisphere.

Notes

1. For a fuller discussion of the Mexican military's role in southern Mexico, see César Seréseres, "The Mexican Military Looks South," in David Ronfeldt, ed., *The Modern Mexican Military: A Reassessment* (Center for U.S.-Mexican Studies, University of California, San Diego, 1984), pp. 201–13.

2. Miguel de la Madrid H., "Mexico: The New Challenges," *Foreign Affairs*, Fall 1984, p. 71.

3. Margaret Daly Hayes, "Regional Perceptions of the Central American Situation," working paper for the November 8, 1983, meeting of the Study Group on Central America, Council on Foreign Relations.

4. For a more detailed discussion of Colombia and Contadora, see Fernando Cepeda Ulloa, "Contadora, Colombia, y Centroamerica," a paper presented at a conference on Regional Approaches to the Central American Crisis, co-sponsored by El Colegio de Mexico and the International Institute for Strategic Studies, in Toluca, Mexico, May 1985.

11. A Costa Rican Perspective

By OSCAR ARIAS SÁNCHEZ

Focus
Costa Rica is Nicaragua's closest neighbor—a vigorous democracy, the oldest in Central America, and the only Latin American republic without an army. Thus when its president-elect, Oscar Arias Sánchez, announced to an American television reporter in February 1986 that he opposed President Reagan's legislative request for $100 million in aid to the Nicaraguan contras, his words had widespread repercussions. In Western Europe, where most people could barely place his country on the map, journalists, parliamentarians, and political intellectuals seized upon his remark as proof that the Reagan administration was taking the wrong path in Nicaragua; and in the United States Arias's comments were welcomed by the administration's opponents in Congress, the churches, and the press.

In Costa Rica, the reaction was no less strong, though different. Fear and dislike of the Sandinistas is widespread throughout the country. Costa Rica is also the most pro-U.S. of Latin American republics, and the one closest to the United States in political culture.

Several weeks after his initial interview, Arias felt obliged to clarify his remarks to his own people. He reaffirmed his opposition to President Reagan's aid proposal, but more on practical rather than political grounds. $100 million, he said, wouldn't be sufficient "to get rid of" the Sandinistas; such aid merely gave the Managua regime an excuse to be more repressive at home. The solution, in his view, is a multilateral political one—presumably under the auspices of the Contadora countries.

However, Arias also gave some hints that he has greater doubts than most advocates of a negotiated peace in the region. Even if the Reagan administration had not decided to back the contras, he said, the Sandinistas would probably have been just as repressive ("that after all is the nature of Marxism"). While he welcomed the pressure of world public opinion as a force for change in Nicaragua, he was not optimistic ("in the short run"), and warned that "there will never be peace in Central America as long as there is a Marxist regime in Nicaragua with the characteristics of the nine *comandantes*." Thus his differences with President Reagan appeared to be over means ("we're going to make Nicaragua give in, but never by arming a few contras"); exactly how he proposed to accomplish his goals he left unsaid.

Arias's observations are worth comparing with the Sandinistas' own "Seventy-two Hour Document" (appendix C), which has important implications for Costa Rica; with the strategic analysis of Alberto Coll (selection 4); with the views of the Latin American foreign ministers (selection 9); and with Susan Kaufman Purcell's discussion of the Contadora process (selection 10).

Oscar Arias Sánchez became president of the Republic of Costa Rica in May 1986.

QUESTION: *The U.S. Department of State has said that it is perplexed about a recent statement of yours, as reported in the "Washington Post," with regard to the contras. In a press conference three weeks ago you made some remarks on support for the contras. Now you are saying that aid is unwise and should be discontinued. What is your position on this question and on the Department of State's attitude, criticizing what seems to them to be a change in your position?*

ANSWER: At the beginning of this interview you showed to the television audience some of my remarks on the steps of our cathedral. One of them, as it happens, was my commitment on this issue—my commitment to keep Costa Rica out of regional conflicts. The topic of peace was one of the principal points of my campaign. Really, it's very easy, just a question of asking ourselves what the consequences would be of continuing to give arms and money to the contras. If that happens, we'll see ourselves involved in the Nicaraguan conflict, whether we want to be or not.

I've said it a thousand times: what has to be sought is a political solution to Central America's problems, in El Salvador, in Guatemala, and the same with the contras and the Sandinistas as well—a political solution, which means negotiations. By negotiations, I meant that they have to be on the multilateral level. If we keep on looking for a military solution, which with all respect is what President Reagan is seeking—my impression, what I said to the reporter from NBC, is that up to the present time the aid to the contras has served only to give the Sandinistas an excuse to increase their repression of the Nicaraguan people. The aid to the contras has just given them an excuse to abolish civil liberties, to make Nicaragua a continually more authoritarian regime, a more tyrannical and totalitarian regime.

Perhaps without the aid to the contras, they would do just the same. That after all is the nature of Marxism, to close itself off more and more instead of opening itself up. But this aid has served them very well in the court of world opinion. As long as the Americans openly aid the contras, we can't negotiate anything in Contadora. We cannot give in.

What I would say the experience has shown us is that the result is totally

---

From a television interview in San José, February 20, 1986; translated by the editors.

different from what was intended. What is the intention of giving aid to the contras? Is it that they'll be able to get rid of the Sandinistas? With 50, with 80, with 100 million dollars, they're not going to get rid of them. The fundamental objective of President Reagan is to twist the Sandinistas' arm, to get them to give in, but what has happened instead? The reality is that the opposite has happened. The Sandinistas have closed themselves off even more; they've become an even more authoritarian and totalitarian regime, even less disposed to dialogue.

On the other hand, the housing I want to construct, the jobs I want to generate, the development of the northern zone — do you think we'll be able to achieve all that if the contras are entering that area whenever they like, like a dog wandering in and out of its own house? Why don't we think about the consequences, and say that we don't agree with those who think war is the only answer? I never have said I agree with that. On the contrary, all during my campaign the main theme was peace.

We're going to make the Sandinistas negotiate. The world has lost its confidence in them, it doesn't support them. In Western Europe, in Latin America, people who until recently thought more or less well of the Sandinistas, like Carlos Andrés Pérez . . . Now we know what the mission of the Socialist International, which passed through here recently, thinks. Until recently, they blindly believed there was a possibility that Nicaragua would evolve into a democracy. Today they see that as a very remote possibility. We do have to twist the Sandinistas' arm, not with military aid (to the contras), but rather by turning our backs on them, as the Latin American world is now doing.

Now let me tell you that I'm pessimistic. Do you know of any Marxist regime that is disposed to share power? Marxists sharing with democrats in Cuba? I really believe that in Nicaragua, the changes one would like to see in the short run won't actually be achieved in the short run. But neither will they be achieved with more war and more deaths, where some are providing the arms and we, the Central Americans, are providing the dead.

Latin America is aware that there will never be peace in Central America as long as there is a Marxist regime in Nicaragua with the characteristics of the nine *comandantes*. We're going to make Nicaragua give in, but never by arming a few contras. Never. On the contrary, then the Sandinistas will just keep using the excuse that has served them so well till now to make their regime more authoritarian and totalitarian than it was some time ago.

QUESTION: *Some of the incoming National Liberation Party [PLN] deputies have manifested their disagreement with your intention to convert the neutrality proclamation into Costa Rican law. How will you deal with that?*

ANSWER: I have said to the twenty-nine deputies who make up our parliament that I'm not going to twist their arms and make them vote against their consciences.... In the case you're referring to, Fernando [ex-foreign minister Fernando Volio, a newly elected PLN deputy] has always had his doubts about neutrality.... Our own deputies, those of the opposition party and the minor parties as well, are undoubtedly going to suggest modifications, and we are prepared in the friendliest way to accept many changes to the neutrality bill.

QUESTION: *In announcing your trip through Central America, aren't you being inconsistent if you visit Managua, given your own principles on not having any dialogue with Nicaragua?*

ANSWER: Good question. Just after I learned of my electoral victory, a foreign journalist asked me that same question. I spoke about seeking dialogue, about knowing how to agree, and on the other hand I showed myself to be a bit inflexible on Nicaragua. My position is very simple. I've always said that any agreement with Nicaragua has to be in a multilateral fashion and not a bilateral one. It has to be a forum that includes all the Central American countries. If not, if Nicaragua resolves its border problem with us alone, then it will never give in as far as achieving the type of accord proposed, for example, by Contadora. Seeking a more pluralistic society, reconciliation, disarmament, the expulsion or reduction of foreign advisors—these will never be achieved if Nicaragua resolves its problems with Costa Rica bilaterally.

The Latin Americans, and in fact the whole world, want Nicaragua to give in on these points. We most of all, because Nicaragua has deceived us. The Sandinistas betrayed the confidence the world placed in them, and that of the Costa Ricans above all, since we, their neighbors, had given them space here. They didn't repay our hospitality very well. We won't negotiate bilaterally because that would imply that on the multilateral plane they wouldn't have to give in on any other points. We want Nicaragua to change somewhat, as much as it can.

12. The Elections in Guatemala and Honduras

By RICHARD L. MILLETT

Focus The sharp polarization of opinion on Central America, argues Richard L. Millett, has led to extreme optimism or pessimism on elections there. The 1986 elections in Guatemala and Honduras were "a hopeful sign in a region where reasons for hope have been notably scarce in the past decade." But, cautions Millett, elections are not enough: "the basic problems of the region are not amenable to ballot-box solutions."

One of the hopeful signs is that "in both nations the new presidents were far from being the military's choice, yet the armed forces refused to prevent such a result." In Guatemala, often regarded as one of the more repressive societies in Central America, this has led to attacks on the army by the extreme right. In Honduras, the outgoing president tried to persuade the military to prevent the victory of new president José Azcona. Given such reactions, says Millett, we must realize that powerful army officers are "by no means the only obstacle to the development of effective democratic governments in Central America."

But it is also necessary to recognize that the armies in these countries are responding to failures at home and pressures from abroad. The economic crisis in the two countries is so great that without outside assistance both would risk total collapse. Intelligent officers know that U.S. aid will not be forthcoming without steps toward civilian democratic governments.

Can these civilian governments succeed? asks Millett. "It is the weakness of civilian political sectors, as much as the power of the military, that undermines the prospects for success in Central America's experiment with democracy." Almost none of Guatemala's new cabinet members has high-level governmental experience. New president Vinicio Cerezo has an absolute majority in the congress but faces a formidable array of economic and social problems, as well as the ongoing problem of guerrilla insurgency. In Honduras, President Azcona leads a minority government that must struggle against entrenched interests.

Millett concludes, "These governments will need help from the United States in rebuilding their economies, patience in their efforts to construct a more effective and democratic political order, and greater freedom in seeking solutions to regional problems."

Millett's essay should be read in comparison with Susan Kaufman Purcell (selection 10) and the recommendations of the Kissinger Commission (selection 3).

Richard L. Millett recently co-edited *Crescents of Conflict: International Relations in the Caribbean Basin* and has written on Central America for twenty years.

THE INAUGURATION OF new civilian presidents in Guatemala and Honduras in January 1986 gives the Reagan administration additional evidence to support its claim that there is a massive trend toward Western-style democratic governments in Latin America. The argument is strengthened by the fact that Vinicio Cerezo in Guatemala and José Azcona in Honduras both attained power in relatively free and open elections, a trend that was continued in Costa Rica's recent elections. As Elliott Abrams, assistant secretary of state for inter-American affairs, puts it: "Elections are now part of a broad movement toward democracy, a movement that is strengthened and reinforced each time a new election is held." Some critics of administration policies in Central America reject these claims, arguing that the elections are actually carefully managed shows, designed to give the illusion of progress while maintaining real power in the hands of the military and traditional elite families.

The truth, as usual, lies somewhere between these two positions. The elections in Guatemala and Honduras are a hopeful sign in a region where reasons for hope have been notably scarce in the past decade. But elections are not enough; the basic problems of the region are not amenable to ballot-box solutions.

Vinicio Cerezo knows that substituting a civilian for a general in Guatemala's presidency doesn't resolve any of his country's basic dilemmas. The experience of Guatemala's last civilian president, Julio César Méndez Montenegro, who occupied the office from 1966 till 1970, underscores this reality. Méndez Montenegro has been quoted as declaring that throughout those four years, Guatemala actually had two presidents, himself and the minister of defense, who "kept threatening me with a machine gun." Four years of such threats destroyed Méndez Montenegro's effectiveness and credibility. Vinicio Cerezo has indicated that he would resign rather than submit to a similar fate. But he is also a realist, recognizing that assuming office and attaining power are distinct events. He talks of slowly increasing his power from an opening level of approximately 30 per cent to perhaps as much as 70 per cent by 1989.

Reprinted by permission from *The New Republic*, February 24, 1986 (© 1986 by The New Republic, Incorporated).

Foreign observers frequently see the military as the prime obstacle to effective civilian government in Guatemala and, to a lesser extent, in Honduras. The officer corps is portrayed as corrupt, brutal, socially and ideologically allied with the most intransigent right-wing elements in society, and fearful that an effective civilian government might hold them accountable for human rights violations in a manner similar to that now taking place in Argentina. The prime task for the new civilian presidents is seen as taming the military, removing it from the political arena, and purging the officer corps of its worst elements.

The More Complex Reality

The real situation confronting both Cerezo and Azcona is considerably more complex. In both nations the new presidents were far from being the military's choice, yet the armed forces refused to prevent such a result. This was especially notable in Guatemala, where the military's refusal to block the victory of the Christian Democrats contributed to a torrent of attacks on the army from the far right. Like a petulant jilted lover, right-wing politicians suddenly discovered corruption, incompetence, and abuses of power among those officers they has so assiduously courted for the previous years. In Honduras it was the incumbent president who attempted to persuade the military to avert the victory of José Azcona, a member of his own party. The ability of the military to resist such pressures indicates that an intransigent officer corps is by no means the only obstacle to the development of effective democratic governments in Central America.

Economic disaster throughout the region—massive budget deficits, rising unemployment, the debt burden, and a near-total lack of new, private investments—has contributed to a crisis beyond the reach of domestic solutions. Guatemala almost ran out of fuel last fall and was saved from turning off the lights in the capital only by an emergency infusion of U.S. credit. Honduras has become dependent on assistance from Washington to keep its foundering economy from sinking altogether. The armed forces in both countries recognized that only an elected, civilian government could provide access to significant external economic assistance.

Disillusionment with the far right, especially in Guatemala, became increasingly apparent. The right had promised the military that an alliance would produce order, stability, and prosperity. Instead, it had produced conflict, international isolation, and economic collapse. The break in the military's alliance with the far right was a necessary prerequisite to the acceptance of a Christian Democratic victory. It does not, however, mean military support for the Christian Democrats, nor does it end the right's capacity to disrupt the new government's reform programs.

The officers' efforts to maintain power had produced massive domestic as well as international criticism, and had caused increasing dissension within the officer corps. In Guatemala the military wanted out of the direct exercise of political power, and in Honduras the high command was determined not to take on the responsibility for dealing with the chaotic situation left behind by the Suazo administration. Still, the military has not given up real power in either country—only the temporary exercise of some elements of it. Should civilians prove incapable of dealing with the economy, maintaining order, or securing international assistance, the option of a return to the presidential palace is always available. A satirical pamphlet published while Guatemala's Constituent Assembly was drafting that nation's new constitution suggested that an article be included specifying that "civilians would take power whenever the military totally fouled things up, the military would take power whenever the civilians totally fouled things up, etc., etc."

Weakness in the Civilian Parties

It is the weakness of civilian political sectors, as much as the power of the military, that undermines the prospects for success in Central America's experiment with democracy. In Guatemala the Christian Democrats have never held or even shared power, and virtually none of President Cerezo's cabinet has high-level governmental experience. The party suffered severe losses during the bloody political violence of the past decade, and the available talent is painfully thin. Other moderate civilian parties are in even worse shape. There is no Guatemalan tradition of political compromise, no concept of loyal opposition, no recent experience with governing by law rather than by force. There is not even an effective judiciary.

President Cerezo has made improvements in this area one of his highest priorities, but this will put even greater pressures on the already limited human resources available to his administration. The bureaucracy he has inherited is inefficient, riddled with corruption, and not particularly sympathetic to his program. The challenges confronting his administration would be formidable to the most unified and experienced government; under existing conditions they appear almost overwhelming.

Vinicio Cerezo does enjoy some advantages. His party is relatively unified and has an absolute majority in the congress. As a Christian Democrat he can count on assistance from fellow Christian Democrats in Latin America and Europe. The opposite is true in Honduras, where the Liberal Party is bitterly divided between supporters of the former president and his successor. Even if all the factions were able to work together, they would still be one vote short of an absolute majority in the congress. Vinicio Cerezo can point to an overwhelming popular mandate in the runoff election for the presidency (over 68 per cent of the vote). José Azcona, owing to the peculiar Honduran system of holding primary and general elections simultaneously, received only 27 per cent of the vote, and one of his opponents received over 40 per cent. The weakness of civilian political structures combined with the dominance of personal loyalties and ambitions has given Honduras a minority government that will have difficulty governing effectively.

The Guerrilla Threat

If Honduras has anything going for it, it is the lack of a serious domestic insurgency, something with which all three of its neighbors must contend. In Guatemala, the guerrillas are not so strong as in El Salvador, but they do constitute an ongoing threat to the government and a major obstacle to new investments, especially in such vital areas as petroleum.

But an even greater problem may be the heritage of past efforts to crush the insurgents. In the process thousands of innocent Guatemalans, largely Indians, were killed, and many more were uprooted from their homes and forcibly resettled in army-controlled villages. Tens of thousands fled to Mexico, Belize, or Honduras. The image of Guatemala as a nation committing genocide against its own population also contributed to its international isolation, drying up tourism and foreign investment.

The ability of Guatemala's new administration to overcome this heritage is severely limited. Although the insurgency has slowed considerably since the early 1980s, in recent months its has shown some signs of resurgence. The military remains concentrated in Indian areas and is fiercely determined to wage the counterinsurgency campaign its own way. It will brook little interference from the capital, and it appears determined to shield its officers from any effort to hold them accountable for past actions.

The new administration will be under constant pressure to curb military excesses and purge the officer corps of its worst human rights violators. But efforts in this area could jeopardize its ability to confront other problems, and ultimately could even provoke a military coup. The military would be less reluctant to return to power to defend its own institutional interests than it would be to defend the power of traditional civilian elites. Failure to control the military, however, will seriously handicap efforts to end Guatemala's international isolation. It is in this area, where the dangers are greatest, that President Cerezo's options appear most limited.

Guatemala has better prospects in its dealings with the rest of Central America. Since it has no border with Nicaragua, it is not deeply involved in the anti-Sandinista efforts promoted by the Reagan administration. It is less concerned over a Marxist government in Nicaragua than it is with its unresolved territorial claims against Belize and its traditional distrust of Mexico. Cerezo can promote Central American efforts to resolve their own problems, gaining credibility with Europe in the process, though at the risk of strained ties with Washington. For Honduras, no such options are available. Dependent on U.S. aid, fearful of both Nicaragua and El Salvador, and terrified at the prospect of being left with thousands of armed, unemployable Nicaraguan exiles, it faces a series of cruel options, none of which bodes well for its future. Elections do nothing to solve this dilemma. The vital decisions will be made outside Honduras, and its leaders are in a poor position to influence decision-makers in either Washington or Managua.

A similar problem confronts Guatemala and Honduras as they cope with their economies. Interest rates, IMF policies, and commodity prices are all determined on a global scale, with minimal consideration to the needs or desires of small nations. The recent boost in coffee prices may do more to aid the Guatemalan economy than any decision its government could make. But more basic problems—such as reforming the tax structure, stabilizing the value of the currency, curbing government waste and corruption, and dealing with agrarian reform—will remain. In both nations, hopes for increased aid from Washington are more likely to be influenced by American concerns over budget deficits than by actions their governments may take. With these nations' destinies so subject to developments beyond their control, the prospects for effective, democratic governments are severely qualified at best.

Needed: Help and Patience

The installation of elected civilian governments in Central America is cause for hope, but not necessarily for optimism. President Cerezo's administration offers the potential of a less brutal, more just society. But in his post-election press conference he admitted that his party couldn't offer the social and economic reforms it had advocated a decade earlier "because the political situation has deteriorated since then." "We are realists," he emphasized as he outlined his hopes for dealing with the economy, reviving the courts, and reorganizing the security forces. If the new governments of Guatemala and Honduras prove no more capable than their predecessors of producing a better life for their people, the hopes for a democratic Central America could be replaced by a new cycle of repression and civil conflict.

These governments will need help from the United States in rebuilding their economies, patience in their efforts to construct a more effective and democratic political order, and greater freedom in seeking solutions to regional problems. The national preoccupation with the deficit and the impact of Gramm-Rudman will make it difficult to maintain current levels of assistance to the region, much less to fund any new programs. Many in the administration and in Congress who are inclined to proclaim a victory for democracy in most of Central America, and who focus their attention on efforts to isolate and destabilize Nicaragua, ignore the effect such policies will have on the rest of this region. This approach will reduce still further whatever chances these governments will have for success.

In such a case, the elections, far from being a solution to the region's problems, could become only another element in the destruction of these societies.

Part Three
El Salvador

Reprinted by permission from *Latin American Politics and Development* (second edition), edited by Howard J. Wiarda and Harvey F. Kline (© 1985 by Westview Press, Boulder, Colorado).

Chronology

1932	Marxist-inspired uprising by peasants and Indians quelled by General Maximiliano Hernández Martínez. Approximately 20,000 peasants massacred in revolt against landed elite. Martínez continues repressive rule for over a decade. Military regimes follow until 1979.
1969	"Soccer War" over border tensions with Honduras. Honduran president expels 300,000 illegal Salvadoran immigrants.
1972	Christian Democrat José Napoleón Duarte wins plurality in presidential election. Legislature, however, acting within constitution, chooses Colonel Arturo Armando Molina as president. Duarte charges fraud, is arrested and exiled.
1979	Government of General Carlos Humberto Romero overthrown by young military officers in response to decade of rising demands for reform and escalating civil war.
1980	Land reform begun; banks nationalized.
	Archbishop Oscar Arnulfo Romero assassinated while saying Mass, by unknown gunmen.
	Revolutionary Democratic Front (FDR), a rebel political arm, formed. Guerrilla umbrella organization, Farabundo Martí National Liberation Front (FMLN), created with help of Fidel Castro. Three strikes called by rebels in summer fail.
	José Napoleón Duarte made president of four-man military-civilian junta directing government.
	Four American churchwomen in El Salvador murdered; in response, President Carter suspends economic aid to government.
1981	President Carter lifts arms embargo begun four years earlier.
	Rebel forces launch "final offensive" to present U.S. president-elect Reagan with *fait accompli*; fails through lack of popular support.
	U.S. Congress requires semi-annual certification of progress in human rights in El Salvador as condition for military aid.

1982	Elections held under Duarte for Constituent Assembly. Large voter turnout despite boycott, threats, and violence by rebels. Alvaro Magaña named provisional president; is first elected civilian head of government in fifty years.
1984	Duarte elected president; death-squad killings drop off sharply after election; Duarte begins dialogue with rebels.
1985	Rebels kidnap Duarte's daughter; demand and get release of prisoners as ransom.

13. A Culture of Violence

By JOHN KURZWEIL

Focus Writing in 1982, before the three successful national elections, John Kurzweil asserted that the Salvadorans had only three choices: (1) to return to the old repressive military government, (2) to help the rebels install a Marxist dictatorship, or (3) to give elections and the moderate forces on both sides a chance. To capitulate to terrorists of the right or the left would be to cave in to sheer power. Even worse, "it would be to carry on, newly ratified, the ideas of the past that disallow peace but are tailor-made for rationalizing war."

Kurzweil points to the moral and political complexity of the Salvadoran conflict, in which both sides proclaim humanitarian goals but are caught up in what President Duarte has called a "culture of violence." There are democratic and moderate elements both among the guerrillas and in the government. Among journalists and other observers, an all too typical response is despair. To react in this way, says the author, is to acquiesce in the hopelessness that makes people on both sides of the conflict embrace force as the only solution.

Kurzweil believes there is hope. The junta formed after the 1979 coup and the subsequently elected government have opened at least the possibility of a way out of the stalemate, he says. The "massive land-reform programs, bank nationalizations, and coffee-industry takeovers — projects ideal for making enemies of the wealthiest, most uncompromisingly anti-Communist elements in society" show that the government is no longer merely playing violent politics as usual. Reforms are going on, and the only constructive approach is to encourage them.

This article was written during the Duarte presidency

of the military-civilian junta. Duarte was democratically elected president in 1984.

Julia Preston presents more recent developments and a somewhat different analysis of the causes of the Salvadoran conflict (selection 14), and Shirley Christian (selections 15 and 16) describes the difficult divisions in the Salvadoran military and among the guerrillas that democratic elements on both sides face.

John Kurzweil was formerly the editor of *Policy Digest* and a contributing editor of the *National Catholic Register.*

At the beginning of Book III of *War and Peace*, Tolstoy describes Napoleon's invasion of Russia in 1812 as "an event . . . counter to human reason and all human nature." What followed was "such an innumerable quantity of crimes, frauds, treacheries, robberies, forgeries, issues of counterfeit money, depredations, incendiarisms, and murders, as are not recorded in the annals of all the courts of justice in the world, but which, at the time, the men who were committing them did not regard as crimes." Tolstoy devoted the rest of that chapter and, for that matter, *War and Peace* in its entirety to answering the question why so many civilized men simultaneously took up so terrible a work of destruction. Indeed, the question should be asked about any war, particularly by peace-loving men *before* a conflagration actually begins.

The war raging in El Salvador is at least as mystifying as the invasion of Russia in its sheer unrelatedness to the humanitarian goals proclaimed by all involved. The left, filled with indignation over what they consider the "immoral" distribution of El Salvador's wealth and power, conclude that force alone will make the rich share, and so they fight. That such prescriptions as the "expropriation without right to indemnization [*sic*] of all properties in the hands of the oligarchy," their "subsequent redistribution as collective, communal, or state properties," and "management of the national economy on the basis of a system of national planning" embracing "all branches, sectors, and regions"—all demanded by El Salvador's guerrillas—have nowhere led to justice, morality, or peace can be confirmed by asking, among others, the nearest Pole. So why do the guerrillas continue to fight for an all-embracing socialism? It is not because the arguments for it have been irresistibly articulated. Rather, it is because the alternatives, freedom and democracy, have been defended so poorly, when they've been defended at all.

An Associated Press report from San Salvador dated January 25, 1932, read:

> The flower of Salvadoran aristocracy, heavily armed, roamed the streets of this capital city tonight to aid their government in stamping out the last

---

Reprinted by permission from the March 19, 1982, issue of *National Review* (© 1982 by National Review, Incorporated).

vestiges of "Communist insurrection." On the suggestion of a prominent banker, Rodolfo Duke, adult citizens were equipped with rifles and revolvers and received carte blanche to shoot any Communist on sight. More than three hundred sons of the first families, both foreign and native, also were armed and turned loose to snare any radicals still at large.

The occasion for this nocturnal adventure was an uprising, primarily involving the country's Indian population, during the preceding four days or so led by the founder of the Salvadoran Communist Party, Farabundo Martí. Though Martí's Communists managed a fair show of carnage and terror around the countryside and even captured a few towns briefly, the revolt was thoroughly crushed in less than a week. Martí and a large number of his followers were executed.

First Free Election: 1931

The slaughter ended a decisive period in El Salvador's history that had begun optimistically only one year earlier. In January 1931, a liberal (in the nineteenth-century sense of the word) member of a wealthy Salvadoran family named Arturo Araujo was elected president in the nation's first free election. He had campaigned on a platform of education, better transportation, and jobs for ordinary Salvadorans, and industrialization for the nation as a whole. Educated at Oxford, Araujo had seen the way in which the Industrial Revolution had promoted class fluidity and mass prosperity in England, and he wanted the same thing for his own country, then even more thoroughly agricultural than now. Using family money, he built El Salvador's first railroad and toured the land on it, campaigning along the way.

It must have made an interesting spectacle, Araujo's train chugging into town, probably festooned with banners and flags, and the candidate himself puffing away before crowds of illiterate Indians and peasants about competition and the rewards of hard work. It was regarded as somewhat less than edifying, however, by his own class of educated, well-off Salvadorans, who must have thought Araujo incredibly naïve. The poor, everyone knew, were capable of eating and of doing a little unskilled work, which was good because a certain amount of that had to be done. But that was it. Nothing but trouble could come from politicians' stirring the passions of the throngs with impossible dreams.

After he took office, Araujo legalized the Communist Party, and Farabundo Martí began trying to organize his revolution. On December 3, amid predictions that the Communists were about to overthrow the dreamer and seize power, the defense minister, Maximiliano Hernández Martínez, led a successful coup against the president and, with the financial banking of wealthy Salvadorans, took over the government. The United States and neighboring Central American countries, however, refused to recognize the new regime because it had taken power by force. "In this situation," the *New York Times* reported, "the Red elements felt encouraged to make a drive for power." Thus, instead of preempting the revolt, Hernández Martínez may have brought it on.

Martí may have been influenced by the anti-Araujo scare-talk into overestimating his strength. And Hernández Martínez himself, nearly as soon as the revolt began, started soft-pedaling the Red Menace that had loomed so large only two months earlier, before the coup.

"There are no revolutionary movements in El Salvador," Hernández Martínez's junta announced on January 25, 1932 (the same day the "flower of Salvadoran aristocracy" sallied forth to shoot Communists on sight). "What happened was that Communist groups in certain towns of the republic promoted disturbances which the government has energetically repressed. The capital city is undisturbed. The government is unanimously backed by all Salvadorans."

The following February, the *Panama Star and Herald* took up the theme in an editorial that described Martí's rebels as possessing too little fidelity or philosophy to claim membership in any party, and added that, had these "revolutionaries" turned up in Russia a few years earlier, Lenin would probably have had them "shot as thieves." If such opinions as these had turned up in print a few months earlier, democracy might have survived in El Salvador.

From the perspective of Hernández Martínez and his supporters, the real danger had never been from the masses' will to revolt—that, they thought, was in any case unavoidable, like hurricanes or crop failures—but from what they considered Araujo's naïveté and unwillingness to meet the rebels' challenge effectively: which meant, of course, with bullets. Now that Araujo was out, the real danger was past. As the present war in El Salvador shows, however, it was Hernández Martínez, rather than Araujo, who was naïve.

What Araujo saw was the potential of the poor to learn and grow and become productive. His enemies saw only a transparent plot to take their land and dissipate the nation's wealth in a frenzy of redistribution that would bring chaos and ruin to El Salvador. In effect, the Hernández Martínez coup ratified the left's view of the human predicament. With the overthrow of democracy, the new government registered its tacit agreement with the revolutionaries that the only way the poor could improve their lot was to take wealth from the rich. And for the rich to retain what they had, the poor would have to be kept poor. The distribution of political power, not the production of wealth, was the key, and that distribution, both sides also now agreed, would be determined first and foremost by brute force. Whatever silly notions about law or authority or majority rule the people might have picked up from Araujo, power was what mattered. The view is tailor-made to justify and encourage violence, and that is exactly what it has done.

Over the years since Araujo's ouster, as the officer corps became increasingly corrupt through the complex of political machinations, cliques, and bribery that replaced merit as the road to advancement, wealthy Salvadorans cooperated to protect their personal monopolies in land and industry by controlling the avenues to wealth. Social, economic, and political distinctions based on ancestry, education, nationality, or some other irrelevant characteristic, usually beyond the individual's control, provided endless sources of friction. The present leader of the Communist Party in El Salvador is a man named Shafik Handal, of Palestinian ancestry. Arabs, who make up a small minority of the country's population, have traditionally been excluded, along with most of the rest of the people, from opportunities to improve their economic circumstances.

It should come as no surprise, therefore, that large numbers of people, reasoning that the sole road to prosperity is to take and keep it from someone else (and who has taught them otherwise?), now make war to accomplish that very thing. Handal is the man who personally arranged the import, through Cuba, of the Soviet-bloc weapons that have transformed a sporadic insurgency into a full-fledged civil war.

The 1972 Election Fraud

Over the years, the left and its opponents in the government—military men taught to govern in the Hernández Martínez tradition—have served to justify each other's ideas and violent methods. In 1972, for instance, Christian Democrat José Napoleón Duarte was elected president, beating the candidate of the National Conciliation Party (PCN), the political arm of El Salvador's military. The PCN had been ruling the country for nearly forty years at the time and was disinclined to relinquish power simply because of some unfavorable ballot totals. Duarte was picked up, beaten by police, and forced to flee the country. The presidency was then given instead to yet another reliable military man.

Each such "lesson" helps El Salvador's extreme, anti-democratic left convince more of its countrymen that war is the only answer. Each subsequent terrorist attack carried out by the left then convinces other Salvadorans that violence and fear alone will suffice to preserve order in the country. The guiding principle is thus passed to each succeeding generation that one's enemies are irrational brutes who must be done unto before they do.

"Some elements in the security forces," said Bishop Pedro Aparicio of San Vicente in an interview, "have become enraged at seeing the bodies of their mothers and sisters raped and mutilated just because they are their relatives. They have found the bodies of their younger teen-age brothers mutilated with the inscription on their chests: Traitor to the FPL (Popular Liberation Forces). When they confront the guerrillas they are like wild stallions. They take matters into their own hands without authority."

1979: The 'Young Military' Coup

In 1979, with terrorist violence spreading out of control and even its staunchest allies abandoning the PCN, a group of young army officers ended the party's forty-five-year rule by overthrowing the presidency of the universally recognized incompetent Carlos Humberto Romero. The coup brought to power a junta composed of and backed by divergent factions, including moderate democrats, socialists, and Marxists of various shadings. In addition, a large number of powerful military men who had served under Romero survived the coup and stayed on.

The far left elements quit the government within a few months and, for the most part, joined or threw their support to the guerrillas who had been fighting since 1972 to establish a Marxist-Leninist regime. After a number of regroupings, a new governing coalition was formed, composed of ex-Romero officers interested in their own security and Christian Democrats who wanted elections and a mixed bag of economic reforms, including, in some cases, greater state control, and, in others, more freedom. Duarte, now back from exile, was made president.

Marxists, it should be recalled, really believe their own propaganda. When the new junta did not immediately begin dismantling Salvadoran society and rebuilding it on the Soviet and Cuban models, the only ideologically admissible explanation for the left was that the government was dominated either by the same old "oligarchs" or by some new manifestation of fascist repression. Both explanations have been used to reach the same conclusion: the junta is an inhuman, bloodthirsty beast that must be crushed before any hope of progress and justice is possible.

This message is broadcast to American audiences through such left mouthpieces as T. D. Allman, writing in *Harper's* magazine. "Anything they could find in their huts or fields," Allman reports (from "behind guerrilla lines, somewhere in El Salvador"), "or take from the forest that might be of use, the *campesinos* [peasants] had gathered together and attempted to interpose between themselves and the jeeps and armored cars of the soldiers who came, periodically, like blight on the coffee harvest or typhoons from the Pacific, to torture their lives at moments they could not predict, and for reasons of which they had no understanding."

During the Vietnam era, anti-war activists chided the U.S. military for projecting a "dehumanized" image of the Vietcong that blunted the American people's normally sympathetic reactions to the plight of the downtrodden rising in revolt. But Allman goes that one better. Not satisfied with obscuring the humanity of Duarte and the Salvadoran army, he transforms them into a blind, mindless force for evil. One doesn't *understand* or reason with the coffee blight or the typhoon, any more than one reasons with Christian Democrats. Suddenly, we're back on familiar ground: there is no solution but war. But if El Salvador's Marxists are barred by their ideology from seeing anything good in El Salvador's government, surely that is *their* problem. The problems of the Salvadoran people, meanwhile, are a good deal more complex than that. If thoughtful Americans wish to understand them, they'll require better information than is found in Allman's superficial melodrama, entitled "Rising to Rebellion."

In Support of Reform

To begin with, the Salvadoran tradition of political violence must be overcome, a job that won't be done by American journalists who write about it as if it were an indigenous, permanent characteristic of the people. Nor will it be ended merely by overwhelming Castro's guns with more and better American guns. The situation might be helped, though, by seeking out and supporting those individuals and factions within El Salvador that favor elections and a free society.

No one, except the guerrillas, denies there are some such good people in the government—Duarte himself for one—and in the military, but genuine Salvadoran democrats are usually written off as too few and too weak to matter. The spirit of Hubert Humphrey would not recognize his liberal brethren today, so burdened with doubt and hopelessness have they become. Efforts toward reform *are* going forward in El Salvador, alongside the revolutionary and reactionary violence. These efforts should be supported if for no other reason than that to do otherwise is to become like the killers in their despair.

"We're not changing a system that goes back fifty years, but one that goes back five hundred years," said Salvadoran minister of education Carlos Aquilino Duarte (no relation to the president). Duarte's nationally broadcast speech spelled out his ministry's plans for reforming the country's educational system. The changes to come in education, he said, would be integrated with those taking place throughout El Salvador, including the land-reform program and the scheduling of elections.

"As things have been done till now," he said, "if a light bulb burns out in a school in San Miguel, that school's principal must request that the maintenance department of the Ministry of Education in San Salvador purchase a light bulb and go to the school to change it. No more!"

The minister decried the inefficiency that used the country's schoolrooms at 20 per cent of capacity. (The educational TV channel that carried his speech was operating at only 30 per cent of its potential.) Duarte criticized the system's "pyramidal, centralized structure" that "kept teachers from developing," and outlined a program of "basic education for all adults and youth" that was of crucial importance, he said, because "a democracy is impossible with one and a half million illiterates — education will allow them to make intelligent choices in a democratic society."

Practicing Democracy

A good deal of rhetorical energy has been expended to deflate the hope that the junta's talk of democracy is more than window dressing. "Democracy, El Salvador style," Juan Vásquez wrote in the *Los Angeles Times,* "is a joke." But must it always be so? The Salvadoran education ministry has been sponsoring local elections of teacher representatives to a new national body that will advise the ministry on education policy. The country has been divided into four hundred school districts in which local teachers select three nominees for the national delegation. All adults then vote to elect their district's delegate.

"We wish to acquaint people with the way elections work, or fail to work, if that is the case," said José Interiano, an assistant to the education minister. "If irregularities occur, and some have, the election is done over." Why aren't such stories written up in the American press? Why are our journalists in love with gloom and despair?

The editorial blurb introducing Christopher Dickey's *Playboy* piece on El Salvador, "Death as a Way of Life," represents the triumph of a confidence game unusually transparent even for this age of credulity. "The reporter went down to El Salvador," it reads, "with the most absurd notion—he thought there would be *reasons* for all the killing." Though some editor at *Playboy*, and to a considerable extent Dickey himself, has succumbed to the "all life is absurdity" syndrome, the reporter actually did find the reason, which he duly relates:

"A goal of the terrorism all along had been to make the people cry out, '*¡Basta ya!*'—Enough—bring us peace, no matter what you have to do." The first, and ultimately the only, demand of the terrorists is that power replace authority as the legitimizing characteristic of government. Elections, the very symbol of government by invested authority, have no place. Now, the remarkable thing is that while the Salvadoran people have yet to cry "Enough!," American liberals have been yelling "*¡Basta ya!*" to the terrorists in droves, declaring elections "unworkable" and democracy "a joke" at every opportunity. There are approximately five thousand leftist guerrillas operating in El Salvador. Suppose, to give a generous estimate, there are about the same number in the anti-Communist death squads. These ten thousand killers, then, amount to less than two-tenths of 1 per cent of the population. For every Salvadoran they've killed, by the most gruesome estimates, 275 remain alive. Shouldn't these more than five and half million people be given the opportunity to repudiate terrorism by voting for a government of their own choice? Haven't enough died for the survivors to have earned the right to conduct free elections?

But the elections will be rigged, it is said, candidates shot, and the people deprived of opportunities to hear all sides. And for the first 132 years of our republic, half the citizens of the United States were denied the vote. Fourteen per cent were slaves until 1863, and after the Civil War the new freemen stood a good chance of being shot or hung if they tried to vote, much less run for office. To this day, several areas of the country have yet to turn in entirely valid ballot returns. Should we cancel all elections every time some such abuses turn up? The answer to electoral tampering, as to terrorism and blackmail, is to renounce and eliminate it, not to capitulate. It's a con game. The killers will never allow elections without a violent challenge, but there *are* ways to defeat them.

Improved Government-Education Relations

Under PCN [the military political party] governments, an intense animosity—at times resembling a state of war—developed between Salvadoran educators and the military government, a situation the left exploited to gain control of the nation's major teachers' union. Since the 1979 coup, however, government-educator relations have improved markedly, to the point where last summer [1981] a previously unthinkable meeting of university and government officials was broadcast over educational television. The two sides agreed on several compromises between the claims of educational autonomy and the government's legitimate prerogatives on campus. State intrusion onto campuses, even in pursuit of criminal suspects, had caused considerable friction in the past. Just by meeting with the ministry people, university officials tacitly recognized the junta's right to rule, itself a major breakthrough in a country where governing authority traditionally extends as far as the rulers' capacity to destroy their rivals and no further. And now a new, moderate teachers' union has formed to compete with the old left-dominated organization. Teacher strikes, previously endemic in El Salvador, are far fewer and less political than before.

"Lastly, and most important," the education minister told his countrymen after listing the various resources their nation possessed, "we have the people of El Salvador, who want to achieve through peaceful means the goals of the new society. Through education we must achieve a profound change."

What are we to make of all this? In the estimation of Cayetano Carpio, alias Commander Marcial of the general command of the Farabundo Martí National Liberation Front (FMLN), it's all part of the junta's "bloody reformist measures . . . used as a smokescreen to cover up genocidal practices."

Shafik Handal [head of the Salvadoran Communist Party] dismisses the whole affair as the work of the "murderous fascist military–Christian Democratic junta."

The question is why a regime that "is fighting the entire Salvadoran people," as Carpio revealed in April [1981] over Radio Moscow, would use precious broadcast time to attack the mass illiteracy that, if Carpio is right, is presumably one of its greatest allies. Why, if you are part of a regime characterized by "institutionalized criminality, exploitation, and oppression" (Commander Roberto Boca over the guerrillas' clandestine Radio Liberación), do you spend twice as much ($150 million in 1981) on education as on defense ($75 million)? Why institute massive land-reform programs, bank nationalizations, and coffee-industry takeovers—projects ideal for making enemies of the wealthiest, most uncompromisingly anti-Communist elements in society—when all you're interested in is crushing the revolutionaries? And why, on the other hand, would you undertake the mass slaughter of your own people, as Carpio claims, when that would alienate irrevocably the media and citizens of the one nation, the United States, upon whose support all your hopes depend?

Three Choices for Salvadorans

The Duarte government is not universally loved in El Salvador. Neither is the Reagan administration here. Nor was Carter, Ford, or any other U.S. president ever. But as things stand, the people of El Salvador can choose either (1) to go back to the old PCN-Hernández Martínez style of government (a Maximiliano Hernández Martínez Brigade competes with the Farabundo Martí left in committing terrorist atrocities), (2) to fight with the FMLN to install a Marxist dictatorship, or (3) to give elections a try.

Virtually no one wants to return to the old way. In any event, a right-wing coup would mean a cutoff of U.S. aid and a fall to the left as inevitable as was Somoza's once Carter abandoned him. For the people of El Salvador, the only real choice, at least for the foreseeable future, is between elections and an imposed settlement giving some or all power to the left.

There is little support for the left among ordinary Salvadorans. Their resistance to the January 1981 "final offensive" was only one of the more dramatic instances of the people's repudiation of the guerrillas. Repeated calls for a general strike have been ignored. During the offensive, guerrillas hit towns and villages in fourteen areas of the country, aiming specifically at security posts and garrisons. In only one city—Santa Ana, the country's second largest—did government troops switch sides. But, though an army colonel and several commanding officers joined the insurrection there, the *townspeople*, armed with handguns, fought the rebels. They denied them control of the town until the army arrived to capture the rebellious officers and drive the guerrillas back to their hideouts in the hills.

The Cost of Resistance

The best chance the people have had to show their support for the left came when the revolutionaries were demanding a general strike. It was again ignored—or perhaps resisted is a better word, for failure to strike cost some Salvadorans dearly. For one example, a man—we'll call him Carlos (some of his relatives still live in El Salvador)—ran a coffee factory on the outskirts of San Salvador before the offensive. Carlos was thirty-two, had an attractive young wife and two small children. He stayed away from politics, had a good sense of humor, and was liked and respected by his employees, whom he had unionized in the mid-seventies.

In December 1980, a few days before those employees left for a two-week Christmas vacation, Carlos addressed them at a meeting. Leftists outside the factory had been distributing leaflets and turning up at employees' homes calling for worker participation in a national strike to be held in concert with a "final offensive" against El Salvador's government. Carlos told the workers—for whom the company had established pension and profit-sharing plans and scholarships for their children's higher education—that the strike, if successful, would hurt them more than anyone. Without production, he said, there would be no jobs and no pay.

A few days later, as he was driving to the factory, Carlos was stopped and dragged from his car. A telephone call informed his family he'd been made a "prisoner of war" by the "popular forces." There was no further word of Carlos's fate until the first week of January, when a "communiqué" was delivered to the San Salvador newspapers. It listed the names of several kidnapped businessmen, including Carlos, and threatened to kill those on the list and to take more such "POWs" should resistance to the general strike continue. One week later, a second "communiqué" told the factory workers they'd never see their boss again if they insisted on working after January 9. They went to work.

Within a week, Carlos's body, savagely beaten and shot once, was found on a country road leading to the port city of La Libertad. He'd been castrated and his testicles taped inside his mouth to prove—what? That Carlos was an "enemy of the people"? Or was the point to convince the workers that justice and mercy no longer existed and that war alone remained? It is no coincidence that El Salvador's terrorists chose the names of Maximiliano Hernández Martínez and Farabundo Martí. These men of violence, symbols of the past, lived by power and died by it. But the people of El Salvador have never wanted their country run that way.

In the course of solidifying their control over Russia, Aleksandr Solzhenitsyn told Americans in 1975, the Bolsheviks "reduced twenty provinces of our country to utter famine. This was in 1921, the infamous Volga famine. It was a typical Communist technique: to struggle for power without thinking of the fact that the productivity is collapsing, that the fields are not being sown, that the factories stand idle, that the country is sinking into poverty and famine...."

The guerrillas' struggle for power in El Salvador has reproduced all of these classic traits. Since the collapse of the final offensive, they've concentrated on blowing up electrical power stations, periodically blacking out large sections of the country and shutting down industry and agriculture in the process. Without power, patients in hospitals cannot receive proper treatment. Some become sicker; others die. Fires set by leftists destroy the coffee crop. Sabotage, kidnappings, and million-dollar ransoms force businesses to close, drive foreign investment from the land, and provide the guerrillas ammunition for propaganda as they point to the misery they have caused and blame it on the junta. But then the aim was never to improve the lot of the people anyway. Power was all, from the beginning.

"Shortly before his assassination," said Bishop Aparicio, referring to Archbishop Oscar Romero, who was shot while saying Mass in March 1980, "he realized the Marxists' thirst for power was stronger than their desire for social justice."

The guerrillas, as Aparicio described them, are "well-trained terrorists.... We see that they have been active at night when we travel the highways early in the morning and find first the heads and then, further along, pieces of bodies blocking the road....

"Ever since the leftist guerrillas lost the final offensive — because the people did not support them — they have turned their anger on the people, especially *campesinos*."

These are the people who Mexico and France, among others, now proclaim have earned the right to govern their fellow citizens. They are to be included in a new government according to a "political solution" reached through negotiations, a course routinely advocated (at least since it became clear the left would lose the final offensive) in contrast to the evil of a "military solution." But a new government including any faction or party unable to win representation through free, fair elections would precisely constitute a military solution. The junta would have caved in to the guerrillas solely to avoid further violence and bloodshed. Their "right" to govern would be that of conquest. And for the left, any other road to power would be hypocritical anyway. If anyone remains unaware of the fact, let it be known that Marxists, deep down, are not democrats. Their ideology presupposes inevitable class warfare, and it would be absurd, according to every principle of Marxist-Leninist theory, to relinquish control of a country to the "genocidal fascist" enemy simply because a majority asked them to do so.

Their "right" to participate in running the country, the right endorsed by France and Mexico, is morally indistinguishable from that proclaimed by Maximiliano Hernández Martínez. To allow them to hold power simply because they've proven capable of mounting a creditable war effort—because they can endanger the lives of innocent Salvadorans day or night—would be to repudiate the very principles of legality, democracy, and freedom on which every opponent of the Salvadoran regime predicates his criticism. It would be to endorse the very political despotism and intolerance the left itself insists it is fighting to end.

Worst of all, it would be to carry on, newly ratified, the ideas of the past that disallow peace but are tailor-made for rationalizing war.

14. What Duarte Won

By JULIA PRESTON

Focus "Duarte and the United States have had greater successes than their critics predicted," says Julia Preston, "but they will be presiding over war in El Salvador for a long time." Contrary to most of the pre-election analyses in the U.S. press, José Napoleón Duarte won not only legislative support in the 1985 Salvadoran elections but also a degree of momentum to effect some change in his war-troubled country.

To begin with, the military refused to support the extreme right's demand for a new election after Duarte's Christian Democrats won a solid majority. Though the military's attitude was clearly intended to attract continuing U.S. aid, it also caused a steep drop in right-wing death-squad activity. Previously, the death squads had operated with tacit army support; after the elections there were no moves to bring death-squad murderers to justice, but as a U.S. official told Preston, "the High Command's deal is, we'll protect you for what you've done so far, but try anything new and we'll get you."

At the same time, civilian casualties in army operations have decreased, though not so much as the death-squad activity. In part, the army is performing better because it is better trained. But there has also been greater pressure to reduce abuses from officers with an eye on U.S. aid.

Over the same period, guerrilla numbers and support have been dwindling owing to the democratic opening. Duarte has gone so far as to meet with leaders of the rebel opposition. While these talks have produced little direct progress, they have sent out a further sign in Salvadoran society that guerrilla warfare may not be the only way to change.

But "beneath the plausible surface of Duarte's political

success, El Salvador remains a violent, almost desperate nation," says Preston. Salvadoran economic growth rates were high until 1972, when oil prices shot up. Since then war damage and uncertainty have kept the per capita income level from returning to the 1972 level. Conservative coffee-growers resent Duarte's land redistribution and economic reforms. Social disruption still occurs regularly where villages are suspected of being rebel sympathizers.

"The best Salvadorans can hope for," says Preston, "is limited, infrequent negotiations to civilize the conduct of the war. Peace will have to be made gradually, by Salvadoran citizens, not only by their leaders: by guerrilla fighters who lay down their rifles and return to their families, or by policemen who adhere to legal procedures instead of brutalizing captured youths they suspect of leftist sympathies."

These observations should be compared with those of ex-guerrilla commander José Napoleón Romero (selection 17).

Julia Preston is a journalist currently covering Central America for the *Washington Post*.

On March 31 [1985], just after the national legislative elections were over, many American reporters in El Salvador seemed close to being in a state of shock. By Salvadoran standards, the vote had been uneventful. The balloting was more or less orderly. Attempts by leftist guerrillas to disrupt the election were scattered and largely unsuccessful. The news that stunned the correspondents came from the Spanish International Network (SIN), a U.S. television company that had contracted to conduct the exit polls. The first SIN results showed that the party of the Christian Democratic president José Napoleón Duarte—described almost universally by the press in the days before the vote as a "beleaguered" leader, with his right-wing enemies closing in on him—had just won thirty-three of sixty seats in the national assembly. Against even his own predictions, Duarte had won the commanding majority he needed to govern.

But the victory went even deeper than that, as Duarte pointed out to the journalists he sumoned to his residence that night. "The people got our message," he said with satisfaction. "They want democracy and peace. This is the same choice the people made in 1972. They reconfirmed it." In his first try for the presidency thirteen years earlier, the army robbed Duarte of victory by fixing the results, beating him up, and driving him out of the country. Duarte went into exile for more than seven years and came back in 1980 to participate in a ruling junta that was steeped in blood. He then stayed quiet until he won the presidency in 1984. By that time, more than 50,000 Salvadorans were dead after nearly five years of civil war.

Many in the press were disconcerted that night not only because they had so badly miscalled the results. Duarte's triumph seemed also to be Washington's, the vindication after four years of a Reagan administration policy that many reporters in El Salvador believed to be based both on gross exaggerations of the rebels' allegiance to foreign Marxist allies and on a high tolerance for violence and venality on the part of the right. The administration had argued it could stop the Marxist insurgency by giving political and financial support—some $1.7 billion in aid during the last four years—to the forces of the political "center." On March 31 it looked as if the

---

Reprinted by permission from the August 15, 1985, issue of the *New York Review of Books*.

administration had been justified. "What happened here," one disconsolate correspondent said, "is that *we* lost."

Strong Show of Military Support

During the following week, the coalition of the two opposition parties, one of them former major Roberto D'Aubuisson's rightist ARENA, presented a petition to annul the vote. The coalition's evidence of electoral fraud—which included claims of interference by the military—was flimsy. But it controlled a majority on the elections council that would pass on the petition. D'Aubuisson's people were in a position to force a new election.

On April 3, the armed forces called a press conference. Into the dreary auditorium at the General Staff headquarters marched every senior commander in the entire military; they formed a wall of olive green heavily decked with stars and shoulder bars. There were officers known by journalists to have commanded operations where dozens of civilians were cut down; officers who had flirted in past years with D'Aubuisson's schemes to carry out a coup; officers suspected of complicity in the killing of American citizens. At the front of the room was the plodding minister of defense, General Carlos Eugenio Vides Casanova, a warhorse whose chief virtue as a commander is his die-hard loyalty to the military as an institution.

"This is no time to be playing around with the will the people expressed at the poll," Vides said, slapping his hand on the table. "While the political parties are entertaining themselves exchanging insults on television, *we* are putting up the bodies. We can't allow the election to be repeated on the whim of a political party as if it were a game of cards."

Within hours, the elections council threw out the annulment petition. Tainted as some of its officers were, the military made a strong show of unity to demonstrate, as Vides said, that it "totally supported the efforts of the Salvadoran people to channel its destiny on a democratic route."

How the Reagan Policy Succeeded

With Duarte firmly in power, Reagan can claim a policy success in El Salvador—a success all the more striking since it seemed so unlikely as recently as eighteen months ago. But on closer inspection the policy that ultimately prospered in El Salvador is not the same one the administration had in mind when it vowed to "draw the line" against Communism at the outset of Reagan's term. Reagan looks successful now in El Salvador largely because his policy-makers eventually incorporated into their planning the criticisms of the administration's most vehement liberal adversaries in Washington and in the press. Reagan, who vowed to free the American people from post-Vietnam fears of intervention, is winning the political battle in El Salvador precisely because his diplomats followed the lessons of restraint the U.S. military learned the hard way during the Vietnam War.

In addition, the Reagan administration owes much to its chief enemies in El Salvador, the guerrillas of the Farabundo Martí National Liberation Front, the FMLN, whose ranks are now estimated to number about 8,500 fighters. In 1983 the rebels' punishing offensives finally forced the Salvadoran military to realize that it had to face either change or defeat. By 1985, the arrogant and hypermilitaristic strategies practiced by key guerrilla leaders estranged many of their former supporters among El Salvador's poor.

In a country where Marxist-inspired radicalism has been a force for some fifty years, the most recent cycle of revolution, which began in 1979, is now over. The FMLN revolutionaries said in communiqués and radio broadcasts this spring that they have postponed their expectations of victory for as long as five years; they will return to gnawing away at the government with a war of small ambushes and booby traps. They are sending their cadre back into the cities to try to revive the urban popular movements that gave rise to the guerrilla armies five years ago. They are reverting to urban terrorism—assassinations and kidnappings—which was their standard practice in the 1970s when they were no more than small clandestine cells. The FMLN has said the killing of four U.S. Marine guards, two American civilians, and seven other people in a sidewalk café in the capital on June 19 [1985] was "only a beginning" of this phase of their war.

Finally, if a successful U.S. policy is one that leaves a country economically sound and autonomous, with anti-government insurgency waning, and people free to express their concerns without arbitrary government retaliation, and with hope for peace, El Salvador today does not fit that description. Most Salvadorans, regardless of their political views, still live with fear, haunted by memories of the terror of the early 1980s. Many show by their words and actions that they no longer believe, as they seemed to in 1980, that the risks of death, exile, or imprisonment are worth taking for a living wage, a decent house, or the prospect of an adequate education for their children—the needs the people now have more urgently than before. Duarte, perhaps inadvertently, was right on election night: his country has an elected constitutional government that falls between the political extremes, but its people are starting again from where they were around 1972.

Combatting the Death Squads

The policy of the Reagan administration in El Salvador began to make some headway when conservatives in Washington and San Salvador confronted the issue of the right-wing death squads. In 1982 it was heresy for news reports to assert that the squads had intimate links to the military, and that the overwhelming number of human rights abuses—people murdered, mutilated, tortured, or "disappeared"—came from the right. Now the chief of staff of the armed forces, General Adolfo O. Blandón, accepts these facts as commonplace. "I began to work against death squads in September 1980, as soon as I returned from being military attaché in Washington," Blandón claimed when I talked to him in June in his windowless office at the General Staff headquarters. "But at that time there was a very dangerous division in the armed forces that I believe permitted the development of the death squads. Very little could be done in practice then."

Blandón is clear about what caused the army to rethink its complicity with rightist paramilitary killing. "We knew that public opinion in the United States and the view of many senators and congressmen opposed to military aid for El Salvador were largely due to our bad image because of the squads," he said. "Knowing that the aid was absolutely vital for us, we concluded we had to take a strong decision to get rid of them."

As Blandón describes it, the change of heart in the armed forces was parallel to, although not induced by, that of American diplomats. The first sign of the Americans' shift came when then U.S. ambassador Deane Hinton met with a group of Salvadoran businessmen on October 29, 1981. No one doubted his anger and conviction when he told them, in his nearly unintelligible Spanish, that "the gorillas of the mafia" had to be stopped. The White House disavowed the speech.

A year later, the FMLN forces started an offensive that swept across northern El Salvador and drove local government constabularies out of dozens of towns. Simultaneously, the best-known death squads, the Secret Anti-Communist Army and the Maximiliano Hernández Martínez Brigade, again became active in the capital. One of them distributed a videotape showing four captured union leaders "confessing" to their leftist sins. Their mangled bodies turned up the following day on a San Salvador street.

In October nine cut-up bodies, one of them of a pregnant woman, were dumped in burlap bags in the rural town of Zaragoza.

U.S. diplomats in San Salvador remember how, one by one, the most powerful conservative policy-makers in Washington changed their minds. By the middle of 1982, the CIA had been asked to look into rightist as well as leftist violence. Intelligence agencies in Washington began to turn up evidence that there were killers both in some rightist political parties and in the security forces. Two conservative advisors circulated an informal policy memorandum to the National Security Council recommending a new emphasis on social justice as a strategy for winning the war and a crackdown on "errant fascist factions." Andrew Messing, then the executive director of the National Conservative Caucus, had a falling-out with members of D'Aubuisson's ARENA party. He felt they did not share the "Judeo-Christian ethic" of American conservatives. A confidential internal memo he wrote setting out his concerns was accidentally distributed to caucus members. When Messing visited El Salvador again, he heard indirectly that one rightist had threatened to kill him.

The Message From Washington

Deane Hinton lost his job in mid-1983, but the new ambassador, Thomas Pickering, arrived with instructions that he could call for a visit from Secretary of State George Shultz if he needed to get the message across that rightist killing was out of fashion. In October when the Kissinger Commission interviewed D'Aubuisson, its members did not believe his assertions that there were no rightist death squads, only a few angry army privates avenging murders of their relatives by guerrillas. "The commission saw through him like Saran Wrap," a U.S. diplomat told me. Fred C. Iklé, undersecretary of defense for policy, was among the officials who visited El Salvador that autumn and went away making biting public statements about rightist murder. On December 11, Vice President George Bush delivered a list of specific demands to the Salvadoran government to curb the violence and told the armed forces that the administration might not push for increased military aid if it did not clean up its image.

"The squads believed they were operating with the protection of the armed forces," General Blandón told me. "When we let them know we would go after them, they came to their senses, and they dissolved."

The U.S. embassy's records, it is true, show only one killing claimed by a named death squad in 1984, and none so far in 1985. Since the intelligence unit of the nefarious Treasury Police was disbanded in mid-1984, accusations of abuse by that force have fallen off as well. U.S. officials note with satisfaction that political killings by the guerrillas have risen to the forefront in the news. "The violence of the left had been constantly submerged in a sea of blood drawn by the right," one American diplomat said.

But Blandón's confident term "dissolved" seems overoptimistic to define the current status of the rightist killers. The archdiocese's legal aid office lists fifty-four politically related cases of civilians who were murdered by nameless plain-clothes assailants during the first three months of this year [1985]. On November 22, the body of a Lutheran pastor, David Fernández, turned up near the eastern city of San Miguel, his face lacerated with a machete. The following week Ambassador Pickering told me categorically that his confidential intelligence sources blamed the guerrillas. But only days after Pickering's statement police in San Miguel arrested an army sergeant and a former private for the murder. Their court affidavits suggest that the sergeant, in a drunken stupor, decided Pastor Fernández had to die because it was said in the San Miguel garrison that he was a guerrilla sympathizer.

Aside from two or three prominent cases that have attracted concern in Congress, the Salvadoran military has an unspoken agreement to overlook the past. "There is hardly an officer who doesn't have some blood on his hands," a U.S. official told me bluntly. "I think the High Command's deal is, we'll protect you for what you've done so far, but try anything new and we'll get you."

Intimidation by the Guerrillas

On April 9 [1985], in the rural hamlet of Santa Cruz Loma, Cecilia Juárez told a group of reporters about the death early that day of her son Daniel. She spoke numbly, factually. Daniel was one of nineteen villagers — including several armed civil militiamen and more unarmed men, women, and children — who were executed or killed in an attack by guerrillas of the Popular Liberation Forces (FPL), one of the five armies in the FMLN, who came into the town posing as army soldiers. Daniel was a militia member, but not on duty on April 9. He was shot at point-blank range. His mother reached into her apron pocket, drew out a flat piece of skull, and held it out to the reporters. "Look what they've done to my son's head," she said. "I found this in the dust at the edge of the road. I couldn't just leave it there. What am I supposed to do with it?"

According to pamphlets the guerrillas scattered around the hamlet, the purpose of their attack was to intimidate the village civil-defense militias and to warn people in the nearby hamlets of what would happen if they allowed new militias to be organized. During 1985, the operations of the guerrillas increasingly resembled the one at Santa Cruz Loma, causing villagers to doubt they are the liberators they claim. Countless passenger and commercial vehicles have been destroyed since February. Ten public telephone offices as well as thirty-three town halls were reduced to ashes by sabotage. The rebels have revealed to the population much about their abilities to destroy, but their actions do little to suggest to Salvadorans outside the zones they more or less control what they might create if they gained a share of power.

Meanwhile, senior Salvadoran and U.S. military officers are full of confidence. They note that the rebels have launched only two significant regular combat attacks in or near any cities in 1985. U.S officers say the 45,000 troops of the Salvadoran armed forces at last have adequately trained, energetic combat leaders, not just for battalions but down to the level of thirty-man patrols as well.

Army Improvements Under Blandón

Since late 1983 two military commanders have dominated the fighting — General Blandón and Joaquín Villalobos, the thirty-four-year-old commander of the ERP, the People's Revolutionary Army, a Marxist force of about 2,500 based primarily in eastern El Salvador.

One correspondent remembers when Blandón, in 1981, canceled a lunch appointment because, he admitted, he was too drunk. Since then Blandón, a shrewd, articulate officer, has pulled himself together. He was appointed chief of staff in November 1983, primarily, it seemed, because his smooth political manner pleased both hard-line anti-Communists and the more moderate officers. But he quickly roused the General Staff from its drowsiness; he created new units to improve communications and centralized command to force listless provincial garrison commanders into action. He broke old rules by promoting officers on the basis of talent, not seniority. He moved the armed forces into a permanent, nationwide offensive, based on cautiously formulated plans covering six-month periods.

Blandón understood that Duarte — loathed and feared by the armed forces for a decade — was the man who could assure U.S. military aid, and he calmed fears of Duarte in the officer corps. More than $403 million has rolled in since he became chief of staff, much of it to increase the air fleet, which now includes some forty helicopters, two AC-47 gunships, nine A-37 jet bombers, and other aircraft. His "heliborne" battalions have been among his most effective units, as some guerrillas will admit. "The armed forces have definitely improved greatly in terms of their firepower and methods," rebel spokesman Salvador Samayoa told me in an interview in Managua. When he was commander of San Salvador's First Infantry Brigade, Blandón always refused to have U.S. advisors around. The general learned much of U.S counter-insurgency theory when he was military attaché in Washington, but he keeps enough distance from American advisors to reassure the nationalist officers under him that he is not merely an American pawn.

Continuing Army Shortcomings

At the same time, Blandón is also a master of propaganda, and he has succeeded in concealing from the public eye shortcomings that continue to plague his forces. He told me that one of his most important moves was to create a new psychological operations and propaganda unit at the General Staff and to improve army press relations. Working together with a Venezuelan Christian Democrat public-relations firm in San Salvador, the armed forces and the Duarte government have been skilled at magnifying their confidence beyond its real proportions. In a gesture typical of his style, General Blandón told me, "Only one of our soldiers has surrendered with his weapon since early 1984." In fact, the FMLN continues to take dozens of prisoners in battle. In late May the rebels attempted to hold a public ceremony in Chalatenango province to hand over twenty-two captured soldiers to the International Red Cross. The event didn't draw much attention because the provincial commander, Colonel Sigifredo Ochoa, blocked the press from the scene.

In a sense, the four U.S. Marines and other civilians who were gunned down in the sidewalk café were victims of the atmosphere of confidence Blandón and Duarte have established in the capital city. The American soldiers momentarily forgot, on a pleasant evening out, that the ugly war still goes on.

The fact is that despite Blandón's improvements, the army is still largely avoiding the aggressive long-range night patrolling by small units that the U.S. military advisors have advocated ad nauseam. Even Colonel Ochoa, famous for mopping up rebel bases in eastern Cabanas province since 1982, is combing through Chalatenango, where he is now, with operations of thousands of troops. The U.S. military advisors are pushing the army to form freshly trained, volunteer civil-defense militias in small villages to keep on the lookout for rebel movements. But one officer familiar with the program admitted it is "very, very difficult to manage." In many towns defense men don't patrol for fear of attracting a heavy guerrilla attack. In at least one village, in central San Vicente province, the defense men confessed they made a pact with local guerrillas to leave each other alone.

Guerrilla Action Under Villalobos

Meanwhile, the boyish-looking Joaquín Villalobos is constantly on the move with his ERP guerrillas through the northeastern mountains. I feel I've come to know him from talks with his followers during all the days and miles I walked in fruitless efforts to meet him face to face.

Once, in 1983, several other reporters and I trekked seven days to northern Morazán province to see the man at the ERP's invitation. Along our route to the rendezvous, we posed hard questions, as journalists do, to all the guerrillas we met, including two young men who had just deserted from the army to join the rebel ranks, and many novice fighters who were in training at the ERP's military school. When word got back to the *comandante en jefe* of our skeptical interrogatories, Villalobos decided not to face them himself. Our ERP guides, forthcoming and confident when they led us into Morazán, were shaken and intimidated as they hurried us back out after their leader's abrupt "no." Later we learned that in the days just before our visit to the military school, the ERP had executed several youths who tried to desert from their courses there.

During the past year the activities of Villalobos's ERP have caused constant headaches for the four other rebel groups in the FMLN. In July 1984 the FMLN general command concluded that they faced a medium-term risk of U.S. intervention because, they reasoned, the Duarte government could collapse under economic pressures before the end of his five-year term. In most of the rebel strongholds, FMLN regulars set about building bomb shelters and stockpiling arms. That wasn't enough for Villalobos. In its redoubt in Morazán the ERP began press-ganging villagers into its ranks; this had the effect of exposing local people whose political loyalties were in doubt and forcing them to flee to refugee camps. When the recruits began deserting—FMLN sources say about 90 per cent of the ERP's forced recruits did so—a few who were caught were executed for making off with their rifles.

On election day the FMLN declared that traffic must come to a halt in the zones it controlled, a small gesture to hamper the vote. Villalobos's troops enforced this by ambushing a priest and a seminary student in San Miguel province, killing the latter. The FMLN had to issue a public apology. More recently, in June, forces mainly from the ERP kidnapped sixteen town officials, killing one, to show everyone how powerful they are in zones where they are the most constant military presence.

In 1984 the FMLN decided on an abrupt change of tactics, trying to adapt to the new U.S.-supplied air power and its capacity for reconnaissance of rebel forces. The FMLN leaders broke down their "columns" of three hundred fighters into more mobile platoons one-tenth that size. In the ERP-dominated eastern part of the country, peasants increasingly reported abuses by petty guerrilla potentates—small-unit commanders who lacked the political and military training the ERP had earlier given to its officers. One high-ranking FMLN leader said that "continuous debates" have taken place during the past eighteen months concerning Villalobos's "tempestuousness" and the ERP's "large errors which affect the civilian population."

Other groups, like the Popular Liberation Force (FPL), the other large army in the FMLN, have been more successful. They disregarded the stern advice of their Cuban counselors to build up their armed forces and keep them separate from their civilian supporters, and concentrated instead on organizing hamlets within the zones they control to defend and govern themselves.

Other FMLN Problems

Beyond factional disputes, however, other signs multiply of an overall deterioration in the FMLN. The FPL is still wrestling with the aftershocks of the gruesome 1983 murder of the group's second-in-command, *Comandante* Ana Maria [Mélida Anaya Montes], ordered by its leader, Cayetano Carpio, who subsequently committed suicide. Several urban splinter groups that broke away from the FPL in disputes over these events have engaged in such senseless terrorism that even the FMLN has disavowed them. A third, more moderate group, the Armed Forces of National Resistance (FARN), has taken a bad beating from the army in its stronghold on central Guazapa Mountain. The armed forces of the Communist Party are rarely heard from. The most recent action of the fifth and smallest group, known as the Revolutionary Party of Central American Workers [PRTC], was the killing of the four U.S. Marines.

During 1984, according to official figures, 1,132 Salvadorans from guerrilla ranks turned themselves in to the armed forces—248 so far this year [1985], although only twenty-eight brought weapons with them. The rest were civilian sympathizers. In May the FPL's top *comandante* in San Salvador, Miguel Castellanos, was taken by the armed forces under confusing circumstances—he says he turned himself in, the FMLN says he was captured. According to both FMLN leaders and military officers, he has been talking as freely to army intelligence as he has to the press about anything they want to know about the inner workings of the FMLN. Castellanos is the highest-ranking guerrilla to go over to the government since the beginning of the war. The information supplied by him and other deserters led the army to at least two sizable rebel arms caches.

The FMLN leaders continue to misread popular feeling in El Salvador. They refuse to acknowledge the small, but nonetheless palpable, comfort Salvadorans derived from their three elections in two years. Duarte's government is still called "*la dictadura*" in rebel radio broadcasts. The FMLN leaders constantly fret over, and even seem to long for, possible intervention by U.S. combat troops, which now seems remote. They persist in believing battlefield prowess is enough to persuade people to trust them; they continue to tell themselves that Salvadorans, by now bone-tired of war, have sufficient confidence in the FMLN's prospects for victory to put up with its grim campaigns of burnings, bombings, and assassinations. They have failed to offer a convincing new argument for revolution now that the armed forces have curbed the reckless slaughter of civilians. They fail to see the significance of the crowds that teem on Saturday afternoons at the Metrocentro, San Salvador's biggest and gaudiest shopping center, where they buy American-made jogging shoes and T-shirts that say "Communism Stops Here."

Continuing Guerrilla Strengths

Nevertheless, just as the government forces hide their failures, the guerrillas have continuing strengths that are not easily visible. Samayoa, the guerrilla spokesman, has some justification when he says, "The Pentagon's idea two years ago was to push us back to the northeast depths of the country and hit us there. What have they achieved? When can the armed forces say they have ever wiped out a single one of our platoons?" During the last eighteen months at least, the army has not dealt a single major blow to the guerrilla forces. The FMLN has moved the war out of its remote northern strongholds into the central and western provinces. The wards of San Salvador's military hospital are newly packed with amputees and other soldiers blinded or maimed by ground mines.

Nearly 70 per cent of the 2,337 soldiers killed or wounded between June 1984 and April 1985 were hit by mines. The mining has greatly reduced the guerrillas' need for ammunition at a time when the armed forces are more successfully impeding resupply from outside the country. It may look from San Salvador as if the FMLN is badly shaken, but its leaders refuse to be pessimistic. "Nobody should think that because we spread out our forces, we aren't preparing some hard blow," Samayoa told me.

To the degree that the Salvadoran army has made headway, the consensus at the U.S. embassy is that it benefited from the limits imposed by Congress on the numbers of U.S. soldiers that can be sent there. One U.S. diplomat now describes the fifty-five-man ceiling, the subject of so much congressional bickering, as a "blessing in disguise." U.S. officials say that even in the darkest hours of 1983, committing U.S. troops was never seriously considered. "It's the lesson of Vietnam," one U.S. official said. "Ultimately the Salvadorans have to solve their own problems."

The FMLN's Foreign Allies

On the matter of ties between leftists in El Salvador and in other nations, however, the administration's original assertions that the FMLN is supplied and influenced by foreign Marxist allies proved factually correct, if distorted in its emphasis. The Pentagon finally completed this spring its long-awaited analysis of the serial numbers of M-16 and AR-15 rifles captured from the guerrillas. It found that about 70 per cent of them were weapons left by American troops in Vietnam, not issued to the Salvadoran army and then seized by rebels. Among the documents found in the backpack of Nidia Díaz, a senior guerrilla commander taken prisoner in combat in April, one, apparently her personal diary, lists thirteen rank-and-file rebels to be trained in 1985 in Vietnam, Bulgaria, or the Soviet Union. The FMLN now says openly that, as Reagan had charged, it maintained its operational command in Managua until early 1983, when Cuban and Sandinista advisors urged that the command be moved to El Salvador. Managua remains an FMLN radio communications center, as well as a meeting place and a refuge for traveling *comandantes* and burned-out *combatientes*.

Castellanos described substantial stockpiles of munitions awaiting transshipment in Managua, some purchased by the FMLN and some donated through Cuba. The FMLN continues to fly small planes back and forth from Nicaragua, and to bring in arms in false-bottomed trucks and by muleback through Honduras and Guatemala and, more rarely, by water from Nicaragua. But Castellanos confirmed what U.S. intelligence reports have suggested: since last year the flow of arms has fallen off and now consists mainly of rifle rounds and explosives.

Relations among different groups of Latin revolutionaries are often strained, FMLN leaders say. Cubans, Sandinistas, and Salvadorans differ about which country is likely to be invaded first and how to negotiate with the United States. In Managua, the Sandinistas have asked the Salvadorans to live far out of town, and haven't given them houses or other amenities. "They look after their interests," Samayoa said. "We look after ours." Even if the United States forces the Sandinistas to cut off aid to the Salvadorans entirely, this will not bring the FMLN down. If the FMLN is crushed, the main reason will be its own political inadequacies.

Discontent Among the Coffee Growers

The weekly meeting of the Coffee Growers' Association in El Salvador is an unhappy occasion. Before 1980, the private growers owned the entire ten-story building known as the "Coffee Company" – one of the tallest in the city. But in early 1980 a series of reforms by the civilian-military junta, of which Duarte was a member, expropriated 426 of the nation's largest haciendas, some belonging to coffee families, and nationalized coffee exporting. Now the Growers' Association has been shunted off to a few offices on one floor, while the state coffee agency occupies the rest.

The board includes people whose family names were formidable during El Salvador's oligarchic past: Francisco García Rossi, Orlando de Sola, and Gerardo Escalón, after whose family San Salvador's most stylish boulevard is named. These men now claim there never was a landed elite in El Salvador. The much-talked-about "fourteen families" were a myth, they say, propagated by socialists in the American government. "We were just a herd of cattle that was fattened up to be slaughtered when the time was right," a prominent fifty-year-old board member, Raúl Calvo, told me.

The coffee growers' lament is that the state coffee agency, INCAFE, has set prices so low that they can't break even on coffee production. Association members as a whole owe $80 million in debts they can't possibly repay. They are, they admit, no longer replanting and fertilizing their coffee groves. "To produce more is to lose more," another board member observed. Duarte recently raised coffee prices and offered the growers loans, but they want profits, not credits.

Unlike the former cotton and sugar barons, who adapted grudgingly to the new system, the coffee growers are holding out in the hope that they can roll back all the reforms. They find it simply insulting that they have to sell their coffee to the government. "I don't work to benefit others," said Raúl Calvo. "I work to benefit myself." They vow not to rest until the coffee trade is denationalized.

Before 1980 the growers were the pillars of anti-Communism in El Salvador. Today they view Duarte as a more formidable enemy than the guerrillas. Most coffee is grown in western El Salvador, where rebel activity has been only sporadic. The growers see the war effort as a waste of money, particularly coffee money, that has been siphoned off by the government but should have come to them.

The 1980 reforms, which were in part designed by the Carter administration, broke the power of rightist domination in El Salvador. But now the growers say they see the United States coming back around to their side. U.S. embassy economic advisors approached them in recent months to discuss ways to increase their control over the industry. "We have seen how the armed forces and the opposition parties have been tamed," said Orlando de Sola. "The only restraint on Duarte's abuses and craziness is provided by the Reagan administration."

Even after the crushing political defeat they suffered in March, rightist politicians and businessmen sense that their time may be coming again. The coffee growers are already moving to strong positions in other sectors of the economy, like real estate and banking. A former oligarch, Roberto Hill, now heads a foundation that has been charged by the U.S. embassy with doling out $7.5 million in aid to the private sector. The ultraconservative Hugo Barrera, once righthand man to D'Aubuisson in ARENA, has formed his own party, sensing that Duarte's predicament, with a near-bankrupt economy, conflicting demands from labor and business, and a possibly insoluble war, will give new legitimacy to anti-statist, anti-Communist views in coming years.

But the coffee growers' meeting ended with ominous words from

Orlando de Sola. He is a striking man, much younger-looking than his forty years, who tends to glance sideways when he talks to a reporter. In 1983 he was accused of raising funds from Miami for rightist death squads. Now back from exile, he makes one doubt that the right has abandoned its interest in organizing private, semi-clandestine armies.

"I think killing is intrinsically bad—with some exceptions," De Sola said. "One exception is self-defense. Right now, in this place at this time, someone may be waiting to kill us. You don't need to wait for a threat to defend yourself. Normally we should be protected by government security forces that we create. But when those fail, as they have in El Salvador, you have to defend yourself."

"Of course we will have our own private security forces," De Sola said bitterly. "We have to."

The Enduring Violence

Beneath the plausible surface of Duarte's political success, El Salvador remains a violent, often desperate nation. On the back of Guazapa Mountain, a longtime rebel stronghold in central El Salvador, there is a hamlet whose name means, inappropriately, "consolation." Its inhabitants can't tell you exactly how often this year U.S.-supplied A-37 jets have made the earth near Consolación shudder with deafening bombs. The days and the bombs have blended together in their minds in a long haze of panic. They can't specify how many people have died this year in Consolación from bombing—maybe fourteen, maybe fifteen.

Marta Alicia Herazo, twenty years old, of Consolación, remembers how the bombing started in the middle of the afternoon of April 22. Soon after, army troops descended on the hamlet, spraying machine-gun fire. Almost every resident has some relative who is a rebel fighter, but the hamlet itself, the residents said, is not an FMLN base. There were no guerrillas around that afternoon.

"The army gets scared they will find guerrillas, so they come in fighting with the chickens and with anyone who tries to run away," I was told by Fidelina Mendoza, a woman of forty-three. Some residents reached the underground bomb shelters they had dug nearby, while others huddled in their houses. The soldiers didn't kill them, but instead corralled them together and over the next two days evacuated them from the hamlet by helicopter to a refugee camp near San Salvador.

Did the soldiers burn houses in Consolación in April? No, Herazo says, the houses had already been burned by the army in 1984. Did they burn crops? No, the crops were burned in an earlier sweep this year. They killed the last fifteen chickens, "and they didn't even eat them," said Mendoza—the final insult.

The army says the people of Consolación—about 270 in all—asked to be "rescued" from the guerrillas. The villagers don't dispute that they left their homes voluntarily. "There was nothing left there for me to hold on to," Mendoza said.

"We were just sitting there waiting for death," Marta Alicia Herazo told me, her thin arms crossed over her stomach.

The armed forces, and President Duarte himself, have said that no A-37 bombing raids are authorized unless they are called to support actual ground combat between soldiers and guerrillas. "There certainly are areas where the army feels the guerrillas are the main inhabitants, and some areas where they don't think there is anything but guerrillas," said one Western military observer familiar with air-force operations. "But I think they're sensitized to the basic point that you don't go shooting at something unless you've got a target that you know is guerrillas, if for no other reason than bombs and artillery rounds are very expensive, and it's really a waste of effort and ammunition to just go shooting stuff out there at nothing. It's not worth it tactically."

But countless statements by refugees point to a systematic effort by the armed forces to remove the population—with bombs, scorched earth, and random mortar fire—from areas where guerrillas are present. When the army is certain that the residents of a town have turned against the rebels, it resettles them. In central El Salvador, stepped-up army sweeps keep civilians who favor the guerrillas on the run in headlong mass flights for days on end. (After five years of war, more than half a million people have been displaced from their homes, though fewer than 20,000 of them are in camps. The army's depopulation tactics are not responsible for displacing many of these people; most of them have just fled from the fighting, whatever side it was coming from.)

In the capital small events mark the continuing uneasiness of daily life. The offices of the anti-government Human Rights Commission and the Committee of Mothers of the Disappeared were sacked on June 12 by intruders who made off with lists of names of the mothers of disappeared Salvadorans, as well as $10,000. Two European relief workers were picked up on charges of collaborating with the left, an unsettling throwback to the early 1980s. In a seemingly quiet middle-class neighborhood in San Salvador stands a modest, middle-of-the-road Lutheran church, a one-room affair. Since the election, the pastor, the Rev. Medardo Gómez, has received a death threat from someone posing as a guerrilla in an attempt to extort some money from him; and he had a warning that the national police believe he is supplying medicines to the guerrillas. Someone called the church and rattled off machine-gun rounds over the telephone. Two church members have fled into exile since the election after threats from the police. "Everyone lives in an extreme state of tension," another Lutheran pastor told me. Among the rapidly growing congregation, dependence on Valium and alcohol is high.

Duarte's Policies

José Napoleón Duarte was an independent-minded, populist reformist when he was robbed of the presidency in 1972. Now, after five years in which he has been the main hope of the United States' policy to defeat the left, Duarte has the power he sought for so many years, but he seems a different, far more conservative man.

The U.S. embassy sees this period as an opportunity to bring him further around to Reagan's politics, urging him to make concessions to business, dismantle state bureaucracies, and return agrarian reform cooperatives to private hands wherever he can. Thus far, Duarte's moves have been consistent with U.S. goals, since he has made it his priority to revitalize the economy by reassuring the private sector, before turning his attention to the desperate demands of the working poor. Economically, El Salvador remains a captive of the United States; without more than $325.4 million in aid this year [1985] the nation would be technically bankrupt.

Duarte is dealing with the rapid resurgence of militant union activity in the capital with a hard hand. He says the strikes are an FMLN ploy to destabilize him; and FMLN leaders proudly acknowledge their inside ties to the teachers', water-workers', and hospital-workers' unions. But while the FMLN fails to see that few workers are still willing to risk their lives in street demonstrations, Duarte for his part does not admit that many rank-and-file demands are legitimate. In 1985, El Salvador's per capita production has not even returned to where it was in 1972. Many workers have had only one raise in five years. Duarte, citing "dangerous disobedience," will negotiate with the unions only on limited issues of wages and hours. If the unions occupy their workplaces, as the hospital workers did recently, he will send troops to take the place back.

But Duarte's ultimate test is whether he can bring peace, as he promised, to El Salvador. The Christian Democrat president had his finest hour when he marched, unarmed and unprotected, into the little church in La Palma last October for his first talks with the FMLN. But now Duarte is pressed by a Salvadoran military that is richer, larger, and freer from constraints than ever before. General Blandón told me in June that his troops are in a position to win "absolute victory" over the FMLN. General Vides, on the day he roared out his defense of the elections, ended by saying: "It's time for the Salvadoran people to join together in an effort to defeat our common enemy, Communist-terrorist subversion." Such talk may tempt the Reagan administration to push for a flat-out defeat of the FMLN. In any case, there is no possibility for the rebels to take a share of power, as they have demanded. But neither are FMLN leaders any closer than they were at La Palma to surrendering their arms to General Blandón.

One sign of change seemed to come after the killings of the U.S. Marines, when some members of one of the non-Marxist political parties in the leftist alliance, the Popular Social Christian Movement, took out ads in San Salvador newspapers to say the attack "certainly does not contribute in any way to the attainment of a just peace in our country." But within days their leader, Rubén Zamora, revised their position, and said that Duarte himself would be a legitimate target for assassination. Leading politicians of the Democratic Revolutionary Front, the non-armed wing of the insurgent alliance, have been outspokenly critical of the FMLN in recent months – but they have not indicated that they are ready to come to any separate agreement with Duarte to return to political life in El Salvador.

The best Salvadorans can hope for, so far as I can see, is limited, infrequent negotiations to civilize the conduct of the war. Peace will have to be made gradually, by Salvadoran citizens, not only by their leaders: by guerrilla fighters who lay down their rifles and return to their families, or by policemen who adhere to legal procedures instead of brutalizing captured youths they suspect of leftist sympathies. Duarte and the United States have had greater successes than their critics predicted, but they will be presiding over war in El Salvador for a long time.

15. Rebel Factions
16. The Divided Military

By SHIRLEY CHRISTIAN

Focus Like John Kurzweil (selection 13), Shirley Christian in these two essays emphasizes the complexity of the struggle in El Salvador and the deep divisions that beset both the governmental and the rebel forces.

The Salvadoran army, says Christian, has been the real source of political power for much of the country's history. This does not mean that there has been only a succession of repressive military regimes. There is also a tradition of reform within the officer corps. The 1979 coup that swept the military dictator General Carlos Humberto Romero from power was one such attempt by the more enlightened military officers to respond to changing circumstances. Reforms were proposed, land expropriations begun, and elections held. The government set up as a result of the coup and subsequent elections continues to have its problems, however, in part because of persistent tensions within the army.

Christian believes that "the Salvadoran military, in large measure, look to the United States to define what is necessary." A clear message from the U.S. side could help certain military leaders take the lead in effecting more far-reaching reforms and in controlling the right-wing death squads. Since 1983, when this article was written, there has been a sharp drop in death-squad killings.

Serious ideological and personal splits also exist within the rebel bands, though the various factions have been united at least nominally under a man who is "apparently Castro's own choice," Joaquín Villalobos. The author urges Washington to consider carefully compromises that the guerrillas have proposed, even though they may be only tactics for gaining time or some other advantage.

But we must harbor no illusions, says Christian. She cautions: "All five guerrilla groups have in the past produced documents or made declarations calling for the creation of governing systems combining the philosophy of Marx and the methods of Lenin." Although in recent years these groups have toned down their ideology in favor of compromise and have proclaimed their desire to remain free from the East-West struggle and Soviet influence, Christian warns that "they still embrace the Leninist concept of internationalism, the worldwide solidarity in which one 'socialist' government or group helps another."

The complex situation analyzed here is often downplayed in proposals for power-sharing or other suggestions for the establishment of a democratic center that will combat extremists. Christian's analysis should be compared with the more recent developments described by Julia Preston (selection 14).

Shirley Christian is a journalist specializing in Central American affairs. She won the Pulitzer Prize for international reporting in 1981.

15. Rebel Factions

ONE EVENING last April [1983], Tomás Borge, a member of the nine-man Sandinista directorate [in Nicaragua], arrived at the surburban Managua home of Salvador Cayetano Carpio, the 63-year-old patriarch of El Salvador's guerrilla movement, with shattering news: security agents working under Borge in the Interior Ministry had gathered conclusive evidence implicating people close to Carpio in the murder the previous week of Mélida Anaya Montes. Anaya Montes had been Carpio's senior deputy in the Popular Liberation Forces (FPL); she had been seeking a negotiated end to the war in El Salvador over his objections. Sometime that evening, Carpio shot himself.

It was two weeks before the FPL revealed Carpio's suicide, saying he had done it out of "revolutionary pain" caused by the circumstances surrounding his comrade's death. But diplomats from several countries with intelligence sources in Managua say Carpio's death occurred "Rommel style," with Borge telling him the choice was between suicide and public revelation of all the names and facts in Anaya Montes's murder, including the possible implication of Carpio himself, and the accompanying damage to the guerrilla movement. If he chose suicide, Borge reportedly told Carpio, the circumstances surrounding the murder of Mélida Anaya Montes would remain an internal affair of the FPL.

Borge kept his promise. Although State Security officials subsequently announced the arrest of Rogelio Bazzaglia, a young member of the FPL Central Command, and five others, no judicial procedures have been started against them, and it is not known whether they are still in prison or even alive.

The killers slipped into Anaya Montes's home south of Managua in the early morning hours of April 6. They stabbed her eighty-three times with an ice pick, then slit her jugular vein with a knife. Carpio, who was in Libya, rushed home. He arrived on April 9, just in time to go directly to

---

Reprinted by permission from the October 24, 1983, issue of *The New Republic* (© 1983 by The New Republic, Incorporated).

her state funeral, which was held in a hot, dusty market plaza on the outskirts of Managua. There were protestations of grief and anti-imperialist rhetoric, but they masked historic divisions in the Salvadoran left, divisions that had now become of concern to Fidel Castro and to the Sandinistas.

The deaths of Anaya Montes and Carpio grew out of efforts to attain unity, and support for negotiations, among and within the five guerrilla organizations that make up the Farabundo Martí National Liberation Front (FMLN). By the time Carpio went to his grave (in an unknown spot in Nicaragua, and without the public tributes given Anaya Montes), he had come to be viewed by his comrades as the chief obstacle to a negotiated settlement—as much as or more so than the Reagan administration. The Sandinistas, themselves besieged by anti-Sandinista guerrillas who have the backing of the United States, had concluded that they would have a better chance of halting these pressures and consolidating their own power if they could promote a negotiated settlement in El Salvador. Along with Castro, they wanted Carpio to turn over the leadership of the guerrilla movement to a younger man more in their line of thinking.

The New Guerrilla Chief

The man chosen to succeed Carpio is Joaquín Villalobos, a thirty-two-year-old former economics student. His path to the top, first of his own guerrilla organization and now of the five-group coalition, has been marked by an expressed willingness to use violence to provoke repression and by the deaths of four guerrilla leaders under questionable circumstances. Despite this history, Villalobos is now attempting to show the outside world that he is a reasonable man, and that the guerrilla movement is eager to negotiate and willing to concede more than ever before in working out the kind of government and military structure that might emerge from negotiations. It may be a sincere move or it may be a feint. Given the confusing and bloody history of this movement, even the man who made the proposals may not know.

In many ways, the war in El Salvador is a product of the original split in the Salvadoran left, precipitated by Carpio's decision in 1970 to leave the Moscow-line Salvadoran Communist Party and form a guerrilla band. Since then, the left has been divided by a progression of issues. When Carpio quit the party, the issue was armed struggle versus what he disparagingly called bourgeois Communism. Then it became prolonged struggle, Mao-style, versus broad-based insurrection—the kind of quick kill in which all the elements unhappy with those in power are brought together, as in Nicaragua in 1979.

The success of the insurrection in Nicaragua was much noted by Marxist-Leninist revolutionary groups throughout Latin America, with their penchant for interminable analysis and self-criticism. Until 1979, they had only two examples to study of how Marxist-Leninists could come to power in the Western Hemisphere. One was Cuba, where Castro came to power at the head of a small guerrilla force and seemed destined to last forever. The other was Chile, where Salvador Allende's coalition of socialists and Communists came to power in 1970 through elections, only to be ousted by the military less than three years later. This convinced most Marxist revolutionaries in the region not to put their faith in electoral politics. On the other hand, for the two decades following Castro's rise, those who tried to emulate his methods failed—in Venezuela, Bolivia, Argentina, Uruguay, Guatemala. In Latin American guerrilla circles, Cuba had come to be viewed as an aberration. Then came 1979, when all the pieces fell into place for the Sandinistas and the dream was reborn.

In the years since 1979, however, the Salvadoran guerrillas have come to realize that El Salvador is not Nicaragua. There was only one Somoza family, the common evil against which it was so easy to unite a disparate opposition. In El Salvador, the struggle is against something faceless and diffused, a military institution and power structure in which good and bad, right and wrong are often inseparable. This realization created a new issue to divide the Salvadoran left: continued struggle versus negotiated settlement.

Origins of the Guerrilla Groups

Historically, the issues that have splintered the Salvadoran left have related to the means of reaching power, not what to do once in power. All five guerrilla groups have in the past produced documents or made declarations calling for the creation of governing systems combining the philosophy of Marx and the methods of Lenin, though such positions have been publicly tempered in recent years as the Marxist-Leninist groups have formed alliances with individuals and groups with Western democratic tendencies. In theory, the Salvadoran guerrillas reject Soviet hegemony, but they seem to do it primarily as a practical matter of survival in this hemisphere. Their argument is that they are a national liberation movement and therefore outside the framework of East-West confrontation or of any kind of accord in which the Soviet Union might promise to stay out of the U.S. neighborhood. However, they still embrace the Leninist concept of internationalism, the worldwide solidarity in which one "socialist" government or group helps another.

The Salvadoran Communist Party claims direct descent from Farabundo Martí, who rode with Sandino in Nicaragua, then returned home and organized the 1932 peasant revolt, to which the military reacted by massacring thousands of people and sending Martí to the firing squad. For the next four decades, the party, formally organized two years before the revolt, concentrated on staying alive. It functioned above ground and below ground, shifting as necessary to accommodate the electoral laws laid down by El Salvador's succession of military governments. The Salvadoran Communists followed Moscow's dictate of seeking power through legal means. They formed front groups, infiltrated labor and student organizations, and, though able to command only a few percentage points of the vote, joined electoral coalitions supporting centrist candidates such as José Napeleón Duarte and Guillermo Ungo. During tough periods, the national university provided them a secure refuge because the Salvadoran government usually (but not always) respected the Latin American tradition of university autonomy, which means the physical inviolability of the campus as much as academic freedom.

This complaisance, this unwritten pact with the establishment, guaranteed a certain anemic well-being. But it rankled some within the party, particularly Salvador Cayetano Carpio. A former bakery worker and union activist, he had joined the party in 1947 and risen to secretary general by the mid-1960s. In the 1950s he had spent two and a half years in Moscow at a school run by the Central Committee of the Soviet Communist Party. By 1969, however, Carpio faced a dispute within the party over his desire to take up arms. He was challenged for the job of secretary general by Jorge Shafik Handal, a son of wealthy Palestinian immigrants, who was then thirty-nine and showing signs of becoming a permanent law student.

The FPL, the ERP, the FARN

The Soviet party gave its backing to Handal and to a continued political approach, so Carpio left the party in early 1970 and formed the Popular Liberation Forces (FPL). The statutes of the new organization accused the

Communist Party of being swept up in opportunism, revisionism, bourgeois reformism, bureaucracy, and other right-wing notions that ignored the needs of the people. Carpio once said that he began the FPL with seven people, including himself, and without any money or even a single pistol.

The People's Revolutionary Army, known by its Spanish acronym ERP, was born about a year after the FPL as the result of the coming together of university activists, among them Joaquín Villalobos, with some other people who left the Communist Party. In 1975, an internal struggle between the "military" and "political" factions of the ERP ended in a bloody purge and the creation of another guerrilla group by the surviving losers—the Armed Forces of National Resistance (FARN). In the process, two members of the losing faction, including its leader, Roque Dalton, were condemned by a guerrilla court-martial and executed. Death threats were made against other dissidents. Once Dalton was dead, the victorious faction claimed that he had been a Cuban agent, a CIA agent, and a revisionist. Five years later, in an interview with the Mexican news weekly *Proceso*, the man who became the leader of the FARN, Ernesto Jovel, accused Villalobos of having personally killed Dalton.

Before the interview was published, Jovel himself died in confusing circumstances. His light plane went down in the Pacific on September 17, 1980, as he flew to Panama for a meeting with friends who were arranging arms supplies for the FARN. Doubts about whether it was an accident were raised, however, by the first report from the FARN command saying he had died in a traffic accident in Salvador, followed by a statement saying the FARN did not blame any other revolutionary organization, then followed by the plane-crash report.

Guerrilla Growth in the Seventies

The guerrilla groups made relatively little impact on El Salvador until the mid-1970s, when they began a series of kidnappings for ransom that netted an estimated $60 million, most of it going to the FPL and the ERP. They also specialized in occupying churches, factories, and government buildings, taking over unions, and manipulating contract bargaining for political gain. Much of this was accomplished through so-called mass organizations, which were created by the guerrilla groups for the street activities. Each of them sought affiliation with dozens of smaller groups, such as organizations of teachers, students, and peasants.

The Salvadoran military, governing through its own political party, played into the guerrillas' hands by its proclivity for repression and its suspicion of any kind of dissent, however peaceful. El Salvador's Marxist-Leninists might have been able to dream their dreams in a vacuum, but they could not have grown and prospered in one. External help aside, they were aided by two key factors inside El Salvador. One was the electoral fraud perpetrated by the military in 1972 and 1977 to prevent victories by the moderate opposition. This served to disillusion people about the prospects for Western democracy and to channel many of them, particularly the young, into the ranks of subversion. The guerrilla groups also benefited from the country's poverty and injustice, which produced uncritical international sympathy for whoever opposed the Salvadoran power structure.

Villalobos, in the foreword of a book written in 1978 by one of his ERP comrades, Ana Guadalupe Martínez, acknowledged the usefulness of these elements to the guerrillas and the need to exploit them. Martínez would not have been able to publish her story of torture and rape in a National Guard prison, Villalobos wrote, if she had not first been willing to take up arms and fight. Such actions revealed to the world the state of human rights in El Salvador, he said. Martínez, the ERP commander in eastern El Salvador, was imprisoned in mid-1976 for the murder of a policeman, but the ERP kidnapped a wealthy industrialist seven months later and secured her freedom as part of the ransom. The industrialist died in guerrilla hands of wounds suffered in the kidnapping.

In April 1979, the Salvadoran Communist Party met secretly and decided to join the armed struggle, reportedly with the agreement of the Soviet Union. Handal has attributed the decision primarily to the Chilean example. However, Allende's downfall had occurred nearly six years earlier. It is more likely that the Salvadoran Communists saw the ranks of the guerrilla groups swelling while the party remained small and static. With the guerrillas and their mass organizations mounting so many antigovernment activities as to make people think an insurrection was imminent, the Communists ran the risk of having no role in the future government if they remained nonviolent. Even so, the Communists delayed in organizing a guerrilla force, because, says Handal, they did not know how to do it.

About the time the Communists were making their decision, a group of army officers was reaching the same conclusion, that insurrection was imminent. The officers moved against the government of General Carlos Humberto Romero, which they judged intransigent and incompetent. On

October 15, 1979, they took power, with a promise to meet some of the demands of the left and to open a dialogue with it. This threw the revolutionary groups into disarray. Led by a junta of two colonels and three civilians, including the social democrat Guillermo Ungo, the new government was joined by Communists and members of other revolutionary groups at the cabinet level. But the major guerrilla groups didn't give an inch. The ERP and the Popular Revolutionary Bloc, the FPL's mass organization, mounted military assaults and takeovers of factories and government buildings in the first few days of the new government. When the junta broke apart ten weeks later, it was not clear whether it was the result of disputes over excessive violence on the part of the military—as some of the civilians said—or of the pressures from outside by the revolutionary groups.

The FDR, the FMLN Umbrella

Almost everybody involved in the Salvadoran drama organized or formed new alignments in 1980. The military made a pact with the Christian Democrats, the largest opposition party, and formed a new government. The right, distrustful of the Christian Democrats and the army High Command, coalesced around Roberto D'Aubuisson, a former army major forced into retirement by the coup leaders. Disaffected center-left politicians who had left the previous government, led by Ungo and Enrique Alvarez Córdova, united with some of the mass organizations controlled by the guerrillas and formed the Democratic Revolutionary Front (FDR), a political group that concentrated on diplomacy in Western nations.

The guerrilla groups, now numbering four, met in Havana and formed a unified military directorate. They later took the name Farabundo Martí National Liberation Front (FMLN). In 1980 the FARN temporarily dropped out of the directorate because of its old dispute with the ERP, but after the death of FARN leader Jovel in September, it returned to the fold under Jovel's successor, Fermán Cienfuegos. At the end of 1980, a fifth guerrilla group came into the FMLN—the Revolutionary Party of Central American Workers, organized the year before with direct ties to the Communist Party through one of its founders, Fabio Castillo.

Despite an awesome organizational structure, the tactics and strategies of the Salvadoran left have been as peppered with mistakes as those of the military and the government. First there were the differences over how to react to the 1979 coup. Then came the inability to capitalize on the assassination of Archbishop Oscar Romero in March 1980. The killing of the archbishop by an unknown gunman sent tremors through the government, which was convinced that it would produce an insurrection. Instead, the left appeared to lose face with the people after the largest of the mass organizations, the FPL's Popular Revolutionary Bloc, disrupted the funeral.

During the same period in 1980 that the guerrilla groups were forming their alliances and unified directorate, two of the four—the Communist Party and the FARN—were secretly, but unsuccessfully, appealing to one of the military officers in the junta, Colonel Adolfo Majano, to stage a palace coup. (Elements on the right were simultaneously trying to convince other military officers to purge Majano.) The FPL, meanwhile, was preparing for a long war from its power base in the mountainous province of Chalatenango on the Honduran border, and the ERP was laying plans to seek victory through insurrection with Villalobos and his lieutenants as the revolutionary vanguard.

After sealing an agreement for Cuban and Sandinista support during meetings in Managua in mid-1980, the FMLN brought off a general offensive in January 1981. It was impressive, but it did not set off the hoped-for popular insurrection, and the army was able to beat it back even before the resumption of U.S. military assistance. Since then, military initiatives have seemed oriented more toward political and diplomatic objectives than toward territorial conquest. Neither side has been able to turn the errors and losses of the other into significant victories for itself. The guerrilla forces have reached an estimated five to six thousand combatants. Until recent months the FPL was considered the largest single group, with at least two thousand. Villalobos's ERP is now thought to have become the largest and strongest, in part because of its easier access to weapons and training through Nicaragua and Cuba.

Proposals for Negotiation

Until the end of 1980, the ERP and the FPL both opposed any suggestion of talking to the other side, apparently convinced of the inevitability of victory. The first of many public calls for talks began in late 1980, with Ungo saying in Mexico that the left wanted to talk with the owner of the circus, not the acrobats—meaning the United States, not the Salvadoran government. The joint Diplomatic-Political Commission of the FMLN and the FDR wrote a "common platform" at the end of 1980 proposing a government based on non-alignment, self-determination, social reforms, democratic representation, a new armed force, continuation of some elements of private enterprise, and freedom of religion. These terms can mean whatever the user wants them to mean, but the platform contained no Marxist-Leninist rhetoric. Nobody ever denied that the guerrilla organizations still had their Leninist programs in mind, backed by reams of documents floating around, some old, some not so old, but the argument was that those were just dreams for some distant future.

Preliminary contact with the United States was subsequently made through a Honduran politician, but the effort ran up against two concurrent events: the change of government in Washington and the big offensive in El Salvador. Since then, the question of negotiations has moved through numerous offers and proposals to today's two sets of contacts, one between the rebels and the special U.S. envoy, Richard Stone, the other between the rebels and a commission named by the Salvadoran government.

The moderates in the left, primarily Ungo and Rubén Zamora, have been arguing in meetings with U.S. congressional delegations that the logic—from a U.S. perspective—of reaching a political settlement to the war, meaning power-sharing or a transitional government in which the left would participate prior to elections, is to prevent Marxist-Leninist hardliners from gaining the upper hand in the government. Conscious of the distaste with which the Sandinista government in Nicaragua is viewed by most U.S. politicians, from conservative Republicans to liberal Democrats, they contend that things have turned out the way they have in Nicaragua because the 1978-79 war against the Somoza dynasty was allowed to continue to the point of a military victory by the insurgents. To avoid this in El Salvador, they contend, it is necessary to reach a political settlement now to give the moderates more clout in a new government. There are some holes in this argument—including the ongoing debate in Nicaragua over whether the Sandinistas really defeated the National Guard or just conned the Western world with their democratic façade. It is also based on the debatable assumption that if the war continues the guerrillas will eventually win. But it is the argument they use.

Negotiations as a Tactic

U.S. diplomats and the Reagan administration have frequently claimed that these offers to talk are just tactics to help the guerrillas gain time or some other advantage that would contribute to total victory. At least in part, the experiences of the past three years confirm that point of view. For example, at the beginning of February 1981, right after the offensive in El Salvador, someone in the Nicaraguan government leaked a document of the joint Diplomatic-Political Commission of the FMLN and the FDR proposing that the left offer to negotiate with the Salvadoran junta if the United States would first terminate military assistance. The objectives of such a maneuver, it implied, were less to reach a settlement than to gain time in the war and improve the standing of the Salvadoran left with European and Latin American governments.

The Salvadoran military and the Christian Democrats used the document as proof of what they considered the endless treachery of the left, but it is also possible that the proposal, since it carried the names of Guillermo Ungo and some other moderates, was part of a maneuver within the left to try to bring the hard-liners into a pro-negotiations stance by whatever means. Six months later, in August 1981, an internal FPL document from Carpio spoke of using dialogue and negotiation as "an auxiliary but strategic factor in our struggle for power." Leftist sources say that during this period Carpio put his name to joint proposals for negotiations only very reluctantly, arguing that a lengthy war was necessary to allow time for the growth of the class consciousness of the masses.

Others in the left compared Carpio to a religious fanatic for his determination to see his method through, no matter how long it took or how much hardship it imposed on the revolutionary movement. But the other leaders were unable to prevail over a man who, at the age of fifty, had been willing to start a guerrilla war with seven people and no weapons. He resisted even the pressures of Castro and the Sandinistas until the bitter end. When Anaya Montes was killed, he was in Libya looking for arms that would allow the FPL to continue the war on his own terms. Between the lines of oration he delivered at her funeral was a pathetic plea for the Sandinistas not to abandon his cause. But the decision to make Villalobos the commander in chief of the guerrilla forces had been made.

A Proposal From Villalobos

Until now, Villalobos has been known primarily as a battlefield tactician, having translated a skill for kidnappings and urban violence into a talent for planning the guerrillas' larger military operations. He also developed a relatively sophisticated knowledge of weaponry. He had talked little about other matters until the beginning of September [1983], when he made a lengthy clandestine radio broadcast putting forward the guerrillas' most conciliatory proposal to date for settlement of the war. Claiming to speak for the entire FMLN, he made four basic points: (1) a call for a new economic and social order but denying any intent to expropriate all private property; (2) a government of three branches that would carry out "truly free elections"; (3) a new national army formed by elements of the existing army and the guerrilla organizations; (4) a non-aligned foreign policy, but one recognizing the strategic necessity of good relations with the United States.

Given the ideological and tactical history of the Salvadoran guerrilla groups, much of what he said may be dismissed as a smokescreen. However, one point seems worth noting. By offering to form a new army made up of rebels and elements of the existing army, Villalobos is trying to address the primary weakness, from the standpoint of non-Marxists, that existed when the Sandinistas came to power in Nicaragua. The Carter administration, in the last days of Somoza, made a panicky effort to salvage part of the old National Guard to merge with the Sandinistas to form a new army in which the United States might retain some influence and which coud serve to strengthen the hands of civilian moderates in the government. The effort failed for a variety of reasons still in dispute, not least of which was the shortage of time. Villalobos, who three years ago was predicting the "moral collapse" of the Salvadoran army, is suggesting that we talk about this now, when neither side appears on the verge of collapse or victory.

In many ways, Villalobos's army proposal is a major concession. He recognizes, for good or for bad, the importance of the army officer corps as a political institution, and seems to accept that it must be part of any settlement. By making the proposal, he is also revealing the left's basic insecurity about its own long-run military capabilities and the uncertainties of continuing supplies and training from Nicaragua and Cuba.

But there is still one major hedge in this—for the Salvadoran left, for the Sandinistas, and for Cuba. It is Villalobos himself. The decision to anoint one man, apparently Castro's own choice, to lead the Salvadoran left both militarily and politically reduces the likelihood of the other major weakness that showed up in Nicaragua after Somoza's downfall—the division of power in the Sandinista Directorate among nine theoretically equal men. Just as Nicaragua's non-Marxists found themselves hampered by a lack of influence in the new military structure, so the Sandinistas found their efforts to consolidate power restricted by their internal divisions and bickering. By putting Villalobos at the top now, the Salvadoran left is in a strong position to deal with whatever comes its way, whether it turns out to be total victory, a piece of the army, or years more of inconclusive struggle.

16. The Divided Military

ONE EVENING in March of 1980, a slightly built man wearing glasses and the three gold stars of a full colonel in the Salvadoran army went on television and told the nation that more than 200 of the largest private farms in the country were being expropriated, as part of the military's commitment to bring social and economic justice to the downtrodden. The next morning, army troops led by officers waving the new decree moved onto the farms to begin setting up cooperatives run by peasants. During the coming weeks, in a temporary operations center at the High Command headquarters, an army major kept track of completed takeovers by placing pins on a large wall map showing most of the farms in the country. Because of the tense atmosphere caused by the brewing guerrilla war and bitter opposition from well-armed land-owners, it was thought that only the Army enjoyed the power and security to set the agrarian reform in motion, a job that otherwise would have been given to a civilian agency.

One night a few months later, uniformed men pulled up to one of the newly created farm cooperatives in an armored vehicle, awakened a dozen or so men—including cooperative members and government specialists assisting them—and shot them to death. Two agronomists died while they were trying to show the troops their government identification cards.

Most of the outside world has come to look on the Salvadoran military as a murderous, repressive, monolithic institution—the problem, if you will. But there is also the other side of the Salvadoran military—the one that is looking for solutions to the country's social, economic, and political problems, and that is willing to break with the past to find them. It is a military that cannot be characterized only with a set of good-bad, black-white images.

When I try to think of episodes or circumstances that capture the essence of the Salvadoran army, it is neither the reforms nor the killings that come to mind. Rather, it is the night three years ago [in 1980] when a captain in his mid-thirties sat before me, a bandage on one shoulder visible through

---

Reprinted by permission of the author, Shirley Christian, from the June 1983 issue of *The Atlantic Monthly.*

his freshly ironed yellow *guayabera* shirt. It was not a guerrilla-war wound that the bandage covered but a wound from the army's own internal warfare. Someone had shot the captain as he drove down the highway from Santa Ana, a provincial capital. He thought it was one of the supporters of Roberto D'Aubuisson, a vehement anti-Communist major who had been invited to leave the Army a few months earlier, because he had refused to turn over to the new military-civilian junta his files on leftist subversion and political prisoners.

D'Aubuisson and about a dozen of his army and civilian friends were being detained for allegedly plotting a *coup d'état* on behalf of rich men who had lost land to the agrarian reform. Troops loyal to Colonel Adolfo Majano, one of the two military officers in the ruling junta, had swooped down on an isolated farmhouse the night before and captured the alleged plotters. The wounded captain was in an agitated state. Majano, who was his colonel, might be in danger; there had been threats from members of the D'Aubuisson camp. The whole officer corps, about 700 men at the time, was in confusion as it began several days of debate on the crisis.

It was tempting to characterize the debate—as the captain did—in terms of Majano, a committed reformer, being under assault from a group of officers serving the interests of big money. But it was just as much, or more, a dispute over the undefined rules under which the officers of the Salvadoran army hold themselves together as the ruling elite. Majano had ordered the arrests without consulting Colonel Jaime Abdul Gutiérrez, the other army officer in the governing junta. Gutiérrez was angry. He too supported reforms, and was not fond of D'Aubuisson, but he thought the way to deal with the problem would be quietly to ship those involved abroad, instead of arresting them and running the unacceptable risk of army officers killing other army officers. The issue of what D'Aubuisson and his friends had, or had not, been plotting became entangled with what Gutiérrez thought of as Majano's questionable methodology.

Gutiérrez appointed a military judge to rule on the charges against D'Aubuisson. In a fence-straddling decision worthy of Salvadoran military tradition, Gutiérrez selected as judge a major who was strongly identified with the so-called Majanista, or reform, sector of the Army but who also had graduated from the military academy in the same class as D'Aubuisson. Gutiérrez hoped that a man with allegiances in both directions might somehow decide the case on its merits. To Gutiérrez that meant a decision avoiding a permanent rupture in the military institution.

Within the week, D'Aubuisson went free and fled to Guatemala, and his alleged co-conspirators were dispatched in various directions. Majano lost a subsequent vote of confidence to Gutiérrez but remained in the junta until he was thrown out of the government, though not the Army, at the end of 1980. My captain subsequently did the unbelievable and took to the hills with the guerrillas. D'Aubuisson returned to relative glory last year [1982], by founding a political party and getting himself elected president of the Constituent Assembly. Gutiérrez saw the government through to those elections, then stepped out of the picture and watched in dismay as some civilian politicians tried to undo the social programs he had helped put in motion.

The Appeal of an Army Career

Where it begins for most of these men is at the Captain-General Gerardo Barrios Military School, a place of waxed tile floors, fresh paint, tropical flower beds, and polite cadets. The teachers talk of rewards that come with loyal service to the nation, and the cadets learn that the welfare of the Army and the welfare of the fatherland are indistinguishable. Most of the cadets come from lower-middle-class families who struggle to put their sons through high school in the hope that they will pass the entrance examinations for the military school, which provides four years of free education and living expenses. Becoming an officer is the most certain way to rise socially for an intelligent, earnest young man lacking family means. It will never put him on the same social level as those whose ancestors built the great coffee estates, but it offers the imprimatur of respectability in a country where that is denied to all but a few. It has traditionally led, at the very least, to influence; to moderate and sometimes great wealth; and to cabinet ministries and maybe the presidency.

Many enter the academy, few finish. Most officers now deciding the future of the country graduated in classes of twelve to twenty men in the late 1950s and the first half of the 1960s. They emerged from the academy with strong alliances and a sense of shared past and future; most received advanced training in the United States, Panama, Taiwan, Argentina, and Chile, and at the Army's own school of high command. By law, a professional military career lasts thirty years, beginning the day a young man enters the academy, which means that most officers retire before they are fifty. Though their paths may cross only occasionally in the years during which they move to seniority and power, no one forgets his classmates.

Together they constitute what Salvadorans call a *tanda*. We might call it a caste, each graduating class a subcaste of the larger caste. If a member deviates too much from a line that nobody can define, he gets a stint abroad for re-education, drumming on a desk in a cubbyhole at a Salvadoran embassy in some country that hardly knows El Salvador exists. Seldom is a member of the caste turned out permanently.

The military in El Salvador is divided into two groups of armed bodies: those traditionally concerned with defense of the national territory and those concerned with keeping internal order. The first group includes the 22,400-man Army plus the Navy and the Air Force, each of which has only a few hundred men. The second group includes the National Guard, with 3,300 men; the National Police, with 3,500 men; and the Treasury Police, with 1,700 men.

Keeping Order Internally

The creation of the internal-security forces is generally linked by historians to the conversion of El Salvador's agricultural economy, in the second half of the last century, to coffee-growing and private ownership of land by *criollos*, Spaniards born in the New World. Such farms needed labor, so the emerging military forces were used to persuade Indians, who had previously farmed in an informal communal system, to work on the farms. When the National Guard was created, it was for the express purpose of carrying out a new law against vagabondism aimed at any Indians who did not want to work for the *criollos*. The Guardsmen also protected private property against thieves or squatters. The Treasury Police was created after the turn of the century to combat trafficking in all kinds of contraband, on which the central treasury was being denied its tax revenue. Specifically, however, it was understood that the Treasury Police agents were to prevent Indians from getting drunk on *chicha*, the local version of corn liquor, and being unable to work. Treasury agents chased the *chicheros* who produced and sold the liquor to the Indians.

Of the three branches of the internal-security forces, only the National Police, which is assigned to handle police functions in the twenty largest urban areas, has dealt with anything remotely connected with protection of human life. Protection of the economic system was always the primary function of the security apparatus. By tradition, the toughest, meanest men in villages and rural townships were selected for the National Guard and Treasury Police, which offered lifetime careers that were attractive to men who had done their army draft duty and needed work. Because of the large size of many estates, groups of Guardsmen or Treasury Police were often based on the farms and worked virtually at the direction of the owner or his manager. No one ever told these men to use finesse in carrying out their assignments. The prevailing philosophy of the security forces was found in a phrase thought to have been brought to the New World by instructors from the Spanish Civil Guard and repeated often in the Salvadoran National Guard: "Authority that does not abuse loses its prestige."

In addition, the National Guard, too shorthanded to cover the entire country, organized canton patrols under the command of sergeants and staffed by men who are not formally a part of the National Guard but are given uniforms and guns. As the war has developed, an additional paramilitary organization, called Civil Defense, has organized patrols in rural battle areas, with only loose connections with the nearest army base. The quality of the manpower, and the attitudes toward individual rights among these two groups, are, at best, on a par with those of the National Guard and the Treasury Police.

The Army developed as a garrison force, and until the war began, more than three years ago, its strength was held to only about a third of its present size. The young conscript soldiers, recruited among the peasants and urban poor for twelve to eighteen months of service, sat in barracks in the fourteen departmental capitals waiting for war with a foreign power, such as the hundred-hour war with Honduras, in 1969, while the academy-educated officers devoted themselves to building the only political party that mattered at the time.

To a large extent, the officers have been the only element connecting these various defense and security forces, and officers have traditionally come from that tight little network of graduates from the Army's military academy. In recent years, there has been some promotion from within the security forces, but the control and leadership of each force has remained with army officers.

The Long History of Military Rule

Newspaper stories often say that El Salvador has been ruled by the Army for half a century. In fact, since Central America became independent from Spain, in 1821, El Salvador has almost always been governed by men whose right to power is based on guns. But historians usually treat 1932 as the watershed year in Salvadoran history. That was the year of a peasant uprising led by Farabundo Martí, one of the first Communists in Central America and the man whose memory the present guerrilla movement invokes in calling itself the Martí National Liberation Front. A military dictator named General Maximiliano Hernández Martínez emerged to quell the uprising by killing a number of people, mostly peasants, put variously at between 7,000 and 30,000. He won for himself the designation of El Salvador's first modern military ruler. Before 1932, the rulers were men who commanded local armies or were combinations of land-owners and warlords. After the bloodbath came a period of modernization. Highways were built, a communications system established, and a national currency created for the first time.

Even counting only from 1932, El Salvador has experienced the longest-running and most institutionalized military rule in Latin America. This rule has been centered in the military itself, in contrast to the personal dictatorships common in many other Latin American countries, where one man—a Somoza, a Trujillo, a Stroessner—rules *through* the military. In El Salvador during the past fifty years, no one individual has ever been allowed to place himself above the military, with the exception, to a certain extent, of General Hernández Martínez, who put the system in motion.

In the late 1940s, the Army organized a formal political party through which it governed the country, though other parties were not prohibited. At the beginning of the 1960s, the party was reorganized and named the National Conciliation Party, but the system of relying on senior army officers for leadership and for presidential candidates remained the same. The officers called elections every five years and established a national assembly. If the National Conciliation Party did not win the elections, the military stuffed the ballot boxes.

The National Conciliation Party and its predecessor were not ideological parties; they existed for the purpose of attaining and holding power behind a façade of legitimacy. An officer had to support the party. It was not something he learned in the academy but something he learned as he went along in his career. If he did not, he passed his days in dead-end hardship posts. The presidential candidate was always a military officer, though civilians were occasionally in the running for the nomination.

In 1966, General José Alberto Medrano, the head of the state intelligence agency (inspired, he says, by John F. Kennedy and the Alliance for Progress), founded a vast rural network called the Nationalist Democratic Organization, known by its Spanish acronym, ORDEN, to promote democratic virtues and to combat Communism. It served as the grass-roots structure for the party. White-collar civilians, particularly business and professional men, were also encouraged to support the party.

Corruption in the Army

The birth of institutionalized army rule in the 1930s came about in tacit agreement with the landed rich, usually referred to as the coffee oligarchy. It was not a hand-in-glove arrangement, in which the rich pulled the military strings, but an unwritten pact to use and abuse each other for mutual benefit. One coffee grower told me that the arrangement guaranteed an "accommodating" attitude by the military toward those with economic power. Another member of his class explained that the "productive sector" agreed to finance the government—i.e., pay taxes and close its eyes to the fact that army officers steal a substantial amount—in return for being left in peace to make money. The rich financed the electoral campaigns and were allowed to name their own kind to the ministries dealing with the economy and foreign affairs. They looked down upon their military partners, who, in turn, felt great social resentment toward those who bankrolled them.

Corruption is still extensive. Officers are routinely bought off or blackmailed by civilians seeking military influence. Some officers receive payoffs from men doing business in their territory; each provincial commander has the opportunity, for example, to make a profit on the monthly food budget for the 1,000 or so troops under his command. In some cases, it is difficult to draw the line between corruption and the granting of favors, such as the offering of bank directorships and jobs in private business after retirement from the military.

Some officers accept only what is dangled in front of them; others aggressively seek payoffs. In 1976, the chief of staff of the Army was convicted in U.S. federal court in New York and sentenced to prison for his part in a scheme to sell $2.5 million worth of submachine guns to American gangsters—guns he was intending to buy in the United States by submitting to the State Department a false certificate saying that the weapons would be shipped to his own army.

Corruption is so much a part of anything related to the Salvadoran military that any time an officer changes his position on any question, Salvadorans automatically assume that someone has bought him. Over the past four years, I have heard so many whispered charges and countercharges of corruption from officers and civilians that I conclude that the alleged corruption adds up to an impossible amount. Even the rare officer who joins the left or so much as proposes talking to the insurgents is likely to encounter the allegation that the guerrillas have offered him money. One theory of why U.S. military assistance is not more successful as a pressure device for ending human rights abuses is that it offers little prospect of individual rake-offs, because very little of it actually comes into El Salvador as money. Most comes as equipment and supplies or in the form of training Salvadoran soldiers in the United States and Panama.

Military Changes From Within

Despite the electoral framework created by the military and its pact with the rich, there have been periodic eruptions from within the military caused by various things: the desire for reform; individual officers' overstepping acceptable bounds of corruption; pressures from younger officers eager for their turn at the top; and external events. Each such eruption, however, has had some lasting effect, because each new group of officers has justified the assumption of power with promises to create a fair society and hold free elections, and has taken at least some steps toward keeping them. Two tumultuous periods of coups and government reorganizations, one in the mid-1940s and another at the beginning of the 1960s, resulted in substantial improvements, relatively speaking, in social and labor laws and the freedom to organize opposition political parties. This freedom led, in turn, to the birth and growth in the 1960s of the Christian Democratic Party, now the strongest single party in the country, though it lacks an outright majority. Some smaller opposition parties to the left of the Christian Democrats also developed, including a legal front organization for the Communist Party. Throughout the 1970s, the Communists participated in elections as part of the opposition coalition, but a split in their party spawned three of the present guerrilla groups, and the party itself opted to become a guerrilla force at the end of 1979.

It was obvious that this gradual opening up of the society would lead to a victory by the opposition, given free elections. When that came close to happening in 1972, the year the coalition led by José Napoleón Duarte got a plurality and possibly an outright majority of the popular vote, the Army went through another eruption. It announced false election results, giving the victory to its own candidate. A month later, several officers, dissatisfied with the fraud, attempted a rebellion. Perhaps because this rebellion raised the ultimate question—whether the military would actually give up power—the rest of the Army put it down with a hundred or more deaths and no significant change in the power structure. Duarte was arrested, beaten, and sent into exile, though he had played no role in organizing the rebellion. Today, many officers, as well as foreign analysts, believe that the failure to allow Duarte his victory contributed to the growth of guerrilla groups and social problems.

In May of 1979, a small group of officers began to meet. They saw a burgeoning leftist movement that not only was raising tens of millions of dollars by kidnapping wealthy Salvadorans or foreign businessmen but could put 200,000 demonstrators in the streets at one time. They looked at Nicaragua, where the Somoza dynasty was in its death throes, and saw that the United States was doing nothing to rescue the Nicaraguan National Guard, a military institution that had been, until recently, as strongly entrenched as that in El Salvador. Finally, they considered the occupant of the presidential palace, General Carlos Humberto Romero, who was isolated from many senior officers, deaf to the pleas of moderate civilians that he take drastic measures to correct national problems, and out of favor with the Carter administration because of the growing number of bodies turning up in trash cans and along the roads. The officers concluded that circumstances were such that the Marxist-Leninist guerrilla groups and their supporting organizations could carry out a successful insurrection by the end of the year. They decided to act before then.

The 1979 Coup

On the morning of October 15, the three senior men in the small group of officers—Colonel Gutiérrez, Lieutenant Colonel René Guerra y Guerra, and Major Alvaro Salazar Brenes—took command of San Carlos, the headquarters of the First Brigade in the capital. Junior officers working with them demanded the surrender of barracks commanders around the country. Gutiérrez telephoned President Romero to request that he leave the country.

Another shaking of the military tree was under way, and everyone involved thought that this one would turn out to be more momentous than any in the past. Salazar Brenes had said during the planning sessions that it would have to be the last military coup in El Salvador for at least twenty years. The political planning that went into it was even more careful than the logistical planning. A proclamation was written containing a heavy dose of theory about the redistribution of wealth—primarily through an agrarian reform — a vague promise to call elections, and a commitment to work to repair the divisions in Salvadoran society, presumably meaning an attempt to patch things up with insurgents. In a country desperately short of skill in political analysis and organization, the three officers represented a remarkably large amount of what skill there was. Gutiérrez, an engineer, had respected administrative and managerial talents. Salazar Brenes had earned a degree in political science at the Central American University after finishing military school, an unusual education for a military officer. Guerra y Guerra, more highly born than most military officers, consulted closely with a relative among the Jesuit priests, who dominate the teaching and administration of the university.

After much jockeying in the final days before the coup, Colonel Gutiérrez and Colonel Adolfo Majano were selected to represent the military in the new ruling junta, which was also to include three civilians. Guerra y Guerra wanted to be a member of the junta, but Gutiérrez insisted that only full colonels should serve, so Guerra y Guerra and the younger officers working with him asked Majano, then deputy director of the military academy, to represent them. He played no role in organizing the coup and apparently hesitated at the last moment, not arriving at the San Carlos barracks until late on the day of the coup.

Majano was then forty-one and Gutiérrez was forty-three; both were part of the small elite that full colonels constitute in a country where few make general. Like the U.S. Senate, the colonels form an exclusive club of people with great influence and status. After the coup, nearly sixty senior officers, including all the generals and the majority of the colonels, were retired or sent abroad. Only about a dozen full colonels were allowed to remain, all of them handpicked by Gutiérrez, though the number was allowed to rise with promotions made in the months after the coup.

A Continuing Military Shakedown

The 1979 coup was not the beginning and end of change in the military. The years since have brought an ongoing shakedown involving both power and ideas. The Salvadoran military has washed its linen in public as no other Latin American military institution has, providing a rare look inside a situation that would be reported with rumor and supposition in other countries. In part, this public display came about because the coup was followed by the assertion of a form of internal military democracy by the entire officer corps; for a while, everybody claimed the right to an opinion and a vote about every government policy. Gutiérrez thought that this was no way to fight a war, and set out to reassert the traditional top-to-bottom command structure. Eventually, some twenty-five commanders, all colonels or lieutenant colonels, assumed the power to make most military decisions, but the lingering effects of the democratization period have made it necessary for commanders to take into account the opinions of lower-ranking officers if they want their barracks to function. There was military unity when the coup was carried out in 1979, but within a few months it began to break down over various issues, and a consensus continues to be elusive today. Among the issues being debated are commitment or non-commitment to the promised reforms; past associations; corruption; relations with, and manipulations by, civilian groups; personal ambition; and, on occasion, conduct of the war.

Guerra y Guerra and many young officers, for example, viewed Gutiérrez as corrupt, because of his past position as head of the state communications corporation, a traditional source of rake-offs. The left regularly dropped the suggestion that Gutiérrez worked for the CIA. Guerra y Guerra was distrusted by Gutiérrez and his friends, who saw him as too personally ambitious and for that reason damaging to the agreed-upon goals. Gutiérrez, a somewhat retiring person, thought that Majano hogged the limelight too much for a man who had done nothing to bring off the coup. Majano, known to friends and detractors alike for honesty, intelligence, and naïveté, thought that as the elected representative of a group of younger officers he had the responsibility to improve the miserable human rights record of the armed forces. Robert E. White, the U.S. ambassador, encouraged him in this role.

In all the allegations of coup attempts and purges during 1980, it was never clear who was trying to do what to whom. Some officers accused Majano of flirting with the guerrillas, whose political front groups were tempting him to make a grab for total power with statements to the effect that they knew him to be "recuperable, not bloodthirsty." At the same time, some officers, particularly those friendly to the ousted Major D'Aubuisson, were viewed as being in the pay of the extreme right.

When the many versions of civilian government that have shared power with the military since the 1979 coup are added to this equation, the machinations and interests involved in any policy decision are multiplied. The first junta, made up of the two colonels and three civilians and backed by a cabinet that ranged from businessmen to Communists, lasted through ten weeks of tears, shouting, and mutual accusations before the inevitable self-destruction. Most of the civilians in the junta and the cabinet wanted Majano to assert the power of the younger officers to remove three senior officers the civilians perceived to be blocking progress: Gutiérrez, Defense Minister José Guillermo García, and Carlos Eugenio Vides Casanova, the director of the National Guard. Those three colonels, on the other hand, claimed that the civilians were being manipulated by the extreme left. Majano was apparently swayed against attempting a takeover by the fear that he might be destroying the military.

When the first junta broke apart, the Christian Democrats joined the military in forming a government, and while they had more collective staying power than the first set of civilians, they were shaken by the unsolved killings of various party activists and the flight of others to exile and affiliation with the insurgents. Though close to Majano in social ideas, the Christian Democrats found him a difficult loner in day-to-day affairs, and decided that Gutiérrez was more realistic and effective.

At the end of 1980, Gutiérrez and Defense Minister García made a written pact with the Christian Democrats that led to restructuring the government in the form that lasted until the elections in March 1982 for the Assembly, which began writing a new constitution. The catalyst for the 1980 restructuring, aside from the power struggles involving Majano, was the murder of four American missionaries by a National Guard patrol. The idea was to give a respected civilian, Duarte, more power by making him president of the junta (there had been none since the coup), and to establish firmer authority lines in the Army and security forces. In the process, García, Gutiérrez, and Vides Casanova became generals. A month later, however, the Reagan administration came into office almost simultaneously with the first big guerrilla offensive. The question of how to fight the insurgency on the battlefield quickly became more important than abuse of authority.

A Tradition of Violence

El Salvador's convulsions of the past four years have drawn attention to the terrible violence that has existed seemingly forever but that has increased as part of the reaction and counterreaction to the insurgency. Somewhere along the line, the general principle that in wars people try to kill their enemies has been replaced in El Salvador with the notion that one kills whoever is easiest to kill. Usually, that has meant any young man between eighteen and twenty-four, families of government troops and of guerrillas, politicians who think it might be a good idea for the sides to negotiate, and nuns and other social activists who become involved with the intention of helping the poor.

The killings and abuses fall into several categories. One is crimes committed by so-called death squads or by individuals in them, which usually single out individual people or families, often those known nationally or in small towns for commitment to a particular cause, revolutionary or otherwise. It is accepted, among military officers and others, that the death squads are commanded by a few middle- or lower-level officers, who, in the pay of civilian groups, recruit gunmen, particularly enlisted men from the National Guard or Treasury Police, to carry out political assassinations. This theory is largely based on supposition, but there are some factual kernels that support it. Papers taken from the briefcase of a captain arrested with D'Aubuisson during the alleged farmhouse plotting three years ago revealed a list of last names of military officers suspected by other officers of receiving payoffs to run death squads.

Distinct from the death-squad killings are mass killings in rural battle zones. The circumstances of these killings are clouded by great confusion and lack of information, such as whether the victims were families of guerrillas and whether they were killed intentionally by government troops, caught in crossfire, or eliminated in a no-holds-barred cleanup sweep. Sometimes what the guerrillas describe as the site of a military massacre the Army will describe as a burial ground for guerrilla combat losses. A third category of killings is related to feuds in small towns and rural areas which are only nominally, if at all, related to any of the issues in the war. In the absence of legal and police authority, those who have guns—which seems to be almost everyone—resolve things in their own way.

Some analysts like to fix responsibility for this violence squarely at the top of the military structure, particularly on General García in his long reign as defense minister, beginning the day after the 1979 coup and ending with his resignation in April 1983, and a few other men in key positions, such as the heads of the National Guard and the Treasury Police. But the structure of the Salvadoran military is so diffuse that there is no such thing as clear order. By tradition, the defense minister presides rather than directs. He is dependent on the willingness of the fourteen departmental commanders and of the heads of the three security forces to obey him. Even the link from the heads of the security forces to their troops is imprecise, because the security-force detachments in the fourteen departments are responsible first to the provincial army commander. When officers are inclined to clean up the units under their command, the old ways are often so imbedded as to prevent it. The two officers assigned to take over the National Guard and the National Police after the 1979 coup, General Vides Casanova and Colonel Carlos Reynaldo López Nuila, sought unsuccessfully in 1980 to be relieved of their posts, because they feared that it was impossible to get internal control of the organizations they were supposed to command. Further removed from the center of power and the command structure is the network of canton and civil-defense patrols in rural zones. These patrols, unpaid or badly paid, appear to take the brunt of guerrilla firepower and, in turn, to bear a large part of the responsibility in mass killings.

Attempts to Deal With Abuses

There have been efforts to deal with these problems, with mixed degrees of enthusiasm and success. The National Police, the National Guard, and the Treasury Police have dismissed several hundred men during the past three years as part of a campaign to weed out those who abuse their authority and to replace them with younger men who might carry out their assignments in a more humane way. Since the time when he wanted to throw up his hands in defeat in his effort to control the National Police, Colonel López Nuila, a lawyer who previously served on the army legal staff, has made some advances in teaching the police how to investigate crimes, particularly kidnappings, and in developing a code of conduct that includes keeping arrest records. Nevertheless, it is still routine for the police to beat up anyone they arrest. The Army High Command has held occasional meetings, which are well publicized, with the leaders of the canton and civil-defense patrols, to plead for better behavior.

A key element in the problems of violence, to which military leaders point as proof that they cannot bear the full responsibility, is the absence of a functioning judicial system. Many people concerned with achieving human rights progress in El Salvador, Americans as well as Salvadorans, believe that until the example of legal punishment is demonstrated, those who commit violent acts, whether they wear uniforms or not, will never change their ways. Some army officers speak bitterly of arresting people and turning them over to the civilian courts for investigation and prosecution, only to find them soon freed on technicalities. Salvadoran judges are known for being easy to buy off and easy to frighten. Bombs, threats, and terrorist attacks are the established methods used by people on all political sides to influence judges. A colonel told me about a large cocaine bust in which he played a significant role several years ago: the defendants, two Peruvian women arrested in a San Salvador hotel, went free after a large amount of money came into the country and, according to the colonel, was generously distributed among key people in the judicial system.

Finally, there is the matter of what José Napoleón Duarte calls the "culture of violence" that prevails in El Salvador. [See also selection 13.] Most Salvadorans are as convinced that extreme violence is part of their national character as they are convinced that corruption is endemic to the military and those who surround it. Government in El Salvador has traditionally been based on the authority of terror, implied even when not exerted. Rumor, cruelty, and ignorance are also at play in many killings among the rural population, which is largely illiterate. Some argue that the issue of military abuse will be solved only as the entire society resolves its violence problem by a combination of education and legal punishment for the guilty.

The Complex Truth

"Each one has his own truth," a colonel commanding a post in eastern El Salvador once told me as he discussed the Army's degree of commitment or non-commitment to social change. Anyone trying to take an objective view will indeed find many truths about the Salvadoran military institution. A few truths are commendable, some are only barely palatable, and some are despicable. Some are simply facts that will not go away. Among them: the Salvadoran military has a lot of innocent blood on its hands, and admits it only reluctantly. It also has an ample historical sense of how its hands got bloody. It has reached a degree of consensus about the need to change the country's social and political attitudes, and to make the military put a high value on human life. But there are sectors in the armed forces not in agreement, men who believe that it is still possible to use the threat of a Communist takeover to justify oppression. There is also disagreement, even among the majority, about how to reach the national goals and how much internal change the military can absorb in time of war. Finally, as Salvadoran military history has shown, conflicts over ideas and policies often get deflected by personal ambition and greed. The error lies in believing only one of these truths about the Salvadoran military, whichever it may be, and ignoring the others. In the end, the military wants to survive, and its leadership wants to do what is necessary to ensure that.

Despite its own soul-searching of the past few years, the Salvadoran military, in large measure, looks to the United States to define what is necessary. The messages it gets are unclear at best, and often contradictory. Trying to interpret the demands coming from the many centers of power and influence in the United States—the White House, the National Security Council, the State Department, the Pentagon, Congress, the press, opinion polls, pressure groups, and demonstrators—leads some officers to conclude that it is enough merely to talk a reformist line, and others to see the disaster ahead if the military does not take the lead in effecting actual reforms. Without a clearer message from the United States, the officers may be unable to agree on what to do next. This is a military that is at war as much with itself as with the guerrillas.

17. Why I Broke With the Guerrillas

By JOSÉ NAPOLEÓN ROMERO

Focus The Salvadoran elections for Constituent Assembly of March 1982 and the presidential elections of 1984 had a profound effect on former guerrilla commander Napoleón Romero: they caused him to leave the rebel forces. "With these actions the dictatorships were left behind that did not allow people through political processes to elect those who would govern them. Furthermore, with the development of the democratic processes came socioeconomic, agrarian, banking, and trade reforms that favored the majority of the weakened populace as well as the power of the minorities."

Romero's personal story helps to explain why by mid-1986 the guerrilla forces were weakened both in numbers and in effectiveness. As a young man in the seventies he joined the rebels for romantic, idealistic reasons. The arms the rebels started to receive in 1980 from Sandinista Nicaragua gave them great hopes. Through the Nicaraguan connection, Romero received training in Cuba and also traveled to a political-military training course in Vietnam by way of Managua, Havana, and Moscow. But his experience of life in totalitarian societies combined with the changing situation at home made him grow disillusioned with the revolutionary cause. He withdrew from the FMLN and surrendered to the Salvadoran government in 1985.

In this account, given to the National Press Club in Washington, D.C., in March 1986, Romero points to three persistent problems with the guerrilla groups that would exist even if the other objections he mentioned did not: (a) internal power struggles among the five main factions, (b) an irreconcilable difference between the guerrillas' military wing, the FMLN, which is Marxist-Leninist, and the political wing, the FDR, which is democratic, and (c) the FMLN's loss of autonomy to the Cubans and Nicaraguans, through which "its objectives acquired a connotation of geopolitical, extra-regional interests."

Romero finally came to believe that democratic, pluralistic means, though slow, offer the best hope for solving El Salvador's social problems.

Romero's account of splits in the rebel forces should be compared with Shirley Christian's (selection 15), and his hopes for Salvador's future measured against the historical context described by John Kurzweil (selection 13) and Julia Preston (selection 14).

I WAS BORN IN San Salvador, capital of El Salvador, on August 1, 1949. I went to the Antonio Najarro School in the city of Mejicanos, north of the capital, and to high school in the General Francisco Menéndez National Institute. I entered the National University after it opened at the end of 1972, studying psychology in the School of Sciences and Humanities.

I was in my third year in 1975 when I was recruited by the FPL [Popular Liberation Forces, one of five rebel groups making up the Farabundo Martí National Liberation Front, FMLN]. They assigned me, along with other cell companions, to create and develop the student movement at the university in accordance with the principles and direction of the "new left." In 1977 I left the university to devote myself to directing clandestine work, and in 1979 I was sent to the province of San Vicente, on the near-central front, as the political-military head of the Zone Directorate. This was before it was divided and the General Staffs corresponding to military structures established.

In March 1980 I went to Cuba for three months of military instruction exclusively for leaders, rejoining my front in June. In late 1980 we received the first weapons from Nicaragua, which enabled us to carry out military missions for the "final offensive" of January 10, 1981, in the provinces of San Vicente and La Paz.

In mid-1981 I was transferred to the Feliciano Ama Western Front, where I was given the rank of front commander and promoted to the Central Committee. In 1982 I was given responsibility for the Metropolitan Front, which comprises the province of San Salvador and nearby cities. My specific position was general secretary of the Zone Committee. Later that year I was promoted to the Political Commission, and since that organism was in Managua, which was where Marcial [Cayetano Carpio, called Commander Marcial, head of the FPL] and Ana Maria [FPL second-in-command] were, I had to be traveling constantly to Managua and from time to time to Havana, Cuba.

In 1983 two important events took place. First, I went to Managua as part of a delegation (along with Salvador Guerra and Leonel González) to investigate the murder of Commander Ana Maria and the suicide of the

---

An address to the National Press Club in Washington, D.C., on March 12, 1986.

commander-in-chief, Marcial. [These incidents are described by Shirley Christian in selection 15, page 233.] The second event was my trip to Vietnam, via Cuba, Moscow, and, of course, Managua, to attend a political-military course and to explain how the cases of the aforementioned commanders were resolved.

I was the political-military head of the Metropolitan Front until April 9, 1985, when I withdrew from the FPL and the FMLN.

Why I Joined the FMLN

My joining this organization was based on my Christian upbringing acquired through my own efforts in my years of junior and senior high and my hope to serve the people.

At the National University, upon learning of Marxism-Leninism and the political-military direction of the clandestine FPL organization, I was overcome by a romanticism, common to youth, in addition to the pressures of my recruiter to join the revolutionary movement as quickly as possible.

Besides the foregoing, I was influenced by the social, economic, and political realities. Social injustice was evident wherein a minority of the social classes, the oligarchy, concentrated the wealth, while the vast majority, the working classes, are unable to meet their basic needs, caught in the depths of poverty. Economically, the increase in unemployment, the high cost of living, and the crisis of the Central American Common Market were contributing factors. Politically, eminently dictatorial governments closed any democratic space, and their only language was repression in order to defend the interests of privileged minorities.

This situation of now more than ten years ago is what gave birth to the political-military organizations and moved people to join groups that applied concepts and means of struggle that many times were mistaken.

Why I Left the FMLN

The causes were political, ideological, and the leadership. Politically, with the coup of October 1979 [overthrow of the government of General Romero by young military officers] a space was opened that created conditions in the following years in which to undertake democratic processes. In March 1982 and 1984, two events occurred that showed concrete steps toward democratization: the election of the Constituent Assembly, and the presidential election. With these actions the dictatorships were left behind that did not allow the people through political processes to elect those who would govern them. Furthermore, with the development of the democratic processes came socioeconomic, agrarian, banking, and trade reforms that favored the majority of the weakened populace as well as the power of the minorities.

Ideologically, I disagreed with the Marxist-Leninist doctrine on which the FMLN is based, which consecrates violence as the midwife of history and holds that to end social injustices it is necessary for the long term to have a dicatorship of the proletariat. I have been able to verify this in my trips to places that have a Marxist-Leninist party in absolute power. It controls the media, it allows no opposition, it denies individual and collective rights, it sacrifices the freedoms of the majorities in large measure, and it denies the people their religious beliefs.

As for policy, the problems occurred at three levels. (1) In the FMLM there was a power struggle among leaders for hegemony and for having more opportunities to make their political and military views prevail. (2) Between the FMLN and the FDR [Democratic Revolutionary Front, the guerrillas' political wing] there was an alliance that had no possibility of being consolidated because the former is Marxist-Leninist and the latter is of a democratic nature. Also, the FDR has consciously carried out the role of political cover for the FMLN, taking away the "red" label, notwithstanding the fact that the FDR tries to carry out its objective of using the FMLN to take advantage of the installation and consolidation, at the outset, of a transition government in which it could have greater hegemony. (3) The political-military organizations gave up their autonomy to the Cubans and Sandinistas because of their need for arms and financial and political solidarity. Upon analysis, we find that the organizations at first responded to correct objectives — to address social injustices in the country — through incorrect methods; but when the FMLN lost its autonomy to the Cubans and Sandinistas, its objectives acquired a connotation of geopolitical, extra-regional interests.

All these concepts and political-military directions are what are leading to the destruction of the country: more than 50,000 deaths produced by the violence between the FMLN and the armed forces, more than half a million displaced persons, the destruction of the infrastructure of the country, and so on.

I believe that violence is not the way to eliminate social injustice and bring about the strengthening of a democratic and pluralistic government. Rather, the way to do this is through peaceful and democratic means, given the conditions that allow for them. At the same time, it is through a political program and plans that reflect the reality of the country and not the interests of the Cubans and the Sandinistas.

18. The State of Human Rights

By the U.S. STATE DEPARTMENT

Focus As a condition for continued U.S. aid to El Salvador, the U.S. Congress ordered the State Department to report every six months on the human rights record of the Salvadoran government in four key areas: dialogue with the insurgents, civilian authority over the military, judicial reform, and land reform. These reports have been the subject of heated debate in the policy community. As might be expected, they emphasize the offenses of the guerrillas and the progress of the government.

During the elections of March 1985, says this April 1986 report, the guerrillas' actions "demonstrated their targeting of noncombatants and undefended civilian facilities. In the six weeks preceding the voting, guerrillas burned more than twenty town halls, attacked the headquarters of several of the political parties, and assassinated political figures and civil defense volunteers." The terror against civilian politicians continued after the elections as well.

Faced with diminishing numbers and lack of popular support, the guerrillas have undertaken more daring actions. In spite of the dialogue begun in October 1984 between President Duarte and the insurgents, in September 1985 they kidnapped Duarte's daughter and demanded as ransom the release of political prisoners. Guerrilla attacks against civilians have been frequent. The report states that "since 1979, insurgent damage to the economy is estimated at $1.5 billion, more than the total amount of U.S. economic assistance provided to El Salvador during the same period." One publication of the Catholic Church in El Salvador has characterized guerrilla behavior as banditry rather than true social revolution.

On the government side, the report quotes a resolution by the U.N. General Assembly: "The government of El Salvador is continuing its policy of attempting to improve the condition of human rights." But that resolution also criticized the Salvadoran judicial system. Another U.N. document cited by the report commends the Salvadoran army for "endeavoring to conduct the war in a more humanitarian manner than in the past and . . . therefore not pursuing a policy of indiscriminate bombing, although in a few cases air and mortar attacks are causing civilian casualties."

The report concludes with details of Salvadoran efforts toward judicial reform and land reform.

This report contains material often underemphasized or overlooked in news reports and policy analyses but should be compared with Julia Preston's picture of problems in the Duarte government (selection 14), Shirley Christian's portrait of divisions within the Salvadoran military (selection 16), and the views of guerrilla defector José Napoleón Romero (selection 17).

ON MARCH 31, 1985, Salvadoran voters went to the polls to elect legislators and municipal officials in the fourth national election in as many years. In all, nine parties participated. After a vigorous and at times acrimonious campaign, 1.15 million persons voted, an estimated 66 per cent of those eligible, in spite of a determined insurgent effort to disrupt the balloting. Voting took place in all but twenty-one municipalities. In 1984, guerrilla actions had prevented voting in forty-three towns.

President Duarte's Christian Democratic Party won over 52 per cent of the vote, capturing thirty-three of sixty legislative seats and 153 of 262 municipalities, including eleven departmental capitals and more than two-thirds of the larger cities. The ARENA [National Republican Alliance] party and the old "official" PCN [National Conciliation Party] ran in coalition; they captured 38 per cent of the vote, giving ARENA thirteen seats and the PCN twelve seats. The new legislators and municipal officials were sworn in on June 1.

The insurgents' attempt to block the March elections demonstrated their targeting of noncombatants and undefended civilian facilities. In the six weeks preceding the voting, guerrillas burned more than twenty town halls, attacked the headquarters of several of the political parties, and assassinated political figures and civil defense volunteers. In the course of their "travel ban" at election time, they machine-gunned a vehicle in which two parish priests were riding, killing one and wounding the other. Attacks against the national electrical grid resulted in a power blackout of eastern El Salvador on March 29 and 30.

Following their failure to block the elections, the insurgents began attacks on the just-elected officials, in some cases before they were sworn into office. On May 1, they killed Christian Democratic mayor Edgar Mauricio Valenzuela in the town of San Jorge in San Miguel Department; his predecessor had been killed by guerrillas in January 1985. On September 26, Salvadoran armed forces personnel found Antonio Hernández, town administrator of San Simeon in Morazan Department, near death after being kidnapped and abandoned by the guerrillas. In all, between the March elections and October 1985, guerrillas kidnapped at least thirty

---

Report to the U.S. Congress by the Department of State, April 1986.

town officials, some of whom were executed by their captors, and assassinated numerous civil defense members.

On June 19, 1985, a terrorist team made up of members of the Revolutionary Party of Central American Workers (PRTC) faction of the FDR-FMLN [Revolutionary Democratic Front–Farabundo Martí National Liberation Front] guerrilla alliance machine-gunned a San Salvador café killing thirteen people, among them four unarmed, off-duty U.S. Marine security guards and two U.S. private citizens. Twelve other people were wounded in the attack, many of them critically. Three of those involved in the slaying were arrested and are currently imprisoned awaiting trial. Unconfirmed reports indicate that the ringleader, the brother of one of those arrested, was killed later in 1985 during a military operation on the Guazapa volcano. The San Salvador slayings demonstrated again the brutal and indiscriminate nature of the tactics employed by the Salvadoran insurgent movement.

The Guerrillas' 1985 Strategy

In 1985 the guerrillas, experiencing a significant decline in their military capability, embarked on a two-part strategy of urban terrorism and rural landmine warfare. With their numbers reduced to about one-half their peak strength by more effective Salvadoran armed forces performance, the insurgents increased assassinations and kidnappings of those they describe as "enemies of the people." In early March a guerrilla splinter group, the Clara Elisabeth Ramírez Front (CERF), killed the armed forces' press spokesman, Lt. Col. Ricardo Cienfuegos. In the same month guerrilla terrorists killed retired general and former politician José Alberto Medrano. On September 10, members of the Salvadoran Communist Party's armed branch kidnapped President Duarte's daughter and a companion as they left a university in downtown San Salvador. Two days after her release, on October 26, the guerrillas kidnapped an air force colonel serving as the director of civil aviation. Other guerrilla terrorist acts during the year included the April 8 massacre of twenty-one civilian men, women, and children in Santa Cruz Loma and the machine-gunning and burning of buses during some fourteen "travel bans," which resulted in numerous civilian casualties.

The September 10 kidnapping of President Duarte's daughter underscored FDR-FMLN terrorist tactics. With this abduction the guerrillas succeeded in drawing government resources and attention away from critical national issues and in forcing the government to come to terms with the kidnappers through the use of blackmail. President Duarte personally directed the ensuing forty-four-day hostage negotiations. Archbishop Arturo Rivera y Damas, assisted by the rector of the Jesuit-run University of Central America, Dr. Ignacio Ellacuría, served as intermediary between the government and the guerrillas.

The negotiations resulted in an exchange on October 24 involving the release of the president's daughter, her companion, and twenty-three mayors and other municipal officials (whom the guerrillas had kidnapped during the previous six months) in exchange for twenty-five prominent guerrillas, imprisoned on criminal charges, plus safe conduct out of the country for 101 disabled guerrilla combatants. The FDR-FMLN also agreed to cease targeting the families of Salvadoran government military and civilian officials. Among the twenty-five prisoners released in exchange for Duarte's daughter were one of the leaders of the terrorist organization that murdered thirteen people in San Salvador on June 19 and the second-ranking member of the Salvadoran Communist Party.

Reneging on the Agreement

The guerrillas failed to fulfill their agreement with the government. While they did free most of the kidnapped local officials, others were withheld in violation of the agreement. In December, Auxiliary Bishop Gregorio Rosa Chavez called on the guerrillas to free the officials they were still holding and expressed his concern that some might have been executed. Rosa Chavez said: "This is not a simple request, but a call to comply with the agreement signed in Panama." On December 30, the clandestine guerrilla radio broadcast that the mayor of Cacaopera, Morazán Department, and others from that town had been executed soon after their kidnapping in July 1984. The town secretary of Villa El Rosario had met the same fate in December 1983. On February 22, 1986, the insurgent radio broadcast an announcement from the FDR-FMLN High Command that they would "no longer be bound" by the agreement not to target family members of government officials for kidnapping and assassination. In March the church strongly criticized the guerrilla repudiation of the agreement. The U.N. Special Rapporteur also called on the guerrillas to respect the agreement and not to target family members.

Indiscriminate guerrilla landmine warfare maimed and killed many civilians in 1985; over half of the victims were children under the age of fifteen. The guerrillas have announced on their clandestine radio stations their intention to continue to plant mines to impede the repair of damaged power installations and to block the coffee harvest in order to damage the government's "war economy." The landmines employed by the guerrillas are homemade and difficult to locate with mine-detecting equipment. On October 7, a guerrilla mine destroyed a Red Cross ambulance.

Church authorities repeatedly condemned the indiscriminate landmine warfare of the FDR-FMLN, most recently in the Easter homily on March 30, 1986. Archbishop Arturo Rivera y Damas made note of the maiming of a man and two of his children and stated: "The indiscriminate use of these devices cannot be justified." In his February 9 homily, Rivera y Damas called upon the FMLN "not to place mines where the civilian population passes through." The archbishop added that in the majority of cases "the victims of the explosions of these mines are innocent." The guerrillas, however, have not desisted from these attacks.

In the only large-scale, rural guerrilla military action in 1985, a major insurgent force attacked the Armed Forces' National Training Center in La Unión on October 10. The guerrillas penetrated the installation and inflicted 113 casualties (including forty-six killed) and damaged two of the trainees' barracks. Quick reaction from many of the 1,700 trainees prevented a higher toll. The guerrillas lost ten killed in action before retreating without accomplishing their primary objectives of killing U.S. trainers and destroying the facility.

Damage to the economy as a result of the conflict remained a serious problem in 1985. The electrical distribution system was particularly hard hit. Public transport also suffered higher losses than in 1984, although damage remained well below the 1979–83 levels. But damage to the major export crops appears to have slackened, despite increased guerrilla presence in the major coffee-producing areas in the west. Since 1979, insurgent damage to the economy is estimated at $1.5 billion, more than the total amount of U.S. economic assistance provided to El Salvador during the same period.

Armed Forces Improvements

The armed forces continued to maintain strong pressure on the guerrillas in the countryside, while improving—with U.S. assistance—their ability to counter urban terrorism and attacks on the economic infrastructure. Morale and confidence within the armed forces remain high, and resources—principally U.S. military assistance—while less than desired, will be adequate to achieve significant military objectives and further reduce guerrilla ranks in 1986. The national plan to defend and revive population centers caught in the war was extended to cover a total of nine of El Salvador's fourteen departments. Progress in establishing new civil defense units moved forward in 1985 but was slowed by an inability to provide the needed weapons and training and by a series of guerrilla attacks specifically targeting civil defense units.

Throughout 1985 the Salvadoran armed forces consolidated military gains, strengthened command of the battlefield, and continued improving human rights practices. Employing a mix of large-unit operations and smaller, patrol-size tactics, they often kept the guerrillas on the move and unable to mass. Six years into the conflict, the armed forces displayed a better understanding of the importance of increased civic action, psychological [warfare], and other operations resulting in increased popular support and larger numbers of guerrilla defections.

The armed forces developed a new tactic called *relámpago* (lightning strike) to enhance offensive capability. Blending significantly increased mobility for ground troops with aerial fire support, this tactic helped the armed forces' effort to regain control of traditional guerrilla strongholds and seize important guerrilla documents. *Relámpago* scored one of the major successes of the year on April 18, 1985, with the capture of PRTC guerrilla leader Ana Maria Valladares, known as *Comandante* Nidia Díaz.

The number of guerrillas dropped from a high of 9,000–12,000 in 1982–83 to an estimated 5,000–7,000 by late December 1985. The decline has forced the insurgents to consolidate or dissolve some units as well as to disperse their dwindling ranks into the countryside, adversely affecting their command and control. Estimated guerrilla casualties remained at the same level as in 1984. The number of overall Salvadoran armed forces casualties in 1985 jumped 16 per cent from the previous year, although the number of those killed in action declined, owing, in part, to improved medical care provided through U.S. assistance.

The Role of the Church

The Catholic Church in El Salvador has continued to play a key role as a trusted and credible intermediary between the government and the FDR-FMLN guerrilla forces. Archbishop Arturo Rivera y Damas and other church leaders accept the legitimacy of the Duarte government but have maintained the independence and authority of the church, which allow it to act as an intermediary. Church leaders have been outspoken in insisting on respect for the rights of noncombatants and that both sides work toward a peaceful solution to the conflict.

The church has actively stated its concerns about actions in which civilians are killed or threatened. On April 15 Archbishop Rivera y Damas denounced the guerrillas' murder of twenty-one people at Santa Cruz Loma on April 8. The archbishop condemned the guerrillas for capturing and then executing unarmed members of the town's civil defense and then attacking a house inhabited by women and children. He added that this was a human rights violation that raised doubts among the people about the guerrillas' commitment to pursue dialogue. In June, the church newspaper, *Orientación*, issued a strong condemnation of the June 19 massacre of thirteen people. The editorial stated:

> In view of the bloody event perpetrated in the Zona Rosa and claimed by the FMLN, there is room to ask ourselves whether there are still some guerrillas or if perhaps they are not bandits and terrorists who will make the promised revolution. What is happening, guerrillas? Have you invoked the spirits of Trujillo, the Somozas, the Duvaliers, Batista, and Stroessner? The terrorist has neither name nor ideology, nor belongs to any social class. . . . Once he has killed he continues killing for its own sake and for the pleasure of seeing men, women, and defenseless children fall.

In an August pastoral letter, the eight Salvadoran bishops gave their views on the conflict and examined the impediments to its peaceful resolution. They stated in the letter:

> We have, on one side, a constitutional government, endorsed by the massive turnout at the voting urns in four successive elections, which have been practically a repeated "referendum" in favor of democracy; and, on the other side, the FDR-FMLN, who arrogate a representativity of the people which they cannot certify and who, in addition, resort to violence and sabotage as an essential component of their struggle, thus placing themselves in a position which we cannot approve.

The bishops reflected further on the difficulty of dialogue by quoting a reference to the Salvadoran guerrilla groups in a statement made by Pope John Paul II during his visit to El Salvador in 1983. The Pope said that a dialogue will be made difficult and sterile "when some parts are supported by ideologies which, in spite of their declarations, are opposed to the dignity of the human being and his just aspirations . . . ideologies which see the motor of history in battle . . . and . . . the source of right in force."

Since the bishops' August statement, leaders of the church have spoken out frequently in person and through church publications on dialogue and other national issues. In a September 22 editorial, *Orientación* condemned the kidnapping of President Duarte's daughter. In the editorial, the church labeled the abduction a "cowardly, criminal act that constitutes the most despicable act of blackmail." The article added that "the archbishop saw in the action of this kidnapping a dangerous and nefarious sign of the negative attitude of some confronted with reasonable and honest means that must be taken to build peace in our country."

An editorial of December 8 summarized the church's views on the conflict. In the article, the church described the conditions of injustice which prevailed in El Salvador for decades as the root of the conflict and the reason why some took up arms against the system. It went on to note that the "guerrillas lost their cause and evidently their popular support" with the advent of social and economic changes. The editorial continued:

> The actions of the extreme left against the national economy, with grave repercussions for our people, caused them to lose their credibility and sympathy. The revolution thus ceased to be popular. The guerrillas no longer tried to claim the people who, to the contrary, had been given positive hope in the reforms of the social order and, above all, with the democratic experience of elections. It is important to note that in this fight of two armies, representing two ideologies, the people now have demonstrated their preference. Their presence at the voting booths and their response to the call of elections are indicative of the popular will.

The U.N. Human Rights Commission's Special Rapporteur on El Salvador, Dr. Pastor Ridruejo, submitted his report to the General Assembly on November 5. The report noted the attempted disruption of the March 31, 1985, legislative elections by the guerrillas and their policy of economic sabotage. On the latter question, the report expressed "deep concern with these attacks, which help undermine the country's already weak economy and seriously compromise important economic, social, and cultural rights of the Salvadoran people." The report also strongly criticized the Salvadoran judicial system for being slow and ineffective.

In a November 26 address to the General Assembly's Third Committee, the Special Rapporteur expanded on his report by lauding the continuing democratization in El Salvador and the government's commitment to improving human rights observance.

On December 14, the U.N. General Assembly passed a resolution on El Salvador, noting: "The Government of El Salvador is continuing its policy of attempting to improve the condition of human rights." This resolution also labeled the Salvadoran judicial system as "notoriously inadequate." On March 12, the 42nd Human Rights Commission in Geneva passed a resolution recognizing "with satisfaction that the question of the observance of human rights forms an important part of the policy of the present government of El Salvador."

A 'Space' for Labor Unions

Following his election in 1984, one of President Duarte's goals was the creation of a "democratic space" for labor in which unions could express their interests. The Salvadoran government succeeded in this effort; through 1985 and into 1986 labor was highly active. Most labor activity focused on traditional issues—wages and working conditions. Nevertheless, labor, including left-wing labor organizations, also played an active and prominent political role.

Between May 1985 and April 1986, there were numerous strikes, Salvadoran labor's basic bargaining tool. El Salvador's private sector experienced the longest strike in the country's history when workers at the country's largest shrimp-exporting company, Pezca, struck for 196 days. The dispute was settled in July 1985, but only after Pezca had suffered significant foreign exchange losses.

Public-sector labor associations, many of them leftist-controlled, coordinated strike activities last year. In May and June, sewage and waterworks (ANDA) employees, social security (ISSS) workers, and teachers engaged in strikes and work stoppages. The ANDA strike ended June 11 after a labor judge ruled the strike illegal, because the union had not followed legal procedures in calling the strike, and ordered the strikers back on the job. At the urging of the union's leaders, 237 workers disobeyed the judge's order and, as a result, were fired. The labor ministry stripped the union leaders of their leadership status after they were fired on the grounds that they could not be union members since they no longer worked at ANDA. The Supreme Court ruled March 19, 1986, that the labor ministry acted unconstitutionally and that ANDA either had to rehire the fired union leaders or had to pay them through February 12, 1987, one year after their terms as elected union leaders end.

Leaders of the ISSS union also failed to abide by labor laws governing strikes. Their strike in May and June 1985 was ruled illegal by a labor judge. Union members occupied the Central Social Security Hospital and social security clinics. During the occupation, which lasted from May 6 to June 2, social security beneficiaries were refused services and the rate of patient deaths in the hospital was greater than average, even though there were fewer patients. On June 2, security forces entered the hospital and arrested two union leaders. Four policemen were accidentally shot and killed by security forces during the operation. The arrested union leaders were released June 5. On June 7 the strike ended, and union leaders called the settlement terms a victory for the workers.

A spate of public employee strikes took place in October and November when employees at the Finance Ministry, Public Works Ministry, telephone company, Agriculture Ministry, tourism institute, and the municipality of San Salvador walked off the job. Negotiated settlements to these strikes between unions and the government included a large salary increase for all public employees.

Two important new labor umbrella organizations were recently formed. One, the National Salvadoran Workers Union (UNTS), has as its largest member the Communist Party–dominated May First Committee. UNTS has been highly critical of President Duarte's administration. The other, the National Worker-Peasant Union (UNOC), has also criticized parts of the Duarte administration's austere economic adjustment package. UNOC, however, has voiced its support for the democratic process and land and social reforms.

During the six-month period beginning in October 1985, various labor demonstrations took place. In January, several thousand people marched to protest a package of economic measures implemented by the government. On February 21, leftists led 7,000–10,000 people in a demonstration against the economic measures. On March 15, democratic worker and farm-worker organizations led a march of some 35,000 who voiced support for the democratic process, peace, and land and other social reforms. These and other demonstrations in the last year have been peaceful.

Dialogue With the Insurgents

In October 1984, President Duarte began a dialogue between his government and the FDR-FMLN guerrilla groups. The peace offer that Duarte presented at the talks held at La Palma on October 15 called for pacification of the country within the framework of the constitution approved in 1983 by the elected Constituent Assembly, plus guarantees for the reincorporation of the left into the democratic political process. President Duarte offered the guerrillas the opportunity to take their cause to the people by participating in the democratic process.

At the second round of talks at Ayagualo on November 30, the insurgents proposed a phased plan that called for the abrogation of the constitution, the formation of a new government, the end of outside military aid and advisors, a ceasefire based on territorial demarcation, and reorganization of the armed forces. Only after all of this was completed would elections be held. President Duarte rejected the guerrillas' proposal as unconstitutional and illustrative of the left's determination to seek power through violence. He noted that the proposal marked a return to the guerrillas' past intransigence and negated any joint efforts for peace.

Since the failure of the talks at Ayagualo, President Duarte and members of his government have frequently stated the government's willingness to reinitiate the dialogue when the guerrillas demonstrate their intention to engage in serious talks. In his state of the nation address on June 1, President Duarte reiterated his commitment to continue the dialogue and stated that he would meet with the guerrillas again when he saw some sign of a real desire for peace on their part. On August 14, President Duarte restated his desire to continue a dialogue with the rebel groups in order to find a rapid solution to the war in El Salvador. In November, following the release of his daughter by her FDR-FMLN captors, Duarte told reporters in Madrid that his offer of talks with the guerrillas still stood and that he was ready to engage in a serious dialogue "at any moment and at any place."

In contrast, the FDR-FMLN utilized the dialogue issue for propaganda. Although making numerous "overtures," they never deviated from their demand that the constitution be overthrown and the government restructured in an undemocratic manner. In October 1985, while holding President Duarte's daughter kidnapped, they advanced yet another version of the same proposal, signed by FDR president Guillermo Ungo and Communist Party secretary general Shafik Handal; its timing demonstrated the initiative's propagandistic nature.

Duarte's Peace Initiative

In March 1986 President Duarte announced a major peace initiative. Recognizing the critical role played in support of the Salvadoran guerrillas by the Marxist-Leninist government of Nicaragua, President Duarte wrote to the head of the Sandinista regime, Daniel Ortega, and proposed a three-part plan to achieve a peaceful political solution to the conflicts in the region. The plan called for a simultaneous dialogue between the Nicaraguan government and its political and military opposition and between the government and the FDR-FMLN in El Salvador. (Talks between the Nicaraguan regime and its democratic opposition would have triggered bilateral U.S.-Nicaragua talks.) The plan also called for the Central American presidents to meet to discuss integrated solutions to the problems of the region.

Duarte's plan envisioned the creation of a Central American parliament. The parliament would include representatives of all of the political and social sectors of the region and would act as a permanent forum for dialogue and consultation on regional problems. President Duarte stated in his letter to Ortega that his government had initiated a dialogue as a means to achieve peace. He noted his continuing belief in a sincere dialogue as a workable formula to reach a peaceful solution to the conflict in El Salvador.

Spokesmen for the Nicaraguan regime and Salvadoran guerrilla representatives immediately rejected President Duarte's effort to achieve a comprehensive peace in the region. The initial Nicaraguan rejection was made in Moscow by Sandinista *Comandante* Bayardo Arce. In an editorial on March 6, the Sandinistas' newspaper *Barricada* denounced the proposal as part of a strategy engineered by the U.S. government. The Salvadoran guerrilla reaction hewed the same line as the Nicaraguan response. Immediately following Duarte's announcement, a principal political leader of the guerrilla groups, Hector Oquelí, rejected the plan and repeated the false and discredited assertion that the Salvadoran rebels do not depend on Nicaragua. Guillermo Ungo, the president of the guerrilla political arm, said that the proposal to link Salvadoran and Nicaraguan talks was "madness" but did not address the issue of the Nicaraguan government's provision of arms to the rebels.

Sandinista Guerrilla Links

In rejecting President Duarte's peace initiative, the Nicaraguans and the FDR-FMLN either denied the existence of or ignored a key reason for linking talks in El Salvador and Nicaragua: the longstanding and continuing Sandinista intervention in El Salvador's internal affairs. Since its assumption of power in 1979, a key feature of Sandinista foreign policy has been support for left-wing subversive movements in other Latin American countries. The Nicaraguan regime has not wavered from its original commitment to foment revolution in neighboring states. Salvadoran guerrillas have been the prime beneficiaries of this policy. Facilities were set up in Managua in 1979 for the transfer of matériel to the Salvadoran guerrilla groups. Guerrilla training sites were also established. U.S. weapons were shipped from Vietnam to the Nicaraguan government and then provided to the FDR-FMLN. Sandinista subversion of the democratic government in El Salvador continued through 1985 and into 1986.

Sandinista collusion with the Salvadoran guerrillas took place during the negotiations to obtain the release of President Duarte's daughter when guerrilla negotiators in Panama were in regular and open communication with Managua. New public evidence of the continuing supply of matériel to the guerrillas in El Salvador was obtained in December 1985 when a vehicle that crashed in Honduras was found to contain ammunition, grenades, radios, and other communications gear and a manifest listing the call signs of insurgent command posts in Nicaragua and El Salvador. Most recently, Honduran troops discovered a cache of arms that originated in Nicaragua and were stored in Honduras by Salvadoran members of the PRTC guerrilla group.

In contrast to the Nicaraguan and FDR-FMLN reaction, the response to President Duarte's plan from other governments in Central America was highly favorable. On March 15, the presidents of Guatemala and Honduras and the president-elect of Costa Rica asked the Nicaraguan government to accept the proposal to seek a dialogue between the Sandinistas and the opposition. In their statement the three leaders said of the proposal:

> We support it, convinced that it is necessary to mount a broad and very serious effort in concert to induce the rulers of Nicaragua to recognize the urgency of opening dialogue and thus creating propitious conditions for achieving peace in the isthmus and consolidating democracy.

An exchange of telegrams between Sandinista leader Daniel Ortega and Costa Rican president Luis Alberto Monge in late March demonstrated clearly the contrast between the reactions of the Communist government of Nicaragua and the democratic government of Costa Rica to the initiative. In his March 24 message, Ortega wrote:

> I have to express my firm and categoric rejection of the recent declaration signed in Honduras on March 13 supporting the initiative of President Duarte, which in essence involves his government in an act which violates morality, international law, and existing treaties, and promotes the manipulation of the government of El Salvador by the United States. The proposal of President Duarte is directed at intervening in internal

matters of Nicaragua and seeks support for the mercenary forces in service of a foreign power attempting to establish an absurd and immoral symmetry between the civil war in our brother republic of El Salvador, resulting from structural and economic injustices, and a war of aggression imposed by the government of the United States against the people of Nicaragua and condemned by the international community.

In his response to Ortega on March 26, President Monge said:

With respect to your opinion that Costa Rica committed an immoral and illegal act in supporting President Duarte's initiative, I must point out to you that the plan responds to the spirit of the Contadora negotiations, in the sense of moving forward with national reconciliation processes in Central America. I understand that for the current government of Nicaragua, it might be unacceptable to go forward with a process of that nature, but for that reason I cannot accept your criteria of the manner in which Costa Rica should direct its foreign policy, and for that reason I reject those criteria energetically, emphasizing that we have always believed in dialogue as a way of solving political problems, and that if we have maintained that should be the line followed in El Salvador, we believe it is equally indispensable that it should also be so in Nicaragua.

Other support for Duarte's initiative came from the Archbishop of San Salvador, Arturo Rivera y Damas. On March 9, the archbishop responded to Duarte's plan by saying that the church supports all efforts that favor a solution to the Salvadoran conflict through an authentic dialogue. He added that to be effective the dialogue had to encompass three levels: national, regional, and geopolitical.

CIVILIAN CONTROL OVER THE MILITARY

Since the October 1979 coup d'état that overthrew the government of President Romero and the subsequent purge of officers opposed to reform, the military in El Salvador has supported establishment of a democratic political system and a more equitable economic system. The coup itself was the result of the conviction held by many in the military that Romero's removal was a prerequisite to implementing the reforms the country needed. In the period of joint civilian-military rule following the coup, in spite of the opposition of some recalcitrant officers, the military as an institution helped to implement the fundamental changes in the country's social and political system that culminated in the free elections in 1982, 1984, and 1985 and the establishment of a democratic civilian government.

The armed forces remain a major force within the country; they are now, however, subject to a civilian authority elected by the Salvadoran people through a democratic system that many in the military helped to bring about. The military is now defending that democratic government against extremists who would reimpose the rightist dictatorship of the past and against those who seek to establish a permanent left-wing tyranny in the future. The Salvadoran armed forces continue to respect the authority of the elected government and to abide by their constitutional role. The role of the military in the crisis provoked by the kidnapping of President Duarte's daughter demonstrated their respect for the country's civilian authority.

During the October 1985 negotiations between the government and the FDR-FMLN, rightist leader Roberto D'Aubuisson attempted to capitalize on discontent within the armed forces over the concessions to the guerrilla groups by lauding the military's sacrifices and contrasting those with the government's willingness to free those responsible for those sacrifices. On the opposite political extreme, the clandestine guerrilla radio also sought to drive a wedge between the civilian authorities and the military with broadcasts that claimed that the crisis was exacerbating "contradictions" and deepening divisions with the government. These efforts to undermine the military's support of constitutional civilian authority failed.

When one rightist military officer criticized the government's handling of the crisis in a petition to the minister of defense, his criticism was rejected by the military high command and received almost no open support from other officers. His position on that occasion was repeated in January when he disputed the military's full backing for a package of economic reforms proposed by President Duarte. These two episodes plus his subsequent charge that the government was penetrated by Communists led to his reassignment as military attaché in the United States. In response to a question about the military's support for the economic reforms, the chief of staff of the armed forces, General Adolfo Blandón, noted that the government had consulted with the military about the economic package, that rightist doubts about the armed forces' support for the package were unfounded, and that the military had a constitutional function to support the government.

The Salvadoran armed forces continued to make institutional changes in order to eliminate abuses of human rights by government troops and members of the security forces. In a year when air power became a key factor in the conflict, President Duarte's guidelines governing use of aerial firepower near populated areas appear to have been closely adhered to by the air force. These guidelines require that the target of bombing be free of civilians, that the area be clearly visible to the pilot, and that permission to bomb be obtained from the General Staff in San Salvador. Salvadoran pilots are complying with these rules. In a report on the observance of human rights in El Salvador, submitted to the U.N. General Assembly on November 5, 1985, the Special Rapporteur concluded that the "Salvadoran army is endeavoring to conduct the war in a more humanitarian manner than in the past and is therefore not pursuing a policy of indiscriminate bombing, although in a few cases air and mortar attacks are causing civilian casualties."

On January 9, 1986, the Salvadoran armed forces began a major military operation called Operation Fenix to dismantle insurgent headquarters and support facilities on Guazapa, a volcano about seventeen miles north of San Salvador. That area had served as a guerrilla stronghold since the insurgency began in 1979. Guerrilla military operations, sabotage of economic targets, and even the kidnapping of President Duarte's daughter were mounted from Guazapa.

Salvadoran troops involved in Operation Fenix were careful to avoid endangering civilians and prevent civilian casualties. They broadcast warnings to noncombatants to remove themselves from the scene of the fighting and avoided firing into areas where civilians might be located. More than 500 civilians were evacuated from the area of the fighting. The civilians were transferred to a safe area several miles from the combat and were supplied with food, water, shelter, and clothing. They were also provided with medicines and attended by doctors, dentists, social workers, and representatives of the International Red Cross and the Human Rights Commission. Most of these civilians were quickly settled with family or friends or in camps for displaced persons.

San Salvador auxiliary bishop Rosa Chavez stated in his homily of January 26 that he had received "unconfirmed reports" that 1,000 civilians were surrounded in two villages northeast of the Guazapa volcano. On January 27, he celebrated Mass on Guazapa mountain and determined that these reports were unfounded. He made no reference to them in his next homily, on February 2, but did express continued concern for civilians who might still be hiding on the volcano. Bishop Rosa Chavez noted that many civilians had already been safely evacuated by the armed forces. Members of the international press were able to interview civilians evacuated during the Guazapa operation. No credible allegation of mistreatment was published.

JUDICIAL REFORM

The Salvadoran government is pursuing a comprehensive program to reform its system of justice. A ten-member Revisory Commission has been established to conduct a thorough review of the Salvadoran judicial system and identify solutions to the problems it faces. Another commission has also been established to oversee the work of a specially trained unit assigned to investigate major criminal cases. The government is also working to implement plans to establish a judicial protection unit that would be responsible for protecting judges, jurors, witnesses, and other participants in the judicial process from threats or intimidation.

The Revisory Commission dates from June 1985, when the Legislative Assembly formally approved the decree creating the commission. Its ten members include two Supreme Court magistrates, representatives of the attorney general, the solicitor general, the Ministries of Justice and Defense, law faculties, and lawyers' professional associations. Once hiring of the technical and expert staff is completed, approximately forty persons will be working under the commission members.

To date, the work of the commission has focused on identifying the judicial areas most urgently needing revision. Three groups of three members each were established to focus on penal, civil, and administrative issues. The plan of action that resulted from the work of these groups was discussed on February 7 in a consultative meeting that attracted over 200 participants, among them Supreme Court magistrates, representatives of several government ministries, members of lawyers' associations and law faculties, and Legislative Assembly deputies and other representatives of political parties. The plan presented to this gathering was revised in twenty-two areas on the basis of observations made during the forum.

The commission's priority for penal law is a comprehensive review of the state of emergency legislation known as Decree 50. The commission's review will include an in-depth study of all of the cases currently before the special tribunals and a revision of the appropriate penal procedures relating to the suspension of constitutional guarantees, including the study of the amnesty issue. In addition, the commission will seek to make changes in current laws that are needed immediately such as the jury selection process and the procedures relating to the bail system. Commission members expect to complete their work on Decree 50 and related issues and submit proposed legislation in five to six months. Anticipating the commission's recommendations, in February the Supreme Court submitted a proposal to the Legislative Assembly that would augment the number of Courts of First Instance in order to deal with the backlog of Decree 50 cases. The measure was unanimously passed by the Legislative Assembly.

Looking Into Judgeships

In the administrative field, the commission will focus on the National Council on the Judiciary and judicial career legislation. The 1983 constitutional mandates that a National Council be formed to ensure that the selection of judges is based on ability and experience and not on political considerations. A draft of the legislation needed to implement this constitutional requirement was submitted to the Legislative Assembly by the Supreme Court in 1984. However, because of opposition in the current court, the proposed legislation was shelved.

As a result, the commission took the initiative to develop an alternative proposal. Commission members intend to accompany the proposed National Council legislation with a proposed judicial career law governing assignments and sanctions of judges; identifying standard requirements for service as a judge; and proposing salaries, benefits, and hours of work, which are currently half-day only. The work on these drafts of legislation is scheduled to be completed in August or September.

In the area of civil law, the extraordinary number of common-law marriages and children born out of wedlock and the inequitable treatment that these Salvadorans face before the law led the commission to focus on family law. The commission's work will include a reform of the laws governing the rights of illegitimate children and of the partners in informal marriages. The reforms that the commission contemplates could bring about fundamental changes in Salvadoran society. The proposed legislation in this area is expected in October 1986.

A New Investigating Commission

The Commission for Investigations was created in July 1985 by legislative decree. It is headed by the minister of justice, with the vice minister of interior and a designee of the president as the other members. The commission directs the activities of an executive unit, a twenty-three-member investigative unit, and a seventeen-member forensic unit. The investigative unit is currently working on several major criminal cases, including the Sheraton murder case, the Armenia well case, the Las Hojas massacre, the Sullivan murder case, the Romero assassination, the murder of an attorney and related adoption racketeering, and the killing of the former head of a government land reform agency, Juan Pablo Mejia. This unit was also involved in the investigation of the kidnapping of President Duarte's daughter and in coordinating the security force task force that identified and arrested some of those involved in the massacre of thirteen people on June 19, 1985.

The commission's investigations unit has accumulated and reconciled the evidence available on the cases it is handling, interviewed witnesses, and reinterviewed others who had testified previously and pursued new investigative leads. On March 9, a group of five investigators traveled to Costa Rica to interview ten witnesses who may be able to shed light on the role of Capt. Eduardo Avila in the Sheraton case and, possibly, the Romero assassination. Unit investigators are also looking into allegations that Walter Antonio Alvárez, a former National Guardsman who was killed in 1981, was involved in the murder of the archbishop. A reversal of the provisional dismissal of charges against the suspects in the multiple murder known as the Armenia case was recently obtained. Efforts are also under way to obtain a judicial order to exhume the remains of the victims from the well into which they were believed to be thrown. The commission investigators are also pursuing the Las Hojas case in which eighteen people were murdered by an army patrol in February 1983. The unit will be involved in developing evidence to support the testimony of two witnesses who have recently come forward with previously unknown eyewitness accounts of the murders.

During this period, the case of two gunmen who committed the murders at the Sheraton Hotel in 1981 went to trial. The two former National Guardsmen, Santiago Gómez Gonzáles and José Valle Acevedo, were each convicted on February 13 on three counts of aggravated homicide. The jury reached its verdict after hearing the prosecution's argument that the gunmen were members of a "death squad" within the National Guard that carried out political murders and was responsible for acts of terrorism that must not go unpunished. In the case of these gunmen, the weak Salvadoran judicial system was able to overcome its deficiencies and render a just decision in a notorious case.

Beyond that, however, this case is significant because of the government prosecutor's appeal to the jury to convict the two gunmen for the violence they perpetrated as members of a death squad. The determination of the government to put an end to the brutality of some of those within the army and security forces was accurately and effectively summarized in the prosecutor's message. That determination was seconded by the five jurors who agreed that the two gunmen should be punished for their actions. Despite reversals before the courts, Salvadoran government prosecutors are continuing their efforts to develop evidence against one of those who ordered the two gunmen to commit the murders, Capt. Eduardo Avila.

LAND REFORM

El Salvador's agrarian reform is now in its sixth year of implementation. Progress has been slow but steady and has resulted in changed land tenure patterns and new opportunity for the rural poor. The reform's three phases currently affect 26 per cent of the rural poor and 22 per cent of the farmland. To date, Phase I of the land reform has transformed 469 large farm properties into 517 cooperatives, benefiting more than 31,000 cooperative members. Under Phase III, more than 240,000 acres of farmland have been granted to 65,782 beneficiaries, who were formerly tenant farmers or sharecroppers. Under Phase II of the reform, landowners have until December 1986 to sell properties in excess of 605 acres or face expropriation without prior compensation.

Phase I (properties in excess of 1,250 acres): A major reorganization of ISTA, the Salvadoran government's land reform institute, was undertaken in 1985 in order to focus its activities largely on land acquisition and titling. This reorganization came after President Duarte ordered ISTA to resolve remaining titling and compensation cases by the end of 1986. The result has been a near doubling of the rate at which cooperative titles have been issued by ISTA, compared to the year before the reorganization.

Two hundred and nine professional managers and accountants have been placed on cooperatives to date; forty-one since the previous reporting period.

The single most important factor affecting the financial viability of Phase I cooperatives is the agrarian reform debt. As many as 95 per cent of the Phase I cooperatives are unable to meet their debt service obligations on an estimated $800 million in agrarian land debt, emergency credits, and accumulated investment and production loans. In this regard, the Salvadoran government's Advisory Council on Agrarian Reform continues to explore possible means for the government of El Salvador to ease the cooperatives' debt burden by reducing interest rates on the debt, extending the grace and amortization periods, approving a moratorium on payments for 1980-81 emergency production credit, and generally improving the liquidity of cooperative financial accounts.

The government of El Salvador is also working to increase the independent status of Phase I cooperatives as private enterprises through enhancement of beneficiary rights and by strengthening the roles and responsibilities of the beneficiaries in the management of their enterprises.

U.S. legislation encourages the use of local currency for agrarian reform activities including the titling/compensation process. The 1986 economic support fund (ESF) balance-of-payments program currently under negotiation should result in the government of El Salvador making available up to 200 million colones ($40 million), including 140 million colones from ESF local currency generations ($28 million), to pay obligations due to former land-owners in the land transfer process. The estimated cost of the cash portion of agreed, but still unpaid, compensation settlements, plus interest and redemption payments due on agrarian bonds, is estimated at $88 million.

During the reporting period, the Phase I implementing agency ISTA provided compensation to former owners of forty-two properties, raising the number of properties compensated to 329. ISTA issued final titles on forty-five more cooperatives for a total of 141.

The armed conflict continues to affect the reform cooperatives. As many as fifty cooperatives have been totally or partially abandoned, and others have incurred direct and indirect losses because of the war. As long as the violence continues, it represents an additional obstacle to the financial well-being of the reform cooperatives.

Phase II (properties between 605 and 1,250 acres): In accordance with the Salvadoran Constitution of December 1983, land-owners have until December 1986 to sell land in excess of 605 acres or holdings over the limit can be expropriated without prior compensation. Approximately 41,000 acres of land may become available under Phase II private land sales. While implementing legislation has not been submitted to the Legislative Assembly, land in excess of the 605-acre limit is being bought and sold on the open market.

Phase III (land to the tiller, up to seventeen acres): Recently passed changes in El Salvador's Registry Law should accelerate the Phase III titling process by the National Agricultural Land Financing Institute, FINATA. With definitive titles, beneficiaries should be more able and motivated to secure credit and technical assistance resulting in increased productivity and standards of living for agrarian reform beneficiaries.

Between the 1982-83 and 1984-85 crop years, much progress has occurred on Phase III lands resulting in increased production yields and investment. Specifically, beneficiary land holdings have increased by 18.3 per cent, fixed assets have increased by 200 per cent, indicating that there are profits to reinvest and incentives to expand production of Phase III lands resulting from land security. In addition, basic grain production increased by over 200 per cent and is now equal to one-quarter of the national production. Use of hired labor increased 400 per cent during this period.

During the reporting period, an additional 224 provisional titles were issued under the Phase III program, bringing total provisional titles issued to 65,900. Also, 2,341 definitive titles were issued for a total of 17,569. An additional 310 former land-owners received compensation for their properties, for a total of 1,622.

Part Four

Nicaragua

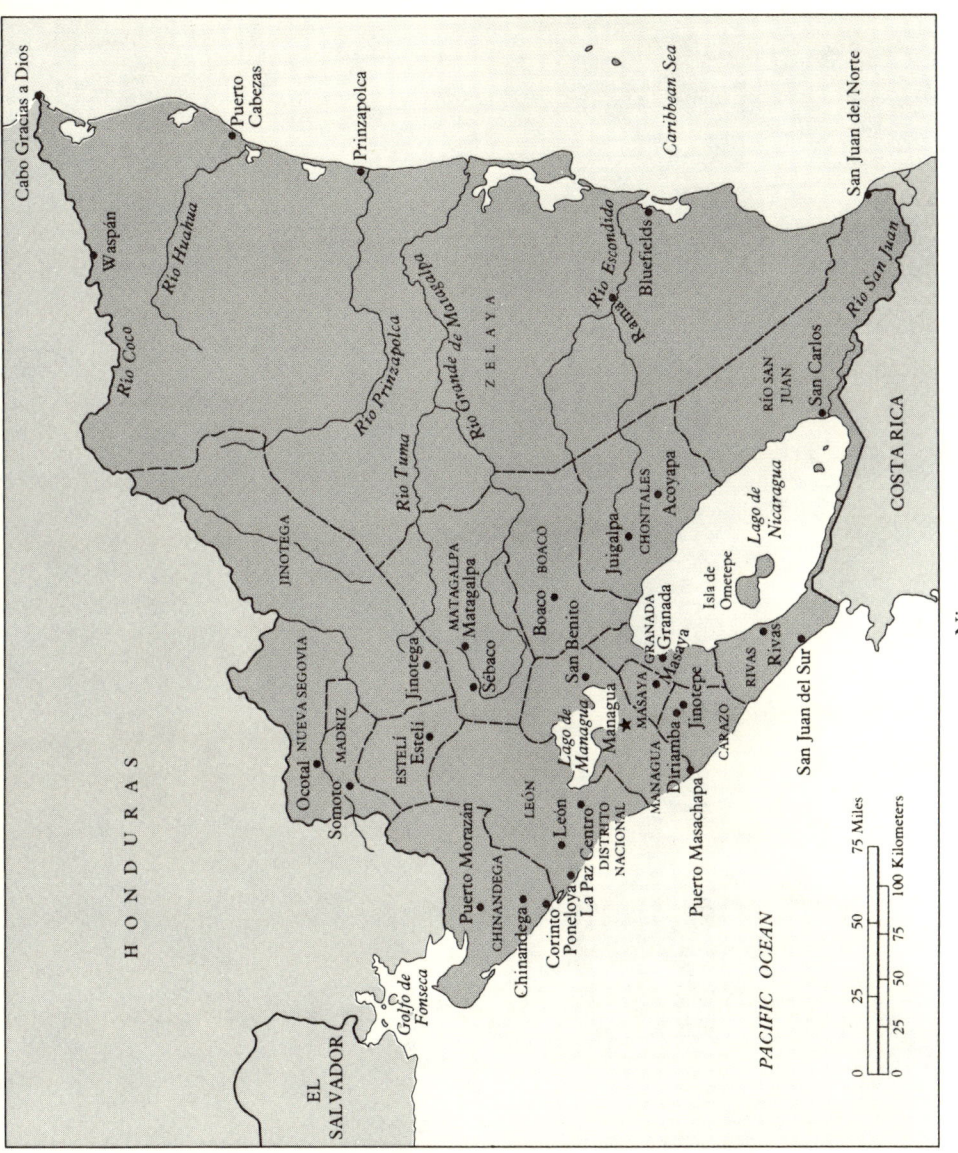

Chronology

1909	Dictator José Santos Zelaya overthrown. Chaos and instability follow, leading to U.S. financial and military intervention (1912-33).
1927	Peace accord among fighting factions provides basis for U.S. occupation and subsequent elections. General Augusto C. Sandino refuses to accept peace accord and leads guerrilla force against U.S. Marines.
1933	General Anastasio Somoza García named director of new "nonpartisan" National Guard. U.S. Marines withdrawn.
1934	Sandino assassinated by National Guardsman; Somoza seizes power.
1937	Somoza officially becomes president.
1956	Somoza assassinated; sons Luis and Anastasio Jr. continue family domination.
1961	Sandinista National Liberation Front (FSLN) founded.
1967	Anastasio Somoza Debayle elected president.
1972	Earthquake devastates Managua; Somoza's mishandling of crisis and of international relief funds increases antipathy to regime.
1974	Election fraud ensures Somoza's reelection to six-year term.
1977	Popular unrest intensifies. U.S. suspends credits to Somoza government through votes at World Bank and Inter-American Development Bank.
1978	U.S. and Organization of American States fail in mediation attempts; U.S. suspends military aid to Somoza.
1979	Marxist FSLN (Sandinista National Liberation Front) supported by other opposition fronts overthrows Somoza.
1980	President Carter suspends economic aid to Sandinista government because of its arms shipments to rebels in El Salvador.
1983	Pope John Paul II visits Managua; his public Mass is disrupted by Sandinistas.

1984 After major opposition leaders object to Sandinista restrictions on campaigning and withdraw, Daniel Ortega elected president.

1985 President Ortega visits Moscow immediately after a vote against contra aid in U.S. Congress; angry Congress approves aid in response.

1986 Radio Católica closed by Sandinistas.

After U.S. Congress approves $100 million in aid to contras, Sandinistas close last independent newspaper, *La Prensa*, expel Catholic bishop Pablo Antonio Vega, and bar return of Cardinal Obando y Bravo's assistant to the country.

19. Somoza, Sandino, and the United States

By MARK FALCOFF

Focus
"If the history of U.S. relations with Nicaragua over the period 1912 to 1979 establishes anything, it is that on the few occasions when it tried, Washington was unable to make that country behave like a democracy—even in the limited Latin American sense of the term." Mark Falcoff says that a careful study of U.S.-Nicaraguan relations over the past half century is called for. This research will not be helpful, however, if its main purpose "is to excuse the conduct of the present revolutionary regime in Nicaragua as a wholly justifiable reaction to past U.S. policies there."

In Falcoff's view, the main problem in Nicaragua has been not so much the exercise of U.S. power there as the lack of it. He traces the complex web of events in and outside Nicaragua and finds many American errors, but not as clear a pattern of U.S. behavior as is normally assumed. The United States supported the Somozas only fitfully, usually under the pressure of external events. The Somozas *claimed* strong American backing and were able to use the claim to their advantage. Against the accepted view, Falcoff maintains that "had Washington been able fully to control its putative 'alliance' with Managua, Nicaragua's political history would have been vastly happier—for the immense majority of its people."

According to the author, events developed as they did for the most part because the United States was much of the time preoccupied with weightier events: Nicaragua was only "a very small part of the international picture

... and at best only a modest amount of foreign policy energy could be devoted to it." World War II gave the Somoza dynasty a chance to consolidate its power.

Americans have a strong desire to be fair in their foreign policy, and that is why many commentators on the current situation often refer to our past real or alleged misdeeds in Nicaragua. Falcoff argues that because of this tendency, "it is as much a matter of public policy as moral house-cleaning to set the record straight."

Mark Falcoff, now a professional staff member with the Senate Foreign Relations Committee, was a resident fellow at the American Enterprise Institute when he wrote this article.

THE EMERGENCE in Nicaragua of a regime hostile to the United States and allied with Cuba and the Soviet Union was bound to send many Americans to their history books. Yet two quite different purposes can and do motivate such exercises. One might hope to learn from past errors, with a view to preventing "other Nicaraguas" in the future. The scope of that effort is a very large one, with ample room for honest differences of opinion over precisely where U.S. policies went off track—and what might have been done to get them back on. No one can doubt that a careful, dispassionate examination of U.S.-Nicaraguan relations over the past half-century and more is in order.

The other "course of study" is quite different, in both spirit and substance. Its effect, if not intent, is to excuse the conduct of the present revolutionary regime in Nicaragua as a wholly justifiable reaction to past U.S. policies there. Some of what has been written under this rubric tries to pass itself off as history, when it is really nothing more than the manipulation of past events (or pseudoevents) in the service of some very current agendas. Fragments of this approach can be found in declarations by academic caucuses, in the editorials of the prestige and religious press, and even in pronouncements by members of Congress. In its purest form, this line of argument was stated by Richard Fagen in *Foreign Policy* magazine:

> In 1912 after three years of unsuccessful attempts by Washington to stabilize Nicaragua by political and diplomatic means ... the U.S. Marines were landed. At stake were the outstanding loans of U.S. and European creditors, ... also the possibility of canal-building rights through southern Nicaragua....
>
> Only in 1933 did the occupying troops finally depart, leaving in their stead the U.S.-created National Guard headed by General Anastasio Somoza García. For the next forty-six years the Somoza family never relinquished direct control of the Guard, and seldom gave up the presidency....
>
> The senior Somoza ruled Nicaragua as a personal fiefdom, with the Guard as his private army and enforcer and with the continuing support and approval of the United States.
>
> From the outset, the dynasty was welcomed in Washington as a solid pillar of pro-American and anti-Communist strength in an otherwise

---

Reprinted by permission of the author from the Fall 1983 issue of *This World*.

troubled area.... Until the early 1970s ... the Washington-Managua alliance seemed unshakable....

So close was the identification of Washington's interest with the continued rule of the Somozas, however, that little actually changed ... until the Carter administration took office.

On the other hand, the new administration also feared any alternative to Somoza that would not be firmly controlled by the most conservative of anti-Somoza forces. Meanwhile, Somoza's powerful friends in the U.S. Congress and elsewhere were doing everything in their power—in the name of anti-Communism and hemispheric stability—to insure that the four-decades-old policy of U.S. support for the dynasty continued.

It is hard to imagine a more indiscriminate indictment; it spares no President since William Howard Taft, and very pointedly includes Jimmy Carter. Admittedly, this is the way many Nicaraguans—by no means all of them Sandinistas—have seen the history of their country. However, insofar as the United States is concerned, it happens to be quite false. The facts are these: The U.S. intervention in 1912 was *not* principally inspired by the motives offered; Somoza did *not* rule with the "continuing support and approval of the United States"; the dynasty was *not* welcomed by Washington "from the outset ... as a solid pillar of pro-American and anti-Communist strength"; and the Carter administration did *not* insist on restricting the alternatives to Somoza to "the most conservative of anti-Somoza forces," unless, of course, one chooses to label anyone who is not a Marxist a conservative, and an extreme conservative at that.

What Fagen rather disingenuously withholds from his readers—and what many who repeat his argument in a watered-down form simply do not know—is the vastly complicated dynamics of Nicaraguan politics. This prevents us from reaching the conclusion that typically overwhelms those who bother to study the subject: that the problem in Nicaragua has not been U.S. power so much as a lack of it—an inability to shape developments there according to our own values and preferences. For when all due tribute has been paid to Nicaraguan nationalism and the right of self-determination, it is still true that had Washington been able fully to control its putative "alliance" with Managua, Nicaragua's political history would have been vastly happier—for the immense majority of its people, if not precisely for the particular political sect of which Fagen happens to approve.

In the present context, the history of U.S.-Nicaraguan relations is more than a matter of mere academic interest. The reason is quite simple. Many countries are capable of formulating and executing foreign policy without excessive reference to their national conscience. The United States, however, is not one of them. If we conclude that we have inflicted a great wrong on a small and defenseless people, we invariably ask ourselves, "Who are *we* to criticize the way its present leaders put things right?," or even assert, "We're just getting what we deserve." History thus used and abused leads to guilt, guilt to immobility. That is why on the subject of our present relations with Nicaragua some commentators make recurrent reference to the past—or to what they imagine the past to have been. That is also why it is as much a matter of public policy as of moral house-cleaning to set the record straight.

Pre-1912: Seeking Stability and Solvency

During the nineteenth century, U.S. interest in Nicaragua was dominated by a peculiar fact of geography—the existence of a huge volcanic lake comprehending approximately a quarter of the country's breadth—that made Nicaragua a logical site for an isthmus canal. A short trench incised from the lake's western shore to the Pacific, and a somewhat longer one in combination with the San Juan River to the Atlantic port of Greytown, would have produced an inter-oceanic route, and at a cost presumably far lower than at any other point of the isthmus, since elsewhere total excavation would be required. Moreover, long before the capital and technology necessary to produce this miracle were readily available, a shipping and passenger service across Nicaragua was in operation through a combination of steamer and stagecoach under the patronage of Commodore Cornelius Vanderbilt.

Vanderbilt's experiment was of short duration—begun in 1851, destroyed in 1855 by a flooding of the San Juan River, and supplanted by the Panama Railway the following year. The idea of a Nicaraguan canal nonetheless persisted into the early years of the present century. A commission created by the U.S. Congress reported in 1897 that it was technically feasible, and President McKinley even recommended its construction in his annual message to Congress in 1898. For reasons extraneous to the present narrative, the Congress decided in 1902 to build the canal in Panama instead. Construction began in 1904, and the facility opened ten years later. Thus in 1912, when Marines first landed in Nicaragua, the question of an inter-oceanic route had already been settled—elsewhere.

With the new route fully operational in Panama, U.S. policy in Nicaragua became virtually undistinguishable from its policy elsewhere in the region—to promote the basic stability and solvency of governments. Lacking both, these tiny nations (and therefore the approaches to the canal itself) might fall into the hands of some hostile power. Outright annexation was thought unlikely, but as Africa and China had recently demonstrated, there were other ways in which European powers could establish naval and strategic—not to say commercial—presences without the full encumbrances of formal colonialism.

In this connection the internal political life of the Central American republics (and Haiti and the Dominican Republic in the Caribbean) offered ample grounds for concern. Perennial outbreaks of revolution endangered the lives and property of European residents, whose home navies were wont to demand pecuniary damages in an extremely forceful fashion. On one occasion German gunboats even threatened to destroy an entire complex of government buildings in the Haitian capital of Port-au-Prince if $30,000 were not collected within a matter of hours. Political instability also provoked serious interruptions in economic life, making it impossible for the states to service their foreign debts. Default was an open invitation for European creditors to seize customs houses and port facilities, as prologue—many Americans and Central Americans feared—to a more permanent political presence.

Factions in Conflict

Thus at the heart of the region's international problems were an economic backwardness and a political backwardness that reinforced each other. Ostensibly, public life was a contest between "Liberal" and "Conservative" parties; in reality, it was a conflict among contending clans, families, and their retainers—typically organized along regional or provincial lines. Because the resources at stake were so scarce, the struggle was one in which quarter was neither asked nor given. No ruling party could afford the luxury of losing an election, and so its opponent was left with no other recourse than the crucible of civil war. "It too often resorted to savage reprisals when it came to power," diplomat-historian Dana C. Munro has written. "The cruelties practiced on political enemies engendered factional hatreds which were passed on from father to son and helped to keep the revolutionary spirit alive."

The State Department archives and also the published correspondence found in successive volumes of *Foreign Relations of the United States* for the years 1898 through at least 1914 unambiguously establish that in Central America and the Caribbean, U.S. statesmanship was obsessed with the search for policy instruments capable of breaking this vicious circle. All manner of devices were tried—"preventive intervention" under the Roosevelt Corollary to the Monroe Doctrine, customs receiverships, debt refundings. After World War I, the emphasis shifted to non-recognition of governments that had come to power by force, and an attempt to replace private, party armies with a non-partisan constabulary.

None of these mechanisms were warmly appreciated by the governments concerned. Nor were they particularly effective—at least in the middle and longer term. But they were not inspired by uniquely sordid or selfish motives. The United States did not land troops or seize customs houses principally to protect its investors and bankers, for the rather undramatic reason that before 1914 U.S. economic involvement in the area (apart from Cuba) was insignificant, and the major creditors remained to an overwhelming degree European. Doubtless such considerations existed, but they were unquestionably minor, Munro concludes, "compared with the desire to avert the danger that disorder would invite European intervention."

THE ERA OF INTERVENTION: 1912-33

Nicaragua was a particularly notable example of the failure of U.S. policy to achieve its announced goals—and for means and ends to stray rather farther from each other than proportion and good sense should have tolerated. Nonetheless, U.S. military intervention there must be divided conceptually into two quite distinct periods. The first began in 1912, when Marines were landed to stabilize a country torn by civil conflict (in the process, shoring up an incumbent Conservative government that was unpopular and probably unrepresentative even in the narrow terms of the day). It ended in 1927 with the Peace of Tipitapa, when the United States, in the person of Secretary of War Henry Stimson, negotiated a truce between Conservative and Liberal politico-military chieftains.

These years represent opposite ends of a learning curve for U.S. policymakers and diplomats. At the beginning, reliance was indeed placed upon force alone. But by 1927 certain realities of Nicaraguan life managed to impose themselves, fostering a serious effort to address what today would be called the "structural" causes of instability. The first of these realities was that the Liberal party, supposedly less friendly to the United States than the Conservatives, could not permanently be denied access to power. Second, since no defeated party could ever accept the results of falsified elections, the Marines would have to remain for several years to assure the integrity of elections. And finally, since no victorious government could escape an armed challenge from its defeated rivals, private military and paramilitary forces would have to be disarmed and disbanded. In their place the armed Marines would train a non-partisan constabulary to preserve public order once the U.S. expeditionary force had departed. In effect, the United States proposed to give Nicaragua the national army it had never possessed.

From 1927 to 1933 the United States tried to put these hard-earned lessons into practice. The process turned out to be so nettlesome that even if the Depression had not eventually intervened to force a drastic reduction of overseas commitments, by 1933 Washington would in all likelihood have been ready to withdraw its troops from Nicaragua. One very large problem was the refusal of dissident elements of the Liberal party to recognize the Peace of Tipitapa. Led by General Augusto C. Sandino, they retained their arms to pursue a guerrilla campaign against U.S. and Nicaraguan forces for six years. Although Sandino's movement was centered largely in the mountain fastness of Nueva Segovia, in the northwestern part of the country, at several points it managed to threaten key cities, including toward the very end the capital, Managua.

The Sandino Legacy

Today Sandino is a brooding presence in Nicaragua — mutely peering down from dozens of walls, with others speaking on his behalf. But his real identity remains enshrouded in myth and misunderstanding. The Coolidge administration repeatedly referred to him and his followers as "bandits," which was patently untrue. But neither was he the Marxist social revolutionary depicted both by U.S. Secretary of State Frank Kellogg and, many years later (in a curious coincidence of needs), by a Nicaraguan government bearing his name.

In reality Sandino was an adventurer, a born leader of men, and a clever Nicaraguan politician much given to self-dramatization. But he was also what he often represented himself to be — a man of principle, forced to defend his country against what he regarded as a humiliation of its national sovereignty. From the very beginning he promised to lay down his arms the moment the last Marine departed Nicaragua — and he kept his word. Even more significantly, Sandino refused to be used by forces extraneous to his cause. Thus, although for a time in the late 1920s he received rhetorical (and some small material) support from both the U.S. and Mexican Communist parties, he steadfastly refused to follow Moscow's dictates, and even denied that a social revolution was necessary in Nicaragua. This eventually led him to sever personal and political relations with Farabundo Martí, a Salvadoran Communist who for a time served as the Comintern's envoy to Sandino's forces.

Although Sandino "won" only a few of his encounters with the Marines, his constant hit-and-run tactics succeeded in making Washington's policy of pacification in Nicaragua very expensive—in blood and treasure, as well as in Latin American and even domestic U.S. opinion. This made all the more urgent the formation of a professional military force in Nicaragua to take over from the Marines, but that was the other large problem. For neither party in Nicaragua was particularly anxious to have a constabulary above politics—were such a thing even possible. Eventually Washington compromised with this reality as well, accepting a bipartisan officer corps in the hope of forestalling what it feared—and what eventually came to pass: a force led by politicians of the party in power.

Formation of the National Guard

The National Guard of Nicaragua was thus organized under the twin pressures of time and circumstance. At first the infant force had American Marines as officers, but by 1931 and 1932 most of these had been replaced by Nicaraguans quickly trained at the new La Loma Military Academy. Since most of the enlisted men were drawn from Nicaragua's underclass, there was no "training up" into the commissioned ranks. Instead, officer candidates were drawn from civilian life, which made their indoctrination into non-partisanship a rather quixotic exercise.

The frantic search for reliable professionals to direct the Guard led the Americans to Anastasio Somoza. A Liberal general and politician, Somoza had studied at business school in the United States, and though of undistinguished social origins, had managed to marry into an aristocratic Nicaraguan family. During the 1920s he had been a consul in Costa Rica, deputy minister of foreign affairs, and, finally, minister of foreign affairs. During the last phase of the Marine occupation he was named chief director-designate of the National Guard. "The last appointment was partly due to the patronage of the American minister in Nicaragua," Neil

Macaulay writes in *The Sandino Affair*. "The minister and his wife were impressed by Somoza's absolute mastery of the American language, and were captivated by his effervescent personality." And, he adds in an acid afternote, "Mrs. Hanna thought Tacho Somoza a smooth tango and rumba dancer." Somoza was also, however, an experienced, disciplined public official who put in long hours, scrupulously kept appointments, and in general impressed the Americans with his industry and serious attention to detail. The decision to make him director of the National Guard was far from illogical.

SANDINO, SACASA, AND SOMOZA: 1933-36

When the last American Marine departed in 1933, the deeper realities of Nicaraguan politics rapidly floated to the surface, sweeping away what positive legacies remained of U.S. involvement. Things had begun well enough: the elections of 1932, supervised by the Marines, were the freest and fairest in the nation's history. And shortly after his inauguration on New Year's Day 1933, President Juan Sacasa received Sandino in Managua to work out the details of a peace accord. Sandino agreed to "morally support" Sacasa's administration, in exchange for which he was allowed to keep a small remnant of his private army, and his followers were assured of preferential employment on future public works projects. Disbandment of Sandino's main force then followed, and the rebel general himself returned home to Nueva Segovia.

Almost immediately it became clear that General Somoza and the National Guard constituted a new kind of threat to peace and order in Nicaragua. Relations between Somoza and Sandino—never good in the best of times—rapidly deteriorated as Guard units harassed the guerrilla leader's former followers. And as early as November 1933, the American Legation in Managua began to receive information that Somoza was planning a coup to oust President Sacasa. In February 1934, Sandino came to Managua to discuss his differences with both the government and the Guard; a few evenings later he was brutally murdered by Somoza minions shortly after leaving a dinner with Sacasa in the presidential compound. Two years later, Somoza deposed Sacasa and seized the presidency for himself.

No one can dispute that these exact events could never have taken place in Nicaragua without U.S. intervention in 1912. On the other hand, the record is clear also on this: there was no direct relationship between the

United States and the murder of Sandino, the overthrow of Sacasa, or even the creation of the Somoza dictatorship. None of these events figured in U.S. plans or policies, nor—even more importantly—were these events greeted by the State Department with satisfaction or even tacit approval. What is true is that beginning with the murder of Sandino, Somoza and, later, his sons and political heirs habitually *represented* their actions as having prior U.S. assent. For different reasons, both opponents and supporters of the regime found it convenient to accept this explanation, and both tirelessly propagated it in various forms for four decades.

A Shift in U.S. Policy

What many Nicaraguans failed to notice—and what Somoza quickly learned to exploit—was a decided shift in U.S. policy just about the time that these events were unfolding. Over a rather long period Washington gradually recognized that constitutional democracy of the Anglo-Saxon type was not exportable to Nicaragua, or, for that matter, to Haiti, the Dominican Republic, or Mexico; and further, that attempts to impose constitutional democracy in tropical lands were both costly and counterproductive. Despotism and military rule seemed the inevitable fruits of the Caribbean environment, and, U.S. officials reasoned, we had best stop attempting to contravene the experience of history. As Arthur Bliss Lane, U.S. minister to Nicaragua 1934–35, confided to a friend toward the end of his mission:

> The people who created the G.N. [National Guard] had no adequate understanding of the psychology of the people here. Otherwise they would not have bequeathed Nicaragua with an instrument to blast constitutional procedure off the map. Did it ever occur to the eminent statesmen who created the G.N. that personal ambition lurks in the human breast, even in Nicaragua? In my opinion, it is one of the sorriest examples on our part of our inability to understand that we should not meddle in other people's affairs.

Of course, it was far easier to reach such conclusions in 1935, informed not only by the wisdom of hindsight but also by the shift in economic and naval power in the area, than in 1912. For after World War I, the threat of European intervention in the Caribbean had virtually disappeared, and political instability—far from being, as it once had been, an "international" problem—could now be regarded simply as a local matter. Somoza was no improvement over what the United States had sought to replace, but by the time he seized power, Washington had virtually abandoned its attempts to reform the Nicaraguans. Having struggled so hard to get off the treadmill of intervention, the United States—beset by the manifold ills of the Depression—was not about to get back on it.

Somoza also benefited indirectly from a broader change in U.S policy toward revolutionary governments, or more precisely, governments which emerged from the extra-constitutional use of force. Before about 1930 Washington had attempted to discourage violent political change in the area by withholding recognition from *de facto* regimes. In 1907 and again in 1923 it had even sponsored treaties—to which all Central American governments were signatories—to this effect.

Over time it became apparent that the punitive use of diplomatic recognition put the United States in a serious bind. As historian William Kamman puts it, "Washington had to do more than just decide which government was in control, it had to determine the legitimacy of [that] government." This meant, perforce, that if the only regimes worthy of recognition were those which issued from the ballot box, then to have diplomatic relations at all with many Central American republics, one would have to insure that elections occurred in the first place. This led almost unswervingly to military intervention, with all of the attendant unpleasantries. It also provoked much nationalist resentment throughout Latin America, where the United States was not acknowledged to have the right to determine the appropriate form of political change for its neighbors.

The Estrada Doctrine

On this subject the Mexicans were particularly vehement, and in 1930 that country's foreign minister, Genaro Estrada, went so far as to call grants of recognition "an insulting practice." According to what became known as the Estrada Doctrine, only *states* could be recognized; when a new government came to power—by whatever means—its *bona fides* was not subject to the value judgments of others. Of course, the Mexicans had in mind their own revolution of 1910, which was very different from the upheavals in Nicaragua, since it went far beyond a periodic shift in the fortunes of contending elites. That upheaval had swept away an entire host of social and economic institutions, and in the process inflicted serious damage—both physical and legal—upon foreign property and investment, much of it belonging to American nationals. For nearly a decade Washington attempted to influence events there by withholding (or granting) recognition to the various governments that succeeded the dictator Porfirio Díaz. Extrapolating from their own experience, the Mexicans declared conditional use of recognition an offense to sovereignty and the right of weaker peoples to self-determination.

Other Latin American nations picked up this theme, and it quickly became part of a package of demands for "non-intervention" thrust at the United States during the Havana Pan American Conference in 1928 — the first such meeting at which American delegates were forced to confront a serious and unified opposition. The events of that meeting plunged senior State Department officials into a mood of sober reappraisal, and during the next four or five years there was a gradual reconsideration of U.S. policy. Matters were helped along by the coming of the Great Depression, which suddenly made the United States more attentive to its image in Latin America, whose markets — some New Deal planners imagined — held the key to domestic economic recovery. Under both the Hoover and Roosevelt administrations, there was a gradual turnaround generally associated with the Good Neighbor Policy. The Marines were withdrawn not only from Nicaragua but from Haiti as well, and at the Montevideo meeting of American states in 1933, and above all at the Buenos Aires Conference in 1936, the United States definitively renounced intervention as an instrument in its relations with other American states.

Meanwhile, in 1934 the Central American nations quietly abandoned their commitments under the 1923 accords to withhold recognition from *de facto* regimes and subscribed instead to the Estrada Doctrine. Between the Montevideo and Buenos Aires conferences, the United States followed suit; given the circumstances, it had no choice. But in some quarters of the State Department, serious doubts persisted to the very end. One official pointed out, for example, that even if non-recognition had not succeeded in preventing revolutions, unconditional recognition would surely encourage them. It would also reinforce the temptation to back "any strong man who came along," with the attendant risk of identifying the United States too closely with a tyrant who would eventually fall. By 1935 or 1936, such apprehensions were overwhelmed by other considerations. The United States signed the Buenos Aires accords, tacitly accepted the Estrada Doctrine, won plaudits from "liberal" Latin American publicists and statesmen, and indirectly strengthened strongman regimes, such as that emerging in Nicaragua.

The Somoza Dynasty: 1936–79

Somoza seized the presidency of Nicaragua in 1936 and remained in office through successive "elections" in 1939 and 1947. He had just accepted his party's nomination for yet another term when he fell victim to an assassin's bullet in 1956. His tenure, by far the longest in Nicaraguan history, was made possible in the first instance by the National Guard. Unlike the Liberal and Conservative armies it replaced, the Guard was more or less professionally organized and equipped, and because it retained a monopoly of arms, there was no force in the country capable of challenging it. In this sense alone Somoza was Nicaragua's first "modern" president. What was striking and unique, however, was the way he adapted modern institutions—not just a professional constabulary, but eventually a rationalized administration, a central bank, public works, and economic development generally—to suit his dynastic needs.

The Somoza regime could thus be described as a patrimonial police state—but it was also something else: a peculiar kind of social revolution. Before 1936, Nicaraguan politicians tended to be gentlemen of property and refinement, recruited from the land-owners and professional class of the country's two major provincial cities, León (for the Liberals) and Granada (for Conservatives). Their views on political and social issues were probably no larger or more responsible than Somoza's, but theirs was necessarily a more impersonal approach to the business of government. Then, too, precisely because Nicaragua had been so unstable before 1936, opportunities in public service or diplomacy had been passed around rather generously, if a bit sporadically. Now all the lines of political ascent ran directly through one man, his family, and their retainers. As the regime consolidated itself over decades, it absorbed an increasing share of the perquisites of power—bribes, kickbacks, and concessions. Corruption became less democratic—and therefore, more hateful.

This was a change; so indeed was the kind of man with whom the dons of León and Granada had to deal. Crude and brutal, Somoza possessed a sort of raffish charm that captivated some foreign admirers but represented for the more traditional political class in Nicaragua the triumph of *mala educación*. The people he brought into government with him—with rare exceptions—were of equally undistinguished antecedents or personal qualities. If the U.S. legation in Managua held a somewhat jaundiced view of the opposition during Somoza's early years of power, it was partly because memories of the old system were so fresh, and partly because it was too easy to evaluate the claims of displaced aristocrats at their true value. These men were not anxious to restore democracy to Nicaragua, merely to get back on the take (which was what *they* meant by democracy). The United States never accepted Somoza's charges that his opponents were agents of Nazism (before and during World War II) or Communism (thereafter). But it was not about to land Marines to return things to the *status quo ante* 1927.

U.S.-Somoza Ups and Downs

Over the twenty-year dictatorship of the elder Somoza, relations between the United States and Nicaragua were far less cordial—or even consistent— than the term "Washington-Managua alliance" suggests. During the years 1936 to 1939, for example, U.S. diplomats maintained a discreet distance from the regime and repeatedly turned down its most frequent request— for military assistance. What suddenly brought Washington around was World War II. Somoza himself was invited to Washington, and eventually Nicaragua received $1.3 million in equipment under Lend-Lease. (In exchange, the United States obtained temporary rights to a naval base in Corinto.)

Once the conflict ended, however, the United States pointedly refused Somoza's plea for allotments on a more continuing basis. One Pentagon official pointedly voiced the War Department's determination not to "burden the country with armaments," and added gratuitously that "military missions from foreign countries" in such places as Nicaragua "should be avoided at all costs." A further attempt by Somoza to purchase arms on a cash basis was blocked by the State Department. "Any arms which we might ship to him at this time," the relevant memorandum read, "could only be taken by him, the Nicaraguan public, and by the other republics of Central America and of the hemisphere as a demonstration of complete support for his plans." This impression "would not only be erroneous, but extremely embarrassing."

In 1947, when Somoza prepared to run for "re-election," Assistant Secretary of State Nelson Rockefeller called in Somoza's ambassador in Washington to impress upon him the Truman administration's acute displeasure, and warned that such an eventuality "might create difficulties ... which would seriously affect relations between the two countries." To show that it meant business, the State Department once again blocked the sale of weapons to the regime, and even managed to pressure Canada and Great Britain into joining the embargo.

This was a nimble procedure, but Somoza was nimbler still. He withdrew from the race in favor of a puppet candidate, Dr. Leopoldo Argüello, who was "elected" in the usual fashion. Somoza, of course, retained control of the Guard. The opposition in Nicaragua tried to persuade the United States to refuse recognition to the new government, but Washington opted for a different course, partly because the new president had quietly assured the American ambassador that he intended to be his own man.

Once in office Argüello did in fact make serious attempts to curb Somoza's power. The two men fell to quarreling over who was in charge — of the Guard and of the country. President Argüello eventually demanded Somoza's resignation and (in a fit of almost inconceivable daring) his departure from the country. Somoza's response was to overthrow his own putative puppet.

The United States, abruptly departing from its own recent adherence to the Estrada Doctrine, now withheld recognition. Even a crude attempt by Somoza to exploit anti-Communism (in a new "constitution" that also made it easier for the United States to establish military bases in Nicaragua) left the State Department unmoved. But Washington changed course some months later, when other nations in the area either had recognized Somoza or were preparing to do so, and when it became clear that any sanctions short of actual military intervention were bound to prove ineffective. (For instance, having refused to sell the dictator warplanes, the United States found it impossible to block his acquisition of B-24 bombers from Brazil.)

Guatemala: The Arbenz Regime

Then, once again, international events converged to bring about a thaw in the diplomatic chill between Somoza and the United States. In 1944 a revolution in Guatemala had brought to power a generation of young officers and intellectuals imbued with vaguely leftist ideals. By 1952, however, under President Jacobo Arbenz, the principal prop of the Guatemalan regime had become the Communist-led Labor Federation.

There is still considerable controversy over the exact nature of the relationship between the Arbenz government and the Soviet bloc. At the time, however, it was perceived by Washington as the opening wedge for Soviet penetration of the Caribbean, and operatives of the Central Intelligence Agency, working with right-wing Guatemalan exiles, staged a coup that overturned Arbenz in 1954.

By cooperating with the CIA in the Guatemalan affair—at least to the extent of acting as a conduit of arms to exile forces—Somoza was able to neutralize some of the opposition to him in the State Department. On the other hand, he still could not obtain approval of his plans to purchase heavy military equipment from the United States; he circumvented the continued American embargo by turning to Sweden for P-51 fighters. Further, when he began to menace Costa Rica with his new weapons, Washington promptly dispatched Navy planes from the Canal Zone to convince Somoza that—whatever unpleasantries might have been necessary in the case of Guatemala—it would not tolerate his aggressive conduct against a democratic neighbor.

The Next Somoza Generation

After Somoza's assassination in 1956, the regime moved into a qualitatively different phase. It was still undemocratic and dynastic, but it became more complex and even—at least to 1972—more popular. The fallen dictator's two sons, Luis and Anastasio Jr. (who was called "Tachito"), were forced to share power. Luis was elected by the Nicaraguan congress to fill out the unexpired portion of his father's term, and "re-elected" in 1957. Tachito, who had been sent to American military schools and West Point, assumed control of the National Guard.

Since the two Somozas had very different notions of how to discharge their legacy, they were continuously at odds until Luis's death in 1967 ended the rivalry and left Tachito in complete control. Unlike his brother, Luis Somoza was a man of some political imagination, who envisioned for Nicaragua a modified "Mexican" solution. The Somozas would retain, perhaps even increase, their power and wealth, but the formal leadership of the country would devolve into the hands of a succession of puppet presidents. In 1959 Luis even restored to the Nicaraguan constitution an earlier article prohibiting consecutive presidential terms and also succession to the presidency of any relative of the incumbent. In 1963 he selected Dr. René Schick to be the first of a new series of chief executives.

Luis also believed in governing with a somewhat less heavy hand than his father (or, as time would show, his brother). Restrictions on the press and on opposition political activity were loosened; the role of the Nicaraguan military was played down and its budget actually reduced. Some new programs of economic development—financed, to be sure, with foreign loans, and often subsidizing inefficient Somoza family industries—nonetheless created thousands of new jobs and therefore broadened the regime's base of support. These years also coincided with the rise of Castro in Cuba, the Bay of Pigs invasion (1961), and the missile crisis (1962), so that in addition to some marginal political improvement within Nicaragua, the Kennedy administration had other, more pressing reasons for dealing with the Somozas. It was just about this time that the United States began a serious program of military assistance to Nicaragua.

Even before the end of Schick's term, however, it was clear that a more impersonal form of Somocismo would not work. Schick attempted to rein in Tachito and the Guard as long as he dared; thereafter, he lapsed into impotence and alcoholism. In 1966 Tachito finally arranged his own election to the presidency, and few observers doubted that he meant to remain in office for life. It was precisely this determination to withdraw his brother's modest concessions to pluralism that aroused so much resentment in the opposition, and even in the Liberal party, to which Somoza nominally belonged. At the same time, there was much resentment of the tendency to enlarge the family's financial holdings at the expense of the state and other entrepreneurs.

1972: The Beginning of the End

During Tachito's first term, a boom in international commodity prices and the ready availability of foreign credit muted some of the opposition to his rule, even to his fraudulent "re-election" in 1971. The real breaking point came in 1972, as the result of an earthquake that devastated the city of Managua. During the first critical days of the calamity, Guard discipline virtually disintegrated, and troops openly looted stores and warehouses. (Many of the stolen provisions later appeared on the Guard-dominated black market.) Somoza himself pocketed millions of dollars' worth of emergency relief from abroad; preferential allotment of what remained went to Guard families and government employees. The government's handling of this crisis created new centers of opposition in the church and the business community, and by 1974 or 1975 the regime had entered a decline from which it was never to recover.

It was in this first half of Tachito's presidency that the United States seemed most strongly to support the regime, largely because of the obsequious conduct of Ambassador Turner Shelton, whose excessive identification with the dictator created a scandal in Nicaragua and ripples of opposition within the State Department and his own embassy. Of course, many Nicaraguans could not be blamed for thinking that Somoza now had a blank check from the United States to do anything he wished, since this was the inevitable impression that the ambassador gave and Somoza himself rebroadcast far and wide. Also, they were not privy to the relevant diplomatic correspondence, which told another story. But after Shelton's recall in 1975 and his replacement by James Theberge, Tachito began to note a decided shift in the political winds from Washington.

No doubt to the end of his days Somoza was mystified by the change, largely because his knowledge of this country was distant and dated. Although he was largely educated here, his English was never as good as he thought it was, and it did not improve with time. His picture of the United States was as dated as his contacts were unrepresentative of the U.S. mainstream: a 1940s collage of conservative Roman Catholic prelates, military officers, right-wing businessmen from Texas and Florida, and a handful of congressmen—the most vocal and active of whom was Congressman John Murphy, with whom Somoza had gone to private military school in New York (and who is now in federal prison following his conviction in one of the "Abscam" cases).

Further, Somoza's own diplomats and advisors in the United States were unrealistic and ill informed. His ambassador in Washington, Guillermo Sevilla-Sacasa, had been in place since 1943, and—though dean of the Washington diplomatic corps—had never managed to learn English. As to the dictator himself, with few exceptions his visits to Washington were fleeting and generally incognito. Thus he was never able to appreciate the degree to which he benefited from Americans' benign neglect and sheer ignorance of his country, which also explain the success for some years of the tiny "Somoza lobby" in the House of Representatives.

The Intensifying Opposition

After his fall, Somoza tried to credit the shift in U.S. policy to sinister forces in Washington. In fact, President Ford's instructions to Ambassador Theberge to distance himself from the dictator reflected nothing more than a sober awareness that since the earthquake in 1972, a dramatic shift had occurred in Nicaraguan politics. Opposition to the regime was more widespread than ever before and growing, and it was largely unrelated to the then-tiny Frente Sandinista de Liberación Nacional (FSLN, or "Sandinistas"). Rather, it embraced virtually every respectable interest outside the Somoza machine, including businessmen like Adolfo Calero and clerics like the archbishop of Managua, Monsignor Miguel Obando y Bravo. What Somoza never grasped was the degree to which such people (whose English was sometimes better than his own, and whose knowledge of American democracy was far more profound) were able to reach the State Department and Congress on their own.

From 1975 on, U.S. policy was clearly aimed at getting Somoza to restore some integrity to Nicaragua's political institutions, through dialogue with the opposition and free elections. When it became obvious that the dictator intended to do neither, Washington, in conjunction with other countries of the region, began to pressure him to resign. This telescopes, of course, a long and very complicated process. Over three years' time Somoza played cat-and-mouse with the opposition and the United States, in turn encouraging and then dashing hopes of a peaceful and negotiated solution.

During these tense and difficult months, relations between the United States and the Nicaraguan opposition became rather frayed. The opposition wanted Somoza out as expeditiously as possible, and at the beginning at least could not understand why the United States could not easily accomplish this, since in their view his regime was utterly dependent for its very existence upon Washington's good will. The State Department and the U.S. Embassy in Managua were equally anxious to see Somoza depart, at least after 1978, but also wished to avoid a power vacuum in which the radical elements in the revolution (that is, the Sandinistas) could seize power. That is why, for example, all of Washington's draft proposals included retention of the National Guard in some form or another. At the beginning the opposition largely shared these apprehensions; but as time wore on, it decided that even jumping into a void was preferable to continued rule by Somoza.

The State Department and the White House meanwhile debated to what degree it was possible or even proper to intervene in Nicaraguan events. This led, in the words of a former Carter administration official, to "policy paralysis." In the end, Washington's modest proposals were rejected by the opposition and voted down in the council of the Organization of American States (OAS), which had become involved in the mediation process. While the opposition quarreled among itself and with Washington, the FSLN closed ranks and projected an image of coherence and unity of purpose.

After the last mediation effort in early 1979, it was obvious that in the event of Somoza's departure, the Sandinistas were bound to play a role in Nicaragua's future far out of proportion to their actual numbers. Fidel Castro himself recognized as much and, after having maintained a somewhat platonic relationship with the FSLN over its lean years, began to ship it vast supplies of arms.

Ironically, this was precisely the prospect favored by Somoza himself. By refusing to negotiate effectively with the mainstream of the opposition, over time he pushed them into an alliance with the Sandinistas. This was done very deliberately, so as to confront the United States with only two choices—Somoza's continuance in office, or a Marxist-dominated government in Nicaragua. To the very end, of course, Somoza was convinced that if the two alternatives were thus starkly posed, the United States would be forced to come down on his side. It apparently never occurred to the dictator that Washington might choose to interpret its own national interests differently, or even less, that it would be unable to decide one way or another and would thus lose what control of events it might have had. Somoza's own belief in his carefully cultivated image as Washington's ally may have proven the most critical element in his fall.

Lessons From the Past

If the history of U.S. relations with Nicaragua over the period 1912 to 1979 establishes anything, it is that on the few occasions when it tried, Washington was unable to make that country behave like a democracy—even in the limited Latin American sense of the term. Intervention could eliminate private armies but not the influence of the military in politics; it could assure honest elections at the bayonet point of a Marine—but not one moment beyond it. Moreover, even after renouncing its policy of intervention, the United States was held responsible for every untoward event that subsequently occurred in the history of Nicaragua, simply because at one point the United States had been present as an arbiter of events.

The two policies—intervention and non-intervention—were equally frustrating. Non-intervention won out because it was, quite simply, less expensive, and, at the beginning, more popular, if not with the Nicaraguan opposition, at least with other Latin American countries. In later years, the United States periodically vented its pique with the Somozas by resorting to milder forms of intervention—to no great effect. For example, U.S. arms embargoes tended largely to enrich other suppliers, and even the Carter administration's vote against Nicaraguan loans at the Inter-American Development Bank—while undoubtedly a psychological shock of major proportions—was not sufficient to force the regime to mend its ways.

The Limits of Power

The Nicaraguan experiment also demonstrates the way that vast asymmetries of power operate in international politics. Because the sheer physical and economic dimensions of U.S. power were so overwhelming to Nicaraguans, they simply could not accept the notion that Washington did not possess an equally unlimited capacity to arrange their political life—and this in the face of demonstrated failure. Rather, the outcome of every event in Nicaraguan political history was seen as part of a conscious policy in which the United States always got what it wanted. Understandably, but also unfortunately, Nicaraguans generally did not recognize the role of inertia and drift in the foreign policy of great powers, much less the failure of political will—a failure that occurred more than once across the years, but most devastatingly in the final hours of the Somoza regime.

For the Somozas, it was precisely in the interstices of U.S. policy that they found their vital breathing space. Nicaragua was, after all, a very small part of the international picture of the United States, and at best only a modest amount of foreign policy energy could normally be devoted to it. For the Somozas, of course, it was 100 per cent of *their* energies, and they saw no reason to cooperate with Washington in any measure they viewed as detrimental to their own interests. When conflicts arose, they simply held their breath and waited for a change in the weather. In this they were uncommonly fortunate. World War II, the Guatemalan affair, the Cuban Revolution—each appeared at a critical juncture in the relationship, and each in turn forced the United States to bend in the Somozas' direction. U.S. motives were by no means dishonorable—Hitler, after all, was certainly a greater menace to humanity than the elder Somoza—but this could not prevent the impact of the larger policy from being felt negatively in Nicaragua.

Somoza's luck finally ran out when events in a tiny Asian country more than ten thousand miles from Nicaragua knocked the moral underpinnings out from under U.S. foreign policy. By 1976 or 1977 a new current was abroad in Washington and in the councils of its foreign policy establishment, one that emphasized "the ethics of clean hands" almost to the exclusion of "the ethics of consequences." Gone was the ice-cold pragmatism from which the Somozas had so often benefited in the past. This did not mean that Washington finally sympathized with the Sandinistas; it meant, rather, that U.S. policy-makers had concluded that the threat of Marxism in Nicaragua was no longer sufficient to counterbalance the brutality, the corruption, and above all, the sheer unpopularity of the Somoza regime. The Carter administration hoped to the very end that the FSLN would be swamped by moderates once the dictator was gone. They were, after all, more numerous and more broadly representative of the political forces in Nicaraguan society. It was a pious hope, and sincerely held, but poorly founded: Nicaragua was in the midst of a revolution, not a presidential primary. In the absence of the concrete application of its power, Washington's purposes remained ethereal, and ultimately irrelevant.

The Limits of Hindsight

No doubt there are other lessons to be learned from the Nicaraguan experience, and other historians will have plenty of time to offer them. But one point must be foreclosed: history does not tell us—and *cannot* tell us—precisely when the United States should have shifted its policy gears in Nicaragua, apart from never having landed the Marines in the first place. Intervention during the 1920s was resented, and understandably so, by Latin American publicists and American liberals alike, but so was nonintervention—equally—once the Somozas were in place. Washington should have seen that after 1936 the Somoza regime was moving Nicaragua into a qualitatively different kind of political system, one pernicious even by local standards; but the process of consolidation was slow, and by the time it was fully evident, World War II was upon the United States and indeed the entire world.

The State Department did attempt to rein in Somoza in the 1940s, but by that time the dictatorship was fully fleshed out, complete with U.S. journalistic, financial, and political connections. In the 1950s and 1960s other priorities in the region moderated Washington's zeal for political change in Nicaragua—and in one unfortunate ambassadorial case, made things much worse. Arguably, the biggest opportunity squandered by the United States was the assassination of the elder Somoza in 1956. Had Washington intervened at that point, the regime would have been unable to extend itself into the next generation. However, this would have required much more than an arms embargo or even an economic blockade, and there is no assurance that it would have worked. It also presupposes that the United States would have been able to discard its commitment to nonintervention, for a cause that—whatever one might think of the Somozas—was certainly not a pressing issue of U.S. security.

Ironically, time has proven that the hobgoblin to which Somoza so frequently pointed was real. Events *have* established that Marxism, if not Communism, was the final consequence of his fall. Perhaps it need not have been that way, and it will be left to earnest American liberals and sobered American conservatives to retrace the path that should have—and more importantly, could have—been taken. This is an exercise, however, in which sympathizers of the new Sandinista dictatorship need take no part; they got the outcome *they* prefer. The floor belongs, rather, to those who carry their past concern for the lack of freedom in Nicaragua firmly and consistently into the present—and, if need be, into the future as well.

20. A New Deal For the Nicaraguan People

By GABRIEL JACKSON

Focus
Since the advent of the Sandinista government in 1979, thousands of Americans — mainly though not exclusively teachers, social workers, health workers, and church people — have visited Nicaragua on their own. The vast majority have returned convinced that the new regime is offering the average Nicaraguan better opportunities than he ever had before, and that the statements of U.S. officials, particularly President Reagan, are either lies or gross exaggerations. One of them is Gabriel Jackson, a distinguished historian of Spain who taught at American universities for many years and now lives in retirement in Barcelona.

Professor Jackson visited Nicaragua in April and May of 1985. He found the FSLN a "political-military coalition drawn from various social classes that ... has labored to create a society that is democratic in its social texture, with the full range of political and religious freedoms, a mixed economy, and a non-aligned foreign policy." He defends the "procedural integrity" of the 1984 elections that brought President Daniel Ortega to power, and insists that the opposition parties "possess complete freedom of organization and propaganda." While there have been some Sandinista "errors," particularly with regard to the Miskito Indians and other minorities, these are being "actively corrected." The treatment of prisoners "resembles that which prevailed for blacks and their white allies in the jails of the southern United States during the late 1960s."

Jackson stresses the importance of context: what Nicaraguans had before, and what they have now; what can reasonably be expected of a nation that has no democratic tradition, but whose government is determined to meet its pressing social and human needs. Thus he praises the Sandinistas' approach to education and health, and guardedly criticizes the hierarchy of the Roman Catholic Church—particularly Pope John Paul II—for failing to see that this regime is working in the spirit of progressive Christianity. As he points out, many Sandinistas are themselves practicing Catholics.

Many of the failings of the regime must also be attributed to causes it cannot control, such as the hostility of the United States, the military threat represented by the contras, the flight of Nicaraguan and foreign capital and technicians, and the shortage of foreign exchange.

Jackson found Nicaraguan life to be truly revolutionary: unlike such democratic societies as Spain and the United States, in Nicaragua "I felt as if people really acted as if all men were free and equal." The eventual degree of pluralism that prevails, as well as the economic success of the revolution, "will depend upon the degree to which the United States can tolerate a truly democratic revolution in Central America . . . and to which both Western and Soviet Europe are willing to supply that country with a minimum of technical and economic aid."

Jackson's views on the nature of the regime are worth comparing with those of Joshua Muravchik (selection 21) and Edén Pastora Gómez (selection 30). His assurances about the elections should be balanced against the analysis of Robert Leiken (selection 23), and his different interpretation of church-state relations and human rights, against that of Cardinal Obando y Bravo (selection 24).

Gabriel Jackson is emeritus professor of history at the University of California, San Diego, and is the author of *The Spanish Republic and the Civil War, 1931–1939* (1964).

IN THE SPRING of 1985 I visited Nicaragua for two weeks, spending most of my time in Managua but making brief visits to the nearby provincial capitals—León, Masaya, and Granada—and to the city of Bluefields on the Atlantic Coast. I did not visit the war zones on the northern frontier, in part for lack of time and the difficulties of transport, but also because my particular purpose in visiting Nicaragua was to get some sense of the nature of civic life—political as well as social—nearly six years after the triumph of the Sandinista revolutionary movement. I focused on political development, economic problems, health, education, daily routine, freedom of expression, and personal evaluations of the revolutionary experience.

Nicaragua is governed by the Sandinista Front of National Liberation (FSLN), a politico-military coalition drawn from various social classes that was founded in 1960 to overthrow the dictatorship of the Somoza family. Since coming to power in July 1979, the FSLN has labored to create a society that is democratic in its social texture, with the full range of political liberties and religious freedoms, a mixed economy, and a non-aligned foreign policy.

In contemporary ideological terms, Sandinismo owes as much to Marxism as to the currents of leftist Catholic thought identified with liberation theology, and to the examples of Archbishop Helder Cámara in Brazil and the assassinated Archbishop Oscar Romero of San Salvador. But its fundamental principles can be directly traced to the career and ideology of General Augusto César Sandino, as interpreted by Carlos Fonseca (intellectual father of the FSLN, killed in 1976 in armed struggle with Somoza's government) and by important present-day leaders of the Sandinista government such as Sergio Ramírez and Tomás Borge.

General Sandino operated on the basis of three principles, without seeking the slightest personal recompense in the form of power or money. He created a small army of peasants and miners to defend the Nicaraguan population—in its vast majority illiterate—against the exploitation of the great land-owners and the multinational corporations. He was committed to lay down his arms and accept the authority of a civilian government the moment that the last American Marine departed from occupied Nicara-

---

A translation by the editors from *El País* (Madrid, Spain), July 2–4, 1985.

gua, a promise he fulfilled in 1933. Thereafter he turned to constructing agricultural and mining cooperatives, until he was assassinated in February 1934 by order of Anastasio Somoza, chief of the National Guard, a body trained by the United States to replace the Marines as a military force to maintain order in Nicaragua. From the example of Sandino the collective leadership of the present-day FSLN took three guiding principles: a popular army at the service of the exploited classes, resistance without quarter to foreign intervention, and the search for a non-capitalist economy that would be shaped by the human and geographical circumstances of Nicaragua.

The present system of government corresponds neither to the Soviet system of dictatorship by a Communist party nor to the Western model of parliamentary democracy. The Sandinista Front is a political organization far freer, more heterogeneous, and non-dogmatic than any Communist party. At the same time, Nicaragua is an underdeveloped country that never had the diversified economy, the large middle class, and the experiences of generations of local self-government that in every case preceded the development of parliamentary democracy in Western Europe, Scandinavia, and the Anglo-Saxon world.

Honest Elections in 1984

From July 1979 until November 1984, executive power was exercised by a government junta, presided over by Daniel Ortega, which included about a dozen *comandantes*, the highest officer rank in the revolutionary army. On November 4, 1984, the junta held elections that resulted in the election of Daniel Ortega as president of the republic and of a National Assembly whose charge is to draft a new constitution. The procedural integrity of these elections was attested to by various European observers who were present in all parts of the country. Moreover, as one of the opposition leaders explained to me, "elections take more than a day to complete."

I read and listened to various substantive criticisms with respect to violence and threats of violence exercised against meetings convoked by the opposition parties. The campaign period was extremely short and marked by sporadic censorship that may or may not have been justified by considerations of military security. On April 22, 1985, the principal opposition periodical, *La Prensa*, published a statistical analysis offering strong circumstantial evidence that the Sandinistas had inflated their total vote by 400,000; but even if this were the case, it remains true that the Sandinistas obtained more than twice as many votes (instead of three and a half times as many) as their closest rivals, the Conservative Democrats. Opposition leaders also accused the Sandinistas of having gained unfair advantage by altering the rules of eligibility at the last moment—lowering the voting age from eighteen to sixteen, and allowing soldiers to vote for the first time. But it seems to me difficult to support the democratic cause by denying the vote to sixteen-year-olds (who in underdeveloped countries often carry out tasks associated with adulthood) and to men fulfilling their military obligation. It is also a fact that the Sandinistas lost thousands of potential votes as a result of the action of the contras, who prevented many voters from going to the polls in the frontier regions.

These charges, all of which no doubt have some element of truth but none of which can be quantified, have led to the plausible criticism that the opposition does not possess as many seats in the National Assembly as it should. It is also true that, because of the war emergency, the Assembly has not yet begun to draft the new constitution. But from a democratic point of view, the elections of 1984 can be judged positively or negatively only by considering the context in which they took place. If after a century and a half of undemocratic government, with one corrupt regime following another and real power in the hands of foreign corporations, Nicaragua was supposed to hold elections as clean as those of England or Scandinavia, of course the conclusion would have to be negative. But if one places the elections in the context of the Nicaraguan past, what stands out is the fact that—with all their imperfections—they are the first in which the entire Nicaraguan population was offered a real choice concerning its political future. Whether or not the electoral proceedings become cleaner in the future will depend in a good measure upon the degree to which the Western democracies increase their economic and diplomatic aid to the regime, or accept Reagan's characterization of Nicaragua as a Communist tyranny.

Everyday Political Activity

For me the best evidence of political liberty in Nicaragua was not the debate over the elections or the composition of the National Assembly. Rather, it was evidence of political activity on a daily basis. The criticisms that I read in the press and the arguments I heard on radio and television were as diverse, as pluralistic as any I have encountered in Spain and the United States.

All the negative opinions on Sandinista policy, on the economy, foreign policy, the treatment of the Miskito Indians, violations of human rights, and the like that I had heard outside Nicaragua I also heard in the country itself. I spoke with leaders of the Conservative Democrats, the Social Democrats, and the Socialist and Communist parties (both consider themselves part of the loyal opposition), with various trade union leaders of non-Sandinista federations, and with defense lawyers for persons accused of counter-revolutionary activities. None of them asked to remain anonymous or to have his remarks held confidential. All criticized the recent elections, the courts, the prisons, and economic policy. But none accused the Sandinistas of purges of the type associated with Stalin or Hitler, none accused the government of systematic torture such as practiced recently by regimes in Argentina and Uruguay, and none acted as if he expected violence or arrest as the consequence of his present political activity. The parties possess complete freedom of organization and propaganda. They publish pamphlets, monthly or weekly bulletins of as great a variety as the political literature found in Western Europe.

My conversations with government officials and my careful, frequent reading of the pro-Sandinista dailies *Barricada* and *Nuevo Diario* showed that they, too, often voice the same criticisms as the opposition. Of course, they tend to put a somewhat more favorable gloss on the intentions of the government. This type of daily political experience is what convinced me that the Sandinista revolution has a truly pluralistic character that will remain if the Contadora process finally achieves peace and non-intervention in Central America.

The Agricultural Decline

Nicaragua was a great exporter of coffee, cotton, sugar, and tropical fruits under the Somoza family. It also produced important surpluses of cattle, fowl, and rice. Landed property was strongly concentrated in the hands of a small traditional elite, as well as the ruling family and its immediate allies. Most exports were financed and administered by American companies, and the profits went to those companies and to the local landowners. The peasants earned salaries that barely permitted them to survive at the subsistence level, and they rarely had land of their own.

The revolutionary government distributed the properties of the Somoza family and its closest collaborators, so that the peasants received between 40 and 50 per cent of the cultivated land in the country, properties that since then have been turned into family farms, state farms, and cooperatives. Those who before were landless peasants are today cultivating their own rice and beans, raising their own pigs and chickens, and eating considerably better than they did in the days of Somoza.

But the volume of commercial agriculture, essential for foreign exchange, fell rapidly. Hence in 1984 Nicaragua was exporting one-third of the 1978 quantities. A leader of the Socialist Party explained to me that rice production was twice as high in the private farms as in the state farms, and that the total production of corn had fallen by about two-thirds since 1978. Leaders of the Conservative Party and businessmen corroborated these figures and gave many specific examples of a decline in efficiency and productivity since 1978.

The fact that defense costs absorb more than half the national budget reduces drastically the availability of foreign exchange to buy fertilizers and insecticides, to finance shipments abroad, to repair trucks and agricultural machinery, and so on. A high proportion of men who would otherwise be working in the countryside have been serving in the army. The military activity of the contras has interfered considerably with the gathering of harvests on the frontiers of Honduras and Costa Rica.

But even the government economists with whom I spoke could not assure me that the drops in production and in productivity were wholly due to considerations of war. At least as important were factors intrinsic to the revolutionary process itself. Many agricultural engineers, foremen, shipping agents, and commercial representatives of foreign buyers chose to emigrate to Costa Rica, Honduras, or Florida rather than to accept the uncertainties and the decline in status associated with social revolution. The government nationalized the banks and restricted sharply the possibilities to repatriate profits for the foreign companies operating in Nicaragua. Therefore foreign banks and companies greatly reduced their operations, with a consequent destruction of the commercial network through which Nicaraguan exports were long financed and sold.

While I was in Nicaragua the press announced the return to its legal owners of a cattle ranch, *Las Mercedes*, which had been unjustly confiscated. The business community claims—and I heard various government economic functionaries admit—that there had been too many incidents of this sort. Quite apart from envy, class resentment, unproved allegations of counter-revolutionary activity, and "infantile leftist" dogmas on the virtues of collectivization (views decidedly not reflected in Sandinista policy), many farms and businesses were erroneously confiscated, and their owners have waged a struggle of many months in the courts and directly to the responsible economic ministries to achieve some rectification. Obviously, the climate of uncertainty about property rights under the new regime has inhibited economic efficiency.

Managing the Economy

Another endemic problem of the regime is that of management of the economy, in both public and private sectors. It is understandable that in circumstances of economic crisis the first revolutionary government of Nicaragua was primarily concerned with the welfare of its people and therefore sought to assert control over prices of basic foodstuffs, medicines, and household articles. But economic controls are effective only if they are applied to a few key sectors and can function without excessive paperwork.

Today in Nicaragua, for any commercial transaction, a farmer requires half a dozen permits from the national and regional authorities of two or three different ministries. Banking functionaries and political authorities tell him what crop he will have to plant if he wishes to be eligible for a loan. They carefully check to see if he invests the full measure of borrowed capital and continuously audit his production costs, his profits, his sources of fertilizers, insecticides, and fuel, the number of his employees, and the salaries he pays them. Oversupervision of this kind inevitably leads to a lack of incentives for the producer.

The scarcity of foreign exchange and the virtual destruction of the commercial link with North American business since 1978 have had devastating effects on the use of machinery. In the Oscar Danilo Rosales Hospital, which services the city and province of León, the director took me on a tour of the basement to show me the washing machines paralyzed by the lack of bolts and bearings, the driers immobilized by the lack of replacement parts (condensers), and the ironing presses working at a third of their capacity for lack of pads on which to place sheets and towels.

Great Gains in Education

Although the economic situation poses important long-range problems, the government has taken many very promising steps that are more important than foreign trade or financial stability. After all, this is a country where the people have always been poor and are therefore ready to accept continuing economic difficulties in exchange for their recently achieved political freedom and social improvements.

Since coming to power in 1979, the government has concentrated on the extension of education at all levels. Education receives 10 per cent of the national budget, second only to defense. The total resources devoted to education have increased by 500 per cent over 1978. The number of students is more than double, and the number of teachers, compensated by considerably higher salaries, has quadrupled. In 1978 the pre-school enrollment was about 9,000; in 1984 it was 60,000. A national literacy campaign for adults has reduced non-readers by 50 per cent – to 13 per cent of the population.

The Sandinista Front is unique among modern leftist movements in possessing large numbers of practicing Catholics in its ranks, and also to be completely lacking in any form of anti-clericalism. The government has reached numerous agreements with Catholic schools in poor neighborhoods, to increase enrollment, to improve the physical facilities (at no cost to them), and to augment teachers' salaries by state subsidies. The government's purpose is, on one hand, to assure universal, free public education, and, on the other, to mobilize the skills of both secular and religious teachers toward this end, without requiring the religious schools to change their fundamental orientation.

Errors on the Atlantic Coast

One of the first errors of the revolutionary government, which today is being actively corrected, was its treatment of the population of the Atlantic Coast, specifically the 100,000 Miskito Indians, 25,000 blacks, and 5,000 Sumo Indians. The Sandinista movement and the armed struggle against Somoza were almost exclusively an affair of the mixed-blood population of the Pacific Coast and the mountainous provinces of the northwest, that is Estelí, Nueva Segovia, Jinotega, and Matagalpa. The scantily populated forest zones along the Atlantic Coast were not involved in the revolutionary struggle.

The ethnic minorities of the Atlantic provinces were always culturally different from the majority of the Pacific Coast. English traders and pirates in the eighteenth century, the Moravian Church, and the numerous black communities of the Caribbean in the nineteenth and twentieth centuries created that cultural difference. Traditionally, the Miskitos emigrated in whatever direction they pleased, without taking into account the Honduran-Nicaraguan frontier. The Sandinistas are the first to admit that they underestimated the level of distinctive cultural identity, and for this reason sharply alienated this population. The Miskitos believed themselves to be victims as much of the Hondurans as of the Nicaraguans in the military actions along the frontier. Spokesmen for the United States and Honduras launched totally unjustified accusations of genocide against the Sandinistas, but it remains true that may Miskitos resisted Sandinista efforts to establish them temporarily far from the militarized frontier zone.

Their complaints are presented principally by the MISURASATA coalition led by Brooklyn Rivera. Under the auspices of the government of Mexico, MISURASATA and the Nicaraguan government signed an initial accord to establish peace and mutual confidence between the minorities of the Atlantic Coast and the government. For its part, the government committed itself to permitting the Miskitos to return to their evacuated communities and reestablish their traditional agricultural and fishing communities. It has granted amnesty to dozens of prisoners captured in the first skirmishes between MISURASATA and the government troops. MISURASATA accepted subsequent negotiations, anticipating an autonomous region under the government of President Ortega. The government is building schools where instruction will be offered in the Miskito and Sumo languages. It is too soon to say to what degree the Sandinistas will succeed in achieving reconciliation with the Miskitos, but they are pursuing a policy that will lead to comprehension on the basis of considerable local autonomy.

Improvements in Health

Probably the most important achievement of the Sandinistas, after education, is their health programs. Before 1979, medical attention for the poor rural population was all but non-existent, and the doctors in the cities devoted a maximum of two hours daily to the public clinics. The Sandinistas sent young doctors and medical technicians to the villages and increased the hours of public hospitals to five or six per day. Massive vaccination campaigns have drastically reduced the incidence of malaria, diphtheria, polio, and measles. But hospital authorities who gave us these figures hastened to explain that the most virulent illnesses, especially infant diarrhea and broncopneumonia, continued to afflict much of the population. The army has been used to carry milk, serums, midwives, and mobile first aid units to the most distant villages.

There are hundreds of Cuban doctors in Nicaragua. Cuba's program of medical education and its public health service are very admired as examples of what an underdeveloped country can achieve in this area. Also at work in Nicaragua are hundreds of doctors and nurses from all parts of Western Europe, Canada, and the United States. Certainly in no other area has international aid, both official and private, been so important and so deeply appreciated as in public health. Lack of equipment has limited sophisticated services in many of the hospitals, but in the area of preventive medicine, nutrition, public health, and personal hygiene, matters have improved considerably over the last five years.

The Treatment of Prisoners

As a long-standing member of Amnesty International and a veteran of the civil rights movement in the United States, I was particularly interested in the human rights situation in Nicaragua. I had the opportunity to read a number of complaints by detainees who were awaiting trial before the appeals court in Managua, and to discuss them with the judge charged with reviewing them. I was also allowed to talk with a conservative lawyer who represented the families of various prisoners accused of counter-revolutionary activities.

The documents were in the form of questionnaires completed by the prisoners. All answered that they had received packages and visits from their families; that they could consult with their lawyers; and, in the majority of cases, that they received medical attention when necessary. The complaints were about the quality of food, lack of water and hygiene, crowding of prisoners in cells and passageways, poor ventilation, verbal threats, days passed in solitary confinement, and bad treatment generally, such as being struck by the guards or having their wrists tied with wire. None of them claimed to be imprisoned for political or religious ideas.

The judge who was evaluating the questionnaires thought that many of the specific claims were justified, but he also pointed out that these men were prisoners for genuine counter-revolutionary activity and were not, strictly speaking, prisoners of conscience.

The conservative lawyer, who was also, by the way, a deputy in the National Assembly, began our conversation by saying that there are some 3,000 appeals pending before the regular tribunals, as well as the popular anti-Somocista tribunals that were set up after the revolution, and that only six persons had been released to date. He pointed to his waiting room, where a dozen or so women were waiting to learn the place of confinement of their sons or husbands.

Nobody knows how many prisoners there are, he added, or where they are being held, and their families go from one prison to another looking for missing members, whom they presume to have been arrested. He described his own arrest for alleged corruption. No evidence was produced, no specific charges made. In repeated interrogations he was asked whether he knew Edén Pastora and Arturo Cruz. Of course he knew them, he answered; he had been friends with both for years. After four unpleasant days he was released. But, he concluded, what do you suppose would happen to a less prominent person, not a lawyer, arrested and grilled about his personal associations?

I asked him about mistreatment and systematic torture. He replied that there was much ill-treatment and considerable psychological torture. If the documents I saw and the things I was told are more or less true for the country as a whole, I would say that the situation of human rights resembles that which prevailed for blacks and their white allies in the jails of the United States during the 1960s: wretched conditions of confinement; sporadic mistreatment applied by individual guards; psychological torture; a variety of procedural confusions, delays, and false arrests.

The Regime and the Churches

A final aspect of Nicaraguan life that I wished to learn more about concerned the relations between the churches and the Sandinista regime. The vast majority of the 2.5 million Nicaraguans who live in the Pacific provinces are practicing Catholics. On the Atlantic Coast, in the sparsely inhabited province of Zelaya, roughly half of the some 150,000 inhabitants are Catholic and half are Moravian.

As in all poor countries, the clergy play an important role as teachers, community advisors, health workers, and general psychological and moral counselors. This meant, inevitably, that the priests and ministers would find their traditional functions undermined by the arrival of public schools and teachers, doctors, nurses, and government functionaries intent upon indoctrinating the people with the political philosophy of Sandinismo. Some of the conflicts with the Miskitos could have been avoided if the Sandinistas had been able to establish a correct relationship with the local priests and ministers after they took power in 1979. But in general, and specifically in the Pacific provinces, there was no direct or doctrinal institutional conflict with the church.

A large number of Sandinistas at all levels of the movement are practicing Catholics. Nearly half the clergy in the country sympathize with the regime, for the simple reason that it is the first Nicaraguan government actively concerned with the welfare of the poor majority. The government subsidizes and cooperates with the Catholic schools and hospitals. It does not threaten to replace them. It does not interfere with the religious symbols or the services conducted in the churches.

The pro-Sandinista clergy at times were able to attenuate the conflicts between the pro- and anti-Sandinista forces in the mountains of the north, where the Sandinista soldiers and their contra opponents control neighboring villages and where the local peasants, given the circumstances, are forced to deal with both sides. A Jesuit priest told me about a fellow member of his order who was kidnapped by the contras near the Honduran border. His captors treated him with respect, and kept asking him how a priest could serve Marxist atheists. Throughout many long discussions he persisted in explaining that many Sandinistas were as Catholic as any contra. Finally they permitted him to celebrate Mass in the village, attended by the local inhabitants, a group of uniformed contras, and a group of Sandinista militiamen.

Various priests with whom I spoke expressed disappointment with the fact that, as they expressed it, Pope John Paul II is convinced that the situation in Nicaragua is exactly like that of Eastern Europe in 1945, and therefore has blindly turned his face against the Sandinista regime. This possible parallel exists in the minds of many people, and inspires the following observations.

The Sandinistas have been in power for almost six years. In the first six years of the existence of Bulgaria, Rumania, Hungary, and Czechoslovakia as Soviet-dominated states, opposition parties were almost physically liquidated. The press was completely shackled; the churches were treated with contempt, when not actively persecuted; and bloody purges based on fantastic accusations drastically thinned the ranks of national Communist parties.

In Nicaragua there have been no bloody purges, no attacks on religion. The spectrum of political parties and the possibilities of open political discussion are as great as in the majority of Western democracies. It is unfortunate, to be sure, that the two international figures most powerful in Nicaraguan life, President Reagan and Pope John Paul II, cannot or will not read the clear evidence.

The Texture of Life in Nicaragua

What is life like in revolutionary Nicaragua? These observations are based mainly on my experience in Managua, where I spent most of my time.

The Nicaraguans are people who speak softly and undemonstratively.

The children I saw in the kindergartens were smiling and playful, but not noisy; they did not push or hit one another. In arithmetic or Spanish classes, adolescents whispered to one another, but the teachers never had to raise their voices to be heard, and the atmosphere was friendly. Walking one afternoon through the streets of Masatepe I saw many turned-on television sets through open doors and windows, but the volume was so low that I could hardly make out the sound. I saw packs of dogs but heard very little barking, since dogs tend to imitate their human masters.

I attended a large political meeting in which Tomás Borge addressed the Committees of Sandinista Defense and criticized the greater part of neighborhood volunteer work. Families with small children passed by the plaza. Uniformed soldiers and non-uniformed adolescents bought tacos, fruit drinks, and plates of chicken from roadside stands, and ate their meals while walking around. There was nothing resembling military discipline; there were no loud noises or incidents. All these informal activities were quiet enough that those listening to the speech were in no way distracted.

What really struck me as revolutionary in the behavior of ordinary people was the total lack of servility. Living in a society that is politically democratic but also highly competitive, with a great sense of status, one that at the same time is emotionally repressive, we have become accustomed to fear, to inhibitions, to artificial smiles, to the anxiety-ridden efforts to please that are the distinguishing characteristic of our insecure fellow citizens. In Managua I felt as if people really acted as if all men were free and equal. The bus drivers, the office workers, the waiters, were friendly and helpful, but they did things with their own rhythm, in their own style, without servile gestures or expressions of any type.

It also seemed to me that the people of Nicaragua are tired of defending the Sandinista revolution but determined to do so. Five years is a long time to live with inflation, shortages, and threats of foreign intervention, especially when there is no end in sight. There is considerable confusion concerning how a mixed economy works and how to codify democratic political procedures in a constitution for an eventual period of peace. But there is no ambivalence concerning the repressive Somocista past. There are no doubts about health, education, the possibility of cultivating a few acres of land of one's own or of building a simple house for one's family. This government, liberated from the rigid social hierarchies of the past, has offered effective freedom to the mass of *mestizos* [persons of mixed

European and Indian ancestry] and Indians for the first time since the theoretical accomplishment of Nicaraguan independence in 1820.

The example of General Sandino possesses for Nicaraguans the same moral force as that of Benito Juárez for the Mexicans or Abraham Lincoln for Americans. The eventual degree of pluralism and the development of a viable economy in Nicaragua will depend upon the degree to which the United States can tolerate a truly democratic revolution in Central America and the degree, too, to which both Western and Soviet Europe are willing to supply that country with a minimum of technical and economic aid.

21. The Slow Road to Communism

By JOSHUA MURAVCHIK

Focus Sandinista Nicaragua cannot be accurately described as totalitarian, argues Joshua Muravchik, but it is a country "ruled by Communists, and solely by Communists, whose unanimous and unswerving goal is to turn it into a totalitarian state." In his view, Western journalists and policy analysts who over the years have discovered "moderates" among the Sandinistas are victims both of Sandinista deception and of wishful thinking.

Muravchik bases these charges on Sandinista public statements and expressions of admiration for the Soviet Union dating from long before the 1979 revolution. Only a few months after coming to power, at a time when Nicaragua was still receiving more aid from the United States than from the Eastern bloc, the Sandinistas and the Soviet Communist Party signed an accord and issued a joint communiqué denouncing the Western imperialist attempt to "stifle the inalienable right of the people of ... Afghanistan ... to follow the road of progressive change." At about the same time, a delegation from Polish Solidarity was not allowed into Nicaragua.

Within the country, Sandinista Defense Committees (CDS), which monitor loyalty to the aims of the party and also control ration cards and many privileges, have given the Nicaraguan rulers a tool for total social control. Muravchik observes that the committees show "an intertwining of party and state" that makes any real pluralism impossible. The Sandinista police and State Security outnumber Somoza's National Guard, which also had to carry out the functions that Nicaragua's current 120,000-man army performs.

Trade unions, the churches, and private businesses are under extreme pressures. Press censorship is so taken for granted that a Sandinista censor once explained paradoxically to the *New York Times,* "They accused us of suppressing freedom of expression. This was a lie and we could not let them publish it." The one remaining independent newspaper, *La Prensa,* still operating though strictly censored when this article was written, was subsequently shut down.

Muravchik's indictment of the Sandinistas should be compared with Gabriel Jackson's more positive view (selection 20), Cardinal Obando y Bravo's description of religious persecution (selection 24), the Seventy-two Hour Document (appendix C), and the draft of the Nicaraguan Constitution (appendix D).

Joshua Muravchik is the author of *The Uncertain Crusade: Jimmy Carter and the Dilemma of Human Rights Policy.*

THE VEXING DILEMMAS that confront U.S. policy toward Nicaragua have been needlessly exacerbated by a confused debate over what is really going on there. The confusion has been assiduously encouraged by Nicaragua's Sandinista rulers, and has been compounded by the tendency of all sides here to define Nicaraguan reality in a way that bolsters their own preferred policy choices.

By calling Nicaragua "Communist" and "totalitarian" President Reagan has set up a straw man that critics of his Central America policies have hastened to knock down. The President is guilty of exaggeration, but the critics who argue that Nicaragua may turn out like Mexico—a relatively open, pluralistic society, albeit dominated by one party—or that, as one former national security advisor to a U.S. president wrote recently, there is no way "to make a firm prediction" about how Sandinista Nicaragua will evolve, are averting their eyes from a mound of evidence that leaves little doubt where Nicaragua is heading.

Nicaragua is not now a Communist country, unless that term is stretched beyond its usual meaning. What other Communist country has legal opposition political parties fiercely opposed to the regime; an independent, albeit censored, newspaper; an independent human rights organization that chronicles, as best it can, the regime's abuses; independent labor and business organizations; freedom of emigration; an economy roughly half of which is privately owned; and unfair elections in which, however, the ruling party claimed only two-thirds, not 99 per cent, of the vote? No amount of stretching will make the term "totalitarian" fit this reality without losing the very kernel of the idea of the total state.

On the other hand, Nicaragua is a country ruled by Communists, and solely by Communists, whose unanimous and unswerving goal is to turn it into a totalitarian state. They are, however, proceeding slowly and carefully, ever mindful of the history of U.S. intervention in their country, and possessed of an image of "U.S. imperialism" that makes a new invasion seem more likely to them than it does to most Americans.

The Sandinistas' approach, therefore, is to be, as *Comandante* Henry

---

Reprinted by permission of the author and the publisher from *This World*, Winter 1986.

Ruiz, one of the nine members of the Sandinista National Directorate, put it, "tactically flexible, but strategically intransigent." The policy of tactical flexibility has guided the FSLN (Sandinista National Liberation Front) since 1977 and has been the key to its success.

Rise of the Ortegas

For more than fifteen years before 1977, the Sandinista Front, a tiny splinter from the Nicaraguan Socialist Party (the name of Nicaragua's official Moscow-oriented Communist party), had experienced almost nothing but failure. Then an internal dispute resulted in the ascendance of the *"tercerista"* faction, led by the brothers Daniel and Humberto Ortega.

The other two factions believed in slowly amassing FSLN cadres until the movement would be strong enough to attempt a pure socialist revolution, that is, a grasp for power on its own. The *terceristas* proposed instead a popular-front strategy aimed at the immediate overthrow of Somoza, followed by a struggle to turn the revolution toward socialism.

In 1977, although factional divisions remained, the FSLN as a whole embraced the "insurrectional" strategy advocated by the *terceristas,* issuing a fifteen-thousand-word program entitled "On the General Political-Military Platform of Struggle of the Sandinista Front for National Liberation for the Triumph of the Sandinista Popular Revolution." The platform called for the overthrow of Somoza and creation of a "revolutionary democratic state" that would "assure the structural and superstructural bases for the revolutionary process towards socialism." It explained that "strategic and tactical factors—both national and international—do not allow for the formulation of socialism in an open way in this stage." And it emphasized that the revolutionary movement must "do everything to avoid a new foreign intervention."

The Sandinistas moved quickly to implement the new program, launching every more daring military actions aimed at igniting popular insurrection, while at the same time seeking to forge alliances with other anti-Somoza elements whom the Sandinistas had previously held in open disdain. In retrospect, the Sandinistas have repeatedly acknowledged when speaking among themselves that the main goal of the alliances was to avert U.S. intervention. Two months after Somoza's ouster, the first ever meeting of the FSLN Assembly, a body of the top 100 cadres, was convened in Managua. The report presented to that body by the FSLN National Directorate explained that in 1979 "the alliance [with bourgeois and liberal anti-

Somoza forces] that took the form of the National Reconstruction Government, the cabinet, and, to a major extent, the FSLN's basic program . . . was designed to neutralize Yankee interventionist policies." [See also appendix C.] In his closed-door speech to the Nicaraguan Socialist Party in May 1984, *Comandante* Bayardo Arce explained that it was the U.S. proposal in June 1979 for OAS intervention in Nicaragua that inspired the Sandinistas to announce their "program of national reconstruction" based on the principles of non-alignment, mixed economy, and political pluralism, "three principles which made us presentable in the international context," he said, and which "kept the international community from going along with American policy."

Projecting an Image to the West

Western observers often took the Sandinistas' newfound tactical flexibility as a sign of "moderation," and many even inferred that Sandinista ideology was not Communist but rather some form of nationalistic democratic socialism. The Sandinistas diligently cultivated such interpretations. Daniel Ortega disingenuously complained to the *New York Times* that U.S. opposition to the Sandinistas showed that "Washington accepts social democracy in Western Europe, but not in Latin America." Tomás Borge told a press conference in 1978, "We have some Marxists with us, but the Front is much wider." On the whole, he said, "we are neither Marxist nor liberal; we are Sandinistas." Sergio Ramírez, in his role as member of the original junta of reconstruction, proclaimed the revolution's goals to be: "No right, no left, just Nicaragua." In numerous private conversations with Western reporters, Sandinista leaders reiterated these themes.

Sandinista efforts to project an image acceptable to the West were further strengthened by the emergence of Edén Pastora as the most visible guerrilla leader after he led the daring commando raid that succeeded in seizing the National Palace in the summer of 1978. Pastora obviously relished his sudden celebrity and spoke willingly to reporters, expressing his genuine democratic convictions. The FSLN high command was content to let Pastora serve as the movement's public face, while never giving him a seat on its ruling body, the National Directorate.

These image-building efforts bore fruit. In 1978 the *Washington Post* characterized the FSLN as "hazy in ideology." The *New York Times* called it "politically ill-defined." ABC's Peter Jennings said the Sandinistas' final offensive of summer 1979 "has a single aim: the removal of President Somoza." And syndicated columnist Jack Anderson devoted a series to the Sandinistas based on first-hand reporting by one of his assistants. Anderson said: "Left-wing influence on the Sandinistas is minimal. Of the three main guerrilla groups [i.e., factions] that make up the rebel camp, the only avowedly leftist group . . . appears to have little or no influence."

Western journalists who insistently perceived "moderates" among the Sandinistas were the victims not only of Sandinista deception but also of their own wishful thinking, as was suggested by their reaction to the announcement on the eve of Somoza's overthrow that *Comandante* Tomás Borge would hold the Interior Ministry folio in the incoming revolutionary government. The Ortega-led *terceristas* had been described often during the preceding two years as "moderates" in contrast precisely to the likes of Borge. But the same journalists now found nothing ominous in Borge's appointment. On the contrary, the *New York Times* observed that in his new post, "Mr. Borge should be in a position to control the most radical elements among the rebels"; while the *Washington Post* quoted approvingly anonymous "political analysts" who said that "as director of police functions [Borge] will be in a better position to keep mavericks from his faction in line." In short, it was Borge who was now perceived as the moderate.

In reality, divisions among the Sandinistas have arisen over issues of strategy, and sometimes personality, but never over the question of "moderation" versus "radicalism," a dichotomy that has meaning in U.S. politics but little in the explicitly Marxist-Leninist politics of the Sandinistas. There, it has no more importance than the fact that Stalin was a "moderate" compared to the "radicalism" of Trotsky. Moisés Hassán, widely described in 1979 as the most radical of the three Sandinista members of the revolutionary junta, and even as its only true "Communist," has since suffered two demotions in Sandinista ranks, apparently for taking too seriously the rhetorical ideals of the revolution.

The 'Sacred Cause' of Marx and Lenin

Ironically, although it was the triumph of the *tercerista* line within the FSLN that was so instrumental in persuading American reporters that the Sandinistas were not mere Communists, the very 1977 platform that embodied the *tercerista* triumph was so chock-full of unmistakable Communist formulas as to leave no reasonable doubt about the ideology of its authors. It explained: "The dialectical development of human society leads to the transformation from capitalism to Communism." It declared: "Our cause . . . is the sacred cause of Marx, Engels, Lenin, and Sandino." It foretold that after the fall of Somoza, "our present-day Marxist-Leninist vanguard will be able to fully develop its organic structure and become a strong Leninist party." Where it spoke of the "revolutionary democratic" phase of development, it hastened to add that this did not mean "bourgeois" democracy. It even went so far, in one piece of historical review, as to explain that in the 1930s, "the glorious Russian revolution was in a process of consolidation and combat against counter-revolutionary terror within its own country," as if the Sandinista authors had been weaned on Stalin's version and hadn't yet caught up with Khrushchev's emendations.

Far from harboring any democratic affinities, the Sandinistas positively feared democratization in Nicaragua, for they realized that the existence of Somoza as their foil offered the best hope for the kind of polarization that was essential for their seizure of power. Humberto Ortega has since explained that the FSLN renewed its military offensive in 1977 precisely in order to try to "prevent such maneuvers" as a "democratization plan," which it feared the Yankees would press upon Somoza. Tomás Borge has said much the same thing. And Jaime Wheelock has explained that the FSLN joined the Broad Opposition Front in 1978 in order "to prevent sections of the bourgeoisie and the petty bourgeoisie from . . . convert[ing] themselves into an alternative to Somoza for imperialism."

Perhaps the clearest indication of all of the anti-democratic ideology of the FSLN was its own internal structure and self-conception. The 1977 platform declared: "The task at hand is to make the Sandinista struggle massive without massifying the FSLN. . . . Because of our vanguard's enormous prestige, all the people who are connected to it in some way consider themselves militants of the FSLN. This is exceedingly important and must not be discounted. However, we must be aware that those who are not incorporated into the vanguard structure, although they may feel part of it, do not take on the responsibilities, duties, rights, etc. of actual vanguard militants. In time, the people will begin to understand the difference between the vanguard and the masses. . . ."

'We Have a Project'

The Sandinistas anticipated that when Somoza was overthrown they would have next to wage a bitter power struggle with their "bourgeois democratic" allies, an alliance the FSLN platform had called "tactical and temporary." It was true that other important anti-Somoza leaders were indeed wary of the Sandinistas, but the idea of the bourgeoisie as a self-conscious political force bent on holding power was a Marxist fantasy. Nine months after the revolutionary junta took office, its two "bourgeois" representatives resigned in disillusionment. One, Violeta Chamorro, insisted disingenuously that she resigned only for reasons of health, citing a fractured bone in her foot. The other, Alfonso Robelo, founded the Social Democratic Party. This was hardly the behavior of a class-conscious bourgeoisie.

Thus, when Somoza fell, the Sandinistas were somewhat surprised to discover the extent of their own dominance. As the movement's leadership explained to the Sandinista Assembly two months after Somoza's ouster: "Sandinism represents the sole domestic force.... Our failure to exercise full power has been more pro forma and quantitative than real and qualitative."

Had the Sandinistas been willing to live with the moderate program of the junta that they themselves had helped to write, their pride of place in the broad coalition that had toppled Somoza and in any revolutionary government would have been secure. This would have been assured not only by their military strength but because virtually everyone in Nicaragua recognized their leadership of the anti-Somoza rebellion and admired their courage and self-sacrifice.

But to be leaders of a coalition government with moderate goals, to wield power only within limits, was not for them. As their leaders put it many times in that period, "we have a project." That project was to remake Nicaraguan society according to their particular conception of socialism.

What made the "project" especially difficult is that the FSLN was so small. In their penultimate offensive of September 1978, the Sandinistas had thrown 150 fighters into the battle, acording to Humberto Ortega, their chief military commander. That was almost certainly the bulk of their membership. Hundreds, perhaps a few thousand, flocked to fight under the Sandinista banner during the ensuing months, but though welcomed as combatants, few were accepted as members. On the morrow of the victory a great many Nicaraguans were eager to become Sandinistas or already considered themselves such, but the Sandinistas stuck to the platform's dictum not to "massify" the movement, and to guard its ideological purity. They judged rightly that to admit all who wished to join would be to run the risk of seeing "the project" undermined from within. Prospective members were required to undergo a long period of indoctrination and numerous tests of their loyalty and other capacities.

The small size of the FSLN did not constitute an immediate threat to the Sandinistas' grip on power, but it was a formidable obstacle to their ability to govern effectively, all the more to their plans for remolding society. Other revolutionary groups in similar straits have relied on raw terror in order to cow a population into submission. But this option was closed to them by their fear that a bloodbath would invite U.S. intervention.

The Sandinistas have coped with this dilemma in two ways. One is to import large numbers of cadres from Communist countries, especially Cuba. The other is to extend the tentacles of social control from the bottom up, reaching Nicaraguans where they live, work, study, and shop, while leaving in place the most visible symbols of opposition and "pluralism" so as not to enrage the beast to the north.

The U.S. government estimates that there are 7,500 Cubans stationed in Nicaragua, of whom about 3,000 are assigned to the military and security services, as well as several hundred Russians and East Europeans and several score Libyans and members of the PLO. Cuban military personnel serve with each unit of the Nicaraguan army from the company level up. In the security services, Cubans are reported to have charge of the unit serving as personal bodyguards to the *comandantes* and to provide guidance in all fields except "high tech" intelligence methods, for which East Germans are preferred. In one case, and perhaps more, a Cuban has been given Nicaraguan citizenship and been made one of the official chiefs of Nicaraguan intelligence. Bulgarians serve in the Ministry of Planning as the chief economic advisors.

Non-Communist governments that offered to send personnel to Nicaragua were rebuffed by the Sandinistas. This included not only the United States, which offered Peace Corps volunteers, but also Costa Rica, which offered teachers, and Panama, which offered military advisors. These two Central American governments were rebuffed despite the fact that they provided critical assistance to the FSLN in its war against Somoza, including the trans-shipment and "laundering" of the Cuban-supplied weapons on which the revolution depended.

Sandinista 'Non-Alignment'

This is only one piece of a vast amount of evidence that refutes the Sandinistas' claim to be "non-aligned," as well as the argument of some

Western observers that they are aligned only ambiguously or reluctantly. Six weeks after the FSLN came to power, Daniel Ortega represented Nicaragua at the sixth summit of the non-aligned countries, where he lined up firmly with Cuba in the effort to bring the Non-Aligned Movement into open embrace of the Soviet bloc, a move resisted primarily by President Tito and other leftist governments not in the Soviet orbit.

Six months later a Sandinista delegation to the Soviet Union signed a party-to-party accord between the FSLN and the Soviet Communist Party; the two bodies issued a joint communiqué that closely tracked Soviet policy, including a denunciation of "the campaign by imperialist and reactionary forces ... [to] stifle the inalienable right of the people of ... Afghanistan ... to follow the road of progressive change." This came at a time when Nicaragua was receiving more aid from the United States than from the Eastern bloc.

Wallace Spaulding pointed out in *Problems of Communism* in 1982 that the FSLN had replaced the traditional Nicaraguan Communists (the Socialist Party of Nicaragua) as the sole representative of Nicaragua at the congresses of foreign Communist parties, notably including those of the Warsaw Pact. This practice appears to have begun from the time the FSLN took power and continues today, and applies also to international Communist gatherings.

Each time a Soviet head of government has died, the FSLN has declared three days of mourning. Banner headlines proclaimed Brezhnev "Glorious Son of the Working Class"; Sandinista TV described Chernenko as a "great statesman and untiring fighter for the cause of world peace and solidarity"; and Andropov's death was officially mourned as a "loss ... to mankind." Deaths are not the only occasions for such effusions. The sixty-fifth anniversary of the Red Army was commemorated by this message from Humberto Ortega to Defense Minister Ustinov: "We know that the U.S.S.R. Armed Forces shall always guarantee the policy of peace pursued in the world by your government, your party, and your people."

Nicaraguan bookstores and newsstands are filled with publications from the U.S.S.R. and other Communist countries. American publications are hard to come by, and the works of Trotsky cannot be found. Sandinista television features such fare as long serialized sagas of the heroic struggles of Cuban soldiers in Africa. When General Jaruzelski's government instituted martial law in Poland, the FSLN instructed all of its media "to publish only those facts that have been confirmed by TASS and by the

Cuban Prensa Latina News Service." When a delegation from Solidarity traveled to the Americas, it was denied entry into Nicaragua.

Seven to eight thousand foreign "advisors" does not seem a vast number in a developing country of two and a half million population, but measured against the FSLN's own cadre it is a formidable force. When it came to power, the FSLN comprised only several hundred full members, or "militants." Since then the Sandinistas have hastened to expand the party. Estimates of its current size range from a few thousand to twelve or thirteen thousand, with most estimates falling in the middle of this range, or roughly the same as the number of foreign personnel. But the FSLN leaders must have doubts about the quality and loyalty of the new members generated through their rapid expansion. They must know that such persons are more likely to be opportunists than ideologues, a situation perhaps entirely congenial to a well entrenched party like that of the Soviet Union but not at all satisfactory to a party still trying to solidify its grip on society. The Cuban and East European advisors, on the other hand, are completely reliable, if only because they are firmly subject to their own governments.

Building the Party

The process of building the party is itself one of the important mechanisms of social control. The party is highly hierarchical. Categories of membership begin with "aspirant" and go up through pre-militant, militant, cadre, member of the Sandinista Assembly, to member of the National Directorate. At each level, promotion is by cooptation. A member may not apply for elevation to the next category. He must simply wait until he is raised up, a procedure that involves the assent of his neighborhood Sandinista Defense Committee and the party Base Committee at his place of employment, as well as clearance by State Security, recommendation by some higher ranking party members, and final approval by a committee governing elevations to the rank in question. All of this occurs without the candidate's being notified of his prospective elevation.

The effect of this system is that while every citizen is encouraged to belong to the Base Committee at his job or school, those who want to get ahead in revolutionary Nicaragua must strive to get themselves noticed by party supervisors. To achieve this they are encouraged to demonstrate their exemplary obedience and to help enforce the obedience of their fellows. They must also prove their earnestness by attending party meetings and classes and by volunteering for the militia and for other activities, such as unpaid work brigades that help harvest cash crops, or "turbas," the government-organized "mobs" that assault and intimidate dissidents.

In addition, those hoping to advance must take part actively in the neighborhood Sandinista Defense Committee (CDS). The most important work of these is "revolutionary vigilance," a kind of night-watch duty aimed less at preventing crime or counter-revolutionary activity than at generating anomie by reminding citizens that they are always being observed. The CDS observes who comes and goes, who complains too demonstratively, who is active in church, and who reads the independent daily, *La Prensa*, rather than the approved newspapers. It distributes ration cards for scarce essential commodities, helps supervise draft registration and housing assignments, and provides letters of approval that are necessary for receiving passports, visas, licenses, business registration, loans, scholarships, and many jobs. It also provides manpower, when called upon, for the *turbas*.

Interior Minister Tomás Borge recently acknowledged to the *Washington Post* what had been charged earlier by such observers as Robert Leiken and Linda Wolin—that many local CDS's were run by former Somocistas, who continued their jobs as neighborhood bullies but merely changed masters. Borge said that these officials had gained their positions as a "refuge to avoid punishment and repudiation." But leading Nicaraguan dissidents say that the FSLN deliberately recruited these Somocistas, using their known former affiliations as blackmail to assure their obedience. Since anyone holding an official position in the CDS was certainly checked out by Borge's State Security force (DGSE), and indeed since defectors from the DGSE say that CDS officials report to or are employed by State Security, it is hard to believe that Borge was unaware of the role played by ex-Somocistas. More likely, Borge's belated acknowledgment of that role is prelude to the time-honored Communist practice of purging underlings as scapegoats to assuage popular discontent.

The CDS's and the workplace party Base Committees stamp Nicaragua with one of the distinct characteristics of totalitarian systems—citizens are not allowed to be politically neutral or uninvolved. Merely not to belong to the CDS or Base Committee marks someone as derelict from the Sandinista norms of good citizenship and invites suspicion. The consequences may not be dire, but the act requires courage. Every person thus faces a choice of either participating in the institutions that enforce conformity or being their victim.

Intertwining Party and State

The CDS's also exemplify another feature of Nicaraguan society that severely vitiates its claim to "pluralism." This is the intertwining of party and state institutions. As pro-Sandinista academic Richard Fagen has explained it, the FSLN's definition of its "vanguard" role is "that FSLN hegemony . . . ought to be a structural, not just a temporary, feature of the political economy of the nation." Thus, for example, although the CDS's are party institutions, they distribute ration cards. Salaries for top CDS officials and other party expenditures are paid out of public revenues. In the schools, students are required to sing both the Sandinista and the Nicaraguan anthem and to salute both the Sandinista and the Nicaraguan flag. Moreover, the army is formally a creature of the party, although its ranks are filled by conscription (a power that was exploited during the 1984 election campaign, when many youth leaders of the opposition parties were drafted).

The militarization of society through the creation of an enormous conscript army is, for the Sandinistas, another means of social control. Between the army and the militia, the Sandinistas now maintain some 120,000 men under arms. This amounts to 5 per cent of the population or ten times the size of Somoza's National Guard after Somoza had radically enlarged it at the height of the civil war. The ordinary size of the National Guard, which served as the nation's police and security forces as well as its military, was about seven or eight thousand, all of them volunteers. Today the Sandinista police and State Security alone exceed that size.

The military buildup is presumably motivated in part by the threat posed by the armed resistance, but the impulse to militarize society has much deeper roots in Sandinista ideology. The FSLN's 1969 platform pledged that once in power, the FSLN would "strengthen the new people's army" and imbue its members with "revolutionary ideals." It promised to "establish obligatory military service" and also to create "people's militias." In its report to the Sandinista Assembly two months after taking power, the National Directorate said that "the defeated National Guard cannot possibly organize an attack on us for the time being" and that "there is no clear indication that an armed counter-revolution by the Somocista forces beyond our borders is going to take place." Nonetheless, it spoke of the need to "establish obligatory military service." A year later, still well before the onset of the contra war, when the *Washington Post* asked Moisés Hassán, one of the Sandinista members of the governing junta, "to name the major accomplishments of the first year, [he] listed the organization of the State Security forces, the Army, the militia, and the police."

Education as a Tool for Indoctrination

The Sandinistas also work hard at indoctrination. Soon after coming to power, they launched a national "literacy crusade." It was directed by Fernando Cardenal, who described it as "not a pedagogical project with political implications, but . . . a political project with pedagogical implications." The crusade used a single, specially prepared text, "The Sunrise of the People," with twenty-three lessons, each one on a political theme. Students began with the lesson "Sandino, Guide of the Revolution," progressed through "The FSLN Led the People to Freedom" and "People, Army, Unity: A Guarantee of Victory," and went on to such advanced themes as "A Real Democracy Is the Expression of the Power of the Organized Masses" and "There Is Freedom of Worship for All Churches that Defend the Interests of the People."

At the conclusion of the campaign, the FSLN announced that illiteracy had been reduced from over 50 per cent to a mere 12 per cent of the population, figures that have been repeated by North American admirers of the Sandinistas. But no one really knows whether that many people learned to read, or indeed if anyone did, as a result of the crusade, and the Nicaraguan government has not provided for any independent assessment. On the other hand, there is no doubt that the crusade enabled the Sandinistas to bring their political message to corners of the country that had previously had little exposure to it. And Miguel Bolaños Hunter, a defector from State Security, says that the DGSE also used the campaign to establish a network of informers in remote areas where it had had few or none.

Just as the literacy crusade required a special text, so the Sandinistas have replaced the texts used in Nicaraguan schools with new ones, often published in East Germany, that, as Borge puts it, "are guided by revolutionary principles." Borge explains: "Education is a process of forming individuals in ideology, in a complex system of values and ideas that justifies the interests of the class that wields state power." The "philosophy program" for teacher training puts it this way: "Our education has as its objective the training of new generations in the scientific, political, ideological, and moral principles enunciated by our national leadership, the FSLN, turning them into convictions and habits of daily life."

It is not only political subjects that are imbued with political content. Grade school children learn elementary arithmetic from a workbook that has them add and subtract rifles, hand grenades, and FSLN banners. The reading primer contains lessons on the army, the militia, the border guards, Sandino, FSLN founder Carlos Fonseca, and "our vanguard," the FSLN. Students learn handwriting by copying the phrase, "The FSLN guided and guides the struggles of the people." In later grades they study grammar by analyzing the speeches of the *comandantes*.

Indoctrination also goes on outside the schools. Both television stations, two out of the three newspapers, and most radio stations are government-owned or -controlled. The editor of the principal official newspaper, *Barricada*, doubles as the director of the FSLN's Department of Agitation and Propaganda. Even the non-government radio stations are required to broadcast news prepared by the government, and they, like the one independent newspaper, are severely censored.

In addition, political officers and party groups are spread throughout the army, where much time and effort is devoted to political training.

Orwellian Redefinition

As with other Communist governments, the FSLN's zeal to control definitions of reality leads it to the kinds of ironic inversions or perversions of meaning that we have come to call "Orwellian." Thus the Nicaraguan police and State Security forces are officially dubbed "the sentinels of the people's happiness." In a perfect echo of Stalin's 1936 dictum that the withering away of the state first required its utmost strengthening, Tomás Borge proclaimed in 1985:

> Some day there will no longer be any reason for coercive organs of the state.... When ... human society has been transformed into the reign of justice, when egotism and hatred have been driven out of man's consciousness....
>
> But in the meantime the Ministry of the Interior is indispensable, and ... the only possible alternative is for it to grow in quality and quantity, in organization, in operative capacity, in sharp and forceful response, in unrelenting vigilance over the happiness we have won....
>
> The Ministry of the Interior, ... as we know it now, [is] a powerful, decisive body whose vitality is the very essence of the revolution.

When the Miskito Indians of the Río Coco were forcibly removed from their villages, their buildings and crops burned, their cattle machine-gunned—all because they were believed to sympathize with the contras—

they were driven on forced marches to a complex of isolated, barren relocation camps that the government named "Tasba Pri," the Miskito words for "free land." The government explained that Tasba Pri was created "for the purpose of improving and dignifying the living conditions of the Miskitos" and to "assure ... the defense of their fundamental human rights."

One of the hundreds of articles excised from *La Prensa* last year by the censors was about censorship. The *New York Times* reported the censor's explanation: "They accused us of suppressing freedom of expression. This was a lie and we could not let them publish it."

In addition to the more manipulative and subtle methods of social control, the Sandinistas rely heavily on raw coercion and intimidation. According to defectors, the DGSE numbers about 4,000 officers and the Sandinista police about 5,000. These two forces work "in close cooperation," says Lenin Cerna, the DGSE chief, because "it is sometimes hard to distinguish criminals from counter-revolutionaries."

These forces have broad powers under the law, including that of administrative detention, but in any event they are not much restrained by the laws. As their boss, Tomás Borge, puts it, "in a revolution there is only one power, revolutionary power." Borge himself often extends, shortens, or commutes prison sentences, merely by edict.

The Sandinistas have reactivated the "special tribunals" originally set up to impose "revolutionary justice" on captured National Guardsmen. Each tribunal consists of one lawyer and two representatives of "the people" who are selected from the Sandinista "mass organizations." They dispense a harsh, politicized justice, little inhibited by due process. Few defendants are acquitted by these tribunals, and sentences often run to thirty years. During interrogation, according to DGSE chief Lenin Cerna, "the accused are told that their sentence depends not only on the gravity of the crime they have committed, but also on whether they are still hostile to the revolution or sincerely repentant." In a further effort to eliminate any lingering trace of judicial independence, the government has instituted new exams for candidates for judgeships in the regular courts. These consist of a series of essay questions such as "When and why did Marxist philosophy arise?," "Explain the terms idealism and materialism," "Define social being and social consciousness and the relation between them," and "What does the method of dialectical analysis consist of?"

Treatment of Prisoners

Estimates of the number of political prisoners held by the Sandinistas vary widely. The government has at various times acknowledged holding a total of 5,000 or 7,000 prisoners, but without acknowledging that any or many are political prisoners. The Permanent Commission on Human Rights of Nicaragua estimated 1,700 political prisoners were being held in addition to former National Guardsmen. The U.S. State Department has put the number of political prisoners at 4,200, and some Sandinista defectors have put it at 15,000. In any event, it almost surely exceeds by many times the number that were held under Somoza.

Not only is there no good count of prisoners, there is not even a good count of prisons. It has been repeatedly reported by defectors and Nicaraguan human rights groups that secret prisons exist, and Nicaraguan dissidents who have been arrested for only short periods of time usually report being taken blindfolded so as not to know where they have been held. The International Red Cross and all other human rights groups have been denied access to the prisons of the DGSE. When the International Human Rights Law Group asked for an explanation of this, "Minister Borge explained that [the prisoners] are isolated in order to establish a psychological link between them and their interrogators." Meanwhile, foreign delegations are often shown a model prison where unguarded inmates are constructively rehabilitated while enjoying such amenities as conjugal visits.

The head of State Security is Lenín Cerna, who was given his unusual first name by parents who were devout Communists. (His brother, reports Cerna hilariously enough, was named Krupskaya). An article in *World Marxist Review* quoted from an interview with Cerna: " 'My underground name was Felix. That,' he added with a smile, 'was probably why I was appointed to this job.' " Cerna's reference, of course, was to Felix Dzerzhinsky, the original head of Lenin's secret police, the Cheka. Cerna has emulated some of Dzerzhinsky's methods, notably in the realm of deception and entrapment. Just as Dzerzhinsky created "the trust," an artificial underground opposition designed to entrap those hostile to the regime, so the DGSE initiated a fake insurrectionary group, the sole purpose of which was to set up and justify their murder of Jorge Salazar, the leader of the private farmers and a man regarded by some as the most charismatic figure in the civic opposition. It also lured the priest who serves as spokesman for Radio Católica to the home of a female parishioner, where he was seized, stripped of his clothes, and then pushed out of the house naked to be filmed by a Sandinista TV crew, which just happened to be waiting outside. And it apparently sent a group of agents, posing as representatives of the International Red Cross, to a Miskito village, where they asked to be directed to the hideouts of local Miskito resistance forces, in order to bring them humanitarian aid.

On the other hand, the Sandinistas have indulged in little eye-catching violence. A relatively small number of executions has been attributed to them, and physical torture of prisoners is far less common than psychological abuse. This has distinguished the FSLN from many other triumphant Communist parties and has gone far toward softening Western perceptions of them. Their behavior seems all the more commendable in view of the sanguinary political traditions of Nicaragua, and the fact that the Somoza regime, though in most ways less restrictive than the Sandinistas, had a reputation for crude brutality.

One major exception to this relatively benign pattern of Sandinista behavior has been in their war with the Miskito Indians. Numerous instances of executions and torture, as well as rapes and other abuse of Miskito civilians, have been documented to the satisfaction of all impartial observers. In addition, recent testimony from some DGSE defectors raises questions about whether, in other situations far from public view, the Sandinistas have indulged in more killing and physical torture than has previously been realized.

Intimidation of Dissidents

Although the FSLN has refrained, for whatever reasons, from unleashing an outright reign of terror, it instead conducts a reign of intimidation. Opposition figures are often arrested for brief periods of interrogation, during which they are sometimes subjected to death threats both against themselves and against their families. More prominent ones are denounced in the Sandinista press as CIA agents, a severe though implicit threat because it justifies virtually any kind of retribution against them.

In addition, the *turbas*, stick-wielding, rock-throwing mobs, gather outside dissidents' homes or offices, chanting threats and inflicting minor injuries and vandalism. Homes are defaced with painted threats and accusations—"traitor," "CIA agent," "always watched." Borge and other FSLN leaders have sometimes denied government responsibility for the *turbas*, characterizing them as spontaneous grass-roots outpourings. But the veneer is thin. The mob attack on the home of former junta member Alfonso Robelo that sealed his decision to flee the country occurred at dawn on a Sunday. Government employees and students were reported to have been given the day off to join the mobs that attacked the meetings and rallies held by Arturo Cruz in 1984, when he weighed entering the Nicaraguan election. And when a U.S. embassy official asked for protection against possible anti-Yankee mob violence, Humberto Ortega replied in a speech published in *Barricada* that the diplomat need not fear because "our people . . . have discipline and they are not going to move against any target unless they have been ordered to do so beforehand by the National Directorate."

Often the *turbas* will chant or scrawl, "Go to Miami," and this probably reveals their true aim. The Sandinistas have not significantly restricted emigration, and their goal seems to be to encourage all dissidents to leave the country.

The Private Sector

Another way in which Nicaragua today differs from Communist countries is in the large proportion of the economy that remains privately owned. According to official Nicaraguan figures, the public sector accounted for just 43.5 per cent of the gross domestic product [GDP] in 1983. Other leading Nicaraguans, such as Alfonso Robelo, argue that such figures, whatever their accuracy in their own terms, understate the scope of government intervention. The public sector is comparatively so inefficient, they say, that to produce a given percentage of the GDP it must utilize a much larger percentage of the means of production. But whatever the truth of this, the private sector is still large.

The Sandinistas apparently recognize that the managerial experience of private producers would be difficult to replace. They also calculate, as a Sandinista leader is quoted as having told the Marxist magazine *Monthly Review*, that "the private sector is bait for getting foreign capital."

In addition, the Sandinistas see important political benefits in preserving the private sector as an influence on U.S. perceptions. *Comandante* Jaime Wheelock explains, "The economic considerations of the Nicaraguan revolution are not as important to us as its political aspects." The survival of the private sector helps to maintain national unity, he says, and "unity to confront imperialism is vital."

Nonetheless, as Borge explains, "a mixed economy in Nicaragua is not the same as a mixed economy in Costa Rica or in Uruguay and other countries of Latin America. This is a mixed economy within the revolution."

This means that private entrepreneurs may own enterprises, but their control over what they own is acutely circumscribed. The state maintains a monopoly over banking and foreign commerce and controls most legal domestic commerce. The state supplies credit and most factors of production; controls wages and prices; and in the case of agricultural goods, is the sole purchaser. As President Ortega put it last year, the revolution's progress toward further "social structuring of the economy . . . is perfectly compatible with the mixed economy, so long as the producers agree to produce what the economy needs, under production contracts with the state, and so long as businessmen dedicate themselves to distribution, in association with the mass organizations, and not to speculation." Probably the biggest reason for the shortages in basic commodities that now plague Nicaragua, traditionally a nation that though poor produced enough food for domestic consumption plus export, is the maintenance of prices by the government's agricultural purchasing monopoly near or below the costs of production, thereby discouraging production.

Within the context of the mixed economy, the Sandinistas have used confiscation as a tool of political control. Initially, the vast holdings of the Somoza family were expropriated, followed by those of his close cronies. Banking and foreign commerce were then nationalized in order to give the government control of the "commanding heights" of the economy. But since the early years of the revolution, confiscations have been applied increasingly as punishment against those who dissent politically or fail to cooperate economically with Sandinista policies. The most recent in a long line of prominent victims of such confiscations was Enrique Bolaños Geyer, current president of COSEP, the umbrella organization of private business and professional associations. Bolaños, said *Comandante* Wheelock, "has been involved in acts of aggression against our country."

If the preservation thus far of a substantial private sector distinguishes Nicaragua from Communist countries, the particular model of "land reform" followed by the Sandinistas falls squarely in the Communist tradition. Nicaragua is a sparsely populated country. As Daniel Nuñez, head of the Sandinista association of ranchers and farmers, put it: "The problem in Nicaragua is not a land problem. There is enough land for a million people to work." When the Sandinistas confiscated the holdings of Somoza and his circle, they had or were close to having enough land to provide each landless peasant with a plot of his own. But instead they created huge state farms and government-supervised cooperatives. Only a few private plots have been allocated, and these have come without clear title.

The Future of the Independent Institutions

Probably the most important thing distinguishing Nicaragua today from totalitarian states is the survival of various independent institutions that make for a genuine element of pluralism. These include the newspaper *La Prensa* [shut down by the Sandinistas in June 1986]; the Permanent Commission on Human Rights; two independent labor federations; a variety of business and professional associations linked together under the umbrella COSEP, the Supreme Council of Private Enterprise; several independent political parties, the most important of which work together with the labor and business groups in the Democratic Coordinator; and various churches, most significantly the Catholic Church, led by the staunchly independent Cardinal Miguel Obando y Bravo [see selection 24].

The FSLN's general approach toward these groups was expressed by Borge in a 1980 statement referring specifically to the political parties but applicable to the others as well: "They want to go on living. They stubbornly refuse to retire to a museum. We are not going to prevent them from continuing to live. They are going to die a natural death."

The FSLN's strategy is to do what it can to hasten their "natural death," without assuming the onus of banning the groups outright. Leaders of these groups have often been arrested and roughed up. In custody they are threatened and often pressed to collaborate with the authorities against their colleagues. The DGSE uses blackmail, threats, and bribes to sow division within their organizations. Even Cardinal Obando was seized in his car in a lonely spot by non-uniformed men, but whatever they had in store for him was aborted when he managed to shout into his two-way radio. *Turbas* have attacked the offices and meetings of these groups and the homes of their leaders, as well as the newsstands that sell *La Prensa*, some of which have as a result stopped selling it. There is relentless petty administrative harassment, and sometimes the harassment is more than trivial. Recognition of any new branch of the independent labor unions requires that the names of all members be submitted to the government. These new members then often receive chilling visits from agents of State Security. Leaders of the business organizations have suffered repeated confiscations.

These methods have borne fruit. None of the groups has yet collapsed, but all have been weakened by leadership turnovers and splits as one person after another has found himself unable to withstand the pressure. Many leaders of COSEP have left the country, as have two successive heads of the Permanent Commission on Human Rights, one labor federation head, several party leaders, the editor of *La Prensa*, and various of its reporters and columnists. Some of those who have remained within the country have moved their spouses and children abroad, not wishing them to share the perils.

Parallel Sandinista Institutions

In addition, the Sandinistas have worked to undermine these independent institutions by fostering their own parallel bodies. Most noted of these is the "People's Church," a group of Catholics who dissent from the Cardinal's stance, defy his authority, and embrace "liberation theology." Although it claims an emphasis on the poor, various observers have pointed out that its adherents are mostly foreign priests and middle-class churchgoers, and that its own institutions are far better funded than those of the mainstream church, because the former enjoy not only the favor of the government but large subsidies from left-leaning foreign church bodies. The "People's Church" bears a striking resemblance to the "Living Church," a progressive, schismatic body in the Russian Orthodox Church encouraged and manipulated by Lenin and then Stalin in their successful efforts to bring the main body of the Orthodox Church to heel.

The Sandinistas also have created their own labor federation, the CST, which, because many workers are compelled or pressured to join it, is now far larger than either of the independent labor bodies. But the CST is also a different kind of union. It is affiliated with the World Federation of Trade Unions, the Communist labor international, and it functions like the trade unions of the Communist countries. Its leaders are appointed by the government and, rather than representing the workers, its job is to represent the government to the workers. Much as the Soviet functionary Shelepin a few years back went from being an official of the KGB to head of the Soviet labor movement, so the head of the CST recently moved over to become head of the Sandinista militias. At its national assembly last year, the CST adopted a resolution declaring that "the strike is a form of struggle ... [that] has no place in Nicaragua, because power is in the hands of the workers"; another calling on the government "to put a stop to the incorrect practice of some administrators and directors who encourage wage anarchy" by paying their workers *above* prescribed scales; another calling for *reductions* in the amount of finished goods that each worker is allowed to purchase at cost from his own factory; and another declaring that in the face of hunger, "we workers must push forward family and institutional gardens." The CST resolutions concluded with ringing calls for "More productivity!" and "More discipline!"

The government also created the National Commission for the Promotion and Protection of Human Rights, the role of which, in the words of one of the several of its officers who have defected, is "to discredit the Permanent Commission for Human Rights" and to "make propaganda for the Sandinista government" by focusing on abuses by the contras. It also has created all kinds of businessmen's organizations to parallel existing independent ones, and even a new organization of the Miskito Indians, MISATAN, as an alternative to MISURA and MISURASATA, the authentic Indian organizations. Brooklyn Rivera, one of the Miskito leaders, commented: "They try to control an organization. If that fails, they try to divide it. If that fails, they form another organization with a similar name."

For the moment, the parallel organizations contribute to the process of weakening and discouraging the original ones. In the long term, the Sandinistas may foresee mergers between various of the parallel groups and their counterpart originals as a graceful, relatively non-controversial way for the latter to expire.

Economic Havoc

After more than six years of rule, the Sandinistas have brought ruin to the Nicaraguan economy. According to official Nicaraguan figures, the economy has been shrinking while inflation and foreign debt have been soaring. GNP per capita has fallen to the levels of twenty years ago. Immense increases in prices of food and clothing, without any commensurate wage increases, mean that the average Nicaraguan's standard of living has plummeted. This of course has been exacerbated by the civil war and the U.S. embargo, but its fundamental cause is irrational economic policies that transformed a food-exporting country into a land of severe shortages.

It is not clear how much this distresses the Sandinistas. "Our economy might drop to 1940 levels," said Jaime Wheelock, but "the important thing is . . . the ability to make the revolution prevail" against its enemies. And although the economy drops, the Sandinista rulers themselves don't share in the privations. They have taken for themselves the homes, cars, and luxuries left behind by Somoza and expropriated from other wealthy Nicaraguans. Las Colinas, a luxury neighborhood of Managua, is now largely populated by the Sandinista elite, guarded by a roadblock that keeps ordinary Nicaraguans away. Borge and some of the other *comandantes* are known to have several homes and cars each, justified on the grounds that this improves their security. As in Communist countries, an exclusive hard-currency store has opened in Managua where foreigners as well as members of the emerging Nicaraguan "nomenklatura" may shop for goods otherwise not available.

One result of the transformations wrought in Nicaragua by the FSLN has been a huge exodus. The Sandinistas acknowledge the flight of many middle-class Nicaraguans to the United States, but tens of thousands of others have crossed the borders into Honduras and Costa Rica. These are mostly poor people, and their migration is not legal. Hence there are no exact numbers. But various shreds of evidence suggest that 5 per cent or more of the Nicaraguan population has fled.

The current civil war is itself another major result of Sandinista rule. The rebels, a wholly volunteer force, are now reported to have some fifteen to eighteen thousand men under arms. This probably exceeds the total number fighting on both sides combined in the FSLN's war to overthrow Somoza. It is fifty times as large as the FSLN was a year or less before it came to power. The Sandinistas were mostly romantic student radicals, but today's rebels are mostly peasants. Ironically, the Sandinistas have finally succeeded in generating the kind of mass movement of the poor that they dreamed of for two decades, only its purpose is to oust them from power, not sweep them into it.

U.S. Policy Dilemma

Whether the rebel movement can succeed is of course quite uncertain. This leaves ample room for thoughtful disagreement about U.S. policy. But there is little room for thoughtful disagreement about where Nicaragua is headed under the Sandinistas. No Leninist group has ever changed its course once in power. Djilas is probably the only example we have of an individual leader of such a group who did change, and he knew he had no chance of turning his comrades around. The current situation and ideology of the Sandinistas allow them the special gratification of being at once flagrantly self-indulgent and certain of their own righteousness. It's a hard combination to beat. As long as they face an external threat they are likely to proceed slowly, but unless something stops them, the end of their journey is not in doubt.

Seeing Sandinista Nicaragua through clear eyes does not in itself resolve the policy dilemmas the United States faces, but it does clarify them. The essential question is whether the United States should support (or even undertake) the use of force against the Nicaraguan government. Some say that U.S. support for the Nicaraguan rebels has led to a greater degree of repression there, but this is true only in a trivial way if at all. Their deeply held convictions tell the Sandinistas that forces independent of themselves are anachronisms whose dying out is part of the process of human liberation. Only concern about U.S. reaction deters them from smothering these forces entirely. The same convictions impel the Sandinistas to lend fraternal support to other Central American revolutionaries. Again, concern about U.S. reaction affects the level and visibility of this support. And the Sandinistas have at least once made public their willingness to host Soviet military bases, although the Kremlin quickly nixed the idea.

The Sandinistas' history of coping with the United States by means of deception diminishes whatever small hope may exist that these issues would be amenable to diplomatic solution. The only agreements that would stick are those that the United States would be prepared to uphold by force, such as prohibitions against basing certain weapons. But the United States is already enforcing such prohibitions unilaterally. The "bottom line" issue is whether the costs of trying to remove the Sandinistas outweigh, for ourselves and the Nicaraguan people, the costs of a Communist Nicaragua.

22. North America's Crimes

By DANIEL ORTEGA

Focus
"Every time I have spoken with U.S. journalists and they have attempted to see U.S. democracy as an example, I tell them that we do not really envy U.S. democracy," Nicaraguan president Daniel Ortega told a group of foreigners engaged in a peace march for Central America. Ortega cited the "annihilation" of the American Indians and a continuing effort to exploit and discriminate against blacks as domestic flaws of U.S. democracy.

In its foreign affairs, especially in Latin America, the United States has demanded submission, often engaging in brutal interventions, said Ortega. "The United States is killing Nicaraguans every day, and when a policy of extermination is launched through economic and military means, and political isolation, that is called genocide."

Ortega characterizes his government in Nicaragua as "a democracy that first of all has given the people the right to speak, to express themselves, to criticize, to organize themselves." Fair elections have been held, marred only by the refusal of some parties to participate. Curtailment of freedoms is solely the result of the U.S. military threat, but even these limitations have been legally proclaimed in a formal state of emergency.

The U.S. response to this has been to murder children, women, and workers, says Ortega, because America demands submission and cannot tolerate a truly nonaligned nation in Latin America. The Sandinistas have good relations with the Soviet Union, he says, and would like to have similar relations with the United States if only it would cease its aggression. Too often, in Ortega's view, U.S. congressmen have shown a poorly developed or distorted conscience, debating only which way will best put pressure on Nicaragua rather than how to reach an understanding with that country.

He concludes by asserting that there is absolute freedom of religion in free Nicaragua. The marchers had asked if they could form a human chain between the Soviet and U.S. embassies. Ortega thinks that the struggle in Nicaragua is not an East-West struggle and that it would be better to form a chain between Managua and Washington.

President Ortega's defense of Sandinista Nicaragua should be compared with the generally favorable views of Gabriel Jackson (selection 20) and the criticisms of Joshua Muravchik (selection 21), Robert Leiken (selection 23), and Michael Walzer (selection 27).

Daniel Ortega, for many years a militant fighter against the Somoza regime, was elected Nicaragua's first Sandinista president in 1984.

APPROXIMATELY TWENTY-FIVE to thirty questions have been asked. We always like you to ask questions, and then we make a speech to the group as a whole. We want to make a speech in which all the people play a part. In this case, it is you, the peace marchers, and us, the officials serving the Nicaraguan people.

We know that you are tired. You have had a hectic journey. Many of you have come from countries in time zones that are hours away from Nicaragua's. You are possibly still unused to the time difference. That is why we did not want to exhaust you by answering each question individually. That would have kept us here until daybreak.

It is meaningful that this beautiful gesture you are staging is taking place in December, a month that is so symbolic for humanity. You are calling for peace. You want peace for the world, for the peoples. Peace, however, has not made itself fully present on earth or in Central America.

You are touring the Central American countries during the month of December, as it was done in the days when Saint Joseph and the Virgin Mary were traveling around seeking a place where they would be given shelter so that Christ could be born. [*Applause.*] No one wanted to give them shelter until they came to a humble manger where, according to history, Christ was born.

Nicaragua wants to be a humble manger for you [*applause*] because we really want peace, we want peace. The Nicaraguan people are struggling for peace; they are struggling for peace by shedding their blood every day. This is done because we want to be an independent nation; because we want just and respectful relations with great countries like the United States. We are facing a policy that is mistaken, selfish, arrogant, and is being adopted by U.S. leaders. We want to have a true democracy, and we are working to create it.

Every time I have spoken with U.S. journalists and they have attempted to use U.S. democracy as an example, I tell them that we do not really envy U.S. democracy. How can we envy a regime, a system like the one which

---

Statement to participants in an international peace march for Central America, in Managua, December 20, 1985, as recorded and translated by the U.S. Foreign Broadcast Information Service.

prevails in the United States, which claims to be democratic and yet in the twentieth century, in 1960, violently countered the U.S. blacks' struggle to have their civil rights recognized? This cannot be an example of democracy for Nicaragua. It is a system that has annihilated the Indian population in the United States and has exploited and discriminated against the black population. The struggle continues today, precisely in Philadelphia, where they are trying to deny the black people's rights, where they are repressing the blacks, and where they are always trying to segregate them in the universities. This is a problem which must be solved by the U.S. people by developing their democracy, by building their democracy.

U.S. Violations of Law

What are the United States' relations, as a democratic nation, with countries like Nicaragua? These relations cannot be described as democratic; these relations violate the U.S. Constitution's basic principles. The United States is violating international laws by claiming it has the right to attack Nicaragua. It is also violating the principles of its own constitution, which hypothetically compel the U.S. government to respect international law.

Every time the United States disregards the International Court of Justice's jurisdiction, it is acting in an irrational way, it is acting in a monstrous way, because it is imposing or trying to impose a policy of force over the policy of law and reason. Every time the U.S. Congress discusses how to attack the Nicaraguan people; every time the U.S. Congress approves $27 million to continue developing the U.S. government's terrorist policy against Nicaragua; every time the U.S. authorities state this is all right because the counter-revolutionary forces, the mercenary forces, are being attacked by the Sandinista army's helicopters; when all these criminal actions are carried out, which have already meant the death of more than 11,000 Nicaraguans, that is acting like a monster, and it is an act of genocide. [*Applause.*]

Nicaragua is a small nation, which has little more than three million inhabitants. Since we have still not had a census, we are still not sure whether we are 3.2 or 3.4 million people. Anyway, the United States is killing Nicaraguans every day, and when a policy of extermination is launched through economic and military means, and political isolation, that is called genocide, and we are defending the Nicaraguan people's right to build their democracy.

What kind of democracy are we building here in Nicaragua? A

democracy that first of all has given the people a right to speak, to express themselves, to criticize, to organize themselves. A democracy that for the first time in history gave our people truly free elections, in which for the first time in Nicaragua's history seven political parties participated, including right to ultra-left parties. The parties that did not participate in these elections did not do so because they did not want to.

Now, in my opinion, this is not an East-West conflict. This is what the United States is trying to make you believe. I think it would be better to make a human chain from Managua to Washington. [*Laughter, applause.*]

The Unpayable Debt

We were also asked about the official exchange rate. You must have been changing dollars already. Well, this is a very complex problem, in which we are seeking ways to encourage the productive sector. In fact, we have an exchange rate that is favorable for the productive sector. This is part of the complexities of the international economic crisis, which is particularly affecting the Latin American countries. The debt is a terrible burden that crushes our people's possibilities for development. We fully agree with President Fidel Castro when he says that the debt is unpayable. [See selection 2.] I believe that all of Latin America is in total accord with this even if it does not say so. The debt is unpayable. Therefore [*chuckles*] it is impossible to collect.

The United States deals with this problem by attempting to divide Latin America. Latin America has begun to close ranks in the face of the threat against Nicaraguan sovereignty and around the foreign debt problem. These two great problems are uniting Latin America. The United States is desperately attempting to divide Latin America. It is working to isolate Nicaragua, to find the support of countries other than the Central American countries to intervene in Nicaragua. The United States uses the economic problem, the foreign debt problem, to divide Latin America. They are approaching the Latin American countries one by one to make them negotiate in accordance with the IMF's standards, which are good only for strangling the Latin American peoples' economies.

However, we have a great deal of confidence in the Latin American peoples. The Latin American peoples have mobilized on behalf of Nicaragua because the sovereignty of Latin America is at stake. The Latin American peoples have also rallied round the foreign debt problem. Therefore, we trust that the Latin American governments will respect their peoples' will.

The United States will continue to struggle—as it is doing now—to make the OAS [Organization of American States] regress to what it was in the sixties, when it was party to the move to isolate Cuba and later to the Yankee invasion of the Dominican Republic. The United States is attempting to make Latin American history turn back in time. It has not realized that history cannot be turned back in Latin America or that Latin America will win the battle for sovereignty [*applause*], the battle against the foreign debt, and for peace. [*Applause.*]

A Peace-Keeping Proposal

I forgot to mention a proposal in connection with U.N. troops that would be used in peace-keeping forces in Central America. Our foreign minister has addressed this idea in general terms also. Moreover, we presented a proposal to Costa Rica to post a multilateral force at the border. Those talks began in Paris. The French government expressed its willingness to help us promote this idea. However, the United States opposed this and blocked the proposal. We know that the United States has veto power in the United Nations. Proposals like this one are difficult to implement. We must struggle to change the policy the United States is currently upholding.

We were asked what you can do for this struggle for peace. The attitude of the U.S. government and people must be changed. What are you doing? A great deal. This march for peace is really unprecedented in Central America. I had never heard of a march similar to this one in Latin America. This peace march is bringing together voices and consciences of citizens from all over the world; from New Zealand, Norway, Canada, the United States, Guatemala, Colombia, Panama, and ... how many other countries? [*People in the crowd shout out country names, including Denmark, Finland, Germany, England, Ireland, Australia, the Netherlands, Spain, Belgium, Ecuador, Mexico, Italy, Argentina, Japan. Crowd laughs, applauds as Ortega repeats names of countries.*] These are citizens of the world united in a brotherhood with the Central American peoples, and tonight with the Nicaraguan people, in the struggle for peace.

I assure you that all the Central American people welcome you joyously. I am sure that the Costa Rican people love you because they know that you want peace between Nicaragua, Costa Rica, and all Central America. We are sure that those who sow hate in Central America are few. [*Applause.*] The Central American people sow love. That is why we welcome you with love, and we will continue to struggle and fight with love, and we are sure that you will always stand beside us for the sake of peace.

Consequently, allow me to thank you for this gesture of peace on behalf of my people. [*Applause.*]

This is a democracy that was immediately attacked by the current U.S. leader. As soon as he assumed the government, President Reagan immediately launched actions against Nicaragua. These actions have resulted in the destruction of schools constructed by the revolution, the destruction of health centers built by the revolution, the destruction of centers for children, development centers built by the revolution, of cooperatives promoted by the revolution, of machinery and tractors that were given to peasants who never before had any machinery or tractors, and, the most brutal result, the loss of thousands of Nicaraguan lives—the murder of hundreds of children under twelve years of age, the murder of women, of young people. Nicaragua has been experiencing a real genocide.

A Tradition of Struggle

Now, what can the Nicaraguan people do in the face of this genocide? We have heard about the peaceful resistance struggle, and we admire struggles such as the ones led by Gandhi and Martin Luther King, Jr. However, we have our own historical tradition. We have our own characteristics, and when the first Yankee filibusters invaded Nicaragua in the last century, there was no place for peaceful resistance. The Nicaraguan people carried out an active resistance, and even with stones the Yankees were defeated then in Nicaragua. [*Applause.*]

Then came the U.S. army intervention at the beginning of the century, at a time when the Soviet Union did not even exist. There was the Russia of the czars. What was the pretext when U.S. troops invaded Nicaragua in 1912? There was no Soviet Union then. It could not have been the threat of the Soviet Union—what was the United States' pretext to invade Nicaragua then? The pretext of its arrogance, its colonial mentality. That was their real pretext to invade our country. The Nicaraguan people resisted the U.S. invasion actively. Then came the time of Sandino. At that time, the Soviet Union could be blamed because by then it existed. However, because the Mexican revolution was closer, it was easier to blame the Mexican revolution. There had been no Cuban revolution yet. That is why the Mexican revolution carried the blame. There was active resistance.

The Nicaraguan people have traditionally followed the line of active resistance. We must not forget that Christ, who was a true pacifist, at one time had to raise his whip to drive the thieves out of the temple. We believe that the Nicaraguan people's struggle is in line with non-violent resistance. We are seeking peace. We are defending peace. We are defending it actively. If we did not defend peace with rifles we would lose everything we have accomplished. This is the kind of struggle the Nicaraguan people have carried out. It is within Latin American's tradition of struggle. We have followed tradition and history in defending ourselves.

We respect those who philosophically uphold and practice pacifism and non-violent resistance. And we repeat: We find that non-violent resistance and the effort we are doing through active resistance—which costs the lives and sacrifice of thousands of Nicaraguans each day—are compatible.

Non-Aligned Nicaragua

The Nicaraguan people's struggle is complex and difficult. To harvest or grow coffee in Nicaragua implies risks, including risking one's life. Workers, teachers, and doctors risk their lives. The mercenary forces fire against teachers, doctors, and workers every day. They are attempting to destroy everything that stands for progress and life in the revolution, and, as we said, all this is the work and deed of the U.S. government, which cannot stand to see a small nation be independent and non-aligned.

I was asked whether Nicaragua could remain a non-aligned country. Let me say this: The United States is attacking us precisely because we are non-aligned. The United States would be much more cautious about attacking us if we were part of a military bloc. However, it is easier for the United States to attack a country that is not a member of any military bloc, even though it does attempt to frame the Central America conflict within the East-West confrontation to justify its aggressiveness. This is not an East-West confrontation. This is a confrontation that is taking place within the United States. American consciences are in conflict because the U.S. government is intent on maintaining a policy of force in Central America. The United States cannot allow small countries like Nicaragua to be independent. They begin with the premise that if one is not under their power, one is against them. The United States only accepts submission. It is inconceivable for the United States that a nation as small as Nicaragua refuses to submit itself.

I say that this is a problem for the U.S. conscience because the United States has continued to feel the same as it did in the past century regarding its relations with Latin America. This means that the U.S. conscience either has not completed its evolution or has not even begun to evolve. The U.S. president reflects this poor U.S. conscience, and its deformation. Many times, U.S. congressmen have not discussed the way to reach an understanding with Nicaragua on respectful relations. They have rather discussed the best and most intelligent way to pressure Nicaragua, whether it is the Reagan way or one proposed by others. They have discussed the best way to force the Nicaraguan people to submit to them.

The Contadora Proposals

Of course, we who are near the United States, these Latin American countries, most directly suffer the consequences of this policy. Contadora has been an effort by Latin America and supported by it. Latin America has adopted a just stance and told the United States that a peaceful rather than a violent solution must be sought. But the United States has not accepted the Contadora peace proposals and has applied great pressure to the Contadora countries. The United States has also pressured and threatened the support countries. The United States has even spoken on behalf of the Contadora countries in a number of instances in an effort to jeopardize these countries' policies.

Contadora held discussions and negotiated for a little over two years. We were involved in negotiations for approximately two years and ten months, almost three years. First it was proposed that the discussions be oriented toward a search for gradual solutions. That was a logical proposal that Nicaragua endorsed. However, the United States disagreed with this idea. The truth is that the United States did not agree with any idea. The United States proposed that negotiations be multilateral. At one point in time Nicaragua—to benefit the negotiations process—agreed to multilateral negotiations. Nicaragua was flexible in Contadora on numerous occasions.

Last year, in September, Contadora presented a peace proposal that Nicaragua accepted. The United States—through Honduras, El Salvador, and Costa Rica—rejected that peace proposal. From that moment on the United States worked to distort and alter the proposal that Contadora presented last year. Along with all its actions to pressure the Contadora Group, it staged military actions against Nicaragua. This means that while the negotiations went one way, the United States was escalating its military aggression against Nicaragua. It came to a point when the negotiations were hiding the truth of the escalation, of the military aggression.

The U.S. representatives said that the United States will continue to support the mercenary forces even after the Contadora peace document is signed. They delivered missiles to the mercenary forces after having approved $27 million and the use of those funds for the purchase of aircraft, vessels, and surface vehicles. It was the first time that surface-to-air missiles have been placed in the hands of irregular forces in this hemisphere. There have been irregular forces in this hemisphere everywhere, from Canada to Chile, including in the United States. However, irregular forces in this hemisphere had never been equipped with this kind of weapon. That was a genuine military escalation. The United States openly defended this military escalation.

Under these circumstances, we think that the effort to be exerted by Contadora and Latin America should be aimed at countering this stepped-up military aggression, at talking with the United States so that it will cease this military aggression against Nicaragua; and then the necessary conditions will be created to achieve some progress in the negotiations. We cannot accept the illusion of negotiations and pretend the solution is near, when the truth is telling us that blood is being shed in Nicaragua, that the United States has stepped up its military aggression, that the United States has even advanced in the search for conditions to carry out a direct military intervention in Nicaragua.

This is Nicaragua's position concerning Nicaragua. We think Contadora and Latin America should decisively counter this stepped-up military aggression. Nicaragua maintains good relations with many countries; it would take too long to list all the countries with which Nicaragua maintains good relations. It is much easier to list the countries that have decided to maintain bad relations with Nicaragua, and we would have to say that one country has decided to maintain bad relations with Nicaragua. The day that that country, meaning the United States, changes its attitude toward Nicaragua, two or three other countries will also change their attitude toward Nicaragua.

Now then, we maintain good relations with the Soviet Union and Cuba, and we have stated that we want to have with the United States the same kind of good relations we have with the Soviet Union. There are many non-aligned countries—India for example—that have good relations with the Soviet Union and the United States. Therefore, we continue to defend our right to be a non-aligned country and to maintain good relations with all the countries in the world.

The State of Emergency

This situation of aggression we are withstanding has compelled us to establish a state of emergency. It is true that the state of emergency is a political decision, but it also proves the respect we have for juridical issues, because it would be justifiable if we adopted other kinds of measures, but we have not done so. Instead, we have resorted to a legal document, meaning the state of emergency, to defend the revolution in a legal way. Many governments, including the U.S. government, use the state of emergency to justify their policies and economic embargo against Nicaragua.

However, the state of emergency will disappear in our country the moment the aggression disappears and we have again a normal situation. The aggression has affected the Nicaraguan society and provoked tension among the political forces in Nicaragua, and the United States has offered the military solution. This has provoked expectation among certain Nicaraguans who oppose the revolutionary process, but this is understandable.

Some Nicaraguans have a submissive attitude toward the United States and see the U.S. armed forces as a power that attacks Nicaragua. They assume that the United States will win this battle because it is a powerful nation with innumerable resources and Nicaragua is a small nation; and this creates tension within our country.

When the United States offers the armed solution, many Nicaraguans are easily attracted either because they are gullible or because they have no political experience. They are thus compromised in armed counter-revolutionary actions. This is how some Nicaraguans and Miskito Indians become involved in armed counter-revolutionary actions. Even the Somocista guards who live in Honduras became involved in the armed actions when the United States brought them weapons and paid them salaries. If the United States came to Honduras and, instead of offering weapons and salaries to the guards, offered tractors and plows to till the land in Honduras, there would be no counter-revolutionary forces. The same thing would have happened with the Miskitos if they had been offered food, clothes, and work instead of weapons.

Priests Who 'Do Not Understand'

In addition, with its actions of state terrorism, the United States provoked and has provoked some expectations among some of the Catholic Church hierarchs. However, the truth is that I cannot say that all bishops are against the revolutionary process. There are some priests who do not understand the revolution, and therefore are against the revolutionary process. So the truth is that if we make a comparison, as Father Cardenal has explained, although the Nicaraguan government revoked the residence of ten foreign priests, some bishops in Nicaragua have revoked the Nicaraguan residence of more than 200 priests and nuns. Priests and nuns have been expelled from our country for the crime of identifying themselves with the process of change in Nicaragua.

But of course, this is a political problem, and therefore political positions are in conflict. So there is a polemic, and there are clashes in the political field with those who oppose the revolution in the political field. But on the other hand, there is no religious persecution here. Here the people can practice their religion in complete freedom, and the religious leaders can conduct their activities with absolute freedom.

As for the Miskito population, *Compañero* [comrade] [Ray] Hooker has already mentioned the progress that has been made regarding this problem. *Compañero* Hooker is from the Atlantic Coast; he was kidnapped for several months by the counter-revolutionary forces, and is currently actively participating in the autonomy process.

There is another question here about the use of the Sandinista symbols in the march. I would say that it is your decision, and we recognize your efforts in favor of peace. We are not asking you to say that you support the Sandinista revolution, because the fact that you favor peace, and that Nicaragua is also in favor of peace, makes us feel that you support us through your gesture. [*Applause.*]

We were also asked if the Nicaraguan government would authorize the creation of a human chain from the U.S. embassy to the Soviet embassy. Well, we have no reason to impose any restrictions on you. You are free to do whatever you want here. You are in free Nicaragua. [*Applause.*]

23. The Sandinistas' Tangled Elections

By ROBERT S. LEIKEN

Focus At the end of the Nicaraguan presidential election campaign in 1984, Daniel Ortega warned a large rally of supporters: "The only ones who will not vote would be the enemies of Nicaragua, the traitors, the turncoats, and will expose themselves to the fury of the people at the moment of [U.S.] intervention." His threat was widely publicized by official organs, says Robert Leiken. Nevertheless, as many as 400,000 more Nicaraguans may have abstained from voting than the final Sandinista tallies indicated.

The validity and significance of Nicaragua's 1984 elections continue to be sharply debated. Often the discussion is determined by political considerations having little to do with election conditions per se. Leiken believes the elections were a partial success for the Sandinistas. "The exclusion of [principal opposition candidate Arturo] Cruz and the electoral abuses described in the American press sharply diminished remaining Sandinista sympathies in the U.S. Congress, but the cautiously favorable report of the official observer of the Socialist International ... seemed to satisfy some of its members." However, a prominent member of the Socialist International commented to Leiken about the elections: "We had to endorse them. Reagan endorsed the Salvadoran elections."

According to Leiken, the Sandinistas still have support "among public employees, peasants who have benefited from the agrarian reform, and young activists." Their great fear, however, that candidate Cruz might create a "wave of support that could elude Sandinista control and reveal the erosion of the FSLN's popular backing" led them to impose a number of restrictions on Cruz that eventually led to his withdrawal from the contest. The election process was sufficiently flawed that only minor Western European and Latin American officials were sent to Daniel Ortega's inauguration. "Fidel Castro dominated the ceremonies."

Leiken's intricate account of the events surrounding the Nicaraguan elections should be compared with the very different views of Gabriel Jackson (selection 20) and Daniel Ortega (selection 22).

Robert S. Leiken is a senior associate at the Carnegie Endowment and the editor of *Central America: Anatomy of a Conflict.*

Nicaragua's 1979 insurrection was called the "beautiful revolution." It united the people against the corrupt Somoza dictatorship and promised a "third way" between neo-colonial capitalist exploitation and the Cuban model of socialism. Today, the "new Nicaragua" is sunk in a fratricidal war equipped and financed by the superpowers, while its national aspirations smother. The movement of the Sandinistas toward closer relations with the Soviet Union has left many of their international supporters either publicly critical or else privately embarrassed; some now concentrate on the aggressive policies of the Reagan administration and the contra forces it is backing rather than directly defend the revolutionary government.

The Nicaraguan elections in 1984 were central to what has happened since; yet they remain poorly understood. They seemed to present a promising opportunity. The revolution could recover its democratic legitimacy; the people would have a chance to approve or reject Sandinista leadership and arrive at national reconciliation. But the "first free elections in Nicaraguan history" bore a strong resemblance to those conducted by the Somoza dynasty. They marked only a pause in the civil war, and another episode in the contest between Moscow and Washington. After the elections, the number of Nicaraguan rebels increased, the war grew more intense, and the superpowers stepped up their involvement in it. After six years of Sandinista rule, Nicaragua was more entangled with outside powers than ever before.

There was a moment when independent Nicaraguans tried to intervene in the electoral contest. On August 5, 1984, in Chinandega, thousands came to a rally in support of Arturo Cruz, the opposition candidate. The Sandinistas dispatched a mob to disrupt the meeting, and the independent newspaper *La Prensa* was prohibited from publishing reports of what had happened in Chinandega. After that, the contest between the Sandinistas and the opposition turned into a protracted and largely secret series of negotiations conducted by politicians and diplomats. Those with the least to say in the matter were Nicaragua's voters. The Sandinistas' advertised

---

Reprinted by permission from the *New York Review of Books*, December 5, 1985.

"first free elections" joined the long, inglorious line of Central American "demonstration elections"—a tradition founded by the United States in the earlier part of the century.

Three Sandinista Promises

For the last decade the Sandinistas have relied on their ability to reconcile their private plans with their public image, and their ideology with domestic and geopolitical realities. Nicaragua is a country of many small businessmen, a large but impoverished petite bourgeoisie, a deeply religious peasantry, and a tiny proletariat in a region in which the United States is the predominant power and in which, except among some of the intelligentsia and young people, the Cuban revolution is held in low regard. Democratic aspirations run deep. The Sandinistas, to gain domestic and international support against Somoza in the spring of 1979, made, as *Comandante* Bayardo Arce said last May, "three promises that made us internationally presentable and that were manageable for us from a revolutionary standpoint . . . non-alignment, a mixed economy, and political pluralism."

The same promises were central to the skillful and flexible policy of the moderate Sandinistas—the *"terceristas"*—who became the internationally prominent leaders of the alliance that brought down Somoza. That alliance included the Catholic Church, most Nicaraguan businessmen, a variety of labor leaders, liberals, social and Christian democrats, Communists, and *La Prensa*.

The 1979 insurrection was mainly an urban struggle made possible by new social forces that were unleashed by thirty years of sustained growth. As export agriculture became modernized, dispossessed peasants flocked to urban shantytowns, labor unions were organized, and from a rapidly growing student population arose not only radical activists but a technocratic and commercial middle class stifled by Somoza's dynastic rule. Indeed, the Nicaraguan revolution was set off by the assassination of Pedro Joaquín Chamorro, editor of *La Prensa* and the leader of the broad-based coalition named UDEL—not by any action of the Sandinistas, whose forces had languished for years in the northern mountains.

For Daniel Ortega, who was elected president on November 4, 1984, and for the other *comandantes,* participation in the broad alliance was from the first "tactical and temporary," as was stated in the 1977 "General Platform" of the *terceristas*. In 1977, Ortega's brother Humberto, a leader of the "moderate" *tercerista* faction and now defense minister, identified the "civic bourgeois opposition" to Somoza as a "reactionary force"—in the same category, he said, as Somoza's followers and Yankee imperialists.

Within six months after taking power the Sandinistas succeeded in removing their unreliable revolutionary partners from the most important cabinet posts. In May 1980 the Sandinista National Liberation Front (FSLN) stacked the quasi-legislative Council of State with its own supporters, leading two prominent democrats—Alfonso Robelo and Violeta Chamorro—to resign from the five-person revolutionary junta.

During the year and a half before Ronald Reagan took office, the Sandinistas turned to the Soviet bloc for help in building a large military force, in setting up a tight internal security apparatus, and in training large numbers of party, government, and military personnel.

In 1981 the regime intensified press censorship and stepped up its harassment of the political opposition, independent trade unions, Miskito Indians, and the church. Expropriations of the property of many non-Somocistas, official corruption, mismanagement of public enterprises ranging from the coffee processors to the national airline, and unsound agricultural commodity pricing estranged hitherto generous lending institutions such as the World Bank. The Reagan administration did its best to encourage this estrangement.

Organizing the Opposition

Then in November 1981 the Reagan administration began to equip and train counter-revolutionary groups—a decision that for many transformed Nicaragua's internal conflict into one between Washington and Managua. But well before the contras became a significant military force, political and economic discontent was already creating its own recruits for counter-revolution. Factories were closing, peasants were balking at imposed state purchases, the supply of foreign exchange and imported industrial goods was dwindling, and consumer goods had become scarce.

These developments were seized on by hard-liners in Washington, especially in the CIA and the National Security Council, who were determined from the outset to cripple and ultimately destroy the Sandinista regime. And indeed, U.S. support of armed insurgents greatly contributed to Nicaragua's economic difficulties, fostered a siege mentality among the Sandinistas, and provided an excuse for a military buildup and internal repression in Nicaragua.

By 1983, the Nicaraguan economy was in serious trouble and the country was on a war footing. The Soviet Union was willing to furnish oil and counterinsurgent weapons but not to resolve the economic crisis or provide guarantees of Nicaragua's security. The favorable U.S. domestic reaction to the intervention in Grenada shattered the Sandinistas' confidence in the strength of political opposition in the United States to an invasion of Nicaragua. They then turned for support to Western Europe and Latin America—only to find that there, too, their prestige had deteriorated.

Closer to home, El Salvador's guerrillas, on whom the Sandinistas had counted to provide them with a "geopolitical shield," were making little progress, and many of the Salvadoran insurgent leaders with whom I spoke blamed the Sandinistas' ultra-left policies for their difficulties in winning non-Marxist backing. Nicaragua's increasingly radical politics, together with the Reagan administration's pressures, also helped to shift the center of political gravity to the right in Costa Rica and Honduras, further isolating the Sandinistas.

Within Nicaragua itself, both armed and peaceful opposition was growing. The decision to institute compulsory military service in the fall of 1983 was vastly unpopular. I interviewed three hundred Nicaraguans from many different occupations and political groups during two recent visits, and most of them told me that they had become fed up with the regime.

In these circumstances, many Sandinista leaders came to see elections, promised grudgingly in 1979, as convenient, even welcome. "Elections are a nuisance, as are a lot of things which make up the reality of the revolution," Bayardo Arce, one of the most powerful *comandantes*, said during a meeting last May with the Marxist-Leninist Nicaraguan Socialist Party (PSN), at which he represented the Sandinista National Directorate. "If it were not for the state of war forced on us . . . elections would be absolutely inappropriate," Arce said, confuting the widespread opinion that military pressure had prevented the Sandinistas from fulfilling their commitments to pluralism. What is needed, he continued, is not "bourgeois formalities but the dictatorship of the proletariat." Nonetheless, he argued, these "bourgeois details" can become "arms of the revolution," in the same way as it has been "useful, for example, to be able to point to an entrepreneurial class and private production in a mixed economy while we get on with our strategic goals."

Sandinista Factions

Along with Tomás Borge, Bayardo Arce is a leader of the radical faction of the Sandinista party, the Sandinista National Liberation Front (FSLN).

Today's factional struggle dates back to the mid-1970s, when Jaime Wheelock led a small group of younger Sandinistas into the "Proletarian Tendency." Wheelock wanted the Sandinistas to organize without delay "a vanguard party" based on the urban proletariat. The Sandinista old guard, led by Tomás Borge and Henry Ruiz, favored "accumulating force" in the countryside, and they became known as the Protracted People's War (GPP) tendency. In 1977, a third "tendency" (hence *"tercerista"*), led by Humberto and Daniel Ortega, seemed to break with the doctrinaire position of Wheelock and Borge and began to organize a broad tactical alliance to prepare for an insurrection. Yet the 1977 "General Platform" of the *terceristas* did not question the common Sandinista objective of Cuban-style socialism but argued against announcing this "in an open way."

The divisions among the Sandinistas gave rise to fierce recriminations, and they accused one another of being "petit bourgeois," "capitulationist," and "CIA agents." Unlike the Salvadoran revolutionary groups during the 1970s, the Sandinistas steered clear of the fundamental ideological debates then taking place in the international Communist movement. The Sandinistas argued about tactics for gaining power, not over what to do once they took power. In Havana in March 1979 the three groups were formally reunited.

Little more than a year before the final offensive in 1979, the total number of militants in the three factions was probably less than three hundred. When the Sandinistas gained power, the three tendencies, now no longer those of small marginal groups, began to struggle over the spoils and instruments of power. The divisions among the Sandinistas have often produced puzzling and self-destructive policies. Many observers attribute the Sandinistas' failure to hold elections during the first several months after coming to power, when their popularity was at its height, to an inability to unite behind a candidate. Sharp infighting between the moderates and the hard-liners also preceded Daniel Ortega's ultimate approval as the party's presidential candidate in July 1984.

Making Use of Elections

In his talk to the Nicaraguan Socialist Party in May 1984, Arce made it clear to his "fellow Communists," as he called them, that the Nicaraguan elections were designed from the beginning to appeal to Western liberals, especially U.S. congressional Democrats, European social democrats, and the Contadora countries. Elections would enable the FSLN to "disarm the international bourgeoisie" and perpetuate the "internal neutralization of the United States."

Arce argued that the international demand for elections could be turned to the Sandinistas' domestic advantage:

> Imperialism demands three things of us: to abandon interventionism, to abandon our strategic ties with the Soviet Union, ... and to be democratic....
>
> We cannot cease to be internationalists without ceasing to be revolutionaries. We cannot cease our strategic relationships without ceasing to be revolutionaries....
>
> But the superstructural aspects, so-called democracy, bourgeois democracy, have something that we can manage and even profit from for socialist construction.

He went on to explain that elections could "legitimate" the construction of a "Red constitution." By approving of the elections, social democrats and liberals would, in Arce's words, provide "the arms" for "terminating this whole artifice of pluralism ... which has been useful up to now, but has reached its end."

"This artifice of pluralism" was a telling phrase. After the American Marines occupied Nicaragua in 1912, the United States now and then sponsored "free elections" while building up the Nicaraguan National Guard under Anastasio Somoza and helping it to suppress the rebels led by Augusto Sandino. The last Somoza, Anastasio Somoza Debayle, a West Point graduate who spoke English better than Spanish, also staged elections while monopolizing political power. He tolerated a noisy but impotent opposition, censored the press, and enriched himself with international earthquake relief funds.

The 1979 Sandinista revolution was supposed to end all that. Nicaragua was to be free from plunderers, from corruption and "national betrayal," from foreigners claiming to bring the benefits of Christianity and democracy. But this was not to be. After four years of Sandinista rule and three of Reagan's, Somoza and the big powers cast long shadows over Nicaragua's future.

The Opposition and the Elections

In July of 1983, Daniel Ortega, on behalf of the governing junta, invited Arturo Cruz to return to Nicaragua for conversations. "Daniel was visualizing my becoming the opposition's presidential candidate—credible but meek," Cruz believed. A former member of the Sandinistas' junta, then its ambassador to the United States, Cruz broke with the Sandinistas in November 1981 in protest against what he called the increasingly repressive methods of the ruling Sandinista National Directorate.

As a young man Cruz participated in two unsuccessful coups against Somoza and was imprisoned by him. Later he worked with Pedro Joaquín Chamorro, the leader of UDEL, the "bourgeois" civic opposition movement. The UDEL coalition included trade unions and opposition parties (among them the Nicaraguan Socialist Party), as well as business, student groups, and community organizations. When the *terceristas* formed "The Twelve"—a group of prestigious Nicaraguans created to legitimize the armed struggle—the FSLN considered Cruz a natural for membership. Even today Cruz still has, as he told me, "a hangup on the Sandinistas." "I came to admire them because they fought bravely, risking their lives against the Somoza tyranny."

When Cruz broke with the Sandinistas, he returned to his previous job with the Inter-American Development Bank in Washington. The Sandinistas later made much of this in order to portray Cruz as "Washington's candidate." But if he had anyone's support in Washington, it was not the Reagan administration's. In fact, he said repeatedly that the administration's militaristic policies were making things more difficult for the beleaguered political opposition in Nicaragua.

The opposition—a loosely organized coalition of political parties, trade unions, and business organizations called the Coordinadora, the short name for National Democratic Coordinator (CDN)—was at a disadvantage in challenging the Sandinistas. The FSLN controlled the cabinet, the State Security apparatus, the army, the militias, the police, state TV, and radio. The local block committees (the Sandinista Defense Committees—CDS), in charge of such basic functions as ration cards, visas, and applications for public jobs and housing, had become extensions of the Sandinista party. Opposition groups had been forbidden to hold outdoor rallies since early 1981; political and trade union activists were frequently detained or imprisoned; opposition offices were attacked by Sandinista mobs called *turbas*; pamphlets and newspapers were confiscated. The Sandinistas encouraged people loyal to them to join the opposition parties and trade unions and form factions with them.

In November 1983 the traditional anti-Somoza Democratic Conservative Party split apart. The government declared that the party could be legally represented only by a minority faction that agreed to participate in the elections under the Sandinistas' ground rules. The rest of the party, the majority, was stripped of its legal status despite demands from other parties that a party assembly be held to determine which of the factions held the majority.

CDN Internal Disputes

The Coordinadora was itself torn by internal disputes. It had gradually come to include most of the UDEL and other groups that had opposed Somoza but then came to oppose the Sandinistas as well. Its right wing was dominated by the landholders of the old anti-Somoza Conservative Party and the leaders of the business council (COSEP). On the left were three groups: the Social Christians (reform-minded Christian Democrats who are close to the Catholic hierarchy); the "progressive" Conservatives (many of whom admired Cruz); and a militant anti-Somoza labor federation composed mainly of stevedores and factory workers. In the center were another labor federation, representing skilled workers, truckers, and independent tradesmen, and the small Constitutional Liberal and Social Democratic parties. The Sandinistas' decision to hold elections put this fragile coalition under great strain.

The older Conservative Party politicians and some of the more prominent business leaders, for example, were by now convinced that only force could move the Sandinistas—preferably American invasion. They were in touch with leaders of the largest group of contras—the Nicaraguan Democratic Force (FDN), which had been trained and financed by the CIA. The leaders of the FDN, along with hard-liners in the National Security Council and the CIA, encouraged the right wing of the Coordinadora to believe that Arturo Cruz was a potential *zancudo*, the term that had been used for those who, for a price, had collaborated in Somoza's staged elections. They reminded them that Cruz's aim, as he wrote in *Foreign Affairs* in 1983, was to "moderate," not to "challenge Sandinista power," and that he favored "dissidence," not "counter-revolution." When he was in the Sandinista government and after he quit, Cruz wrote, he wanted to "reconcile the revolutionary family," and he spoke out against the contras.

But after several weeks of bickering, the CDN nominated Cruz on July 20, 1984, three days before he returned to Managua from Washington. The right wing of the CDN still distrusted Cruz but reluctantly agreed that he would be the most popular candidate the opposition could present. The CDN's delay in nominating Cruz left him little more than a week to hold public meetings. The Sandinistas, still at that time anxious to have Cruz take part in the elections on their own terms, agreed to extend the registration period until August 5 to provide the time for negotiating the conditions under which the CDN would participate in the campaign. If the CDN did not register by August 5, the government said, it would be allowed only to hold meetings indoors with active CDN members.

CDN Conditions for Participation

In December 1983 the CDN had stated nine conditions for its participation in the election. These included demands for separation of the state and the FSLN party, respect for human rights, lifting the February 1982 state of emergency, an amnesty law, trade union and religious freedom, judicial independence, and legal safeguards such as *habeas corpus*. They also called for a "national dialogue" among all Nicaraguan factions including the armed opposition. Such a "dialogue"—the word has become central to Central American politics—would recognize that those who took part in it had a legitimate place in Nicaragua's future. Cruz put emphasis on the last point, and it was on this issue that talks with the Sandinistas broke down on August 3, 1984.

The FSLN claimed that the CDN, by insisting on the legitimacy of the rebels, would be using the elections to promote the war against the government. Some in the CDN—especially the Social Christians and the unions—wanted to take part in a political contest that could begin to democratize Nicaragua. They were caught between implacable extremes—the Sandinista hard-liners, with Cuban and Soviet backing, and the CDN right, with its friends supported by the CIA. Those with guns had the most powerful patrons.

The CDN right wing may well have supported the demand for talks with the rebels while expecting it to be rejected. For Cruz, the demand for talks was consistent with his support of the two attempts by the rebel commander Edén Pastora to reach a political settlement between 1982 and 1984, as well as with the position of the Nicaraguan bishops in their appeal of April 1984. Cruz also found the demand consistent with the proposals of the Contadora group for "national reconciliation." But, in view of the Sandinistas' categorical rejection of talks, the CDN's demand appeared quixotic at best and, at worst, an attempt to discredit the elections. It thus proved to be a political blunder, permitting the Sandinistas to brand the CDN a "contra front." As Daniel Ortega put it, the CDN's program confused the minimum conditions for participation in elections (such as freedom of the press, absence of harassment, access to the public media, and guarantees of personal safety) with issues that belonged in the CDN's campaign platform.

The Rally in Chinandega

Before the date for Cruz's registration had passed, the CDN, despite threats from the police, organized a series of rallies throughout Nicaragua. These came to a climax on August 5 at the rally in the historically pro-Sandinista city of Chinandega. Several thousand people turned out to support Cruz. A mob of *turbas* organized by the Sandinistas disrupted the Chinandega meeting.

A public surge of support for the opposition did not figure in the Sandinistas' electoral plans, and they prohibited *La Prensa* from publishing reports from Chinandega. Had the news of what had taken place there reached Nicaraguans in other cities, they might have been emboldened to do likewise. The memory of what had happened in Chinandega remained during the rest of the contest between the FSLN and the CDN—as a promise for some, and a menace for others.

Cruz won the next round in what, after Chinandega, became a diplomatic struggle with the FSLN, conducted behind closed doors. In late August he was officially received by the presidents of Colombia, Venezuela, Ecuador, Costa Rica, and El Salvador. That he was welcome in Venezuela, whose ruling Acción Democrática is the largest Latin American party in the Socialist International, underscored the desire of leading Latin American social democrats to have him included in the elections.

President Belisario Betancur of Colombia, the de facto leader of the Contadora group—which includes Mexico, Colombia, Panama, and Venezuela—accepted Cruz's proposal that he mediate the conflict over the elections. Now Cruz became central to any evaluation of the elections' legitimacy. By September, the presidents of the neighboring democracies were in effect telling Cruz: "You were right not to register—at least some of your conditions for participation are valid." From September on, Betancur and the Socialist International were continually trying to act as brokers in a deal between the Sandinistas and the opposition.

In December 1984, looking back on the events before the election, Betancur told me, "It was obvious that Contadora's fate might well hinge on the Nicaraguan elections. Peace not only in Nicaragua but in the whole region was at stake." He suggested to the Sandinistas that representative elections were their "best defense against any possible U.S. intervention" and perhaps the only way to head off a civil war into which Costa Rica and Honduras were already being drawn.

The Contadora group was then negotiating an agreement to limit arms and troop levels in Central America as well as military installations and exercises, foreign bases and advisors, and support for insurgents. But many in Costa Rica, Honduras, and El Salvador regarded an effective political opposition in Nicaragua as a guarantee of their own security. They were unlikely to sign the Contadora agreement without such a safeguard. Thus Betancur told me he was prepared not only to mediate but to be "blunt with the FSLN" and to urge Cruz "to be flexible."

In early September, along with Betancur and the "Latin" members of the Socialist International (including Spain and Portugal), a number of prominent U.S. Democrats—including House Majority Leader Jim Wright, Senator Edward Kennedy, Representative Michael Barnes, and House Deputy Whip William Alexander—telephoned Sandinista leaders urging them to make a deal that would bring Cruz into the elections.

In mid-September the Sandinistas agreed to reopen the candidate registration period, void the outlawing of the CDN political parties, and allow the CDN more time on the radio and television. Now the main sticking point was the CDN's request to postpone the elections. The CDN argued that the remaining six weeks before the elections was insufficient for them to mount a national campaign. At a minimum the CDN wanted Cruz to appear one Sunday in the capital of each of Nicaragua's sixteen departments, and some are in remote regions.

On Wednesday, September 19, President Betancur telephoned Cruz to tell him that the Sandinista candidate for vice-president, Sergio Ramírez, had promised postponement of the election. Cruz replied that this was good news; the bad news, he told Betancur, was that after a small indoor meeting in León he and other CDN leaders had just been attacked physically by two thousand *turbas*. They had hit Cruz with a stone, spat on him, and pulled his hair. Later that same week Daniel Ortega said: "We are not ashamed to be *turbas*, because to be part of the *turba* is to be part of the people." The literature distributed by the government to election observers portrayed the attacks as a "spontaneous popular repudiation" of Cruz's candidacy. Residents of Masaya told me, however, that an attack on a Cruz meeting there was carried out by outsiders trucked in by the government.

Like Betancur, Brent Budowsky, Representative Alexander's legislative aide, also received word that the elections would be postponed. However, on September 21, *Comandante* Tomás Borge, a leader of the radical faction, returned from a three-week visit to several Soviet-bloc countries. At the airport he declared that "it would be wrong to postpone the elections." Borge went directly to a meeting of the Sandinista National Directorate in which, according to rumors circulating in Managua, a harsh dispute erupted between radicals and moderates. The directorate announced they would not postpone the elections but would sign a draft of the Contadora treaty instead.

The Reagan administration quickly dismissed the signing as "hypocritical," thus managing to appear hypocritical itself, since it claimed to be supporting the efforts of the Contadora group. However, some Contadora leaders—as well as some Democrats in Congress—were also wary. They noticed that the Sandinistas' signing of the draft was conditioned on its not being amended by other Central American countries, and that, in any event, it could not go into effect before November 15, that is, after the elections. Thus the Nicaraguan elections would not be bound by the Contadora treaty's requirement of "impartial elections" to include "all representative currents of opinion." In simultaneously signing the draft and postponing the elections, the Sandinistas again appeared to be trying to fend off pressures for internal democracy with clever public relations.

During the next week, between September 24 and 28, Sandinista officials attempted to convince congressional Democrats that Cruz was to blame for the breakdown in negotiations. Congress was about to reconsider aid to the contras, and the Sandinistas wanted to encourage opposition. At this point the CDN blundered again, proposing that the elections be postponed until February 24. The Sandinistas immediately claimed that this was evidence of the CDN's bad faith. When Budowsky asked Cruz about this, Cruz told him that the February date was open to negotiation and that mid-January would be acceptable. Budowsky then told this to the Sandinista authorities. Nonetheless, Budowsky later recalled to me, "the Sandinistas spent the next five or six days telling everybody that February 24 was Cruz's answer, and that it was non-negotiable. I began to question the good faith of the Sandinistas."

The Rio Agreement

On September 30, members of the Socialist International met in Rio de Janeiro. The leaders of the southern or Latin wing, including the Socialist

International's vice-president Carlos Andrés Pérez of Venezuela, President Mário Soares of Portugal, and Elena Flores of the ruling Spanish Socialist Workers' Party, arranged a meeting between Bayardo Arce and Cruz and other members of the CDN. President Betancur was in close touch by telephone.

After four long sessions, an agreement in principle was reached on October 2. The Sandinistas made a key concession—they would postpone the election if Cruz yielded to several of their demands. Cruz agreed to ask the insurgents to declare a ceasefire and to surrender their arms to international authorities. The Sandinistas knew this would put the CDN in a difficult position. By interceding with the contras, the CDN could be portrayed as linked to them. Moreover, Cruz also agreed that if the contras did not lay down their arms, the elections would take place November 4 as scheduled.

Cruz had not come to Rio expecting to negotiate. Since he was not authorized to do so, he told me, he had to consult by telephone with his colleagues in Managua. Daniel Ortega, then touring the United States to publicize his candidacy, told several newspaper editors that the Sandinistas had tapped the opposition's phones and were aware that the CDN right wing was reluctant to accept the Rio conditions. By the same means, the Sandinistas also learned that officials in the CIA were urging the rightists in the CDN to torpedo the Rio agreements.

The Arce Walkout

Bayardo Arce seemed startled when Cruz accepted the demands. A member of the Socialist International who was present at the meeting told me, "On Tuesday, October 2, at 5:00 P.M. everything appeared to be settled. Suddenly at 5:40 Arce got up and walked out." Arce announced to a press conference that Cruz's request to return to Managua to get the CDN's agreement was unacceptable. Some European socialists at Rio found Arce's attitude inexplicable. "If," one of them told me, "Cruz is unable to get the CDN to sign on, why not let him return and try? If he failed, the Sandinistas would be vindicated. Do the Sandinistas fear the CDN?" In fact, when Cruz returned to Managua he did obtain, after one stormy meeting, the CDN's approval.

If the Sandinistas feared Cruz, their fear was not of losing the election—they controlled the electoral process too tightly—but of "two, three, many Chinandegas": a wave of support that could elude Sandinista control and reveal the erosion of the FSLN's popular backing. By tying Cruz's hands in Rio, the hard-liners in the Reagan administration, working through its allies in the CDN, provided the Sandinistas a convenient way out of the impasse.

Arce's walkout caused considerable consternation among the members of the Socialist International. This led Willy Brandt, the Socialist International president, to ask both parties to return to the negotiations, and he offered to travel to Nicaragua to "mediate" the conversations.

There was consternation in Washington as well. Budowsky told me, "The Sandinistas wouldn't accept their own offer as soon as it seemed that Cruz's people would. We are talking about stopping a war, about a democratic election, about the Contadora process, about the future of a country. All this was not worth a three-day wait?"

The next week Congress was to vote on covert action. A number of Democrats decided against pushing for a complete cutoff of funds to the contras in order to maintain pressure on the Sandinistas to negotiate. But when Congress voted to suspend covert action, with renewal subject to approval by both the House and the Senate, the Sandinistas cheered, and their position continued to harden.

Betancur told me he had still hoped that "we could work out something" at the inauguration of the new Panamanian president on October 11. Cruz waited with Socialist International leaders and President Betancur to meet with Daniel Ortega in Panama, but Ortega never arrived; he sent instead the FSLN candidate for vice-president, Sergio Ramírez, who told SI officials that Brandt should not "meddle in our internal affairs." When he got to Managua Brandt made no effort to mediate at all. He pronounced the elections "a positive step" and left.

Other Opposition Parties

While international attention was concentrated on the duel between Cruz and the Sandinistas, the six small registered opposition parties mounted vituperative campaigns. Three of those parties are Marxist-Leninist, the most important being the Nicaraguan Socialist Party (PSN), which formerly had open support from the Soviet Union. The Popular Social Christian Party and the Conservative Democratic Party were originally pro-FSLN factions, but many of their activists became estranged from the Sandinistas because of harassment duing the campaign. The Independent Liberal Party (PLI), which included a pro-FSLN faction, had a larger following. The PLI was led by Virgilio Godoy, a former labor minister who quit the government in April 1984. When his party registered for the elections it announced that it would withdraw if the Sandinistas did not keep their promises to restore freedom of movement and expression.

After the attacks on Cruz's indoor meetings in September were reported in the international press, the *turbas* were reined in. Nonetheless, the registered opposition parties continued to complain that party activists were being harassed and jailed, and that the Sandinistas were not keeping their promises. They charged that the FSLN was using state resources and the CDS (Sandinista Defense Committees, which controlled not only food rations but travel visas and eligibility for public housing and employment) for its campaign, and that the electoral council was not providing the opposition parties with their share of internationally donated campaign supplies (such as paper, ink, and paint).

They also claimed that legislation lowering the voting age to sixteen, combined with Sandinista control of the army and militias, provided the FSLN with a captive voting bloc. The voting age had been lowered to sixteen in February 1984. According to Douglas W. Payne's *The Democratic Mask*, the Sandinistas commissioned a secret survey by the Strategic Institute of Spain which showed that they would obtain 35 per cent of the vote if the voting age remained at eighteen, but that the vote would increase significantly if the voting age were lowered to sixteen. (See also Dennis Volman's article on the effects of lowering the voting age in the *Christian Science Monitor*, March 2, 1984.)

Nonetheless, the Sandinistas allowed these parties to run campaigns denouncing Sandinista abuses and corruption. The parties deplored the numerous former Somocistas in the leadership of the CDS and named a good many of them. They claimed that Sandinista mismanagement of the economy had turned Nicaragua, in Godoy's words, into "the country of *no hay*" ("there isn't any"). Opposition candidates denounced the draft for "obligating Nicaraguan youth to fight for a party, not for their country." Some charged that the Sandinistas were reproducing "Somoza-style elections" in which the opposition could make noise but had no chance of winning.

Withdrawals From the Election

On October 21, by a four-to-one-majority, Godoy's PLI voted to pull out of the elections for "lack of minimum conditions." Godoy told me that party campaign workers had been harassed and arrested and that the Sandinistas failed to fulfill their promise of "freedom of the press, of movement and assembly, and [honoring] the rights of *habeas corpus* and injunction." But *La Prensa* was stopped from publishing news of PLI's withdrawal. Godoy told me later that though the PLI suspended all publicity, "suddenly there were more PLI advertisements than ever before" in the pro-government press, radio, and TV. The Supreme Election Council upheld the PLI's minority, saying it was too late to reprint the ballots. Godoy then announced he was participating "under duress."

The elections at this point presented an odd spectacle: one opposition candidate, Cruz, couldn't get in, and another, Godoy, couldn't get out. But the Reagan administration's ineptness succeeded in obscuring what was actually happening. Two days before the PLI voted to withdraw, the American ambassador to Nicaragua, Harry E. Bergold, following State Department orders, paid a visit to Godoy to restate the U.S. position that the elections were not representative. Bergold, a senior U.S. diplomat told me, felt the State Department's instructions were unwise. Godoy is well known in Nicaragua as a radical critic of the United States, and the ambassador's visit did much to help the Sandinistas disparage his reputation. Once again Washington and Managua seemed, in effect, to be working hand in hand.

On October 28, the Democratic Conservatives were also on the verge of voting to withdraw. Several dozen young Sandinistas broke up the party's convention. Shortly thereafter the other non-Marxist opposition party, the Popular Social Christians, voted to participate only "provisionally," proposing new elections "within a year." Only the Marxist-Leninist parties took part in the elections unconditionally, and one of them, as we shall see, had serious reservations.

The banning of Cruz, the coercion of the registered opposition, press censorship, attacks by *turbas* — all these produced an unfavorable impression overseas. Colombia's President Betancur told me he had shown his "disappointment" by declining to send official government observers. Indeed, none of the Contadora countries sent official observers. Nor did any of the Europeans, except for the Dutch.

November 4: The Election

What happened on Sunday, November 4? Or which account is one to believe? A visiting group of American academics sponsored by the Latin American Studies Association (LASA) — opposed to Reagan and generally sympathetic to the Sandinistas — found the elections an "impressive beginning." Whatever the FSLN's "abuses of incumbency," they "did not cast doubt on the validity of the electoral process." The same general view was taken by Lord Chitnis, a British Liberal, who wrote his own report. This was not the impression of the Dutch official observers or of most U.S. reporters who were there; nor was it my own.

In the *Los Angeles Times*, Dan Williams reported widespread rumors "that people who did not vote would be black-listed for government jobs, passports, and other benefits." Julia Preston of the *Boston Globe* wrote that some Nicaraguans, "in defensive whispers," told of "fears and aggravations for those who didn't want to vote." The Dutch observer team "repeatedly heard people remark that they did not want to vote but feared that to abstain would be interpreted by the CDS as support for the counter-revolutionaries."

I heard similar stories. Members of artisan cooperatives in Masaya and Diriamba told me they felt obliged to vote because the government controlled the distribution of leather and other supplies they badly needed. Adolfo Evertsz, the candidate for vice-president of the Marxist-Leninist Nicaraguan Socialist Party, told me that the Sandinistas had "prepared a campaign to confuse and frighten people.... The poor were convinced that if they did not vote they would have problems with their ration cards and jobs." In a highly publicized speech before a huge rally closing the campaign, Daniel Ortega warned: "The only ones who will not vote would be the enemies of Nicaragua, the traitors, the turncoats, and will expose themselves to the fury of the people at the moment of [U.S.] intervention."

The LASA report claims that on election day "voter turnout was heavy." Julia Preston of the *Boston Globe*, one of the most experienced American reporters in Central America, reported that "in some key cities, lines had dwindled to nothing by 10:00 A.M." The greatest display of enthusiasm I saw was at the Hotel Intercontinental, where "international observers" boarded government buses to visit polling places. According to the official Dutch report:

> A certain confusion arose because of the presence of official and not-so-official observers, i.e., private individuals and groupings who had been invited by the Nicaraguan government but could not be regarded as representatives of foreign governments or parliaments.... Some, who acted more in the guise of performers than observers, were prepared as soon as they were off the aeroplane steps to make all kinds of statements about the nature and the exemplary functioning of the Nicaraguan elections, which could give rise to some embarrassing situations for the official observers.

In the eleven voting places I visited in Masaya, Monimbo, and Managua, the turnout averaged 40 per cent. Voting appears to have been lighter in outlying districts. In small rural villages, residents later told me that between 20 and 35 per cent had voted. A Socialist Party politician told me that a concerned Soviet diplomat summoned a party leader to the embassy residency Sunday afternoon to ask why so many Managua polling places were desolate by 3:00 P.M. In the late afternoon there was a small flurry of voting activity after Sandinista activists made house-to-house visits in many neighborhoods.

The Election Results

After nine days the official results were announced: nearly 1.1 million Nicaraguans had voted, a turnout of 75 per cent, with 67 per cent voting for Daniel Ortega and 64 per cent for Sandinista National Assembly candidates. Sandinista officials, who had earlier publicly anticipated a 90 per cent turnout, predicted 80 per cent just before the elections. At that time, a Sandinista National Assembly candidate had added that if the Sandinistas did not win 80 per cent of the turnout "we will have to reconsider our methods and the quality of our party members."

By their own count the Sandinistas received only 47 per cent of the registered votes—against a majority consisting of those who abstained, annulled their ballots, or voted for the opposition. The FSLN, in my view, still has support among public employees, peasants who have benefited from the agrarian reform, and young activists. But Rafael Solis, the FSLN party official in charge of the elections, frankly acknowledged that "the results show that we have problems in some areas. A significant number of Nicaraguans obviously do not understand or support what we are doing."

There is no way of determining whether the official vote count was accurate. Manipulation of election results is traditional in Central America, and certainly few Nicaraguans I talked to took the results literally. Those international observers who did not depart the day after the voting eagerly awaited disclosures of partial and final results. Like the numerous foreign observers in El Salvador's 1982 elections, they assumed they were attending a protracted "election-night vigil" in a tropical setting. Meanwhile Nicaraguan journalists, academics, and opposition leaders described the waiting period in terms more reminiscent of a smoke-filled room at a U.S. party convention.

Leaders of two registered opposition parties (the PLI and the PSN) told me that the opposition parties had participated in a pre-election agreement with the FSLN to allocate the votes. Godoy claimed that the PLI's portion would be reduced as "punishment" for seeking to withdraw from the elections. Several well-placed Nicaraguans told me that the Sandinistas' own factional fight affected the results that were announced. Radical Sandinistas, who had opposed Ortega's nomination, wanted his vote kept low so as to prevent his emerging as the Sandinistas' undisputed leader.

The opposition party leaders I spoke to said the results would award the registered parties with enough votes to maintain themselves as a visible opposition but not enough to challenge the FSLN in the National Assembly. The elections, they argued, were held almost exclusively for international consumption, and the results would have to establish that Nicaragua was not "an Eastern European dictatorship," thus ensuring a continued flow of international assistance. The announced turnout, they predicted, would be high enough to declare victory over those who had illegally advocated abstention but not so high as to seem implausible in view of the visibly disappointing actual turnout.

No one produced documentary evidence of a pre-electoral pact or of tampering with the ballots; nor has anyone done so during the last year. Opposition poll watchers were present at fewer than 20 per cent of the polling sites. However, Jaime Chamorro, the new editor of *La Prensa*, compiled a statistical analysis of the partial and complete official registration and election figures. (He was allowed to publish only a part of it.) He noted numerous discrepancies and concluded that the FSLN padded the registration count by 400,000. These votes, he argued, were later added to the FSLN election totals.

Sandinista Post-Election Activity

In the tradition of Somoza's demonstration elections, the November election results preserved the appearance of pluralism but ensured the Sandinistas effective control over the National Assembly. They did not hesitate to use it to consolidate their power and to cripple the opposition still further.

What has happened since the elections has offered little encouragement for Willy Brandt's view that the elections were a "step forward." Shortly after the elections, prominent church officials and opposition political, labor, and business leaders were prevented from traveling outside the country. Censorship of *La Prensa* increased dramatically (nearly 50 per cent of its articles were soon being censored). *La Prensa*'s former editor, Pedro

Joaquín Chamorro, Jr., went into exile in Costa Rica. A Sandinista government source acknowledged to the *Washington Post* (December 3, 1984) than an "intimidation campaign" was under way.

The *Post* also reported that two provincial officials of the Social Christian Party were arrested shortly after the election, one charged with collaborating with the rebels. Later a prominent human rights lawyer, Roger Guevara Mena, was jailed without charges and kept *incommunicado* for nine days, but the authorities usually picked for their reprisals inconspicuous mid-level opposition activists from provincial towns like Matagalpa and Chinandega.

Before the elections the Sandinistas agreed to a "national dialogue" among all political parties to take place after the elections. After the elections, the FSLN refused to hold any such meeting. In early January 1985 all Nicaraguan political parties—with the exception of the FSLN and the tiny ultra-left MAP (ML) but including the Nicaraguan Socialist and Communist parties as well as the Coordinadora—signed a proposal to "renew the national dialogue." The November 4 elections, the proposal said, had not solved the country's main political problems; the "national economic crisis" had sharpened with mounting inflation; "workers' salaries have plummeted, and poverty and indigence prevail among the masses." Only a renewed national dialogue could "restore peace, tranquility, and stability."

Manipulating the Assembly

The Sandinistas asserted that discussion of such issues could occur only in the National Assembly. But suspicions of the opposition parties that the Assembly would mechanically endorse Sandinista policy were soon confirmed. In February, against the vigorous objections of the parliamentary opposition, the Sandinistas and minority pro-FSLN factions in other parties pushed through legislation that granted Ortega broad emergency powers, curtailed discussion of the budget, prohibited either discussion or reduction of defense spending by the Assembly, and virtually denied the minority parties their right to propose legislation. Socialist deputy Luis Sánchez said the legislation "violates the main principles of the revolution" and "brings back ugly memories" of Somoza's rule.

When some of the parliamentary opposition proved refractory, the Sandinistas on March 7 imposed rules stipulating that all proposals, including the new constitution, must be approved by a 60 per cent majority. That meant that even if the entire opposition walked out, the Sandinista delegation could continue to run the legislature and approve a constitution.

A commission was formed to draft the constitution. It was composed of FSLN delegates along with docile members of the opposition, some of whom, opposition-party sources have claimed to me, are on the government dole. The president of the Social Christian Party, Augustín Jarquín, said that the Sandinistas' evident intentions to dictate the constitution furnished "further proof that the FSLN does not intend to allow political pluralism." Other opposition leaders said the Sandinistas were fulfilling Bayardo Arce's vow to draft "a Red constitution." [The draft constitution is in appendix D.]

On March 21 the National Assembly approved an internal statute granting broad powers to the executive. Virgilio Godoy said the rules meant that "now the National Assembly has more members but less power" than the defunct Sandinista-dominated Council of State. According to the *New York Times* (May 10), "opposition deputies . . . said they no longer believed [the Assembly] could serve as a forum for serious debate." Under present rules all motions must be submitted weeks in advance to Sandinista *comandante* Carlos Nuñez, who can reject any proposal he considers "notoriously out of place." According to the *Times* report, "up to now nearly every bill has been approved in the exact form in which it was proposed by the Sandinistas."

Another blow against pluralism was struck on March 6 when the Supreme Court upheld the government's decision to deny legal status to the traditional anti-Somoza Conservative Party. In May the PLI newspaper announced that it was ceasing publication because of "excess censorship." Finally, on October 15, Daniel Ortega announced the suspension of virtually all civil liberties, including the rights to assemble, to move about the country, to strike, and to criticize the government publicly.

Though the Sandinistas apparently had urged other countries to send high-ranking delegations to Daniel Ortega's inauguration on January 15, in contrast to recent inaugurations in Panama, Uruguay, and Brazil, Western Europeans sent minor officials. No Contadora or other Latin American president attended, not did other Central American countries send delegations. Fidel Castro dominated the ceremonies. His presence was made particularly conspicuous by the absence of the other leading patron of the revolution, former Venezuelan president and Socialist International leader Carlos Andrés Pérez. Declining an invitation to the inauguration, Pérez wrote Ortega: "Those of us who believe we have done so much for the

Sandinista revolution feel deceived because sufficient guarantees were not provided to assure the participation of all political forces."

Effect on the Political Climate

There is bitter retribution for U.S. policy in the Sandinista elections. They were no worse but no better than those we have sponsored for half a century in Central America. For decades we backed El Salvador's military regime and applauded "elections" in which the military party, the Party of National Conciliation, like the FSLN, controlled the state apparatus, the army, the police, and the election council, and routinely received the seats necessary to dominate the National Assembly.

The elections were a partial success for the Sandinistas. The exclusion of Cruz and the electoral abuses described in the American press sharply diminished remaining Sandinista sympathies in the U.S. Congress, but the cautiously favorable report of the official observer of the Socialist International, Thorvold Stoltenberg of Norway, seemed to satisfy some of its members, especially those from West Germany, France, and the Scandinavian and Low Countries. When I expressed my own reservations to a leading member of the Socialist International who had just publicly endorsed the Nicaraguan elections, he replied: "But we had to endorse them. Reagan endorsed the Salvadoran elections."

The elections left much bitterness among the Nicaraguan people—not only toward the Sandinistas but toward the opposition as well. Many Nicaraguans who hoped the elections would help to resolve the national crisis, or at least to expose the Sandinistas' failings, criticized the opposition forces for not having participated in the campaign, even under unfavorable conditions, and for their disunity and indecisiveness. They felt Cruz had let himself be manipulated by the right wing of the Coordinadora instead of capitalizing on the moral authority he had gained from the rallies in Chinandega and elsewhere. Had he persisted, he might have posed a strong challenge to the regime. The Cruz campaign, too often conducted through behind-the-scenes negotiations rather than through direct appeal to the Nicaraguan people, left the opposition without a coherent political structure.

After the elections the dissident Nicaraguans withdrew what confidence they had from the Coordinadora. The undisputed political leader of the opposition has become Miguel Obando y Bravo, the archbishop of Managua, who was made a cardinal last spring [1985; see his statement, selection 24]. When he returned from Rome in June he was greeted by huge crowds, and many thousands have come to hear him as he has held Masses throughout the country. He has implicitly criticized the regime by calling for a "national dialogue" and by asserting that the Nicaraguan people "want neither capitalism nor Communism." (The popular responses to Cardinal Obando—along with recent protests organized by Christian Democrat, Socialist, and Communist unions against bonus cuts—were apparently the main reason for the regime's emergency decree of October 15.)

During the year following the elections, thousands of Nicaraguans left the country, some to join the rebels, whose ranks quickly grew.

24. The Sandinistas Have Bound and Gagged Us

By MIGUEL OBANDO Y BRAVO

Focus "I would explain to those who have ears to hear the sensitive situation of our church and the serious danger we place ourselves in simply by speaking out," says Miguel Obando y Bravo, cardinal archbishop of Managua. He does not wish to confuse his pastoral mission with politics or journalism, he explains, but "as a man, as a citizen, as a Christian, and even as a bishop, I have certain duties that I must fulfill."

The cardinal describes the Nicaraguan church as being without public outlets—Radio Católica was closed, and the printing press for the church publication "Iglesia" was confiscated. Even church bulletins have been suppressed. Obando's weekly article in the independent newspaper *La Prensa* has been censored. (*La Prensa* itself was shut down two months after this article was written.) Virtually the only place from which the church can now reach the people, he says, is the pulpit. Hence his agreement to write this article for the *Washington Post*.

The Sandinistas have been asking why Obando has not issued a condemnation of U.S. aid to the contras. Citing the New Testament story in which Christ was asked if it was lawful to pay taxes to Caesar, Obando argues that in both cases the question was not asked to gain an answer. The Nicaraguan Conference of Bishops "has already stated that it was against any outside interference, whether by the United States or the Soviet Union (pastoral letter of April 22, 1984). The intention is to use the statement to manipulate. While no effort was spared in suppressing our earlier statements, this statement would be given international publicity. Not for the faithful—but for the U.S. Congress."

The Nicaraguan bishops desire withdrawal of both foreign superpowers, recognition of legitimate grievances among those Nicaraguans who have joined the contras, and dialogue leading to national reconciliation. To embark on this path, says Obando, the Sandinistas would have to confess that they have become just as much a tool of Soviet interests as the contras have of U.S. interests. They would also have to recognize that Sandinista violations of human rights have produced the contra force. But the Sandinistas have censored the bishops' texts explaining this.

Obando's views should be compared with those of Gabriel Jackson (selection 20), Joshua Muravchik (selection 21), and Robert Leiken (selection 23).

Miguel Obando y Bravo is the Roman Catholic cardinal archbishop of Managua, where he has been active in the struggle for justice under both Anastasio Somoza and the Sandinista regime.

YOUR MESSAGE ASKING ME for an article arrived on Sunday, April 13, just as I finished celebrating Mass, and my first decision was not to grant your request. I must not confuse my pastoral mission with others, however worthy, such as politics or journalism, which are different from the mission that our Lord has entrusted to me. But I am not obligated to keep silent either. As a man, as a citizen, as a Christian, and even as a bishop, I have certain duties that I must fulfill, and these duties compel me to grant your request.

In the Mass I just celebrated, I had to announce, with great sorrow, that some of the offices of the Curia, occupied by the State Security police since October 1985, had been confiscated by government order, despite the fact that they were built on land occupied by the apostolic nunciature.

In these offices there was a small printing press donated by the German Bishops' Conference, which was used to print our bulletin "Iglesia," a strictly intra-ecclesiastical publication. Both the press and the bulletin were seized by the State Security police, along with all the files, including baptismal records and my own personal seal.

During the Mass, I read the pastoral letter that we, the bishops of Nicaragua, had written for Holy Week. The pulpit was now our only means of disseminating information, because the letter was totally censored and pulled from the pages of the newspaper *La Prensa*, the only private newspaper in the country, which attempted to publish it but in vain. We believe that the reason for the censorship was that for the second time we called all Nicaraguans to reconciliation and dialogue as the only way to peace.

It was also announced that the Sunday bulletin with the prayers and texts for the day would not be available because it was confiscated, and that my Sunday address would not appear in *La Prensa* as, under the heading "The Voice of Our Pastor," it had for many years, because it too had been censored, despite the special care taken to exclude from it anything that could serve as the remotest excuse for censorship.

"Radio Católica," the only Catholic radio station, had been closed by the state several months earlier. It was at this point, when the church was gagged and bound, that your request arrived.

Reprinted by permission from the *Washington Post*, May 12, 1986.

The reading for the day, taken from the Acts of the Apostles, was about an incident that pricked my conscience. The Sanhedrin sent for Peter and John, intending to force them into silence. "But Peter and John said to them in reply: 'Is it right in God's eyes for us to obey you rather than God? Judge for yourselves. We cannot possibly give up speaking of things we have seen and heard'" (Acts 4:18–20).

I felt then that I ought to tell the truth and speak as a prophet speaks, even at the risk of being a "voice that crieth in the wilderness." I would explain to those that have ears to hear the sensitive situation of our church and the serious danger we place ourselves in simply by speaking out.

An Attempt to Use the Bishops

I am reminded of the incident related in the twenty-second chapter of Matthew: "Then the Pharisees went away and agreed on a plan to trap him in his own words." The method they chose was to appeal hypocritically to his spiritual authority, saying: "Master, you are an honest man, we know; you teach in all honesty the way of life that God requires.... Give us your ruling on this: are we or are we not permitted to pay taxes to the Roman emperor?" Jesus was aware of their malicious intention and said to them: "You hypocrites! Why are you trying to catch me out?"

History repeats itself, and this is the situation of the Nicaraguan bishops, a situation that we denounced in our recent pastoral letter. An appeal is made to our moral authority and to our position as spiritual leaders of the people. We are asked to make a statement on an extremely sensitive political matter, but the real objective is not to seek moral guidance, but rather to use our statement to manipulate opinion.

If Jesus had answered that taxes should be paid to Caesar, he would have become a collaborator of the occupying Roman imperialists. If he had answered no, he would have become a criminal and an agitator who violated the laws of the land. If he had not answered at all, he would have lost his authority in the eyes of the people.

We are asked to issue a statement against U.S. aid to the insurgents. The state-controlled communications media, the organizations of the masses in the service of the system and their allies in the so-called People's Church, and the minister of foreign affairs, Father Miguel D'Escoto, are all clamoring for our statement. But, as I mentioned, it is not moral guidance that is sought, since on several occasions our Conference of Bishops has already stated that it was against any outside interference, whether by the United

States or the Soviet Union (pastoral letter of April 22, 1984). The intention is to use the statement to manipulate.

While no effort was spared in suppressing our earlier statements, this statement would be given international publicity. Not for the faithful—but for the U.S. Congress. But we are not pastors to the Congress of the United States.

If we were to support military aid to the insurgents, we would be persecuted as traitors. If we opposed aid, we would be accused of taking sides, which would automatically disqualify us as pastors to all of the people. If we remained silent, our silence would be considered guilty, the silence of complicity.

It can be argued that the U.S. Conference of Bishops has more than once issued statements on political matters. But there is one big difference: the U.S. bishops' statements are made freely, they are addressed to their own people, and their purpose is to provide moral guidance. They can make such statements in complete freedom, and they can give their reasons, with full access to the communications media. Their words are not censored, twisted, or distorted. But above all, their statements do not make them criminals and traitors to their country.

An 'Ingenious Distortion'

In Nicaragua any dissident from the Sandinista cause can be placed outside the law through an ingenious distortion of the truth.

The government, with all the media under its control, has taken great pains to convince the outside world that what is happening is essentially a direct attack by the United States on our country. That there is a war, open or covert, between the two countries, and, consequently, any form of assistance to the enemy, whether material or moral, is punishable by law.

Along the same lines, and with equal insistence, it rejects both the idea that an East-West conflict has made of our country a disposable card, a pawn in the game between the superpowers, and the reality of a civil war: an enormous number of Nicaraguans oppose with all their might the turn taken by a revolution that has betrayed the hopes of the Nicaraguan people and even its own promises.

To accept the reality of an East-West conflict would be to admit that the Sandinistas are just as much the tools of Soviet interests as the insurgent forces are of the United States. If this is accepted, aid from the one is equally as deplorable as aid from the other. It would necessitate the withdrawal of the Soviet and Cuban advisors, as well as the withdrawal of all U.S. military aid.

If the reality of an internal conflict between Nicaraguans is admitted, the conclusion could not be avoided that the insurgent dissidents are now in the same position that the Sandinistas themselves once occupied, and, consequently, that they have the same right that the Sandinistas had to seek aid from other nations, which they in fact did request and obtain in order to fight a terrible dictatorship.

To accept this would mean giving the insurgents the title of "rebels," a title that the Sandinistas proudly gave to themselves in former days.

The only possible argument against this is that unlike the Somozan dictatorship, which the Nicaraguan people fought almost unanimously, this is a democratic government, legitimately constituted, that places the interests of the Nicaraguan people above any ideological struggle or international cause, seeks the welfare and peace of the people, and enjoys the support of an overwhelming majority.

Unfortunately, this is not true either. To accept this as the indisputable truth is to ignore the mass exodus of the Miskito Indians, who, on numerous occasions, fled in the thousands, accompanied by their bishop, Salvador Schlaeffer. It is also to ignore the departure of tens of thousands of Nicaraguan men and women of every age, profession, economic status, and political persuasion. It is to ignore that many of those who are leaders or participants in the counter-revolution were once leaders or members of the Sandinista front or were ministers in the Sandinista government. It is to ignore the lack of any justification for the most terrible violation of freedom of the press and of speech in the history of our country. It is to ignore the progressive and suffocating restriction of public liberties, under the cover of an interminable national emergency law, and the continual violation of human rights. It is to ignore the expulsion of priests and the mass exodus of young people eligible for military service.... None of this is true of a government that has the sympathy and general support of the people.

The Bishops' Message

And this is what the Nicaraguan bishops wish to state:

"It is urgent and essential that the Nicaraguan people, free of foreign interference or ideologies, find a way out of the situation of conflict that our country is experiencing.

"We reaffirm today, with renewed emphasis, what we said in our pastoral letter on Easter Sunday, April 22, 1984:

"Foreign powers are taking advantage of our situation to promote economic and ideological exploitation. They view us as adjuncts to their own power, without respect for our persons, our history, our culture, and our right to determine our own destiny.

"Consequently, most of the Nicaraguan people live in fear and are uncertain about the future. They feel deeply frustrated. They cry out for peace and freedom, but their voices go unheard, drowned out by militaristic propaganda on every side.

"We feel that any form of assistance, regardless of the source, which causes the destruction, suffering, and death of our families, or which sows hatred and discord among the Nicaraguan people, is reprehensible. To choose annihilation of the enemy as the only possible way to peace is inevitably to choose war."

The church proposes reconciliation through dialogue as the only real solution, the only way to peace, and maintains, in the words of His Holiness John Paul II, in his visit to El Salvador in March 1983, that this dialogue "is not a delaying tactic to strengthen positions prior to continuing a fight, but rather a sincere effort to respond, by seeking appropriate solutions to the anxiety, the pain, the weariness, and the fatigue of the many who yearn for peace. The many who wish to live, to rise again from the ashes, to seek warmth in the smiles of children, free from terror and in a climate of democratic cooperation."

This is the text that was censored by the Sandinista government.

We are asked to issue a statement against aid, the church, and the position of our Conference of Bishops, which is trying to guide the church through turbulent waters, more by the spirit than by the natural sciences and politics of man, which do not seem to hold any solution for such difficult problems. We are in a difficult situation, but we place our faith and trust in the Lord Jesus, the Prince of Peace and the Lord of History.

25. The Nature of the Insurgency

By MICHAEL S. RADU

Focus According to Michael Radu, the Nicaraguan conflict is not between a group of guerrillas and an established government that they are trying to overthrow. It is a civil war. "Neither class antagonisms nor political history satisfactorily explains the Nicaraguan civil war—the political culture of Nicaragua and the circumstances of the revolutionary victory of July 19, 1979, serve far better."

Contrary to Sandinista claims, their movement was never of the people or the masses. Like the leadership of the contras, the Sandinista leaders come from middle- or upper-middle-class backgrounds. Sandinista followers tend to come from the cities on the Pacific Ocean side of the country, contra followers from the rural peasantry and the Atlantic Coast. "The civil war represents an intra-elite leadership conflict and an urban-rural polarization among the rank and file."

The early anti-Sandinista insurgent groups were small and, though often composed of former National Guardsmen, cannot be characterized as simply followers of Somoza, says Radu. Their cause might well have gone nowhere except for the "dramatic shift in Nicaragua's internal politics by 1980–81."

The increasingly obvious internal repression and the drift toward pro-Soviet and pro-Cuban positions caused many people, including some Sandinista leaders, to join the insurgents. The FDN, one of the contra groups, cannot be made up of National Guardsmen, says Radu, because only about 6,000 of the Guardsmen escaped but the FDN numbers about 15,000. "Moreover, all available evidence indicates that among the FDN regional and task force commanders there are more former Sandinistas (twenty-seven, or 48 per cent) than former Guardsmen (thirteen, or 23 per cent)."

"Despite Sandinista claims to the contrary and the labeling of all insurgents as 'mercenaries,' the overwhelming majority of recruits to both ARDE [another contra group] and the FDN receive no payment," says Radu. He concludes that the tragic polarization of Nicaragua has just about reached its limit, and the only likely resolution of the conflict is "all-out victory for one side or the other."

Radu's characterization of the anti-Sandinista forces should be compared with those of Gabriel Jackson (selection 20), Nicaraguan president Daniel Ortega (selection 22), and Jaime Chamorro (selection 29).

Michael S. Radu is a research associate at the Foreign Policy Research Institute, Philadelphia, Pennsylvania.

THE INVOLVEMENT OF the United States in Nicaragua's civil war threatens to obscure the indigenous sources of that conflict, pushing its nature into the shadow of domestic ideological and partisan debates. Arguments over Washington's and Moscow's role in Nicaragua have wildly distorted and grossly oversimplified the very complex historical and sociological antecedents of this war. This essay is an attempt to provide a fuller picture of both what is behind the Nicaraguan civil war and what is at stake in it.

Like most civil wars, Nicaragua's is far bloodier than a conventional conflict between two regular armies under the control of national governments pursuing their separate interests. Nicaragua is a society tearing itself to pieces. Families are torn by conflicting loyalties that supersede blood ties. Former comrades are murderously divided. Neither class antagonisms nor political history satisfactorily explains the Nicaraguan civil war—the political culture of Nicaragua and the circumstances of the revolutionary victory of July 19, 1979, serve far better.

While claiming to represent "the people" or "the masses" of Nicaragua, the leaders of the ruling Sandinista National Liberation Front (FSLN) are overwhelmingly from the middle or upper-middle class. David Nolan has commented, "The Sandinismo of the FSLN proper . . . was never a lower-class phenomenon. It was, instead, the ideology of a group of young people, mostly middle or upper class in origin."[1] The insurgents' political leaders come from a similar background. On both sides in this conflict, most followers are from "the people": in the FSLN, from among the marginal urban youth; in the largest insurgent group, the Nicaraguan Democratic Forces (FDN), and among the ethnic insurgents of the Atlantic Coast, from the whole population. The civil war thus represents an intra-elite leadership conflict and an urban-rural polarization among the rank and file.

Geographically, members of the insurgent forces are largely recruited among the peasantry of the north and northwest, in the departments of

---

Reprinted by permission of the Foreign Policy Research Institute from the Winter 1986 issue of *Orbis*. Notes for this essay begin on page 429.

Nueva Segovia, Madriz, Estelí, Jinotega, Chinandega, and Matagalpa. The FSLN popular base lies in the more urbanized departments of Managua, León, Granada, Masaya, and Carazo on the Pacific Coast. These are traditionally the most politicized areas of the country, historically divided between the Liberal center of León and the Conservative Party's Granada stronghold. The central departments of Boaco and Chontales and the eastern departments of Zelaya and Río San Juan, with their small populations, tend either to be receptive to the insurgents or, in the case of Zelaya, to be distinct from the rest of the country in population (ethnic minorities) and history. In a country whose population barely exceeds three million, such cleavages indicate a complex socio-political background that is not reflected in the terminology of public discourse—"freedom fighters," "counter-revolutionaries" ("contras"), Communists or democrats, Somocistas or revolutionaries. Recent, as well as more remote, history helps explain the origins and the trends in the civil war.

Collapse of the Anti-Somoza Coalition

The almost universal perception, in Nicaragua and around the world, was that the July 1979 victory over the Somoza regime was the result of an entire people's rising up against an isolated tyrant. Among the overwhelming majority of the Nicaraguans who fought Somoza, either with arms or through strikes and through propaganda abroad, the prevailing hope was that expressed by Ramiro Gurdian, a prominent private-sector representative: "I thought that we were going to have a free society, with a free press, with elections, with a very good legal system."[2]

As Gurdian and innumerable other non-Sandinista participants in the revolution have claimed, this optimism sprang largely from the apparent support of the Carter administration and Latin American democracies for the revolution. If the United States and Venezuela were against Somoza, the Sandinistas could not be committed Marxist-Leninists as Somoza had claimed.[3] When the post-revolutionary grand coalition collapsed, the myth of the "betrayed revolution" was born and has resisted historical reality until the present.[4] The myth survives despite the FSLN's consistent, though not always public, decision to retain absolute control after victory: "We seek to conserve the political hegemony of the FSLN, and in this way, as our platform signifies, we avoid the possibility of the bourgeoisie becoming the political leader of an anti-Somoza front.... We assign a tactical and *temporary* character to this front."[5]

The FSLN–non-Marxists coalition that triumphed in 1979 could therefore not have lasted. Some non-Marxists realized this almost immediately; for others, like Alfonso Robelo, it took almost a year; and for some, the process was far longer. In December 1981, Arturo Cruz, who replaced Robelo in the National Reconstruction Junta in 1980, was still speaking out about "the supposed Marxist-Leninist leanings of the revolution" and hoping that "the Nicaraguan revolution can become a political model of internal stability and a stabilizing force in Central America."[6] By mid-1982 Cruz realized that "the moderates were also very useful for tactical reasons to those who already had the intention of making it [Nicaragua] a totalitarian system."[7]

By 1980 the unraveling of the grand anti-Somoza coalition had become obvious to objective observers. From the first day of the revolutionary regime, the five-member junta, controlled by the three FSLN members (Daniel Ortega, Moisés Hassán Morales, and Sergio Ramírez), received direct orders from the nine-member FSLN National Directorate. The National Guard was immediately replaced by the Sandinista Popular Army (EPS), and the only government institution not then under direct Sandinista control was the Council of State, a quasi-legislative body of thirty-three members, of whom twelve were open FSLN members. On May 4, 1980, the FSLN National Directorate decreed an increase in the membership of the Council of State to forty-seven seats, twenty-four allocated to the FSLN and its auxiliary "popular organizations."[8] Thus, fewer than ten months after the revolution, any policy-making role for non-Sandinistas were eliminated.

With the FSLN controlling the military, the police, the Council of State, the governing junta, all the key ministries, most of the media, and the economy by May 1980, Nicaragua's political "pluralism" resembled the "multiparty" systems of East Germany, Poland, and Hungary. Then, as now, the FSLN claimed that over half of the economy was in private hands; but the regime controlled the banks, foreign and internal trade, and currency exchange rates, making formal ownership largely void of content.

The National Guard Under Somoza

Pushed from political power and at the mercy of the FSLN economically, growing numbers of the anti-Somoza activists of 1978–79 began to discover that the old regime had always been more than a one-family kleptocracy. While it is not surprising that foreigners, particularly hurried journalists, should have reduced the Somoza regime to the family of the dictator, it is amazing how many Nicaraguans did so, at least in the enthusiastic days of 1979, forgetting their own history and dismissing reality and common sense.

Somoza was indeed a dictator, and a greedy one. Yet the Somoza family and the Liberal Party could not have ruled for more than four decades without a degree of popular support. Almost two generations of National Guard (GN) members had a profound impact on many communities, particularly in the northern departments, through family ties, a vested interest in a regime that favored them, and traditional Liberal loyalties dating from the nineteenth century. The numbers themselves are significant in this respect: according to some calculations, in 1978 one out of every 250 Nicaraguans was in the National Guard, or one out of every 166 was in the Guard, police, or Treasury Guard.[9] As late as September 1978, when Somoza defeated the first massive insurrection in Estelí, León, Masaya, and Chinandega, Nicaraguans were still attracted by service in the National Guard, which had increased its strength from approximately 7,000 to 15,000 by the beginning of 1979.[10]

The GN soldiers were reportedly attracted by the relatively high salaries,[11] but mercenary considerations fail to explain the loyalty of the military at the very last hours of the regime. Neither can money alone completely explain the success of the GN in establishing an extensive system of informers and local representatives, in attracting the loyalty of peasants in certain regions such as Nueva Guinea, or in denying the FSLN significant peasant support in most areas. These successes can be partially explained by the growing professionalism of the GN, its training and esprit de corps, acknowledged even by its critics.[12] This professionalism resulted in loyalty to the state among the rank and file, and support for the national security doctrine among the officer corps. Although the National Guard was not a fully professional army in 1979, it was close enough to be prepared to transfer its loyalties from the person of Somoza to his legitimate replacement as defined by the institutional interests, the perceived national interest, and the individual field commanders' decisions. As subsequent events demonstrated, such a replacement could even be anti-Somoza.

Guardsmen After the Fall

At its defeat in July 1979, the National Guard was top heavy with trained and experienced officers; some were relatively new to their senior positions, a result of Somoza's mid-1970s decision to retire entire graduating classes of senior officers (the last such mass retirement occurred in the fall of 1978).[13] Thus there were two generations of relatively young, experienced anti-guerrilla commanders available to replace the casualties suffered in the civil war. Most of these commanders had received extensive training abroad, largely in the United States, Panama, Argentina, and Chile: between 1970 and 1975, for instance, fifty-two Nicaraguans graduated from U.S. military academies, and 303 from the School of the Americas in the Panama Canal Zone.[14]

The GN elite anti-insurgency troops, the Basic Infantry Training School (EEBI, led by Somoza's son), were largely concentrated on the Southern Front, around Rivas, at the end of the war,[15] and were led by the army's best and most respected field commander, Major Pablo Emilio Salazar ("Bravo"). Not only did Salazar stop the FSLN's largest armed unit—by preventing its commander, Edén Pastora, from reaching Managua ahead of his colleagues, thereby decisively and permanently upsetting the balance of forces within the FSLN itself[16]—but he saved most of his force, transporting them by barge to El Salvador and Honduras.

At the time of victory, the FSLN claimed to have captured some 7,500 former GN members;[17] some 500 EEBI members were captured while fighting their way out of the country.[18] These figures remain controversial, with the FSLN claiming to have freed 3,000 former Guardsmen,[19] while the unofficial Permanent Nicaraguan Human Rights Commission alleges that "during the first months, from July 1979 until February 1980, the Sandinistas executed in jail no fewer than two thousand prisoners."[20] Referring to members of his own State Security services, Tomás Borge admitted that often they hit prisoners or killed prisoners.[21] Conservatively, it appears that as many as 6,000 former GN members may have escaped abroad during the first year after the revolution, most to Honduras but many to Guatemala and El Salvador; a disproportionate number of these were former officers and elite troops.

Ripe for Reorganization

Three major factors appear to have precipitated the reorganization of former GN members in exile. First, many experienced economic and family hardships in their new jobs, such as security personnel, in El Salvador, Guatemala, and Honduras; second, the loss of friends, harsh treatment by the FSLN's "people's tribunals," including often exaggerated data on secret killings of captured Guardsmen, galvanized action; and third, many felt the desire to return home or to avenge the loss of property and lifetime savings.[22] Although the government did not legally proclaim the National Guard "a criminal organization," it treated GN members as criminals. Having abolished the death penalty, the government nonetheless acknowledged the continued executions of former Guardsmen.

Thus the capricious nature of FSLN justice served to politicize and to unify most of the former officers and soldiers who had escaped. Personal fear of the long arm of the FSLN prodded many former GN officers into activity. In their opinion, as well as the opinion of others, the murders of Pablo Emilio Salazar in Tegucigalpa, Honduras,[23] in October 1979 and of Somoza in Paraguay less than a year later bore the stamp of FSLN vengeance. In addition, simple friendship, the remaining esprit de corps, and FSLN threats at home and abroad helped the most active among the émigré officers to attract their erstwhile colleagues and subordinates to the cause of counter-revolution.

Presumably, of the GN members who managed to escape Nicaragua before the Cuban-led and -trained Sandinista secret police made escape extremely difficult, only some later became politically active. Among these were a large proportion of officers, elite anti-insurgency troops (including many NCOs), and some regular soldiers. The latter were mostly new recruits (after the fall of 1978) from northern Nicaragua, particularly the department of Nueva Segovia, the GN's traditional recruiting grounds. Since the northern departments were barely touched by the 1978–79 civil war and the FSLN had little support and even less recruiting success there, the traditionally strong family ties in the north were undisturbed by the political polarization that unsettled the more modern semi-urban or urban areas along the Pacific Coast. The Guardsmen's families helped their kinsmen flee to Honduras and often resented FSLN attempts to depict them as monsters and criminals.

The First Counter-Revolutionary Groups

The first organizations were born in the three major concentrations of former GN members: Guatemala; Tegucigalpa, Honduras; and Miami. One such group comprised about forty-five officers under Francisco Urcuyo Maliaño, who had succeeded Somoza as president for forty-two hours. Urcuyo founded the Revolutionary Nicaraguan Front (FRENICA) in Guatemala immediately after his pathetic loss of power in Managua.[24]

and similar small organizations were founded in Honduras and Miami. Most of these groups joined to form the "Legion of the 15th of September" (named after Nicaragua's Independence Day), which organized training – or retraining – camps in Honduras in 1980. The retraining was intended to transform an effective anti-insurgency force (the former GN) into an equally effective insurgent force. This process was made easier by the GN's ability to conduct small patrols that lived much like guerrillas. They also benefited from the experience of the Khmer Rouge in Kampuchea (first guerrillas, then regular government army, and, since 1979, guerrillas again) and the pro-Portuguese forces in Mozambique and Angola (first anti-insurgents, then guerrillas).[25]

Leadership of the Legion of the 15th of September was in the hands of former senior officers of the Guard, such as Salvador Argüello, a former colonel, who ran a training camp in Florida through 1980; Emilio Echaverry, later known as "El Fierro"; and Colonel Ricardo Lau, called "El Chino." Funds came largely from wealthy Nicaraguan refugees in Miami, Guatemala City, and San Salvador, and from the wealthier members of the Cuban exile community in Florida.[26] Cubans also helped retrain the members of the Legion and of another organization of exiled former GN military, the National Liberation Army (ELN). It appears – though this is difficult to prove – that the nationalist and "liberation" terminology of these groups came from their links with the Guatemalan National Liberation Movement of Mario Sandoval Alarcon, patriarch of the Central American far right.

The total membership of the ELN, the Legion of the 15th of September, and other small groups is best approximated at 600–800 men before mid-1981. Until then these nascent groups differed very little from the émigré groups of other times and regimes fallen to Marxism-Leninism – White Russians, Miami Cubans, and Kuomintang Chinese. Nor were their chances of having an impact any better. What changed their fate, and soon their structure, membership, and role, was the dramatic shift in Nicaragua's internal politics by 1980–81.

Politicians in Exile

By the end of spring 1980, the post-revolutionary fervor that had infected even normally level-headed politicians – prompting, for instance, Violeta Chamorro, member of the first junta after July 19 and owner of the newspaper *La Prensa*, to scream "On to El Salvador"[27] – was clearly over.

Both Chamorro and Alfonso Robelo left the junta in disgust and disappointment. Robelo's Nicaraguan Democratic Movement (MDN) was persecuted and prevented from operating normally, while the two new non-FSLN junta members, Rafael Cordoba Rivas and Arturo Cruz, Sr., had no power base of their own (unlike Violeta Chamorro's *La Prensa*, which was worth a party in its influence, or Robelo's MDN). Then, as now, Rivas was usually unwilling to criticize the Sandinistas, and Cruz was then harboring illusions over the ideological nature of the National Directorate.

While both Robelo (until 1981) and Chamorro (to this day) remained in Nicaragua as the loyal opposition in the hope of free elections soon, other politicians, having decided on all-out opposition, fled into self-imposed exile. By late 1980, the most prominent of those was José Francisco Cardenal ("El Chicano"), a former deputy president of the Council of State immediately after the revolution. Together with Edgar Chamorro, Mariano Mendoza, and Mariano Martínez, Cardenal founded the Nicaraguan Democratic Union (UDN) in Miami by the end of 1980.[28] At that time, the UDN wanted nothing to do with the former Guardsmen, then already led by Enrique Bermúdez Varela, a former Somoza military attaché in Washington. Fernando Chamorro ("El Negro"), a veteran anti-Somoza fighter, left Nicaragua in 1981 and re-established his own Nicaraguan Revolutionary Armed Forces (FARN), a small but very effective and committed force totally loyal to "El Negro." FARN enjoyed some popular support in Managua and in the central departments of Chontales and Boaco.[29]

As a result of Nicaragua's political history, small armies, or more often pseudo-armies, each led by one person, mushroomed until 1985, with each self-appointed leader trying to distinguish his movement from all the others. A "Nicaraguan Liberation Movement" under Roberto Ponce Torres was proclaimed in Tegucigalpa in June 1984, claiming 2,500 fighters.[30] A "Third Way Movement" (M-3) under self-styled "commander" Sebastian González claimed to have started operations on November 1, 1983.[31] Edén Pastora Gómez, the fallen deputy minister of the interior and then of defense in the Sandinista government, has had a record of attracting marginal opposition groups in exile since his defection in April 1982. To a large extent, this personalistic approach to resistance to the Managua regime appeared even among the ethnic minorities of the Atlantic Coast, despite their general status as small minorities, racially divided between black Creoles and full-blooded Indians.

Opposition Among the Ethnic Minorities

No other factor has damaged the FSLN's carefully cultivated image as much as their treatment of the Atlantic Coast populations: Miskito, Rama, and Sumo Indians, and black Creoles. The extent of the damage to their credibility abroad has even prompted prominent Sandinista leaders to acknowledge "errors" in handling the Indian question: Daniel Ortega described the forced relocation of the Indians from along the Río Coco at the beginning of 1982 as such an error, while Tomás Borge described the FSLN Indian policy as a series of "stupid errors" and concluded that "we have driven the Miskito into the arms of the CIA."[32] As Steadman Fagoth Müller, the first prominent leader of the Miskito resistance, stated, for his people the issue that forced them into armed opposition was the preservation "of our identity, our customs, our traditions, and our lives in face of ideological, political penetration by Marxism Sandinism."[33] Collision between Managua's nature and interests and the Atlantic Coast populations' history caused a rapid deterioration in their relations.

During the Somoza years, the Atlantic Coast (Zelaya department) was largely neglected, except for a number of timber and mining activities in the northern half of the region. These industries more often provided jobs than disruptions in the lives of the inhabitants. The Atlantic Coast populations, perhaps as many as 160,000 Indians (the large majority Miskito) and about 70,000 black Creoles, were culturally isolated from the rest of the country. They spoke English and Indian languages rather than Spanish, were Protestant (mostly Moravian) rather than Catholic, and were historically distrustful of the Pacific Coast population. The Atlantic region was geographically isolated as well, with only one road linking its port of Bluefields with the Pacific, and it was economically oriented toward the Caribbean rather than toward the rest of the country. Somoza's benign neglect of the Atlantic Coast reinforced its isolation and established a de facto autonomy rarely disturbed until 1979. The civil war leading to Somoza's fall barely touched Zelaya; extremely few Indians were involved in any way.

Once in power, the FSLN immediately initiated radical changes on the Atlantic Coast. Traditional leaders (councils of elders) and practices were scorned, and communal lands were often nationalized. The ubiquitous Sandinista Defense Committees (CDS), huge networks of informants rapidly growing on the Pacific Coast, began "mobilizing" the villagers, while the Moravian Church, historically uninvolved in the Christian Marxism of "liberation theology" highly favored by the FSLN, was persecuted as a creation of North American "imperialism."[34] The "literacy crusade," begun in Managua as a mass indoctrination exercise, was imposed upon the linguistic minorities of the Atlantic Coast in Spanish, involving a heavy use of Cuban teachers. While "the metaphors and terminology of the campaign were purposefully military—'The National Literacy Crusade: Heroes and Martyrs for the Liberation of Nicaragua,' 'the war on ignorance,' 'the cultural insurrection,' and 'the second war of liberation' "[35]—the distinction between the campaign's symbols and substance escaped the blacks and Indians. Such misapprehensions were helped by the heavy presence of the EPS (the Sandinista army) in the region—in contrast with the absence of military units throughout the Somoza regime and during the 1978–79 war—and by Managua's heavy-handed treatment of all Indian leaders, including those few, like Steadman Fagoth Müller, active in the anti-Somoza opposition before 1979.

In mass demonstrations in October 1980, blacks in Bluefields protested the presence and behavior of the Cuban teachers.[36] The violence that ensued was brutally quelled by the military, and the leaders of the spontaneous uprising were jailed. Other than isolated forays by former Guardsmen across the Honduran border, the Bluefields uprising was the first major expression of violent opposition to the FSLN.

The Atlantic Coast minorities were not alone in their strong resentment of the presence of "internationalists" in their country. These internationalists— whether Soviet-bloc and Cuban personnel, assorted free-lance revolutionary ideologues, or terrorists from Chile, Uruguay, Argentina, Colombia, El Salvador, Guatemala, Western Europe, and the Middle East—are seen by many Nicaraguans as alien invaders who care little for local customs and sensibilities.[37]

By the end of 1979, under direct pressure from Daniel Ortega, the Indian organization ALPROMISU (The Alliance for the Progress of Miskito and Sumo Indians), founded in 1975, was "sandinized" into MISURASATA (Miskito, Sumo, Rama, Sandinista Unity).[38] In September 1979, a Miskito leader, Lyster Athers, was arrested and killed in the Puerto Cabezas jail by the authorities.[39] By 1980 communal forests had been nationalized, as had communal lands around Puerto Cabezas. In light of the essential role played by Cuba in the survival of the Sandinista regime, the FSLN's strategic interest in securing the Bluefields, Puerto Cabezas, and El Bluff harbors on the Atlantic is understandable, as is Indian resistance.

By March 1980 the Indians had begun their exodus to Honduras. The exodus increased after the arrest, subsequent release, and escape to Honduras of Fagoth Müller. There, amid nearly 25,000 Indians, he established MISURA (MISURASATA without the Sandinista label). Another leader, Brooklyn Rivera, maintained his own faction, as well as the MISURASATA name, and fled to Costa Rica. In search of allies, both MISURA and MISURASATA entered into alliances with larger insurgent groups: the FDN and ARDE, respectively. Subsequent squabbling among the Indian organizations, the apparent downfall of both Steadman Fagoth Müller, because of heavy-handed treatment of his followers, and Brooklyn Rivera, expelled for misguided and fruitless attempts to negotiate with Managua, did not diminish Indian determination to fight for autonomy.

At least 2,500 Indian fighters are now in Zelaya, posing a serious threat to Sandinista communications with the Caribbean coast, and preventing the exploitation of the mines and forests, while discrediting Managua's human rights claims. Although they are proportionally the most effective of the insurgents opposing Managua today, their small numbers and the isolation of their region prevent an Indian victory. Meanwhile, their experience with the Sandinistas both in war and in negotiations appears to preclude any large-scale acceptance of the amnesty offered them by the government.

Formation of ARDE

On April 15, 1982, Edén Pastora Gómez, then deputy defense minister in charge of the formation of the Sandinista popular militias, and previously deputy interior minister, held a press conference in Costa Rica to announce his departure from the Nicaraguan government, and to accuse the members of the National Directorate of treason. Pastora denounced their betrayal of the revolution because of their Marxism-Leninism, and their betrayal of Nicaragua because of the dominant role permitted the Cubans and Soviet-bloc personnel. In September 1982, Robelo's Nicaraguan Democratic Movement (MDN), then Nicaragua's largest and most prestigious non-Marxist party; Brooklyn Rivera's MISURASATA; Fernando "El Negro" Chamorro's Nicaraguan Democratic Union–Nicaraguan Revolutionary Armed Forces (UDN–FARN); and Pastora's own Sandinist Revolutionary Front (FRS), proclaimed the formation of ARDE, the Democratic Revolutionary Alliance.[40]

From the beginning, ARDE differed from all other groups involved in the insurgency, in that it included former anti-Somoza activists. Their having taken arms against Somoza initially endowed FARN and FRS with greater legitimacy than that of the opposition centered around José Francisco Cardenal's UDN. From the outset ARDE claimed to be *the* true Sandinista heir, to Sandino's ideas that had been betrayed by the FSLN. That both Pastora and Robelo had held high positions in the post-revolutionary regime, while Rivera and Fernando Chamorro both cooperated with the FSLN, demonstrated the depth of their revolutionary commitment.

However, the seeds of ARDE's destruction were sown at the beginning: the organization was little more than a convenient umbrella for four strong leaders, each with his own following, goals, and priorities. ARDE's main goal, proclaimed in its founding declaration as "the rescue of the original project of the Nicaraguan Revolution,"[41] was articulated in its slogan: "Without totalitarianism nor return to the past." ARDE's program was intended to attract all those anti-Somoza fighters who were disaffected after their coalition collapsed. The story of one of ARDE's first prominent recruits, Salvador Aranda Mairena, typifies the motives of those who joined the organization and illuminates their background:

> I joined the Frente [FSLN] during the last years of the struggle against Somoza. The contact was established through my two brothers, who were Sandinistas.... When the uprising began in 1979, I was actively involved in the takeover of the military posts at Malpaisillo, El Sauce, and Las Mojarras on the Río Grande.... Even after July 19, I remained active in the CDS [Sandinista Defense Committees]. But that's when the problems began.... I had personal problems with some people who had been Somoza supporters before and now played the big supporters of the revolution. Some of them were given good positions—in the UNAF [Unión Nacional de Agricultores], the CDS, and even the military. That burned me. Damn it, I had participated in the armed struggle, taken a clear position, and now I had to watch while the same people as before skimmed the cream off the top.[42]

Most of ARDE's recruits were veterans of Pastora's Southern Front against Pablo Emilio Salazar in 1979, or were from among Robelo's middle-class followers, including many students, from small cadres of committed supporters of Fernando Chamorro, and from Brooklyn Rivera's small faction of MISURASATA.

Weakening of ARDE

ARDE began operations along the southern border of Nicaragua in 1983, taking advantage of Pastora's experience in the region. More important, ARDE exploited Pastora's and Robelo's extensive network of contacts within the establishment and the population of Costa Rica. However, ARDE never managed to establish a northern front from Honduras, chiefly because of Pastora's hatred for the FDN, whom he has consistently accused of being "Somocistas," coupled with his own negative image among the Honduran military.

From the beginning, Pastora was the main leader of ARDE's military activities, and his errors and merits have largely decided the fate of the organization. After initial disappointments in the attempt to attract Sandinista military and militiamen to their side, ARDE became a rapidly growing force of about 500 by the end of 1983, and numbered nearly 3,000 fighters by 1984.[43] However, by then the group was already rent by the conflict between Pastora's confused proclamations and Robelo's pragmatic approach to the FDN. The rift put a halt to recruiting and, by the end of 1984, resulted in a public break. Robelo and Fernando Chamorro's FARN joined the FDN, while Pastora tried to establish his own politico-military group, the Southern Opposition Bloc (BOS).

By the end of 1985, after a year of continuous EPS pressure against ARDE and the latter's loss of its main bases at La Penca and Sarrapiqui, Pastora's forces numbered fewer than 1,000 fighters, his field commanders actively cooperated with FDN forces in the field,[44] and the FDN was actively recruiting entire ARDE units from the southern border areas. Even Adolfo Chamorro (exaggeratedly) defined ARDE, at the end of 1985, as "5,000 armed men who do not respond to any individual leadership or a single will."[45]

Pastora's military failure—not surprising, considering his lack of success as a commander of large forces in 1979—and ARDE's perhaps fatal weakening do not indicate any lack of support for Pastora or, more important, for those center-left elements in Nicaragua and in exile who are unhappy with the FDN or at least with some of its field commanders. The list of organizations constituting the BOS is impressive, though most are in exile: the Union Committee of Nicaraguan Workers and Peasants in Exile; ARDE (under Adolfo Chamorro Cardenal); Unity of Nicaraguan Professionals in Exile; Association of Nicaraguan Professionals in Exile; The Christian Workers' Solidarity; and the Nicaraguan National Rescue Conciliation Movement.[46] What makes some of these groups significant is less their strength in exile and their role in the insurgency than their followings within Nicaragua (in the cases of Pastora, "Popo" Chamorro, and Alfredo César of the National Rescue and Conciliation Movement) and their still extensive external connections with democratically minded Latin American governments, parties, and individuals.

The 'People' and the Insurgency

Both the Managua regime and the insurgent leaders claim to represent "the people" of Nicaragua: against a "counter-revolutionary, Somocista clique" and against a "Marxist-Leninist clique," respectively. The fact that the insurgents fight mostly against other Nicaraguans and are not yet close to winning—coupled with the flawed results of the 1984 elections—shows that the Sandinistas still have significant support, albeit from a decreasing minority. On the other hand, Managua's claims that the insurgents are "CIA mercenaries" and "Somocista gangs" have no credibility. Even Sandinista sympathizers in the United States are now forced to acknowledge that the "FDN and U.S. government claims that the FDN is largely a 'peasant army' of Nicaraguans disaffected with their government are accurate."[47]

Simple arithmetic invalidates Sandinista claims that the FDN, with approximately 15,000 fighters, is made up of "National Guardsmen," of whom no more than 5,000–6,000 could have escaped in 1979. Moreover, all available evidence indicates that among the FDN regional and task force commanders there are more former Sandinistas (twenty-seven, or 48 per cent) than former Guardsmen (thirteen, or 23 per cent).[48] Moreover, former GN members, though prominent at higher levels, make up less than 2 per cent of the total FDN membership.[49] The main issue regarding the Nicaraguan insurgency relates to the motives of those thousands of peasants who join the FDN or smaller groups and risk their lives against the government's impressive army.

First, brutal government intrusion into property, authority, and belief traditions—land seizures, forced cooperativization-collectivization of villages, repression of Indian elders or local peasant leaders in the northern areas, and persecution or exile of non-revolutionary priests—has alienated significant numbers of the population. The mistreatment of Catholic clergy (other than "liberation theology" supporters) was at the root of the spontaneous uprising in the Monimbó district of Masaya in November 1982. That was the first urban uprising on the Pacific Coast and occurred in the very place that has symbolized anti-Somoza rebellion since 1978.[50] The protest spread to fourteen high schools in five cities, and a number of people, mostly youth, were killed by the army.[51]

Second, the Sandinistas' Patriotic Military Service (SMP), a compulsory draft, helped focus resistance. While one might have expected draft evaders to be unwilling to fight, the FSLN polarization of the society actually forced many of those fleeing the SMP to join the insurgents. As one of them put it, "Sure, I have joined an army [the FDN] anyway, but at least that is of my own will."[52] Draft evasion is widespread,[53] even epidemic in certain areas.[54] In Managua, half of the young private school students threatened by the SMP fled.[55]

Most important, because of their multiplying effect upon the insurgents' recruiting capabilities, are the reactions of the families of those drafted or threatened by the SMP. In the small town of Nagarote, an EPS (Sandinista army) recruiting drive resulted in open street fights with the population.[56] Clearly, it is among such furious and threatened groups that the insurgents find recruits and informers, while the FSLN finds only "counterrevolutionaries." To potential draftees and their families who join the insurgents rather than fight for the regime are added recruits from among the newly arrived slum-dwellers of Managua, León, and Granada, and the almost 100,000 peasants from northern Nicaragua forcibly relocated by the military to "protect" them from the insurgents.[57]

Nature of the Insurgents

As far as the Sandinistas are concerned, all insurgents are either hardcore "CIA mercenaries" and "Somocista criminals" or people under the influence of "religious sects" such as the Moravians, Mormons, Jehovah's Witnesses, or Seventh Day Adventists.[58] According to Captain Roberto Calderon, an EPS commander, the insurgents "use different methods in recruitment, such as involving kidnapped peasants in the crimes they commit.... They recruit thirteen- to fifteen-year-old children, who are subjected to a 'conversion' process to turn them into real beasts."[59] Nevertheless, Calderon admitted that "there are also elements who conscientiously help the 'contras,' particularly farmers who respond to counterrevolutionary propaganda."[60] Sandinista repression of Protestant churches has also provided many recruits to the insurgents,[61] and in some areas, lay religious workers cooperating with the regime and its allies among the revolutionary clergy are favorite targets of the insurgents.[62]

Among the insurgents in general, and the FDN in particular, women are at least as numerous as they are among the Sandinista leadership. The difference is that while the Sandinista women are almost exclusively from the middle or upper-middle class (such as Nora Astorga, Monica Baltodano, Leticia Herrera, Dora Maria Tellez), the insurgent women are peasant or working class in origin. Many of these women are seen by their male comrades as "stronger" than the men,[63] and their commitment is at least equal to that of the men. Some still fight, often in command roles, even when pregnant.[64] At least one woman reached the rank of FDN task force leader (and was killed in combat), and many, like Marta Luisa Martínez, arrested in Río Blanco in August 1982, were actively recruiting other women to the insurgent cause.[65]

Despite Sandinista claims to the contrary and the labeling of all insurgents as "mercenaries," the overwhelming majority of recruits to both ARDE and the FDN receive no payment, and only a few leaders receive support for their families. Although some cases of forced recruitment, including kidnapping by the insurgents, are well documented, most fighters join voluntarily. Thus, a government prisoner, Uriel Navarette Medrano of Chinandega, stated that only a dozen FDN guerrillas were needed to escort as many as 500 willing peasants into Honduras.[66] Testimonies of Sandinista prisoners affirm that guerrilla groups coming from Honduras swelled as they penetrated southward, mostly because of local recruits who joined spontaneously. Some of these recruits, like eighteen-year-old José Sarmiento, whose brother was in the EPS, joined because "it was more fun than going back to my family,"[67] but most joined for weightier reasons.

The high degree of motivation, almost ferocity, of the Nicaraguan insurgents was abundantly demonstrated from the start of military operations. On the one hand, real and alleged Sandinista atrocities against captured insurgents[68] are presumed to be real by the fighters in the field[69] and result in an extremely low level of captures by the EPS, even in the official claims. Thus, in January 1986, Captain Roberto Calderon claimed that 1,400 "counter-revolutionaries" were killed during 1985 but only "over 100" were captured.[70] Or the other hand, there is little mercy on the part of the insurgents for Sandinista cadres, including CDS members, revolutionary priests and lay preachers, or government officials. As far as the insurgents–

with the exception of ARDE—are concerned, few prisoners are taken, in part because the guerrillas cannot guard, feed, or carry prisoners, but also because of the hatred involved.

A Purge of Guardsmen

Their military training and experience in small-unit operations as counterinsurgency fighters made it absolutely necessary for former Guardsmen not only to belong to but initially to lead the Nicaraguan insurgent groups. But by 1982, through the internal dynamics of the insurgency—particularly the successful recruiting of former Sandinista sympathizers—as well as the need to present a better image abroad, especially in the U.S. Congress, a massive purge of former senior Guardia officers occurred. At least three of the most important ones—FDN chief of staff Emilio Echaverry, intelligence chief Edgar Antonio Hernández ("Abel"), and field commander Pedro Pablo Ortiz Centeno ("El Suicida")—were shot for atrocities against their own troops and civilians, and for rebellion or theft.[71]

The removal of those elements, combined with the influx of non-Guardsmen into the ranks of the FDN, and most of all the association of the fighters with such prominent, often liberal, and known anti-Somoza leaders like Arturo Cruz, Alfonso Robelo, and Adolfo Calero, all contributed to the growing recruiting strength of the insurgent organizations. Whether they will ever succeed in making active resistance fighters of all those Nicaraguans, in the country or abroad, who do not support the regime is unclear and probably depends on their ability to show they can win.

On the other hand, FSLN policies, usually on purpose but sometimes by mistake, have resulted in the increasing polarization of Nicaraguan society. In the words of Mariano Montealegre, a former squadron leader in the Sandinista air force, who defected to Costa Rica and joined ARDE in 1982, "There are only two options: either you are with the FSLN or against it."[72] Since then, alternatives have further diminished, and nothing remains to prevent an all-out war among Nicaraguans, with neutrals forced to take sides.

Outlook for the Future

Steadily since July 19, 1979, and rapidly since 1981, the nature of the Nicaraguan state and of Sandinista rule has changed. The opposition has also changed. The total politicization of Nicaraguan society created a self-perpetuating polarization. Each Sandinista crackdown on the opposition provoked more violent responses that were answered with escalating state violence, more crackdowns, and more responses. In 1986, the regime has accused even Cardinal Miguel Obando y Bravo, archbishop of Managua, of being an imperialist agent, and the still legal opposition groups—including Conservatives, Social Democrats, Christian Democrats, Stalinists, Trotskyites, and pro-Moscow Communists—have formed a coalition, if not an alliance, directed against the FSLN.

The trend toward polarization and the translation of that polarization into more clearly divided armed camps has almost reached its climax in Nicaragua. As in many civil wars, polarization has a limit, after which the two sides are reduced to their hard-core, immovable strength. Those Nicaraguans with a vital stake in the continuation of FSLN rule are well defined by now, and their fear of losing everything should the FSLN collapse will make them fight to the finish.

It is equally clear that the insurgents will continue to fight irrespective of external factors, such as the U.S. Congress or the Honduran military. What does depend on those factors is not the continuation of the civil war but its nature and duration. The Sandinista style of rule implies absolute control over the state apparatus, the military, and the economy, rendering any distinction between the party and the state meaningless. Therefore, every aspect of the state has become a natural target of the insurgent forces, because they are all mutually reinforcing and strengthening the FSLN's grip on the country. State-owned cooperatives, state-controlled or -dominated factories, the CDS, Fernando Cardenal's "literacy crusaders," and the revolutionary priests and their lay pupils, whether native or foreign—all are strands in a single fabric, the FSLN's fledgling totalitarian system. The Christianity of the insurgents is incompatible with that of Fernando Cardenal or of Foreign Minister D'Escoto, just as their nationalism is incompatible with the FSLN's outspoken internationalism.

Although political or economic differences between people can often be solved by negotiations, deep chasms between beliefs are seldom negotiable. As a prominent exile active in the insurgency leadership has defined it, the insurgent "is fighting for no other reason than to preserve his way of life, to protect his traditions from the voracious appetite of a Leninist vanguard determined to transform him—against his will—into a 'new man.' "[73] For this reason, there is no room to hope for any solution of the Nicaraguan civil war other than all-out victory for one side or the other.

Notes

1. David Nolan, *FSLN: The Ideology of the Sandinistas and the Nicaraguan Revolution* (Coral Gables, Fla.: University of Miami, 1984), p. 22. A multitude of sources, including many FSLN documents, indicate the same phenomenon.
2. Quoted in Shirley Christian, *Nicaragua: Revolution in the Family* (New York: Random House, 1985), p. 185.
3. Ibid.
4. A typical articulation of this myth is found in Humberto Belli, Adolfo Calero, and Haroldo Montealegre, *Three Nicaraguans on the Betrayal of their Revolution* (Washington: The Heritage Foundation, 1985).
5. Humberto Belli, *Breaking Faith: The Sandinista Revolution and Its Impact on Freedom and Christian Faith in Nicaragua* (Westchester, Ill.: Crossway Books, and The Puebla Institute, 1985), quoting Daniel Ortega.
6. Arturo Cruz, "Nicaragua Needs U.S. Tolerance," *New York Times*, December 9, 1981.
7. Cf. Christian, *Nicaragua*, p. 278.
8. See Douglas Payne. *The Democratic Mask: The Consolidation of the Sandinista Revolution* (New York: Freedom House, 1985), p. 26.
9. Eduardo Crawley, *Nicaragua in Perspective* (New York: St. Martin's Press, 1979), p. 167.
10. Adolfo Gilly, *La Nueva Nicaragua* (Mexico City: Editorial Nueva Imagen, 1980), p. 112.
11. George Black, *Triumph of the People: The Sandinista Revolution in Nicaragua* (London: Zed Press, 1981), p. 51.
12. Crawley, *Nicaragua in Perspective*, p. 168; Black, *Triumph of the People*, p. 53.
13. Black, *Triumph of the People*, pp. 47–48.
14. Ibid. A typical case is that of "Pecos Bill," a middle-level FDN field commander, who graduated from the Valley Forge Military Academy in Pennsylvania and the School of the Americas in Panama, joined the U.S. Navy, and received further training in Israel. See Dieter Eich and Carlos Rincón, *The Contras: Interviews with Anti-Sandinistas* (San Francisco: Synthesis Publications, 1984), pp. 189–90.
15. See Edén Pastora's own complaints on the matter, in "Testimony of Edén Pastora Gómez," in Uri Ra'anan et al., *Hydra of Carnage, International Linkages of Terrorism: The Witnesses Speak* (Lexington, Mass.: Lexington Books, 1986), pp. 325–26.
16. Ibid., p. 326, one of the few truly reliable claims made by Pastora.
17. Christian, *Nicaragua*, p. 133.
18. Crawley, *Nicaragua in Perspective*, p. 173.
19. This provoked general skepticism, except on the far left, where the reaction was to accuse the Sandinistas of irresponsible weakness. See D. Fogel, *Revolution in Central America* (San Francisco: Ism Press, 1985), p. 199.
20. See *The Voice of Nicaragua*, January 1986, p. 7, for Red Cross testimonies. Other accusations of summary executions of captured Guardsmen are in Belli, *Breaking Faith*, p. 127; Christian, *Nicaragua*, pp. 132–34.
21. Quoted in Belli, *Breaking Faith*, p. 121.

22. "Pecos Bill," in Eich and Rincón, *The Contras*, p. 189, as an example of the thirst for revenge. For the depth of the desire to return home and live a normal life and its role as a motive for joining the insurgents, see the testimony of former GN lieutenant colonel Jorge Ramírez Zelaya, for whom "the actual goal is returning to Nicaragua" (ibid., p. 39).

23. For details on the liquidation of Pablo Emilio Salazar, and the direct role played in it by Tomás Borge and then secret police chief Lenín Cerna (now ambassador to Bulgaria), see Christopher Dickey, *With the Contras* (New York: Simon and Schuster, 1985), pp. 64–67. Most of the information was confirmed by this author's own research in San Salvador and Tegucigalpa in 1983.

24. "Pecos Bill," in Eich and Rincón, *The Contras*, p. 187.

25. Ibid., pp. 184–85.

26. *New York Times*, December 23, 1981; Eich and Rincón, *The Contras*, p. 45.

27. Edgar Chamorro with Jefferson Morley, "Confessions of a Contra," *The New Republic*, August 5, 1985, p. 19.

28. Ibid., p. 20; and Eich and Rincón, *The Contras*, p. 137, for the testimony of Pedro Espinosa Sánchez, leader of the FDN "internal front." Sánchez's testimony (while in captivity) is in doubt since he claims that it was José Fernando Cardenal, rather than the real José Francisco Cardenal (see also Christian, *Nicaragua*, pp. 176–77), who founded the UDN. That is a strange error for a person claiming to know Cardenal well, particularly in light of the latter's fame in Nicaragua.

29. For the origins of FARN, see *Nicaragua Hoy*, August 10, 1985.

30. *La Prensa Libre*, Guatemala City, June 23, 1984, p. 4.

31. See *FBIS-LAM (Foreign Broadcast Information Service-Latin America)*, November 21, 1983, p. P18.

32. Quoted in Fogel, *Revolution in Central America*, p. 109.

33. Steadman Fagoth Müller, "A Witness to Genocide," AFL-CIO, *Free Trade Union News*, March 1982, p. 3.

34. Belli, *Breaking Faith*, pp. 106–17.

35. These are the words of former Jesuit Fernando Cardenal, Nicaragua's minister of education, in his "Nicaragua 1980: The Battle of the ABCs," in Stanford Central America Action Network, *Revolution in Central America* (Boulder: Westview Press, 1983), p. 450.

36. Roxanne Dunbar Ortiz, "Miskitus in Nicaragua: Who is Violating Human Rights?," ibid., p. 469; also see Payne, *The Democratic Mask*, p. 29.

37. See for instance, "Sandinistas Attract a Who's Who of Terrorists" and "From Italy to the PLO, World's Leftists Find Haven in Nicaragua," by Juan Tamayo, in the *Miami Herald*, reprinted by the Cuban American Foundation, Washington, D.C., 1985. There are consistent reports of Salvadoran, Guatemalan, Costa Rican, and Chilean guerrillas participating in anti-insurgency operations against both the FDN and ARDE, and some were killed in combat.

38. Fogel, *Revolution in Central America*, p. 93. It is highly significant that Dunbar Ortiz, a committed supporter of each and every action of the FSLN, as well as Fogel, a critic of the Sandinistas from the far left, had to acknowledge the mistreatment of the Indians, as did Penny Lernoux in *The Nation*.

39. Fagoth Müller, "Witness to Genocide," p. 2.

40. Text in ARDE, *Propuesta de Paz en Nicaragua, para la Paz en Centro America*, January 1983.

41. Ibid.

42. See the testimony of Salvador Aranda Mairena, in Eich and Rincón, *The Contras*, pp. 107–8; for the role of former Somoza supporters in the CDS, see also Robert Leiken, "Nicaragua's Untold Stories," *The New Republic*, October 8, 1984, p. 17.

43. Pastora's deputy, Adolfo "Popo" Chamorro, made the implausible claim that ARDE had 6,000 combatants by the end of its first year, in Adolfo Chamorro, "Balance Militar del Frente Sur de Nicaragua," *Foco Centroamericano*, 2nd quarter of October 1985, pp. 1, 4.
44. See the statements of Manuel Urroz, alias "Julio Bigote," a Pastora lieutenant, in *FBIS-LAM*, December 15, 1983, p. P14.
45. Adolfo Chamorro, "Balance Militar," p. 4.
46. *La Nación*, San José, Costa Rica, July 28, 1985.
47. Reed Brody, *Contra Terror in Nicaragua* (Boston: South End Press, 1985), p. 133. It is an interesting fact that Brody and other pro-Sandinista accusers of the insurgents never try to explain why simple peasants would engage in atrocities against other peasants.
48. U.S. Congress, House, Committee on Foreign Affairs, Subcommittee on Western Hemisphere Affairs, *U.S. Support for the Contras*, 99th Cong., 1st sess., April 16–18, 1985, p. 358.
49. Ibid.
50. Humberto Belli, *Nicaragua: Christians Under Fire* (Garden City, Mich.: The Puebla Institute, 1984), pp. 49–51; see also Payne, *The Democratic Mask*, p. 37.
51. *Christian Science Monitor*, August 19, 1982; *New York Times*, August 18, 1982.
52. *New York Times*, February 18, 1985.
53. Ibid., June 26, 1984.
54. Leiken, "Nicaragua's Untold Stories," p. 20.
55. *New York Times*, August 31, 1983.
56. Ibid., February 15, 1985.
57. Ibid., February 18, 1985.
58. See statement by Tomás Borge, in *FBIS-LAM*, July 16, 1982, pp. P9–10.
59. *Barricada*, Managua, August 18, 1985, p. 7.
60. Ibid.
61. Perhaps as many as 20 per cent of the insurgents are evangelical Christians, a proportion far higher than among the general population; see U.S. Congress, House, *U.S. Support for the Contras*, pp. 297, 309.
62. A fact much deplored by revolutionary priest Teófilo Cabestrero, an FSLN activist, in his *Blood of the Innocent: Victims of the Contras' War in Nicaragua* (Maryknoll, N.Y.: Orbis Books, 1985), pp. 9, 15.
63. See Eich and Rincón, *The Contras*, p. 99.
64. Ibid., p. 65.
65. *Barricada*, August 24, 1982, p. 12.
66. Eich and Rincón, *The Contras*, p. 89, testimony of Emerson Uriel Navarrete Medrano.
67. Ibid., p. 169.
68. "If fifteen [insurgents] are captured, two will be taken to Managua for debriefing, where they will be put on TV, and the rest will be killed. Often they are killed by stabbing, but there is also the 'vest cut.' In this, the prisoner's arms and legs are cut off while he is alive, and he is left to bleed to death. It is an old technique used by Somoza and Sandino." Miguel Bolaños Hunter, "Nicaragua: A View From Within," in Mark Falcoff and Robert Royal, eds., *Crisis and Opportunity: U.S. Policy in Central America and the Caribbean* (Washington: Ethics and Public Policy Center, 1984), p. 390, reprinted from Heritage Foundation *Backgrounder* #294. Bolaños was a member of the Sandinista counter intelligence.
69. See Eich and Rincón, *The Contras*, p. 180.
70. *FBIS-LAM*, January 30, 1986, p. P18.
71. See Eich and Rincón, *The Contras*, pp. 150–51; U.S. Congress, House, *U.S.*

Support for the Contras, p. 318. The most detailed examination of the execution of "El Suicida," together with three of his lieutenants, is in Dickey, *With the Contras*, pp. 250–51.
72. *La Nación*, May 7, 1982, p. 1A.
73. Arturo Cruz, Jr., "Managua's Game," *The New Republic*, March 10, 1986, p. 19.

26. Nicaragua and International Law

By JOHN NORTON MOORE

Focus "The United States has supported peace efforts through the Contadora process," claims John Norton Moore, but it will not "simply accept a parchment barrier while the Nicaraguan secret war on its neighbors continues in violation of at least twelve important legal charters and resolutions."

In this paper written before the World Court's June 1986 decision that U.S. support of the anti-Sandinista insurgents was illegal, Moore cites several congressional, Central American, and other studies that find that the Sandinistas, by providing military and logistical support to guerrilla movements, pose an active threat to El Salvador and the rest of Central America. "This pattern of aggression constitutes an armed attack justifying the use of force in collective defense under Article 51 of the United Nations Charter and Article 3 of the Rio Treaty. Indeed, Article 27 of the OAS Charter declares that such an attack is 'an act of aggression against . . . [all] the American States,' and Article 3 of the Rio Treaty creates a legal obligation on the United States to assist in meeting the armed attack."

While some concede these legal points, says Moore, they argue that support for the contras is disproportionate to the threat. (The World Court accepted this reasoning in its findings against the United States.) But the Sandinistas' clear intention to overthrow the democratically elected government of El Salvador and the eventual threat to Costa Rica make a similar threat to the Sandinista regime, in Moore's view, a just response. He sees as menacing the remark of Sandinista foreign minister

Miguel D'Escoto: "You may look at us as five countries, six now with Panama, but we regard ourselves as six different states of a single nation in the process of reunification."

Moore's analysis of the legal situation in Central America should be compared with the views of President Daniel Ortega (selection 22) and the qualified criticisms of Michael Walzer (selection 27).

John Norton Moore has served as a special counsel for the United States in the case of *Nicaragua v. United States* before the International Court of Justice (World Court).

THE SECRETARY GENERAL of the United Nations, Javier Pérez de Cuellar, once said that "an extended and tolerable future for all humanity ultimately depends upon our success in making the purposes and principles of the Charter of the United Nations the basis of day-to-day relations of governments and peoples." There is now, sadly, a grave threat to those principles in Central America. That threat is not, as some would have us believe, from the United States and its allies. Rather it is from the ongoing repudiation by the nine Sandinista *"comandantes"* of the provisions for self-determination, human rights, and the non-use of force in the charters of the United Nations and the Organization of American States (OAS).

I will briefly examine the factual background of the conflict in Central America, then turn to a brief legal analysis, and finally discuss two recurrent misperceptions about the conflict.

THE FACTUAL BACKGROUND

The history of the Sandinista regime includes these facts:

- The United States cut off military aid to Somoza during the revolution and voted for an OAS resolution endorsing the revolution.
- The United States actively sought good relations with the new Sandinista government when it took power in 1979.
- The United States gave $118 million in economic assistance to the Sandinistas during their first two years in power—more aid than it had given to the Somoza regime in the preceding twenty years.
- The United States supported $292 million in World Bank and Inter-American Development Bank loans to the Sandinistas.
- The United States offered a substantial Peace Corp commitment, but the Sandinistas rejected American helpers in favor of thousands of Cuban, Bulgarian, East German, Libyan, PLO, and other Soviet-bloc and radical-regime advisors. (There are approximately 10,000 such advisors today in Nicaragua.)
- President Carter invited Daniel Ortega to the White House.
- The bipartisan Kissinger Commission found that the United States

---

An address to the American Society of International Law, April 1985.

"undertook a patient and concerted effort to build a constructive relationship of mutual trust with the new government."

In response to these overtures of friendship, the nine *comandantes* instituted three policies that are the root causes of the challenge to charter principles in Central America.

Abandoning Pluralism and Non-Alignment

First, they began consolidation of a Leninist vanguard party to control Nicaragua and reneged on their 1979 pledge to the OAS to build a democratic, pluralist society that would be non-aligned and supportive of human rights. Their actions included:

- The nine *comandantes* — three from each of the three Nicaraguan Marxist parties, chosen at a 1979 meeting in Havana — began a purge of the many genuine democrats, such as Arturo Cruz, who had fought against Somoza.
- The *comandantes* began a massive campaign against the Miskito Indians. This included attacks on villages, destruction of houses, crops, and livestock, arrest of Indian leaders, disbanding of the Indians' organization as "counter-revolutionary," and some brutal killings. Of approximately 100,000 Indians at the beginning of these atrocities, some 20,000 have fled Nicaragua and another 20,000 have been moved to "relocation camps."
- The *comandantes* began to put in place the depressingly familiar apparatus of a totalitarian police state, including suppression of labor movements, attacks on the church and religious freedom, press censorship, an internal security system down to the block level, a merger of the party with the state, suspension of *habeas corpus*, and detention of growing numbers of political prisoners without charges. The Pope was insulted by carefully orchestrated mobs when he sought to bring a message of peace to Nicaragua.
- Within nine months of taking power — as massive U.S. aid continued — the Sandinistas made their first pilgrimage to Moscow. Their official anthem pledges, "We shall fight against the Yankee aggressor, the enemy of humanity."
- In their voting record the Sandinistas are aligned with the Soviet bloc. For example, in the 1983–84 session of the U.N. General Assembly they voted for the Soviet-Cuban position 96 per cent of the time. They voted for the Vietnamese invasion of Kampuchea, and they refused to condemn the Soviet invasion of Afghanistan.

- Although human rights abuses were legendary under Somoza, 120,000 Nicaraguans who stayed under Somoza had fled the Sandinista revolution by 1984.

The Military Buildup

The second major challenge to charter principles is that the *comandantes* began a massive military buildup even as the United States poured in economic assistance. Before any contra threat they had built up the Nicaraguan armed forces to nearly six times the size of the Somoza National Guard.

Today the armed forces are nine times that level and still growing. They have some 350 tanks and armored vehicles. In contrast, there were three tanks under Somoza. There are currently none in Costa Rica, sixteen armored reconnaissance vehicles in Honduras, and fewer than thirty armored personnel carriers in El Salvador—a nation with a substantial military insurgency. A major airfield capable of taking the largest aircraft in the Soviet arsenal is being built at Punta Huerta, and Nicaraguan MIG pilots are being trained in Bulgaria.

'Revolution Without Frontiers'

Third, and the factor most important for our legal analysis, as the revolution in Nicaragua was consolidated, the Cubans and Sandinistas began active support for a "revolution without frontiers" in neighboring Central American states. Remember in this connection that Cuba had supported insurgencies and other operations for the overthrow of indigenous Latin and Caribbean governments in some seventeen nations during the first twenty years of its existence, beginning in 1959 with attacks against Panama and Nicaragua. Cuba was condemned by the OAS for its serious attacks against Venezuela. Ché Guevara's own diary detailed the unsuccessful attack in Bolivia and elsewhere in Latin America.

The evidence of the 1979 "revolution without frontiers" attacks on neighboring Central American states from Cuba and Nicaragua is clear. (We will look at the meaning of "attack" in the second section of this article.) By late 1980 the Carter administration, alarmed by the evidence, had suspended U.S. economic assistance to the Sandinistas and had begun a program of emergency military assistance to El Salvador and neighboring states. This evidence included the following:

- In December 1979 and May 1980, Castro held meetings in Cuba to organize competing Salvadoran insurgent factions into a unified command following a Moscow line.

* In 1980, leaders of the Salvadoran FMLN (Farabundo Martí National Liberation Front) traveled to Moscow, East Germany, Bulgaria, Ethiopia, and Vietnam to obtain arms and supplies for the insurgency. In response they received a major shipment of ammunition and arms—primarily U.S. arms taken in Vietnam and Ethiopia—a total of over 700 tons.

* Weapons serial numbers and defectors' reports show conclusively that the preponderance of weapons used by the insurgents are trans-shipped from Soviet-bloc sources through Cuba and Nicaragua. Moreover, it is easy to show that they are not captured locally: the insurgents were equipped with M16 rifles and M60 machine guns before the Salvadoran army had them, and the Salvadoran army has regularly captured more arms from the insurgents than it has lost to them. The U.S. Department of State issued detailed reports on weapons intercepts in February 1981, March 1982, May 1983, and July 1984. The governments of El Salvador, Costa Rica, and Honduras have confirmed this information. Of particular importance is the 1980 report of the Costa Rican Special Legislative Commission detailing the arms flow to Costa Rica and Salvadoran insurgents.

* Command and control of the Salvadoran insurgency—with orders on a daily basis—come from a headquarters complex near Managua, Nicaragua. The Kissinger Commission stated that "the guerrilla front has established a unified military command with headquarters near Managua."

* The statements of Sandinista leaders themselves confirm these intentions and assistance. As early as May 1980, well before the U.S. government ended its aid to the Sandinista regime, no less an authority than Foreign Minister Miguel D'Escoto said: "You [the U.S.] may look at us as five countries, six now with Panama, but we regard ourselves as six different states of a single nation in the process of reunification."

In short, there is convincing evidence that Cuba and Nicaragua are involved in the instigation, organization, training, financing, arms supply, command and control, and political and technical support of the insurgency in El Salvador.

That insurgency is neither temporary nor minor. It fields forces roughly one-fifth the size of the Salvadoran army, operates sixty-seven support offices in thirty-five countries, and has inflicted more than $1 billion in direct war damage on the economy of El Salvador.

These are not the conclusions of the U.S. Executive Branch alone. The governments of Costa Rica, Honduras, and El Salvador have documented Sandinista subversive efforts. The bipartisan Kissinger Commission found that the Sandinistas together with the Cubans and Soviets "committed all-out support" to the Salvadoran insurgents.

Moreover, the U.S. Congress has repeatedly made similar findings. For example, Congress stated in the Intelligence Authorization Act of 1983 that "activities of the governments of Cuba and Nicaragua threaten the independence of El Salvador and threaten to destabilize the entire Central American region, and the governments of Cuba and Nicaragua refuse to cease these activities." A May 1983 report of the House Permanent Select Committee on Intelligence found:

> The insurgents are well trained, well equipped with modern weapons and supplies, and rely on the sites in Nicaragua for command and control and for logistical support. The intelligence supporting these judgments provided to the committee is convincing. There is further persuasive evidence that the Sandinista government of Nicaragua is helping train insurgents and is transferring arms and financial support from and through Nicaragua to the insurgents. They are providing the insurgents bases of operations in Nicaragua. Cuban involvement, especially in providing arms, is also evident.

And Congress asserted in the Intelligence Authorization Act of 1984:

> By providing military support, including arms, training, logistical command and control, and communications facilities, to groups seeking to overthrow the government of El Salvador and other Central American governments, the Government of National Reconstruction of Nicaragua has violated Article 18 of the Charter of the Organization of American States.

It is important to keep in mind two other points. First, the Sandinistas' armed attacks against their neighbors began in August 1979. There was no "contra" response until the spring of 1982, more than two and a half years later.

Second, the Sandinistas have simply lied about their secret war against neighboring states. As one sample: Foreign Minister D'Escoto filed an affidavit with the World Court declaring, "I am aware of the allegations made by the ... United States that my Government is sending arms, ammunition, communication equipment, and medical supplies conducting a civil war against the Government of El Salvador. Such allegations are false."

The Law

The Cuban-Nicaraguan activities described above in attacking third states in Central America violate:
- Article 2(4) of the United Nations Charter;
- Articles 3, 18, 20, and 21 of the Revised Charter of the Organization of American States;
- Article 1 of the hemispheric Rio Treaty;
- Articles 1, 2, 3, and 5 of the U.N. "Definition of Aggression";
- Article 3 of the 1949 U.N. General Assembly "Essentials of Peace" resolution;
- Article 1 of the 1950 General Assembly "Peace Through Deeds" resolution;
- Article 2 of the 1954 International Law Commission "Draft Code of Offenses Against the Peace and Security of Mankind";
- The 1965 General Assembly "Declaration on Inadmissibility of Intervention";
- The 1970 General Assembly "Friendly Relations" declaration;
- The 1972 "Principles Agreement";
- Principle 5 of the Helsinki Accords;
- Articles 1, 2, and 6 of the Soviet "Draft Definition of Aggression."

Meaning of 'Armed Attack'

This pattern of aggression constitutes an armed attack justifying the use of force in collective defense under Article 51 of the United Nations Charter and Article 3 of the Rio Treaty. Indeed, Article 27 of the OAS Charter declares that such an attack is "an act of aggression against . . . [all] the American States," and Article 3 of the Rio Treaty creates a legal obligation on the United States to assist in meeting the armed attack. This obligation is parallel to that owed by the United States to NATO under Article 5 of the NATO Treaty in the event of an attack on a NATO member, and to Japan under Article 5 of our Mutual Defense Treaty with that country, should it be attacked.

A response in defense may lawfully be overt, covert, or both, as has been the case in virtually every conflict in which the United States has fought in this century. In World War II no one regarded Allied support for partisan forces or covert operations in Germany as illegal in responding to Axis aggression. Such activities in defense against an armed attack have never been and are not now "state terrorism." Indeed, to make such a charge is to undermine the most important distinction in the United Nations and OAS Charters—that between aggression and defense.

Some have argued that a covert attack cannot amount to an armed attack justifying response in defense under Article 51 of the U.N. Charter. This is wrong both as a matter of law and as a matter of policy.

Kelsen writes, "Since the Charter of the U.N. does not define the term 'armed attack' used in Article 51, the members of the U.N. exercising their right of individual or collective . . . defense may interpret armed attack to mean not only an action in which a state uses its own armed forces but also a revolutionary movement which takes place in one state but which is initiated or supported by another state." This conclusion is broadly and strongly supported by McDougal and Feliciano in perhaps the best scholarly treatment of the subject, *Law and Minimum World Public Order* (1961).

Indeed, even the Soviet "Draft Definition of Aggression" says, "That State shall be declared the attacker which *first* commits support of armed bands . . . which invade the territory of another State, or refusal, on being requested by the invaded State, to take in its own territory any action within its power to deny such bands any aid or protection." And within this hemisphere the principle that states may respond with the use of force to a covert attack through assistance to insurgents was affirmed at the Ninth Meeting of Consultation of the Ministers of Foreign Affairs serving as the Organ of Consultation under the Rio Treaty, in response to the earlier problem of Cuban covert attack.

U.S. Response: Disproportionate?

Some have conceded that the United States may respond in defense but have argued that its support for the contras is disproportionate. But why is it disproportionate for the United States to respond to the Sandinistas' armed attack on a democratically elected government aimed at the overthrow of that government—by not ruling out that same objective—i.e., overthrow of the government—against the Sandinista military junta?

Remember, Nicaragua in its attack on El Salvador has no Boland Amendment or funds cut-off. That attack is aimed at replacing the government of El Salvador before proceeding to Costa Rica as, in the words of *Comandante* Borge, "the dessert."

Two Misperceptions

There are two recurring misperceptions of U.S. behavior in Central America. The first is that the United States has violated the non-intervention Articles 18 and 20 of the Revised OAS Charter. This is not so. Article 22 of the Revised Charter specifically says, "Measures adopted for the maintenance of peace and security in accordance with existing treaties"—in this case Article 3 of the Rio Treaty—"do not constitute a violation of the precepts set forth in Articles 18 and 20." And Article 21 of the OAS Charter says, "The American States bind themselves in their international relations not to have recourse to the use of force, except in the case of self-defense." Articles 27, 28, and 137 of the Revised OAS Charter support the same legal point, that actions in defense under the Rio Treaty and the U.N. Charter are not illegal.

The second misperception is that the United States is simplistically seeking military solutions in Central America or aligning itself against social change. The facts are these:

- Approximately four out of five U.S. dollars to the region go for economic assistance, in sharp contrast to the Soviet practice of emphasizing military assistance.
- The United States has strongly supported land reform and genuine democratic processes in Central America and has vigorously opposed human rights abuses from all sides.
- During the 1970s the number of U.S. military advisors in Latin America declined from 516 to 70, while Soviet and Soviet-bloc advisors were increasing greatly. By 1981 the Soviet Union had fifty times more military advisors in Latin America than did the United States.
- From 1962 to 1982 the Soviets provided more than twice as much security assistance to Latin America as did the United States—roughly $4 billion from the U.S.S.R., compared to $1.5 billion from the United States.
- In 1984 the Soviet Union gave $4.9 billion in assistance to Cuba and Nicaragua—nearly six times the $837 million in U.S. assistance to all of Central America. Indeed, the Soviet Union gave considerably more military assistance to Nicaragua in 1984 than the United States gave to all of Central America combined.
- There are 2,000–3,000 Cuban military advisors in Nicaragua, and only 55 U.S. advisors in El Salvador. There are more East German military advisors in Nicaragua than U.S. military advisors in El Salvador.

U.S. policy in Central America continues to include four elements pursued simultaneously: support for democracy; economic aid to improve living conditions; active diplomacy; and security assistance. The United States has supported peace efforts through the Contadora process. It will not, however, simply accept a parchment barrier while the Nicaraguan secret war on its neighbors continues in violation of at least twelve important legal charters and resolutions.

27. An Alternative to Contra Aid

By MICHAEL WALZER

Focus Given the alternatives, Michael Walzer recommends "a policy of hostile neglect" toward Nicaragua. "The greatest benefit we can confer upon the Nicaraguan people is to foster democracy and economic development among their neighbors."

Walzer bases this recommendation on his judgment that the $100 million in aid to the contras cannot do anything more than continue a bloody struggle against the Sandinista regime. Under just war criteria, war cannot be carried out where there is no hope of success: "War is mostly a waste anyway. Without some hope of a military and political victory, waste is all it is. And we have no right to waste Nicaraguan lives."

He makes it clear, however, that his moral opposition to fighting an unwinnable war does not imply approval of the Sandinista regime, which he sees as dominated more and more by extreme left-wing elements. Without a strong popular uprising, Nicaragua's future is likely to be a typical Third World authoritarianism: "political mobilization, intermittent brutality, economic stagnation, and, over the long run, the social decay that follows upon every betrayal of revolutionary idealism."

Since the Sandinistas seem bent on using the United States as a scapegoat to consolidate their power, we should remain their enemies. "The hardships of repression and censorship, and of scarcity and rationing, are not like the hardships of war: the Nicaraguans have brought the former, but not the latter, on themselves. They will have to find their own escape."

"Someday there will be a Nicaraguan Solidarity movement or a revolutionary rather than a counter-revolutionary resistance," predicts Walzer, "and then it will be time enough for us to involve ourselves again."

Walzer's views on contra aid should be compared with those of Ronald Reagan (selection 1) and Daniel Ortega (selection 22).

Michael Walzer is in residence at the Institute for Advanced Studies in Princeton, New Jersey.

WHAT IS the policy of the Reagan administration in Nicaragua? That is an odd question to ask at this late date, when so many people (myself among them) have already declared themselves opposed to that policy. And yet it isn't at all easy to figure out. The measures that administration spokesmen urge upon Congress don't come close to matching the threat they describe. Nor is it clear what is supposed to happen after those measures have been enacted by Congress, signed by the President, put into effect in Central America, and their usefulness, whatever that is, exhausted. What comes next? Perhaps the President has adopted the revolutionary maxim *on s'engage et puis, on voit;* perhaps he has a secret plan that can't yet be revealed.

I have a hunch about the Reagan administration that seems to explain most of its actions to date. The administration's aim, I think, is to sponsor a small war in northern Nicaragua and southern Honduras for as long as it can find anyone willing to fight. A small war, since $100 million won't buy anything more and is probably only a down payment on that. The point of the war is to put off for as long as possible the moment when President Reagan must choose between acknowledging that Nicaragua is "lost" and sending in the Marines. I don't think that he wants to send in the Marines. Some people in Washington may be practicing their trumpet calls, but Reagan and his chief advisors seem to me entirely honest when they say that the point of aiding the contras is to avoid more direct American involvement. In all probability, the contras can't win, but all that matters is that they not lose. So long as the war continues, the President can say that he is standing tall, fighting Communism, defending the hemisphere (and cheaply, too). If some future Democratic president gives up on the contras, he is the one who will have "lost" Nicaragua.

This view helps to explain the otherwise odd indifference of administration officials to the political character of their military cohorts. I don't think that all of them find Colonel Enrique Bermúdez [former National Guardsman who is now a military leader of the anti-Sandinista FDN] congenial. Nor are they misled or ill-informed about the actual power of Arturo Cruz

---

Reprinted by permission from the April 28, 1986, issue of *The New Republic* (© 1986 by The New Republic, Incorporated).

and his friends vis-à-vis the colonel and his friends. They just don't see the contras as the future rulers of Nicaragua. This is not the next government; the contras won't replace the Sandinistas, so why worry about their politics? What matters is staying power and grim endurance, which Bermúdez, and no one else, has demonstrated. Everyone else has come and gone; he has stuck fast.

All this may seem a bit too cynical for so ideologically committed an administration. Perhaps I have underestimated the extent to which its members, or some of them, have adopted the Communist doctrine of protracted struggle. Perhaps they are committed to some world-historical theory: history is on the side of the contras! But I am inclined to think that for most of them the protraction of the war is a political convenience. What ideology rules out is direct negotiations with the Sandinistas, for that would concede the (relative) permanence of their regime. The contras make it possible to avoid the concession.

An Unacceptable U.S. Policy

Assuming for the moment that this is an accurate picture, what should we think of such a policy? That is an easier question, for there isn't any account of war and morality (or even of war and prudence) that will justify what the administration proposes. It is just too bloody-minded. Too many people will die, and from the point of view of the likely victims, there is painfully little to be gained.

If there is to be a protracted struggle in Nicaragua, it would be nice to find some evidence of popular support for the insurgents. There is in fact very little evidence. The contras have been able to recruit some thousands of soldiers among relatively small groups of Indians and northern peasants, but after five years of hard fighting they do not seem to have become the focus of discontent among any substantial segment of the Nicaraguan people. They don't appear to have urban cadres or a rural infrastructure anywhere in the country. They have not made themselves the symbols of heroic resistance. The visible opposition in Managua is not (despite Sandinista claims) a contra front. The contras have not even been able to attract the sons of the middle-class exiles—not, at least, to the actual business of fighting. Anti-Communist zeal, even democratic zeal, may run high in Washington and Miami, but not along the Honduran border. The struggle feeds on other passions, not strong enough to carry it to victory.

I would feel different about a genuinely popular struggle, but given the struggle that exists, our encouragement of an indefinite war, whatever its functional value in American politics, is an act of willful cruelty toward the Nicaraguans. War is mostly a waste anyway. Without some hope of a military and political victory, waste is all it is. And we have no right to waste Nicaraguan lives.

The Hard Left Is Winning

This argument is in no sense an apology for the Sandinistas. I am not claiming that a popular insurgency is impossible in Nicaragua, only that it hasn't yet begun. Nor am I claiming that there is anything admirable about the Sandinista party/regime. It looks from here as if the hard left is winning out among the Sandinistas—and probably would be winning out even if there were no contras and no "Reagan Doctrine," whatever that is. The state of emergency and the military buildup make the task of the hard-liners easier, but it is always possible to counterfeit emergencies when the real thing doesn't exist. Totalitarian movements feed on imagined as much as on real crises, past as well as present enemies. Were we to forswear every intent to intervene, the present Sandinista leadership would campaign against our previous interventions. It is best to have no illusions about this: the *comandantes* count on American enmity to consolidate their power, and will have that enmity whether we provide it or not. But that's not a reason for providing it in military form. The past is not so glorious, our record of interventions is not so wonderful, that we need to repeat it.

The hard left is winning out, but winning out is not the same thing as having won. The Sandinistas have not yet taken on the Catholic Church in the full-scale confrontation that would be necessary for a totalitarian victory. Nor have they set out systematically to destroy the urban and rural middle classes. And they may well do neither of these things, if only for tactical reasons. A war with the church would undercut their legitimacy, and the destruction of the middle classes would ruin the economy—they probably can't count on a Russian bailout.

So some internal opposition will persist, in the shadow of a repressive regime. Even if one were to accept the long-dark-night theory of totalitarianism (I don't . . .), that is not Nicaragua's prospect. Something more like the dimness of Third World authoritarianism is more likely: political mobilization, intermittent brutality, economic stagnation, and, over the long run, the social decay that follows upon every betrayal of revolutionary idealism.

What, then, should our policy be? That is the hardest question, for there is no step or set of steps that will bring us, within some measurable time, to a more pleasant place than the contra camps in Honduras or the committee rooms of the *comandantes*. For too many years, in too many countries, we underwrote regimes like Somoza's, and the predictable consequence is a revolutionary politics like that of the Sandinistas. Cory Aquino's victory in the Philippines was a piece of extraordinary luck, but she is running only just ahead of an Asian version of the Sandinista Front. To open up hope for something else in Nicaragua requires patience now, and the long view.

The Contadora negotiating process, endorsed by congressional Democrats, represents only the barest beginning. Its conclusion would guarantee against a Soviet military base in Nicaragua—not a likely prospect in any case—and also against continued material support for the insurgents in El Salvador (and then it follows as the night the day that there must be no material support for the insurgents in Nicaragua: reciprocity is what any negotiation is about).

This achieved, however, the Sandinistas will remain our enemies; and we should remain their enemies. Insofar as we can make things hard for them, politically or economically, we should do that. If they can't expect a Russian bailout, they certainly can't expect an American bailout. The hardships of repression and censorship, and of scarcity and rationing, are not like the hardships of war: the Nicaraguans have brought the former, but not the latter, on themselves. They will have to find their own escape.

Focus on the Other States

Our focus, as the president of Costa Rica recently argued, should be on the other Central American states. We have an interest now in seeing to it that they do better than Nicaragua—and that they do better with our help. That last point is not as obvious as it sounds. Many of these countries might well have done better in the past without our help. The oligarchs and the colonels have been our friends, but that doesn't make us a friendly power. We have supported, often helped to create, the sorts of regimes that breed their own Sandinos. Now we have to do something else, and it is not at all clear that we can find something else to do, a policy, that is, that benefits neither the oligarchs we know nor the *comandantes* we fear.

Such a policy would have two aspects: a form of economic aid that reaches ordinary people, and a form of political pressure that aims at pluralism and openness. It may be too much to press immediately for our own version of democracy, but we have to press for something well this side of the routinized indifference and the fits of murderousness that have marked the politics of most of our Central American "friends."

An alternative model, with decency here and now and at least a tendency toward democratic government: that should be our goal. In countries where masses of people live in misery and destitution, elections don't make a democracy, but we should insist nonetheless on elections whenever we can. They are wonderfully educative, and they sometimes have unexpected results. We also have to help end the misery and destitution, with favorable trade terms, technical assistance, and genuinely humanitarian aid. We should train Central American engineers and farmers with the zeal currently reserved for the training of soldiers. And we should send our own people. The old Peace Corps model was a good one—technicians, agricultural experts, schoolteachers, doctors, and nurses. CIA operatives and military advisors may be necessary too sometimes, but they should never be our only representatives in countries where we have some hope of encouraging a democratic politics.

And in Nicaragua? Perhaps there should be Americans there too, though I am inclined to think it better if they are sponsored by private groups like the Catholic Church than by the American government. If things open up in Nicaragua, we should be prepared to resume trade and economic assistance. But the built-in tendencies of Nicaraguan politics right now move the country toward greater and greater closure.

In the face of these tendencies, I can only recommend a policy of hostile neglect. Someday there will be a Nicaraguan Solidarity movement or a revolutionary rather than a counter-revolutionary resistance, and then it will be time enough for us to involve ourselves again—with public support and (if such a thing is possible) covert aid. How effective we are then is likely to depend upon how effective we are now in countries like El Salvador and Honduras.

The greatest benefit we can confer upon the Nicaraguan people is to foster democracy and economic development among their neighbors. That will take a lot more than $100 million. It will also require political intelligence and a long-term commitment. Given these two, it may even be possible that history is on our side.

28. The Newest Political Pilgrims

By PAUL HOLLANDER

Focus
The Sandinista revolution in Nicaragua has revived "a grotesque and embarrassing tradition in Western intellectual-political history," says Paul Hollander: "the reverential pilgrimage to highly repressive Communist countries by educated people, beneficiaries of considerable political freedom and material well-being."

Hollander points out that Sandinista Nicaragua is not as repressive as Stalin's Russia or Mao's China—two earlier destinations for political pilgrims. But he agrees with the distinguished Mexican writer Octavio Paz that in Nicaragua "the process of Sovietization is quite advanced."

In light of the effect of Vietnam on the American psyche, the Sandinistas have sought to maximize the effects of foreigners' visits, making sure that some of the *comandantes* and other high officials meet with every group. Since Nicaragua cannot possibly resist an all-out military attack by the United States, the struggle for the moral high ground is all the more important. As Interior Minister Tomás Borge put it: "Nicaragua's most important war is the one fought inside the United States.... The battlefield will be the American conscience."

The Sandinistas have been very adept at appealing to several aspects of this conscience. A *New York Times* reporter noted that they tailored their message to various groups of visitors: church and university groups were told the revolution is humanistic, while left-wing visitors heard of "scientific change."

For Hollander, all this is a sad repetition of other

events of this century. "Today's new pilgrims demonstrate the same tenacity of belief, the willful inability to learn from history, and above all the hostility toward our own society that have repeatedly predisposed certain groups and individuals to admire and idealize political systems opposed to ours, especially when they are run by revolutionaries acting in the name of Marx."

Hollander's views of Nicaragua and its supporters should be compared with those of Gabriel Jackson (selection 20), Joshua Muravchik (selection 21), and Daniel Ortega (selection 22).

Paul Hollander is a professor of sociology at the University of Massachusetts, Amherst, and a fellow at the Harvard Russian Research Center. His books include *Political Pilgrims: Travels of Western Intellectuals to the Soviet Union, China, and Cuba* (1983).

MARXIST-LENINIST NICARAGUA has in the last few years emerged as the new destination of political tourists from the United States who have revived a grotesque and embarrassing tradition in Western intellectual-political history: the reverential pilgrimage to highly repressive Communist countries by educated people, beneficiaries of considerable political freedom and material well-being.

By 1979 this tradition had temporarily fallen into discredit. Following the death of Mao in 1976, his successors' revelations about Chinese society largely demolished the worshipful accounts the pilgrims to China had brought back earlier. Mao himself ceased to be deified and (even before the official Chinese rejection in late 1984 of Marxism as an infallible guide to the future) the new Chinese regime began moving toward more free enterprise and better relations with the United States.

By the early 1980s, a number of developments had also reduced the glamor and reputation of another Communist country, Cuba. On the one hand, Dr. Benjamin Spock still believed that "the Castro government . . . has made remarkable, admirable progress in education, in housing, in . . . health care—for all citizens," and for a publication of the United Methodist Church, Cuba, as of 1981, still represented "a vision of the future." On the other hand, the appeal of Cuba to its American admirers was sharply reduced by the outpouring in 1980 of 125,000 refugees (most of them poor, and young, and dark-skinned), the persecution of homosexuals, the growing militarization of the society, the stationing of tens of thousands of troops abroad, and the increasingly intimate relationship between Castro and the Soviet Union (which had lost its own attraction decades earlier when even its most ardent supporters were jolted out of their faith by the celebrated revelations of Khrushchev about the reign of Stalin).

As for Communist Vietnam, it was one thing to celebrate it when American bombs were raining down and its heroic guerrillas were defying American military might, but it was something else again to sing its praises after over a million people had escaped under extremely hazardous conditions from the southern portion of the newly united country.

Reprinted by permission of the author and the publisher from *Commentary*, August 1985.

In these circumstances the rise of Marxist-Leninist Nicaragua could not have been better timed. Here was a small country that had earlier been dominated by the United States, run by a corrupt pro-American dictator, and redeemed by an authentic revolution, the culmination of years of guerrilla war. The new regime came complete with a youthful leadership, most of them former guerrilla fighters, some of them intellectuals of sorts (among the top leaders, Daniel Ortega, Ernesto Cardenal, and Sergio Ramírez had poetic-literary leanings or credentials), and others among them devotees of liberation theology. There was also something for the feminists in the person of Nora Astorga, the deputy foreign minister celebrated for helping to trap and kill a general of Somoza. ("Oh, God," said an American woman described by the *Washington Post* as a political activist, "to try to get the guy to bed and then kill him! Fantastic. It's like a Western. That's my dream, to do that to Reagan, George Bush, go right down the line!")

Replaying the Sixties

For many American sympathizers, events in Nicaragua represented a replay of the 1960s—there was, at any rate, an appealing resemblance. "Here," said *Playboy*, "was a place seemingly run by the kind of people who were sixties radicals. Wherever we went, people were young, singing political folk songs and chanting, 'Power to the People.' One night there was even a Pete Seeger concert in town!" Elsewhere the leaders of the regime were described as "Rock 'n' Roll Rebels . . . into baseball, beer, and Bruce Springsteen."

No wonder, then, that the roster of prominent supporters of the Sandinista regime included so many well-known veterans of the radical movement of the 1960s: William Sloane Coffin, Ron Dellums, Ramsey Clark, Linus Pauling, George Wald, Benjamin Spock, Allen Ginsberg, and Abbie Hoffman. The National Sponsors of USOCA (U.S. Out of Central America), a major pro-Sandinista lobby, included Eqbal Ahmad (of the Institute for Policy Studies), Noam Chomsky, Harvey Cox, David Dellinger, Douglas Dowd, Richard Falk, John Gerassi, John C. Leggett, Robert McAfee Brown, Bertell Ollman, Ruth Sidel (author of a glowing report on welfare in China under Mao), Pete Seeger, Leonard Weinglass, Adrienne Rich, Jessica Mitford, the Berrigan brothers, and many other Vietnam-era radicals.

People of this political stripe were, somewhat paradoxically, reinvigorated by the 1980 victory of Ronald Reagan ("the best organizer we have," as one of them said during a demonstration against the administration's policies in El Salvador). Reagan was the exponent of everything the Left detested: faith in capitalism, simple patriotism, an expressed willingness to use force in the defense of American interests abroad, and an unapologetic anti-Communism. Far from killing off the Left, then, the election of Reagan stimulated a resurgence of political energies, especially in the universities, the churches, and the media.

The Pilgrimage Promoters

Knowing that it had this substantial reservoir of sympathizers on which to draw, and making good use of the lessons of Vietnam—the main one being that public opinion in the United States has great influence on foreign policy—the Sandinista regime began organizing and encouraging tours to Nicaragua almost immediately after the triumph of the revolution in 1979. "Now that the rebels are victorious," wrote a *New York Times* correspondent, "there is a new rush of assorted politicians, journalists, academics, and 'revolutionary groupies' eager to witness . . . the first popular revolution on the continent in twenty years."

Throughout the early 1980s the tours gathered force. As another *Times* correspondent wrote in 1982: "So many Americans and Western Europeans have descended on Nicaragua to study and work with the Sandinista government that a word, *'internacionalistas,'* has been coined to refer to them." A year later, in 1983, the *Times* reported: "Over the past year the Managua government has been a near-permanent host to American fact-finding missions, ranging from church delegations to doctors, students, and senators, who are warmly received, briefed, and shown projects."

The scope of the new pilgrimages may be gauged in part from the number of organizations promoting the tours. They include Marazul Inc. (specializing in trips to socialist countries; in January 1985 alone, Marazul sponsored thirteen tours to Nicaragua); National Network in Solidarity with the Nicaraguan People (with branches in seventy-five American cities); Nicaragua-Honduras Education Project (which "sponsors trips to Nicaragua, mostly for state and local opinion-makers such as elected officials"); Nuevo Instituto de Centro America (which organizes five-week courses of language study); the *Guardian* (a weekly radical newspaper that has organized tours since 1980); Tropical Tours (the official representative of Tur-Nica, the Nicaraguan national tour agency); Tur-Nica itself; U.S.

Out of Central America (a "national group with representatives in more than 100 cities actively opposing U.S. policy ... in Central America. Work includes lobbying elected officials, tours, and donations of medical supplies, ... teach-ins, and a traveling slide show"); and Witness for Peace (supported by the Quaker American Friends Service Committee, with 100 chapters nationwide).

Careful preparations have preceded the tours. According to a story in the *Christian Science Monitor*:

> At a conference in Mexico City, Rosario Murillo, the wife of Nicaraguan junta leader Daniel Ortega Saavedra, asked a well-connected American, Blase Bonpane, to organize delegations of prominent American celebrities to Nicaragua....
>
> Mr. Bonpane, a former Maryknoll priest and professor of Latin American history at the University of California at Los Angeles, is a liberation theologian sympathetic to the Sandinistas. He understood ... the impact Hollywood stars could have on American public opinion.
>
> By now American liberals have created a virtual industry of delegations to Nicaragua.... More than 2,500 Americans have taken part in such missions....
>
> Delegations of church activists, college professors, architects and planners, artists and photographers, nurses and health-care workers, journalists and media-professionals, Vietnam veterans and average citizens ... have headed south....
>
> Many of the most visible critics of U.S. policy come from Hollywood—celebrities like Ed Asner, Mike Douglas, and Susan Anspach.
>
> Much of the Hollywood interest in Nicaragua can be traced back to Blase Bonpane, who helped organize a nine-city tour ... with singer Jackson Browne, actors Mike Farrell and Diane Ladd, former Georgia state senator Julian Bond, and others. The tour was aimed at rallying opposition to U.S. intervention in Nicaragua.

Comandante Viewing

The extraordinary political importance attached to the tours has also been indicated by the readiness of the Sandinista leaders to make themselves available to the visitors. In the words of a *Miami Herald* account:

> Almost any visiting American official, no matter how low his rank, can now expect to meet with at least two of the nine *comandantes*.... Nonofficial American visitors ... can count on at least one *comandante* and a well-worn tour of revolutionary highlights.
>
> There are visits to the neighborhood Sandinista Defense Committees, tours of schools, and clinics, and trips to the northern town of Jalapa to

witness the damages wreaked by CIA-backed anti-Sandinista guerrillas....

"When they return to the United States they have a multiplier effect on the public opinion of your country," [Interior Minister Tomás] Borge said.

The experience of James C. Harrington, Texas Civil Liberties Union legal director, was typical:

We met with Sergio Ramírez (a novelist and member of the three-member junta ...), two department directors, with Deputy Foreign Minister Nora Astorga (a charming heroine of the revolution), ... with the Minister of Culture (Father Ernesto Cardenal), and with two of the three Electoral Commission members....

We broke mid-day bread with three Supreme Court members....

Claudia Dreifus, who interviewed members of the Sandinista Directorate for *Playboy*, also found them most accessible:

After the interviews were under way, some of the Nicaraguan leaders began inviting Marcelo [the photographer] and me, well, to hang out with them. Things we did in Managua: go with Borge to a prison farm for Miskito Indian counter-revolutionaries; watch Father Cardenal put on an all-day Latin American song festival, in Revolutionary Square ... dinner at Ramírez's house.

The Nicaraguan public-relations campaign has been appropriately described by the *Miami Herald* as "a low-key but relentless sales job, subtle but effective, high in moral tone but aimed right at the guts of the Americans' conscience." For as Minister Borge has said: "Nicaragua's most important war is the one fought inside the United States.... The battlefield will be the American conscience."

Accordingly, the regime has tailored its message to different audiences. As John Vinocur of the *New York Times* has noted:

To American visitors, frequently from church and university groups, the revolution is described as a humanist one, a struggle against misery. To other visitors, with left-wing views, the talk is of "scientific change" with no interest in achieving "perfect democracy," but a revolution aimed at a "total social transformation."

Not all visitors have been mere sightseers. The Washington law firm Reichler and Appelbaum, which is the Nicaraguan government's official registered agent in the United States (and is reportedly paid about $320,000 per year for its services), has sent hired investigators who have been provided "in-country transportation, boarding, housing, office space [and] staff" to help collect information on atrocities committed by the contras.

Other visitors, like their predecessors in Cuba who cut sugar cane (the Venceremos Brigade), have volunteered to work on various projects such as picking coffee beans. However, the "central thrust is what each volunteer does when he or she returns to the United States." In other words, to quote Diane Passmore, national coordinator of the National Network in Solidarity with the Nicaraguan People, "The major goal is to have them return and tell others about the country and their experiences."

Back Home: Spreading the Word

And so they have. For example, following a ten-day visit, Republican state senator Jeanette Hamby from Oregon and her fellow women tourists returned with "the fervor of new converts." Reported Colman McCarthy in the *Washington Post*:

> In Oregon, Hamby and her friends have been speaking regularly before political, civic, and church groups. They are seeking to persuade people . . . that our policies there [in Nicaragua] are politically wrong and morally corrupt.

So too, Michael Harrington, the well-known author and chairman of the Democratic Socialist Organizing Committee, came back from Nicaragua feeling, as he wrote,

> more ashamed of my country than at any time since the Vietnam war. The Nicaraguans are a generous people, a poor and often hungry people, who want to make a truly democratic revolution, and it is we who work to subvert their decency.

Similar feelings about both the Nicaraguan revolution and American policy were expressed by other prominent American writers. William Styron joined a group of fellow novelists from Europe and Latin America in protesting American threats to the "modest but profound achievements of the Nicaraguan revolution." The poet Adrienne Rich described Sandinista Nicaragua as "a society that took poets seriously" and approvingly quoted someone who told her: "You'll love Nicaragua. Everyone there is a poet."

This remark recalled the news brought back from North Vietnam by Tom Hayden and Staughton Lynd in 1966:

> We knew . . . what the Vietnamese contribution to a humane socialism would be: it was evident in the unembarrassed handclasps among men, the poetry and song at the center of man-woman relationships, the freedom to weep practiced by everyone. . . . Here we began to understand the possibilities for a socialism of the heart.

Other echoes of past pilgrimages to Communist regimes could be heard in comments about Nicaraguan prisons:

The prison we visited was the first of seven prison farms. Former National Guardsmen willing to cooperate are moved through a series of more and more relaxed prison settings. The prison we saw had thirty-eight inmates, no armed guards, conjugal visits.... The man speaking had high praise for the government and said if freed he would go to fight for the FSLN [the Sandinistas] in the north. Money made from the crops is put back into improvements for the prison.... As part of the routine the men attend classes in literacy and agriculture. Many who previously had no skill but shooting a gun now have plans to become farmers.

Church Groups: The Most Avid Supporters

This, from a group of American churchmen. Indeed, of all the pilgrims to the Marxist-Leninist regime in Nicaragua, it is church groups who have become its most active and dedicated supporters (perhaps because, as former President Jimmy Carter put it in announcing his endorsement of a project "to build homes for landless peasants" in Nicaragua, "We want the folks down there to know that some American Christians love them").

Thus: Maryknoll nuns have returned from Nicaragua to lobby in Washington and have exerted considerable influence on House Speaker Thomas P. O'Neill. The Reverend William Sloane Coffin (who had earlier affirmed the decency of the North Vietnamese Communist regime) now assured readers of the *New York Times* that the Nicaraguan regime could not possibly be Marxist-Leninist since it included Roman Catholic priests (all of whom, incidentally, were on record asserting the compatibility of Marxism and Christianity). In any case, Coffin was satisfied that the goals of the Sandinistas were "to stop the exploitation of the many by the few and to end foreign domination." A reporter for the *Catholic Worker* sensed "an atmosphere of youth, vitality, and hope throughout Nicaragua." Father Richard Preston of Lansing, Michigan, reached the conclusion that "the reign of God has arrived in Nicaragua" as well as "the reign of truth, hope, and justice." A member of the Quaker Witness for Peace group disclosed that he had "never been in a society so permeated by religion" as Sandinista Nicaragua, and David Sweet, a founder of Witness for Peace, emphasized "the Christian nature of the Nicaraguan revolution" and insisted that "the revolution is drawing its strength from Christians...." The German novelist Günter Grass agreed. After visiting a Sandinista prison in the company of Minister of the Interior Tomás Borge, Grass decided that "in this tiny, sparsely populated land, ... Christ's words are taken literally."

On this point too the echoes of past pilgrimages are loud. For example, D. F. Buxton, an English Quaker, wrote of the Soviet Union in 1928: "In the emphasis they place on the spirit of service, the Communists have taken to heart some of the most important maxims of the New Testament. ... Their society is a more Christian one than ours." An American Quaker, Henry Hodgkin, proposed in 1932: "As we look at Russia's great experiment in brotherhood, it may seem to us that some dim perception of Jesus' way, all unbeknown, is inspiring it." Hewlett Johnson, the dean of Canterbury, regarded Stalin's Russia as "singularly Christian and civilized." And to a group of Christian theologians, Mao's China "has come to exert some particular impact on our understanding and experience of God's saving love."

Deception and Self-Deception

It is not being suggested here that Nicaragua today is nearly as repressive or violent a country as the Soviet Union under Stalin or China under Mao. But on the other hand, as Octavio Paz, the eminent Mexican writer, puts it, "the process of Sovietization is quite advanced" in Nicaragua today. Even when allowances are made for the overpowering effects of favorable predisposition and the inherent limitations of learning about a country through a short conducted tour, the credulousness of the pilgrims to Nicaragua remains staggering. Not only do they ignore the lessons of similar pilgrimages and tours in the past; they also blind themselves to the abundant information and testimony available about Nicaragua—much of it coming from Nicaraguans who are untainted by any association with the Somoza regime and were in fact supporters of the revolution that deposed him—that belies the image projected by the Sandinistas and carefully cultivated through the tours.

Edén Pastora is one such prominent leader who first fought against Somoza and is now fighting the Sandinistas. He writes:

> Sadly, the revolution's bright promise has not been realized. The Sandinista directorate has replaced the Somozas with a totalitarian tyranny....
> The government has emasculated the country's independent labor unions.... Freedom of the press has been practically extinguished.... The directorate has set up a powerful secret-police apparatus.... [The regime] remains silent in the face of the Soviet invasion of Afghanistan and acts as an apologist for the ... crackdown in Poland.
> ... Despite ... loans and outright grants totaling over $1.5 billion, the economy is in shambles.... Living conditions are deteriorating. The real wages of Nicaragua's working class have plummeted 60 per cent during last year.

Domingo Sánchez Delgado, "a dedicated Marxist-Leninist" and nominee of the Socialist Party for president, says:

We are not Sandinistas.... We don't want a country where the press is not free ... where power is abused ... where young people can't go to the movies because they are afraid they will be captured for military service.
... There is arrogance and abuse of every sort. This is hardly revolutionary conduct....

Virgilio Godoy Reyes was minister of labor in the Sandinista government from 1979 until 1984. He has reached the conclusion that

these five years have shown the great error we made in giving our confidence to those who think of nothing but the interests of their party.... After so many dreams, disillusion. Instead of liberty, new forms of oppression. To say that the workers and peasants are in power is a monstrous lie.... The only equality we are achieving is equality in misery.

Arturo Cruz, former Sandinista ambassador to the United States and the most prominent democratic critic of the regime, writes:

The Sandinistas are evidently determined to ignore the democratic yearnings of the Nicaraguan people.... The problem of Nicaragua is not MIGs and assault helicopters. It is, fundamentally, the absence of liberty — the character of the government that will put such weapons to use.

There has also been criticism from some former American admirers of the regime. Robert S. Leiken of the Carnegie Endowment is one of them:

For one who has sympathized with the Sandinistas, it is painful to look into the house they are building.... Each succeeding trip to Nicaragua drains my initial reservoir of sympathy for the Sandinistas....
One of the most depressing aspects of our trip was to hear from so many that their lives are worse today than they were at the time of Somoza.
... A Sandinista *nomenklatura* has emerged. Party members shop at hard-currency stores, dine at luxury restaurants restricted to party officials, and vacation in the mansions of the Somoza dynasty, labeled "protocol houses" [as in Cuba].... Vans pull up daily at government and party offices to deliver ... delicacies unavailable elsewhere.
... Ration cards are confiscated for non-attendance at Sandinista meetings.
... Draft resistance has become a mass movement in Nicaragua.

Senator Edward Kennedy, generally not a harsh critic of the Sandinistas, has had this to say about their policy toward the Miskito Indians:

... The Sandinistas' treatment of the Indians continues to be unconscionable. One-third to one-half of the 90,000 Indians on the coast have been displaced. Some 20,000 fled to Honduras to escape the Sandinistas' scorched-earth policy.... 10,000 are confined to resettlement camps. ... Most disturbing of all, 3,000 to 5,000 have lived for two years in forced-labor camps which resemble concentration camps.

The treatment of the Indians is not the only manifestation of the repressive policies pursued by the regime. Contrary to the claims of American sympathizers, the Sandinistas (according to the Nicaraguan Commission of Jurists) carried out over 8,000 political executions between July 19, 1979, and December 12, 1982. This and many other examples of political violence and human rights violations have been extensively documented in what probably is the single best compilation of the true record of the Nicaraguan regime, *Breaking Faith*. Its author, Humberto Belli, used to be a supporter of the Sandinistas and editorial-page editor of *La Prensa*.

In the light of such information, and against the background of known precedents, the current political pilgrimages to Nicaragua emerge as a remarkable example of the confluence of deception and self-deception. This, indeed, is in part the message that Michael Massing intended to convey in an article in *The Nation* ("Hard Questions on Nicaragua," April 6, 1985), a rather mild demurral from the Left's blind enthusiasm for the Sandinista regime for which, predictably, he was then heavily pilloried in that magazine's letters section. As that exchange once again underscores, today's new pilgrims demonstrate the same tenacity of belief, the willful inability to learn from history, and above all the hostility toward our own society that have repeatedly predisposed certain groups and individuals to admire and idealize political systems opposed to ours, especially when they are run by revolutionaries acting in the name of Marx. The only question is—and it may not be premature to raise it, since as we have seen there are already signs of disillusionment with the Sandinistas—who will be next?

29. Don't Abandon the Nicaraguan People

By JAIME CHAMORRO

Focus
Jaime Chamorro, the editor of Nicaragua's only independent newspaper, *La Prensa*, until it was shut down by the Sandinistas in June 1986, says that the main problem in Nicaragua is not the curbing of political pluralism and freedom of expression, economic stagnation, or religious repression. These ills, he says, have been known in Nicaragua and Latin America before. The basic problem is that the Sandinistas "are taking a national movement and turning it into a beachhead for Communist expansion. And they have sacrificed the national interest for the benefit of this cause."

To avoid this outcome, Chamorro argues that Nicaraguans who desire freedom have the right to seek aid from wherever they can get it. Such aid would not interfere with Nicaragua's right to self-determination as some have argued, says Chamorro: "The same Sandinistas received direct military aid from other countries when they were fighting to overthrow the Somoza dynasty . . . and no one accused those countries of being guilty of aggression toward Nicaragua. The reason is that the Somoza regime, like the Sandinistas today, did not represent the will of the people."

In the United States, many have asserted that tiny Nicaragua cannot be seriously regarded as a military threat. But Chamorro sees this as short-sighted: the struggle over Nicaragua is an important test of the democracies' willingness to defend themselves. "Managua is filled with internationalists from Latin American countries who wield influence in this revolution and whose aims are the expansion of Communist influence and Soviet domination in the region."

The result of a spreading pro-Soviet influence in Latin America could be catastrophic for the United States: "When Latin America, or much of Latin America, is under the influence of the Eastern bloc, NATO will no longer be in Europe; it will be in San Antonio, Texas."

Negotiations might be possible, says Chamorro, but the United States is not in a strong position to conduct them with Congress's constant wavering over aid to the contras. Writing before Congress approved contra aid in 1986, he said, "In negotiations one concedes something in exchange for something else. The Sandinistas have a lot to give. Reagan has nothing left to offer; Congress has already offered it all." The result may be a much higher price-tag to deal with problems in the future.

Chamorro's views should be compared with those of Ronald Reagan (selection 1), Fidel Castro (selection 2), Daniel Ortega (selection 22), and Michael Walzer (selection 27).

Jaime Chamorro, a member of the distinguished Chamorro family of Nicaraguan journalists, was the editor of the independent Managua newspaper *La Prensa* until it was closed by the Sandinistas on June 26, 1986. He has become one of the most prominent figures in Nicaragua's democratic opposition.

A S THE QUESTION of sending $100 million in aid to the anti-Sandinista rebels was being discussed in Congress, the bishop of León, Nicaragua, Monsignor Julian Barni, made the following comment:

"While in the United States they are discussing the $100 million, the Soviet Union has already given $100 million and much more without any discussion at all." Bishop Barni added: "What is necessary is that both imperialist powers, not one alone, stop complicating matters in Nicaragua. The Nicaraguan people have fought to establish a true democratic regime and hope to achieve one. This is what matters most."

Nicaragua's problem, in effect, is not only a problem of the Nicaraguan people—their loss of freedom, of civil and political rights. The problem is not only the total absence of democracy and political pluralism or the suppression of freedom of expression. Nor is it just the problem of discontent that prevails as a result of the same kinds of disastrous social and economic conditions that brought on the revolution. Nor is it only the persecution of the church, as if we have never seen this in the history of our country. Nor is it the 10,000 political prisoners.

In addition to these disgraces, which in one form or another we have seen appear and disappear in most Latin American countries, there emerges a particularly grave situation: the Sandinistas are transforming the Nicaraguan revolution, fought for by all Nicaraguans, into a revolution that serves the purposes of Marxism-Leninism. That is to say, they are taking a national movement and turning it into a beachhead for Communist expansion. And they have sacrificed the national interest for the benefit of this cause.

Before the Sandinistas reach this goal, those Nicaraguans who are fighting for democracy have the right to ask for help from wherever they can get it. It is a cause far too important to lose. For the Nicaraguan people, the issue at hand is of such transcendental importance that they cannot vacillate at all in choosing the right position. The future of the freedom of generations of Nicaraguans hangs in the balance.

Those who argue that to give aid to the Nicaraguan rebels would be a violation of the "principle of a people's right to self-determination" are

Reprinted by permission from the *Washington Post*, April 3, 1986.

mistaken. These people seem to ignore or perhaps forget deliberately that self-determination applies to peoples, not oppressive governments that do not legitimately represent the will of the people.

They try to forget as well that the same Sandinistas received direct military aid from other countries when they were fighting to overthrow the Somoza dynasty. And despite the fact that the Sandinistas were receiving aid in the form of arms from other countries, no one accused those countries of being guilty of aggression toward Nicaragua. The reason is that the Somoza regime, like the Sandinistas today, did not represent the will of the people.

The free peoples of the world, and particularly those in America, both North and South, must not at this critical time abandon the Nicaraguan people, because their struggle is also the struggle for the future of the Western democracies. Nicaragua has become an important point of East-West confrontation. That Nicaragua in the long term could determine the balance of forces between the East and the West and ultimately the security of the United States and the Western Hemisphere as a whole may seem an exaggeration. But everything depends on future actions and the capacity of the democracies to defend themselves.

A Threat to U.S. Security?

In the United States, the debate centers on whether the Sandinistas represent a serious threat to U.S. security. President Reagan argues firmly that they do. Nicaraguan president Daniel Ortega has declared that he is prepared to discuss matters of regional security, but he refuses to speak with anyone regarding Nicaragua's internal situation.

A short time ago, two members of the U.S. Congress debated on television whether to give the $100 million to the Nicaraguan rebels. One of them, who opposed aid, asked: How is it possible that such a small country with a population of only three million could pose a security threat to a great military power such as the United States? Against a power like the United States it would be impossible for even a single plane or tank to reach San Antonio, Texas, without being destroyed.

When I heard the congressman's statement I couldn't believe he was serious. The danger is not military: naturally, when we speak of the military, we think of a war between the United States and Nicaragua. The danger is that the Sandinista revolution is not a revolution of the Nicaraguan people. Managua is filled with internationalists from Latin American countries who wield influence in this revolution and whose aims are the expansion of Communist influence and Soviet domination in the region.

The Real Sandinista Strategy

Nicaragua with its army of 60,000 men (Somoza's army had only 7,000) cannot be a military threat, nor can Cuba, whose army and militia consist of more than a million men. This absurd idea of a direct military threat from the Sandinistas is an attempt to obscure the real danger of the Sandinistas.

Their strategy is to prop up their Communist regime in Nicaragua by sacrificing the freedom of the Nicaraguan people while they inspire, aid, and arm, from Managua, insurgencies throughout Latin America, "movements of national liberation" that will convert the entire continent into an immense base of insurrection.

Perhaps now the idea of Nicaragua's becoming a serious military threat to the United States seems absurd, but in the future it could take on a far more serious air. Sooner or later, in twenty or thirty years, Latin America is going to succumb to one form or another of Communist domination. Mexico is not necessarily an exception. It might one day be the country most likely to fall. Moreover, Mexico is considered by the Communists to be the country that best fits into their strategy.

If all of this comes to pass, the balance of power between East and West will be definitively in favor of the East, and spending $100 million or a billion dollars will not reverse it. It could bring a world war to the doorstep of the United States. When Latin America, or much of Latin America, is under the influence of the Eastern bloc, NATO will no longer be in Europe; it will be in San Antonio, Texas.

No Sandinista Concessions

But if the president of Nicaragua wants to have a dialogue on the subject of U.S. security, why not do it? We believe that dialogue is necessary. It should not be a dialogue solely on U.S. security but also on our democracy and freedom—something that repels the Sandinistas, because making concessions by restoring democracy and freedom in Nicaragua will be their political death. The negation of the system that has been established will be the end of their internationalist and expansionist aims.

In addition, the Sandinistas have no reason or motivation to negotiate because the counter-revolution is in a ruinous state. This is because Reagan has not been and will not be able to, as a result of congressional opposition, give effective aid so that the resistance can achieve its objective. In negotiations one concedes something in exchange for something else. The Sandinistas have a lot they can give. Reagan has nothing left to offer; Congress has already given it.

Daniel Ortega hopes to achieve the total elimination of the counterrevolution in exchange for the promise not to be a military threat to the United States or to Nicaragua's neighbors, not to allow the Soviets to install military bases, and to remove all Cuban advisors. With this the Sandinistas could achieve their consolidation and a free way to continue their expansionist aims through non-military, but not less dangerous or effective, means.

As Jean-François Revel, in his book *How Democracies Perish*, writes: Democracy "awakens only when the danger becomes deadly, imminent, evident. By then, either there is too little time left for it to save itself, or the price of survival has become crushingly high."

30. A Revolution Betrayed

By EDÉN PASTORA GÓMEZ

Focus
Edén Pastora Gómez, the famous "Commander Zero," was the most charismatic leader of the Nicaraguan revolutionary army that defeated Anastasio Somoza Debayle in 1979 and installed a revolutionary government. Almost immediately after the victory, however, Pastora felt that the Sandinista rulers were betraying the original aims of the revolution. He voiced his criticism, was ignored, and left the government to work quietly for a true Nicaraguan democracy. In April 1982 he made public his break with the Sandinistas and issued the statement below.

Eventually Pastora began an armed struggle against the Sandinistas. In 1983 his group of contras, whose bases are in southern Nicaragua near the Costa Rican border, joined forces with another army of freedom fighters in northern Nicaragua. Later that year the two groups separated again over political differences. Most of his commanders left him to join the forces of the United Nicaraguan Opposition (UNO) in 1986. He then withdrew to Costa Rica.

Pastora's views, as this statement makes clear, are strongly nationalistic. Like Augusto César Sandino, the rebel leader for whom the Sandinista movement is named, Pastora is little attracted to ideology. His concern is for Nicaraguan freedom.

Nicaragua must be a truly non-aligned state, says Pastora. "Our Sandinismo cannot allow us to be dragged into the East-West conflict, since that is contrary to national interests." He denounces "U.S. imperialism" but also insists upon a withdrawal of the many Cuban and Eastern-bloc "advisors" from Nicaragua. "The time has come for those who are not engaged in activities strictly contributing to health and education to leave us alone."

Several serious internal deficiencies must be remedied as well, says Pastora. He calls for respect for the Nicaraguan Indian groups, a free economic system, political pluralism, free elections, "strict respect of individual rights and demands for workers' rights," true freedom of worship ("not just a mere declaration . . . a reality warranting the deepest respect"), and freedom of the press.

Pastora's views conflict strongly with those of the Sandinista president Daniel Ortega (selection 22).

Edén Pastora Gómez has spent over twenty-five years fighting for the freedom of the Nicaraguan people.

I WILL REMAIN ON GUARD so that the revolution will not be subordinated or betrayed." I said this back on that day of 20 July 1979 at the Plaza de la Revolución in Managua, Nicaragua.

Historical circumstances place responsibilities on men. Those circumstances oblige me to come and fulfill an obligation as a Nicaraguan Sandinista. It was my lot to have been born in the darkness with which Somocismo disgraced and degraded my fatherland, Nicaragua. When I was seven years old I lost my father, who was murdered by the oppressors of my people. As I grew up and learned, I realized that many other Nicaraguan families were enduring the same sorrow as mine. Later, thanks to the opportunities for education my mother provided for me, I discovered the sad reality that the sovereignty of my country had been injured many times by U.S. imperialism and that the vast majority of my fellow citizens were victims of the most degrading social injustice. In the course of my education I also learned that there was a patriot who deeply loved Nicaragua, and who gave up his life in the struggle for the liberation of the Nicaraguan people. That man, Augusto César Sandino, is the fundamental source of inspiration in my life as a citizen.

From the time I was very young I made the decision to be a revolutionary. I understood clearly that it was necessary to take up arms to overthrow the tyranny, and I gave up my medical studies in Guadalajara, Mexico. With the maturity acquired during years of struggle, I became increasingly convinced that a lasting peace could be achieved only by establishing democracy and by doing away with exploitation and with all kinds of injustice. Since I come from a family of working men, I alternated my periods of armed struggle in the mountains with periods of work in cattle-raising, farming, business, and fishing. It is possibly to that experience that I owe my firm conviction as to the need to establish guarantees and incentives for production and investment as the bases of economic development. The despotism of the system that reigned for more than forty years awoke in me a hatred for arbitrary command and a love for individual freedom. Those principles make up the foundations of my revolutionary ideals, and I would like to make it clear once and for all that I have never been concerned about doctrinaire labels.

Guided by those principles during my revolutionary struggle, in 1959 I became one of the founders of the Sandino Revolutionary Front, the first revolutionary movement to proclaim General Sandino as the immortal leader of our resurgence as a sovereign people. Subsequently, in 1961, I reaffirmed my Sandinista, anti-imperialist, democratic, and popular ideals by being one of the first to forge the Sandinista National Liberation Front, to which I have the high honor of having contributed twenty-one years as a disciplined and loyal member.

In 1976 I put an end to a peaceful break in my life, working side by side with my beloved wife and children, to begin yet another period of struggle in answer to another call from my Sandinista comrades. On this occasion I went to meet them on the battlefields, bursting with enthusiasm because it was the beginning of a transcendental crusade in the history of my people: the unification of all the national sectors in order to expel the dynastic tyranny from the fatherland forever and to establish a social system of complete revolution—an eminently just revolution, with participation by all, with hatred toward none, driven by justice and ready to defend national sovereignty. . . .

[In several paragraphs omitted here Pastora pays tribute to many "martyrs and heroes" who took part in the struggle to overthrow Somoza.]

'Rash Actions and Errors'

At the moment of triumph, I went with enthusiasm to render my services to consolidate the revolution, filling any post that the national leadership of the Sandinista National Liberation Front ordered me to assume. However, from the first moment of triumph I noted with sorrow what in my opinion are deviations that endanger the revolutionary process and even the very security of the Nicaraguan state. Fulfilling my duty, I pointed out to my superiors the dangers to which those rash actions and errors might expose the country. I did so with a desire for rectification and with revolutionary loyalty. When I did not get a response, I thought it best to separate myself from the government and to channel my revolutionary ideals within Internationalism as a continuation of Sandinismo. I made that decision with deep sorrow and without resentment. My dissidence and my cooperation have been, are, and always will be within the framework of the revolution to which I am completely devoted. I have kept silent, confident that patriotism would prevail among the leaders of the revolution.

After I joined the Internationalist movement my exhortations were never heard, and in answer I was politically attacked by those whom I considered to be my brothers. Today, following ten months of prudent silence, I am obliged to break that silence to make public a statement of my attitude toward the governmental disaster and at the same time to express clearly my categorical repudiation of any aggression against my people and to say that I am ready and willing to fight from my trenches against any violation of the fatherland.

The Nicaraguans who truly love Nicaragua, and who wish for the good outcome of a fair revolutionary process, look upon Mexican president José López Portillo's peace initiative with satisfaction. I include myself among those Nicaraguans.

Nationalism and Non-Alignment

Peace for our people is achievable to the extent that we are truly non-aligned. There can neither be contradictions nor ambiguities in Sandinismo: the invasion of Vietnam was as imperialist as the invasion of Afghanistan. Just as imperialist are those who support a fascist junta in El Salvador as those who support a totalitarian regime in Poland. Our Sandinismo cannot allow us to be dragged into the East-West conflict, since that is contrary to national interests. Within this nationalist policy, we know that injustice and class exploitation are the roots of the tragedy that Central America is experiencing, and we must combat these roots with determination. Today, as yesterday, the people have the obligation to free themselves from oppression and exploitation.

We must promote Central American brotherhood, respecting the right of each fraternal nation to seek social transformation by whatever means are most suited to its own realities and interests. In that context, we must aspire to our revolution's being truly Nicaraguan, as the Mexican revolution is Mexican and the Cuban revolution Cuban. And I pay tribute to them. There are in both positive achievements that would enrich our revolution, while preserving its genuine and Nicaraguan character.

I am an Internationalist because I am a free man and I wish to contribute to the liberation of all men. The selflessness and total commitment of Commander Ernesto Ché Guevara are cause for inspiration to me. I am grateful, as I am sure most of my fellow citizens are, for the support that the International comrades of Panama, Costa Rica, Cuba, and other fraternal peoples have given us yesterday in war and today in peace, which is in danger. At this time I am interpreting the feeling—and the reason for that feeling—of that majority of Nicaraguans when I say that the time has come for those who are not engaged in activities strictly contributing to health and education to leave us alone. As a lover of my people, I will honor Sandino's ideas, calling on all Nicaraguans to put themselves on a war footing as long as there is one foreign soldier on our native soil. I know that the ranks of the Sandinista People's Army and the Sandinista People's Militia are made up of men and women of honor and love, and that they constitute the only guarantee that the revolution is irreversible. Today I am calling on that honor and love.

The Necessary Freedoms

The national economy, vital to the revolution, will begin a process of free recovery only if we create a political climate that stimulates production and investment within a mixed economy system. A policy that generates both internal and external peace can only be one in which democracy enjoys the real attributes befitting it, without omitting political pluralism, the practice of free elections, strict respect of individual rights and demands for workers' rights. Freedom of worship is not just a mere declaration. It must be a reality warranting the deepest respect. The revolution does not need to limit freedom of the press, since, if it does, even the walls in the jails would be converted into newspapers.

The fundamental statute of the republic, the statute on the laws and rights of Nicaraguans, and the government's national reconstruction program are not being complied with when, in broad daylight or under the cover of night, the seizures, expropriations, and confiscations overwhelm Somocistas and anti-Somocistas, counter-revolutionaries and revolutionaries, guilty and innocent. In the jails the counter-revolutionaries rub elbows with the Marxist revolutionaries, the latter being punished for the grave offense of interpreting Marx by different criteria from those of their comrades with power. I have with sorrow seen that among my people there is anxiety, distress, fear, the bitterness of frustration, and personal insecurity, when they see our Miskito, Sumo, and Rama Indians persecuted, jailed, or murdered, without a press or radio which might denounce to the world this reign of terror prevailing on the Atlantic Coast and throughout Nicaragua by the already feared State Security.

By all that is stated here, I leave no doubt as to my disagreement with the way the national leadership is conducting the process. If it continues in the present fashion, the people will have to pay a very dear price, possibly even going back to the past unless the armed people expel from power those whom Sandino's condemning and accusing finger points to as traitors and murderers.

Long live the people's revolution.
Long live Nicaragua. Long live freedom, long live Sandino.
Free fatherland or death.

APPENDIX A

Caribbean Basin Initiative

President Ronald Reagan introduced his plan for economic recovery of the Caribbean and Central American countries in the following address to the Organization of American States in Washington, D.C., February 24, 1982.

The principles which are embodied by the Organization of American States —democracy, self-determination, economic development, and collective security—are at the heart of U.S. foreign policy. The United States of America is a proud member of this organization. What happens anywhere in the Americas affects us in this country. In that very real sense, we share a common destiny. We, the peoples of the Americas, have much more in common than geographical proximity. For over 400 years our peoples have shared the dangers and dreams of building a new world. From colonialism to nationhood, our common quest has been for freedom.

Most of our forebears came to this hemisphere seeking a better life for themselves. They came in search of opportunity and, yes, in search of God. Virtually all descendants of the land and immigrants alike have had to fight for independence. Having gained it, they've had to fight to retain it. There were times when we even fought each other.

Gradually, however, the nations of this hemisphere developed a set of common principles and institutions that provided the basis for mutual protection. Some twenty years ago, John F. Kennedy caught the essence of our unique mission when he said it was up to the New World "to demonstrate . . . that man's unsatisfied aspiration for economic progress and social justice can best be achieved by free men working within a framework of democratic institutions."

In the commitment to freedom and independence, the peoples of this hemisphere are one. In this profound sense, we are all Americans. Our principles are rooted in self-government and nonintervention. We believe in the rule of law. We know that a nation cannot be liberated by depriving its people of liberty. We know that a state cannot be free when its independence is subordinated to a foreign power. And we know that a government cannot be democratic if it refuses to take the test of a free election.

We have not always lived up to these ideals. All of us at one time or another in our history have been politically weak, economically backward, socially unjust, or unable to solve our problems through peaceful means. My own country, too, has suffered internal strife including a tragic civil war. We have known economic misery and once tolerated racial and social injustice. And, yes, at times we have behaved arrogantly and impatiently toward our neighbors. These experiences have left their scars, but they also help us today to identify with the struggle for political and economic development in the other countries of this hemisphere.

Out of the crucible of our common past, the Americas have emerged as more equal and more understanding partners. Our hemisphere has an unlimited potential for economic development and human fulfillment. We have a combined population of more than 600 million people; our continents and our islands boast vast reservoirs of food and raw materials; and the markets of the Americas have already produced the highest standard of living among the advanced as well as the developing countries of the world. The example that we could offer to the world would not only discourage foes, it would project like a beacon of hope to all of the oppressed and impoverished nations of the world. We are the New World, a world of sovereign and independent states that today stand shoulder to shoulder with a common respect for one another and a greater tolerance of one another's shortcomings.

Some two years ago when I announced as a candidate for the Presidency, I spoke of an ambition I had to bring about an accord with our two neighbors here on the North American continent. Now, I was not suggesting a common market or any kind of formal arrangement. "Accord" was the only word that seemed to fit what I had in mind. I was aware that the United States has long enjoyed friendly relations with Mexico and Canada, that our borders have no fortifications. Yet it seemed to me that there was a potential for a closer relationship than had yet been achieved. Three great nations share the North American continent with all its human and natural resources. Have we done all we can to create a relationship in which each country can realize its potential to the fullest?

Now, I know in the past the United States has proposed policies that we declared would be mutually beneficial not only for North America but also for the nations of the Caribbean and Central and South America. But there was often a problem. No matter how good our intentions were, our very size may have made it seem that we were exercising a kind of paternalism.

At the time I suggested a new North American accord, I said I wanted to approach our neighbors not as someone with yet another plan but as a friend seeking their ideas, their suggestions as to how we would become better neighbors. I met with President López Portillo in Mexico before my inauguration and with Prime Minister Trudeau in Canada shortly after I had taken office. We have all met several times since—in the United States, in Mexico, and in Canada. And I believe that we have established a relationship better than any our three countries have ever known before.

Economic Health of the Caribbean Basin

Today I would like to talk about our other neighbors—neighbors by the sea—some two dozen countries of the Caribbean and Central America. These countries are not unfamiliar names from some isolated corner of the world far from home. They're very close to home. The country of El Salvador, for example, is nearer to Texas than Texas is to Massachusetts. The Caribbean region is a vital strategic and commercial artery for the United States. Nearly half of our trade, two-thirds of our imported oil, and over half of our imported strategic minerals pass through the Panama Canal or the Gulf of Mexico. Make no mistake: The well-being and security of our neighbors in this region are in our own vital interest. Economic health is one of the keys to a secure future for the Caribbean Basin and our neighbors there. I'm happy to say that Mexico, Canada, and Venezuela have joined in this search for ways to help these countries realize their economic potential. Each of our four nations has its own unique position and approach. Mexico and Venezuela are helping to offset energy costs to Caribbean Basin countries by means of an oil facility that is already in operation. Canada is doubling its already significant economic assistance.

We all seek to insure that the peoples of this area have the right to preserve their own national identities, to improve their economic lot, and to develop their

POTENTIAL BENEFICIARIES OF
THE CARIBBEAN BASIN INITIATIVE

Total Population: 39 million
Total GDP (Gross Domestic Product): $45 billion

Country	Population (millions of persons)	GDP ($ millions)	Exports to U.S. ($ millions)	Imports from U.S. (% of total)
Bahamas	.22	1,267	1,382	51
Barbados	.25	815	96	28
Belize	.15	165	60	40
Cayman Islands	.15	—	3	—
Costa Rica	2.24	4,847	356	36
Dominican Republic	5.43	6,733	786	55
Eastern Caribbean (Anguilla, Antigua and Barbuda, British Virgin Islands, Dominica, Grenada, Montserrat, Saint Christopher-Nevis, Saint Lucia, Saint Vincent and the Grenadines)	.65	500	37	45
El Salvador	4.50	3,484	427	30
Jamaica	2.19	2,402	383	29
Guatemala	7.26	7,852	435	38
Guyana	.79	524	120	25
Haiti	5.01	1,453	252	89
Honduras	3.69	2,538	419	40
Netherlands Antilles	.27	—	2,564	—
Nicaragua	2.70	1,566	211	28
Panama	1.94	3,511	330	48
Surinam	.39	109	1,030	30
Trinidad and Tobago	1.14	6,708	2,378	39
Turks and Caicos Islands	.07	—	3	—

political institutions to suit their own unique social and historical needs. The Central American and Caribbean countries differ widely in culture, personality, and needs. Like America itself, the Caribbean Basin is an extraordinary mosaic of Hispanics, Africans, Asians, and Europeans, as well as native Americans.

At the moment, however, these countries are under economic siege. In 1977, one barrel of oil was worth 5 pounds of coffee or 155 pounds of sugar. To buy that same barrel of oil today, these small countries must provide five times as much coffee (nearly 26 pounds) or almost twice as much sugar (283 pounds). This economic disaster is consuming our neighbors' money, reserves, and credit, forcing thousands of people to leave for other countries—for the United States, often illegally—and shaking even the most established democracies. And economic disaster has provided a fresh opening to the enemies of freedom, national independence, and peaceful development.

Proposed Economic Program

We've taken the time to consult closely with other governments in the region, both sponsors and beneficiaries, to ask them what they need and what they think will work. And we've labored long to develop an economic program that integrates trade, aid, and investment—a program that represents a long-term commitment to the countries of the Caribbean and Central America to make use of the magic of the marketplace, the market of the Americas, and to earn their own way toward self-sustaining growth.

At the Cancún summit last October, I presented a fresh view of a development which stressed more than aid and government intervention. As I pointed out then, nearly all of the countries that have succeeded in their development over the past thirty years have done so on the strength of market-oriented policies and vigorous participation in the international economy. Aid must be complemented by trade and investment.

The program I'm proposing today puts these principles into practice. It is an integrated program that helps our neighbors help themselves, a program that will create conditions under which creativity and private entrepreneurship and self-help can flourish. Aid is an important part of this program because many of our neighbors need it to put themselves in a starting position from which they can begin to earn their own way. But this aid will encourage private sector activities, not displace them.

First. The centerpiece of the program that I am sending to the Congress is free trade for Caribbean Basin products exported to the United States. Currently, some 87 per cent of Caribbean exports already enter U.S. markets duty free under the generalized system of preferences. These exports, however, cover only the limited range of existing products, not the wide variety of potential products these talented and industrious peoples are capable of producing under the free trade arrangement that I am proposing. Exports from the area will receive duty-free treatment for twelve years. Thus, new investors will be able to enter the market knowing that their products will receive duty-free treatment for at least the payoff lifetime of their investments. Before granting duty-free treatment, we will discuss with each country its own self-help measures.

The only exception to the free trade concept will be textile and apparel products because these products are covered now by other international agreements. However, we will make sure that our immediate neighbors have more liberal quota arrangements.

This economic proposal is as unprecedented as today's crisis in the Caribbean. Never before has the United States offered a preferential trading arrangement to any region. This commitment makes unmistakably clear our determination to help our neighbors grow strong. The impact of this free trade approach will develop slowly. The economies that we seek to help are small. Even as they grow, all the protections now available to U.S. industry, agriculture, and labor against disruptive imports will remain. And growth in the Caribbean will benefit everyone with American exports finding new markets.

Second. To further attract investment, I will ask the Congress to provide significant tax incentives for investment in the Caribbean Basin. We also stand ready to negotiate bilateral investment treaties with interested basin countries.

Third. I'm asking for a supplemental fiscal year 1982 appropriation of $350 million to assist those countries which are particularly hard hit economically. Much of this aid will be concentrated on the private sector. These steps will help foster the spirit of enterprise necessary to take advantage of the trade and investment portions of the program.

Fourth. We will offer technical assistance and training to assist the private sector in the basin countries to benefit from the opportunities of this program. This will include investment promotion, export marketing, and technology transfer efforts, as well as programs to facilitate adjustments to greater competition and production in agriculture and industry. I intend to seek the active participation of the business community in this joint undertaking. The Peace Corps already has 861 volunteers in Caribbean Basin countries and will give special emphasis to recruiting volunteers with skills in developing local enterprise.

Fifth. We will work closely with Mexico, Canada, and Venezuela, all of whom have already begun substantial and innovative programs of their own to encourage stronger international efforts, to coordinate our own development measures with their vital contributions, and with those of other potential donors like Colombia. We will also encourage our European, Japanese, and other Asian allies as well as multilateral development institutions to increase their assistance in the region.

Sixth. Given our special valued relationship with Puerto Rico and the U.S. Virgin Islands, we will propose special measures to insure that they also will benefit and prosper from this program. With their strong traditions of democracy and free enterprise, they can play leading roles in the development of the area.

This program has been carefully prepared. It represents a farsighted act by our own people at a time of considerable economic difficulty at home. I wouldn't propose it if I were not convinced that it is vital to the security interests of this nation and of this hemisphere. The energy, the time, and the treasure we dedicate to assisting the development of our neighbors now can help to prevent the much larger expenditures of treasure as well as human lives which would flow from their collapse.

One early sign is positive. After a decade of falling income and exceptionally high unemployment, Jamaica's new leadership is reducing bureaucracy, dismantling unworkable controls, and attracting new investment. Continued outside assistance will be needed to tide Jamaica over until market forces generate large increases in output and employment, but Jamaica is making freedom work.

Threats to Security

I've spoken up to now mainly of the economic and social challenges to development. But there are also other dangers. A new kind of colonialism stalks the world today and threatens our independence. It is brutal and totalitarian. It is not of our hemisphere, but it threatens our hemisphere and has established footholds on American soil for the expansion of its colonialist ambitions.

The events of the last several years dramatize two different futures which are possible for the Caribbean area: either the establishment or restoration of moderate, constitutional governments with economic growth and improved living standards; or further expansion of political violence from the extreme left and the extreme right resulting in the imposition of dictatorships and inevitably more economic decline and human suffering.

The positive opportunity is illustrated by the two-thirds of the nations in the area which have democratic governments. The dark future is foreshadowed by the poverty and repression of Castro's Cuba, the tightening grip of the totalitarian left in Grenada and Nicaragua, and the expansion of Soviet-backed, Cuban-managed support for violent revolution in Central America.

The record is clear. Nowhere in its whole sordid history have the promises of Communism been redeemed. Everywhere it has exploited and aggravated temporary economic suffering to seize power and then to institutionalize economic deprivation and suppress human rights. Right now, six million people worldwide are refugees from Communist systems. Already, more than a million Cubans alone have fled Communist tyranny.

Our economic and social program cannot work if our neighbors cannot pursue their own economic and political future in peace but must divert their resources, instead, to fight imported terrorism and armed attack. Economic progress cannot be made while guerrillas systematically burn, bomb, and destroy bridges, farms, and power and transportation systems—all with the deliberate intention of worsening economic and social problems in hopes of radicalizing already suffering people.

Our Caribbean neighbors' peaceful attempts to develop are feared by the foes of freedom because their success will make the radical message a hollow one. Cuba and its Soviet backers know this. Since 1978, Havana has trained, armed, and directed extremists in guerrilla warfare and economic sabotage as part of a campaign to exploit troubles in Central America and the Caribbean. Their goal is to establish Cuban-style Marxist-Leninist dictatorships. Last year, Cuba received 66,000 tons of war supplies from the Soviet Union—more than in any year since the 1962 missile crisis. Last month, the arrival of additional high-performance MiG-23/Floggers gave Cuba an arsenal of more than 200 Soviet warplanes—far more than the military aircraft inventories of all other Caribbean Basin countries combined.

For almost two years, Nicaragua has served as a platform for covert military action. Through Nicaragua, arms are being smuggled to guerrillas in El Salvador and Guatemala. The Nicaraguan government even admits the forced relocation of about 8,500 Miskito Indians. And we have clear evidence that since late 1981, many Indian communities have been burned to the ground and men, women, and children killed.

The Nicaraguan junta cabled written assurances to the OAS in 1979 that it intended to respect human rights and hold free elections. Two years later, these commitments can be measured by the postponement of elections until 1985; by repression against free trade unions, against the media and minorities; and—in defiance of all international civility—by the continued export of arms and subversion to neighboring countries.

Two years ago, in contrast, the government of El Salvador began an unprecedented land reform. It has repeatedly urged the guerrillas to renounce violence, to join in the democratic process—an election in which the people of El Salvador could determine the government they prefer. Our own country and other American nations through the OAS have urged such a course. The guerrillas have refused. More than that, they now threaten violence and death to those who participate in such an election.

Can anything make more clear the nature of those who pretend to be supporters of so-called wars of liberation? A determined propaganda campaign has sought to mislead many in Europe and certainly many in the United States as to the true nature of the conflict in El Salvador. Very simply, guerrillas, armed and supported by and through Cuba, are attempting to impose a Marxist-Leninist dictatorship on the people of El Salvador as part of a larger imperialistic plan. If we do not act promptly and decisively in defense of freedom, new Cubas will arise from the ruins of today's conflicts. We will face more totalitarian regimes tied militarily to the Soviet Union; more regimes exporting subversion; more regimes so incompetent yet so totalitarian that their citizens' only hope becomes that of one day migrating to other American nations, as in recent years they have come to the United States.

I believe free and peaceful development of our hemisphere requires us to help governments confronted with aggression from outside their borders to defend themselves. For this reason, I will ask the Congress to provide increased security assistance to help friendly countries hold off those who would destroy their chances for economic and social progress and political democracy. Since 1947, the Rio Treaty has established reciprocal defense responsibilities linked to our common democratic ideals. Meeting these responsibilities is all the more important when an outside power supports terrorism and insurgency to destroy any possibility of freedom and democracy. Let our friends and our adversaries understand that we will do whatever is prudent and necessary to insure the peace and security of the Caribbean area.

In the face of outside threats, security for the countries of the Caribbean and

Central American area is not an end in itself but a means to an end. It is a means toward building representative and responsive institutions, toward strengthening pluralism and free private institutions—churches, free trade unions, and an independent press. It is a means for nurturing the basic human rights that freedom's foes would stamp out. In the Caribbean we above all seek to protect those values and principles that shape the proud heritage of this hemisphere. I have already expressed our support for the coming election in El Salvador. We also strongly support the Central American Democratic Community formed this January by Costa Rica, Honduras, and El Salvador. The United States will work closely with other concerned democracies inside and outside the area to preserve and enhance our common democratic values.

We will not, however, follow Cuba's lead in attempting to resolve human problems by brute force. Our economic assistance, including the additions that are part of the program I've just outlined, is more than five times the amount of our security assistance. The thrust of our aid is to help our neighbors realize freedom, justice, and economic progress.

We seek to exclude no one. Some, however, have turned from their American neighbors and their heritage. Let them return to the traditions and common values of this hemisphere, and we all will welcome them. The choice is theirs.

The Need for Assistance

As I have talked these problems over with friends and fellow citizens here in the United States, I'm often asked, "Why bother? Why should we try to help?" I tell them we must help because the people of the Caribbean and Central America are in a fundamental sense fellow Americans. Freedom is our common destiny. And freedom cannot survive if our neighbors live in misery and oppression. In short, we must do it because we're doing it for each other.

Our neighbors' call for help is addressed to us all here in this country—to the Administration, to the Congress, to millions of Americans from Miami to Chicago, from New York to Los Angeles. This is not Washington's problem; it is the problem of all the people of this great land and of all the other Americas—the great and sovereign republics of North America, the Caribbean Basin, and South America. The Western Hemisphere does not belong to any one of us—we belong to the Western Hemisphere. We are brothers historically as well as geographically.

Now, I'm aware that the United States has pursued good neighbor policies in the past. These policies did some good, but they're inadequate for today. I believe that my country is now ready to go beyond being a good neighbor to being a true friend and brother in the community that belongs as much to others as to us. That, not guns, is the ultimate key to peace and security for us all.

We have to ask ourselves why has it taken so long for us to realize the God-given opportunity that is ours. These two great land masses north and south, so rich in virtually everything we need—together our more than 600 million people can develop what is undeveloped, can eliminate want and poverty, can show the world that our many nations can live in peace, each with its own customs and language and culture but sharing a love for freedom and a determination to resist outside ideologies that would take us back to colonialism.

We return to a common vision. Nearly a century ago a great citizen of the Caribbean and the Americas, José Martí, warned that "mankind is composed of two sorts of men—those who love and create and those who hate and destroy." Today more than ever the compassionate, creative peoples of the Americas have an opportunity to stand together; to overcome injustice, hatred, and oppression; and to build a better life for all the Americas.

I have always believed that this hemisphere was a special place with a special destiny. I believe we are destined to be the beacon of hope for all mankind. With God's help, we can make it so. We can create a peaceful, free, and prospering hemisphere based on our shared ideals and reaching from pole to pole of what we proudly call the New World.

APPENDIX B

Contadora Proposals For Peace in Central America

The following "document of objectives" adopted by the Contadora group (Mexico, Venezuela, Colombia, and Panama) was presented to the secretary general of the United Nations on October 6, 1983, by the foreign secretary of Mexico, Bernardo Sepulveda.

WHEREAS:
 The prevailing situation in Central America, characterized by an atmosphere of tension which threatens security and peaceful coexistence in the region, requires for its solution the observance of the **principles of international law** that regulate relations among states, particularly:
- The free determination of the peoples.
- The nonintervention.
- The equal sovereignty of states.
- The peaceful settlement of controversies.
- The abstention from resorting to threats or the use of force.
- The respect for territorial integrity of states.
- The pluralism in its various manifestations.
- The enforcement of democratic institutions.
- The promotion of social justice.
- The international cooperation for development.
- The observance and encouragement of human rights.
- The proscription of terrorism and subversion.
- The eagerness to reconstruct the Central American fatherland through the progressive integration of its economic, legal, and social institutions.
- The need for economic cooperation among the Central American states, in order to fundamentally contribute to the development of their peoples and strengthen their autonomy.
- The commitment to create, promote, and strengthen democratic systems in all countries of the region.
- The unjust economic, political, and social structures that intensify the conflicts in Central America.
- The need to stop the tensions and establish the bases for understanding and solidarity among countries in the area.

- The arms race and the increasing traffic of arms in Central America, which deteriorate political relations in the region and divert economic resources which could be used for development.
- The presence of foreign advisors and other forms of foreign military interference in the zone.
- The risk of using the territory of the Central American states to undertake armed and political destabilizing actions against others.
- The need for political compromise to facilitate dialogue and understanding in Central America, to dismiss the danger of generalized conflicts and set into motion mechanisms which can ensure harmonic coexistence and security for its people.

HENCE:
They express their intention to achieve the following **objectives:**
- To reduce tension and end situations of conflict in the area, abstaining from any action which may endanger political confidence or jeopardize peace, security, and stability in the region.
- To ensure strict compliance with the principles of international law previously outlined, since nonobservance will determine responsibilities.
- To respect and guarantee the observance of human, political, civil, economic, social, religious, and cultural rights.
- To adopt measures conducive to the establishment and, in some cases, the improvement of democratic, representative, and pluralistic systems, which would guarantee effective popular participation in decision-making and ensure free access of the different currents of opinion to honest and periodic electoral processes, which should be based on a total respect for citizens' rights.
- To promote national actions towards reconciliation in cases of deep social divisions, allowing participation in democratic political procedures according to the law.
- To create political conditions directed to guarantee international security and the integrity and sovereignty of the states of the region.
- To halt the arms race in all its manifestations and to initiate negotiations on the subject of control and reduction of the current arms inventory and actual number of arms.
- To forbid the establishment in the region of foreign military bases or any other form of foreign military interference.
- To concert agreements to reduce, and eventually eliminate, the presence of foreign military advisors and other forms of foreign military and security actions.
- To establish internal mechanisms of control for the prevention of the traffic of arms from the territory of one country of the region to another.
- To eliminate the traffic of arms, within the region or from abroad, forwarded to persons, organizations, or groups attempting to undermine Central American governments.
- To prevent the use of their own territory by, and neither to lend nor to allow military or logistic support to, persons, organizations, or groups attempting to destabilize Central American governments.

- To abstain from promoting or supporting acts of terrorism, subversion, or sabotage in the countries of the area.
- To create mechanisms and coordinate systems of direct communication aimed to prevent or, if necessary, to resolve incidents among states of the region.
- To continue with the humanitarian aid directed to help Central American refugees who have been displaced from their country of origin, providing also conditions suitable for their voluntary repatriation, in consultation or cooperation with the high commissioner of the United Nations—UNHC—and other interested international organizations.
- To undertake economic and social development programs with the purpose of achieving a higher standard of living and a more equitable distribution of wealth.
- To revitalize and normalize the mechanisms of economic integration in order to achieve a continuous economic development based on solidarity and mutual benefit.
- To negotiate the acquisition of external monetary resources which will guarantee additional means to finance the reactivation of intraregional commerce, overcome the severe difficulties in the balance of payments, secure working capital funds, support programs for the expansion and restructuration of the systems of production, and promote short- and long-term investment projects.
- To search for a greater and wider access to international markets in order to expand the commercial flow between Central American countries and the rest of the world, in particular with industrialized countries, through a revision of commercial practices and elimination of tariffs and non-tariff barriers, and while assuring profitable and fair prices for the products exported by countries of the region.
- To promote mechanisms of technical cooperation to plan, program, and execute multi-sectorial projects of investment and promotion of commerce.

The ministers of foreign relations of the Central American countries initiated, with the participation of the Contadora group countries, consultations with the purpose of preparing the conclusion of agreements and adopting the mechanisms necessary to formalize and develop the objectives contained in this document, and to ensure the establishment of appropriate systems of control and verification. To that effect, the initiatives presented will be taken into account in the meetings summoned by the Contadora group.

APPENDIX C

The Seventy-two Hour Document

Two months after the Sandinista victory in July 1979, the leaders of the FSLN (Sandinista National Liberation Front) met in secret for three days to lay plans to consolidate their power. Their detailed report on the meeting, issued on October 5, 1979, and intended to be circulated only among party members, soon became well known outside the FSLN.

Analysis of the Situation and Tasks of the Sandinista People's Revolution[1]

I. INTRODUCTION

BROTHERS:

The First National Assembly of Cadres of the Sandinista National Liberation Front took place in Nicaragua on September 21, 22, and 23, 1979. Although not all leaders and rank-and-file cadres were in attendance, there was sufficient representation among the comrades present to give us a fairly good idea of the situation in our country.

The National Directorate called this assembly, which bore the name of the national hero, Rigoberto López Pérez,[2] in order to have a direct exchange of ideas with responsible, intermediate cadres on the national problems and on the internal activity of the organization.

As a result of these three days of work, and after analyzing the national situation, guidelines were drawn for the purpose of formulating concrete proposals for the different areas of work and for the different sectors involved in our revolutionary process.

We need to underscore the transcendental nature of this assembly in the history of our organization, as, by unanimous consensus of the Sandinista delegates, it was agreed to call in the future our top body [the] National Directorate of the FSLN. In fact, this was the first time that the leaders, cadres, and militants of our organization were gathered together. This assembly confirmed in a definitive manner the indestructible unity of our vanguard organization, which, led by the National Directorate and unanimously supported by all our militant and revolutionary membership and our people, once more

---

Translated and published by the U.S. Department of State, February 1986. Notes for this document are on page 517.

confirms that our people, led by the FSLN, are victoriously marching toward the sun of our historical and total liberation.

For obvious reasons, in a report which we want to circulate widely to all our militants, both within the country and abroad, we cannot divulge as we would like to the fundamental aspects of what was discussed. We are certain that within the party structure, the political guidelines and analyses can be expanded upon and dealt with at greater depth. All our militants should devote time to study these guidelines and look for creative ways to apply them in their respective areas of work, while, at the same time, through proper party channels, they should convey their opinions, ideas, and contributions which could better define and enrich the guidelines in this circular.

II. THE PRESENT SITUATION

A. *The Sandinista Revolution and the Question of Power*

Over the past two years, the struggle for power in Nicaragua essentially centered on seeking the overthrow of the Somoza dictatorship through a military defeat of its principal means of support: the *Somocista* [National] Guard. The strategy of our organization for the armed struggle can be said to be based on three vital objectives: (a) the national and international isolation of the dictatorship; (b) a bold policy of national alliances of a combative character; and (c) the development of all forms of insurrectional participation of the masses. Through a decisive combination of political and armed struggles, our organization, particularly since the second half of 1977, by promoting and utilizing the growing participation of the masses in the political and military struggle, turned the structural crisis of the *Somocista* system of oppression of our people into an ever deepening and uninterrupted crisis.

From the moment of the unleashing of the political crisis for the regime, the Sandinista National Liberation Front brought back to the surface the power system that imperialism and the local reactionary forces had created during the 1930s for the purpose of resolving through the creation of a puppet military regime the failure of the military intervention which had been humiliated politically and militarily by the patriotic forces led by our national hero, Augusto C. Sandino. From the very beginning of the crisis of *Somocismo,* we realized more clearly that the true enemy we would have to confront was the imperialist power of the United States and, to a lesser degree, the treachery and demagoguery of the local reactionary bourgeoisie.

We should make special mention, in order to clarify the issue of the nature of the power which emerged with the triumph of the revolution, of the spectacular rise of the struggle of the masses. The last two years, from the middle of 1977 on, were decisive in the overthrow of the dictatorship, because during that period our people began to involve themselves more and more in the strategy for the conquest of power as implemented by our organization.

The class struggle was taking a massive, all encompassing, revolutionary character. Actually, our people understood and comprehended with absolute clarity that, in order to satisfy their enormous needs, the dictatorship had to be overthrown by a popular revolutionary movement.

The masses were increasing their heroic participation in the struggle, not retreating a single step in the face of the regime's genocidal repression, toughening their spirit and forms of struggle, seeking a confrontation with the dictatorship, and overcoming all obstacles. These included the efforts to overcome the subjective conditions which served to limit the power of our vanguard, that is to say, the problem of the different factions and that of deviations from the strategic line.[3] Our organization was faced with two crucial problems in securing the military defeat of the dictatorship: on the one hand, solving the material problems of a type of war which was extraordinarily complex because of its diverse forms of combat, its intensity, its scale, and its extensiveness; and, on the other hand, neutralizing through an adroit combination of internal and external alliances and a spectacular diplomatic struggle of worldwide extent the interventionist policies of imperialism intended to make our Sandinista revolution fail.

In the final months especially, it was over one point that all those who for different circumstances found themselves involved in the Nicaraguan conflict became enmeshed in an obsessive struggle: the retention or dissolution of the National Guard, although clearly between these two extremes there was a variety of intermediate positions. Actually, the Sandinista Front had all the advantages. We can say that the historic trap that imperialism and the local reactionaries had set for the Sandinistas in 1933 and 1934 by the substitution of a native interventionist force allowed the Sandinista movement, under today's conditions, to draw imperialism and the reactionary bourgeoisie into a colossal ambush which proved extremely effective. With the combination Sacasa–Nicaraguan Guard,[4] they succeeded in cutting short for Sandino the continuity of the struggle using the banners of national liberation, especially since the Yankee troops, with the greatest of cynicism, had withdrawn early in 1933, without the political and economic domination having been resolved in favor of our people.

The military dictatorship, which was founded as a consequence, created, with the passing of the years, sharp contradictions and was rejected by all the "democratic" segments of the population. The Sandinista movement of today, facing the Somoza–Genocidal Guard combination, was able to wage a true struggle of national liberation by raising the highly unifying anti-Somoza banner while at the same time routing the military underpinnings of the bourgeois system of domination, with the help of the bourgeoisie itself.

In order to clarify further the question of power, it is necessary to assess more carefully the significance of the defeat of the National Guard. Imperialism in Nicaragua—with the model that it imposed on us, just as on the Dominican Republic, Cuba, Venezuela, El Salvador, and so on—saw its domination assured through the National Guard. *Somocismo* in Nicaragua, rather than an accident, was a historic necessity that resulted from the meshing of a militarist model of imperial domination with the characteristics of a traditional society, strongly paternalistic, where the influence of the landowning aristocracy heightened the power of family clans. But the Guard was really the essence of power. With the defeat of the Guard, the substance was attacked, and, of course, the form, *Somocismo,* fell to pieces.

On the other hand, the military dictatorship model was applied in Nicaragua under socioeconomic conditions that could not allow imperialism to establish its domination by using the national bourgeoisie as a direct intermediary—as it was able to do in other societies such as Argentina and Chile. The bourgeoisie in Nicaragua was just beginning to come to life when it was uprooted by the intervention of 1909. And at the time of the crisis of imperialist power in 1927 and 1933, this same bourgeois class was nearly wiped out economically by the impact of the great world depression. There was no alternative other than that of installing a direct military dictatorship without class intermediaries. For this reason and the natural weakness of the native bourgeoisie, the political and economic power of the Somoza dictatorship attained a markedly monopolistic character. The bourgeoisie in Nicaragua did not really pursue its own policy but was limited to developing its role of accumulating material possessions, while in reality it was represented by the dictatorship in the political field. This explains why, when the dictatorship was collapsing as an instrument of domination, the bourgeoisie, lacking parties and political know-how, resorted to trade unions and economic organizations to strengthen its political participation.

In reality, we helped bring about the fusion of the crisis of the capitalist model with that of the dictatorship, so that the crisis of the latter became, of necessity, the crisis of the economic order, the exhaustion of a dependent capitalist system, based on the superexploitation of labor, which had made of the military dictatorship a historical necessity.

For this reason, the overthrow of the dictatorship by the revolutionary action of the masses and their vanguard historically opened the doors not only to a new political regime but also, and most importantly, to a new and different socioeconomic plan of transition, the base necessary to build the new revolutionary power, the expression of the interests of the workers, peasants, and all the other oppressed sectors of our people.

It is important to emphasize this here, because by defeating the National Guard and overthrowing the dictatorship, we also dealt a decisive blow to the power of the bourgeoisie.

B. On the Correlation of Forces

The Sandinista victory of July 19 erased all the question marks. The pressure of the imperialist circles and international reactionaries was of no avail in saving what for some was mainly the support of their geopolitical interests and for others the preservation of the bourgeois democratic system. The National Guard was not even disbanded by decree as some had hoped; after having suffered successive humiliating defeats, the National Guard collapsed like a house of cards and fled in disgrace with its tyrants, its commanders, and its false heroes. Few victories in the annals of revolutionary war have been as complete as the Sandinista victory. All the events that usually accompany such a defeat occurred at a dizzying pace one after another: military defeat in the war fronts, the takeover of urban centers, the rout of the commanders, the flight of the high command, the capture *en masse* of prisoners of war, the general disarming, and, as the culmination of the wickedness, the total rout. Nothing was left of that army but shame, smoke, and ashes. It was totally routed.

The Government of Reconstruction—the result of a special class alliance but principally the political alternative organized by the Sandinista Front to neutralize Yankee intervention—entered triumphantly into Managua under conditions totally different from those which had existed at the time of its creation. The war had been won by *Sandinismo,* and the people recognized above all the total victory of *Sandinismo.*

It is true that in the situation prevailing in 1977, the alliance with the democratic elements of the bourgeoisie was skillfully aimed at the main objective of isolating *Somocismo* and widening the forces of the Sandinista Front. It was an alliance for internal neutralization. Nevertheless, the alliance that took the form of the Government of National Reconstruction, the Cabinet, and, to a large degree, the same basic program of the FSLN, under the circumstances of the new insurrectional offensive, was dictated by the need to neutralize Yankee interventionist policies in light of the imminent Sandinista victory.

Actually, the selection and organization of the government was a relatively easy task, as it did not have to be negotiated with the opposition parties of the bourgeoisie, but merely involved appointing patriotic figures who were somewhat representative. Thus, in practice the Government of Reconstruction began its administration in a situation different from that which had given rise to it. The presence of known Sandinista figures in the government compensates for the lack of consistency between the political system which the government put in place and the hard facts of the Sandinista revolution and the crushing military victory.

The alliance that the MPU[5] represented also was somewhat affected by our revolutionary triumph. In a few days the MPU disappeared and the Sandinista Front emerged as the hegemonic force of the Nicaraguan revolution, lending momentum to the growth of mass organizations. A partisan army without precedent began to be organized within a state which nevertheless still had vestiges of old institutions; a Sandinista people; and, finally, the red and black flag[6] covers the national territory. We can assert, without fear, that internally there is no force other than that represented by *Sandinismo.*

We can nevertheless state that since July 19, the FSLN exercises the control of power in the name of the workers and other oppressed sectors or, to put it another way, that the workers control power through the FSLN. However, despite its sweeping victory, *Sandinismo* has not made radical moves to transform all this power once and for all into the power of the workers and peasants, because political expediency dictates that more favorable conditions be developed for the revolution and requires that first the more urgent task of its political, economic, and military consolidation be obtained in order to move on to greater revolutionary transformations.

Thus, two months of government have netted the revolution few results that we could consider sweeping. We Sandinistas are engaged in military and political organization, consolidating our revolutionary bases, but we have not yet advanced with the same energy in the area of in-depth economic and social transformations which this time would change, in historical terms, the relations of power between workers and capital.

With regard to the economic project in itself, of course, our economy is still in a state of deterioration, and overall production levels are down because of the war, among other things, but mainly because of the economic disaster into which Somoza plunged the country, leaving it a foreign debt of around $1.6 billion.

In spite of this, certain economic measures have been taken in order to place the economy on a course which could give the people the independence which they really need. These fundamental measures for the economy of the country are:

a. The expropriation of the property of Somoza and the *Somocistas.*
b. The nationalization of banks.

c. The creation of the Agrarian Reform Institute.
d. The expropriation of unoccupied houses and lands.
e. The creation of the Ministry of Foreign Commerce.

Of course, we will not see the results of these steps in the short term but rather in the medium and long term. The Somoza dictatorship caused economic damage of unbelievable consequences.

With regard to the expropriation of the property of Somoza and *Somocismo*, we can say that the Agrarian Reform Institute has in its possession six million manzanas[7] of the finest farmland of the country, farmland which once belonged to *Somocismo*.

There are no fewer than 140 enterprises clamoring for qualified personnel and financial resources to be able to keep this process moving forward and to prevent industrial production from grinding to a halt.

But, with the factories and lands of the *Somocistas*, we have a starting point for the economic transformation of the country. To those we should add the immense wealth of the state which was previously in the hands of individuals and corporations who took for themselves whatever they could and exploited it for their personal gain. This has stopped. Our projects are ambitious, and the results of the initial investigations indicate that, despite disproportionate and uncontrolled exploitation of our natural resources, we have prospects for obtaining substantial amounts of foreign exchange by making optimum use of the resources of the state for production.

The nationalization of banks will enable us to begin monitoring funds entering the country and to manage them properly. Government financing will be determined by the real needs of those who request it in accordance with the interests of the people.

Another important economic measure which will benefit the masses is the rent freeze, which will tend to eliminate landlords in such a manner that negotiations can begin for the state to take over all rental housing and implement a policy of readjustment of rents whereby the tenant will pay the state a given percentage of income.

However, it is not only through the Agrarian Reform Institute that the first tasks of the revolution will begin to be implemented in the countryside. At present, there are two kinds of production units: the large farm administered directly by the state, and the cooperative sector which also is managed by INRA [the Agrarian Reform Institute] and consists of the various agricultural cooperatives that are being organized.

Six million manzanas of land have been taken from *Somocismo* and placed under the direct responsibility of INRA. In León alone, there are 45,000 farm workers in eighty-four production units run either by cooperatives or by the state.

INRA itself has under its control 23 per cent of the coffee production, placing the state in a position of direct influence in this important sector of production. As of now, INRA expects to receive $23 million in aid from other governments and a loan of $800,000 from the IDB [Inter-American Development Bank].

Finally, the creation of the Ministry of Foreign Commerce marks the beginning of an open trade policy with all the peoples of the world, without any considerations other than those arising from our own people. This will allow the centralization and control of imports and exports pursuing a suitable policy of giving priority to imports which are strictly necessary and of exporting products which will earn us the foreign currency to meet the needs of our own development as a revolution.

With regard to the agricultural sector, despite the widespread smuggling and thefts that have occurred in some parts of the country, it is estimated that for 1979, that is to say during the last months of the year, it will be possible to export some 30 million pounds of meat more than *Somocismo* had, reaching a total of 90 million pounds, which will bring in approximately $100 million.

Concerning grain production, it is estimated that there is a 44 per cent shortfall, including rice, beans, corn, and sorghum. The biggest problems are with corn. Some 125,00 manzanas were planted, whereas about 190,000 were planted previously, and the crop is not expected to satisfy the needs of the country. Only 10,000 manzanas of beans have been planted, when usually 25,000 were sown before, but with a late harvest, the needs of the country will be met.

There are no great problems with rice, but the supply of sorghum will not satisfy national demand, as only 30,000 [manzanas] were planted compared to 90,000 sown under *Somocismo*.

We should clarify that during the Somoza era, both the government and private enterprise inflated and exaggerated the figures in order to make production costs appear higher and thus make bigger profits.

With regard to cotton, between 40,000 and 45,000 manzanas were planted compared to approximately 250,000 planted previously. This would mean a decrease of foreign exchange earnings to only $100 million, the same as from beef, with the difference that with beef 80 cents of every dollar remains in the country, while with cotton 80 cents of every dollar is spent on imported inputs. When we speak of an estimated $100 million, we also include cotton byproducts (seed, twine, etc.). The decreased cotton production will have grave consequences for the revolution because of the unemployment it will cause among the peasant masses.

We already have lopped off a strategic portion of the economic power of the bourgeoisie, reinforcing the material bases which strengthen the position of the exploited classes. Nevertheless, we can assert without ambiguity that only a change in the relations of production which begins in this area of the social economy of the state administration will really tilt, this time in depth, the balance of power between classes in favor of the oppressed, who already count on—this should not be discounted—the power of the arms of the Sandinista People's Army which assures from now on the irreversible character of the conquests and goals achieved so far.

It is important to note, and it is a matter on which for different reasons the FSLN and the bourgeoisie appear to agree, that the dominant factor which dictates the rules in matters of politics in the alignment of forces at the international level, and, more specifically, the influence exerted at the continental level by imperialism and its allies. In other words, under the present circumstances, although it would be wise to maintain a skillful posture of neutralization with respect to imperialism, the FSLN appears instead to have adopted an instinctively defensive posture which has placed us in a conservative position without the benefit of a definite policy for this phase. Meanwhile, the bourgeoisie, contrary to the conservative role it played in the past, finds itself in an excellent position to take advantage better than we can of the machinery of the state, its own economic base, and its channels to enhance the contingency policies of imperialism in order to affect our revolutionary process.

Imperialism lost its armed instrument in Nicaragua and lacks secure means to set up in the immediate future any reactionary movement. The kind of military victory achieved over the dictatorship makes it impossible for now, from a practical point of view, to organize aggression by the defeated GN [National Guard], mainly because it would require the solid support of a border or at least nearby state. But Honduras, forced to maintain a neutral position while it is going through a complex internal situation, and El Salvador and Guatemala, which are facing problems of social upheaval, could not embark on such a chancy venture. Probably some GN detachments who maintain contacts with hardcore leaders and could eventually obtain the support of unofficial right-wing military groups or gangs like the "MANO BLANCA"[8] can engage in very limited terrorist or banditry activities. In addition, subversive acts organized by saboteurs of the ultra left or lumpen [proletariat] elements infiltrated in our ranks could contribute in some way to a spontaneous counter-revolutionary uprising.

Without downplaying the need for a strong army capable of assuring the National Defense, it should be noted that at present there are no clear indications of an armed counter-revolution by *Somocista* forces from abroad which actually threatens our stability. Actually, what merits our attention, from this point of view, is domestic matters. From another point of view, it appears far more likely that for some time to come counter-revolutionary action from abroad will be in the form of financial pressure organized by imperialism to destabilize the social and economic foundation of the Sandinista revolution.

Up to now, the rousing momentum of our resounding, historic victory plus the confidence of the masses in their vanguard, the FSLN, have enabled us to maintain a considerable degree of leadership over our people. Moreover, a determined political pragmatism practiced by the FSLN has won us the overwhelming support of the middle classes of the population. It can be said that the substance of the FSLN's policy since July 10 translates to a large degree into a policy attractive to the patriotic elements of the nation, as reflected by the influence of various factors which have affected our decisions, such as:

 a. The need to gain ground to consolidate our army.
 b. Keeping a high degree of social cohesiveness, particularly with the bourgeoisie.
 c. Expectation of financial aid from the Western bloc.
 d. The need to eliminate any legitimacy from imperialism's tactics of undermining our position.
 e. Common sense (pragmatism) in matters of political direction on the part of our organization's leadership. After all, it is a positive development that this "intermediate" situation is helping to stimulate desires to merge with the FSLN which have been expressed by "middle-of-the-road" political groups such as the PLI [Independent Liberal Party], the PS [Nicaraguan Socialist Party] of Ramírez, the Progressive wing of the MDN [Nicaraguan Democratic Movement], the PC [Communist Party of Nicaragua], and the PSC [Social Christian Party], while, at the same time, the bourgeois reaction remains politically bankrupt. On the other hand, however, this type of institutionalization will give rise to contradictions, the signs of which are already beginning to surface. Moreover, Sandinista energies have been devoted to bringing together all those social sectors which in the past had been oppressed in its mass organizations, the only means

through which they can guarantee the realization of their most heartfelt aspirations. The impact of the revolution has penetrated deeply into the revolutionary masses, because they were the principal actors in the struggle, the force behind the triumph. Nevertheless, our people are still going through a truly trying situation, at a stage during which we are working to create the indispensable foundation for the new regime to function and to bring about the necessary conditions for solving the acute economic and social problems that afflict the population.

But it is evident that sixty days after the triumph the masses have advanced qualitatively in political consciousness, in organizational experience, in education, and in combative spirit further than other revolutions. In this time alone, the workers and the peasants, the social base of the revolution, have organized themselves in great numbers in the Sandinista Workers Central and the Rural Workers Association, acquiring a strength never before seen in our country. The people's organization—CDS [Sandinista Defense Committees][9]—operates nationwide; the youth and the women, like other social sectors, are rapidly organizing themselves for the purpose of consolidating and defending the revolution. Nevertheless, greater efforts are required to show the organizations their true role now that the contradiction between people and dictatorship has been resolved. Now the issue is to defeat the new enemies, those who are against the revolution and the reconstruction of the country in accordance with the aspirations of the oppressed and exploited masses. And it is in the area where our people, despite all vicissitudes, are demonstrating with great fervor their unbreakable will to defend its revolution and to follow the leadership of the FSLN.

Another danger facing the masses and specifically the workers' movement is posed by the efforts to divide, confuse, sabotage, and boycott undertaken by the right and the ultra left. In the case of the latter, its efforts are expressed not only in the political and organizational field but also take the form of armed action. Although they are not sufficiently strong to take power, they aim to create an image of instability about our country in the international community and to confuse some backward sectors of our people such as the peasants by taking advantage of the freedoms instituted by the revolution through the government.

Instead of going into a detailed explanation, we will cite some examples. The labor relations between employers and workers have remained practically intact, and with minimal changes the Ministry of Labor maintains the same structure that it had under the dictatorship. Unemployment is high in both the cities and the country. Wages have not been adjusted, and the rate of inflation is really hurting the grass-roots segments of the population, while the most important measures of the revolution are of a structural character whose effects can only be felt in the long run.

In the meantime, there is fertile ground for the anti-Sandinista agitation conducted by groups such as the Workers Front and the PS [Nicaraguan Socialist Party] of Chaguite [Domingo Sánchez]. Paradoxically, the reactionary sectors of the bourgeoisie can find a magnificent opportunity to confuse the masses and even to organize them in blocs of resistance against the measures taken by the government. This is the case with the Large Coffee Growers Cooperative, where reactionary sectors were able to bring together thousands of small producers who today are effectively manipulated by reactionary pressure. This type of situation demands that rather than a policy which up to now has been characterized by a series of realistic actions which are not always coherent, we adopt policies which fall within a strategic concept of the revolutionary phase which has been opened with the Sandinista victory.

C. The Problem of the Character of Our Revolution

We should avoid unnecessary theroretical arguments and attend directly to the matter which in effect is endangering the success and deepening of our Sandinista People's Revolution. It is evident that the military base of imperialism in Nicaragua has been destroyed, for today, there is no interventionist aggression knocking at our door. The reactionary bourgeoisie is defenseless, knowing by class intuition that its fate can depend upon a telephone call. There is broad consensus about the need for sweeping changes. However, we Sandinistas are not exercising all the power that the victory on July 19 gave us. This failure of ours to exercise our power has been more pro forma and quantitative rather than real and qualitative, but, in any event, it is evident that we have to strive to lay the foundation of a system of power that will not endanger the stability of our revolution.

The conduct of the bourgeoisie in these last weeks, in addition to certain moves of imperialism in the financial field, gives us an important clue about how to determine, if not the character of our revolution in a global sense, at least the frame of reference for formulating a political strategy for the current phase.

Through the dictatorship and its hub, the GN [National Guard], something defended imperialism in Nicaragua. This something is an economic system which, since its establishment, represents one cog in the movement of the overall machinery of imperialism. It is the continuity of this system that constitutes the primary objective of imperialist policy, and, today in our country, despite the revolution which has had a principally political and democratic effect, the bases exist for an imperialist alliance with groups of traitors for the purpose of undertaking a counter-revolutionary plan. The worst of all is the fact that both imperialism and the bourgeois traitors can avail themselves of the Nicaraguan state itself to carry out their plans.

The fact is that the economic and financial sector of the state, with the exception of the agrarian reform—and with certain limitations even in this case—are in the hands of the bourgeoisie. This situation could afford the opportunity for the most reactionary elements of the bourgeoisie and for imperialism first to rebuild and then to consolidate a model of economic development with the following elements:

a. Maintaining dependency with respect to imperialism.

b. Strengthening the "free enterprise" system.

c. Isolating and undermining revolutionary social and economic programs.

d. Strengthening as an economic and political class one sector of the bourgeoisie: the "traitorous bourgeoisie."

As basic aspects of this model to be promoted with every external resource and internal support, we should mention:

a. Promoting in the government the thought of the indispensable need for the "take-off" of the reconstruction to be based on heavy foreign indebtedness, which would bring the Nicaraguan debt to a level of $4 billion. This would lock our country to the international capitalist system with a permanent deficit economy. In other words, we sell cheap what we produce and they sell to us at high prices that which we need in order to produce and to subsist; and, because the balance of trade is not in our favor, they will make us loans to keep on going.

b. Attracting, through financial resources and promises of "renegotiations," the IMF [International Monetary Fund] into Nicaragua. This means shackling our economy to all the extortionist policies of imperialism in matters of control of investments, employment, wages, exchange rate, taxation, and the like, which, of course, are at odds with revolutionary policy.

c. Increasing dependency on technology and supplies originating in the U.S.A. and its allies.

d. Renegotiating the foreign debt, but under political pressures and conditions which are detrimental to the sovereign measures which we can take in economic matters.

e. Through agents infiltrated in the government, injecting substantial financial aid to rebuild and ensure the expansion of "local" capitalism. Also, using "American" banks as bridgeheads in the country to strengthen the "free enterprise" system. Some organization could take over the management of the financial assistance while at the same time playing the role of political leadership.

f. Tying whenever possible the financing to private banks or financial mechanisms protected by the government of the United States, and the Congress, so that, in the event of any nationalization, they could invoke the just compensation clause, which, if not resolved, could lead to the application of an automatic [economic] blockade.

g. Contaminating industry, commerce, and private agriculture with North American capital or joint investments in order to protect the Nicaraguan enterprises by [linking them with] this same blockade mechanism.

h. Curtailing the eventual assistance that could be channeled to the public sector.

i. Supporting the political strengthening of the trade unions, associations, and parties of the bourgeoisie.

In short, in our country the enemies of the revolution are:

a. The traitorous bourgeoisie, the principal instrument of the counter-revolution. **This enemy is personified in the class of the financial oligarchy**, which is trying to entrench itself in industry, commerce, and agriculture (the Fernández Hollmans, the Montealegre Callejas, and the like),[10] the commercial and industrial sector which had not yet become a financial oligarchy but had played a leading role in private inititative, and the class of local agricultural bourgeoisie which is attempting to create alliances with the peasantry for the purpose of creating a counter-revolutionary social base, particularly with the most backward of the peasantry.

b. The vestiges of *Somocismo*, represented by the *Somocista* government officials, members of *Somocista* organizations, paramilitary personnel, *Somocistas* who have infiltrated mass organizations and the army, as well as the corrupt practices which characterized the Somoza regime.

c. The ultra-left sectors who are trying to confuse the people by the use of provocative attitudes against the revolution.

The above does not, of course, exhaust the subject [but] attempts to show that it is through financial means that, for now, the beginning of a tactic of distorting our revolution is being put into effect. For today there are no other reactionary forces to promote, and it is evident that imperialism, after having failed time after time to prevent our victory, is now counting on elements who are at its disposal to continue its persistent action to undermine [the revolution]. In our opinion, this is the main danger that we are facing. That is precisely where we are the weakest and least experienced.

For this reason, we believe that our revolution, if it has a clear democratic content, should at the same time endeavor to achieve our national liberation in the economic field. And this is the essence of one of the tasks most clearly bequeathed to us by Sandino. We should remember that in 1933 he pointed out that while the Yankee invervention appeared to have ended, political and economic intervention remained intact. Politically we have dealt a tremendous blow to imperialism; however, it is in the economic field, where the bonds of domination are maintained and now threaten to become the basis of the rebirth of an axis of counter-revolutionary forces, that in the medium term a serious danger can exist to our revolution.

Consequently our revolution should make qualitative progress in the economic field as well, seeking how to transform the social relations of production in all that area in which we have brought the bourgeoisie to bay, incorporating urban and rural workers *en masse* into the struggle for fundamental changes in Nicaraguan society.

In this way, the nature and character of our revolution will be advancing during this transitional phase, opening all the avenues of power in its dimension which must belong solely to the true creators of social wealth: the workers.

III. Our Tactic

Recognizing fully the harsh domestic and international situation and knowing that the Sandinista People's Revolution is marching toward its definitive emancipation, after completing the democratic transition stage, we need to indicate the political and military course of action that the forces of the revolution ought to pursue under the present circumstances. For a long time, American imperialism, the rabid enemy of all peoples who are struggling to achieve their definitive liberation or who are in the process of achieving it, established by force bonds of political and economic domination in our country through various means. By eliminating forever the political-military tool created to exercise this domination, our people have succeeded in breaking the bonds that tied them to the imperial dominion. They did not, however, do away with the economic dependence fostered for years by the dictatorship and the bourgeoisie. Therefore, our revolution must have a strong national, anti-imperialist emphasis, stressing efforts to achieve national liberation in an economic sense without neglecting its political and military consolidation at the domestic and international levels.

The specific circumstances which resulted from the events in Nicaragua leading up to the fierce battle in which the dictatorship was toppled have given the Sandinista Front and its people an extraordinary degree of power, capable of imparting a markedly democratic, popular, and anti-imperialist quality to the process. They also are an important factor in shifting the correlation of forces in our favor and moving the revolutionary process forward in its transitional phase. An undertaking such as this requires a correct tactic in the different fields and a skillful channeling of all revolutionary forces and their allies against their enemies, that is to say, the traitorous bourgeoisie, the vestiges of *Somocismo*, and the ultra left at the domestic level and American imperialism at the international level.

Attracting our friends and forming with them a solid bloc to neutralize the moves of the reactionaries and to isolate and crush our enemies implies performing the following tasks during this stage:

1. Isolate the traitorous bourgeoisie, the ultra left, and the vestiges of *Somocismo* from the democratic sectors; and organize the driving forces of the revolution and place all forces under the leadership of the FSLN.

It is extremely important for our vanguard to unite all sectors of the nation around the defense and the consolidation of the revolution. Its main strength lies with the workers and peasants, the petty bourgeoisie and the democratic sectors of the bourgeoisie that identify with its political blueprint, and it is from these groups that it must extract all of the energies that it needs to achieve its objectives. The organized revolutionary masses are the inexhaustible source of power, the sole force that can preserve the revolution and spur it on to greater revolutionary transformations. Only they can go the distance precisely because they carry inside themselves the power to transform capitalist society. Although it is true that our main concern is to unite all democratic, progressive, and revolutionary sectors to consolidate the revolution, it is much more important to ensure the influence, education, organization, and guidance of the most revolutionary classes, turning them into the driving force of the revolutionary process.

Preventing the dispersion of the worker-peasant movement and of the masses in general in a country in which certain organizations for their own interests have traditionally striven to keep them dispersed is a complex and difficult task. Nevertheless, we should aim all of our political efforts in that direction in order to involve the organized masses in the central tasks of the revolution and set them against the main enemy whom we will inevitably have to confront. The position in which the Nicaraguan revolutionary movement finds itself as a result of its victory enables it to take a more advanced stand in this regard, particularly because *Sandinismo* is capable of influencing and establishing its political and military leadership over all segments of the masses. The policy we will have to follow in the future must be for *Sandinismo* to lend greater strength and vigor to activities of the masses and, at the same time, to place left-wing political groups under our leadership with an eye toward gradually absorbing them [into *Sandinismo*] and its mass organizations.

It is in the way that *Sandinismo* is able to show its ability to unite, lead, and rebuild the country that it will be able to keep intact its victory and that the revolutionary process will be able to bring about sweeping revolutionary transformations. The position of the FSLN with respect to the political parties of the left is dependent on the attitude of these parties with respect to the revolutionary process. If their attitude entails an actual danger, these parties will be treated as enemies of the revolution. Such is the case of the groups who, from ultra-left positions, have adopted sabotage and counter-revolutionary positions, such as the MAP [Popular Action Movement] and its organizations and the Trotskyite groups; these groups opposed to the [revolutionary] process must be crushed!

On the other hand, with [regard to] the leftist organizations which show a predisposition to work toward the interests of the revolution, whether through becoming an integral part of the FSLN by dissolving their mass organizations or, in the end, through working closely together under the leadership of the FSLN, we should encourage them to work without rest to maintain the revolution.

But there are other sectors which also need to be brought over to the side of the revolution. The petty bourgeoisie now is coalescing and recognizes the FSLN as the vanguard of the revolutionary process. The same thing is happening with small organizations of this sort and with the democratic sectors of the bourgeoisie who prefer to work within an established framework rather than waste away. We should attract the petty bourgeois masses by giving them their own organizations and by integrating them into the affairs of state, and, keeping in mind the international situation, we should also preserve the micro parties, doing work inside them for the purpose of assimilating into the revolution the most important elements that compose them. Our policy should seek that those micro parties—which instead of representing the petty bourgeoisie are rather groups of organized petty bourgeoisie—remain, especially in order to carry out a policy of changing their opinion of the Council of State, which should have a real base in the political activity of the organized working masses. With some of these groups we can be frank and explain the situation; with others we should be cautious in order to achieve the desired objectives.

On the other hand, we must isolate from the democratic sectors the traitorous bourgeoisie, which blindly persists in trying to keep our country subject to the economic dependence of imperialism. Our policy is to achieve this isolation through an appropriate political tactic that responds to the situation presented by the revolutionary process. We should hit it not by attacking it as a class, but by attacking its most representative elements as soon as they give us the first opportunity. By striking political and economic blows, we will greatly reduce its power and its capacity for counter-revolutionary maneuvering. The same kind of isolation should be used with ultra-left groups which persist in organizing activities of sabotage and confusing the masses. Pursuing this policy facilitates the identification of the enemies of the revolution, making it possible for the masses to direct the heaviest blows, to annihilate the counter-revolutionary enclaves of the traitorous bourgeoisie, the remnants of *Somocismo*, and the ultra left.

With the Catholic Church and Protestant Church, we should strengthen relations on a diplomatic level, maintaining, generally, a careful policy which seeks to neutralize as much as possible conservative positions and to strengthen our ties with the priests sympathetic to the revolution, while at the same time we are stimulating the revolutionary sectors of the church. With the Protestant Church, which is generally formed by North American religious sects, we should adopt a restrictive policy, conduct an intelligence operation on them, and, if they are caught, arrange for their immediate expulsion.

Finally, with the former National Guardsmen who did participate in some measure with the FSLN or who surrendered before they were called upon to do so, we should follow a policy of rapprochement, while keeping files on them and preventing them from obtaining positions of responsibility in the Sandinista People's Army or in the government. Obviously, exceptions should be made for those who, by possessing certain technical skills and an acceptable record, are indispensable.

2. **Make the State Sector the focus of the national economy and guarantee the effective participation of the mass organizations.**

In order to achieve our objectives we should make use of the political forces of *Sandinismo*, of the mass movement, and of the governmental structure, placing its economic policy at the service of the working masses and the allied sectors who, on a national level, show a willingness to support the cause of the revolution. The hub of the economy in our country should be the State Sector, because it is through it that we can let the organized masses participate.

At the same time we should implement a production system which takes into consideration, first and foremost, the interests of the nation as a whole, which establishes a new kind of social relations of production, and which stimulates the democratic sectors of the bourgeoisie to produce within the framework established by the economic policy. In this respect, the mass organizations, particularly those involved in the organization of the workers and peasants, should understand perfectly that their political action is to be channeled toward the reinforcing of the different policies formulated on the governmental level by the Sandinista National Liberation Front through its National Directorate, to educate the masses on how to use the power they have conquered, to consolidate the revolution, to rebuild the country, and to defend the conquests [already] achieved from the actions of the reactionary forces which are attempting to reverse the revolutionary process.

Our organizations must clearly distinguish the forces that are on their side from those that are against them. The relations of production cannot be viewed in the same way they were before the overthrow of the dictatorship.

First of all, we must distinguish between the State Sector and the economy promoted by the sectors of private enterprise. The first consists of all the property seized from the *Somocistas* both in the countryside and in the cities which now has come under state administration. Consequently, instead of considering the state as the owner, the class organizations should participate directly in production, in reconstruction, in vigilance so that the plans of the government for the economy are carried out effectively, and in purging the remnants of *Somocismo* from state institutions. They should also provide skilled workers to make the state enterprises function and solve the unemployment problems of the workers by finding employment for them in the production centers of the state as new places of work open. In other words, [they should] be convinced that the State Sector is at the service of the popular interests and, in addition, it gives birth to a production system which allows it to rely on its own resources in order to break the ties of economic dependence on imperialism.

Secondly, we should pressure the progressive sectors of the bourgeoisie in order to bring their level of production in line with the standards of the new regime, producing mainly what is in the national interest. Conversely, we must not allow the traitorous bourgeoisie any opportunity to take advantage of its ties with imperialism because we know that instead of following an economic policy in accordance with the most urgent needs of the masses and all the country, they prefer to export products to increase their wealth, even if the people starve to death and remain permanently unemployed. All this means that in the economic as well as governmental field, we must address ourselves to the following tasks:

On the Economic Level—

a. Our economy must adhere to comprehensive national planning whose hub must be the State Sector, through which we can establish in the field of production a strong base of social relations of production and organization as a function of our historic and total liberation.

b. The national economy must try to become independent of the system of extortion and subordination imposed by imperialism worldwide which limits us to a role of suppliers of raw materials and buyers of manufactured products and forces us to depend on cyclical imperialist financing.

c. Establish economic policy measures in the fields of production and export, international trade, and the use of techniques and financing in order to break imperialism's hegemony in the national economy.

d. Break away from the concept of production for profit which uses a high degree of imported components and try to attend to our own economic realities which demand that we utilize our work force (much of which remains unemployed because of labor-saving trends whose justification is to maintain "competitiveness").

e. Base our industrial and economic development on the use of our raw materials.

f. Reject the notion of reconstruction based on massive infusions of foreign capital, [and instead] help ourselves through a national effort, complemented by financial aid, by applying an austerity policy, especially with regard to products that require foreign exchange.

g. Avoid the spread of labeling and canning industries while stimulating industries with a high domestic value added.

h. Establish fiscal, taxation, custom, and credit policies based on nationalist and popular orientation.

i. The organization of state exploitation of our natural resources (minerals, forests, and fishing).

j. Promote industrial development under state control in areas of production that are of strategic importance to the country's economic development.

On the Government Policy Level—

a. Develop bolder social plans in the fields of education, health, and housing in order to bring the revolution to the masses. Give priority to the peasant population, particularly on the northern border and the ATLANTIC COAST.

b. Effectively control the banking and financial sectors, both by government decrees and through politically trustworthy cadres. Forbid foreign banks from making loans to the private sector.

c. Create state enterprises to organize fishing, industry, and mining. At the same time, the Trusts should disappear, giving way to corporate enterprises that will administer and direct them.

d. Support the Agrarian Reform's plans for expansion.

3. Our international policy seeks to secure the support of friendly countries, governments, and organizations and to neutralize the reactionary sectors.

The foreign policy of the Sandinista People's Revolution is based on the full exercise of national sovereignty and independence and the principle of revolutionary internationalism. The objective of the FSLN's foreign policy is to achieve the consolidation of the Nicaraguan revolution as this will help to strengthen the Central American, Latin American, and world revolution. The consolidation must be achieved through the solution of the military and economic problems, principally because with the solution of the first we are strategically preparing to repel any aggression and with the second we can make headway in severing the ties of economic dependence on North American imperialism. This concept will govern our foreign policy as expressed in the following guidelines:

a. Develop political and diplomatic relations which will strengthen our process of military consolidation and economic independence.

b. Stimulate and strengthen the formulation of a national anti-imperialist and democratic policy, both internationally as well as on the continental level, and in the Caribbean area in particular.

c. Contribute to and promote the struggle of the peoples of Latin America against fascist dictatorships [and] for democracy and national liberation.

d. In the Central American region, because of its immediate strategic value, the same principles will apply, emphasizing the need to neutralize, through the proper handling of their internal contradictions, the aggressive policies of the military dictatorships of Guatemala and El Salvador and the differentiation with the special situation in Honduras and the friendly conduct of Costa Rica and Panama.

4. On the organizational situation of the masses.

Beginning with the cadres conference, "Rigoberto López Pérez," the role of the Secretariat of the Masses and all its affiliates was clearly defined. This allows us to better undertake the tasks of organizing the masses and to carry out the work correctly, and to grasp the full scope of the role of the Party's Departmental Directive Committees and the nationwide tasks of the Secretariat of the Masses. To begin with, we should say that the Departmental Directive Committees of the FSLN are the political instruments of the FSLN through which proper guidance of the work is assured. In the specific field of mass organization, they are charged with watching and assuring that the organizational line is adhered to in every way as well as [providing] the proper guidance to all the militant forces involved in these matters in the Departments. The policy of the FSLN toward the masses should pursue the following objectives:

a. Make every effort to unite the revolutionary masses around the vanguard.

b. Strengthen and promote the mass organizations which are the real expression of the people's will.

c. Create legal instruments through which the mass organizations can participate in the decision-making of sectors of the government when necessary.

d. Within the organizational lines, the FSLN gives priority to the revolutionary mass organizations: workers and peasants of the CST [Sandinista Workers Central], ATC [Rural Workers Association], and any other peasant organization, so that these organizations may be the defenders of the revolution. Secondly, we should promote the organization of the democratic sectors of the petty bourgeoisie.

e. Give priority to work within the CST and the ATC in the state enterprises, guaranteeing them, in accordance with their development, participation in the decision-making of the enterprise and offering the organized masses the possibility of improving their technical knowledge.

f. Devise [two] different lines of political work, one for the state workers' unions and another for the unions in the private sector. In the latter, the unions should do surveillance and exert pressure.

We should also broach the tasks which should be taken up immediately by the Departmental Directive Committees related to mass organization. We must work hard to educate our people and its most advanced sectors on the practical significance of the tasks of national reconstruction, spurring production and promoting of the various organizations that they have to build to consolidate the revolution. Failure to do so could create serious and perfectly foreseeable political problems. We state this because we already know of excesses committed by heads of mass organizations which practically nullify the authority of the representatives of the government. They demand measures which have nothing to do with the guidelines issued; rather, they make the mass organizations the sole judges of how things should be run without taking into consideration the character of the revolution and the policy of alliances which we should follow.

Actually, in some cases Sandinista leaders have attempted to become managers of enterprises and to establish administrative policy, thus creating political problems for us, instead of playing their proper role, which is that of control, vigilance, and demanding that the state policy drawn up by the FSLN is followed to the letter. The policy of the mass organizations must take into account the objective reality of the revolution; from the economic point of view we have state enterprises and firms which belong to the private sector. Therefore, our policy must take into consideration these situations, these conflicts and these relations, because otherwise, contrary to our doctrine, we will be promoting anarchy. We will find ourselves bogged down in problems of our own making and unable to attend to the fundamental problems which truly we ought to solve. In view of the above, our activities among the masses should be governed by the following guidelines:

a. Form national organizations with the participation of delegates from those mass organizations which already have developed a structure in the departments. Where no structures have yet been formed, it is up to the party organs in charge of such work, as it is up to this national organization, to counsel and guide those affiliated with these organizations. The CST, the ATC, and the CDS have priority in the structuring of these national bodies of the organization.

b. Draw up a draft charter for the mass organizations, emphasizing their bylaws and their declaration of principles. The former will include the organizational concept of the mass organizations, and the latter the political aims of the organization. For this purpose, the Secretariat of the Masses is in the process of forming the teams who will take charge of accomplishing this task.

c. The Secretariat of the Masses will transmit, through the national bodies, the policy the mass organizations should be required to follow. These same bodies will go through the channels of the Departmental Directive Committees through the Executive Commission. The purpose of this is to begin to differentiate the role of the National Secretariat of the Masses from that of the party leadership organizations in the departments. It also has the same aim of strengthening internal order.

THE SEVENTY-TWO HOUR DOCUMENT 511

d. Once the necessary documents have been drafted, a procedure would be established through which the departmental organizations would be consulted, and a Constitutional Congress of the Mass Organizations would be convoked at a national level.

e. In the departments where the [organizational] work is just beginning, it is necessary to build the departmental mass organizations, keeping in mind the democratic participation of the masses so that they themselves can put in their most advanced representatives. Once this is done, we must select the delegate who will be part of the national body and send him to the National Secretariat of the Masses.

f. Mobilize the masses to bolster the production process, especially in those areas of the economy where our government and FSLN are most deeply involved.

g. Establish connection between delegates of the mass organizations and the state bodies in order to give a stronger impetus to the economic policy and to the relations that should be maintained.

h. See to it that the majority of workers are drawn, by means of their class organizations, into state enterprises. In other words, the CST and the ATC, under the new conditions, should resolve the unemployment problem through the ties they have with the state and thus assure the resumption of industrial and agricultural production. The case of the firms in the private sector is different because there it involves the worker-owner relationship. Nevertheless, we must know how to advise our organizations as to what kind of relationship they should adopt and to turn to state bodies in order to clear up their problems of vigilance and control so that these businesses produce that which is in the interest of the nation, and not to take radical measures unless they are necessary because any measure that tends to paralyze overall production is a serious blow to the efforts to overcome the economic crisis.

i. Hold assemblies with delegates of the national and departmental organizations and with the organized workers in order to show the latter their tasks.

j. Make full use of mass cadres to extend the organization to all departments (including municipalities).

k. Support the efforts of our organization in the struggle to suppress counterrevolutionary pockets.

5. Build, strengthen and educate the Sandinista People's Army, while cultivating its loyalty to its people and its revolution, whose vanguard is the FSLN.

The Sandinista People's Army is the armed organization *par excellence* of the revolutionary masses of Nicaragua. The triumph of our revolution makes it possible for the Sandinista People's Army to be recognized as the Constitutional Army of the Republic. For the same reason, it is the mission of the FSLN to assure the loyalty of its members to the revolution and to the leadership of the historic vanguard: the FSLN. This revolutionary loyalty should be assured through the following mechanisms and tasks:

a. A permanent effort of political education within the armed forces.

b. The organization of the FSLN's vanguard structure which would guarantee the transmission and application of our organization's policies and would assure the political activity of our militants in the army.

c. The FSLN exerts its influence and its political leadership through the directive committees and internal groups of militants within the armed forces. The DN [National

Directorate], through the military committee, assures the political education policy through the military chain of command and will be the organization in charge of the FSLN party structure within the Sandinista People's Army.

d. The party structure should carry out its mission by seeking to strengthen and respect always the military structure and chain of command.

e. It is the task of the FSLN to strengthen the political education section of the Sandinista People's Army, which must be composed of militants of the vanguard with recognized revolutionary qualities.

Other Tasks Within the Armed Forces Are:

a. Strengthen the military leadership in zones of strategic importance and see to it that highly sensitive regions be under the command of a member of our DN [National Directorate]. Specifically the North, South and Atlantic zones.

b. Purge the army at all levels, eliminating those elements who are incompatible with revolutionary measures.

c. Institute mandatory military service.

d. Draw up an emergency plan to take care of the vital needs of the comrades in the Army.

e. Issue military laws and regulations.

f. Establish military regions in accordance with a strategic approach to national defense, eliminating the urban militia type of army. Maintain law and order in the cities with the police and place the forces [of the army] in the countryside or the periphery. Prohibit the carrying of large weapons of war in the cities as well as the display of grenades, with exceptions.

6. The task is: Reorganize the FSLN and transform it into the party of the Sandinista People's Revolution.

We could not face the tasks related to the burning issues of the revolution if our organization did not recognize that an important objective is the building of the revolutionary party. This party, which has a definite class position, a unique political principle, a scientific ideology, and a correct strategy and tactic, places itself at the forefront of all society and embodies the political and military leadership of all revolutionary forces which struggle and work to carry the revolution toward imcomparably greater achievements.

For nearly four years, the FSLN was shaken by the problems created by the political crisis of October 1975. During this time, the styles, the practices, and the strategic-tactical concepts that prevailed in each of the factions served to foster a climate of political mistrust among the factions, resulting from the serious divisions within the Sandinista Front. More than once we were in danger of not being able to carry forward the strategic plan for the insurrection and to bring about the necessary conditions in order to unify the different tendencies under one single, monolithic leadership. The imperatives of the political situation at the end of May, the urgency to enter combat as united as possible, the necessities of the war, the vital need to oppose the enemy with the maximum of forces and weapons, and the historic duty to lead our people to victory allowed the uniting, in many places, of a great number of forces under a single leadership. Generally, they followed the political and military instructions of the constituted leadership and fought tremendous battles against the *Somocista* guard until they ground it to dust.

Nevertheless, the realities of today are different. We are an organization which, at the head of its people, has seized power, and that allows us to implement the political plan proclaimed for so many months. This is a necessary condition for advancing toward a higher stage of the struggle where power will definitely be in the hands of the people. In order to assure a correct revolutionary leadership, the leadership of all the forces, to promote the most varied range of organizations, to raise the level of political consciousness of our people, to efficiently fight the traitorous bourgeoisie who have begun mobilizing to oust us from the state apparatus and take over the economy of the country while they are trying to organize themselves politically—that is to say, in order to discharge such responsibilities, we need to count on a vanguard detachment which can, first of all, eradicate from within the Sandinista Front all remnants of sectarianism and place the organization under a single recognized politico-military leadership and, secondly, rapidly begin building the revolutionary party.

It is impossible to successfully accomplish the task of consolidating the Sandinista People's Revolution without being able to count on that instrument of the vanguard, without this political apparatus which constitutes the best known collective leadership of the society. It has an organizational aspect, it works out the contradictions that arise as the process evolves and solves the problems that systematically appear; it leads the class struggle and guides the whole nation down the road strewn with victories. Without this vanguard, without this revolutionary party which is the highest form of organization of the workers and their most characteristic leader, it would be much more difficult to face the crucial tasks, to maintain power, and to place [that power] at the service of the revolution.

The most serious internal danger facing the FSLN is the maintenance of divisionist, sectarian, or factional positions which in actuality serve to boycott and sabotage the internal cohesion of the organization, weakening any position of unity the FSLN could adopt with respect to other revolutionary organizations. To speak of internal unity within the organization means to remove forever the original causes of the political crisis and to make efforts to build within the organization the party mechanisms for resolving the contradictions so as to strengthen the vanguard. An organization that does not stimulate collective discussion, the education of its militants, the participation of its members in the burning issues of the movement, is an organization that ages quickly, loses its vigor and force, and is liquidated politically. It should be understood that it is not a matter of implementing within the organization a non-critical approach, the ultra-democratic way, and excessive centralism, but to function scientifically in accordance with the revolutionary principles that govern an organization.

Everyone realizes that we are going through a period when our biggest efforts are devoted to the most efficient redeployment of the militant forces. Some of these forces still show their own tendencies, styles and practices, political immaturity, and ideological weaknesses. These traits are destined to disappear permanently, but this will not be achieved without the participation of and the conscious will of the militants to overcome the present limitations once and for all.

To speak of monolithic unity from now on will mean to change all the militant forces, which now are divided and without direction, into a powerful and organized force which is the political guarantor of the revolutionary process. This unification, which can in no way resemble the unity in action that characterized the activity of the political factions of the FSLN in the past, should take into account the specific situation in which we find ourselves at present. That is to say, we are in an organization which through insurrection has overthrown the *Somocista* dictatorship, taken power, and installed a type of democracy particularly representative of the popular interests whose main duty is to prepare itself for the new struggles that are approaching.

We must fulfill with maturity our people's historical imperative of having a strong, capable, and monolithic vanguard. We must deal critically, and not with mistrust, with all those manifestations of sectarianism, competitiveness, supremacism, and organizational disintegration and consistently struggle to crystallize and create the organic political and ideological unity of Sandinista militants. We must constantly and systematically spread [our message] and educate our brothers in the revolutionary principles that govern a vanguard, which, at the same time, are the strongest guarantee of unity of the organization. We must fight to the death against amateurish organizational practices and theoretical, dogmatic, and liberal approaches in Sandinista militants. We must claim as ours all lessons learned as a result of the political crisis of the FSLN, analyzing them with a positive spirit and, above all, learning to be conscious of the fact that it is necessary to struggle every day and with all our forces in order to keep our vanguard united.

These are extremely important, unavoidable tasks and the formidable challenge facing Sandinista militants in order to erase the memories generated by the political crisis of the FSLN. This is the only way to keep the organization intact and to infuse it with the powerful energy displayed by its militants. Nobody can, at this time, divert their efforts in order to implant sectarianism or to live conspiring against the unity of the organization. This would mean lowering our guard and preparing fertile ground for divisions while the enemy is preparing, joining forces, and working feverishly to develop his political apparatus in order to struggle to gain control of the political process.

It must be understood that, generally, in every organization there are currents that run against the tide. They create contradictions, but this is something quite logical, quite natural, part of every political organization when within the organization a correct ideological struggle takes place against currents alien to the revolutionary ideology. It is thus that greater strength and political consolidation are obtained. And, if this struggle is fought within the organic framework of political participation within the organization, nothing can destroy the organization; it is invincible.

But this is one thing, and it is something quite different to believe that it is possible to carry on political activities outside the organization, that any militant, on the basis of his own beliefs, can continue to promote factional positions without regard to the political guidance of the central bodies of the FSLN. Many of our brothers have a tendency to attempt to put into practice their particular experiences based on a purely mechanical approach, imposing unrealistic methods by using altogether theoretical arguments. They attempt to undermine the political authority of comrades who belonged to a different faction in the past. This is nothing less than an attempt to ignore the development of the FSLN, its historic foundation, the objective reality that faces us, and the political and organizational objectives we are pursuing at the present stage.

We can affirm that the organizational objectives for which we currently are striving are the following:
1. Reorganize the militant forces of the FSLN and unite all the scattered forces under a single, sound political and military leadership, creating leadership bodies at every level of the organization whose overall leading body is the National Directorate.
2. Eliminate factions within the FSLN and educate the militants on a basis of a single set of political principles under one strategy and one tactic, and starting from a single internal organizational policy.
3. Make the best use of the cadres and the militants, attending to the most urgent needs at the national level.
4. Begin building the revolutionary party whose ideology is none other than the one that embodies the Sandinista heritage and the contributions of the world revolution.

On the other hand, before determining the tasks concerning organizational matters, we should make clear their political content. We must say that under the new conditions, all organizational criteria have greater flexibility. We are an organization whose greatest aspiration is to maintain revolutionary power, not to conquer it. Consequently, our goal is to work to educate our people to recognize their vanguard and the tasks it has proposed, beginning from the fundamental premise that the FSLN is the legitimate organization to lead the revolutionary process. On the basis of this premise, it is of paramount importance to point out this reality to each of the organizations that are politically and organically independent by clearly explaining the FSLN policy of integrating people into the vanguard and the need for counting on a single set of organizations with a clear revolutionary content in order to accomplish the appointed objectives.

After the years of struggle during which our organization suffered brutal repression, new perspectives are opening in our country for giving the masses a true vanguard, which, taking into account our own organizational experience and the lessons taught and learned through revolutionary theory, can form a solid organization. In it, on one hand, the political structure of revolutionary leadership is guaranteed, and, on the other hand, the participation of the most advanced elements of the people. At the same time, this will strengthen the FSLN's organization politically and ensure the class approval of the exploited and oppressed sectors of the nation.

Toward this end, the organizational policy of the FSLN seeks primarily to continue organizing the militants into select organizations that can guarantee effective guidance for the revolutionary tasks, subject to strict standards of militancy that seal the revolutionary content of *Sandinismo*. It also enlightens all the militants as a whole. On the other hand, it should allow access to the vanguard by the numerous advanced elements of the people who, following a policy of tightly regulating individual membership, will remain in their mass organizations and extend more widely the influence of the Sandinista Front within all the organized and non-organized sectors of the country.

The lines of organization of the FSLN serve to achieve the following objectives:
1. Strengthen the leadership of the National Directorate as the highest body of the FSLN and of the revolution as well as analyze the tasks adequately so as to get down to the orientation of the work in every field. Toward this end, our leadership has been organized into three commissions: Governmental, Military, and Executive. The latter sees to it that the strategic conduct, the guidelines, and the policies in the different fields and

the agreements arrived at by the National Directorate are put into practice in such a way as to advance the process and the vanguard to new, qualitatively better situations. This in no way means that the Executive Commission is hierarchically higher than the rest of the members of the DN [National Directorate], but that it had been constituted to facilitate the smooth execution of the tasks.

2. Maintain the secretariat as an auxiliary consultative and advisory instrument formed by cadres of proven revolutionary caliber, loyal to the revolution and with long histories within the organizaton. It is they who will promote the various policies nationwide. This group of cadres heads the secretariats created by the DN, and one of their major responsibilities is to see that the purity of the party line is maintained in their specialized fields, to advise the Directive Committees in the departments, and to prevent the rise of deviations of any kind.

3. The State Commission will be in charge of promoting the governmental policy of the FSLN and the organization of Sandinista forces in matters regarding the central government. The Military Commission will have among its functions taking charge of the political work and the organization of Sandinista militants in the armed forces on a national level.

4. Put together as soon as possible the Departmental Directive Committees using the most distinguished cadres, regardless of the area in which they currently work. It is a matter of giving to these leadership bodies the greatest authority possible and converting them into the supervisors of tasks in the departments. In this way, the militant cadres of the FSLN who are engaged in the areas of internal organization, of the masses, the army, and the like, will be perfectly capable of becoming part of the Departmental Directives, devoting the bulk of their energies to the work of leading Sandinista forces. The Directive Committees will maintain ties with the Executive Commission and will receive their instructions from it.

5. Reproduce in the departments the organic framework that will be under the direction of the Directive Committees of the FSLN, which basically entails the creation of Sandinista organizations in the areas of masses, propaganda, education, and the state. We will thus be able to count on a complete political and organizational apparatus through which we can pursue, in an organized way, the extraordinary tasks that have fallen on our shoulders.

6. Organize the membership, resolving first the situation of many comrades, especially those who joined the struggle in the heat of battle and developed great qualities, and who today consider themselves Sandinista militants. A condition for membership is participation in any of the mass organizations and acceptance with revolutionary discipline of the requirements which will be imposed in this category.

7. Immediately select the rank-and-file militants who should be sent to strengthen the organizational work among rural and urban workers and the peasants. We all should be guided by the need to strengthen as soon as possible the Sandinista Workers Central (CST) and the Rural Workers Association (ATC) with militants and cadres. At the same time, we point out to these Sandinista groups the tasks to be achieved and the direction the workers' movement should take with regard to production and the real participation, not subjective or abusive of power, of the class organizations in the revolution.

8. Create organization bases in the municipal administrations in the departments,

sending to accomplish this comrades with recognized authority and broad organizing experience.

9. Place those Sandinistas who are state employees under the direction of the Departmental Directive Committees, at the same time guaranteeing greater political involvement in the tasks of organizing the masses during their free time.

10. Have orderly control over Sandinista militants as well as over those whose organic situation within the organization is being clarified.

Finally, in order to bring to its conclusion this Circular #1, we need say that the different National Secretariats are involved in drafting specific plans to implement our practical policies in each of the fields.

Again, we would like to convey our greetings to you. We have already taken the first step by overthrowing the dictatorship. From now on, we expect our tasks to be more arduous, much more difficult, with stumbling blocks that we will surely overcome. The battle has not yet ended, and while our enemies by their actions are digging their own graves, we Sandinista Revolutionaries continue advancing tirelessly, winning new victories, loyal to the revolution, faithful to our people, developing greater unity, struggling, building the new fatherland and our definitive liberation.

Free Fatherland or Death
NATIONAL DIRECTORATE
Sandinista National Liberation Front
"From the Fatherland of Sandino"—October 1979

NOTES

1. The following translation conforms as closely as possible to the original Spanish text. Material in brackets rather than parentheses, e.g., interpretations of initials or abbreviations, has been inserted to assist the reader. Similarly, minor revisions have been made in the format; e.g., capitalization, paragraph spacing, and indentation, in order to make the translation more readable. Footnotes have been added to clarify certain references in the text.

2. Rigoberto López Pérez assassinated President Anastasio Somoza García in September 1956.

3. In the mid-1970s, the FSLN split into three feuding factions: the Prolonged Popular War faction, led by Tomás Borge; the Proletarian faction, led by Jaime Wheelock; and the Third Force or Insurrectionalist faction, led by Daniel and Humberto Ortega.

4. Juan Bautista Sacasa was president of Nicaragua in the early 1930s.

5. The United People's Movement (MPU), an alliance of twenty-two political, labor, and mass organizations of the left, was formed in July 1978 and was pledged to bring down the Somoza regime.

6. Red and black are the colors of the FSLN flag.

7. One manzana = 1.75 acres.

8. The MANO BLANCA is a right-wing terrorist organization.

9. The CDS are "block committees" modeled after the Cuban Committees for the Defense of the Revolution.

10. These are prominent families in Nicaragua's private sector.

APPENDIX D

The Nicaraguan Constitution – First Draft

This draft constitution was presented to the Nicaraguan National Assembly in February 1986. It is divided into thirteen sections, called Titles, and each Title has one or more Chapters. After the Title numbering reaches ten, it repeats the last three numbers. This English text was furnished by the Embassy of Nicaragua in Washington, D.C. Inconsistencies in capitalization and spelling have been retained.

Title I: Preamble

SOLE CHAPTER: FUNDAMENTAL PRINCIPLES

Article 1—The principles enumerated in this Chapter constitute the interpretive spirit of the National Constitution of the Republic of Nicaragua.

Article 2 – Nicaragua and Nicaraguans Venerate the Heroes and Martyrs. Nicaragua and its people will remember, with gratitude, veneration, and respect, the Heroes and Martyrs of our country. Present and future generations will be educated by their exemplary legacy of heroism and generosity.

Article 3 – The Forces Upon Which Revolutionary Power Rests. Revolutionary power lies in the people: city and rural workers, women, youth, patriotic agricultural and industrial producers, artisans, professionals, technicians, intellectuals, artists, and members of religious orders, all of whom together constitute the majority of the nation's (social) forces and who are the guarantors of the irreversible character of the National and Democratic Revolution in Nicaragua.

Article 4 – Democracy. Democracy is understood to be a combination of the concepts of liberty and equality, just as Sandino dreamt it: "Effective Democracy and Social Justice." In other words, the construction of a society with the real participation of the people where the right to elect and to be elected is affirmed; the right to expression; the right to organize; the right to demonstrate; the right to decent shelter; the right to education, to health, to work. In sum, the right to live with dignity.

A democracy where all the political, economic, and social sectors of the country may participate toward concrete goals and objectives, and where those sectors propose to reestablish and develop the country's economy in order to protect it from destruction and war, to make possible the people's happiness, to eradicate misery, hunger, destruction, and unemployment, and to promote the social development of Nicaragua.

Article 5 – Political Pluralism. Political pluralism means the existence and participation of all political organizations without ideological restrictions except for those that seek a return to Somocismo or advocate the establishment of a political system similar to that of Somocismo.

Article 6 – Mixed Economy. A mixed economy means an economic model where diverse types of property may exist and associate: state-owned, private, mixed, and cooperative ownership, where all have, as their principal objective, the benefit of the people, together with the establishment of reasonable profit margins.

Article 7 – Non-Alignment. Non-alignment is understood to be the principle that guarantees independence from centers of power and the active peaceful co-existence of all States, through our moral solidarity with the struggles of peoples against imperialism, colonialism, apartheid, and racism.

As Nicaraguans we also express our opposition to the existence of military blocs and alliances and recognize the urgent need, through the establishment of a new international economic order, for a restructuring of international relations based on just principles.

Article 8 – Anti-Imperialism. The basis of our anti-imperialism is our country's historic struggle for independence and sovereignty. For this reason we reaffirm our right to self-determination and we reject unjust commercial trade relations that function against developing countries; we reject consideration of Latin American countries as geopolitical reserves and the military, political, and economic intervention against the legitimate sovereign rights of peoples.

Article 9 – Latinamericanism. We understand Latinamericanism to be the ideal of Bolívar and Sandino of achieving the unity of Latin American countries to strengthen and fortify our peoples.

Article 10 – Anti-Interventionism. Nicaragua subscribes to the principle of non-intervention in the internal affairs of other States.

Article 11 – Defense of the Nation. We understand the defense of the nation as the participation of all the people in this defense and in the struggle to preserve the peace as indispensable to the social and economic development of the country.

Article 12 – Sovereignty and National Independence. Sovereignty resides in the People, the legitimate owners of the nation, of its territory, and of its natural resources, all to be used toward the progress of the nation and the social well-being of all Nicaraguans.

Title II

SOLE CHAPTER: GENERAL PROVISIONS

Article 13 – On the State. Nicaragua is a free, sovereign, independent, and unitary State.

Article 14 – Form of Government. Nicaragua is a democratic, participatory, representative, and non-aligned Republic. The organs of government are the Legislative, Executive, Judicial, and Electoral Powers.

Article 15 – Sovereignty. The Nation's sovereignty is one, indivisible, and inalienable: it belongs to the people, who will exercise their sovereignty according to the norms provided by this Constitution.

Article 16 – National Territory. Nicaragua is the territory delimited by the Republics of Honduras and Costa Rica and the Atlantic and Pacific Oceans. The soil, the subsoil, the continental platform, the territorial sea, the underwater insular shelves, the airspace, the stratosphere, the adjacent islands and keys are all part of the national territory. Treaties and the law will determine the parts of the territory that are not delimited.

Article 17 – Supremacy of the Constitution. This national Constitution is the fundamental law of the Republic: all other laws are subordinated to the Constitution. Acts of government bodies, as well as laws, decrees, regulations, orders, provisions, or treaties that explicitly or implicitly oppose the Constitution or alter its provisions will be void.

Article 18 – Nationality. All those so considered by law or treaty are nationals.

Article 19 – Language. Spanish is the official language of the State. The diverse ethnic groups have a right to the free use and development of their languages, since they belong to the national culture.

Article 20 – Capital and Seat of Government. The City of Managua is the Capital of the Republic of Nicaragua and the seat of the State's Powers: they can be reestablished in another part of the national territory if required by exceptional circumstances.

Article 21 – National Symbols. The National Symbols are: the Flag, the Coat of Arms, and the National Anthem established by law. The law determines their characteristics and their use.

Article 22 – The State has no official religion.

Title III

SOLE CHAPTER: THE RIGHTS OF THE NICARAGUAN PEOPLE AS OF PEACE AND SOCIAL ORDER

Article 23 – Defense of the Country and Peace. It is the right of all Nicaraguans to fight for the defense of the Nation and for Peace for the integral development of the Nation.

Article 24 – Right of the Nicaraguan People to Free Determination. The Nicaraguan people have the right to self-determination in the political, economic, social, cultural, and all other spheres of life.

Article 25 – Right of the People to Dispose of Their Natural Resources. The Nicaraguan people have the right to freely dispose of their wealth and natural resources, without prejudice to the obligations derived from international cooperation based on the principles of reciprocal benefit, solidarity, and international law. In no case may the Nicaraguan people be deprived of their own means of substance.

Article 26 – Removal of Obstacles That Hinder Citizen Equality. It is the obligation of the State to remove, by all the means within its reach, the obstacles that effectively hinder the equality of Nicaraguans and their participation in the political, economic, and social life of the country.

Article 27 – Right of the People to Organize. In Nicaragua the urban and rural labor, women, youth, patriotic agricultural and industrial producers, artisans, professions, technicians, intellectuals, artists, and members of religious orders have the right to form organizations to participate in the building of the new society.

Article 28 – Right of the People to Participate in State Affairs. All citizens have the right to participate in the management of the country's public matters and in the fundamental affairs of the State at all levels.

Article 29 – Legal Effect of Human Rights. The State guarantees all unqualified respect, promotion, and protection of Human Rights, as well as the full effect of the Human Rights law subscribed to in the Universal Declaration of Human Rights; the International Agreement on Economic, Social, and Cultural Rights; the International Agreement on Civil and Political Rights of the United Nations; the American Declaration on the Rights and Duties of Man; and in the American Convention on Human Rights of the Organization of American States, all of which are wholly incorporated into this Constitution.

Title IV: National Economy

Chapter 1: Fundamental Principles

Article 30 – Strategic Nature. The Economy is a strategic element of the Nation's development. Its propelling force is derived from labor as the main source for production of wealth.

Article 31 – Satisfaction of Material and Spiritual Needs. The Economy of the Nicaraguan Republic is a strengthening factor for National Sovereignty and for consolidating Democracy. It is directed at the material and spiritual needs of Nicaraguans.

Article 32 – Policy-making Affairs of the State. The direction of the Economy corresponds to the State, which plans and gives orientation to economic activity in order to guarantee national development.

Chapter 2: Forms of Property

Article 33 – The Function of Property. Property, be it individually or collectively owned, fulfills a social function by virtue of which it can be subject to limitations on its title, enjoyment, use, and alienability whether for reasons of security, public interest or utility, social interest, for reasons relating to the national economy, national emergencies or disasters, or for the purpose of agrarian reform.

Article 34 – People's Property. People's property is constituted by all these goods and means of production that have been entrusted to the State for their administration.

Article 35 – Private Property. Private property consists of all those goods and means of production that belong to one or more persons, to the exclusion of others. No one may be deprived of their property unless they are indemnified in accordance with the law.

Article 36 – Mixed Property. The goods and units of production utilized by the State with the participation of other persons, natural or legal, are mixed property.

Article 37 – Cooperative Property. Cooperative property is the voluntary organization of workers for the joint utilization of goods and units of production according to law.

Chapter 3: Agrarian Reform

Article 38 – Objective. Agrarian reform is a fundamental instrument of the economy and of revolutionary transformation. By means of agrarian reform the active participation of farm workers in the economic and social development of the country will be guaranteed.

Article 39 – Latifundia. The State will secure, according to the terms established by the Agrarian Reform Law, the transfer of both the land and the means of production used in its development to the person or persons working that land, through the appropriation of latifundia.

Article 40 – Guarantees to Real Property. The Agrarian Reform will guarantee proprietary rights to the land to those efficient farmers who use it as an instrument of their work, as established by law.

Article 41 – Agricultural Cooperatives. The State will promote the voluntary formation of cooperatives for the development of the land.

Article 42 – Financing. The State will furnish financial and technical assistance to agricultural and cattle-raising production in the People's Property Areas, and in private, mixed and cooperative or other forms of property.

Article 43 – Farm Laborers Participation. In the application of Agrarian Reform and in the organs created by the State to that effect, the participation of agricultural laborers and producers through their organizations is established.

Chapter 4: Commerce

Article 44 – Domestic Trade. The State has the obligation to regulate and oversee domestic trade in order to guarantee consumer defense. The law will establish the scope of State action.

Article 45 – Foreign Trade. The State formulates, carries out, promotes, and oversees Foreign Trade policy in order to secure the country's development and the diversification of markets to promote economic independence.

Article 46 – The State will promote active participation in international organizations associated with foreign trade, especially with Central and Latin American countries.

Chapter 5: Foreign Investment

Article 47 – Foreign investment complements domestic investment. Likewise, it shall contribute to the country's development, conform to the law, and not damage National Sovereignty.

Article 48 – The State will ensure that technical knowledge derived from foreign investment will be transferred to it or to its subjects and that the State or its subjects adequately participate in the ownership and administration of the enterprises.

Chapter 6: Regarding the Budget of the Republic

Article 49 – Objective. The Nation's General Budget will monitor all income and its declared sources; expenditures will be structured in such a way as to agree with the production of goods and services in order to determine the expenditure limits of State Bodies.

Article 50 – Fiscal Year. The Public Sector Budget year begins on January 1st and ends on December 31st. The Budget will be drafted, and then approved by the President of the Republic by means of the Annual Budget Law.

Article 51 – Its Consideration. The budget will be considered by the National Assembly.

Chapter 7: Tax System

Article 52 – System of Taxation. The Law will determine the system of taxation, which shall take into account the distribution of wealth and income as well as the needs of the State.

Article 53 – Tax. Taxes shall be created by the law that will establish the incidence of taxation, the type of taxation, and the taxpayer guarantees.

Article 54 – Tax Evasion a Crime. The non-payment of taxes due and tax evasion are crimes.

Article 55 – Prohibition. The State will not demand payment of taxes that have not previously been established by law.

Title V

Sole Chapter: National Defense

Article 56 – Nature. The nature of national defense is defined by the Nicaraguan people's dedication to peace and their unyielding will to permanently and integrally defend the vital interests of the Nation and the triumph of the Revolution.

Article 57 – Social Basis of Defense. The social basis of the integral defense of the Nation are all levels and social sectors that make up Nicaraguan society.

Article 58 – Popular Participation. National Defense against military, political, or economic aggression, either external or internal, is guaranteed by means of popular organized participation.

Title VI: Rights, Duties, and Guarantees of the Nicaraguan People

Chapter 1: Individual and Civil Rights

Article 59 – Inviolability of the Right to Live. The right to live is inviolable and inherent to the human being. In Nicaragua there is no death penalty.

Article 60 – Personal Liberty. All persons have the right to individual liberty and security. No one may be subjected to arbitrary detention or imprisonment, nor deprived of their freedom, except for causes determined by the law and in keeping with legal procedures.

Article 61 – Protection of and Respect for Private Life. All persons shall have the right to private and family lives, to the inviolability of their residences, their correspondence or communications, to their honor and reputation.

Article 62 – Equality Before the Law. All persons are equal before the law and have a right to equal protection.

Article 63 – Freedom of Expression. All Nicaraguans have the right to express their thoughts.

Article 64 – Freedom of Movement. Anyone on national territory shall have the right to move freely and to select a place of residence. The Nicaraguan people shall have the right to enter and leave the country freely.

Article 65 – Freedom of Conscience, Thought, and Religion. All persons have the right to freedom of conscience, of thought, and of professing a religion or not. No one may be the object of coercive measures that might impair the right to hold or adopt the beliefs of his/her choosing.

Article 66 – Retroactivity of the Penal Law Benefit the Offender. The Penal Laws retroactive effect in favor of the offender.

Article 67 – Principle of Legality. No functionary has more authority than that established by the Constitution and the Laws. No one is obliged to do that which is not required by Law, nor is hindered from doing what the Law does not forbid.

Article 68 – Right to Criminal Procedure Guarantees. All persons have the right of individual freedom and personal security. No one may be subjected to arbitrary detention or imprisonment, nor be deprived of freedom, except for the causes determined by Law and in keeping with legal procedure.

Consequently:

1. Detention can occur only by virtue of the written order of a competent judge or of the authorities expressly designated by law, except in the case of a flagrant crime.

2. All persons detained shall have the right:

    a. To be informed without delay and in detail, in a language or tongue they understand, of the nature and causes of the accusation made against them.

    b. To be brought, within the time established by Law, before the competent authority or to be freed.

    c. To obtain reparations in case of illegal detention.

Article 69 – Everything else being equal, all defendants shall have the following minimal guarantees:

    a. They are presumed innocent until their guilt is proven in conformity with the law.

    b. They are guaranteed participation and defense from the beginning of the process.

    c. They are not obliged to testify against themselves or their relatives, nor to make a confession of guilt.

    d. They may not be tried for a crime for which they have already been condemned or acquitted by a definitive sentence.

    e. They may not be tried or condemned for an act or an omission which at the time of its commission had not previously been expressly and inequivocably designated by law as punishable offense, or be sanctioned with penalties not foreseen in the law.

Article 70 – Minors may not be subjects or objects of judgment, nor be subjected to any judicial proceeding. The law shall regulate this area.

Article 71 – Prohibition of Degrading Punishment. No one shall be subjected to torture or to penalties or treatment that is cruel, inhuman, or degrading. No punishment may be imposed for more than 30 years.

Article 72 – Respect for Physical, Psychological, and Moral Integrity. All persons have the right to respect their physical, psychological, and moral integrity. *The penalty shall affect only the defendant's person.*

Article 73 – Habeas Corpus Appeal. The Remedy of habeas corpus shall be presented before a competent Court in accordance with the law by the persons designated under that law.

Article 74 – Writ of Prohibition *(recurso de amparo)**. The Writ of Prohibition is established, whereby all citizens whose rights and liberties as recognized under the present Constitution shall have been affected, may present an appeal for a writ of prohibition in accordance with the Law.

Article 75 – Prohibition of Slavery, Servitude, and Trafficking in Persons. No one shall be subjected to slavery and servitude. Any kind of slavery and trafficking in persons is prohibited in all its forms.

Article 76 – No Imprisonment for Debt. No one shall be imprisoned solely for failure to comply with financial obligation, whatever its origin.

Article 77 – Right to Enjoy Constitutional Guarantees. The State respects and guarantees the rights and guarantees established in this Constitution to all persons who are in its territory and are subject to its jurisdiction.

Chapter 2: Political Rights

Article 78 – Citizenship. All native or naturalized Nicaraguans having reached the age of 16 are citizens. Citizens enjoy the political rights subscribed to by the laws in force.

Article 79 – Right to Petition. All Nicaraguans have the right to petition the State or any authority and to obtain a prompt answer and resolution.

Article 80 – Right to Assemble. The right to peacefully assemble on private property does not require prior permission.

Article 81 – Right to Public Meeting or Demonstration. The right to a public meeting or demonstration shall be regulated by the respective Law.

Article 82 – Right to Elect and to Be Elected. All citizens have the right to elect and to be elected.

Article 83 – Right to Be a Candidate for Public Office. All citizens shall have the right to be candidates for public office.

Article 84 – Right to Organize Political Parties. All citizens shall have the right to organize political parties with the object, among others, of aspiring to obtain political power to carry out a program that responds to the needs of national development.

Political parties are institutions of public law. They shall be regulated in accordance with the Law.

Article 85 – Right to Asylum. In Nicaragua the right to asylum is guaranteed to those

---

*A constitutional provision peculiar to Mexico which resembles United States writs of prohibition, certiorari, injunction, and habeas corpus.

who are persecuted for struggling for peace, justice, and the recognition or extension of human, civil, political, social, economic, and cultural rights.

The Law shall define who is a political exile or refugee.

Article 86 – Prohibition of Extradition. In Nicaragua there is no extradition for political offenses or common offenses connected with them according to Nicaraguan definition. No Nicaraguan may be the object of extradition from the national territory.

If for some reason the expulsion of a person who has been granted asylum is agreed to s/he shall never be sent to the country in which s/he was persecuted.

Extradition shall be regulated by Law and by International Treaties.

Article 87 – Suspension of Political Rights. Political Rights are suspended or lost on the grounds established by the respective laws.

CHAPTER 3: SOCIAL RIGHTS

Article 88 – Right to Religious Worship. All persons both individually and collectively have the right to express their religious beliefs in public or in private, through worship, the celebration of rites, practices, and teaching, all in conformity with the laws.

No one may invoke religious beliefs or disciplines in order to elude compliance with the laws or to impede others from exercising their rights.

Article 89 – Right to Information. The right to information is a social responsibility and shall be exercised without impairing the right of those informed nor the values of the Nicaraguan people.

Article 90 – Social Security and Welfare. All persons have the right to Social Security and Welfare in accordance with the law in that area.

Article 91 – Protection of Combatants. The State guarantees attention through all its programs to the Nation's Combatants and to the families of those who have fallen in the defense of the nation, in accordance with the laws.

Article 92 – Right to Nourishment. The Nicaraguans have the right to be protected from hunger. The State shall promote programs that will assure an adequate availability and an equitable distribution of food.

Article 93 – Right to Health. All Nicaraguans have the right to health. The health of the Nicaraguans constitutes a public good.

The State shall provide free health care to Nicaraguans and has the obligation to adopt measures so that Nicaraguans enjoy optimal conditions of physical and mental health.

Article 94 – Health Services (*journadas de salud*). The State shall promote community health services through the corresponding organization with the participation of the people.

Article 95 – Right to Housing. The Nicaraguans have the right to decent housing, in conditions of hygiene, comfort, and security that guarantee family privacy.

Article 97* – Protection, Recovering, and Conservation of the Environment. All persons have the right to freely meet or associate with others for licit ends.

Nicaraguans have the right to establish and promote popular, community, neighborhood, and rural organizations.

**Editors' Note:* There is no Article 96 in the text, and the heading of Article 97 does not seem to belong to the provisions.

Article 98 – Right to Recreation and Relaxation. The Nicaraguans have the right to recreation and relaxation. The State guarantees these rights through specific programs and projects.

Chapter 4: Rights of the Family

Article 99 – Protection of the Family. The family is the natural and fundamental nucleus of society and has the right to be protected by the society and the State.

Article 100 – Right to Form a Home. The right of the Nicaraguans to constitute a family is recognized. It can be constituted through marriage or a *de facto* union.

Article 101 – Equality of the Couple. Family relations rest on the absolute equality of rights and responsibilities between men and women.

Article 102 – Patria Potestas. Patria Potestas shall be exercised in accordance with the law of Relations Between Mother, Father, and Children. Parents must maintain their home and the formation of the children through their common effort.

In turn, children are obligated to respect and help their parents.

Article 103 – Protection of Maternity. The State shall give special protection to mothers during pregnancy. During the pre- and post-natal periods working mothers must be given paid leaves and adequate benefits of social security. Parents have the right to expect the State to care for their minor children while the parents are at their work places.

Article 104 – Equality of Children. All children have equal rights. No discriminatory designations shall be used with regard to parents-child relationships.

Article 105 – Protection of Minors. All minors have a right to protection measures required by their age, or the part of their families as well as society and the State.

Article 106 – On Paternity. The State protects responsible paternity. The right to investigate paternity in accordance with the Law is established.

Article 107 – Right to Adoption. All legally capable Nicaraguans have the right to adopt minors, exclusively in the interest of the minor's integral development, in accordance with what has been established by Law.

Article 108 – Family. The State guarantees the establishment of family patrimony, as inalienable, unattachable, and exempt from all public encumbrances; the law shall determine its function.

Chapter 5: Economic Rights

Article 109 – All workers have the right to participate in the elaboration, oversight, and execution of all the major economic and social measures that the State may promote.

Article 110 – Duty of the State to Remove Obstacles That Hinder Economic Equality. The State shall promote the economic well-being of the Nicaraguans to eliminate the obstacles that impede economic equality.

Article 111 – Equitable Distribution of Wealth. The State shall set forth the necessary corrective measures in order to achieve an equitable distribution of wealth and income among all citizens.

Article 112 – Decent Material Life. The State shall try to guarantee the harmonious development of all productive forces and the just distribution of the national product in order to guarantee a decent material life to the Nicaraguan people.

Title VII: Labor Rights

Article 113—Right to Work. Work is a right and a social responsibility of all persons. It is the obligation of the State to procure full and productive work for all Nicaraguans under conditions that guarantee the fundamental rights of human beings.

Article 114—Participation of Workers in Their Places of Work. All laborers through their organizations have the right to make use of diverse forms of participation in their places of work, in conformity with the law.

Article 115—Workers' Rights. All workers have the right to enjoy equitable and satisfactory working conditions that especially guarantee them:

    a. *Equal wages for equal work.* Equal wages for equal work in identical conditions of efficiency and adequate to their social responsibility with no discrimination by reason of sex, that will assure a well-being compatible with human dignity.

    b. *Payment in legal tender.* To receive wages in legal tender.

    c. *Unattachable minimum wage.* An unattachable minimum wage, except for attachments toward the protection of the laborer's family in accordance with the law.

    d. *Workday, weekly rest, vacations.* A limited workday, a weekly rest, and vacations regulated by the law.

    e. *Work stability.* Workers have the right to stability in their work in conformity with the law.

Article 116—Right to Strike. The right to Strike is recognized, and is to be exercised in the matter established by law.

Article 117—Right to Social Security. The State guarantees the right of workers to Social Security with all the benefits and protections contemplated by the law; and which can be added to. The law shall also regulate the progressive integration of all levels of society.

Article 118—Work of Minors. Work by minors is prohibited, when incompatible with their physical capabilities or dangerous to their moral development.

Article 119—Right to Training. Laborers have the right to cultural and technical skills training. The State shall facilitate this through special programs.

Article 120—Right to Freely Associate in Unions. Laborers are guaranteed the freedom to associate in unions; in exercise of this freedom they may establish unions at all levels. No laborer shall be forced to belong to a specific union.

Article 121—Autonomy of Unions. Laborers are guaranteed autonomy to establish those organizations they may deem necessary.

Article 122—Individual Contract and Collective Agreement. Laborers are able to execute contracts, and collective agreements with their employers, subject to the provisions of the law.

Title VIII: Education and Culture

Article 123—Education. Education has as a goal the development in Nicaraguans of a critical and liberating consciousness under the principles established in the Constitution. It must also be scientific, based on a knowledge of history and the national reality, on the domain of science, or participation in the development of the revolution, on social justice, and on human solidarity.

Article 124 – Educational Policy. The State in directing education shall promote the democratization of education and its conditions, so that, through the means available to it, it may contribute to the development of the personality and the establishment of a democratic society with social justice.

Article 125 – Right to Culture. It is the State's role to stimulate all expressions of literacy, artistic, craft, and folkloric production, so that a truly popular Nicaraguan culture may be built.

Article 126 – Academic Freedom. The State guarantees academic freedom in conformity with the plans and programs approved by the State and in accordance with law and public order. Primary education shall be obligatory.

Article 127 – Secular Education in State Schools. In public schools education shall be secular.

Article 128 – Religious Education in Private Schools. Non-obligatory religious teaching is authorized in private schools.

Article 129 – Obligations of Parents. Parents have the obligation to contribute, along with the schools, to the educational process of their children.

Article 130 – Free Education. Education shall be free at all levels; university education shall be regulated in accordance with the law.

Article 131 – Literacy. A permanent literacy and adult education campaign shall be maintained, with the goal of raising the educational and cultural levels of the Nicaraguans.

Article 132 – Academic Autonomy and Liberty. Education, administrative, and economic autonomy of the Universities is guaranteed, in order that they respond to the country's need for transformation within the national plans for development. The State will provide the necessary economic support so that they may develop a creative curriculum and scientific research appropriate to the national reality. Academic and research freedoms are guaranteed as essential principles of education at all levels.

Article 133 – Coordination of Higher Education. In order to coordinate higher education there will be a National Council for Higher Education. The law shall determine its composition and attributes.

Article 134 – Copyright. The State guarantees authors' copyright, and that of inventors, and artists. The law shall regulate in this area.

Article 135 – Cultural and Historic Patrimony. The State shall have the obligation of preserving, maintaining, and conserving all monuments, paleontological, archaeological, historical, cultural, and artistic objects of the country, situated in the territory of the Republic, whoever their owner may be. The law shall determine the provisions for their conservation, restoration, maintenance, and restitution.

Article 136 – Right to Sports. The practice of physical education and sports shall be stimulated by all means as a part of the integral development of the person.

Title IX: Citizens' Duties

Article 137 – All persons have duties with regard to family, community, the Nation, and Humanity. The rights of all persons are limited by the rights of others, by security, and by the just demands of the common good.

Article 138 – Service to and Defense of the Nation. It is the duty of all Nicaraguan citizens to fight for the defense of the Nation and for the maintenance of Peace.

Article 139 – Military Service. All Nicaraguans have the duty to serve in the military in accordance with law.

Article 140 – Observance of the Constitution. It is the duty of all citizens to respect and obey the provisions contained in the Constitution and in the laws in force.

Article 141 – Contribution to Public Expenditures. All Nicaraguans have the duty to contribute to public expenditures through the payment of taxes created by the law.

Article 142 – Efficient and Honest Performance in Public Office. All citizens who hold public office in the Government or in State institutions are obligated efficiently and honestly to fulfill their duties.

Title X: On the Organization of the State

Chapter 1: General Principles

Article 143 – On the Powers of the State. The Powers of the State are: the Legislative, the Executive, the Judicial, and the Electoral. The Functions of the State Powers are determined in this Constitution.

Article 144 – Independence and Interrelation. In the exercise of their functions, each one of the State Powers shall have its own activities, but they shall collaborate among themselves in accomplishing the State's goals.

Chapter 2: Legislative Power

Article 145 – Exercise. The Legislative function is exercised by the National Assembly.

Article 146 – Composition. The National Assembly shall be composed of ninety Representatives of the nation with their respective alternatives. In addition, candidates for President and Vice President of the Republic shall be part of the National Assembly as seatholder and alternate respectively, as long as they have obtained in the national territory a number of votes equal or superior to the average of the regional quotients.

Article 147 – Qualifications. In order to be a Representative in the National Assembly, the following qualifications are required:

    a. To be a native of Nicaragua and in full enjoyment of his/her rights.

    b. To be over 21 years of age.

Article 148 – Terms of Office. The representatives of the National Assembly shall be elected for a term of six years.

Article 149 – Attributions. The responsibilities of the National Assembly are:

    1. To elaborate and approve laws and decrees as well as to reform and repeal the existing ones. It shall also have the authentic interpretation of the law.

    2. To decree amnesty and pardons of penal sanctions, as well as commutations or reductions of sentences in conformity with the Law of Pardon.

    3. To solicit reports and examine the Ministers or Vice Ministers of State, Presidents of Autonomous Entities, and Directors of Governmental Entities, as well as summon them to appear.

4. To grant and cancel the legal personality of civil or religious entities.

5. To consider the General Budget of the Republic in conformity with the procedure established in the present Constitution.

6. To enact laws regulating inversions by foreigners.

7. To acknowledge and accept the resignation of Representatives.

8. To ratify, or not ratify, international agreements, treaties, or negotiations.

9. To regulate everything relating to the national symbols (the Flag, the Coat of Arms, the National Anthem).

10. To create Honors and Distinctions of national character.

11. To receive [in] solemn session the annual report of the President of the Republic.

12. To delegate legislative powers to the President of the Republic, except for those powers which relate to the laws of the Republic.

13. To create permanent and special commissions.

14. To appoint research commissions for any matter of public interest or to delegate that work to the appropriate permanent commissions.

Their conclusions will not be binding for the courts, nor will they affect judicial resolutions; the result of the research will be communicated to the Minister of Justice for proper action if necessary.

The National [Assembly] has power to issue subpoenas; the law will regulate what actions can be taken to deal with non-compliance.

15. To grant pensions and honors to individuals for outstanding services to the Nation and to humanity.

16. To reform the political and administrative division of the Nation.

17. To fill presidential and vice presidential vacancies, if both are definitive vacancies.

18. To authorize the President of the Republic to leave the national territory if his absence should last more than two months.

19. To acknowledge and resolve complaints presented against public officials who enjoy immunity.

20. To appoint the Magistrates of the Supreme Court of Justice and the members of the Supreme Electoral Council, selected from slates of three candidates proposed by the President of the Republic.

21. To determine its own statute and internal rules.

Article 150 – Election. Representatives shall be elected by means of a popular, secret, and direct ballot, according to the system of proportional representation in judicial districts determined by law.

Article 151 – Immunity. Representatives will be free from responsibility for their opinions and votes in the National Assembly and will have immunity in accordance with the law.

Article 152 – Executive Committee. The National Assembly will be presided by an executive committee formed by one president, three vice presidents, and three secretaries.

Article 153 – Commissions. There will be two types of commissions: permanent and special. Permanent commissions shall be responsible for studying and ruling on drafts of legislation submitted to the National Assembly for consideration. Special commissions shall perform occasional functions, which will be determined by the National Assembly upon their proposal by the Presidency. Both types of commissions shall be appointed by the President of the National Assembly, after consultation with the Executive Committee.

Article 154 – Introduction of Bills. The Representatives of the National Assembly and the President of the Republic may introduce Bills. The Supreme Court of Justice and the Supreme Electoral Council may also do so in matters of their competence.

Article 155 – Bills presented by the President of the Republic, the Supreme Court of Justice, and the Supreme Electoral Council in agreement with the preceding article will be sent directly to Commission.

In case of emergency concerning Bills from the Executive, the President of the National Assembly will submit them immediately to the whole Assembly for discussion, if the Bill had been given to the Representatives forty-eight hours in advance.

Article 156 – Procedure and Debate. The regulations and general statute of the National Assembly shall determine the procedure in regard to Bills and the method of conducting debates in the sessions.

Article 157 – Sanction, Promulgation, and Publication. Once a Bill is approved by the National Assembly, the final text, after discussions and revision, shall be written in three original documents. All three shall be signed by the president and the secretary of the National Assembly, with the date of the Bill's approval. One of the documents shall be filed in the National Assembly archives; the other two shall be sent to the President of the Republic for sanction, promulgation, and publication. The President will return one of them to the National Assembly to be filed. The length of time allowed for the sanction shall be fifteen days.

Article 158 – Veto. The President of the Republic shall have the right to veto any Bill, rejecting it totally or partially, within fifteen days of the date of receipt.

Article 159 – If the President does not exercise the right to veto in the established period of time and does not promulgate the law, the President of the National Assembly shall promulgate the law and order its publication.

Article 160 – A Bill totally vetoed by the President of the Republic shall be brought back by the Secretary to the National Assembly to be debated in the plenary session. The President of the Republic, at the time, shall state the reasons for his veto.

If the veto of the President is rejected by vote by 60 per cent of the attending representatives, the National Assembly shall sanction, promulgate, and publish the law.

Article 161. If the President of the Republic partially vetoes a Bill, and proposes reforms, suppressions, or additions to it, the Bill shall be returned to the National Assembly by the Secretary, with an explanation of the reasons for such proposed changes.

In all cases, the Bill shall be sent to the President of the Republic for its sanction, promulgation, and publication. If this is not done in fifteen days, the process established here shall be followed.

CHAPTER 3: EXECUTIVE POWER

Article 162 – Exercise. The executive power belong to the President of the Republic of Nicaragua. The President of the Republic is the head of the State and the Commander in Chief of the Armed Forces.

Article 163 – The Vice President of the Republic. The Vice President of the Republic shall perform the functions delegated to him by the President and shall replace the President if a temporary or definitive vacancy occurs in the Presidency.

Article 164 – Election. The President and Vice President shall be elected by relative majority of votes, obtained by popular, direct, and secret ballot.

Article 165 – Qualifications. To be elected President or Vice President the following qualifications are required:

   a. to be a Nicaraguan national in full possession of all his rights.
   b. to be over 25 years of age.
   c. not to be a member of a religious order.

Article 166 – Term. The presidential term will last six years from the date of inauguration, by oath or affirmation before the National Assembly.

Article 167 – Substitution for Temporary Absence. If a temporary and simultaneous absence of the President and Vice President should occur, the President shall appoint one of the Ministers, according to regulations, to act in his place.

Article 168 – Substitution for Definitive Absence. If a definitive absence of both the President and the Vice President of the Republic should occur, the National Assembly shall determine how to proceed.

Article 169 – Prerogatives of the President. The President of the Republic has the following attributions:

1. To enforce the Political Constitution and the laws.
2. To exercise the power of introduction of Bills as established in this Constitution.
3. To formulate executive orders considered as laws when they are:
   a. of fiscal and administrative nature.
   b. related to international economic or political agreements, including those related to foreign debt.
   c. for developing and approving the General Budget of the Republic.
4. To appoint Ministers as Delegates of the Government in all geographical jurisdictions included in the national territory.
5. To appoint the Mayor of the capital of the Nation.
6. To assume the legislative power that the National Assembly shall delegate during its period of recess.
7. To conduct the foreign relations of the Republic and sign international treaties and agreements.
8. To declare a state of emergency on occasions foreseen by this Political Constitution. The state of emergency shall be ratified by the National Assembly within ninety days. In case of war such ratification is not necessary.
9. To appoint or to remove from office Ministers and Vice Ministers of the State, Presidents of Autonomous Entities, and other officials whose appointments or dismissal is not otherwise determined by the Constitution or by law.
10. To appoint the Heads of the Diplomatic Missions.
11. To totally or partially regulate the laws, according to their context or purpose.
12. To sign agreements of national interest.
13. To declare war.
14. To establish by decree additional credits to the Budget and send it to the National Assembly for acceptance.

15. To award national Honors and Decorations.
16. To direct the Public Administration.
17. To propose slates of three candidates to the National Assembly for the election of Magistrates of the Supreme Court of Justice and of members of the Supreme Electoral Council.
18. To present information or special reports to the National Assembly, either personally or through the Vice President.
19. All other attributions noted in the Constitution or regulated by law.

Section I: Ministers of the State

Article 170 – Function. In the exercise of his duties, the President of the Republic shall be advised by Ministers, Vice Ministers, Presidents of Autonomous Entities, and other officials considered appropriate for the welfare of the public administration.

Article 171 – Qualifications. To be a Minister, a Vice Minister, or a President of an Autonomous Entity, the following qualifications are required:
  a. to be a Nicaraguan.
  b. to be over 21 years old.
  c. to have the full exercise of political and civil rights.

Article 172 – Responsibility. Ministers are responsible for their actions, as stated in this Constitution and in the laws.

Article 173 – Number and Organization of Ministries. The law shall determine the number and organizations of the Ministries of State and Autonomous Entities, as well as their respective competences.

Article 174 – Duties of the Civil Servants. Public and civil servants in the exercise of their functions must strictly fulfill their duties to the State. The use of State resources for purposes other than public functions is forbidden. All activities related to any political party cannot be carried out during working hours.

Section II

Article 175 – General Controller of the Republic. The duties of the Public Controller of the Republic are to audit, control, and supervise the income, expenditures, and national or connected goods, as well as all operations related to all the above.

Article 176 – Organization and Operation. The law shall determine the organization of the Office of the General Controller of the Republic.

Section III: The Sandinista Armed Forces

Article 177 – Nature. Because of its highly popular and democratic nature, the Sandinista Armed Forces are the strategic instrument of national defense and revolutionary gains, of public security, and for the preservation of inner stability. The People in Arms, as basis of the Sandinista Armed Forces, guarantee the sovereignty and territorial integrity of the nation.

Article 178 – The Sandinista Armed Forces are strictly governed by this Constitution, by its constitutional laws, and by all other military laws and regulations.

Article 179 – The Sandinista Armed Forces are the only armed body of the nation. The organization and operation of any other armed groups is forbidden and shall be penalized by the laws of the Republic.

Article 180 – Structure, Command, and Operation. The Sandinista Armed Forces have a national, patriotic, and popular nature. The Law shall regulate its structure, command, and operation.

The Sandinista Armed Forces are organized according to the principle of a single and vertical command that shall be exercised in accordance with the established hierarchical structure.

Article 181 – Civil Defense. The civil defense shall be organized by the Sandinista Armed Forces with active participation of the people. The Law shall regulate its actions and operations. Its main objective shall be to serve the population in case of war or natural disaster.

Section IV: State of Emergency

Article 182 – The President of the Republic may declare a state of emergency for a limited or extended period of time in all or in part of the national territory. The decree must be ratified by the National Assembly within ninety days. In case of war such ratification is not necessary.

Article 183 – Reasons for a State of Emergency. The state of emergency may be declared:

1. If the nation were engaged in international war or in imminent danger of a foreign invasion.
2. If natural disasters occur, such as earthquakes, flooding, epidemics, or any other public calamity.
3. If maintenance of peace or national security are in danger for any reason.

Article 184 – Guarantees That Cannot Be Suspended. The President of the Republic shall not have the power to suspend the Rights, Duties, and Guarantees established in the following articles of this Constitution: 59, 62, 63, 65, 67, 69, 70, 71, 72, 75, 76, 82, 83, 85, 86, 88, 90–115, 117–142.

CHAPTER 4: JUDICIAL POWER

Article 185 – The People, Source of Justice. Justice emanates from the people and shall be enforced in their name and as their delegates by the Courts of Justice determined by Law.

Article 186 – Legality and Human Rights Guarantee. The administration of justice guarantees the principle of legality and protects and guards all human rights through the enforcement of the Law in matters of its competence.

Article 187 – Judicial Power. The judicial power is represented by the Supreme Court of Justice and other agencies established by Law.

Article 188 – Supreme Court of Justice. The Supreme Court of Justice is the highest Court of the Republic and holds the representation of the Judicial Power.

Article 189 – Popular Participation. The administration of justice shall be organized and shall operate with popular participation. Appropriate laws shall determine such participation.

Article 190 – Characteristics of the Courts of Justice. The Courts of Justice shall be formed by three or more members in accordance with the law, which shall also determine the qualifications of their members.

Article 191 – Term of Service. The term of service for the Magistrates of the Supreme Court of Justice shall be the same period of time determined for the members of the National Assembly. The law shall decide the length of term of service for members of all other Courts.

Article 192 – Dismissal. The members of the Supreme Court of Justice may only be dismissed during their term of service by a just cause duly proven.

Article 193 – Election of Magistrates. The National Assembly shall elect the members of the Supreme Court of Justice from slates of three candidates presented by the President of the Republic.

Article 194 – Special Laws. The organic law of the Courts of Justice shall rule in any matter not included in this Constitution and pertaining to the Judicial Power.

Article 195 – Principle of Independence. The Judicial Power is independent from any other power of the State.

Article 196 – Unity and Exclusiveness. The Courts of Justice form a unitary system where the Supreme Court of Justice is the highest organism. The exercise of jurisdiction belongs exclusively to the Courts, excepting what the law regulates in military and agricultural matters and in matters related to maintaining the security of the State.

The Supreme Court of Justice shall be notified, by means determined by law, of any official appeal against a decision of the Court.

Article 197 – Judicial Profession. The Judicial profession is established according to the law of the matter.

Special Section: Constitutional Control

Article 198 – Appeal Because of Unconstitutionality. The appeal because of unconstitutionality is established against any law, act, or regulation that is contrary to what is prescribed by the Constitution.

Article 199 – Competent Body. The Supreme Court of Justice is the competent body to deal with appeals because of unconstitutionality.

A corresponding law will determine how to proceed.

Article 200 – Persons Who Can Legally File an Appeal. An appeal because of unconstitutionality may be legally filed by:
  a. The President of the Republic.
  b. The President of the Supreme Electoral Council in matters of his competence.
  c. Forty-nine representatives in the National Assembly.
  d. The signatures of thirty thousand citizens duly verified according to law.

Article 201 – Individual Appeal. The individual appeal is established against any disposition, action, or resolution, and in general against any action or omission of any official, authority, or any of their agents, that violate or show intent to violate the rights and guarantees asserted in the Constitution. The corresponding law will determine how to proceed.

CHAPTER 5: ELECTORAL POWER

Article 202 – Electoral Power. The organization, management, and control of all actions related to voting are the exclusive competence of the Supreme Electoral Council.

Article 203 – Composition. The Supreme Electoral Council shall be formed by five members and their respective substitutes, elected by the National Assembly from slates of three candidates proposed by the President of the Republic.

Article 204 – Qualifications. To be a member of the Electoral Council the following qualifications are required:
  a. to be a native of Nicaragua.
  b. to be over 25 years old.
  c. not to be a member of a religious order.
  d. to have full exercise of political and citizen rights.

Article 205 – Attributions. The attributions of the Supreme Electoral Council are:
  a. to initiate the electoral process.
  b. to appoint the members of all electoral bodies according to the electoral law.
  c. to enforce constitutional and legal dispositions related to the electoral law.
  d. to know the outcome of the resolutions adopted by subordinate electoral bodies.
  e. to institute the necessary measures so that, according to law, the electoral process be developed with full guarantees.
  f. to be in charge of the final count of votes in the presidential and vice presidential elections, and in the elections of representatives to the National Assembly and other authorities.
  g. to give the final results of the election of the President and Vice President of the Republic, and of the Representatives to the National Assembly and other authorities in the period of time determined by law.
  h. to issue its own bylaws.
  i. all other functions indicated by law.

Article 206 – Term of Service. The members of the Electoral Council shall serve for a term of six years.

Title VIII: Political Administrative Division of the Nation*

CHAPTER 1

Article 207 – Criteria of Territorial Division. For administrative purposes, the national territory shall be divided into several geographic circumscriptions. The following criteria will be adopted:
  a. strategic location from the point of view of national defense and economy.
  b. dedication to culture and production.
  c. population density.
  d. historical tradition.
  e. special circumstances.

The law of the matter shall determine the number of circumscriptions, and their organization, structure, and operation.

Article 208 – Municipality. The municipality, considered as the basic unit of the political administrative division of the nation, shall be organized according to what is es-

---
*Editors' Note: The last three Titles of the Constitution repeat the numbers of the previous three; there are therefore two Titles called VIII, two IX, and two X.

tablished by law. The government and administration of municipalities shall be the responsibility of local authority with autonomy, but in cooperation with the central government. The law shall regulate how the election of local authority must proceed.

Article 209—Integral Development. The state guarantees the establishment of integral development among the different areas of the Nicaraguan Territory.

CHAPTER 2: AUTONOMY OF NATIVE PEOPLE AND COMMUNITIES IN THE ATLANTIC COAST

Article 210—Native peoples and communities of the Atlantic coast of Nicaragua have the right to preserve and develop their cultural traditions, their historical and religious heritage; the right of free use and development of their languages; the right to organize their social and productive activities according to their values and traditions. The culture and traditions of native peoples and communities of the Atlantic coast are part of the national culture.

Title IX*

SOLE CHAPTER: CONSTITUTIONAL REFORM

Article 211—To Initiate Reform. The National Assembly may partially reform this Constitution at the request of the President of the Republic, or at the request of forty Representatives to the National Assembly, or by a petition with forty thousand signatures duly verified.

Article 212—Proceedings. The proceedings shall be the following:
  a. The reform proposal must contain the text of the articles to be reformed and a rationale of the motives in which the proposal is based.
  b. The proposal shall be sent to a special commission appointed by the president of the National Assembly.
  c. The commission shall adopt a resolution within sixty days.
  d. After presenting the resolution, discussion of same will be held following the established procedures for the adoption of laws. A consitutional reform must be approved by 60 per cent of the whole membership of the National Assembly.

Article 213—Veto. The President of the Republic may use the right to veto as established in the Constitution.

Article 214—Article That May Be Considered for Reform. No constitutional reform may be considered in matters related to the popular nature of the Revolution, to democracy, to the National defense, to anti-imperialism, to non-alignment, to anti-interventionism, and to Latino-Americanism.

Title X*

SOLE CHAPTER: FINAL AND TRANSITORY DISPOSITIONS

Article 215—Validity. The Fundamental Statute and the Statute of Rights and Guarantees shall be in effect until this Constitution is adopted and promulgated. Then where it says "State Council" it shall be read "National Assembly" and where it says "Commission for National Reconstruction" it shall be read "President of the Republic" in all the laws of the Republic.

Article 216—Executive Order. All executive orders issued by the Commission for National Reconstruction and by the Government of the Republic since July 19, 1979, are recognized as valid and effective.

Article 217—Publication of the Constitution. This constitution shall be published and widely distributed in the official language. It will also be translated into the ethnic languages of the Atlantic coast for its distribution there.

Article 218—Body of Laws. Pending its modification or repeal, the existing body of laws shall be maintained, as long as it is not contrary to the Constitution.

Article 219—Organization of the Judicial Power. The present structure and organization of the Judicial Power shall be maintained so long as a law for a new organization is not enacted.

Article 220—Present Political and Administrative Division of the Nation. The existing political and administrative division of the National Territory shall remain until a law of the matter be enacted.

Article 221—Manuscripts. Four manuscripts of this Constitution shall be signed by the President of the National Assembly, by Representatives of the National Assembly, by the President of the Republic, and by a Nicaraguan mother on behalf of the mothers of the heroes and martyrs of the nation. Each one of the four manuscripts shall be respectively kept in: the Presidency of the National Assembly, the Presidency of the Republic, the Presidency of the Supreme Court, and the Presidency of the Electoral Council. Each manuscript shall be considered to be the original text of the political Constitution of Nicaragua. The President of the Republic shall have it published in *La Gaceta*, the official newspaper.

This draft of the Political Constitution has been presented by the Special Constitutional Commission to the Plenary Session of the National Assembly on February 21, 1986.

Bibliographical Essay

PRIOR TO THE Nicaraguan and Salvadoran revolutions of 1979, there were very few academic experts on Central America and the Caribbean in the United States, and their scholarly production was neither copious nor particularly distinguished. Most university departments preferred to hire specialists on the Latin American "majors" (Argentina, Brazil, Mexico, Chile, and Peru); ambitious graduate students took note and oriented their projects accordingly. This explains why much of the outpouring of writing in the past seven years has been the work of self-styled or "instant" experts, and why great care is needed to identify reliable scholarship.

SOURCES OF RECORD. Three invaluable source books appear on an annual basis: Jack W. Hopkins, ed., *Latin America and the Caribbean Contemporary Record* (New York: Holmes and Meier), brings together articles on individual countries by leading specialists. Richard Staar, ed., *Yearbook on International Communist Affairs* (Stanford, Calif.: Hoover Institution Press), does the same for Communist and other left-wing movements worldwide, though the volume actually covers much more than the title suggests. James Wilkie et al., eds., *Statistical Abstract of Latin America* (Los Angeles: Center for Latin American Studies, University of California, Los Angeles), provides many hard data on national economies, nutrition, education, and demographics.

PERIODICALS. The quality and quantity of coverage has steadily improved over the last few years. National dailies that give the most serious attention to the region are the *New York Times,* the *Washington Post,* the *Christian Science Monitor,* and, in Spanish, *Diario de las Américas* (Miami). Those wishing to follow the Central American and Caribbean press can do so conveniently through *Foreign Broadcast Information Service (Latin America),* published five times weekly by the U.S. Information Service.

Many weekly, monthly, and quarterly (w, m, q) periodicals devote considerable attention to the region. These include *America* (w), *Catholicism in Crisis* (m), *The Christian Century* (w), *Christianity and Crisis* (w), *Commentary* (m), *Foreign Affairs* (five times yearly), *Foreign Policy* (q), *Inter-American Economic Affairs* (q), *Journal of Inter-American Studies and World Affairs* (q), *National Catholic Register* (w), *National Catholic Reporter* (w), *The National Interest* (q), *The New Republic* (w), *Sojourners* (m), *Strategic Review* (q), and *Times of the Americas* (w). The National Catholic News Service publishes both *Origins* (w) and *Catholic Trends* (bi-w).

U.S. GOVERNMENT DOCUMENTS. These are generally produced by the U.S. Department of State, Bureau of Public Affairs; they include *Current Policy, Department of State Bulletin, Gist,* and *Special Report.* Of growing relevance are the volumes now produced annually by the Arms Control and Disarmament Agency, *World Military Expenditures and Arms Transfers*. See also the Kissinger Commission findings, *The Report of the President's National Bipartisan Commission on Central America* (New York: Macmillan, 1983).

Regional and Global Perspectives

SEVERAL EXCELLENT SURVEYS provide useful historical background. Sir Eric Williams's *From Columbus to Castro: The History of the Caribbean, 1492-1969* (New York: Random House, 1983) provides a synoptic vision of the development of the French, British, and Spanish-speaking nations. The author, onetime prime minister of Trinidad, was an important figure in English Caribbean politics for many years. Ralph Lee Woodward's *Central America: A Nation Divided* (New York: Oxford University Press, 1976) emphasizes continuities over time and also between the republics. Dealing only with the period 1900-1921, Dana G. Munro's *Intervention and Dollar Diplomacy in the Caribbean* (Princeton, N.J.: Princeton University Press, 1964) passes into careful review the policies of the United States during the period of its maximum intervention in the region. Munro was a career diplomat who served in Haiti and Nicaragua during these years. Carrying the story forward is Bryce Wood, *The Making of the Good Neighbor Policy* (New York: Columbia University Press, 1961), which traces Washington's disillusionment with earlier policies and the evolution of the doctrine of "absolute non-intervention."

For the period from World War II to the Nicaraguan revolution there is almost nothing for the student to consult except two studies dealing with the "Guatemalan affair" of 1954, both highly critical of the U.S. role in deposing the government of President Jacobo Arbenz: Stephen Kinzer and Stephen Schlesinger, *Bitter Fruit: The Untold Story of the American Coup in Guatemala* (New York: Doubleday, 1983), and Richard H. Immerman, *The CIA in Guatemala: The Foreign Policy of Intervention* (Austin, Tex.: University of Texas Press, 1983). Also of interest are the sections dealing with Guatemala and the Dominican Republic in David Atlee Phillips's remarkable memoir, *The Night Watch: Twenty-Five Years of Peculiar Service* (New York: Morrow, 1977).

Of the many studies produced since 1979, probably the best is Howard J. Wiarda, ed., *Rift and Revolution: The Central American Imbroglio* (Washington: American Enterprise Institute, 1984), the work of more than a dozen specialists under the direction of a distinguished scholar. It combines history, politics, and economics and explores both regional and global perspectives.

Of equal interest is Robert S. Leiken, ed., *Central America: Anatomy of Conflict* (Pergamon Press for the Carnegie Endowment for International Peace, 1984), which was intended to be "the Democratic alternative to the Kissinger Commission report" but is stronger on analysis than on concrete policy recommendations. Particularly important are chapters by Arturo Cruz Sequeira ("The Origins of Sandinista Foreign Policy"), Richard Feinberg and Robert Pastor ("Far From Hopeless: An Economic Program for Post-War Central America"), Richard Millett ("Praetorians or Patriots? The Central American Military"), and Morris Rothenberg ("The Soviets and Central America").

H. Michael Erisman and John D. Martz, eds., *Colossus Challenged: The Caribbean Struggle for Influence* (Boulder, Colo.: Westview Press, 1982), and Richard E. Feinberg, ed., *Central America: International Dimensions of the Crisis* (New York: Holmes and Meier, 1982), offer left-of-center interpretations. Rear Admiral (ret.) Thomas H. Moorer and Georges Fauriol, *Caribbean Basin Security* (Washington: Center for Strategic and International Studies, 1984), provides the traditional strategic perspective that informs present U.S. policy.

Barry Levine's compendium *The New Cuban Presence in the Caribbean* (Boulder, Colo.: Westview Press, 1983), originally a prize-winning special issue of the *Caribbean Review*, brings together an international team of authors to explore the implications of Castro's foreign policy for almost all the nations of the Caribbean Basin, including the English Caribbean. The diversity of perspectives is useful as a corrective to the largely apologetic Pamela Falk, *Cuban Foreign Policy: Caribbean Tempest* (Lexington, Mass.: D. C. Heath, 1986).

Robert Wesson, ed., *Communism in Central America and the Caribbean* (Stanford, Calif.: Hoover Institution Press, 1982), though slightly dated, provides a comprehensive survey of individual countries by an ideologically mixed group of academic specialists. Despite its title, Communism is only one of the themes explored.

The short-lived Bishop regime in Grenada and its implications for the region are the subject of Jiri Valenta and Herbert Ellison, eds., *Grenada and Soviet/Cuban Policy: Internal Crisis and U.S./OECS Intervention* (Boulder, Colo.: Westview Press for the Kennan Institute for Advanced Russian Studies, 1986). This volume has the virtue of placing Marxism in the English Caribbean in a larger international context and also of reproducing, in a lengthy appendix, key documents captured by the U.S. and OECS forces that liberated the island in 1983.

El Salvador

HISTORICALLY, U.S. INVOLVEMENT in El Salvador has been limited, and little was written about the country by U.S. scholars before 1979. Much of the really valuable analysis to have appeared since then is found in scattered periodicals rather than in books.

The most important historical monographs are Thomas P. Anderson, *War of the Dispossessed* (Lincoln, Neb.: University of Nebraska, 1981), a study of the so-called soccer war between El Salvador and Honduras in the 1970s as an expression of the tensions inherent in both societies; Enrique Baylora, *El Salvador in Transition* (Chapel Hill, N.C.: University of North Carolina Press, 1982), a survey by a distinguished Cuban-born political scientist; and Stephen Webre, *José Napoleón Duarte and the Christian Democratic Party in Salvadoran Politics, 1960-72* (Baton Rouge, La.: Louisiana State University Press, 1979).

Both T. S. Montgomery, *Revolution in El Salvador: Origins and Evolution* (Boulder, Colo.: Westview Press, 1982), and Marvin Gettleman et al., eds., *El Salvador: Central America in the New Cold War* (New York: Grove Press, 1981), emphasize indigenous factors and reject the focus on Cuban and Soviet involvement, while R. Bruce McColm, *El Salvador: Peaceful Revolution or Armed Struggle?* (New York: Freedom House, 1982), analyzes the totalitarian nature of the FDR-FMLN. In a fashion reminiscent of Alexis de Tocqueville, Joseph P. Mooney, writing in *Inter-American Economic Affairs* (Autumn 1984), asks, "Was it a worsening of economic and social conditions that brought violence and civil war to El Salvador?" He finds that deterministic "sociological" explanations are grossly deficient.

The emergence of a new Christian Democratic government since 1983 has not stilled the waters of controversy. Enrique Baylora, "Dilemmas of Political Transition in El Salvador," in *Journal of International Affairs* (Winter 1985), is a worthwhile guide to the present situation, as is Alberto Coll's brief, pungent "Political and Military Losers, Salvador's Leftists Opt for Terror," *Wall St. Journal,* October 18, 1985. The distinguished liberal journal *The New Republic,* which had supported military and economic aid to the Provisional Government before Duarte's election, comments ironically on the unexpected turn of events there in "Good News from El Salvador," June 10, 1985.

The policies of the Duarte administration, supported by the Reagan administration, have aroused the ire of conservatives north and south. See, for example: Claudia Rosett, "Economic Paralysis in El Salvador: What the Guerrillas Don't Destroy, Central Planning Does," *Policy Review* (Fall 1984); Mario Rosenthal, "Is El Salvador on a U.S.-Subsidized Road to Serfdom?," *Wall St. Journal,* January 31, 1986; and Tom Bethell, "But Who Gets the Land?," *Washington Times,* May 4, 1983. But Rhoda Rabkin responds with "A Conservative Case for Land Reform," *National Review,* July 12, 1985.

Kerry Ptacek, *The Catholic Church in El Salvador* (Washington: Institute for Religion and Democracy, 1981), casts light on a vital social institution whose role has often been misrepresented or misunderstood.

Nicaragua

BECAUSE OF THE INTENSE involvement of the United States in its internal affairs, there is considerable U.S. literature on the history of Nicaragua and especially on the rise and reign of the Somoza dynasty. Absolutely indispensable for understanding this period is Neill Macaulay, *The Sandino Affair* (Chicago: Quadrangle Books, 1967); the author reviews Nicaraguan political history from 1912 through 1934, when in rapid succession the U.S. Marines withdrew from the country, the elder Somoza murdered Sandino, and a family dynasty began. A balanced diplomatic history is William Kammen, *A Search for Stability: U.S. Diplomacy Toward Nicaragua, 1925–33* (Notre Dame, Ind.: University of Notre Dame Press, 1968). Other studies relevant to the U.S. role during this period are Marvin Goldwert,

BIBLIOGRAPHICAL ESSAY 545

The Constabulary in the Dominican Republic and Nicaragua: Progeny and Legacy of U.S. Intervention (Gainesville, Fla.: University of Florida Press, 1962); Dana G. Munro, *The United States and the Caribbean Republics, 1921–33* (Princeton, N.J.: Princeton University Press, 1974); and John J. Tierny, *Somoza and Sandinistas: The United States and Nicaragua in the Twentieth Century* (Washington: Council for Inter-American Security, 1982).

The indispensable source for the Somoza period is Richard Millett, *Guardians of the Dynasty: A History of the U.S.-Created National Guard and the Somoza Family* (Maryknoll, N.Y.: Orbis Books, 1977). Less reliable is Eduardo Crawley, *Dictators Never Die: A Portrait of Nicaragua and the Somoza Dynasty* (New York: St. Martin's Press, 1979). Written at great speed to capitalize on the sudden interest in Nicaragua, Bernard Diedrich's *Somoza and the Legacy of U.S. Involvement in Central America* (New York: E. P. Dutton, 1981) is slipshod, wrong on many important points of fact, and dull. The posthumous autobiography of the deposed Nicaraguan dictator Anastasio Somoza Debayle (written with Jack Cox), *Nicaragua Betrayed* (Belmont, Mass.: Western Islands, 1980), is an utterly unconvincing *apologia pro vita sua;* its only real interest is an appendix of conversations (clandestinely taped) with U.S. officials who journeyed to Managua in 1978 and 1979 in a vain attempt to convince Somoza to step down.

Shirley Christian, *Nicaragua: Revolution in the Family* (New York: Random House, 1985), is probably the best single volume on the events that brought down Somoza and led to the establishment and consolidation of the Sandinista regime. The author, a Pulitzer-prize winning correspondent of the *Miami Herald*, has succeeded in combining scholarship and journalism in an impressive fashion. A complementary volume is David Nolan, *FSLN: The Ideology of the Sandinistas and the Nicaraguan Revolution* (Miami, Fla.: Institute of International Studies, University of Miami), which traces the ideological evolution of the FSLN and explores the significance of internal divisions within the revolutionary leadership; it also contains maps, chronologies, and a useful biographical appendix of all the *dramatis personae.*

Omar Cabezas, *Fire From the Mountain: The Making of a Sandinista* (New York: Crown Publishers, 1985), is a literary *tour de force,* the witty, charming battlefield memoirs of the man who is now Nicaragua's vice-minister of the interior. Xavier Argüello, an old friend and associate of Cabezas who is now in exile in Costa Rica, objects to the book's representation of persons and events in "A Guerrilla and His Pen," *The New Republic*, February 24, 1986.

Since events in Nicaragua have taken a turn for the worse, there has been much controversy over how much the decline in civil and political rights is a response to U.S. provocations and how much it follows a logic of its own. The human rights situation itself is discussed authoritatively and with care by Martin Kriele, a West German Social Democrat, in "Power and Human Rights in Nicaragua," *German Comments*, April 1986. The exact sequence of events in Nicaragua, as provided by Douglas W. Payne, *The Democratic Mask: The Consolidation of the Sandinista Regime* (New York: Freedom House, 1985), strongly suggests that the U.S. role has been marginal. A somewhat similar interpretation is offered by Humberto

Belli, *Breaking Faith: The Sandinista Revolution and Its Impact on Freedom and Christian Faith in Nicaragua* (Westchester, Ill.: The Puebla Institute, 1985). Belli, an ex-Sandinista, became an editorial writer on the opposition daily *La Prensa* and now lives in exile. His book is also important for its extensive discussion of the relation of the Sandinista regime to the Catholic Church in Nicaragua and the role of Protestant and Catholic missionary organizations there.

Perhaps the best single case study of economic policy in Nicaragua since 1979 is Forrest D. Colburn, *Post-Revolutionary Nicaragua: State, Class, and the Dilemmas of Agrarian Policy* (Berkeley: University of California Press, 1986). Among other things Colburn shows how ideology, politics, and economic realities have clashed and forced the Sandinistas continually to revise policies that so far have been disastrous. Theodore Schwab and Harold Sims look at "Revolutionary Nicaragua's Relations With the European Communist States" in *Conflict Quarterly* (Winter 1985). John Felton's "Sanctions on Nicaragua," *Congressional Quarterly*, Winter Report, May 11, 1985, emphasizes the limited impact of U.S. economic pressures since the imposition of the embargo.

Two books that present the Sandinistas in the best possible light are Tomás Borge and others, *The Sandinistas Speak: Speeches and Writings of Nicaragua's Leaders* (New York: Pathfinder Press, 1982), and Thomas Walker, ed., *Nicaragua: The Land of Sandino* (Boulder, Colo.: Westview Press, 2nd rev. ed., 1985). The latter is also a good example of the kind of "committed" scholarship that dominates much of Latin American studies in the United States today.

Index of Names

Abrams, Elliott, 183
Acción Democrática (Venezuela), 386
Acta (draft Contadora treaty), 155–56, 165
Adams Doctrine, 139–40
Adams, Grantly, 135
Adams, Tom, 139–40, 143
Afghanistan, 33–34, 90, 105
AFL-CIO, 119–20
Africa, 23, 30–32, 35
African National Congress (ANC), 31
Afro-Asian People's Solidarity Organization, 61
Agribusiness Promotion Council, 121
Ahmad, Eqbal, 456
AID, *see* United States Agency for International Development
Alexander, William, 387–88
Alfonsín, Raúl, 25
Allende, Salvador, 235, 238
Allman, T. D., 202
ALPROMISU, 420
Alvárez, Walter Antonio, 286
Amnesty International, 331
Anaya Montes, Melida (Ana Maria), 68, 222, 234, 242, 263
Anderson, Jack, 342
Anderson, Thomas, 74
Andropov, Yuri, 346
Angola, 30–31, 62, 64, 66, 137, 417
Anguilla, 95–112 passim
Anspach, Susan, 456
Antigua, 95–112 passim, 130–46 passim
Aparicio, Pedro, 201, 208
Aquino, Corazon, 450
Arafat, Yasser, 17
Aranda Mairena, Salvador, 422
Araujo, Arturo, 198–200
Arawak Indians, 98
Arbenz, Jacobo, 312–13
Arce, Bayardo, 279, 341, 378, 380–31, 389, 397
ARDE (Democratic Revolutionary Alliance), 421–24, 426–27
Argentina, 25–26, 138, 184, 235, 247, 326
Argüello, Leopoldo, 312
Argüello, Salvador, 417

Armed Forces of National Resistance, *see* FARN
Arriola, Lopez, 69
Aruba, 95–112 passim
ASEAN (Association of Southeast Asian Nations), 33
Asner, Edward, 458
Associated Press, 197
Association of Southeast Asian Nations, *see* ASEAN
Astorga, Nora, 426, 456, 459
Athers, Lester, 420
Australia, 34
Avila, Edward, 286–87
Azcona, José, 183–88

Bahamas, 95–112 passim, 130–46 passim
Baltodano, Monica, 426
Baltodano, Prudencio, 13
Barbados, 95–112 passim, 130–46 passim
Barnes, Michael, 387
Barni, Julian, 467
Barrera, Hugo, 226
Barricada, 279, 326, 355
Barrios, Captain-General Gerardo, Military School, 247
Basic Infantry Training School (EEBI), 415
Batista, Fulgencio, 40
Bay of Pigs, 314
Bazzaglia, Rogelio, 233
Bear (Soviet bombers), 14
Belize, 186–87
Belli, Humberto, 462
Bergold, Harry E., 392
Bermuda, 95–112 passim, 130–46 passim
Bermúdez Varela, Enrique, 418, 447
Best, Lloyd, 100, 103
Betancourt, Romulo, 135
Betancur, Belisario, 154, 162–64, 386–87, 389–90, 392
Bible, 403–4
Bimini, 137
Bishop, Maurice, 24, 137, 138
Blaize, Herbert, 134
Blandón, Adolfo O., 216–20, 230, 282
Boca, Roberto, 205

547

Boland Amendment, 441
Boland, Christopher, 67
Bolaños Hunter, Miguel, 71–72, 350
Bolivia, 235, 437
Bolsheviks, 207
Bond, Julian, 458
Bonpane, Blase, 460
Borge, Tomás, 233, 334, 342–43, 348–49, 350–53, 357, 360, 380–81, 388, 415, 419, 441, 459, 461
BOS (Southern Opposition Bloc), 422–23
Bosch, Juan, 99–100, 135
Boston Globe, 393
Botswana, 32
Brandt, Willy, 390, 395
Brazil, 12, 25–26, 98, 135, 312
Brezhnev, Leonid, 346
British Honduras, 131–46 passim
Brock, William, 126
Browne, Jackson, 458
Brown, Robert McAfee, 456
Budkowski, Brent, 388, 390
Buenos Aires Conference (1936), 309
Bulgaria, 16, 64–65, 68, 345, 350, 437
Burma, 107
Burnham, Forbes, 134, 137–38
Buxton, D. F., 461

Cabanas Province, 221
CABEI, CACMF, CADC, CADO, *see* Central American...
Calderon, Roberto, 425–26
Calero, Adolfo, 316, 427
Calvo, Raúl, 225–26
Camara, Helder, 323
Cambodia, 62
Canada, 108, 110, 124, 312, 368, 372
Cardenal, Ernesto, 456, 459
Cardenal, Fernando, 428
Cardenal, José Francisco, 418, 422
Caribbean Basin Initiative (CBI), 28, 47, 107, 115–28, 479–87
Caribbean Common Market (CARICOM), 125, 134–35
Caribbean Council of Churches, 125
Caribbean Group for Economic Cooperation and Development, 124
CARICOM, *see* Caribbean Common Market
Carpio, Cayetano, 205–6, 222, 233–34, 236
Carter, Jimmy (administration), 107, 206, 226, 243, 299, 316–17, 319, 412, 435, 461
Castellanos, Miguel, 233

Castillo, Fabio, 239
Castro, Fidel, 15–16, 62, 64–66, 69, 101, 108, 132, 160, 162, 198, 202, 235, 367, 397
Catholic Church, 13, 79–90, 273–75, 323, 329, 332–33, 357–58, 378–379, 403–7, 449, 451, 461
Catholic Worker, 461
Cayman Islands, 95–112 passim, 130–46 passim
CBI, *see* Caribbean Basin Initiative
CDN (National Democratic Coordinator, or "Coordinadora"), 383–90, 396, 398
CDS (Sandinista Defense Committees), 347–50, 383, 390, 393, 419–20, 422, 426–28, 458–59
Central American Bank for Economic Integration (CABEI), 45
Central American Common Market Fund (CACMF), 44–45
Central American Development Corporation (CADC), 48–49
Central American Development Organization (CADO), 48–49, 55
Central Intelligence Agency, 25, 67, 255, 312–13, 345, 354, 379, 381, 384–85, 389, 419, 424–25, 451, 459
Cerezo, Vinicio, 183–88
CERF (Clara Elizabeth Ramírez Front), 270
Cerna, Lenín, 312, 353
Cesaire, Aimé, 99
César, Alfredo, 423
Chamorro, Adolfo, 423
Chamorro, Edgar, 418
Chamorro, Fernando, 421–22
Chamorro, Jaime, 395
Chamorro, Pedro Joaquín, 378, 383, 395–96
Chamorro, Violeta, 344, 379, 417–18
Chernenko, Konstantin, 346
Chile, 12, 235, 247, 312, 372
Chinandega, 379, 386–87
China, People's Republic of, 34, 455, 462
Chitnis, Lord, 393
Chomsky, Noam, 456
Christian Democrats (El Salvador), 198, 201–2, 252, 256, 269
Christian Democrats (Europe), 27
Christian Democrats (Guatemala), 184–86
Christian Democrats (Venezuela), 220
Christian Science Monitor, 391, 458
Churchill, Winston, 17
Cienfuegos, Ferman, 239
Cienfuegos, Ricardo, 270

INDEX OF NAMES   549

Clara Elizabeth Ramírez Front, see CERF
Clark, Ramsey, 456
Cline, Ray, 104
Coffee Growers' Association, 225
Coffin, William Sloane, 456, 461
Colombia, 63, 124, 153-73 passim, 386-87
Columbus, Christopher, 98
Committee of the Mothers of the Disappeared, 228
Conference of Bishops, 404-5
Conservative Democratic Party, 326
Conservative Party, 303, 384, 390, 392, 397, 412
Consolación, 227-28
Constituent Assembly (Guatemala), 185
Constitutional Liberal Party, 384
Contadora Group, 25-26, 57, 82-83, 87, 149-50, 153-73, 177, 179, 281, 326, 371-72, 385-88, 390, 392, 444, 450, 489-91
Coolidge, Calvin (administration), 304
Coordinadora, see CDN
Cordoba Rivas, Rafael, 418
COSEP (Nicaraguan Businessmen's Association), 356-58, 384
Costa Rica, 12, 25, 70-71, 75, 122, 133, 154, 156, 166-67, 170, 177-79, 183, 280, 286, 313, 327, 345, 355-56, 360, 368-69, 371, 386-87, 427, 437-39, 441, 450
Council of State (Nicaragua), 379, 397, 413
Cox, Harvey, 454
Cruz, Arturo, 156, 332, 355, 377, 382-92, 398, 413, 418, 436, 447-48, 463
Cuba, 11-18, 20-40 passim, 61-76, 86-87, 95-112 passim, 131-46 passim, 159, 161, 163, 170-72, 178, 196, 198, 225, 243-44, 263, 265, 299, 303, 330, 345, 347, 367-68, 373, 377, 381, 405-6, 420, 437-38, 442-43, 455, 460, 469-70
Cuban Missile Crisis, 62
Cuban Revolution, 84, 108, 318, 378, 475
Curacao, 95-112 passim
Czechoslovakia, 62-63, 68, 333

Dalton, Roque, 237
D'Aubuisson, Roberto, 241, 217, 226, 239, 246-47, 255, 257, 282
De la Madrid, Miguel, 160
Dellinger, David, 456
Dellums, Ronald, 456
Demas, William, 99, 101
Democratic Conservative Party, 383-84

Democratic Revolutionary Alliance, see ARDE
Democratic Revolutionary Front, see FDR
D'Escoto, Miguel, 404, 428, 438-39
De Sola, Orlando, 225-27
Development Group for Alternative Policies, 125
DGSE (State Security Forces of Nicaragua), 348-49, 352-54, 357
Díaz, Nidia, see Valldares, Ana Maria
Díaz, Porfiro, 308-9
Dickey, Christopher, 204
Dole, Robert, 125
Dominica, 95-112 passim
Dominican Republic, 28, 95-112 passim, 118-19, 123, 130-46 passim, 131, 302, 368
Douglas, Mike, 458
Dowd, Douglas, 456
Dreifus, Claudia, 459
Duarte, Carlos Aquilino, 199, 203
Duarte, José Napoleón, 27, 88-89, 160-61, 178, 200, 202, 209-26, 252-53, 256, 270, 276-80, 282-83, 287
Duke, Rodolfo, 198
Duvalier, "Papa Doc" and "Baby Doc," 25, 101, 274
Dzerzhinsky, Felix, 353

East Germany, 16, 64-65, 345, 350, 443
Echaverry, Emilio, 417, 427
Ecuador, 12, 386
EEBI, see Basic Infantry Training School
Ellacuría, Ignacio, 271
ELN (National Liberation Army), 417
Enders, Thomas, 126, 171
EPS (Sandinista Army), 420, 423-24, 426
ERP (People's Revolutionary Army), 219, 221-22, 236-37, 238-40
Escalón, Gerardo, 225
Estrada Doctrine, 308-9, 312
Estrada, Genaro, 308-9
Ethiopia, 32, 62, 64, 66-67, 96
Europe, 301-3, 307, 341
European Economic Community (EEC), 38
Evertz, Adolfo, 393
Export-Import Bank, 123

Fagen, Richard, 299-300, 349
Fagoth-Müller, Steadman, 419-21
Falk, Richard, 456
Fanon, Frantz, 99
Farabundo Martí Liberation Front (FMLN), see FMLN
FARN (Armed Forces of National

550 INDEX OF NAMES

Resistance), 22, 222, 236–37, 239–40, 418–19, 421
Farrell, Mike, 458
FDN (Nicaraguan Democratic Forces), 384–85, 411–12, 423–24, 426
FDR (Democratic Revolutionary Front), 239, 242, 265
FDR-FMLN, 265–70, 278
Fenix, Operation, 353
Figueres, José, 135
Flores, Elena, 389
FMLN (Farabundo Martí National Liberation Front), 68–69, 88, 201–2, 205, 215–16, 218, 221–24, 227, 229–30, 234, 239–40, 242–43
Fonseca, Carlos, 323, 350–51
Ford, Gerald (administration), 206
Foreign Affairs, 384
Foreign Assistance Act, 52
Foreign Relations Committee, U.S. Senate, 117–18
FPL (Popular Liberation Forces), 197, 201, 218–19, 220, 222, 233, 236–40, 242, 263–66
France, 101, 208–9, 368
Free Trade Area, 117–19, 126–28
French Guiana, 95–112 passim
FRENICA (Revolutionary Nicaraguan Front), 416–17
FSLN (Sandinista National Liberation Front), 316–17, 319; and 323–35, 340–61, 378–99, 411–28 passim

Gairy, Eric, 100, 138
Gandhi, Indira, 33, 35
Gandhi, Mahatma, 309
Gandhi, Rajiv, 33, 35
García Márquez, Gabriel, 163
García Rossi, Francisco, 225
Generalized System of Preferences (GSP), 117
George Meany Institute (AFL-CIO), 47
Gerassi, John, 456
Ginsberg, Alan, 456
Godoy, Virgilio, 390–92, 394, 397, 463
Gómez Gonzáles, Santiago, 286
Gómez, Mercado, 229
Gonzáles, Leonel, 263
Gonzáles, Sebastian, 418
Good Neighbor Policy, 309
Gorbachev, Mikhail, 22–23
Grass, Günter, 461
Great Britain, 101, 134, 142, 161, 312, 325
Greece, 16–17, 75

Grenada, 23–24, 95–112 passim, 130–46 passim
Gromyko, Andrei, 12–13
Guadeloupe, 95–112 passim
Guardian, 457
Guatemala, 12, 24–25, 52–53, 62, 71, 89–90, 118, 123, 159, 166, 169–70, 177, 183–88, 225, 235, 280, 313, 318, 415–17
Guatemalan National Liberation Movement, 417
Guazapa Mountain, 283–84
Guerra, Salvador, 263
Guerra y Guerra, René, 253–55, 263
Guevara, Ché, 62, 437, 475
Gurdian, Ramiro, 412
Gurkhas, 26
Gutiérrez, Jaime Abdul, 246–47, 253–56
Guyana, 95–112 passim, 131–46 passim
Guzman Bolaños, Miguel, 72

Haig, Alexander, 107
Haiti, 28, 95–112 passim, 122, 302, 307, 309
Hamby, Jeanette, 460
Handal, Shafik Jorge, 63, 194, 200, 238, 278
Harper's, 202
Harrington, James C., 459
Harrington, Michael, 460
Harvard University, 106
Hassán Morales, Moisés, 342, 349–50, 413
Hayden, Tom, 460
Helms, Jesse, 127
Helsinki Accords, 440
Herazo, Marta Alicia, 227–28
Hernández, Edgar Antonio, 269, 427
Hernández Martínez, Maximiliano, 194–200, 206–7, 209, 216, 250
Herrera Campíns, Luis, 116
Hill, Roberto, 226
Hindus, 96
Hinton, Dean, 216–17
Hitler, Adolf, 318
Hodgkin, Henry, 462
Holland, 107, 142, 392
Honduras, 12, 25–26, 71, 89, 123, 133, 154, 156, 166–70, 183–88, 280, 313, 327, 360, 371, 380, 387, 415–17, 437–39, 451
Hooker, Ray, 374
Hoover, Herbert (administration), 309
House of Commons (U.K.), 142
Hull, Cordell, 104
Human Rights Commission (El Salvador), 228

INDEX OF NAMES   551

Human Rights Commission (Geneva), 276, 283
Humphrey, Hubert, 199, 203
Hungary, 68, 333

IMF, see International Monetary Fund
INCAFE (El Salvador state coffee agency), 225-26
Independent Liberal Party, see PLI
India, 33-35, 142
Industrial Revolution, 198
Inglesia, 403
Intelligence Authorization Act of 1983, 439
Inter-American Development Bank, 46-47, 318, 383, 435
Intergovernmental Commission for Migrants, 90
Interiano, José, 203
International Court of Justice (World Court), 366, 439
International Law Commission, 440
International Monetary Fund (IMF), 29, 46-47, 367
International Red Cross, 283
Israel, 32, 105
ISTA (El Salvador land reform agency), 287-88

Jackson, Henry, 17
Jagan, Cheddi, 142
Jamaica, 28, 95-112 passim, 112, 130-46 passim
James, C. R., 99
Japan, 22, 33, 440
Jarquín, Augustín, 397
Jaruzelski, Wojciech, 346
Jehovah's Witnesses, 425
Jennings, Peter, 341-42
Jesus Christ, 365, 370, 404, 461
John Paul II, 83, 274, 333, 407, 430
Johnson, Lyndon (administration), 106-7
Joval, Ernesto, 237
Juárez, Benito, 335
Juárez, Cecilia, 218

Kamman, William, 308
Kellogg, Frank, 304
Kennedy, Edward, 387, 463
Kennedy, John F., 17, 250, 324
KGB, 104, 358
Khmer Rouge, 417
Khomeini, Ayatollah, 16-17
Khrushchev, Nikita, 61-62, 343
King, Martin Luther, 369
Kirkland, Lane, 13

Kissinger Commission, 62-63, 75-76, 217, 435-36, 438-39
Knight, Franklin, 95
Kommunist, 63
Korea, North, 16, 33
Korea, South, 33

Ladd, Diane, 458
La Loma Military Academy, 305
La Nación, 70
Lane, Arthur Bliss, 307
La Prensa, 324, 348, 352, 358, 377-78, 386, 395, 403, 418, 464
Latin American Economic System (SELA), 26
Latin American Studies Association (LASA), 392-93
Lebanon, 32
Leggett, John C., 456
Legion of the 15th of September, 417
Leiken, Robert S., 348, 463
Lenin, Nikolai, 195, 199, 343, 358
León, 387, 412
Lesotho, 31
Lesser Antilles, 130-46 passim
Lewis, Arthur, 99
Liberal Party (Honduras), 186
Liberal Party (Nicaragua), 414
Libya, 31-32, 65, 233, 242, 345
Lincoln, Abraham, 17, 335
Linton, Neville, 125
Llovio Menéndez, José Luis, 72
Lomé Agreement, 47
Loomis, Francis Butler, 106
López Niula, Colonel, 258
López-Portillo, José, 160, 473
Los Angeles Times, 203
Luce, Clare Boothe, 17-18
Lynd, Staughton, 458

Macaulay, Neil, 305-6
Mackinder, Halford John, 104
Magaña, Alvaro, 161
Mahan, Alfred Thayer, 104
Majano, Adolfo, 246-47, 254-56
Manley, Michael Norman, 101, 135, 137
Mao Tse-tung, 455
Martí, Farabundo, 198-99, 207, 236, 250, 305
Martí, Farabundo, Liberation Front, see FMLN
Martí, José, 39
Martínez, Ana Guadalupe, 238
Martínez, Mariano, 418
Martinique, 95-112 passim

Marxism-Leninism, 73–5, 138–39, 141–42, 178, 195–205, 213, 215, 235–36, 238, 240–41, 253, 264, 317, 341–45, 413, 417, 424
Marx, Karl, 476
Masaya, 367, 425
Massing, Michael, 464
Mauricio Valenzuela, Edgar, 269
McCarthy, Coleman, 460
McKinley, William, 301
MDN (Nicaraguan Democratic Movement), 418, 421
Medrano, José Alberto, 250, 270
Mejia, Juan Pablo, 286
Méndez Montenegro, Julio César, 183
Mendoza, Fidelina, 227
Mendoza, Mariano, 418
Mengistu, Haile Mariam, 32
Messing, Andrew, 217
Methodist Church, 453
Mexico, 11, 16, 44, 101, 105, 108, 110, 124, 133, 135, 153–73 passim, 186–87, 208–9, 307–8, 339, 387–88, 469, 475
Miami Herald, 456
MISATAN, 359
Miskito Indians, 325, 329–30, 351–52, 359, 373–74, 379, 406, 418–19, 436, 459, 463–64, 476
MISURA, 359, 421
MISURASATA, 330, 359, 420–22
Mitchell, James, 134, 141
Mitford, Jessica, 456
Monge, Luis Alberto, 70, 280–81
Monroe Doctrine, 62, 302
Montealegre, Mariano, 427
Montenegro, Alejandro, 69–70
Monthly Review, 355
Montserrat, 95–112 passim, 130–46 passim
Moravian Church, 420, 425
Morazán Province, 221
Mormon Church, 425
Mozambique, 62, 417
Mugabe, Robert, 35
Muñoz Marin, Luis, 100, 135
Munro, Dana C., 302
Munroe, Trevor, 141
Murillo, Rosario, 458
Murphy, John, 351

Naipaul, V. S., 97, 99
Namibia, 30–31
Napoleon, 197
Nassau, 137–38
National Assembly (Nicaragua), 324–25, 331, 394, 396–97

National Conciliation Party, *see* PCN
National Democratic Coordinator, *see* CDN
National Democratic Organization, *see* ORDEN
National Directorate, 233, 243, 340–41, 347, 349, 413, 418, 421
National Guard (El Salvador), 248–49, 257–58, 286–87
National Guard (Nicaragua), 85, 241, 299, 305–13, 316, 349, 352, 413–15
National Liberation Army, *see* ELN
National Liberation Party, *see* PLN
National Network in Solidarity with the Nicaraguan People, 457
National Police, 248–49, 257–58
National Reconstruction Junta, 413
National Salvadoran Workers Union, *see* UNTS
National Security Council (NSC), 217, 379, 384
National Worker-Peasant Union, *see* UNOC
Nation, The, 462
NATO, 15, 22, 26, 75, 440, 469
Netherlands Antilles, 95–112 passim
New International Economic Order, 29–30
New York Times, 199, 341, 352, 397, 457
New Zealand, 34
Nicaragua-Honduras Educational Project, 457
Nicaraguan Businessmen's Association, *see* COSEP
Nicaraguan Commission of Jurists, 464
Nicaraguan Communist Party, 396
Nicaraguan Democratic Forces, *see* FDN
Nicaraguan Democratic Movement, *see* MDN
Nicaraguan Democratic Union, *see* UDN
Nicaraguan Revolutionary Armed Forces, *see* FARN
Nicaraguan Socialist Party, *see* PSN
Non-Aligned Movement, 31–32, 35, 162–63, 346
North Korea, 16, 65
Norway, 75
Nuevo Diario, 326
Nuevo Instituto de Centro America, 457
Nuñez, Daniel, 356

Obando y Bravo, Miguel, 13, 357, 398–99, 428
Ochoa, General, 66
Ochoa, Sigifredo, 220
Ogarkov, Marshal, 13
Ollman, Bertels, 456

INDEX OF NAMES   553

ORDEN (National Democratic Organization), 250–51
Organization of African Unity (OAU), 31
Organization of American States (OAS), 56, 115, 117–18, 154, 163, 316, 341, 368, 435–37, 439, 440–42
Orientación, 275
Ortega, Daniel, 17, 84, 256, 271, 280–81, 324, 340–41, 356, 378, 381–82, 385–87, 389–90, 393–98, 413, 419, 435, 454, 456, 466
Ortega, Humberto, 340, 343–44, 346, 355, 378, 381
Ortiz Centeno, Pedro Pablo, 427
Orwell, George, 351–52, 357
Osgood, Robert, 73–74
Overseas Private Investment Corporation, 122–23
Oxford University, 198

Pakistan, 32–33
Palestine Liberation Organization, *see* PLO
Panama, 118, 122–23, 153–73 passim, 247, 280, 302, 345, 390
Panama Canal, 11, 104–5
Pan American Conference (1928), 309
Panama Star and Herald, 199
Pasmore, Diane, 460
Pastora Gómez, Edén, 167, 332, 341, 385, 415, 418, 421, 423, 462
Patriotic Military Service (SMP), 425
Pauling, Linus, 456
Payne, Douglas W., 391
Paz, Octavio, 462
PCN (National Conciliation Party), 196–98, 200–2, 205, 250, 269
Peace Corps, 121, 345, 435, 451
People's Church, 404
People's Revolutionary Army, *see* ERP
Pérez, Carlos Andrés, 161, 178, 389, 397
Pérez de Cuellar, Javier, 435
Permanent Nicaraguan Human Rights Commission, 415
Peru, 26
Pickering, Thomas, 217–18
Pinochet, Augusto, 25
Playboy, 204, 456, 459
PLI (Independent Liberal Party), 390–92, 394, 397
PLN (National Liberation Party), 178
PLO (Palestine Liberation Organization), 11, 17, 32, 345
Poland, 90, 346–47
Polisario Front, 32
Ponce Torres, Roberto, 418

Ponomarev, Boris, 63
Popular Liberation Forces, *see* FPL
Popular Social Christian Party, 390, 392
Portugal, 387
Preston, Julia, 393
Preston, Richard, 461
Price, George, 134
Protracted People's War, 381
PRTC (Revolutionary Party of Central American Workers), 223, 270
PSN (Nicaraguan Socialist Party), 340–41, 380–82, 390, 393–96
Puerto Rico, 95–112 passim, 127, 131

Qaddafi, Muammar, 11, 17
Quakers, 461

Radio Católica, 403
Radio Liberación, 69
Radio Martí, 39
Radio Moscow, 205
Radio Venceremos, 69–70
Ramírez, Clara Elizabeth, *see* CERF
Ramírez, Sergio, 323, 341, 387, 390, 456, 459
Reagan Doctrine, 449
Reagan Peace Plan, 158, 163
Reagan, Ronald (administration), 12, 20–40 passim, 107, 109–10, 115–28, 157–58, 162, 178, 187, 206, 213–15, 229, 234, 239, 241–42, 325, 339, 377, 379, 383, 388, 389–90, 392, 423–24, 442–43, 447–51, 457, 468
Red Brigade, 11, 14, 16–17
Reichler and Appelbaum, 459
RENAMO, 30–31
Revel, Jean-François, 470
Revolutionary Democratic Front, *see* FDR
Revolutionary Nicaraguan Front, *see* FRENICA
Revolutionary Party of Central American Workers, *see* PRTC
Rich, Adrienne, 456, 460
Ridruejo, Pastor, 275
Rio Treaty, 388–89, 440–42
Rising to Rebellion, 202
Rivas, Rafael Cordoba, 418
Rivera, Brooklyn, 330, 359, 421
Rivera y Damas, Arturo, 271–74, 281
Roach, John R., 84
Robelo, Alfonso, 344, 355, 379, 413, 418, 421–22
Rockefeller, Nelson, 311
Romania, 333
Romero, Carlos Humberto, 201, 281

Romero, Oscar, 208, 239, 285–86, 383
Roosevelt Corollary, 104, 303
Roosevelt, Theodore, 23, 106–7, 309
Rosa Chávez, Gregorio, 271, 283
Rosales, Oscar, 328
Rostenkowski, Daniel, 125–26
Royal Commonwealth Society, 143–44
Ruiz, Henry, 339–40, 381

Sacasa, Juan, 306
St. Kitts-Nevis, 95–112 passim, 130–46 passim
St. Vincent, 131–46 passim
Salazar Brenes, Alvaro, 253–54
Salazar, Pablo Emilio, 415–16, 422
Salvadoran Communist Party, 194, 198, 234
Samoya, Salvador, 220, 223–25
Sánchez Delgado, Domingo, 461
Sánchez, Luis, 396
San Miguel Province, 222
San Vicente Province, 197, 221, 263
Sandinista Army, see EPS
Sandinista Defense Committees, see CDS
Sandino, Augusto César, 304–7, 323, 350–51, 369, 382, 473–74
San Miguel, 203, 218–19
Santa Cruz Loma, 218–19
Santo Domingo, 24
Savimbi, Jonas, 30
Schick, René, 313–14
Schlaeffer, Salvador, 406
Seaga, Edward, 100, 106, 108, 141
Seeger, Pete, 457
SELA, see Latin American Economic System
Seventh-Day Adventists, 425
Seventy-two Hour Document, 15
Sevilla-Sacasa, Guillermo, 315
Shelton, Turner, 314–15
Shultz, George, 115, 149, 150
Sidel, Ruth, 456
Simmons, Kennedy, 134, 141
Soares, Mario, 381
Social Christians, 384, 396–97
Social Democratic Party (Nicaragua), 326, 384
Socialist International, 178, 386–87, 389–90, 398
Sol, George, 125
Solidarity, 346–47
Solis, Rafael, 394
Solzhenitsyn, Aleksandr, 103–4, 207
Somoza Debayle, Anastasio ("Tachito"), 16, 19, 67, 83, 154–55, 158–59, 206, 239,
241, 243, 274, 313–20, 340, 343, 345, 356–57, 360, 377–79, 382–84, 395–96, 412, 414–16, 436–37, 450, 462–63, 468
Somoza García, Anastasio, 299, 305–12, 324
Somoza, Luis, 313
South Africa, 30, 31
Southern Opposition Bloc, see BOS
South Yemen, 62
Soviet Union, 11–18, 22, 50–51, 61–76, 81–82, 86–87, 102, 141, 161, 195, 198, 224, 235, 283–84, 324, 335, 343, 346, 369–70, 373, 382, 405–6, 435–43, 462
Spain, 387
Spalding, Warner, 345
Spanish International Network (SIN), 213
Spock, Benjamin, 454–55
Springsteen, Bruce, 456
Sri Lanka, 107
Stalin, Josef, 326, 342–43, 351, 358
State Security Force of Nicaragua, see DGSE
Stimson, Henry, 303
Stoltenberg, Thorvold, 398
Stone, Richard, 241
Strategic Institute of Spain, 391
Stroessner, Alfredo, 25, 250, 274
Suazo Cordova, Roberto, 185
Supreme Court (El Salvador), 85, 276, 284
Supreme Court (Nicaragua), 397
Supreme Election Council, 392
Surinam, 95–112 passim
Sweet, David, 461

Taft, William Howard, 106–7, 300
Taiwan, Republic of China on, 247
TASS, 356–57
Tegucigalpa Act, 156–57, 169
Theberge, James, 315
Tipitapa, Peace of, 303–4
Tito, Marshal, 346
Tolstoy, Leo, 197
Torríjos, Omar, 154, 164
Treasury Police, 218, 248–49, 257–58
Trinidad and Tobago, 95–112 passim, 130–46 passim
Tropical Tours, 457
Trotsky, Leon, 342
Trujillo, Rafael, 96, 250, 274
Truman Doctrine, 17
Truman, Harry (administration), 17, 312
Turbay, Julio César, 162
Turkey, 75
Turks and Caicos Islands, 130–46 passim